RURAL HAUSA
a village and a setting

RURAL HAUSA
a village and a setting

POLLY HILL

Fellow of Clare Hall, Cambridge

Cambridge
at the University Press
1972

Published by the Syndics of the Cambridge University Press
Bentley House, 200 Euston Road, London NW1 2DB
American Branch: 32 East 57th Street, New York, N.Y. 10022

© Cambridge University Press 1972

Library of Congress Catalogue Card Number: 75-161287

ISBN: 0 521 08242 0

Printed in Great Britain
at the Aberdeen University Press

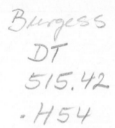

Contents

Tables

Tables

Illustrations

FIGURES

We are grateful to Methuen and Co. Ltd for permission to reproduce the map from p. 357 of W. B. Morgan and J. C. Pugh's *West Africa* (Fig. 1); and to the editor of *Man* and the Royal Anthropological Institute of Great Britain and Ireland for permission to reproduce the graph from *Man*, vol. 4, p. 397 (Fig. 10).

PLATES

(Between pp. 144 and 145)

Illustrations

Preface

This book consists of two separate, but related, sections. The fourteen chapters are concerned with analyzing the socio-economic affairs of a single village in Nigerian Hausaland; the long alphabetical Commentary provides that village with a general setting of rural Hausaland and is partly intended as a separate browsing ground. Just as this multi-purpose book has not been designed to be read through from start to finish, so I have not had any particular 'class of reader' in mind. I hope that the book will appeal, at the one extreme, to readers with no particular interest in Hausaland (even as a demonstration of the relevance of detailed village studies to wide general questions of rural economic under-development) and, at the other extreme, to those who want to know more about country life in their homeland. As mentioned in the Introduction to the Commentary (p. 201), which is not repeated here, one reason for splitting the book into two sections is to enhance readability: the development economist may ignore the Commentary, while the reader in search of 'background' may leave most of the chapters unread.

The first of the fourteen chapters serves as a brief introduction to all of them. Plain facts and figures relating to socio-economic life in our village (Batagarawa) are given in Chapter II, where the impossibility of distinguishing cash and subsistence sectors is also emphasized. Supporting lineages (and concepts of 'family land') are lacking in Hausaland, and Chapter III deals with the means by which fathers and sons seek to relieve their individual insecurity through the farming relationship known as *gandu*. The dominant theme of economic inequality is introduced in Chapters IV and V, and further pursued in Chapters VI, VII and VIII, which relate to farm-selling, migration and farm-labouring. Chapter IX is a necessary digression on village price fluctuations (seasonal and otherwise). Summarized case material emphasizing the contrasting situations of poorer and richer individual farmers is given in Chapters X and XI. The most important conclusions on the village are provided in Chapters XII and XIII, which analytically-minded readers may peruse, if they wish, immediately after scanning Chapters I, II and IV. Chapter XIV is a postscript on the causes of general poverty, not a summing-up of my findings.

The material in the Commentary derives exclusively from my research in Batagarawa and from published and (to some limited extent) Nigerian archival sources. Although I am only too well aware that in covering so large a field so rapidly some errors will have crept in, I must implore readers (however angry) who find that 'things are different in their village' not to condemn me for this reason alone, but to remember that I have merely done my utmost to summarize *that which has been recorded*. The reference material in the Commentary is no more comprehensive than an assemblage of footnotes: it's a question either of publishing now (and enduring the consequences) or of spending many years organizing the collection of much fuller information. I hope that the little that I have been able to do will stimulate others to do much more. It is this hope that partly justifies my constant harping on the theme that we (the literate community) are far more ignorant than we think. Apart from serving as a repository of reference material and as a glossary, the Commentary includes (as separate entries) short essays on such important topics as: economic regulations, *fatauci* (long-distance trade), granaries, groundnuts, manure supplies, market-places, marriage-expenses, migration, permanent cultivation, ploughing, taxa-tion, usury and women (economic position of).

In the course of my future research in Hausaland, I hope to explore the dis-tinction between 'rural' and 'urban', a matter which receives scant attention in this book. The old Hausa terms *birni* (a walled or capital city) and *gari* (a town), were always somewhat relative and are now quite outmoded in this analytical connexion. We cannot use a definition based on population-size, as the boundaries of town enumeration areas, for census purposes, usually include outlying por-tions of countryside. While working in Kazaure town, in 1971, where most farmers store their grain in rooms (*soro*), not in granaries, it occurred to me that grain storage methods might provide one useful distinction between 'rural' and 'urban'. Certainly (as in Yorubaland) many farmers are urban-dwellers: but (in contrast to Yorubaland) a very high proportion of farmers lives wholly in the countryside.

However, my present inability to define 'rural' should not invalidate my general approach, which is partly an endeavour to invert normal procedures by regarding Hausaland *from within a village*, rather than *vice versa*: it is also an affirmation that village communities are *not* cities in microcosm, but quite different places – see, in particular, Chapter XIII. The notion that rural Hausa-land is the essential Hausaland (that it is the cities which are anomalous), takes much support from a recent article by Prof. Abdullahi Smith, in which he argues that Hausa cities are cosmopolitan communities which 'emerged not so much as a result of the natural increase of a single community but rather as centres of immigration'. (*Journal of the Historical Society of Nigeria*, December 1970, p. 341.)

Prof. Smith's article appeared after my bibliography had gone to press. Several other important works, which will appear before this book, are omitted for the same reason. Also, there would have been much more reference to the fundamental and extensive research of members of the Rural Economy Research

Unit at Ahmadu Bello University (particularly that of D. W. Norman) had it not happened that their publication programme substantially overlapped with my own; one cannot cull citations from unfinalized drafts (such as were kindly made available to me), if only because pagination is due to be changed.

Acknowledgments

It would be impossible for me to exaggerate the debt of gratitude I owe to Mohammed Sabi'u Nuhu who, in my absence, collected much of the material in this book. In 1966, when on vacation from Ahmadu Bello University, M. S. Nuhu worked as my assistant on an enquiry on trade and marketing, and happened to suggest a visit to Batagarawa, his home village. Somehow it came about that the whole direction of my research was soon changed and in 1967 I returned to live for six months in Batagarawa in an excellent, newly-built, traditional-style house in the centre of the village. M. S. Nuhu, ably assisted by Usuman Salisu (whom I found a most interesting companion), continued to organize my work with his accustomed efficiency and kindness. In October I concluded my fieldwork, only to realize a few months later that there were many very serious gaps. Fortunately M. S. Nuhu had promised to continue our work; during 1968 and 1969 he made many visits to Batagarawa for this purpose and also lived there for about six months. He not only dealt with all my queries with speed, accuracy, efficiency and imagination, but also organized many statistical and other enquiries entirely on his own initiative. All the material in this book which is dated later than 1967 (and much else besides) was collected by M. S. Nuhu. (Unless otherwise stated, our statistics relate to 1967, which seems sufficiently recent to justify the use of the present tense.)

So kind and friendly were the people of Batagarawa that my stay there was one of the most enjoyable times of my life. Mallamawa, the District Head, had no hesitations about welcoming me, and his benign approval transmitted itself throughout his entire District, so that no introductions were necessary in more remote hamlets, where I met many interesting people, including Abubakar Labo, erst-while long-distance trader. My warmest thanks go to Mallamawa personally, as well as my apologies for any unwitting misrepresentations. I am also most grateful to Magaji (the Village Head), to M. Tukur (formerly District Scribe), to Alhaji Barau (especially for organizing the building of my house), and to Mukaddas (the Hamlet Head).

So many Batagarawa citizens helped me, or contributed to the enjoyment of my stay, that it is impossible to mention most of them. My special thanks are due to Mati Na'ida, who as an inspired and thoughtful commentator and observer, was particularly helpful over our detailed enquiry on the history of transactions in farmland. Among others I am particularly grateful to are: Alhaji Nuhu and his senior wife (parents of M. S. Nuhu), M. Abubakar, Bila,

Galadima Ruga, Kaura, M. Mamman, Mande, Sani Ruga, Sule Magini and my next-door neighbours Danjuma Drummer and his wife Mairo. Especially on my evening strolls through the farmland, I enjoyed the companionship of many schoolchildren, who were most welcoming to my daughter Susannah Humphreys and my niece Alison Hill.

During the many arduous months entirely devoted to writing this book my chief encouragement came (yet again) from Prof. Ivor Wilks, then in Cambridge; although we spent so much time in discussion and he read most of the typescript at various stages of drafting, he (like all the others who helped me) bears no responsibility for the final result. I am also particularly grateful to Murray Last and A. H. M. Kirk-Greene for reading earlier drafts of the Commentary and for numerous suggestions and corrections; to Prof. Joan Robinson, my teacher of long ago, for reading and criticizing the chapters and for generously appreciating the relevance of my approach; and to Barbara E. Ward for her most constructive criticisms of Chapters XII and XIII. Prof. Meyer Fortes, Thomas Hodgkin, John Lavers and Renée Pittin are among the other friends I must thank for criticizing certain sections.

My research in rural Hausaland was made possible by the Center for Research on Economic Development, at the University of Michigan, Ann Arbor: I am extremely grateful to the Center and in particular to Prof. W. F. Stolper, for their remarkably enlightened financial support (over as long as four years), which gave me entire freedom to pursue research in Nigeria, as and where I wished. I am very glad that I decided to work in rural Hausaland and I am very grateful to the Nigerian Institute of Social and Economic Research (NISER), at the University of Ibadan, for their active support at such long range, particular thanks being due to Dr Onitiri, the Director, and to Mr A. Ijose, Administrative Secretary.

Finally, I wish to thank members of the staff of the Cambridge University Press for their unfailing courtesy, helpfulness and tolerance of the waywardness of authors; and the administrators of the Smuts Fund for a grant for typing.

My insistence that rural (Nigerian) Hausaland is, socio-economically, *the* great under-explored region of West Africa, echoes through the pages of this book. Yet, anyone who ventures into this field derives extraordinary help from as many as five great authors, and why should they not find a place in a list of acknowledgments? They are the famous explorer Henry (Heinrich) Barth (1857); the lexicographer G. P. Bargery, whose dictionary (1934) is a mine of encyclopaedic information on rural Hausaland to which one never turns in vain; the doctor–scientist J. M. Dalziel whose *Useful Plants* (1937) is, ethnographically, so much more than a botanical compendium; and the social anthropologists M. G. Smith and G. Nicolas who, more recently, have laid the foundations for all subsequent socio-economic work in rural Hausland.

July 1971   POLLY HILL

Abbreviations and Conventions

After some earnest debate, which took account of printing costs among other factors, it was finally decided not to use the three Hausa 'hooked' letters – the implosive 'b' and 'd' and the 'k' which is modified by being forcibly ejected and accompanied by glottal stop.

Most Hausa words that appear in the chapters are included in the Commentary: to facilitate reference, isolated nouns usually take their singular form, even when the sense requires the plural. The letters 'q.v.' after any word, tell the reader that there is an entry in the Commentary under that word if he cares to refer to it. Similarly, any words in semi-bold type in the chapters refer to contextually relevant entries in the Commentary. (See, also, pp. 201–2.)

References such as Last (1970, pp. 346–7) relate to entries in the bibliography – in this case M. Last's article of 1970.

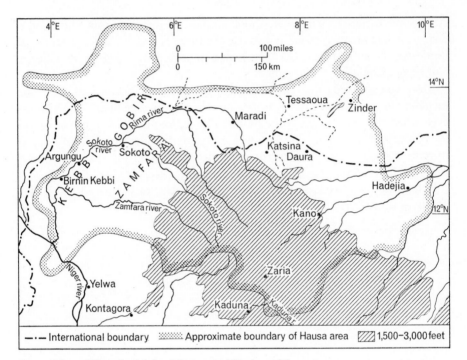

Fig. 1. Map of Hausaland (after Morgan and Pugh, 1969)

CHAPTER I

Introduction

As most publications relating to Hausaland have long historical introductions, there is good reason not to follow suit. So this book, on socio-economic life in a Hausa village, opens with no more than a few general observations on historical, administrative, ethnic, linguistic and other background matters, the general reader being referred to a number of specialist studies, such as those from which citations have been drawn, where far more detail may be found.

The Hausa people are settled mainly between $10\frac{1}{2}$ and $13\frac{1}{2}$ degrees North and 4 to 10 degrees East (see Fig. 1) in a huge area, mainly in the north of Nigeria but also in the south of the Niger Republic, which essentially consists of the basin of the Sokoto river and its tributaries to the west, and of a great plateau to the east.

The Hausa enjoy a high degree of cultural, linguistic and religious uniformity; the differing patterns of social and economic organization relate rather to the contrast between rural and urban life than to ethnic differentiation. Politically, Hausaland has for long comprised a number of emirates owing a common allegiance to the Caliph (Sultan) of Sokoto. Each emirate was centred upon a capital town (*birni*) in which the Emir (*sarki*) resided. The ruling-class was predominantly Fulani in origin. The high degree of cultural assimilation of this ruling-class with the culture of Hausa commoners has, however, mitigated against the continuance of ethnic exclusivity.

The Fulani assumed a position of political dominance in the aftermath of the *jihad* (q.v.) called by 'Uthman dan Fodio in 1804. The extraordinarily complex nature of the movement that culminated in *jihad* makes any brief description impossible. Suffice it to note that the movement, in the later eighteenth century, drew much of its strength from the discontented rural population – whether sedentary Hausa farmers or nomadic Fulani pastoralists: Hausa rulers had become increasingly oppressive over such matters as taxation and compulsory labour (military and otherwise), with a resultant fall in the standard of living of the free peasantry. In the course of the *jihad*, however, the movement appears to have passed under the control partly of Fulani clan leaders and partly of certain scholars who were particularly closely associated with 'Uthman. It was the members of these élites who created the structure of the emirates which has survived to the present time – see Last (1970, pp. 346–7).

Almost a hundred years after the *jihad*, the caliphate (with its component emirates) was incorporated into the British Protectorate of Northern Nigeria, under Sir Frederick Lugard as High Commissioner. In 1900, when Lugard first assumed this office, there was, as Perham has noted, nowhere in sub-Saharan Africa to compare with –

the political and cultural sophistication of these ancient Hausa states, with their walled red cities, crowded mosques, literate mullahs, large markets, numerous crafts in metal and leather, far-ranging traders, and skilled production of a wide variety of crops. Served by cattle, camels, horses and donkeys, and by slaves whom early travellers to Kano reckoned as half the popula-tion, not only the ruling class but the more prosperous of the Hausa had some of the luxury of leisure coupled with a standard of living very rare in tropical Africa.

Perham (1960, pp. 33–4)

The policy of the colonial administration was based upon the conservation of the older political structure. As J. A. Burdon, the first Resident of Sokoto, argued:

What is the attitude of the British Administration towards these states? Briefly, it is con-struction, not destruction. Our aim is to rule through existing chiefs...to enlist them on our side in the work of progress and good government. We cannot do without them. To rule directly would require an army of British magistrates...My hope is that we may make of these born rulers a high type of British official, working for the good of their subjects in accord-ance with the ideals of the British Empire, but carrying on all that is best in the constitution they have evolved for themselves, the one understood by, and therefore best suited to the people.   (Burdon, (1904), cited by Crowder (1966, pp. 212–13))

As a result of this attempt to create continuity, Hodgkin has observed that

The two major empire-building movements which marked the beginning and end of the [nineteenth] century – Fulani and British – had more in common than is sometimes realised. Both succeeded in imposing, by a combination of diplomacy and military force, the authority of a single government over a large, politically heterogeneous, region. Both derived their dynamic from a missionary impulse – the idea of the construction of an Islamic state, on the model of the early Caliphate, in the one case; of the spread of Christian civilization, European commerce, and British justice, in the other. For both this sense of mission was accompanied by a certain contempt for the institutions of the supposedly 'backward peoples', whose moral and social standards it was the conquerors' duty to raise.   Hodgkin (1960, p. 51)

In 1914 the Northern and Southern Protectorates of Nigeria were amalga-mated, Lugard being appointed Governor-General – see Kirk-Greene (1968). In 1954 Nigeria became a full federation of three regions (North, East and West), with a federal capital at Lagos. In 1960 Nigeria became an independent country, and 1967 saw the creation of twelve separate Nigerian states, six of them in the former Northern region, three of them (Kano, North Central and North Western) being the homeland of most Nigerian Hausa. (See Fig. 2.)

In a typical emirate the Fulani ruling-classes and their Hausa subjects con-tinued to owe common allegiance to the Sokoto Caliphate. M. G. Smith has drawn attention to the extent to which Islam provided an ideology which minimized tension, especially at a societal level, between the Fulani ruling-class and their Hausa subjects: 'As Muslims, both groups...belong to the Malikite school or rite. Both emphasize agnatic kinship in descent and domestic life, both practise polygyny with easy divorce, both hold common judicial and administrative institutions, and, formerly a common system of slavery' – Smith (1965, p. 231).

'Hausa' is a linguistic not an ethnic term, and refers to those who speak the Hausa language by birth: many groups whose sole language is Hausa have little or nothing in common ethnically. But the Fulani ruling-class (Hausa-speaking though it is) constitutes a separate group, as is emphasized by their use of the name 'Habe' (singular 'Kado') to denote an 'indigene'. The Hausa proper are, also, often differentiated from the pagan Hausa-speakers, the Maguzawa (q.v.), who are scattered throughout the centre of Hausaland. It may be that there are some 15 million Hausa-speakers in the northern states today: certainly there is no other 'linguistic group' in the whole of sub-Saharan Africa with as many 'members' (see **Hausa**).

The fact is that ethnic classifications 'remain fluid according to the social context' – Smith (1955, p. 3). Even the settled Fulani (*Filanin gida*), from whom the ruling-class is drawn, are apt to describe themselves as 'Hausawa' to the outsider, but –

although they have lost most of their independent culture, all their language but the greetings, most of their cattle and, through intermarriage and concubinage, some of the Fulani physical traits, among themselves they draw sharp distinctions not only between the dominant Fulani and subject Hausa, but between Fulani members of ruling families and other settled Fulani.

(*ibid.*, p. 3)

But despite the complexity of its ethnic structure, the society and the economy of Hausaland (and of the kingdom of Bornu to the east) have an 'underlying uniformity':

Here the local rural community, despite its self-sufficiency in food and in most other commodities, has long formed part of a wider administrative and economic framework. Tax-collectors and traders have for centuries been transporting the rural surpluses to the political capitals and the tradition of surplus production for distant centres of consumption, through trading, taxation and levies is deeply implanted. Forde (1946, p. 119)

While Hausa has long been a literary language, most Hausa works have been religious, poetical, or historical in content; or have been renderings of traditional folk tales, animal fables, proverbs and so forth. There are few sources which touch on the day to day economic affairs of ordinary people – on craftwork, rural slavery, trade, markets and so forth. Literary-minded British administrators (such as E. J. Arnett, J. A. Burdon, F. Edgar, H. R. Palmer, R. S. Rattray, A. J. N. Tremearne and others) compiled many documents on history and customs, languages and folk lore, their contribution, according to M. G. Smith (1969, p. viii), being outstanding in its 'depth, quality, variety and volume'.

Since those times, history, politics and administration have continued to be the subjects on which books have been written. Apart from M. G. Smith's *The Economy of Hausa Communities of Zaria* (1955) and the fascinating auto-biography of Baba of Karo recorded by Mary Smith (1954), no books have been written about rural Hausaland, though Forde's section of a book edited by Perham (1946) is a most useful compendium of archival material. The results of such fieldwork as has been done in rural areas since the last war now mainly rest in inaccessible, or out-of-print, articles and officially published pamphlets. It is this extraordinary neglect of socio-economic affairs over the centuries which has prompted the gathering together of so much reference material in the Commentary of this book. The opportunity has also been taken of emphasizing our ignorance on many matters, such as rural slavery, craftwork, or the cloth trade, on which somehow there is always assumed to be a wide corpus of knowledge. Often it seems that the great traveller Henry Barth, who was in West Africa 120 years ago, is the most modern of all observers of the rural scene.

Although the chapters of this book mainly relate to certain aspects of socio-economic life in a single Hausa village (Batagarawa in Katsina Emirate), and although the single theme of economic inequality dominates the whole analysis, these chapters, together with the accompanying Commentary, partly represent a tentative demonstration of the possibilities of arguing from the particular to the general in this enormous, sociologically unexplored, region. Put in general terms the idea is that the analysis of the detailed findings in a single village, set against the background of similar work elsewhere, enables the for-mulation of hypotheses, or the presentation of mere ideas, relating to the identity of some of the salient socio-economic variables associated with the posited 'uniformity' in Hausaland – hypotheses and ideas which may then be tested elsewhere.

The adoption of such a procedure does not involve the idea that there is anything especially 'representative' or 'typical' about the chosen Hausa village – although it is necessary to insist, for reasons given below, that Batagarawa is the centre of a considerable area of dispersed settlement and not a mere suburb of nearby Katsina city. In a part of the world where rural population densities vary enormously (and where high proportions of the population live respectively in very densely and very sparsely populated localities), and where hosts of other ecological or geographical factors also show immense variation – examples being the depth of the water-table, soil fertility, the proportion of marshland (*fadama*), accessibility to markets, availability of firewood, extent of good grazing land, incidence of trypanosomiasis – the very notion of a representative village is obviously absurd. Different though ten Hausa villages in as many widely-flung areas might happen to be, there is no need to decide which of them is the most representative when analysing why they have 'more in common' than (say) any pair of villages one of which is Tiv, the other Hausa.

This book is also an attempt to demonstrate that when studying the structure of socio-economic life in a small West African rural community, there are places and circumstances in which an approach based on isolating economic factors within a sociological framework may be even more illuminating than one of wider and more sociological scope. Low though the standard of living in Batagarawa is, it may yet be the kind of place where economic factors have more influence than kinship on the choice of marriage partners.

But any method of fieldwork which leans so heavily on the study of the economic behaviour of individual farmers (*qua* individuals) must be based on a theme (or set of themes) relating the individuals to one another, differentiating their functions, enabling one to observe the workings of the economy as a whole and so forth. It was by sheer accident that the theme of economic inequality first emerged towards the end of the present writer's six-month stay in Batagarawa in 1967 when grain was very scarce, and it was only gradually, as analysis of the detailed material proceeded, and as additional information came in from M. S. Nuhu, that it began to appear that a single-theme approach, based on the classification of farmers into four 'economic-groups' in accordance with their living standards, provided a workable framework.

While this framework proved much more useful than had been expected, its artificiality, as a mere device on which to hang the detailed findings, must be strongly emphasized. It is true that a man's general economic standard is closely related to his success as a farmer and that some farmers are generally regarded as notable successes and others as dismal failures; yet the ordinary man-in-the-street does not look at society in this mechanistic kind of way. In a society where neither land nor labour are scarce factors, the present writer is not in the least obsessed by the topic of economic inequality as such, but has rather experimented with the use of a tool which is seldom used in such an environment. It is quite likely that some other approach would have proved more relevant to the primary aim of tentative generalization.

But this approach is certainly a forceful demonstration of the dangers of regarding any farming community as composed of a group of 'average farmers' – together with (as one must always nowadays assume) a few 'progressive farmers'. It is not merely that a few farmers operate on a much larger scale than others, but that there are many richer farmers who have entirely different economic aims from many poorer farmers. As for the 'failed farmers', those who in our terminology are 'too poor to farm', they do not deviate from the 'norms' set by more successful men, 'but live in a looking-glass world of contrariety' (p. 160).

The Hausa people are much less urbanized than the members of many of the other important West African 'ethnic groups' (such as the Yoruba or the Ashanti), it being likely that at least four-fifths of those in the homeland are largely dependent on farming for their livelihood (see p. 297) – though many who travel abroad to Ghana, southern Nigeria and elsewhere, congregate in cities. Yet nearly all administrators and research workers (except for a few missionaries and others who have studied the pagan Maguzawa) have been based on cities and large towns, like the fief-holders in the nineteenth century. A mass of valuable village assessment reports and similar material, compiled by young and enthusiastic District Officers, who travelled around the country-side 'on tour', must still lie unexplored in the National Archives. But most publications suffer from severe 'urban bias' – hallowed conventional notions about the 'mass of the peasantry' (*talakawa*) passing from one respectable author to another. A few pertinent citations are presented here without com-ment; many similar citations from more recent sources are criticized elsewhere in this book.

First there was (and is) the idea that where land is plentiful 'there could be no natural supply of wage-labourers' – Perham (1960, p. 41), so that 'to obtain workers it was necessary to resort to force' – Meek (1925, p. 287); tied up with this was the belief in the 'rudimentariness' of rural economic systems. 'There was only a rudimentary monetary and exchange system and the ruling class, or men of exceptional enterprise, could hardly obtain the labourers their activities required except by compulsion' – Perham (1960, p. 41). Lugard's policy of abolishing the *legal status* of slavery, while permitting owners to retain the slaves they already owned, was readily justified, as follows: '...thus slavery was built into the Hausa economic system which would have been completely disrupted by wholesale manumission, and hordes of unemployed people who had lost their lands and their tribes would have been thrown out to starve or to thieve' (*ibid.*).

Secondly, there was (and is) the presumption that given 'freedom from fear', benign evolutionary processes automatically come into play in the countryside:

Freedom from want, as far as ever it entered colonial plans, was thought of as something that followed in due though slow course from the freedom from fear that the Pax Britannica provided; unharassed by tribal wars and slave raids, and by fiscal extortion, the people could be left to develop their natural resources in their own way.   Mahood (1964, p. 7)

Thirdly, there was (and is – see p. 136) the belief that farmers lacked foresight or the incentive 'to work more than the low standards of well-being demand' – Perham (1960, p. 41). In reference to the early years of British administration Heussler (1968, p. 150) recently asserted that 'everyone knew that the peasant was in the habit of planting just enough to see him through from one harvest to the next'. Hastings, who first arrived in Northern Nigeria as a Political Officer in 1906, readily confirms this viewpoint:

Nigerian farmers are not provident, they never take thought about the morrow, or keep a reserve in hand for times of scarcity. The average man just sows and reaps for present needs. He has to feed himself and his wife and children for a year and keep enough grain for next year's seed, for paying his tax and a bit for charity and hospitality. That is all the great majority bother about. In an abundant year they will have an extra surplus, but it is by God's will, not their own effort, that they gain it. At first sight it is difficult to understand why they do not guard against the rainy, or in Nigeria the non-rainy day, but they have their reasons, and one can suppose they know best what suits them. Constitutionally they are lazy, and will not work more than they need, though while they are at it they work hard. Another thing they know is that rain shortage is rare on the whole, and they trust to luck and Allah.

Hastings (1925, pp. 112–13)

In reference to the (then) new policy of 'mixed farming' (see **Ploughing**), another colonial official, asked: 'What is the use of increasing his [the farmer's] productivity eight-fold? What can he do with the crops? He already has as much food as he wants, and sells such surplus as he has with difficulty' – Crocker (1936, p. 132).

Fourthly, most writers are burdened by the presumption that 'ordinary farmers' compose the great bulk of the population – a belief which, as already mentioned, it is our particular purpose to demolish. This idea is so deep-seated that it is seldom made explicit, except in relation to 'mixed farming': thus 'the ordinary farmer normally cultivates only about 3 or 4 acres' – Faulkner and Mackie (1936, p. 94).

Given the persistence of beliefs of this kind, and of important misconceptions about more specific matters such as the cultivation of manured farmland and farm-selling, it is no wonder that the reports of most outside experts who have been asked to advise on methods of increasing agricultural output are informed by profound pessimism. The experts are in a cleft stick. On the one hand, Hausa rural economies are assumed to be in such stable (natural) equilibrium that no outside intervention could make any significant impression on them; on the other hand, this equilibrium is presumed to be so fragile that any reform which happens to help some farmers more than others is bound to lead to immediate disaster – particularly to the emergence of a 'landless class'. The author would like to think that her findings will assist the adoption of some stance intermediate between these two extremes.

The concept of a typical Hausa village is necessarily absurd. Yet certain villages may be regarded as notably atypical if it is certain that only a small proportion of the total Hausa population lives in similar environments. Thus, a village situated on a river bank which is so suitable for onion-growing that most farmers cultivate this crop, might be considered atypical for this reason alone. Again, it is arguable that villages in the Kano and Sokoto Close-Settled Zones, where population densities are so great that bush-farms have been entirely eliminated from the agricultural landscape, are notably atypical – although the realization that there are many localities where farmers *choose* to cultivate most of their farms every year despite the availability of nearby bush-land, has some-what reduced the strength of this case. However this may be, it is necessary to avoid misconceptions by insisting that Batagarawa is not notably atypical owing to its proximity to the famous city of Katsina.

Owing to the small scale of most population-density maps, it is often assumed that Katsina city is entirely encircled by a densely-populated zone, but the large-scale published dot-map compiled by R. M. Prothero on the basis of the 1952 census shows that this zone is a mere segment running from north-east, through east, to south-east, densities elsewhere being quite low, though variable. As Fig. 3 and Plate 33 show, a forest reserve lies between Batagarawa and Katsina city; and early travellers (see **Batagarawa**) commented on the wild state of the country to the south of the city. The Batagarawa Hamlet (*unguwa*) extends some miles to the west, north-west and south of the village and includes much un-cultivated, though cultivable, bush.

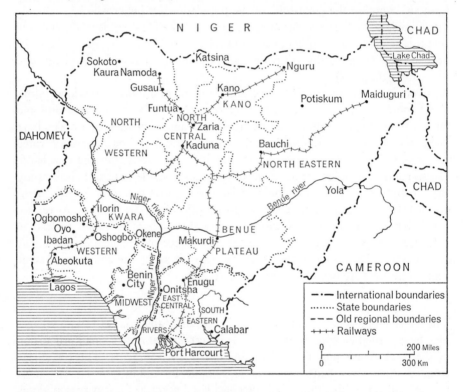

Fig. 2. Map of Nigeria, showing state boundaries

The farmers of Batagarawa have a preference for growing most of their crops on permanently cultivated manured farmland, although many of them also own some bush-farms; but unlike many farmers in the Kano Close-Settled Zone – see Mortimore and Wilson (1965) – they obtain no manure, in the form of compound sweepings, from the nearby city.

This physical separation is reflected in an absence of close sociological ties between the indigenous inhabitants and the city – only the members of the ruling-class and one other man having their origins there. Only 7 out of 303 farmers' wives in Batagarawa are of Katsina city origin (Table VII.1, p. 96). Nor is there much outward migration by men to the city, as Chapter VII makes clear.

Batagarawa is the capital of Mallamawa District which, as its name suggests, may formerly have been renowned for its Malams; however, the town was in Yandaka District until 1928 and, as local people nowadays insist, is not a notable centre for religious studies.

The great proportion of present-day inhabitants of Batagarawa count themselves as 'indigenes', tracing their descent back through several generations of local farmers. Although historical enquiries would doubtless reveal the population to be very mixed ethnically (including many of slave origin), there are few people who normally care to denote themselves as Kanuri, or members of other northern ethnic groups, apart from a very small number of men in dispersed farmhouses in a part of Batagarawa Hamlet known as Kauyen Yamma, whose fathers or grandfathers were Fulani pastoralists who migrated to the area to take up farming. (The settled Fulani pastoralists who nowadays provide the town with milk, live outside Batagarawa Hamlet.) So Batagarawa cannot be regarded as notably unrepresentative for reasons connected with the ethnic origin of the population (see **Mallamawa District**).

Batagarawa is, of course, most unrepresentative in being the seat of a District Head, the highest level of chief under an Emir. However, as most of the farms cultivated by members of the ruling-class are situated in other Mallamawa Hamlets, the ruler's presence has no significant effect on such economic matters as the distribution of Batagarawa farmland.

CHAPTER II

Batagarawa

The Hausa village called Batagarawa is situated in the north of Katsina Emirate, in the North Central State of the Federation of Nigeria, some six miles south of Katsina city, on a minor road – see Fig. 2, p. 8 and Fig. 3. It is the seat of the District Head of Mallamawa, the smallest of the twenty Districts (other than Magajin Gari, the Katsina city 'Home District'), into which the emirate is divided for administrative purposes. The District Head (*hakimi*), who bears the same title as his District, lives in the village, as does one of his three Village

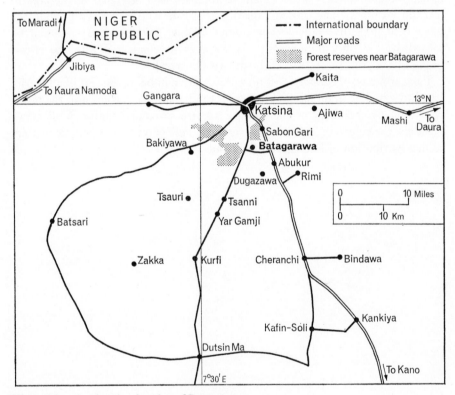

Fig. 3. Map showing the situation of Batagarawa

Heads (Magaji Batagarawa) and one of the latter's sixteen Hamlet Heads (Mukaddas).

In the mid-nineteenth century Batagarawa (q.v.) was listed by the explorer Henry Barth as being one of the principal towns of Katsina Emirate – otherwise

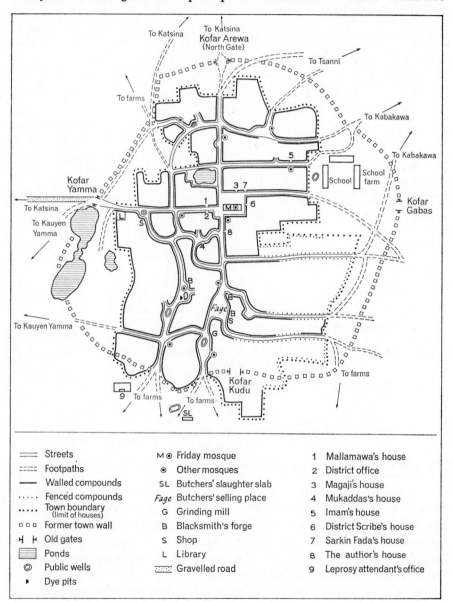

Fig. 4. Sketch-plan of Batagarawa *gari*, 1967 (not to scale).
Originally drawn by Usuman Salisu

nothing is known to have been recorded of its history before the British occupation. As elderly informants' earliest memories go, the town was possibly somewhat more populous in the first decade of this century than it is today. It was a walled town (always known as a *gari*, not a *birni*), with gates at the principal points of the compass.

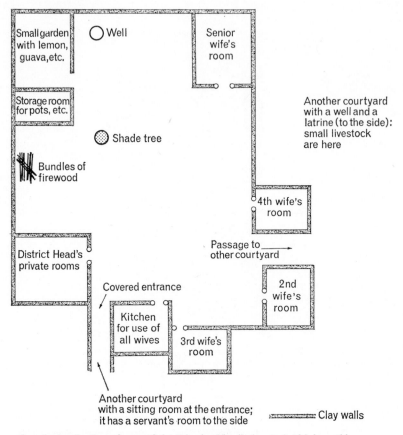

Small garden with lemon, guava, etc.

Well

Senior wife's room

Storage room for pots, etc.

Another courtyard with a well and a latrine (to the side): small livestock are here

Shade tree

Bundles of firewood

4th wife's room

District Head's private rooms

Passage to other courtyard

Covered entrance

2nd wife's room

Kitchen for use of all wives

3rd wife's room

Another courtyard with a sitting room at the entrance; it has a servant's room to the side

Clay walls

Fig. 5. Rough sketch-plan of part of the District Head's house (*gida*) in 1966

The walls – which within living memory were maintained by free men, not slaves – have long since collapsed; but the houses remain concentrated within the same circle today – see Fig. 4. In 1967 all the various structures which comprise a house or compound (*gida*) – see Fig. 5 – were made of reddish sunbaked earth (or clay), and all had thatched or clay (not corrugated iron) roofs; most of them were surrounded by high clay walls which effectively cut off the wives, who are in full Muslim seclusion (*kulle*), from the public gaze. With its narrow, walled streets, or alleys, which link the houses (see Plate 12); with its square roofed, entrance-huts (*zaure*) and numerous one-roomed mosques; with its public (as well as its private) wells; with its prominently situated school buildings; with its small central square, which is surrounded by the concrete-built 'Friday mosque', the houses of the chiefs and the District Office; with its lack of gardens – the *gari* resembles a densely-packed, miniature city.

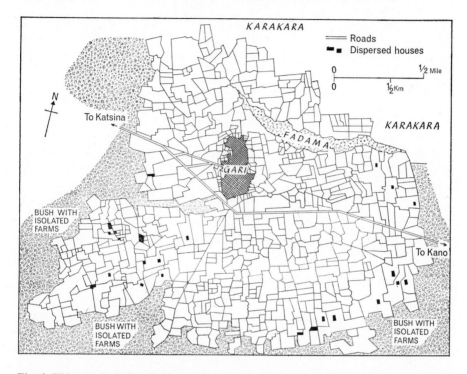

Fig. 6. This map includes all the so-called 'mapped farms' and most of the manured farms (*gonakin karakara*) owned by Batagarawa farmers in their Hamlet, the boundaries of which are not precisely determinate. A few of the houses in Kauyen Yamma (the western village) are too close together to be shown separately. Originally drawn by M. S. Nuhu. See p. 63.

This *gari*, with its population of some 1,160 people, is the centre of a considerable area of mainly dispersed settlement which extends for varying distances of up to five miles or more, to the east, south and west, but not at all far to the north where, as already mentioned, uninhabited bush and a forest reserve lie between the village and Katsina city. Some of the homesteads in this area, which has a much larger population than the central *gari*, stand isolated within their own farmland (see Fig. 6); more of them form small 'coagulated groups'; the residents of one Hamlet (Kaukai) have been partially resettled, on a modern grid-iron pattern, near the main Katsina to Kano road (see Fig. 7). (Kaukai was one of three Mallamawa Hamlets – Makurdi and Autawa being the others (see Figs. 8 and 9) – where farms were mapped for comparative purposes.)

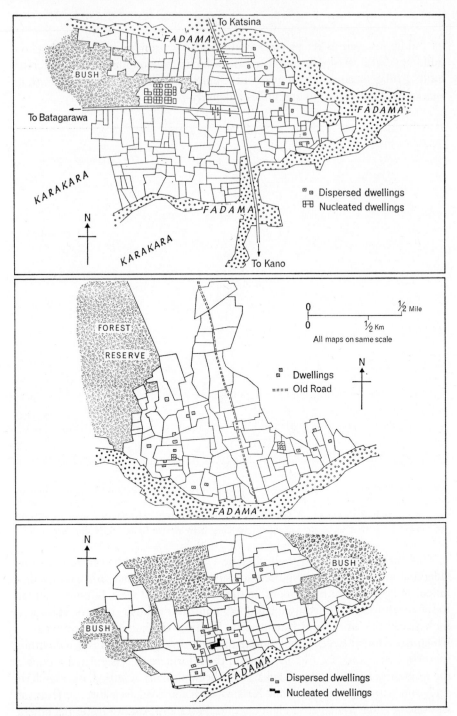

Figs. 7, 8 and 9. Farm maps of parts of Kaukai, Makurdi and Autawa Hamlets, respectively. All originally drawn by Usuman Salisu

The limits of this area are not set by modern administrative, or territorial, factors, but mainly, as one must suppose, by earlier population movements. That it is a cohesive area within which people flow conveniently, mainly on foot or donkey-back, is indicated by the fact that only 14% of all Batagarawa wives (see Table VII.1, p. 96) originated outside it.

For the purposes of this book the name 'Batagarawa' includes that portion of this area of dispersed settlement which lies within the Batagarawa Hamlet Area (*unguwa*), being under the authority of Mukaddas the Hamlet Head. There are about 230 people living dispersedly within the zone of manured farmland (*karakara*) around the *gari*, but none elsewhere in the *unguwa*, which extends west north-west for some miles, the boundary in that direction probably being indeterminate (see **Hamlet boundaries**).

Although Batagarawa is the administrative and social centre of Mallamawa District, it is not the centre of economic life to anything like the degree which might be expected. Its weekly market, which was established as recently as 1968 (see **Batagarawa Market**), is of little significance; there is an ancient, though small, market in Dugazawa, a dispersed hamlet a few miles south – and local grain-traders ('*yan kwarami*), whose wives retail the produce from their houses, are found in every hamlet. Just as much of the countryside in the general neighbourhood of Katsina city is not economically peripheral to the *birni*, but rather the general matrix within which settlements of various sizes have crystallized out, so the Mallamawa hamlets are not peripheral to the *gari*.

Population density

According to the 1966 tax registers the population of Mallamawa District was then about 15,000, a figure which has since risen owing to the enlargement of the District in 1967. As there are no official maps showing District boundaries, the area of Mallamawa District cannot be reliably estimated. However, any population density figure relating to the District as a whole would have little relevance to the Batagarawa Hamlet, which includes a larger proportion of uninhabited bush than many Mallamawa hamlets. Even if the area of this Hamlet were known, the corresponding population density figure would probably be misleadingly low, considering that many of the bush-farms (q.v.) cultivated by Batagarawa farmers happen to be situated in other, more densely populated, neighbouring Hamlet Areas.

But although the actual figures of population density are lacking, two conclusions, which are based on aerial photographs, observation and local information, are quite certain. These are, first that population densities in Mallamawa are nowhere so high that bush-farms have been entirely eliminated from the agricultural landscape, as around Kano city, or in parts of certain other Katsina Districts, such as Bindawa to the south; and second that the failure to cultivate much of the bush-land within two or three miles of the *gari* is unrelated to questions of fertility – such land being surplus to requirements.

The ruling-class

For the purposes of this enquiry, four men were classified as *masu-sarauta*, or members of the ruling-class: they were Mallamawa the District Head or Hakimi (Alhaji Dalhatu), Magaji Batagarawa the Village Head, Alhaji Barau the District Head's eldest son, and the District Scribe (Malam Tukur – see each name in the Commentary. Alhaji Barau was included because of his prominence as a farmer, organiser and personality, not by virtue of his office – which is that of Village Scribe. The District Scribe, who is not a member of the ruling-family, was included partly because of his position, but mainly because he and the other three *masu-sarauta* are the only Batagarawa men whose farms are mainly situated in other hamlets. Ibrahim Mukaddas, the Batagarawa Hamlet Head, is not a member of the ruling-family, is never regarded as *mai-sarauta*, and unlike the other men is himself a working farmer, who cultivates local farms – see p. 157: the same reasons justify the exclusion of the present Sarkin Fada, whose late father was a prominent man in Katsina city who removed to Batagarawa, being then appointed Sarkin Fada.

Alhaji Dalhatu is a son of Ibrahim who was the first District Head of Mallamawa (q.v.) to have had his headquarters in Batagarawa (q.v.). A member of an aristocratic family of Katsina city, Ibrahim had earlier been a touring judge (*alkali*); his father (Dalhatu) and his paternal grandfather (Hambali) had also been Katsina *alkalai*, who owned farm-estates at Makurdi (q.v.). When Ibrahim died he was succeeded by Murtala (the late father of the present Magaji Batagarawa), who was in turn succeeded by his younger brother Alhaji Dalhatu.

In terms of his status (see Chapter XIII), Mallamawa stands far apart from his people: but his general style of living is similar (see Fig. 5) – even though all his affairs, including his farming, are conducted on a much larger scale. Apart from his official farm, near the centre of the *gari*, Mallamawa owns farms in about ten other Batagarawa Hamlets on which he produces huge quantities of grain. Unlike the other *masu-sarauta*, he relies, to some extent, on labour services (including ploughing) voluntarily rendered by some of his people, in return for some reward. Although the *masu-sarauta*, as well as Mukaddas and some other prominent men, find it easier than most farmers to attract men to undertake communal farmwork for them for a small reward (*gayya* or *taimako*), they all employ farm-labourers proper (*'yan kwadago*).

All the sons (and some of the daughters) of the *masu-sarauta* attend the Batagarawa primary school, mixing on an entire basis of equality with their schoolmates, with whom they are to be found at most times of the day. Many of the boys and a few of the girls proceed to higher education and thence to occupations in the modern economy. A sample of 138 ex-schoolboys included 18 sons of the ruling-family (among them sons of the late District Head), all save one of whom were either at secondary school or university, or were civil servants, or professional men (see p. 103).

Unlike nearly all other citizens, all the *masu-sarauta* have 'servants' and/or clients attached to them (see *Bara*) most of whom have domestic or farming duties.

Population and housing

According to our 1967 count of the Batagarawa population (which was probably nearly complete except for the omission of a few men with no fixed sleeping-places), there were 1,395 people living in the Batagarawa Hamlet, of whom about 1,163 lived in the *gari* and 232 in dispersed farmhouses. There were found to be about equal numbers of men and women (386 and 399 respectively); and children (of whom there were 610) amounted to 44% of the entire population.

For the purposes of this survey it is appropriate, as will be seen, to regard most members of the population as belonging to a 'farming-unit' – a domestic group, or set of groups, headed by the farmer in charge of cultivating the set of farms on which the group, or groups, depend. Of the 171 farming-units which were distinguished, 48 were defined as *gandaye* (sing. *gandu*) because they included a married male dependant (usually a son or brother) of the head of the farming-unit, who worked on his relative's farms. (Most sons remain in *gandu* with their fathers after marriage – see Chapter III – but fraternal *gandu* is uncommon.) The 1,226 people in these 171 farming-units accounted for 88% of the population (see Table II.1, p. 32), the balance including 64 people in the households of the four *masu-sarauta*.

The structure of the population comprising the 171 farming-units was very simple when analysed in terms of the relationship of individuals to the head of the farming-unit – Tables II.2 and II.3 (p. 33). The 171 heads of farming-units and their 144 sons comprised nearly 90% of the total adult male population, almost all the remainder being brothers (20), sons' sons (11) and brother's sons (6). The 216 wives of heads of farming-units comprised nearly two-thirds of the adult female population, most of the remainder having been son's wives (63 of them), widowed or divorced mothers (32), or brother's wives (13). As many as 32 farming-units included widowed or divorced mothers, probably mainly the former, as it seems that women have higher life expectancies than men (see **Age-structure**).

Over a third of all farming-units (Table II.4, p. 33) had no more than 5 members, and over a half had between 6 and 10 members; nearly all the 140 units in these two size-groups were simple families, or childless married couples, some of them also supporting widowed mothers. At the other extreme there were 4 farming-units, all of them including married sons, with between 20 and 30 members. Half the entire population was in the farming-units with between 6 and 10 members.

Allowing for the 11 heads of farming-units who were retired, the total number of youths and adult men in the 171 farming-units who were available for (though not necessarily performing) agricultural work was 343 (Table II.5, p. 34) – an average of about 2 per farming-unit. But as many as half of the so-called 'heads of farming-units' were in fact single-handed farmers, of whom about three-fifths were estimated to be under forty years old, being unlikely for this reason to have sons of working age. About a quarter of all farming-units included 3 or more working-men – about one half of all working-men being in those units.

The population cannot be satisfactorily classified into domestic-groups, based on either co-residence or shared cooking, as practices vary greatly. When a young man first marries, his wife joins him in the house to which he is already attached, this always being his father's house, if the latter is resident and surviving; apart from the building of a separate sleeping-hut (*daki*) for the bride, the internal structure of the house will remain unchanged, and the bride will assist her husband's mother with the cooking, as though she were a junior co-wife. Later on, there may or may not come a time when the father partitions off a separate section of his house, which will always be approached through the entrance-hut (*zaure*), for the son and his growing family, or the son may or may not remove into an entirely separate house – and this irrespective of whether or not he remains in *gandu*. Thus a father with several sons-in-*gandu* may happen to occupy either one unpartitioned house, or one partitioned house, or several separate houses. Nor does this matter of residence necessarily have much influence on the existence, or otherwise, of separate cooking-groups (see Chapter III).

Furthermore, many houses, especially in the over-crowded *gari*, provide accommodation for more than one farming-unit. Thus, brothers often remain together in the same house, following their father's death, although they do not form a fraternal *gandu*; and house-sections may be sold or rented to non-kin. In fact only 22 of the 56 separate house-sections in Batagarawa are inhabited by sons or brothers in *gandu* – see Table II.6, p. 34.

The enumerated population occupied altogether 184 houses (*gida*), of which 158 were in the *gari*: 39 of these houses were partitioned into two or more separately-occupied sections, the total number of separate sections or living-units being 240 (Table II.7, p. 35).

Over a half of all the living-units (Table II.7) housed between 3 and 6 people. About a seventh of all the units housed only 1 or 2 people, those housing 10 or more people being about the same proportion. Nearly a third of the whole population was in the large living-units housing 10 or more people, the corresponding proportion for the units with 5 to 9 people being about a half.

The word '*mai gida*' (pl. *masu gida*), which is the common and respectful term of address (and reference) for men and husbands, has the literal meaning of 'house-owner', the corresponding term for a woman being *uwar gida* – lit. 'mother of a house'. Insofar as the senior man in a house inhabited by several married men is regarded as the sole *mai gida*, this is owing to his seniority, not his ownership of the house. Little significance attaches to the question of which son lives in a deceased father's house, and in cases where two brothers, who are not in *gandu*, share an unpartitioned house, questions of ownership hardly arise so long as they continue together – each son repairing his own section.

Rainfall and crops

Much emphasis will be placed in this book on the precariousness of economic life in a farming community where (see **Rainfall**) the rainy season (*damuna*) usually lasts for no longer than four to five months; where there is a two-month variation in the date of the planting rains; where crop yields are often adversely affected by insufficient rain or poor distribution within the rainy season; and where manured soils are badly leached by violent storms. Hausa communities vary greatly in the extent of their reliance on marshland (*fadama*) which may be cultivated during the dry season (*rani*). Batagarawa has little *fadama* – see Fig. 6, p. 13 – and nearly all agricultural operations, apart from the application of manure and the clearing of bush-farms, are carried out during the short rainy season and in the few following weeks when guinea corn, late millet and cowpeas are harvested.

The main crops grown by the Batagarawa farmers are grains, cowpeas or beans (*wake*) and groundnuts (*gyada*). The grains – chiefly early millet (*gero*) and guinea corn (*dawa*), but also late millet (*maiwa* or *dauro*) – as well as the cowpeas, are grown both for 'own-consumption' and for sale. The groundnuts are mainly sold to licensed buying agents of the Marketing Board (q.v.) for export overseas, but considerable quantities are used for making groundnut oil – the only type of cooking-oil which is available for local consumption. Subsidiary crops include: tobacco (*taba*), sweet potatoes (*dankali*), cassava (*rogo*), henna (*lalle*), numerous small vegetables, pepper, various tree fruit and seeds (notably locust beans, *dorowa*), rice (*shinkafa*) – this mainly on the small area of *fadama* – and hemp (*rama*). All the tobacco is sold outside Batagarawa; other crops which are sold both inside and outside the village, include sweet potatoes, henna and cassava.

Crop storage

The Hausa farmer not only grows nearly all the produce on which the rural and urban population subsists, but he is also responsible for most of its long-term storage, his traditional receptacles (see **Granary** and Plates 6 to 8) being far more serviceable than any other methods of storage generally available in Hausaland, e.g. city sheds in which bagged grain deteriorates much more rapidly – but see *Soro*. As many as 571 granaries (all here denoted such, whether used for storing grain or other produce) were counted in Batagarawa in 1969, of which 445 were owned by independent farmers, 108 by their dependent sons (see Table II.9, p. 36), 13 of the remainder being owned by the four *masu-sarauta* (most of whose storage was undertaken elsewhere) and 5 by women. Allowing for a few which possibly went uncounted, and for the fact that some storage is undertaken in country areas outside Batagarawa, not only by the ruling-class but also by grain-traders and others, the community possibly owns nearly one granary for each 2 members of the population. About one-third of these granaries were used for storage of early millet (*gero*), another third for guinea corn (*dawa*), the remaining one-third containing groundnuts, cowpeas, fodder, tobacco or crop-mixtures (see Tables II.9 and II.10 p. 36).

Most granaries are inside, or near, the house-compounds, their siting in the *gari* causing much congestion. Grain is stored unthreshed in bundles (*dami*) – see Plate 2 – and groundnuts are stored unshelled. As no one save the owner or sometimes his son, may look inside a granary, it was unfortunately impossible to estimate granary stocks, fundamental though this matter of storage is to any understanding of the working of this economy (see Chapter XII).

Farmland

The bulk of each Batagarawa crop, with the exception of late millet (*maiwa*), is grown on permanently cultivated manured farmland (*karakara*) around the *gari*. All the farms in this zone, with the exception of those in the small area of *fadama*, were mapped with the aid of an air photograph, following ground inspection (see p. 63) and, for the sake of convenience, are sometimes referred to as 'mapped farms' (see Fig. 6, p. 13). Many farmers also cultivate unmanured bush-farms (*gonar daji*) scattered outside this zone, which it was impracticable to map (see **Bush-farms**). The curious shape of the mapped zone mainly results from the proximity of certain neighbouring Hamlets: thus, to the north the zone is bordered by similar manured farmland owned by farmers of Tsauni and other Hamlets.

Despite the fact that land is plentiful, individual farmers prefer to concentrate their farming in the manured zone and some of the most successful of all farmers do not trouble to cultivate any bush-farms. The main types of manure (q.v.) are compound sweepings, including the droppings of small livestock (sheep, goats and donkeys) which are of fundamental importance in this economy, and cattle dung which is partly provided by cattle owned (or cared for) by Batagarawa people (see **Cattle**), partly by non-resident Fulani pastoralists who are paid for bringing their cattle to graze on the farms after harvest. Imported chemical fertilizers (see **Fertilizers**) are very popular, and increasingly applied, but are as yet of little importance relative to natural manures, including latrine manure.

Nearly all writers on rural Hausaland during this century have implicitly, or explicitly, assumed that permanent (or intensive) cultivation only occurs in localities where the population is so dense that farmers are obliged to farm all the cultivable land every year. But there is much evidence for the view – see **Permanent cultivation** and Hill (1970a) – that Batagarawa is not a special case, and for believing that this agronomic *system*, which has been practised for centuries, does not necessarily lead to progressive deterioration of yields. So vast is the extent of permanently cultivated, manured, farmland, that rural Hausaland is certainly unique in West Africa: not even in the densely-populated areas of the 'groundnut basin' of Senegal – see Pelissier (1966) – is there anything comparable.

As has been well known since M. G. Smith undertook his pioneering work in rural Zaria, there are no corporate lineages in Hausaland and accordingly no concept of lineage, or family, land over which lineage members have permanent rights. For practical purposes (see **Farm-selling**) all the manured farmland (as distinct from the land as such) in the Batagarawa mapped zone may be regarded as effectively owned by individuals, *qua* individuals, people who do not even have to consult their immediate relatives if they propose to sell a farm. Men farmers (other than the *masu-sarauta*) own about 92% of the mapped farmland; the *masu-sarauta* (whose farmland is mainly elsewhere) own only 4%; the remaining 4% is owned by women – see **Women farmers**.

In addition to their farms in the mapped zone, a few Batagarawa farmers cultivate manured farms elsewhere, for instance in the intensively cultivated zones around neighbouring hamlets. As these manured farms could not be mapped, they have had to be included in the category 'bush-farm', and our statistics relating to acreages of manured farmland are consequently somewhat deficient.

Most farmers own several separate (non-contiguous) plots (always known as 'farms') in the manured zone, a farmer's holding (or farm-holding) comprising all his plots – see **Farm-holding**. If very small plots of some fifth of an acre or less are omitted (on the grounds that most of them are abandoned house-plots – *kufai*) and if farms owned by sons are included, the proportions of all farming-units which owned 1, 2, 3, 4, or 5 farms are 22%, 30%, 20%, 11% and 9%. The total number of mapped farms owned by the 171 heads of farming-units (together with their male dependants) was 455 (see Table II.11, p. 37) of which 20%, 37%, 18%, 10% and 14% fell into the size-ranges 0·3 to 0·9 acres, 1 to 1·9 acres, 2 to 2·9 acres, 3 to 3·9 acres and 4 acres or more – i.e. more than half of the farms were between 1 and 3 acres (see also Table C.2 on p. 233). The corresponding proportions of the *total area of farmland* which fell into these size-ranges were 5%, 22%, 19%, 14% and 40% (Table C.2. II, p. 233): thus, over half of the acreage consisted of farms of 3 acres or more.

Similar patterns of farm-holding are probably very common in old-established farming areas in Hausaland. The basic reason why most holdings consist of several farms is simply that the farms are not usually established all at once, but gradually over time, often in response to the growth of a farmer's family. When a farmer decides to clear additional farmland it commonly happens that his neighbours have already started to cultivate the land adjoining his own, so that he has to expand further away from his homestead. Although, as will be seen, manured farmland is commonly bought and sold, the same does not apply to land (as such), which is not privately owned; consistently with this, new settlers cannot stake out an advance claim, on their arrival, to a tract of land sufficient for their longer-term requirements.

The same consideration partly accounts for the large number of farms under 3 acres: it seems likely that everywhere in West Africa where farm-plots represent annual clearings by individual farmers, high proportions of farms are in the size-range 1 to 3 acres, and this irrespective of the type of inheritance system. Although in Hausaland (see **Inheritance**) a man's farmland is divided between his sons on his death, it may be that the smaller plots often pass intact to one or other son: if one son then happens to receive less than his fair share he may be financially compensated by his brothers. While some of the smaller farms are portions of larger plots which were divided on death, it is interesting (see p. 185) that very few of the smallest farms, those under one acre, represent portions of larger farms which had been divided on the death of the present owner's father: gifts and loans of farm *portions* largely account for the existence of so many small farms.

Batagarawa farmers are well aware of the superiority of larger farms: better-off farmers often create large farms by buying, or exchanging, plots adjoining their own (see p. 87), and farmers often sell farms to their brothers when they migrate – see Chapter VII. Given the possibilities of migrating for farming and of enlarging the manured zone, there is certainly no need to presume that farms would necessarily become smaller if the population of Batagarawa were to increase.

Marriage, divorce and Muslim seclusion

Virtually all women of child-bearing age in the *gari*, but not (see *Kulle*) in the dispersed farmhouses, are in full Muslim seclusion, to the degree that during the course of a normal day they do not emerge from their compounds. Although some husbands permit their wives to go visiting after dark, and there is more running about than husbands like to suppose, yet as a householder (*uwar gida*) in the centre of the *gari*, the present writer rarely saw a younger woman in the street, unless some special event, such as celebration of the Prophet's name-day, occasioned her release – see Plate 25. Fifty years ago only the wives of practising Malams were in purdah in the *gari*, but now (see **Marriage-types**) purdah-marriage (*auren kulle*) enjoys such prestige on quasi-religious grounds that, for practical purposes, there is no need to distinguish it from other types, as was necessary even as recently as twenty years ago when M. G. Smith worked in Zaria villages.

M. G. Smith has also classified marriages according to various, somewhat overlapping, non-religious criteria. Although the incidence of these types was not studied in Batagarawa, it seems unlikely that 'cousin-marriage' is generally preferred, though very poor men may occasionally be obliged to marry close kin in order to avoid high marriage expenses (q.v.) – see p. 151. The incidence of one type of parallel-cousin marriage, which Smith states (1954a, p. 21) is preferred in Islam, is definitely very low: in a sample of 67 marriages involving partners who were both of Batagarawa origin, there were only 3 unions of brothers' children.

As commonly in West Africa, polygyny is an ideal which many men fail to achieve, or to hold. The main determinant of the average number of wives per husband is the age at which young men first marry, for every girl necessarily marries for the first time when she is about fourteen or fifteen, widows and divorcees are quick to remarry (but see *Takaba*) and there are no bachelors – i.e. men, other than the very young, who have never tried marriage. In Batagarawa where, as already noted, there is a rough balance of the sexes (as there is in Mallamawa District as a whole), only a small degree of polygyny (namely 1·3 wives per head of farming-units, and 1·1 wives per (dependent) man-in-*gandu*) is consistent with men marrying some five to ten years later than women: if, as is always stated, men are marrying earlier than formerly, the average number of wives has, of course, been reduced. So about two-thirds of all husbands who are heads of farming-units, and most men-in-*gandu*, have to make do with only one wife (Table 11.12, p. 37), all but five of the remainder having no more than 2 wives.

In rural Hausaland generally the evidence is that divorce (q.v.), which may be sought by either party, is extremely common, but statistics are fragmentary. Although M. G. Smith has estimated (1954a, p. 26) that 'divorce occurs on average two or three times during a woman's life', this tells us very little, as many women spend their whole married life with one husband, and others are divorced and remarried every few years. As for divorce rates among men, average figures may again be very misleading if our sample of 13 young men for whom divorces were recorded (see p. 150) is at all representative: 7 of these men had contracted one marriage, while 4 others had between them contracted 16 marriages, most of which had ended in divorce. Certainly the general average is high: Smith found that a sample of 89 men in rural Zaria had recorded (1955, p. 21) as many as 24 divorces during the previous three years. In Batagarawa, as elsewhere, remarriage of the same partners often follows divorce.

The initiative in seeking a divorce often comes from the wife, though official records do not necessarily reflect this. Presumably many more wives would seek divorce were it not that husbands have the right, which they often exert (especially in the case of their sons), to claim their children as soon as they have been weaned. 'The man whose wife brings to his home her child by a former marriage (*agola*), under law and social practice cannot retain the child after its genitor demands it, and makes no effort to do so' – Smith (*ibid.*). A wife who is dismissed, maybe on impulse, by her husband, is in similar plight to one who runs away with another man, in regard to her lack of rights over her children.

The physical isolation of women is not quite as complete as the extraordinary combination of general wife-seclusion with a low incidence of polygyny might be thought to imply. Although nearly three-fifths of all Batagarawa wives have no co-wives, only one woman in seven lacks adult female companionship in the house in which she lives.

Of course men tend to justify the strictness of purdah in terms of the women's preference for being freed from heavy household tasks, such as the carrying of water and firewood – they say little about farming obligations, possibly because (see p. 41) the wives of 'heads of farming-units' (unlike sons' wives) did not formerly work alongside the slaves on the *gandu* farms. (In Kauyen Yamma nowadays the unsecluded women mainly work on their own, not their husband's, farms: but they do little farming – see **Women farmers**.)

Such strict rural wife-seclusion occurs nowhere else in Muslim West Africa: perhaps it would not have become so prevalent in rural Hausaland were it not for the high water-table (which permits of the building of many wells) and the ubiquity of the donkey (q.v.), so that without inconvenience to themselves men could excuse women from their traditional function as beasts of burden. Certainly it is necessary to emphasize that these restrictions on personal freedom, which are so much at variance with modern notions of individual rights, are innovatory, not traditional.

Aspects of family life

Few Batagarawa men have any part of the house (*gida*) which they may call their own, other than the entrance-hut (*zaure*) – which is usually little more than a roofed passage, is freely entered by passers-by and shared by all men in the house, and which can seldom be used for storage. Many schoolboys, youths and unmarried men, have no proper sleeping place, unless a relative, such as a grandmother, provides one; they are often obliged to roam the streets at night, perhaps sleeping in gangs in a *zaure* or under a tree. Each wife has her own thatched hut (*daki*), where she keeps her bed, clothing and other possessions, and where infants and other girls also sleep. Husbands join their wives in their huts at bed-time; those with two or more wives sleep with each of them in strict rotation, commonly for two successive nights, but sometimes for one or three. Although, in principle, cooking duties follow the same rotation, in practice the various women in a house, including sons' wives, tend to work together when cooking the evening meal (*tuwo*), especially during the farming-season (*damuna*) – see p. 50.

It is the husband's duty to provide all the grain and meat (as well as firewood) required by his dependants, and to give his wife a daily sum in cash (*kudin cefane*) for the purchase of other ingredients such as groundnut oil, vegetables, locust-bean cakes (*daddawa*), salt, natron, etc., which are usually bought from secluded women house-traders (see **House-trade**) – a wife may even buy from herself. If a husband cannot provision his dependants from his own granaries, then it is his duty to buy the necessary grain himself or to provide cash. But these are mere norms and many wives help their husbands to meet their food expenses and many male dependants in poorer households fend for themselves, buying cooked food.

When discussing grain allocations (*dauki*), informants always state the quantities in terms of the numbers of *tiya* – a standard measuring bowl – issued daily. But as grain which a farmer has grown himself is always stored unthreshed in bundles in granaries and as the quantity threshed on any occasion is usually sufficient for several days, if not for as long as a week, many husbands are in fact unaware of the exact quantities (in threshed grain equivalents) which they extract from their granaries, but trust their wives to store the threshed grain in their huts, and to measure the appropriate quantity daily.

Husbands partake of their meals separately from other members of their households. Women, young children and girls of all ages, eat together. Older boys, youths and unmarried men often consort with age-mates in any convenient place. After the evening meal, which is the main repast of the day (see *Tuwo*), the sexes remain separated until it is bed-time, the husbands chatting outside their compounds with other men.

Husbands and wives are never seen together in public and avoid addressing each other by name. Although the life-long avoidance-cum-shame relationship (*kunya*) between either parent and their first-born son or daughter remains extremely strong, and also involves reciprocal name-avoidance, this takes particular expression in the presence of others. Non-reciprocal name-avoidance involves certain affines (*suruki*) (see also *Abokin wasa*).

Child adoption (*tallafa*) is common in rural Hausaland, almost always involving close kin. For the purposes of this book there has been no statistical need to distinguish between a man's own children, adopted children (*tallafi*) and wife's children (*agola*), all of whom are dependent on him so long as they remain in his household.

A man's wives (*mata*) are ranked in the order in which he married them, the senior being the *uwar gida*, the junior being known as *amarya* (lit. 'bride') however long she has been married. Although the word for a co-wife is 'the jealous one' (*kishiya*), the capacity of many secluded co-wives to co-operate harmoniously, although constantly in each other's presence, is often much more remarkable than their jealous bickering. Of course it is often the wives themselves, especially the older among them, who urge their husbands to marry additional women, for the sake of the work-sharing and companionship.

'Babies are from the father, merely housed by the mother in her womb until birth' (personal comment by Murray Last) and accordingly a man's property (see **Inheritance**) is divided equally among his sons on his death without regard to whether they had different mothers. As, in addition, the question of whether men are full or half brothers appears to have little bearing on *gandu* organization, all sons of the same father are denoted 'brothers' in this book (see **Kinship terminology**).

The role of cash

Such is the stage of the present debate, that were Batagarawa to be denoted, without more ado, as a village with a 'cash economy', this would amount to an acceptance of the practicability of distinguishing it from a 'subsistence economy'. The objection to such a dichotomy is not merely that virtually all West African rural economies are 'mixed' (the relative size of the subsistence sector being, almost by definition, extremely hard to evaluate), but also that 'subsistence' is a word of so many connotations. Thus, even if it were accepted that 'subsistence versus cash' is a matter of degree, there remains the issue of whether to measure the ratio in terms of, for instance: (a) the degree to which different physical outputs are *conceived of* as having relative cash values (this involving quantification as well as valuation); (b) the extent to which agricultural and other output is actually sold for cash; (c) the size of the market for the factors land and labour; or (d) the degree of self-sufficiency of the economy, whether defined as a single village or a wider community. In the West African context, a community like Batagarawa would be likely to have a high cash to subsistence ratio on some of these criteria and a low ratio on others. If emphasis were placed on the degree to which the output of goods and services of women working at home was sold for cash by the women themselves, to their own husbands as well as to others, then Batagarawa might even rate higher than the United States.

However, it is still possible that the idea of separate subsistence and cash sectors *within* the economy might be analytically useful, or that cash and subsistence *farmers* might be distinguished. Would either of these approaches be analytically helpful in Batagarawa?

There are many farmers in Batagarawa who are subsistence farmers in the narrow sense that they consume all the grain that they grow. Some of these farmers – the proportion in any season depending mainly on the weather – may happen to be neither grain-buyers nor grain-sellers; others may be both grain-buyers and grain-sellers, for instance buying grain at harvest when it is cheap and storing it for resale when the price has risen; others, again, may be grain-buyers only. So different are the circumstances of such subsistence farmers (as defined) that the category is not a useful one.

Alternatively, the subsistence farmer might be defined as one who grew (or even aimed to grow) all the grain required for his own consumption. But the class of non-subsistence farmer would then include both richer farmers who prefer to buy some grain for their own consumption from the proceeds from selling groundnuts, as well as those who rely on bought grain because they farm on too small a scale to meet their own needs – and the latter group are hardly 'cash farmers'.

Thirdly, a cash farmer might be defined as a man who sold some part of his produce. Again, this would involve the grouping together of richer farmers who sell grain surplus to their requirements and poorer farmers who are forced to sell grain at harvest, owing to lack of cash, to pay the community tax (*haraji*), meet their debts, etc. Besides, virtually all farmers who grow some groundnuts (and groundnuts are grown by rich and poor alike) would then count as cash farmers, for nearly all the groundnuts produced (other than those retained as seed) are sold either for export, or for oil-making, or as seed for other farmers.

So, it would not be logical to distinguish cash and subsistence farmers. The arguments against isolating cash and subsistence *sectors* of the economy are equally strong. Crops which are grown mainly or entirely for selling include (non-commercial) tobacco, groundnuts, cassava, sweet potatoes and henna. But grains and cowpeas, which are produced by virtually all farmers, are grown either for self-consumption, or for selling, the actual ratio for any individual often depending on unforseeable circumstances, such as yields, seasonal price variations and expectations, irregular types of expenditure and so forth. Although there is, at all seasons, an active market in grains, groundnuts and cowpeas (a market which is no less effective because it happens not to be conducted in a market-place), this does not mean that conventional notions about the wisdom of growing grains for self-consumption are lacking: certainly all better-off farmers aim at producing a considerable proportion of their grain requirements, and readily justify this in terms of the dire consequences of widespread breaking of this rule. (Farmers are also very well aware of the dangers, for climatic reasons, of concentrating on one crop.) But individual conformity to a convention which is partly based on notions of the common good, does not imply the existence of a subsistence *sector*.

Of course, as in all societies, some subsistence *activities* may be distinguished. Insofar as men-in-*gandu* receive no cash wages, being rewarded in terms of grain (or foodstuffs) for their own consumption, they are subsistence producers. Then husbands have an obligation to provide their wives with basic foodstuffs, in return for their cooking, child-rearing and sexual activities. But the note-worthy fact is not the existence of these subsistence activities, but the freedom possessed by both the man-in-*gandu* and the woman-in-marriage to engage in cash-rewarded activities outside their contractual obligations.

Four possible bases for measuring the 'degree of subsistence' were mentioned above (p. 26), on which some qualitative notes will now be made, starting with (a) and (b). The first point to note is that barter or exchange (q.v.) is both uncommon and casual, mainly involving women in somewhat furtively exchanging types of produce, mostly grain, issued to them by their husbands for household cooking. (Nor is the unimportance of barter necessarily anything new, cowries (q.v.) having been a very practical form of currency for small purchases throughout the nineteenth century.) Secondly, it is not only true that almost everything in Batagarawa is conceived of as having a cash value, but that almost everything is apt to be bought and sold. Household sweepings and the droppings of small livestock and birds are sold as manure. Cornstalks, various types of grass, groundnut haulms and shells, twigs, fodder-leaves, bran, wood, palm fronds... all are useful as raw materials for building and craftwork, as fodder, or as firewood for cooking – and all command a price. Cattle (q.v.) are not reared for the sake of prestige, but for selling to butchers. Small livestock – sheep and goats – as well as fowls (*kaza*) are mainly reared for selling; and eggs, which are nowadays much relished by some people, command a very high price. Only donkey-meat, which is subject to Muslim taboo, goes to waste.

So far as concerns homogeneous, measurable produce, such as grains, groundnuts and cowpeas, retail price is always expressed in terms of the standard measuring bowl (*tiya*) and the prices ruling on any day (see Chapter IX) are well-known to the general populace, including children who play an important role in linking the secluded women house-traders. Seasonal price fluctuations are both severe and erratic and are earnestly studied by the entire population.

In many West African communities most farmers provide most of their own seed and planting material. But in Batagarawa (as elsewhere in Hausaland) many farmers store no groundnuts and buy or borrow all their seed, mainly from other local farmers. Many farmers lack grain seed at planting-time, their granaries being then empty.

Turning to (c), the market for land and labour, the selling of manured farmland is an old practice which is becoming increasingly common (see Chapter VI), though prices are still often very low in relation to annual yields. Farm labour employment (*kwadago*), involving the employment of one farmer (or farmer's son) by another – there is no landless labouring-class – is quite common (see Chapter VIII). Considerable employment (likewise known as *kwadago*) is also provided by builders, who require earth to be dug, transported, mixed and handled.

Then, women are much given to employing each other for payment (*aikatau*), both on ordinary domestic tasks such as threshing, winnowing, grinding or pounding of grains and on the processing of groundnut oil and locust-bean cakes (*daddawa*) for sale: they also pay certain specialists, such as hairdressers, for personal services. Farmers pay women (including their wives) for many tasks, including de-stalking threshed groundnuts, winnowing mechanically-shelled groundnuts, vegetable-picking and rice-boiling. Men, also, pay each other for many types of service rendered, including clothes-washing, barbering, house-repairing and donkey transport.

On the final question, that of the self-sufficiency of Batagarawa as an 'island community', the village's principal exports are such groundnuts as are sold to licensed buying agents, for eventual export overseas. Minor 'export crops' include cowpeas, sweet potatoes, cassava, etc., which are sold for consumption by Nigerians outside Batagarawa, as well as tobacco, some of which is destined for consumers in the Niger Republic. Except possibly in years when harvests are quite unusually good, grains (mainly from nearby areas) are presumably one of the two main types of 'import', cloth and clothing (the former mainly manufactured in factories in northern Nigeria) being the other; a great variety of other types of ware for local general consumption (such as salt, natron, kerosene, soap, kola-nuts, matches, cigarettes, cooking-pots, mats, hurricane lamps, torches, batteries and grindstones) are purchased in Katsina city, in neighbouring markets, or from visiting traders.

Other miscellaneous points bearing on the cash-orientation of this economy may be mentioned here. There is a large trade in cooked foodstuffs prepared by secluded women, these consisting not only of numerous tasty snacks (see **House-trade**), but also of complete evening meals. Then, most items of capital equipment are hired out for cash (some of them even being acquired for this purpose alone), the list including imported ploughs, groundnut decorticators and bicycles, but not motor vehicles, of which there are none in Batagarawa. House and house-sections are sometimes rented – though more usually sold. Farms are rented for cash (*aro*), share-cropping not being practised.

The surprise usually registered by 'Europeans' when they learn that Hausa people who are related by kinship or marriage habitually pay each other for goods or services rendered, not necessarily expecting special terms owing to their relationship, is based on a failure to realize that rural Hausa do not share the pejorative European attitude to cash (*kudi*) as filthy lucre, or regard 'working merely for monetary or other reward' in the derogatory sense of 'mercenary'. 'Cash' is a positive good, and there is no reason why personal relationship should create any inhibitions about giving or receiving it. A woman who makes groundnut oil for sale is in business on her own account and there is nothing immodest about buying groundnuts from her husband at the market price, or about buying oil from herself with her 'housekeeping money' (*kudin cefane*). It is true that there is a great deal of secrecy about the sale of farms by fathers to sons (which is very common), but this is involved with doubt about the extent of a father's well-recognized duty to give farmland to sons-in-*gandu*. (Husbands and wives readily admit to selling farms to one another, the point being that neither party ever has an obligation to give farms to the other.) The very practical, unemotive, positive attitude to cash is well illustrated by the fact that a brother who migrates for farming is never expected to give his farmland to a brother, only to offer him the first refusal of buying it for cash at the market price. Then, cash contributions are usually an important component of all types of ceremonial expenditure (see **Marriage expenses, Naming-cere-mony**) and there is never anything derogatory about slipping someone a sum in cash on occasions when most participants donate foodstuffs. The relationship between female bond-friends (*kawa*) is largely cemented by cash contributions – see *Biki* (see also *Adashi*).

One reason why most men have one or more non-farming occupations (which may be pursued all the year round, or during the dry season only) is that these provide them with the possibility of raising cash for purchasing foodstuffs, for use in emergencies, or for financing their farming, both when their granaries are empty and when, owing to low seasonal prices, the sale of stored produce would be unwise. About a fifth of the 171 heads of farming-units (see Table v.1, p. 72) had trading as their primary non-farming occupation; about a seventh were craftsmen; about a seventh were firewood-collectors or makers of such goods as thatches or cornstalk beds, which are made from materials which may be freely collected; the remainder included 'servants' (*bara*) – mainly employed by the *masu-sarauta*, – labourers, butchers and Koranic teachers (see **Malam**).

This is not to say that remuneration is always in cash and never in kind: thus, farm-labourers are paid partly in cash and partly in porridge (*fura*) which is served on the farm, and are sometimes offered the alternative of grain rather than cash; and women who harvest cowpeas may be allowed to retain all that they pluck after a certain time of day. Domestic servants, most of whom have sought refuge from their poverty by a partial withdrawal from the economy, are mainly remunerated with food. Nor is the communal labour system (*gayya*), which declined in importance as farm-labour employment (*kwadago*) increased, at all likely to vanish altogether.

There is no shortage of labour in Batagarawa, in the sense that (see Chapter VIII) individual farmers with cash available, may recruit, at the standard wage, all the daily labourers they require, without detriment to other farmers or to the farming undertaken by the labourers themselves. Nor, as has been seen, is there any shortage of farming-land. So any diagnosis of poverty in terms of 'scarce factors' must classify the Batagarawa economy as suffering from a shortage of working capital, but not of land or labour. There is nothing subtle about such a practical conclusion, but rather everything that is appropriate to a cash-orientated economy, based on the intensive cultivation of manured farmland.

It is argued elsewhere (see **Usury**) that much standard economic behaviour in a rural economy like Batagarawa is necessarily usurous according to Muslim law. But it is doubtful whether formal, legal or official attitudes to such matters as interest-taking have much effect on the day-to-day workings of this rural economy, if the wide economic framework within which it is operating are taken for granted. From the angle of economic development the real question (which lies right outside the scope of this book) is whether official attitudes to usury prevent the introduction of government reforms, relating for instance to grain-trading or storage, which would raise the living standards of the rural populace – see **Economic regulations** and Chapter xiv.

Modernization

Some of the main socio-economic changes that have come about since the British occupation, such as the strict seclusion of women, have already been discussed, and others will emerge in the course of this book. At this stage it is only necessary to emphasize that despite some measure of 'modernization', there are many ways in which economic life remains basically unchanged – see **Farm-tools.** Farm-tools (other than the oxen-drawn plough (q.v.) which is a most important innovation) are still made by local blacksmiths. The donkey is mainly used for transporting crops, manure and trade goods – there are no carts. Houses, granaries and domestic wells are of traditional construction, there being only a small usage of manufactured (as distinct from local) cement. There is no piped water, modern sanitation, electric light, telephone or post office in the *gari*. Despite the establishment, as long ago as 1946, of an excellent primary school, which has recently enabled many young men to enter higher education and to take up jobs in the modern sector (see p. 103), there is a fairly low level of literacy in Hausa and English, except among present-day school-children and recent school-leavers – see literacy statistics on p. 287 – and most of the many ex-schoolboys who remain in the village (see pp. 98 and 100) keep few records in connexion with trading and other kinds of business transactions, including farm-selling. (Almost all 'reading' is still Koranic and Arabic is taught in the school.)

Apart from the single mechanical grinding mill (which is apt to fall out of order for long periods), and the 15 (or so) groundnut decorticators (q.v.), which are mainly used for shelling nuts destined for export, food processing methods are as laborious and time-wasting as ever, mainly involving the hand grindstone and the pestle and mortar. (However, it must be sadly admitted that were women to be liberated from this traditional drudgery, other kinds of output would hardly increase, as the area within which they can trade is so severely limited by their seclusion.)

The introduction of the lorry has greatly reduced the risk of famine, by extending the area from which grain supplies may be drawn; but this vehicle has not proved an unmixed blessing to the people of Batagarawa if, as seems likely, it has led to long-distance trade being much more urban-based than in the old days of the donkey-caravan (see *Fatauci*). Improved availability of many manufactured goods, especially cloth, may be on balance beneficial, but an offsetting factor is the associated decline of traditional crafts, such as weaving and dyeing, which have been replaced by few modern crafts or industries.

The northern Nigerian economy as a whole has undoubtedly benefited from the huge expansion of groundnut-growing for export. But (taking one year with the next) there is no agronomical evidence that in a locality like Batagarawa groundnuts often yield a higher net return than grains per unit of effort, with export duties, which are effectively paid by the farmer, at their present high level – see **Marketing Board**. Then, massive groundnut exporting may be deleterious nutritionally, if it has resulted in raising the price of groundnut oil (q.v.), above the level which can be afforded by many poorer farmers.

It cannot be taken for granted that (the risk of famine apart) general life expectancies are higher than in former times. Certainly smallpox is controlled by vaccination and leprosy will soon be a scourge of the past; but if the incidence of acute rural poverty is higher than formerly, death-rates might have risen. Certainly, most Batagarawa citizens receive no modern medical attention before they die; however, cyclists can nowadays carry messages quickly to Katsina city and an over-worked ambulance is occasionally summoned successfully.

All of which speculation is intended to say no more than that rising standards of living in rural areas follow no more automatically from the small degree of 'modernization' so far achieved, than did 'freedom from want' from the Pax Britannica.

STATISTICAL TABLES

TABLE II.I. *Classification of Batagarawa population*

Households	Men	Women (Numbers)	Children[a]	Total	%
Masu-sarauta[b]	7	17	40	64	5
Farming-units[c]	354	341	531	1,226	88
Other[d]	25	41	39	105	8
Total	386	399	610	1,395	100
	28%	29%	44%	100%	

(a) Including all unmarried girls and all schoolboys and boys of school-age.
(b) See p. 16.   (c) See p. 17.
(d) Including 66 members of households which made no appreciable attempt to maintain themselves by farming, the heads of which included certain 'servants' (*bara*) and musicians (see **Maroki**) as well as a few retired men and older husbandless women. The investigator, her family, and assistants, are excluded.

TABLE II.2. *The relationship of adult male dependants to heads of farming-units*

Relationship to head of farming-unit	Number of men	%	
Heads of farming-units			
active	160 ⎫ 171	45	
retired	11 ⎭	3	
Sons[a]			
married	58 ⎫ 144	16	
unmarried	86 ⎭	24	
Brothers	20	6	
Sons' sons	11	3	
Brothers' sons	6	2	
Other	2	1	
Total	354	100	

(a) See p. 25.

TABLE II.3. *Women dependants of heads of farming-units*

Relationship to head of farming-unit	Number of women	%
Wives	216	63
Sons' wives	63	18
Brothers' wives	13	4
Other wives	3	1
Total wives	295	86
Mothers[a] (widowed or divorced)	32	9
Others with no resident husband[b]	14	4
	46	13
Total	341	100

(a) Including one mother's mother.
(b) Mainly daughters who were temporary visitors as a result of childbirth or divorce.

TABLE II.4. *Size of farming-units*

Number of persons per farming-unit	Number of farming-units	%	Total number of persons	%
1	5 ⎫		5 ⎫	
2	10 ⎪		20 ⎪	
3	15 ⎬ 65	38	45 ⎬ 233	19
4	12 ⎪		48 ⎪	
5	23 ⎭		115 ⎭	
6–10	80	47	597	49
11–15	15	9	188	15
16–20	9	5	157	13
21–30	2	1	51	4
Total	171	100	1,226	100

TABLE II.5. *Size of family work-groups*

Number of men in work-group	Number of farming-units	%	Total number of working men	%
1	80	47	80	23
2	47	27	94	27
3	25	15	75	22
4	9	5	36	10
5	7	4	35	10
6	1	..	6	2
7	1	..	7	2
10	1	..	10	3
Total	171	100	343	100

NOTES

(i) The table relates to the potential farming labour-force available to each farming-unit.

(ii) Boys of school-age and retired fathers are excluded.

(iii) All heads of farming-units, save the old and infirm, are regarded as 'working', with two exceptions.

TABLE II.6. *Relationship of heads of house-sections to heads of houses*

(Number of house-sections)		
Sons-in-*gandu*	20 ⎱	22
Sons not in *gandu*	2 ⎰	
Brothers-in-*gandu*	2 ⎱	16
Brothers not in *gandu*	14 ⎰	
Brothers' sons not in *gandu*		7
Father's brother's sons not in *gandu*		2
Sister's son, not in *gandu*		1
Unspecified elderly kinsman		1
Non-kin		
retired drummer	1 ⎱	
heads of farming-units	3 ⎰	7
sanitary inspectress	1	
other	1	
Total		56

NOTE. For the purposes of this table a house-section is defined as any section partitioned-off by the house-owner – the latter's own portion being excluded. See p. 18.

TABLE II.7. *Population by house and house-section*

Number of persons in house or house-section	Number of living-units			Number of persons		
	Undivided houses	House-sections	Total	Undivided houses	House-sections	Total
1	8[a]	4	12	8	4	12
2	11	10	21	22	20	42
3	18	21	39	54	63	117
4	16	11	27	64	44	108
5	19	12	31	95	60	155
6	20	8	28	120	48	168
7	11	7	18	77	49	126
8	14	8	22	112	64	176
9	4	3	7	36	27	63
10–14	20	9	29	227	95	322
15–19	4	1	5	69	15	84
22	—	1	1	—	22	22
Total	145	95	240	884	511	1395

NOTES

(a) Most of these are not houses (*gida*) proper.
(i) See Note on Table II.6. For the purposes of this table the house-owner's portion of a divided house *is* regarded as a house-section.

TABLE II.8. *Ownership of granaries*

Number of granaries per farmer	Granary owners		
	Heads of farming-units	Men-in-gandu (Number of owners)	Total
1	35	22	57
2	64	21	85
3	30	5	35
4	20	1	21
5	5	3	8
6 or more	11	..	11
Total	165	52	217

NOTES

(i) Exclusive of those who own no granaries.
(ii) The granary count was made in 1969.
(iii) Exclusive of granaries owned by: the *masu-sarauta*; men who are not members of farming-units; and women.

TABLE II.9. *Ownership of granaries by type of produce stored:* (*A*)

	Owners		
Type of crop	Heads of farming-units	Men-in-*gandu* (Number of granaries)	Total
Sole crops			
Millet (*gero*)	158	35	193
Guinea corn (*dawa*)	143	34	177
Groundnuts (*gyada*)	31	7	38
Late millet (*maiwa*)	11	—	11
Cowpeas (*wake*)	4	2	6
Tobacco (*taba*)	2	—	2
Crop mixtures			
Millet and guinea corn	36	19	55
Other	47	9	56
Fodder	13	2	15
Total	445	108	553

NOTES

(i) See notes on Table II.8.
(ii) See also Table II.10.

TABLE II.10. *Ownership of granaries by type of produce stored:* (*B*)

	Owners		
Sole crops and mixtures	Heads of farming-units	Men-in-*gandu* (Number of granaries)	Total
Millet (*gero*)	197	56	253
Guinea corn (*dawa*)	193	58	251
Groundnuts (*gyada*)	50	7	57
Late millet (*maiwa*)	35	4	39
Cowpeas (*wake*)	21	4	25
Tobacco (*taba*)	2	—	2
Fodder	14	—	14
Not known	9	—	9

NOTES

(i) See notes on Table II.8.
(ii) The table shows the total number of granaries used for storing each particular crop, whether as a sole crop or as a mixture. Granaries containing mixtures are, therefore, counted more than once, and no grand total is shown. See also Table II.9.

TABLE II.11. *Ownership of manured farms by farm-area*

Acreage range	Heads of farming-units (1)	Men-in-gandu (2)	Cols. (1) + (2)	*Masu-sarauta*	Other men farmers	Women farmers	Total
			(Number of farms)				
0·3–0·9	70	21	91	3	3	26	123
1·0–1·9	134	36	170	1	9	19	199
2·0–2·9	75	8	83	2	2	2	89
3·0–3·9	38	9	47	1	—	—	48
4·0–4·9	13	3	16	2	1	—	19
5·0–9·9	37	2	39	3	1	—	43
10·0–14·9	6	1	7	—	—	—	7
15·0–18·9	2	—	2	—	—	—	2
Total	375	80	455	12	16	47	530

NOTES

(i) Very small farms under about 0·3 acres are omitted, most of them being former house-plots (*kufai*).
(ii) See p. 21.

TABLE II.12. *Number of wives per husband*

Number of wives of husband	*Masu-sarauta*	Heads of farming-units[a]	Men-in-gandu	Total
		(Number of husbands)		
1	—	108	68	176
2	—	48	4	52
3	3	4	1	8
5	1	—	—	1
	4	160	73	237
		(Total number of wives)		
8	—	108	68	176
2	—	96	8	104
3	9	12	3	24
4	4	—	—	4
	13	216	79	308
Average number of wives per husband	3·2	1·3	1·1	1·3

(a) Excluding the 11 heads of farming-units (most of them young men) who were unmarried.

CHAPTER III

Fathers and sons in *gandu*

The Hausa institution of paternal *gandu* is a voluntary, mutually advantageous, agreement between father and married son, under which the son works in a subordinate capacity on his father's farms in return for a great variety of benefits including a share of the food supplies. Nowadays in Batagarawa the *gandu* group usually, though not invariably, dissolves within a year or two of the father's death, when each son appropriates a portion of the *gandu* farmland and sets up as an independent farmer.

Starting with a general historical introduction, this chapter deals mainly with paternal *gandu* in Batagarawa. It lists the numerous rights and obligations which reciprocally link fathers and sons and considers the extent to which actual practices deviate from stated norms. It is concerned with the incidence of *gandu* and the circumstances in which sons leave *gandu*. It presents material relating to the 'private farming' of sons-in-*gandu*. It examines the fragility of fraternal *gandu*. But consideration of many wider related issues is postponed until later chapters.

The word 'gandu'

The word '*gandu*' has many different meanings. It may denote a farm (or farms), a group of men, the relationship between the men concerned, a condition of trust, a large farm, a farm owned by a chief in virtue of his office, tribute (or tax), or a store of money (*gandun kudi*). The word in its present-day usage among Muslim Hausa should never be identified, in the manner of several writers, with the 'extended family', nor with 'ancestral land'.

In relation to farming organization, the word is colloquially used in many expressions, which are often literally translatable. The question 'Are you in *gandu*?' is literally rendered '*Kana cikin gandu?*'; and 'I am in *gandu* with my father' is '*Ina gandu tare da mahaifina*'. The relationship between father and son is reciprocal to the degree that either party may describe themselves as 'in *gandu*' (*cikin gandu*) with the other. A son who wishes to convey that it was he who left *gandu* against the wishes of his father may say '*Na fita gandu*' (lit. 'I left *gandu*') – and a father who took the initiative in dismissing his son may use the verb '*sallama*' ('leave to depart') as a euphemism for 'driving out'.

'*Gandu*' and the Maguzawa

Greenberg's study of certain pagan Hausa (Maguzawa) in Kano Emirate throws much light on the evolution of *gandu* among Islamised Hausa. With the Maguzawa 'the ancestral land, known as *gandu*' – Greenberg (1946, p. 17) – was usually held collectively by a number of brothers, 'being considered as a trust placed in the care of the oldest brother, who may not alienate or sell any of it without the consent of his fellows'. Most brothers remained in *gandu*, working with their wives and children for four days a week during the farming-season, being free to work on their private plots (*gayawna*) – which had been 'temporarily separated from the *gandu*' – on other days and in the evening. The wives of the *gandu* head and his married sons also received private farms. The grain stored in the *gandu* granary might not be touched during the dry season, and those with private farms were required to take turns in feeding the *gandu* head during this time, often doing so with the help of their wives. The *gandu* head was expected to sell grain to meet the marriage expenses of *gandu* members. Younger brothers usually left this fraternal *gandu* when their own sons had grown up. It was 'a rare, and scandalous situation for a son to leave his father's compound during the latter's lifetime' – Greenberg (1947, p. 194).

In some instances 'cousins related only through a common grandfather or even great-grandfather' inhabited a large compound of perhaps a hundred people, but sooner or later such groups broke up owing to 'their unwieldiness and through a lack of sufficient arable land in the vicinity' (*ibid.*, p. 194). The land cultivated by members of the same compound was 'considered to belong to the patrilineal core collectively', the 'compound head being merely the administrator with well-defined privileges and obligations'.

An earlier, detailed and serious study of Maguzawa in southern Kano by Krusius (1915), suggests that the institution of *gandu* had changed little during the thirty years before Greenberg was in the field. At the earlier date, members of the family had worked for four days a week on the *gandu* farm, and all *gandu* produce was separately stored – being used (*ibid.*, p. 302) for paying tax, buying clothes, entertaining visitors, making beer, 'raising children' and nourishing the entire family during the farming-season.

'*Gandu*' and slavery

In the nineteenth century slaves and sons worked together on the *gandu* farms, as do sons and paid labourers ('*yan kwadago*) today. But the literature on farm-slavery is extremely scanty, this rather reflecting the dearth of relevant material in Hausa and Arabic manuscripts, than dis-interest on the part of present-day historians. (There are scarcely any references to farm-slavery in the various collections of oral stories such as *Tatsuniyoyi* – see Skinner (1969) – perhaps partly because many of them pre-dated rural slavery.) Then, Barth unfortunately took note rather of the food crops than of those seen cultivating them.

However, when Clapperton was at Sokoto in 1826 he made some detailed observations on rural slavery – Clapperton (1829, pp. 213–14). At the age of eighteen or nineteen, farm-slaves were given a wife and sent to live in the country, being provided with their food until harvest. They were allowed to 'enclose' portions of land for their own use and, having laboured on their master's farms in the morning, might work on these plots if they wished. Allocations of grain were made to them at harvest. During the farming-season, if not at other times, slaves were 'fed the same as the rest of the family', with whom they appeared to be 'on an equality of footing'.

However many slaves there were in Hausaland (and it is difficult not to believe – see **Slavery** – that some observers made inflated estimates), their distribution must have been very uneven, so that many free farmers lacked slave labour. Yet the traveller Staudinger (1889) gives the general impression (see, e.g., p. 608) that the slaves of the richer farmers did most of the farming in Hausaland, and even asserts (p. 579) that the Hausa pursued agriculture only as a side-line! Whatever the importance of huge slave estates in some localities (e.g. parts of rural Zaria), common sense suggests that many, if not most, farm-slaves may have been employed by ordinary farmers (corresponding, for example, to a few of the richest farmers in Batagarawa today) whose small numbers of slaves were an adjunct (not an alternative) to their family labour-forces – Krusius (1915, p. 299) referred to master and slave as working alongside each other.

Given the lack of source material, the following brief description of *gandu* at the end of the nineteenth century is necessarily based only on *Baba of Karo* – Mary Smith (1954) – to which has been added oral information obtained from Abubakar Labo (q.v.) of Kaukai near Batagarawa.

Abubakar Labo, who was born soon after 1880, insisted that *gandu* had existed in the time of his father's father. The word, as employed in his youth, had most of its present connotations, but was also applied (as it is not today) to non-farming occupations, so that a son who accompanied his father on long-distance trading (*fatauci*) was in *gandu* with him. To this informant two special connotations of '*gandu*' were 'obedience' and 'trust': 'a slave has got to obey before he is trusted, so from obedience comes trust' – which is to say that, having become trustworthy, the slave is *cikin gandu*.

Sometimes slaves and sons-in-*gandu* were accorded similar treatment (the latter being regarded as in training for future responsibility), sometimes the sons were treated more leniently. Sometimes the master himself did not work, but rather, as Baba humourously put it (*ibid.*, p. 44), donned his best clothes 'and sat in the shade and watched'. A well-trusted slave, known as *sarkin gandu*, was often in charge of the farmwork, having authority over sons and slaves alike, and maybe himself avoiding heavy work. When *sarkin gandu* married, he would be given a farm and a house and although he might be freed from slavery, he would never be released from *gandu*. When the master died the sons continued to respect *sarkin gandu* and to consult him in all they were doing. *Sarkin gandu* might also be *sarkin gida*, then being responsible for provisioning his master's house.

Slaves-in-*gandu*, like sons, were obliged to work on the *gandu* farms until the afternoon prayer (*azafar*), but the sons had two off-days when they were free to work on their private farms (*gayauna*) or to pursue any other occupation. As in Clapperton's time, slaves often had *gayauni*, being free (like the sons) to work on them in the evening – or, as Baba reported (*ibid.*, p. 41), in the very early morning. (In the second edition of C. H. Robinson's *Hausa Dictionary*, 1906, *gayauna* was, indeed, defined as 'a farm given by a master to his slave on which he works on Sundays and Thursdays'.)

The question of the extent to which free women cultivated the *gandu* farms is quite obscure, as is that of women's participation in farming generally. Perhaps there were times and circumstances when the following extract from a poem, which was said to have been reduced to writing about 1866, was more than romanticisation:

> Farm-work is not becoming for a wife you know; she is free,
> you may not put her to hoe grass (as a slave).
>
> Robinson (1896c, p. 6)

Certainly M. G. Smith reports (1960, p. 92, fn. 1) that in Zaria in 1865 free-born women did no farming; and Meek (1925, p. 233) goes so far as to assert that '...among the Muslim peoples generally only slave-women formerly engaged in farming operations'. In reference to the position of Maguzawa women, Krusius asserted (1915, pp. 298–9) that they worked hard unlike their Muslim sisters.

According to Abubakar Labo, although the wives of the *gandu* head were not required to work on the *gandu* farms, sons' wives (like slaves' wives) were so required, though they were allowed to break off work earlier than the men in order to attend to their domestic tasks. A son could not excuse his wife from working on his father's farm; and on his off-days his wife worked with him on his *gayauna*, unless she had a plot of her own.

On these farms, as Baba relates (Mary Smith, 1954, p. 41), 'everyone grew guinea corn, cotton, millet, cowpeas, sweet potatoes, pumpkins, groundnuts, peppers, bitter tomatoes, sugar-cane, rice, *iburu*, okras, tomatoes and green peppers'. Both slaves and sons were free to dispose of their farm produce as they wished. The sons and slaves received food and clothing in return for their farming work and were assisted in numerous other ways. Porridge (*fura*) was served on the farm and wives received grain to cook for themselves. In the evening, according to Baba, all members of her grandfather's dependent families, who lived in a separate hamlet (*rinji*), came to his house where they partook of a meal which had been prepared with the help of the dependent wives.

First-generation slaves who had been bought in the market were permitted to do nothing but farm, but their sons (*dimajai*) pursued independent craft-work: according to Baba (*ibid.*, p. 42) 'Some wove on the men's narrow loom, some were brokers in the market, some were salt-sellers, some sold kolanuts or sugar-cane or sweet potatoes or cotton, or other things. Some were dyers, some grew onions or sugar-cane in marsh-plots.' According to Smith (1955, p. 104) *dimajai* sometimes worked entirely on their own farms, handing over a fixed portion of the produce (*murgu*) in lieu of *gandu* service.

Sons, unlike slaves, might leave *gandu*, but (according to Abubakar Labo) they seldom left 'until they were rich', by which time their own sons were usually old enough to work on their farms. Sons-in-*gandu* were reluctant to consume any of the produce from their *gayauna*, preferring rather to sell it and to buy livestock with the proceeds, thus preparing, over the years, for their ultimate economic independence. Fathers were quickly aroused to jealousy if their sons became 'too rich' and no son-in-*gandu* might have more than one wife. When, ultimately, a son did leave *gandu* his father gave him a farm additional to his *gayauna*, and he might remove from his father's house if it had become congested. But the break was not complete: the son would continue to help his father with the weeding when special need arose and, as Labo put it, 'he would use his father's property without permission': his father admonished him to be kind to his brothers and to be available for consultation.

On the father's death the *gandu* slaves, as well as the *gandu* farms, passed to the sons. Perhaps much more commonly than today, the sons might decide to remain together for a limited term, forming a working group under the authority of the eldest; sometimes, if there were many wives and many sons, the sons of each wife would establish their own *gandu*, in which case the most senior son would co-ordinate the work of the separate groups. Baba volunteered (*ibid.*, p. 40) that the sons of wealthy men more commonly divided the inheritance between themselves. She vividly described (p. 39) the break-up of her paternal grandfather's *gandu*: 'the family was wailing because he [the grandfather] was dead and the slaves saw their chance and ran away'; 80 of the 130 slaves fled, each son taking a share of the remainder to work on his portion of his father's farmland.

The extent to which slaves and their descendants were ultimately assimilated, *by virtue of their 'gandu' position*, as kinsfolk of the *gandu* head, was probably quite limited, owing to the break-up of most *gandu* estates by the time the grandsons had reached marriageable age, if not before. But the near-equality of slaves and sons as agricultural workers must have promoted much intermarriage between the two groups and, for that reason, and also because of the partial economic independence of *gandu* slaves (especially *dimajai*), one may agree up to a point with Hiskett that in many, though not in all, areas 'the *gandu* system enabled the slave population to become almost entirely absorbed' into Hausa society (1968, p. xxvii).

With Lugard's abolition of the 'legal status' of slavery, slaves had legal power to assert their freedom and all children born after 31 March 1901 were free at birth. But as it was not illegal to possess a slave, and as many slaves had little objection to their status or were too poor to establish themselves satisfactorily as independent farmers, slave labour was common in some areas until the mid-1920s – see Meek (1925, p. 133) – after which the number of surviving able-bodied ex-slaves rapidly diminished.

It is conceivable that the manpower gap resulting from the slaves' departure was at first partly filled by the wives of *gandu* heads, for elderly Batagarawa informants spoke of them as having been in *gandu* with their husbands within living memory, just as are Hausa wives in parts of rural Niger today (see *Gandu*). Meek did not comment on the contrast with former times, when he reported in 1925 that 'women usually join in all farming work except the heaviest forms of hoeing and reaping' (*ibid.*). But, even if wives resident in towns and compact villages had not gone increasingly into seclusion, it is possible that this trend would have been reversed, as the practice of employing hired labourers gradually increased; as constantly emphasized, the unsecluded women in Mallamawa hamlets today are not in *gandu*.

Paternal *gandu* may be regarded as a set of ascribed and mutually interacting rights and obligations characteristic of rural Hausa society, which reciprocally link fathers and sets of sons. The following list sets out the various rights and obligations which commonly regulate the *gandu* relationship in Batagarawa; it is based on observation of economic behaviour as much as on informants' statements, which are quite inexplicit on certain subjects. It is followed by some discussion of the way things tend to work out in practice.

RIGHTS

Father's rights	*Son's rights*
1 During the farming-season (*damuna*), a father is entitled to insist that his sons (and any sons' sons) should work on the *gandu* farms without payment, as required, for up to about five hours in the morning. These rights extend to carrying produce off the farm, but not to any form of processing, apart from groundnut shelling – for which, however, the father should give his son 'something' (*goro*); the rights do not cover any non-farming work.	1(a) A son has the right to refuse to work for his father during the dry season (*rani*), though he may be expected to transport manure to the farms if not otherwise occupied. 1(b) A son is entitled to at least one (some would say two) off-days every week when he may do as he wishes. (Little, if any, regard is paid to the fact that Wednesday and Friday are the traditional off-days). 1(c) If a son is asked to work on the *gandu* farms in the evening, he should be paid as

2   As an alternative to morning work on the *gandu* farms, the father has a right to instruct his son to work on the farms of others, and is himself free to take such work. Even if the son has taken the initiative in finding such work, the father is always entitled to most of the earnings.

3   A father may dismiss his son from *gandu* if his work is unsatisfactory, his dependants too numerous, or for other good reason. He is, however, entitled to expect that a dismissed son should remain civil to his brothers and himself and assist them with very urgent farmwork.

4   A father may exercise discretion on whether to readmit a son who has left *gandu* or migrated, except that any son who migrated as a Koranic student should be automatically readmitted.

5   A father is entitled to sell any of the *gandu* farmland, whether inherited or self acquired, and to retain the proceeds.

6   A father's rights over the contents of the granary in which the *gandu* produce is stored include the right of sale.

7   A father's right to sell compound sweepings as manure, if not applied to the *gandu* farms, cannot be gainsaid.

8   A father is entitled to close the *gandu* granary during the dry season.

though he were a hired labourer (*dan kwadago*).

1(d)   A son has the right to take up work of any kind, in any place, during the dry season.

3(a)   The father's rights to dismiss his son are paralleled by the son's right to leave *gandu* against his father's wishes.

3(b)   A dismissed son is entitled to retain any *gayauna* which has been formally alloted to him by his father.

(3c)   While a dismissed son has the right to demand that his father should give him a portion of the *gandu* farmland on his departure, the father may make difficulties about this.

4.   If a son's circumstances have changed for the worse he has a right to expect that he will be readmitted to *gandu* at least once, unless he originally left against his father's wishes.

5   A son who considers that his father is selling farms unnecessarily, or recklessly, may appeal to the *masu-sarauta*, though his appeal may not improve the situation.

6   A son has complete control over the produce in any granary he may own privately.

7   If a son lives in a separate house, he has a right to utilise his compound sweepings on his private farms.

OBLIGATIONS

Father's obligations

9   During the farming-season the father should do his best to provide all the food required by the son and his family for their evening meal, either in the form of *tuwo*, or as grain allocated either at harvest or at intervals thereafter. Sons should be treated equally, which means that in allocating grain, or food, account should be taken of the size and composition of the son's household.

10   Millet porridge (*fura*) should be served on the farm when the son works there. (This obligation does not necessarily extend, as in the days of slavery, to the provision of millet for the son's wife.)

Son's obligations

9(a)   Any grain allocated to a son should be used for 'own consumption' and not sold.

9(b)   If *tuwo* is provided, the son's wife should help her mother-in-law with the cooking. (If she pounds or grinds grain she may keep any bran (*dusa*) for her own livestock.)

9(c)   If a father is short of grain a son should help him from his private granary if possible – this applying to all seasons.

10   A son does not necessarily feel obliged to provide his wife with millet for *fura* if his father does not do so: he may rather leave his wife to fend for herself and her children.

11 While a father is emphatically not obliged to give his son any portion of the *gandu* groundnut crop (not even seed for his *gayauna*) – part of the proceeds of which are conventionally devoted to paying the community tax, see (12) – a father should give his son 'something' to finance clothing purchases, etc.

12 A father should pay his son's annual community tax (*haraji*), although it is always levied in the son's name.

12 If a father is unable to meet the tax, the son should secretly give him the money if he can.

13 A father should, on request, give his son a portion of manured farmland for his own use (*gayauna*); he should permit him to work there on his off-days and in the evenings and to dispose of the proceeds as he wishes. (Such a gift is usually permanent, being regarded as 'outside inheritance'.)

13(a) A son should not sell any *gayauna* given to him by his father.

13(b) If a son buys a farm from his father, he should be discreet about this.

14 A father should provide his son with adequate housing for himself and his family, but he is not required to allot him separate quarters.

14 A son should not sell, without permission, any house given to him by his father.

15 A father should do his best to meet his son's marriage expenses (q.v.), especially in the case of his first marriage, and to make a large contribution to the costs of naming-ceremonies (q.v.).

16 A father should provide the tools required for work on the *gandu* farms and should permit his son to use them on his private farms and for *kwadago*; if he owns an ox-plough he should allow his son the free use of it on his private farms.

16 A son should take good care of the tools provided by his father.

17 A father should provide his son with grain-seed for his *gayauna*, but he is not obliged to provide groundnut seed.

18 When, through illness, old-age, or decrepitude, a father can no longer farm, he should delegate his authority to his eldest son, whose brothers will then effectively be in *gandu* with him.

18 A son should defer to the wishes of a retired father and he should not sell any *gandu* farms: if the *gandu* acreage is inadequate he should find some other means of maintaining his father.

19 Unless aged or infirm, a father should usually work alongside his sons on the *gandu* farms.

The incidence of paternal 'gandu'

Before discussing these rights and obligations further, it is necessary to deal with the incidence of paternal *gandu*. At first glance this incidence seems low, for only 41 out of the 171 farming-units include married sons. But the following figures show that actual incidence is high in relation to potential incidence. Firstly, only 10 of the total of 69 married sons resident in Batagarawa have left *gandu* and started farming on their own account, and they are the sons of only six fathers. Secondly, there are only 2 heads of farming-units, *all* of whose resident married sons have left *gandu*. Thirdly, there are not many cases in which the lack of a *gandu* is accounted for by the migration of sons: of 51 heads of farming-units estimated to be over forty years old who have no married working-sons (23 of whom also had no unmarried sons), only 7 are known to have had sons who migrated.

The fact that less than a quarter of all farming-units are organized as *gandaye* is largely accounted for by two demographic considerations: these are the youthfulness of many (fatherless) heads of farming-units (two-fifths of all heads of farming-units are estimated to be under forty, see Table v.8, p. 80) and the high proportion of men of forty and over who have no adult sons. High mortality rates (in middle age, as well as in infancy) thus mainly account for the low proportion of *gandaye*.

Such are the formal figures. But when account is taken of the number of *gandaye* which cannot be regarded as strong or viable farming-units, a rather different picture emerges. As many as 10 of the 41 *gandaye* are so weak (see Chapter XII, pp. 170–2) that neither fathers nor sons can effectively exert their rights or meet their obligations. This weakness, as will be seen, is due to poverty, not to the flexibility of the '*gandu* rules', so that in considering this flexibility the 'failed *gandaye*' must be ignored.

Finally, it should be noted (Table XII.1, p. 170) that as many as 8 of the 29 strong (or viable) *gandaye* somewhat resemble fraternal *gandaye* in that they are headed by elderly fathers who have retired from farming.

The numerical strength of the total *gandaye* labour-force is greater than the above figures might suggest. Of the total of 343 married and unmarried working-men (Table II.2, p. 33), nearly half (162) are in those farming-units which are organized as *gandaye*.

RIGHTS AND OBLIGATIONS IN PRACTICE

1 *The father's right to his son's farmwork*

The father continues to exert his rights throughout the farming-season until the guinea-corn harvest is completed – which may be up to two months after the cessation of the rains. These rights do not cover the later harvesting of cowpeas (*wake*), which is women's work – in 1968 this crop was harvested about seven weeks later than guinea corn. If a son has gone away on *cin rani* by the time the tobacco is due to be harvested, the *gandu* head either picks the crop himself or hires paid labour. The last of all the major crops to be harvested (apart, of course, from cassava, which may be dug at any time) is the sweet potato (*dankali*) which may not be ready until February: a son-in-*gandu* should be paid for this work and for digging the storage pits.

There is great variability of practice over such work as farm clearance during the dry season: some fathers pay their sons for this work, others do not. Some fathers are indifferent to what their sons do at this time, while others feel much concerned.

2 *The father's right to his son's 'kwadago' earnings*

Earnings for morning work are probably usually handed over to the father 'except for 3*d*. or so': as a group of labourers commented – 'some of the boys are annoyed about this, some are not'. The sons of better-off farmers seldom work to any extent as *'yan kwadago* – see Chapter VIII. If a poor father has two working-sons he may instruct one of them to work as a labourer.

3 and 4 *Departure from 'gandu'*

Perhaps in former times father and son often mutually agreed to part company when the latter had two or three children, or was proposing to take a second wife. But, partly for reasons of prestige, most fathers nowadays do their best to retain their sons' services, however irritated or troubled they may be by their waywardness, disobedience, laziness and so forth and whatever inconvenience results from a son's large family. A father may even go so far as to sell farmland to spite his son and yet not dismiss him from *gandu*.

It is most uncommon for sons to leave *gandu* against their father's wishes and not to migrate: of the total of 10 resident sons who have left the fold, it seems that only 2 (viz. F and G in the following list) defied their fathers in so doing. Most departures appear to be amicable and mutually agreed, the fathers showing their approval by giving additional farmland to their sons. Even if a son does not better himself by his departure, he may be happier in his new-found freedom, as H (in the list) most certainly is.

Occasionally disputes about departures are referred to the Hamlet Head. The two eldest sons of a prosperous farmer were one day discussing the situation that might arise if their father refused to release any of their younger brothers: they thought that were the matter to be referred to the Hamlet Head he would probably say that so long as they themselves remained in *gandu* their younger brothers should do likewise. If, following such advice, the younger sons had departed, they could not have expected to have been given any farmland.

It is sometimes said that a son who is himself the father of a married son always leaves *gandu:* this could hardly be checked as, owing to short life expectancies, there were only two married men with surviving paternal grandfathers in Batagarawa in 1967 – each of whom was in a three-generation *gandu*.

The following list reviews the circumstances of the 10 resident sons who have left *gandu*.

Son	Father's circumstances	Manner of leaving 'gandu'	Son's independent position
A	The elderly father has 5 married sons who have left *gandu*, 3 of them being A, B and C, 2 others having migrated.	After being in *gandu* for some 15 years, he left by mutual agreement, having a large family, his father giving him farms. He built himself a house opposite his father's. He occasionally works on his father's farms 'out of respect'.	Unable to provide adequately for his household of 13, including 6 young children, he is even poorer than his father.
B	See A.	He was given a farm when he left *gandu*. He has his own house.	He is often away for Koranic studies. He has 2 wives and only 1 child and is not badly off.
C	See A.	He was given a part of one of his father's farms when he left *gandu*. He has continued to live in his father's house.	His manured farms are too small to support his small family of 3, but he works hard at many occupations, including thatch-making, earth-collecting, clothes-washing and *kwadago*.
D	The old father still lives with his son D, having no wife or other dependants save E.	The old father boastfully, if jokingly, asserted that it was he who had recently dismissed his 2 sons from *gandu*: general opinion had it that this was because D was 'very trouble-some'.	He is little interested in farming but is keen on *kwadago* and also does paid building work during the farming-season. He was once a servant. He is very poor.
E	See D.	See D. E has his own house.	He is not so poor as D and has rented one of his farms.
F	A very prominent farmer-trader who has lost the services of 4 out of 5 of his married sons, 2 of whom have migrated.	He and 3 of his brothers left *gandu* because they could not get on with their father. His father gave him no farm. He has his own house.	Despite his youth, he is one of the most successful farmers, having bought many farms. He is an active *dan kwarami*.
G	See F.	Like F, he received no farm from his father. He has his own house.	He has bought many farms. He is a teaching Malam.
H	His elderly father still has one son in *gandu* with him.	Being too independent to remain in *gandu*, he departed amicably, his father giving him a small farm. He has his own house.	A real 'character' who has numerous types of occupation besides farming.
I	One son remains in *gandu* with the father who has retired from farming. Another son has migrated.	He left *gandu* by mutual consent, his father giving him a large bush-farm as well as a manured farm.	Although his farms are insufficient to support 7 dependants, his position is improving slightly. He is contemplating migrating as a farmer.
J	Another son is still in *gandu* with him. Some relatives who have migrated give him much grain.	One of the rare cases in which opinion differs on whether he has left *gandu* or not: he said he was nervous of provoking his father by making a formal break. After a long struggle he has moved into his own house.	He has adequate farmland, having bought two farms. He pays his brother for farmwork.

5 and 6   *A father's freedom to sell 'gandu' farms or crops*

In former times, if the present position of the Maguzawa is any guide, the *gandu* land was considered as, in some measure, 'collective property', though only during the life-time of the *gandu* group, as the wider group which Greenberg denoted the 'clan' had 'no political organisation' and never acted as a unit – Greenberg (1947, p. 197). However this may once have been, nowadays in Batagarawa there is little (if any) sense of collective property so far as paternal *gandu* is concerned, so that the *gandu* farms are best regarded as effectively owned by the father, who, as it were, personally rewards his sons for their labour-services. Just as any farm which a father might buy from the proceeds of some private occupation, such as trading, is automatically regarded as a *gandu* farm, in the sense that the sons have as much right to a share of the crop as in the case of an inherited farm – so a father may sell part of the *gandu* farm-land and the sons-in-*gandu* are no more entitled to make complaints to the *masu-sarauta* than if they were brothers or other relatives. Nor is the house in which sons live with their father in any sense *gandu* property: it will be inherited by the sons whether or not they are in *gandu* at the time of the father's death. See p. 270.

The only type of property, other than farmland, ever to be denoted as *gandu* property consists of those granaries (*rumbun gandu*) in which the crops grown on the *gandu* farms are stored. However, if a father buys and stores grain for a price rise, it is presumably usual for him to deposit it in the *rumbun gandu*, as only four (richer) heads of paternal *gandaye* were reported as owning personal granaries (altogether 17 of them) – corresponding to those owned personally by their sons.

Not only are notions of collective (physical) property virtually lacking, but there is also no concept of '*gandu* funds'. From this aspect, *gandu* appears rather as a relationship than a business, this being one reason for the importance attached to non-farming occupations, which may be as freely pursued by fathers as by sons.

It is doubtful whether the extreme reluctance of farmers to admit to selling any grain of their own production has much connexion with *gandu*, for it applies to farmers generally, not only to those with married sons. It would seem to be rather that farmers are deeply sensitive to taunts, however unjustified, that grain-sellers are necessarily those who neglect their wives and children. In such a cash-oriented economy, the fears on this subject seem curiously anachronistic, especially as grain must often be sold to meet the community tax (*haraji*).

7   *The 'gandu' manure*

Unless they live in separate houses, sons have no right to apply compound sweepings to their private farms, for the father's right to sell such sweepings cannot be gainsaid – this being a right derived from his position as household, rather than *gandu*, head.

8 *Closure of the 'gandu' granary*

The ancient precautionary right which fathers possess to close the *gandu* granary during the dry season, has as its corollary the sons' obligation to maintain their fathers at that time, this being one reason why fathers encourage the private farming of their sons; although it is a right which is falling into desuetude, many fathers are then far less liberal over grain supplies than during the farming-season.

9 and 10 *The distribution of food and grain*

If a son-in-*gandu* lives in the same house as his father, then (irrespective of whether he lives in a separate section) it is very common, especially with well-organized *gandaye*, for *tuwo* (for the evening meal) to be provided for him and his family all the year round, his wives assisting his father's wives with the cooking. If the father's wife is elderly, then the son's wives may assume responsibility for cooking, perhaps in rotation, the father's wife perhaps helping when she feels inclined. In some households the customary rotation of cooking between the father's wives has been dropped, the wives of both generations comprising a cooking team under the authority of the father's senior wife (*uwar gida*). Although in such circumstances the grain ought to come from the *gandu* granary, in practice the son often supplements supplies – especially if he has received a substantial allocation after harvest. When the father is retired the senior son, and/or the son resident with his father, may, or may not, have access to the *gandu* granary.

If the son-in-*gandu* lives in a separate house, then it often happens that he is provided with *tuwo* during the farming-season only, in which case, as a member of a well-organized *gandu*, he will usually receive a share of the guinea-corn crop at harvest, for storage in his own granary. Again, it is usual for sons' wives to assist with the cooking, which may be done in either house – son's and father's houses are usually nearby. But some *tuwo* is cooked in most of the separate houses, whether or not full requirements are met.

As for *fura* (millet porridge) and millet allocations, although practices (like circumstances) vary greatly, it is safe to assert that individual wives often prepare it for themselves and commonly dip into their own pockets to supplement grain supplies. Some fathers prefer to share out millet supplies after harvest, hoping that their sons will make no further demands on them, others allocate (if they can) on demand. (For many of the poorest *gandaye* there can be no rules: everyone lives from hand to mouth, sons and sons' wives largely fending for themselves as best they may, often mainly depending on bought food.)

This general account of food and grain allocation in the better-organized *gandaye* shows that *gandu* cannot be defined, as it often is, as a group of persons who eat from a 'common pot'. It also demonstrates the crudity of common statements such as that co-wives always cook for their husbands, in rotation, on the nights when they sleep with them.

11   *Groundnuts*

No doubt it is partly because of the reticence and embarrassment over grain-selling that it is conventional to insist that the community tax (*haraji*, q.v.) ought to be met from selling groundnuts. However this may be, no father was reported as giving a son any share of the groundnut crop as such, which is only to say that fathers are responsible for selling the groundnuts and for the dis-tribution of the proceeds, in regard to which sons have certain expectations. Many of the poorer farmers fail to produce groundnuts or have small crops.

12   *Community tax*

If a poor farmer has several dependent sons aged sixteen or over the community tax may weigh very heavily on him, the average rate for dependants being little lower than that for heads of farming-units. If, as often happens with poorer farmers, the proceeds from selling groundnuts are insufficient to meet the tax, grain may be inopportunely sold (at low post-harvest prices) and sons may be asked to contribute.

13   *A father's obligation to give his son a 'gayauna'*

Most better-off farmers honour their obligation to give their son a *gayauna*, if he wants one. However, as many as 26 of the 62 sons-in-*gandu* (throughout this book this term includes two brother's sons and one sister's son) are not recorded as owning private farms in the manured zone, and about half of these men have no bush-farms: some sons may own (or cultivate) small portions of farms belonging to their fathers which, being without boundaries, could not be mapped. The total acreage of manured farmland apparently owned by the 36 sons was 142 acres, but the affairs of 3 of them had become so entangled with those of their retired fathers that they are better omitted, in which case 33 sons were recorded as owning 108 acres. A son's holding is typically between 1 and 3 acres, as many as 24 of the holdings falling within this size-range. Three sons have private holdings of between 8 and 12½ acres, one of them being the remarkable case of a son whose manured acreage is over three times as large as his father's, although he is genuinely in *gandu*. Despite their *gandu* obligations, many sons (as will be seen) are notably successful farmers in their own right, some 9 of them (Table VIII.2, p. 109) being significant employers of farm-labourers.

Enquiries suggested that two-fifths of the farms owned by sons were *gayauni* in the sense that they had once been their father's property: however, a considerable proportion had probably been bought by sons from fathers, though no precise estimates could be made. About two-fifths of the farmland had been bought, by about a dozen sons, from non-kin.

Although *gayauni* are usually regarded as permanent gifts 'outside inheritance', which may be retained by sons who leave *gandu*, yet fathers do occasionally reclaim these farms or exchange them for others. However, when a son assumes charge of his retired father's farming the *gayauni* may effectively become pooled with the *gandu* property.

Fifty-three men-in-*gandu* owned 108 granaries (see Table 11.9, p. 36), or nearly a quarter as many as were owned by all heads of farming-units; allowing for the 12 granaries owned by 7 members of fraternal *gandaye*, the total number of granaries owned by 46 sons-in-*gandu* was 96, or about 2 apiece. Nearly all those with private farms own granaries, though there are a few men who store their produce in their father's granaries or elsewhere. Little produce, other than grain, is stored in most of the sons' granaries, though 7 sons own groundnut granaries.

14   *The father's obligation to provide housing*

Batagarawa men have an entirely practical attitude towards house property, as towards farmland, so 'nothing is fixed' about the type of accommodation a father should provide for his sons-in-*gandu*. The symmetry of the set of mutual rights and obligations linking father and sons is nicely illustrated by the case of a father who moved out of his house because his son's dependants were too numerous. Sons sometimes secretly buy houses from their fathers, as in the case of a son who gradually paid for his house over seven years, or they may buy them from non-kin. There is a serious shortage of house-plots in the *gari* and many sons are discontented with their cramped conditions.

About a quarter of all the sons-in-*gandu* are housed entirely separately from their fathers and about a third (see Table 11.6, p. 34) live in separate sections of their father's house. Of the 6 sons who have more than one wife, 5 have separate houses or house-sections – the exception being a son who lives in a large 'country house' where there is space, as seldom in the *gari*, for house expansion.

15   *Ceremonial expenditure*

The father's obligation to assist a son-in-*gandu* to meet his heavy marriage expenses (q.v.), which may amount to as much as £30 or £40 for a girl's first marriage, weighs very heavily with the son when he contemplates leaving *gandu*, the same applying to expenditure on naming-ceremonies (q.v.). Marriage expenses must be paid in full at the due time and the son's possibilities of marrying the girl of his choice are often dependent on his father's generosity, wealth and capacity to call in contributions from his friends (*biki*). Sons of poor fathers, who have weak capacities to help their sons, thus lack one of the great incentives for remaining in *gandu*, and, as will be seen (Chapter VII), more often migrate to take up non-farming occupations, such as domestic service. So complex is the nexus of celebratory expenditure, so varying the circumstances, that it is quite impossible to estimate the proportion of expenses 'normally' borne by the father.

17   Seed for 'gayauna'

Whereas fathers often regard a son's grain crops as effectively contributing to the total supplies available to the *gandu*, if only because the son may try to help his father from his granary if he is in need, the same is not true of groundnuts, which the sons sell for cash: consistently with this, fathers give grain, but not groundnut, seed to their sons.

18   The retirement of fathers

The Hausa farmer, in contrast to the Fulani pastoralist, seldom follows the policy of progressively giving his property away to his sons during his life-time, so that little remains at his death. He may give several farms to a son-in-*gandu* and he may make additional allocations to a son who leaves *gandu* by mutual consent, but otherwise (unless, of course, he is a farm-seller) he holds on to his farmland until his dying day, thus ensuring that the *gandu* is not disbanded. Some elderly fathers graciously hand over entire responsibility to their eldest son, in which case the *gandu* farms may be effectively merged with the son's farms, as has happened in 4 of the 8 cases of *gandaye* which have retired heads; others continue to oversee the work on the *gandu* farms. In 5 cases there was no longer any *gandu* granary, the eldest son having taken over. One retired father had altogether withdrawn from farming, while remaining in full charge of the 9 *gandu* granaries. One son who was in charge of all the granaries, was very strict in observing the rule that *gandu* farms should be cultivated before private farms.

Fraternal 'gandu'

In Batagarawa nowadays most *gandaye* break up soon after the father's death, the sons (see **Inheritance** and pp. 184–5) dividing the farmland among themselves and setting up as independent farmers. In some cases, especially when the father had been poor, the sons immediately start selling their father's farms, as though celebrating their freedom and middle-aged men sometimes use the proceeds to finance their migration as farmers. That sons who had found paternal *gandu* irksome should be even less willing to accept the authority of their eldest brother is not surprising. As for the older members of the more successful *gandaye*, they are apt to be the very men whose private farming is on a large enough scale for them to be viable as independent farmers when they are also in possession of their share of the *gandu* farmland. Material relating to the fragility of fraternal *gandu* is presented here, but discussion of the wider issues is postponed – see Chapters XII and XIII.

Although many middle-aged informants said that they had spent a few years in fraternal *gandu* following their father's death (the incidence of fraternal *gandu* having certainly been somewhat higher than it is today), it has not been common within living memory for brothers to regard this phase as other than temporary. After sampling the experience, and fending off the shock of their father's death, it was usually not long before they mutually agreed to part, usually simultaneously, though sometimes one brother would leave ahead of the others.

Of the 7 fraternal *gandaye* in 1967, 3 appeared to be temporary arrangements, in which division of the *gandu* property was merely delayed, and special circumstances accounted for the persistence of *gandu* in 3 of the remaining 4 cases. It is significant that 2 of these *gandu* heads are blacksmiths, this being the only craft such that sons and junior brothers may effectively work as paid assistants to their fathers and elder brothers – the only other blacksmith in the *gari* has no resident brother and is head of a paternal *gandu*. (In addition there is the unique case of Alhaji Nuhu's paternal-cum-fraternal *gandu*, which had earlier been a three-generation *gandu*, headed by Alhaji Nuhu's father until he died in extreme old age.) There was a total of only 9 (dependent) married brothers in the 7 *gandaye*.

The actual incidence of fraternal *gandu* should be compared with potential incidence. The total of only 7 (or 8) fraternal *gandaye* may be compared with the 30 sets of brothers whose father has died or migrated who are not in *gandu* together. As these numbers are so small, figures for one neighbouring Hamlet are added: in Autawa (q.v.) there is only one fraternal *gandu* to compare with 7 sets of fatherless independent brothers.

Brief notes on the 7 fraternal *gandaye* follow:

(i)   *Temporary 'gandaye'*. (a) and (b)   At the time of the father's death there were 5 brothers: one of them joined the eldest brother who had left paternal *gandu*; one (a youth) joined an elder brother; and one migrated. The *gandu* farms have been temporarily divided between the two fraternal *gandaye*. (c)   The eldest son migrated and vanished for some ten years; when his father was near death's door, the family succeeded in tracing him and he returned home; on his father's death he imposed his will on his younger brothers (another had already left *gandu*), insisting that the farms should not be divided. The eldest son, like his late father, is a blacksmith and one of his brothers assists him.

(ii)   *Infant sons*. (d)   The father died before the youngest son had been weaned and the eldest (then adult) took over. (e)   The father died when one son was an infant, the other unborn; on reaching adulthood, the brothers formed a *gandu*, their mother's second husband having meanwhile died.

(iii) *Migration.* (f) The father migrated taking 3 of his sons with him, the 2 sons who remained behind forming a fraternal *gandu*. The younger brother expressed the strong opinion that sons of a migrated father should remain together during their father's life-time: he assists his brother who is a blacksmith.

(iv) *Straightforward case.* (g) On their father's death the 4 sons formed a *gandu* which appears to be quite stable. They own 2 houses, 2 brothers being in each. All the brothers work, at times, as farm-labourers. The 3 younger brothers own no private farms.

Four of the 9 dependent (married) brothers-in-*gandu* own no manured or bush-farms, being entirely dependent on the *gandu* farms; the remaining 5 brothers own a total of only 14 acres. It is interesting that heads of fraternal (unlike paternal) *gandaye* are quite apt to own 'private farms', acquired since their father's death, which would not be divided among the brothers when the *gandu* breaks and would thus ultimately pass to their sons; dependent brothers work on these farms as though they were *gandu* property, taking a share of the proceeds.

'Gandu' in rural Hausaland generally

The few published sources relating to *gandu* in rural Hausaland are listed in the Commentary, where a brief summary of Nicolas' findings on *gandu* in rural Niger is also to be found. M. G. Smith (1955) provides much the most useful introduction to the subject, dealing fully with the various reciprocal rights and obligations; his statistics of the 'incidence' of *gandu* in rural Zaria are of limited value, actual numbers of *gandaye* not being related to potential numbers, as in this analysis. Greenberg, Reuke and Krusius have dealt with *gandu* among the pagan Hausa (Maguzawa). Goddard (1969) provides statistics relating to *gandu* in three villages in northern Sokoto where population densities are very high; he distinguishes four types of paternal *gandu*, one of them such that sons are responsible for paying their own community tax.

The institution of paternal *gandu* must be presumed to exist everywhere in Hausaland until an investigator reports its absence, which none has done so far. There are so many obvious factors (such as population density, the extent of permanent cultivation, the incidence of short- and long-term migration, the importance of craftwork) which might influence the incidence and strength of paternal *gandu* and the nature of the *gandu* relationship, that there would seem to be little purpose in listing them here. Besides, in accordance with the evidence from Batagarawa, the viability of individual *gandaye* may depend so much on the father's economic situation, that general conclusions as to the strength of the *gandu* institution by locality might usually lack all validity. In addition, it is worth mentioning that certain associated factors, such as the level of marriage expenses, might be *dependent* variables.

As for fraternal *gandu*, the general evidence is that among the Muslim Hausa large three-generational households are everywhere becoming much rarer (the

Hausa of the Niger Republic being no exception), in which case it would be surprising if farming organization, also, were not becoming increasingly based on individuals or on men assisted only by their married sons. Goddard (1969) has reported that fraternal *gandu* is weak in northern Sokoto. In the twenty years which have elapsed since M. G. Smith worked in the Zaria villages, it may be that fraternal *gandu* has declined in importance, so that the numbers of fraternal and paternal *gandaye* are no longer roughly equal there.

A postscript on the Nupe 'efako'

The Nupe institution of *efako*, as described by Nadel (1942), is remarkably similar to *gandu*. The word '*efako*' denotes either a labour-unit of close kin (which occupies a section of a compound) or the farm which it works. The *efako* farm is cultivated jointly by the *efako* group, the produce being stored in the *efako* granaries which are controlled by the *efako* head, who is responsible for paying the tax of all members and for providing tools. He is also responsible for alloting small farms, known as *buca*, to individual dependants (as formerly to slaves), who are free to work on them in their off-time. A general distinction between joint and individual enterprise (*efako* and *buca*) formerly ran right through Nupe economic life, affecting craft organization as well as farming.

A postscript on large households

No more than three miles east of the Kano city wall, immediately bordering the modern residential area of Nassarawa, there is a farming area where a considerable proportion of the (Muslim) Hausa population lives in very large, traditional-style, houses, some of them including fifteen or more married men of three generations. Although preliminary enquiries (1971) have suggested that large complex households (such as are generally associated only with the Maguzawa) may be a common feature of certain very densely populated Muslim areas of dispersed settlement near Kano, it does not follow that *gandu* organisation is strong there: indeed both paternal and fraternal *gandu* seemed surprisingly weak.

CHAPTER IV

The evidence for economic inequality

In a community like Batagarawa where there are no land-owning classes, clans or lineages and no privileged groups with special rights over other scarce factors such as water; where land is plentiful and there is no landless class; where there is no slavery or serfdom or ethnically inferior group; where there is little property of any kind (other than land or houses) with a life of more than a few years – in such a community it might be thought that a man's standard of living would be largely determined by the size of his family labour-force in relation to the number of his non-working dependants. Since most resident married sons remain in *gandu* with their fathers, then (questions of migration apart) farmers would tend to get richer as they got older and had more adult sons. Of course, rich men might have more sons *because* in this polygynous society, where marriage expenses are high and wives are secluded, they could afford to marry, and maintain, more wives – in which case the number of sons is not necessarily an *independent* variable. But the general approach to economic inequality would have to be demographic.

One of the main themes of this book is that such a demographic approach is misleadingly rigid and deterministic – that, for example, there are many reasons why an individual who is the proud father of several sons cannot rely on becoming involved in a benign developmental process as those sons grow up. Nor can the workings of the economy as a whole be analysed in terms of the economic behaviour of that dangerous statistical artefact, the average or representative farmer. It is the complementary relationship between richer and poorer farmers, who have different roles and ambitions, which requires examination. The starting-point for the development of these ideas was the discovery of a very pronounced degree of economic inequality in Batagarawa which was evidently not straight-forwardly 'demographic', the detailed evidence for which is presented in this and the following chapter.

Before attempting to justify the unorthodox approach to economic inequality which was adopted, it is necessary to ask whether a conventional survey of income and expenditure would not have served equally well, had the necessary resources to conduct it been available – which they were not. Certainly, statistics relating to the daily food consumption of the members of each farming-unit would have been very interesting, but even so it is doubtful whether their value would have justified the enormous labour their collection would have involved. Owing to the extreme seasonality of economic life, it would have been necessary for the survey to have related to a whole year – a year which sub-sequent experience might show to have been quite exceptional. (Indeed, annual crop-sizes may be so variable, that it is better not to have detailed figures for a single year, owing to the risk of their enshrinement as 'normal'.) Owing to the severity of seasonal price fluctuations (Chapter IX), it would have been necessary to have valued the grain in some arbitrary way based either on prices at the time of harvest (or purchase) or at the time of consumption. Owing to the importance of the trade in cooked foodstuffs and of private farming by sons-in-*gandu*, it would have been necessary to value the purchases of each member of the farming-unit. Owing to the break-up into separate 'cooking-units' of many of the larger farming-units during the dry season, it would have been necessary to study each nuclear family separately at that time – and to make guesses about those who had temporarily migrated (*cin rani*). Finally, owing to wife-seclusion, most of the field assistants would have had to have been educated Hausa women, who would have been far better employed in other capacities!

It is doubtful whether reliable statistics on income and expenditure (as dis-tinct from production and consumption) could ever be obtained in a Hausa village, if only because of the extreme secrecy that surrounds various trans-actions, including the sale of grain of 'own production'. Then, indebtedness is not a subject which could be explored by direct enquiry; and the study of ceremonial expenditure and contributions would be a colossal task. In a society where husbands and wives are often kept in ignorance of their spouse's economic affairs, how could fieldworkers expect to have the truth, in all its appalling complexity, revealed to them? Certainly, any enquiry would have to be on a sample basis, whereas one of the very great advantages of our approach was that everybody was included.

The starting-point during the fieldwork was the idea that one of the most important elements in a farming-unit's 'standard of living' (however that expression might be understood) was its ability to withstand the shock of a very late, or very poor, harvest. In 1967 the planting rains, and hence the early millet (*gero*) harvest, were very late and in early September, shortly before the harvest, there was obviously much hunger. With the idea of forming a very rough estimate of the number of people who were 'suffering', in the limited sense that they were eating considerably less than was usual *in their case*, three very well-informed farmers, each of whom was especially well placed to know a great deal about the affairs of others, were each independently (and secretly) invited to say which of the 171 farming-units were 'hungry' and which were not. Our informants performed their task so enthusiastically that it was soon decided to ask them to classify each farming-unit in one of 4 'economic-groups': Group 1 consisting of those who, far from suffering hunger, were actively assisting others in their plight by means of gifts or loans; Group 2 of those who were 'neither suffering nor helping'; Group 3 of those who were 'suffering somewhat'; and Group 4 of those who were 'suffering severely'. Each informant was invited to make his own subjective judgments, on the basis of his own knowledge, and he was not asked to justify his assessments. Instructions were reduced to the minimum, the idea being that each informant should rely on his knowledge and common sense. In particular, no instructions were given as to the classification of farming-units headed by poor farmers who were largely reliant on their wives' earnings, except that in cases of real indecision the husband's position should be the main determinant (see **Women, economic position**).

The results of this 'examination' (as it was jocularly called by the 'examinees') were compared and the degree of correspondence between them seemed to justify continuing an exercise which, up to that point, had rather resembled a game. A meeting was held to enable the three men to thrash out discrepancies among themselves; no one was prompted and no statistics were discussed – in any case, most of the statistics, including the farm acreages, had not then been computed. In almost all cases of disagreement on the first round, unanimity was secured without much difficulty on the second round, except for some doubt as to the distinction between Groups 3 and 4: in only a few other cases, most of them perhaps 'border-line', did arbitrary decisions have to be made. Each informant had already been seen to have a very good idea of what he thought he was measuring or assessing; now it began to seem possible that they were all striving towards similar classifications. (It should be noted that one of the three informants was classified by the others as Group 1, two of them as Group 2.)

The enquiry began to look less like an exercise and more like a promising experiment when enquiries made of other informants suggested that hardly any of the heads of farming-units in Groups 1 or 2 (or, as later emerged, their sons) were accustomed to work to any extent as farm-labourers (*'yan kwadago*), although some half of those in Group 3, and some two-thirds of those in Group 4 were reported as doing this work. Then, enquiries about the sale of compound sweepings as manure (q.v.) revealed that nearly all Group 4 farmers in the *gari* were apt to be sellers and that only two of the Group 1 and 2 units were known as such. Although it was conceivable that some farming-units had been classified as Group 3 or 4 *because* their heads were known to be farm-labourers or manure-sellers, it yet seemed possible that this subjective classification reflected genuine economic differentiation.

Without making any alterations to this classification (except to some slight extent on the basis of judgments made by a fourth informant with special knowledge of Kauyen Yamma), numerous simple calculations were later made for each economic-group relating to population, numbers of working-men, acreage of manured farmland, and so forth – preliminary results being published – see Hill (1968 and 1970a). Surprisingly, it was found that nearly *all* the indicators of economic activity (as distinct, for example, from statistics relating to population structure, such as the ratio of working-men in the population) showed that the average Group 1 farming-unit was 'better off' than the average Group 2 farming-unit and so on down the scale. Furthermore, as will be seen in Chapter v, the range of variation within economic-groups was usually very much less than that between economic-groups. Whether or not our three informants had reliably judged who was 'hungry', they certainly seemed to have been measuring 'something significant'.

The original distinction between Groups 3 and 4 had not been sufficiently clear cut. It was therefore later decided to amalgamate these economic-groups and, on the basis of all available information (not of subjective judgment), to select from this list, and to place in a new Group 4, all farming-units which appeared to be desperately poverty-stricken at all times; in this connexion further information was collected in Batagarawa in 1968 by M. S. Nuhu.

Finally, several amendments were made to the original list on the basis of detailed information which made it seem that the subjective judgments *must* have been faulty; 2 farming-units were switched from Group 1 to Group 2 – but (as was subsequently regretted, see Chapter xii, p. 161) there were 3 farming-units wrongly classified as Group 3, which were not upgraded to Group 2, as they should have been; a few other alterations resulted from a reassessment of certain *gandu* relationships. But except for the creation of the new Group 4, the final distribution between economic-groups remained basically unchanged, reflecting the original subjective judgments of our informants.

About two-thirds of all farming-units (corresponding to over half of the classified population) were put in Groups 3 and 4; about one-tenth of all farming-units (17% of the classified population) were classified as Group 1 ('the top 10%'); and about a quarter of the units (28% of the classified population) were placed in Group 2.

The following statistics relate to each of the four economic-groups as a whole: variation within economic-group is dealt with in Chapter v.

Population

Statistics relating to population by economic-group are presented in Table iv.1. They show that:

(2) the proportion of farming-units organized as *gandaye* is much higher for Group 1 (11 out of 17) than for the three other groups (37 out of 154);

(4) and (8) Group 1 farming-units are much larger than other farming-units (12·6 persons per unit, compared with 7·6, 6·1 and 6·1 respectively), this being associated with the higher proportion of *gandaye*;

(10) and (11) the number of working-men per farming-unit is much higher for Group 1 than for other economic-groups; this reflects the greater size of the Group 1 units, for the number of dependants (weighted) per working-man varies little between economic-groups;

(12) the heads of Group 1 farming-units have more wives (1·8 on average) than those of other units (1·3, 1·2 and 1·1 respectively).

TABLE IV.1. *Population by economic-group*

	Economic-group				
	1	2	3	4	Total
(1) Number of farming-units	17	45	68	41	171
(2) – of which *gandaye*	11	13	15	9	48
(3) Population–total numbers	214	344	417	251	1,226
percentages	17	28	34	20	100
(4) per farming-unit	12·6	7·6	6·1	6·1	7·2
(5) Women – numbers	59	92	124	66	341
(6) Children – numbers	92	158	172	109	531
(7) Weighted population – numbers	168	266	332	196	962
(8) per farming-unit	9·9	5·9	4·9	4·8	5·6
(9) Working-men – numbers	61	89	118	75	343
(10) per farming-unit	3·6	2·0	1·7	1·8	2·0
(11) Dependants (weighted) per working-man – numbers	1·8	1·9	1·8	1·6	1·8
(12) Wives per head of farming-unit – numbers	1·8	1·3	1·2	1·1	1·3

NOTES

(3) The population is the total organized in farming-units; see Table II.1, p. 32.
(6) See Table II.1, p. 32.
(7) In weighting the population, children were counted as 'half-adults'.
(9) See Table II.5, p. 34.

Farmland

The distribution of manured farmland between economic-groups is most unequal, as the summary statistics presented in Table IV.2 show:

(5) and (11) the 17 farming-units in Group 1 own 28% of the mapped acreage, compared with 11% owned by 41 farming-units in Group 4; including men-in-*gandu*, the corresponding proportions are 30% and 10%;

(6) and (8) heads of farming-units in Groups 3 and 4 had bought very little mapped farmland, whereas farmers in Groups 1 and 2 had bought about a

quarter of their total acreage. In the case of men-in-*gandu* about two-thirds of the farmland owned by those in Group 1 had been bought (from persons other than fathers or brothers), against about one-tenth for Group 2 (see also Table IV.3, p. 64);

(12)   average acreage per farming-unit (including the acreage owned by men-in-*gandu*) is seen to fall progressively from 19·5 for Group 1, to 8·4, 4·2 and 2·8 for the other economic-groups;

(13) and (14)   average acreage per head of weighted population likewise falls progressively (2·0, 1·4, 0·9, 0·6), as does average acreage per working-man (5·3, 4·1, 2·4, 1·5);

(15)   the farms (plots) owned by farming-units in Groups 1 and 2 are on average larger than those owned by farmers in Groups 3 and 4: 3·8 and 2·5 acres, against 1·8 and 1·6 acres respectively. See also Table C.4, p. 234;

TABLE IV.2. *Ownership of manured and bush-farmland by economic-group*

		Economic-group				
		1	2	3	4	Total
(1)	Number of farming-units	17	45	68	41	171
	Number of mapped farms owned by					
(2)	heads of farming-units	71	132	144	65	412
(3)	men-in-*gandu*	28	27	20	9	84
(4)	total	99	159	164	74	496
(5)	Mapped acreage owned by heads of farming-units	270	328	253	103	954
		(28%)	(34%)	(27%)	(11%)	(100%)
(6)	of which, % bought	27	25	6	3	18
(7)	% inherited	47	64	70	74	62
(8)	Mapped acreage owned by men-in-*gandu*	61	50	34	11	156
(9)	of which, % bought	63	11	..	..	36
(10)	% inherited	20	71	..	..	41
(11)	Total mapped acreage	331	378	287	114	1,110
		(30%)	(34%)	(26%)	(10%)	(100%)
	Mapped acreage					
(12)	per farming-unit	19·5	8·4	4·2	2·8	6·5
(13)	per head of weighted population	2·0	1·4	0·9	0·6	1·2
(14)	per working-man	5·3	4·1	2·4	1·5	3·2
(15)	Average acreage of farms (plots) owned by heads of farming-units	3·8	2·5	1·8	1·6	2·3
(16)	Number of farms per holding	4·2	2·9	2·1	1·6	2·4
(17)	Number of bush-farms owned by heads of farming-units	26	40	68	35	169
(18)	Number of bush-farms per farming-unit	1·5	0·9	1·0	0·9	1·0
(19)	Percentage of heads of farming-units with no bush-farms	29	42	31	37	37
(20)	Number of owners of *fadama* farms	7	10	6	1	24

See notes opposite.

(16)   numbers of farms per holding (exclusive of farms owned by men-in-*gandu*) also fall progressively from 4·2 for Group 1 to 2·9, 2·1 and 1·6 respectively;

(18) and (19)   despite their larger ownership of manured farmland, the Group 1 farming-units own more bush-farms than others – 1·5 per farming-unit, against about 1·0 for others. The proportion of farming-units with no bush-farms is lowest for Group 1;

(20)   most of the marshland (*fadama*) farms are owned by the farmers in Groups 1 and 2.

Means of acquisition of farmland

About three-fifths of all the manured farmland had at one time belonged to the present owner's father: it had either been inherited from the father or had been gifted or bought during the father's life-time – see 'Notes on Table IV.3'. About three-quarters (74%) of the farmland owned by heads of farming-units in Group 4 had been obtained from the father, compared with about one-half (47%) for the Group 1 farmers.

Table IV.3 shows that 82% of the farmland that had been bought by the present owner belonged to heads of farming-units in Groups 1 and 2 and to

---

Notes on Table IV.2

All farm and acreage statistics, other than those in lines (17) to (20), relate to mapped farms within the manured zone (*karakara*) – see p. 13. The farms were mapped using an enlargement, on the scale of about 1 : 12,000, of an air photograph, dated March 1966, which had kindly been lent by the Survey Department, Kaduna – see Plates 33 and 35; although the farm boundaries, which are mostly low grass ridges, are clearly visible on this photograph, it was of course necessary to walk around each farm and to discuss ownership details on the ground. Farm boundaries within the marshland (*fadama*), which (as Fig. 6 shows) is only a small proportion of the acreage, could not be seen on the photograph, so that the farms there could not be mapped, the numbers of such farms only being given in the Table (line 20). Given the small scale of our map, great accuracy is not claimed for the acreage figures: all that is claimed is that they are generally sufficiently accurate for present purposes (see Table IV.3).
(2)   Two or more contiguous plots in the same ownership are regarded as a single farm, irrespective of how they were acquired (see p. 21).
(3)   All separate farms owned by men-in-*gandu* are included – see (8).
(4)   These totals equal (2) + (3). Farms owned by women are excluded.
(6), (7), (9), (10)   See 'Notes on Table IV.3' for particulars relating to the estimation of these figures. 'Inherited' includes farms given by, or bought from, fathers.
(8)   The acreage includes separate farms only; although farm-portions are sometimes given to men-in-*gandu*, they have no boundaries and could not be seen on the air photograph.
(11)   These totals equal (5) + (8).
(12), (13), (14)   These figures are respectively (11) divided by (1), and by (7) and (9) in Table IV.1.
(15)   These figures are (5) divided by (2).
(16)   The figures relate to holdings of heads of farming-units only, and are (2) divided by (1).
(17)   Any unmapped farm outside the manured zone had to be classified as a bush-farm – see p. 21. The figures are very approximate – see **Bush-farms.**
(18)   The figures are (17) divided by (1).
(20)   Most of the farms in the *fadama* (q.v.) are very small. The figures relate only to owners who are heads of farming-units; some owners own more than one farm.

men-in-*gandu* in Group 1 – they had bought 192 acres out of a total of 228 acres. Nearly a quarter of the area owned by heads of farming-units in Groups 1 and 2 had been bought, the corresponding proportion for Group 1 men-in-*gandu* being two-thirds (see Chapter VI).

The 'Notes on Table IV.3' deal with the other means by which manured farmland had been acquired.

TABLE IV.3. *Means of acquisition of manured farmland by economic-group*

	Economic-group					Economic-group				
	1	2	3 (Acreages)	4	Total	1	2	3 (Percentages)	4	Total
Heads of farming-units										
(1) Inherited from (or given by) father	126·7	209·5	178·3	76·6	591·1	47	64	70	74	62
(2) Bought from non-kin	72·4	81·2	15·1	2·8	171·5	27	25	6	3	18
(3) Cleared by present owner	25·7	15·0	25·4	13·2	79·3	10	5	10	13	8
(4) Rented (*aro*)	6·6	3·8	10·6	3·3	24·3	2	1	4	3	3
(5) Other and unascertainable	38·5	18·3	23·8	6·9	87·5	14	6	9	7	9
Total	269·9	327·8	253·2	102·8	953·7	100	100	100	100	100
Men-in-*gandu*										
(1) Inherited from (or given by) father	12·1	35·3	14·8	2·1	64·3	20	71	44	··	41
(2) Bought from non-kin	38·6	5·6	9·7	2·8	56·7	63	11	29	··	36
(3) Cleared by present owner	—	4·0	5·7	1·4	11·1	—	8	17	··	7
(4) Rented (*aro*)	5·7	1·3	1·0	1·8	9·8	9	3	3	··	6
(5) Other and unascertainable	5·0	3·7	2·5	3·3	14·5	8	7	7	··	9
Total	61·4	49·9	33·7	11·4	156·4	100	100	100	··	100
Heads of farming-units and men-in-*gandu*										
(1) Inherited from (or given by) father	138·8	244·8	193·1	78·7	655·4	42	65	67	69	59
(2) Bought from non-kin	111·0	86·8	24·8	5·6	228·2	33	23	9	5	21
(3) Cleared by present owner	25·7	19·0	31·1	14·6	90·4	8	5	11	13	8
(4) Rented (*aro*)	12·3	5·1	11·6	5·1	34·1	4	1	4	4	3
(5) Other and unascertainable	43·5	22·0	26·3	10·2	102·0	13	6	9	9	9
Grand total	331·3	377·7	286·9	114·2	1110·1	100	100	100	100	100

Notes on Table IV.3

After the farms had been mapped with the aid of the air photograph (see 'Notes on Table IV.2'), particulars were obtained as to the means by which each farm had been acquired by its present owner, the opportunity being taken of obtaining as much detailed information as possible on the history of land transactions during the past twenty-five years or so. If a farm had been cleared from bush by its present owner, no further questions were asked: but if, for instance, it had been inherited from the owner's father, then information was sought as to the means by which the father had acquired the farm, and so on back in time. If a farm had been bought, then the name of the seller was obtained; if that seller had bought the farm, the name of the earlier seller was recorded – certain farms had been

Early millet (*gero*) and groundnuts

Immediately after the completion of the early millet (*gero*) harvest in 1967, heads of farming-units and men-in-*gandu* were asked to state the total number of bundles (*dami*) that had been harvested from their various farms. The average number of bundles per farming-unit (Table IV.4) was found to fall progressively from 143 for Group 1 to 45, 22 and 14 respectively for Groups 2 to 4.

TABLE IV.4. *Millet ('gero') production and estimated groundnut acreage by economic-group*

	Economic-group				
	1	2	3	4	Total
Number of bundles of millet					
(1) per farming-unit	143	45	22	14	37
(2) per unit of (weighted population)	14	8	4	3	7
(3) Estimated groundnut acreage per farming-unit 1968	8·7	3·3	1·5	1·1	2·6

NOTES

(i) Figures cover men-in-*gandu* as well as heads of farming-units.

(ii) (1) and (2): the figures for early millet (*gero*) relate to 157 farming-units only – 14, 43, 60 and 40 being in Groups 1 to 4 respectively – and to 39 men-in-*gandu* only. The figures are estimates, some farmers having clearly rounded off their numbers.

(iii) (3): the estimated groundnut acreages are very rough – see **Groundnuts**.

---

bought and resold large numbers of times within recent memory. Much of the information for farms owned by men in the *gari* was obtained from one elderly farmer, who in many cases had a much better knowledge of a farm's 'pedigree' than the present owner, the latter commonly being altogether unfamiliar with the history of earlier transactions: his memory proved remarkably accurate, when his statements were checked with other farmers (see also Chapter VI, p. 86).

By such means, lists of farm-sellers and farm-buyers were obtained (and put to very good use in Chapter VI) and estimates of the proportion of farmland which had been inherited, bought, etc. by present-day farmers were made. While it is hoped that these estimates are sufficiently reliable for present purposes, it should be stressed that memories of transactions which occurred some time ago are inevitably somewhat inaccurate and that particular difficulty was encountered in tracing the history of large 'composite farms' – see below.

(1) Inherited from (or given by) father. All farms which were previously owned by the present owner's father are included here, whether they had been inherited from him, given as *gayauni*, bought from him, etc. For the sake of convenience, such farmland is often referred to as 'inherited' elsewhere in this book.

(2) Farms which had been bought from fathers, brothers or sons are excluded.

(4) The acreage that is rented (*aro*) is certainly somewhat under-estimated as portions of farms (which could not be distinguished on the air photograph) are sometimes rented. However (see *Aro*), most renting involves bush-farms.

(5) Included here are: farms inherited through the maternal line (estimated at a total of 23 acres); farms acquired by husbands from their wives (14 acres); pledged farms (see *Jingina*); and a considerable acreage of 'consolidated farms' (see p. 88) such that the proportions which had been acquired by various means could not be estimated.

The corresponding figures per unit of weighted population fell from 14 bundles for Group 1 to 8, 4 and 3 bundles for Groups 2 to 4, these figures being equivalent to 490, 280, 140 and 105 lbs of threshed grain if the average weight of threshed grain per bundle is put at 35 lb (see p. 222).

The estimates of groundnut acreages shown in Table IV.4 provide a very rough indication of relative groundnut production on mapped farms: these acreages, which relate to 129 farming-units only, are shown as diminishing from 8·7 for Group 1 to 3·3, 1·5 and 1·1 for Groups 2 to 4. As the farms of the better-off farmers are generally much better manured than those of the worse-off farmers, acreage ratios under-estimate the extent of the variation in the volume of production as between economic-groups and the variation in the value of production is even more under-estimated – see **Groundnuts**.

Livestock

As most farmers own no cattle and as it proved difficult to estimate the numbers (other than plough oxen – see **Ploughing**) owned by individual farmers, no figures of cattle-ownership by economic-group are presented here. There is certainly a heavy concentration of ownership among richer farmers – see **Cattle**.

A count of donkeys was made in the *gari* only: of the total of 77, 55 were owned by farmers in Groups 1 and 2 (or their sons). The number of donkeys per farming-unit (Table IV.5) varied between 1·5 for Group 1 and 1·0, 0·3 and 0·1 for Groups 2 to 4 respectively. (The discrepancy between Group 1 and other groups would be greater were it not that some richer farmers, especially those without young children, find it more convenient to hire donkeys than to own them – see **Donkeys**).

Although the sheep and goats were counted in the *gari* towards the end of the farming-season, when most of them were confined to compounds, no great accuracy is claimed for the figures, partly because such animals are sometimes left in compounds other than their owner's and also because one cannot be sure that ownership by men and women respectively was always reliably reported. However, the findings that about two-thirds of the sheep and two-fifths of the goats are owned by women is generally consistent with reports from elsewhere – see **Sheep and goats**.

With regard to sheep and goats, the only ratio in Table IV.5 which shows the consistent downward progression from Group 1 to 4, such as is shown by nearly all the other indicators so far presented, relates to the ownership of sheep by men: the average number of sheep per married man (line 4) is shown as falling progressively from 1·6 for Group 1 to 1·0, 0·2 and 0·1 for the other economic-groups. As for goat ownership by men, it is interesting to note that married men in Group 2 own 3·3 goats against 1·7 goats owned by men in Group 1, the corresponding ratios for Groups 3 and 4 being 0·9 and 1·0.

TABLE IV.5. *Ownership of donkeys, sheep and goats by economic-group*

	Economic-group														
	1			2			3			4			Total		
	Owned by			Owned by			Owned by			Owned by			Owned by		
	Men	Women	Total	Men	Women	Total	Men	Women	Total	Men	Women	Total	Men	Women	Total
1. Number of farming-units in *gari* for whom figures obtained		13			35			54			30			132	
2. Number of donkeys owned by heads of farming-units and their sons		19			36			18			4			77	
3. Number of sheep	41	35	76	41	79	120	16	75	91	3	3	6	101	192	293
%	54	46	100	34	66	100	18	82	100	..	..	..	34	66	100
4. Number of sheep per married man and per woman	1·6	0·8	..	1·0	1·1	..	0·2	0·7	..	0·1	..	..	0·6	0·7	..
5. Number of goats	44	48	92	143	112	255	59	182	241	40	91	131	286	433	719
%	48	52	100	56	44	100	24	76	100	31	69	100	40	60	100
6. Number of goats per married man and per woman	1·7	1·1	..	3·3	1·5	..	0·9	1·7	..	1·0	1·7	..	1·6	1·6	..

NOTE. The figures relate to most of the farming-units in the *gari* (only).

(In passing, it is interesting to note that women in Group 2 own more sheep per head than those in Group 1 (1·1 against 0·8). As for goats (which sell for very much less than sheep) women in Groups 3 and 4 actually own substantially more per head than women in Group 1. See p. 335.)

Ownership of granaries

Although granaries vary greatly in capacity and construction and in the extent to which they are filled with produce, the statistics in Table IV.6 are of interest as showing that over a quarter of all granaries are owned by Group 1 farming-units (including men-in-*gandu*) and that the numbers of granaries per farming-unit and per head of population are higher for Group 1 than for other economic-groups.

TABLE IV.6. *Ownership of granaries by economic-group: heads of farming-units and men-in-'gandu'*

	Economic-group				
	1	2	3	4	Total
Number of farming-units for which figures obtained	17	43	67	41	168
Number of granaries	152	164	156	81	553
%	28	30	28	15	100
Number of granaries					
per farming-unit	8·9	3·8	2·3	2·0	3·3
per head of population	0·7	0·5	0·4	0·3	0·5

NOTE. Some farmers, particularly those in Group 1, may own granaries elsewhere than in Batagarawa, which are not included here. The count was made in 1969.

Machinery

Bicycles (q.v.), groundnut decorticators (q.v.), imported oxen-drawn ploughs (see **Ploughing**) and sewing machines (see **Tailors**) are the main types of machinery owned by Batagarawa men. (In 1967 there was one mechanical grinding mill in the *gari*, but it was owned by a merchant in Katsina city.) In 1967 no resident owned a lorry, car or motor bicycle. Most of this machinery is owned by Group 1 and 2 farmers and by the *masu-sarauta*.

Of the 24 bicycles owned in 1969 by members of farming-units, 12, 9 and 3 were respectively owned by members of Groups 1 to 3. (The poorest owners acquire bicycles exclusively for hiring: they buy after the harvest and sell when in need of cash during the following farming-season.)

All the 15 or so groundnut decorticators (*sarkin aiki*) which were in working order in 1968 were owned by farmers in Groups 1 and 2 or by the *masu-sarauta*: none of the owners lived in Kauyen Yamma.

Of the 14 ploughs owned by farmers in the *gari* in 1968, 2 were owned (or operated) by the *masu-sarauta* and 9 and 3 by members of Groups 1 and 2 respectively – one plough was owned by a farmer in Kauyen Yamma. The corresponding number of plough-oxen was 35, nearly a third of which were owned by non-Batagarawa men – see **Ploughing**.

Of the 9 sewing machines in use in 1968, 2 were owned by the District Scribe, 1 by a woman, 4 by members of Group 1 (of whom 2 were sons-in-*gandu*) – the 3 operated by members of Group 3 may have been owned by others.

Other property owned by men

Hausa men are greatly interested in clothing and there is certainly a close link between a man's economic situation and the quantity and quality of the clothing that he owns: it is abundantly clear that the richest men own many plain or embroidered gowns (*riga*) and that the poorest buy, or are given, second-hand clothing only. However, no statistics on clothing-ownership were collected, intrusive questioning being avoided.

As for other kinds of moveable property, it is clear from the inventory in

TABLE IV.7. *Ownership of moveable property by 44 married men in Group 1*

Item	Number of owners	Number of men who do not own item	Total number of each item owned
Beds – iron	5	39	7
wooden	4	40	4
Mattresses	7	37	10
Pillows	9	35	19
Mosquito nets	5	39	5
Chairs	14	30	23
Tables	2	42	2
Cupboards	1	43	1
Suitcases and trunks	35	9	39
Watches	8	36	8
Clocks	6	38	6
Books	19	25	..
Radios	4	40	4
Hurricane lamps	34	10	35
Torches	29	15	29
Kettles	33	11	34

NOTES

(i) Apart from types of machinery listed opposite, there are of course many other kinds of property owned by men, including farm-tools (q.v.), cooking pots (most, though not all, of which are owned by women), calabashes, well-buckets, and other household utensils.

(ii) With regard to beds, an unknown proportion of wives own iron or wooden beds which they bring with them on marriage; however, the use of cornstalk beds is still very common.

(iii) Clothing and other property is usually stored in suitcases etc., and not in cupboards.

Table IV.7, which relates to Group 1 farmers only, that there can be little variation as between economic-groups in the ownership of such costly items as mosquito nets, furniture (such as chairs and tables), watches, clocks and radios, since very few of the richest men own them.

Such is the first batch of statistical evidence relating to the working hypothesis that our informants knew what they were about in classifying the farming-units. Further material relating to variation within the four economic-groups will now be presented.

CHAPTER V

Further aspects of inequality

Sceptical readers may have been unimpressed by the statistics presented in Chapter IV. It is no wonder, they might argue, that three intelligent and knowledgeable informants should have succeeded in classifying the 171 farming-units in a sufficiently non-random way to ensure that important indicators, such as the average acreage of manured farmland per head, should have shown regular variations between economic-group; considering all the other variables that have received no mention, this degree of inequality between economic-groups is not in the least surprising or interesting. It would have been much more remarkable, or so the critics might add, had all men been found to be 'equal'.

The possibility that this classification did more than indicate the proportion of the population which was suffering from pre-harvest hunger had first been suggested by the discovery that nearly all the farm-labourers were in Groups 3 and 4. The most interesting question is whether there is a general association between types of non-farming occupation and economic-group.

Non-farming occupations

As already noted, nearly all Batagarawa farmers, other than some of those who are decrepit or retired, pursue one or more types of remunerative non-farming occupation, either during the dry season only or (as with butchers, shopkeepers, 'yan kwarami, blacksmiths and others) at all times of the year. A most striking relationship between types of occupation and economic-group is shown by Table v.1, which is presented with no comment, all analysis being deferred until later chapters. (Farm-labouring work – kwadago – is the main paid occupation of some farmers: being a 'farming-occupation' this is not included here, but is dealt with in Chapter VIII.)

PRINCIPAL OCCUPATIONS OF HEADS OF FARMING-UNITS BY ECONOMIC-GROUP (Table v.1)

(i) Summary by occupation

Traders. Three-quarters of all the traders, and all the 'yan kwarami, are in Groups 1 and 2.

(Continued on p. 73)

TABLE V.I. *Principal (and subsidiary) non-farming occupations by economic-group: heads of farming-units*

Type of occupation	Principal occupations Economic-group				Subsidiary occupations (total)
	1 and 2	3	4	Total	
		(Number of men)			
Traders					
(1) 'yan kwarami	8	—	—	8	
(2) shopkeepers, etc.	5 ⎱	2 ⎱	— ⎱	7 ⎱	
(3) sweet potato	3 ⎰ 21	2 ⎰ 12	— ⎰ 2	5 ⎰ 35	21
(4) other	5 ⎰	8 ⎰	2 ⎰	15 ⎰	
Craftsmen					
(5) tailors	4 ⎱	3 ⎱	— ⎱	7 ⎱	
(6) builders	3 ⎰ 12	1 ⎰ 6	2 ⎰ 5	6 ⎰ 23	9
(7) blacksmiths	3 ⎰	— ⎰	— ⎰	3 ⎰	
(8) other	2 ⎰	2 ⎰	3 ⎰	7 ⎰	
(9) Butchers	2	4	3	9	1
(10) 'Free goods'	3	10	13	26	32
(11) Barori (sing. bara)	3	9	3	15	2
(12) Building and other labourers	—	6	4	10	9
(13) 'Services'	2	7	2	11	2
(14) Koranic studies	11	2	—	13	4
(15) Drummers	—	2	3	5	1
(16) Other	7	4	6	17	15
(17) None	1	6	—	7	..
Total	62	68	41	171	96

NOTES

(i) It was sometimes difficult to decide which of a man's several occupations was the principal one, especially as work is often pursued intermittently: of course, nobody thinks in terms of the income derived from an occupation over a fixed calendrical period.

(ii) Groups 1 and 2 have had to be amalgamated and certain detail has had to be omitted in an endeavour to conceal the classification of individuals by economic-group.

(iii) Trading in certain crops (such as cassava) by those who grow them was not regarded as a non-farming occupation.

Occupations

(1) Traders who buy grains, groundnuts etc. in nearby markets and elsewhere for retail sale mainly in Batagarawa. See Chapter IX.

(2) Consisting of 2 shopkeepers and 5 'yan tebur (q.v.).

(3) These traders mainly handle sweet potatoes (*dankali*) grown in Batagarawa.

(4) Those in Groups 1 and 2 are: 2 tobacco traders, 1 trader in small livestock, 1 trader in local fruit and 1 kola wholesaler. Those in Groups 3 and 4 are all traders in local foodstuffs, apart from one grindstone trader.

(5), (6), (7). See Commentary.

(8) These craftsmen are 2 dyers, 2 well-diggers and 3 carpenters (or hoe-handle makers).

(9) See Commentary. One of those in Groups 1 and 2 is virtually retired.

(10) Collectors and manufacturers of 'free goods' – i.e. materials such as grass for thatching which may be freely collected (though they are not then devoid of value), or of manufactures therefrom – such

Craftsmen. Twelve out of 23 craftsmen are in Groups 1 and 2. The 5 craftsmen in Group 4 are 2 builders, 2 carpenters and 1 well-digger.

Butchers. Seven out of 9 of the butchers are in Groups 3 and 4; of the 2 butchers in Groups 1 and 2, one is virtually retired and the other is an anomalous case of a young unmarried (fatherless) man.

'Free goods'. Nearly all the collectors and manufacturers of 'free goods' are in Groups 3 and 4.

Barori. Nine out of 15 of the *barori* ('servants' and others) are in Group 3.

Non-farming labourers. All these labourers are in Groups 3 and 4.

'Services'. Seven out of 11 of those in 'service occupations' are in Group 3.

Koranic teachers and students. Eleven out of 13 of those whose principal non-farming occupation was adjudged to be Koranic teaching or studying are in Groups 1 or 2 (see *Malami*).

Drummers. All those 5 drummers who were regarded as heads of farming-units (there were also a few others) were placed in Groups 3 and 4.

(ii) *Summary by economic-group*

Groups 1 and 2. About a third of all the heads of farming-units in these two economic-groups are traders, 8 of them being *'yan kwarami* (q.v.) and 5 being shopkeepers. About a fifth are craftsmen – 10 out of 12 of whom are tailors, builders or blacksmiths. About a fifth are Koranic teachers and students. A great variety of occupations is pursued by the remaining 17 men – see Chapter XI.

Group 3. No occupation is predominant. Eight men are small-scale traders in local foodstuffs – none of them *'yan kwarami;* 10 are collectors and/or manufacturers of 'free goods'; 9 are *barori;* 7 are in 'service' occupations; 6 are craftsmen (of whom 3 are tailors); and 6 are non-farming labourers.

Group 4. About a third of these 41 men are engaged in collecting and/or manufacturing 'free goods', of whom 8 are firewood-collectors; the remainder are in a great variety of occupations, only 2 being traders. (See Chapters X and XII.)

---

as mats, thatches, ropes, cornstalk beds, etc. (see Commentary). The total of 26 includes 13 firewood-collector/sellers and 5 makers of ropes, thatches, mats, etc.

(11) Includes servants (domestic or other) and clients and retainers – see **Bara.**

(12) Including earth-collectors.

(13) Including 5 barbers, 3 calabash repairers and decorators, 2 washermen and 1 bicycle repairer and hirer.

(14) Including Koranic students as well as teachers and 1 Arabic teacher; 8 of the 9 teachers are in Groups 1 and 2.

(15) See Commentary. (Several drummers are not included here as they are not heads of farming-units.)

(16) Including: the Chief Imam, the Hamlet Head, the Sanitary Inspector; those with several occupations none of which appears to be predominant; and a few men in miscellaneous occupations such as cattle droving, prayer-calling, road work, and cattle management.

(17) All of these men are unable to work through old age or decrepitude, except for one who is an active *dan kwadago.*

SUBSIDIARY OCCUPATIONS OF HEADS OF FARMING-UNITS (Table V.1)

Recorded subsidiary occupations (of which any individual might have one or more) total 96, of which one-third (32) are collectors or manufacturers of 'free goods', 21 are traders and 9 (each) are craftsmen or non-farming labourers: this total is an under-estimate as men may fail to mention such occupations as are pursued casually, intermittently, or occasionally, according to opportunity or inclination. Again, the large number of mentions of 'free goods' came mainly from members of Groups 3 and 4.

OCCUPATIONS OF MEN-IN-'GANDU' (Table V.2)

The relationship between non-farming occupations and economic-group is even more striking for men-in-*gandu* than for heads of farming-units and follows much the same lines.

TABLE V.2. *Non-farming occupations by economic-group: men-in-'gandu'*

Type of occupation	Economic-group			
	1 and 2	3	4	Total
	(Number of occupations mentioned)			
Traders				
'yan kwarami	4 ⎫	— ⎫	—	4 ⎫
'yan tebur	2 ⎬9	1 ⎬4	—	3 ⎬13
other	3 ⎭	3 ⎭	—	6 ⎭
Craftsmen	4	1	—	5
Butchers	1	2	2	5
'Free goods'	—	4	3	7
Barori	—	1	—	1
Building and other labourers	5	4	5	14
'Services'	1	1	—	2
Koranic studies	6	—	—	6
Other	2	5	1	8
Total	28	22	11	61

NOTES

  (i) For notes on different types of occupation see Table V.1.

  (ii) As the difficulty of distinguishing principal and subsidiary occupations was greater than with heads of farming-units, the table relates to *all* recorded occupations followed by those men-in-*gandu* for whom this information was obtained.

  (iii) Assistance given to fathers by sons is omitted, even when payment was received.

Summary by occupation (Table V.2)

Traders. Again, all the *'yan kwarami* are in Groups 1 and 2. No Group 4 man was recorded as being a trader of any type.

Craftsmen. Four of the 5 craftsmen are in Groups 1 and 2, being 2 tailors, 1 blacksmith and 1 builder.

Butchers. Four out of 5 of the butchers are in Groups 3 and 4.

'*Free goods*'. All 7 sellers of 'free goods' are in Groups 3 and 4.

Labourers. This is the only occupation pursued to any extent by members of all economic-groups, as many as 5 out of 14 of the building and other labourers being in Groups 1 and 2.

Koranic studies. All those recorded as being actively engaged in Koranic studies are in Groups 1 and 2.

Summary by economic-group (Table v.2)

Whereas 19 out of 28 occupations mentioned by those in Groups 1 and 2 are trading, Koranic studies and craftwork, no man in Group 4 mentioned these occupations.

Whereas 5 out of 11 of the occupations mentioned by those in Group 4 were 'free goods' or butchering, such occupations account for only 1 of the 28 'mentions' by those in Group 1.

The statistics in the following sections show that the various averages by economic-group presented in Chapter IV did not conceal wide variations within the economic-groups.

Individual holdings of manured farmland

Considering that those responsible for the classification by economic-group had access to no acreage statistics (the figures had not then been computed), a remarkable degree of association between economic-group and the size of the holdings of individual heads of farming-units is revealed by Table v.3, which shows that:

(i) all save one of the farmers with no manured farmland are in Groups 3 and 4, the exception being a retired father whose farms have passed to his eldest son;

(ii) as many as 27 out of 30 of those with holdings of less than 2 acres are in Groups 3 and 4; and that

(iii) all save 2 of those with holdings of 10 acres or more are in Groups 1 and 2.

If the private holdings of men-in-*gandu* are included with *gandu* holdings, as in column (12) of Table IV.2 (p. 62), then (see Table v.4) it is found that roughly three-quarters of all holdings in each economic-group fall within the following ranges: 10 – 29·9 acres (Group 1); 5–19·9 acres (Group 2); 2–9·9 acres (Group 3); 2–4·9 acres (Group 4). Only 3 out of 17 of the Group 1 holdings are less than 10 acres, the corresponding figures for the other economic-groups being 31 out of 45, 65 out of 68 and 41 out of 41.

TABLE V.3. *Holdings of manured farmland by acreage range: heads of farming-units*

	Economic-group				
Acreage range	1	2	3 (Number of holdings)	4	Total
Nil	—	1	5	7	13
Under 1	—	1	4	2	7
1–1.9	—	2	10	11	23
2–4.9	2	9	29	17	57
5–9.9	3	21	18	4	46
10–19.9	6	11	2	—	19
20 and over	6	—	—	—	6
Total	17	45	68	41	171

TABLE V.4. *Holdings of manured farmland by acreage range: heads of farming-units and men-in-'gandu'*

	Economic-group				
Acreage range	1	2	3 (Number of holdings)	4	Total
Nil	—	—	4	4	8
Under 1	—	1	4	2	7
1–1.9	—	2	9	13 } 30	24
2–4.9	1	9	26 } 48	17	53
5–9.9	2	19 } 31	22	5	48
10–19.9	5 } 12	12	3	—	20
20–29.9	7	2	—	—	9
30–39.9	1	—	—	—	1
55.7	1	—	—	—	1
Total	17	45	68	41	171
Average acreage (as per Table IV.2)	19.5	8.4	4.2	2.8	6.5

Production of early millet (gero) by individual farming-units

The figures in Table V.5 show that there is a close relationship between the reported quantity of millet produced by farming-units (exclusive of production on the private farms of men-in-*gandu*) and economic-group. Thus:

(i) all those farming-units which produced no millet at all, or less than 10 bundles, are in Groups 3 and 4;

(ii) as many as 26 out of 29 of those units which produced 50 bundles or more are in Groups 1 and 2. Furthermore, there is reason to think that some Group 4 farmers inflated their figures.

Considering that both late millet (*maiwa*) and guinea corn (*dawa*), for which no production estimates were obtained, are to some extent acceptable substitutes for early millet (*gero*); that family size (and thus grain requirements) varies greatly within economic-groups; and that better-off farmers do not necessarily aim at self-sufficiency in grain – the figures suggest that most farmers aim to produce 'considerable quantities' of millet, though many of the poorer farmers fail to achieve this.

TABLE V.5. *Bundles of millet ('gero') produced by economic-group*

Number of bundles	Heads of farming-units Economic-group					Men-in-*gandu* Economic-group				
	1	2	3	4	Total	1	2	3	4	Total
		(Number of men)					(Number of men)			
Nil	—	—	5	5	10	..	..	..	..	..
Under 10	—	—	6	9	15	—	3	3	2	8
10–19	—	2	23	15	40	2	5	7	1	15
20–49	3	26	23	11	63	6	5	2	1	14
50–99	6	15	3	—	24	—	—	—	—	—
100 and over	5	—	—	—	5	2	—	—	—	2
Total	14	43	60	40	157	10	13	12	4	39

NOTE. See Notes on Table IV.4 (p. 65).

As for millet production by individual men-in-*gandu*, Table V.5 shows that this bears little relation to economic-grouping. Some of the sons of fathers in Groups 3 and 4 who are small grain producers try to make up the deficit by growing millet on bush-farms; some of those in all economic-groups concentrate on groundnuts. (However, the figures are of interest in showing that 2 out of 7 farmers who produced 100 bundles or more are men-in-*gandu;* and that the 16 men-in-*gandu* who produced 20 bundles or more, grew more millet than 65 heads of farming-units.)

Estimated groundnut acreage

The estimates of groundnut acreage are very rough (see **Groundnuts**) and relate to mapped farmland only, but it is worth noting that 26 out of 28 of the farming-units (including men-in-*gandu*) which were recorded as having no (mapped) acreage under groundnuts are in Groups 3 and 4; and that 20 out of 22 of the farming-units with an estimated 4 acres or more under groundnuts are in Groups 1 and 2. See also Tables C.9 and C.10, p. 257.

Ownership of granaries

As Table V.6 shows, 12 out of 17 of Group 1 heads of farming-units own 4 or more granaries, compared with 16 out of 43, 6 out of 67 and 2 out of 41, respectively, for the other economic-groups. The 35 men who own only one granary are all in Groups 3 and 4. The 11 men who own 6 or more granaries are all in Groups 1 and 2.

TABLE V.6. *Ownership of granaries by heads of farming-units*

Number of granaries	Economic-group				
	1	2	3	4	Total
	(Number of farmers, with number of granaries in parentheses)				
Nil	—	—	2 (—)	1 (—)	3 (—)
1	—	—	19 (19)	16 (16)	35 (35)
2	2 (4)	12 (24)	31 (62)	19 (38)	64 (128)
3	3 (9)	15 (45)	9 (27)	3 (9)	30 (90)
4	4 (16)	10 (40)	5 (20)	1 (4)	20 (80)
5	—	3 (15)	1 (5)	1 (5)	5 (25)
6 or more	8 (63)	3 (24)	—	—	11 (87)
Total	17 (92)	43 (148)	67 (133)	41 (72)	168 (445)

NOTES

(i) See Table IV.6, p. 68.

(ii) In a few cases where the *gandu* grain is clearly stored in a son's granaries these are included with the father's granaries.

Economic inequality and age

At this stage it is necessary to ask whether the 'inequalities' we have been observing may not be mainly a function of the age of the head of the farming-unit, as would be required by any rigid demographic approach, relating the scale of a man's farming to his number of working-sons.

The full age-statistics, distinguishing between heads of paternal *gandaye* and of other farming-units, are presented in Table V.7 – to which much reference will be made in later chapters. Summary statistics are given in Table V.8, which shows at a glance that:

(i) the proportion of heads of farming-units aged fifty and over shows no significant variation as between Groups 1 and 2 (taken together) and Groups 3 and 4;

(ii) men in their forties (who are in the prime of life and often have working-sons) make up a somewhat higher proportion of the two higher economic-groups;

(iii) a much higher proportion of Groups 3 and 4 than of Groups 1 and 2 consists of young (fatherless) men under thirty.

The more detailed figures (Table V.7) show that a much higher proportion of farmers in Group 1 than in any other economic-group are aged fifty and over. Certainly, the odds against being 'rich' are particularly heavy for those under

TABLE V.7. *Ages of heads of farming-units by economic-group*: (A)

Estimated age of head of farming-unit	Paternal *gandaye* Economic-group					Other farming-units Economic-group					All farming-units Economic-group					%
	1	2	3	4	Total	1	2	3	4	Total	1	2	3	4	Total	
						(Number of heads of farming-units)										
10–19	—	—	—	—	—	—	1	1	1	3	—	1	1	1	3	2
20–9	—	—	—	—	—	—	1	11	1	13	—	1	11	1	13	8
30–9	—	—	—	—	—	3 (1)(a)	17 (2)	21 (2)	14	55 (5)	3	17	21	14	55	32
40–9	1	2	3	2	8	4 (1)	15 (1)	13 (1)	11	43 (3)	5	17	16	13	51	30
50–9	4	2	4	5	15	—	1	5	4	10	4	3	9	9	25	15
60–9	4	4	4	1	13	1	—	1	1	3	5	4	5	2	16	9
70–9	—	2	1	—	3	—	—	2	—	2	—	2	3	—	5	3
80 and over	—	—	—	1	1	—	—	—	—	—	—	—	—	1	1	1
N.A.	—	—	—	—	—	—	—	2	—	2	—	—	2	—	2	1
Total	9	10	12	9	40	8 (2)	35 (3)	56 (3)	32	131 (8)	17	45	68	41	171	100

NOTES

(a) Numbers of heads of fraternal *gandaye* are shown in parentheses.

(i) The approximate ages of heads of farming-units were estimated mainly on the basis of independent judgments made by 5 educated young men of the village, who consulted their fathers about the older men. When these informants disagreed further enquiries were made.

(ii) The single head of a paternal/fraternal *gandu* is included under the heading 'paternal *gandaye*'.

(iii) One *gandu* head, who is little older than his brother's son who is in *gandu* with him, is included, like the heads of fraternal *gandaye*, under the heading 'other farming-units'.

fifty, only 8 out of 122 of whom are in Group 1 – against 9 out of 47 of those aged fifty and over. But as many as half of the 32 heads of paternal *gandaye* who are aged fifty and over are in Groups 3 and 4.

The really significant conclusion regarding age and economic-grouping which emerges from the table is that older men without *gandaye* seldom prosper. Whereas 19 out of 43 of the heads of farming-units aged 40 to 49 who have no *gandaye* are in Groups 1 and 2, the corresponding figures for those aged 50 and over are 2 out of 15.

Although the association between age and economic-group is generally not close, there are two sets of men whose situation is apt to be particularly precarious: they are those whose fathers died when they were young (and who are not dependent members of fraternal *gandaye*) and those older men who are not *gandu* heads.

TABLE V.8. *Ages of heads of farming-units by economic-group: (B)*

Estimated age of head of farming-unit	Economic-group		
	1 and 2	3 and 4	Total
	(Numbers and percentages)		
Under 30	2 (3%)	14 (13%)	16 (9%)
30–9	20 (32%)	35 (33%)	55 (33%)
40–9	22 (36%)	29 (27%)	51 (30%)
50–9	2 (11%)	18 (17%)	25 (15%)
60 and over	11 (18%)	11 (10%)	22 (13%)
Total	62 (100%)	107 (100%)	169 (100%)

NOTE. See Table V.7.

Numbers of wives

Considering high marriage expenses and the frequency with which 'hunger' is said to account for a wife's initiative in seeking a divorce, the relationship between a man's economic-grouping and his number of wives is not as marked as might be expected, except that (Table V.9) about two-thirds of heads of farming-units in Group 1 have two or more wives, compared with about one-third of those in Group 2, and about one-quarter of those in Groups 3 and 4 respectively. But more detailed analysis shows that this distinction between Group 1 and the other economic-groups applies only to heads of farming-units aged fifty and over.

Whereas Group 1 husbands under fifty do not have significantly more wives than the average (1·3), those over fifty have an average of 2·1 wives – there being no corresponding increase with age for the other economic-groups. We have therefore arrived at the interesting conclusion that only the old and prosperous stand a really good chance of achieving the general ambition of maintaining two wives simultaneously.

TABLE V.9. *Number of wives by economic-group*

Number of wives	Economic-group				Total	Total number of wives
	1	2	3	4		
			(Number of husbands)			
	Heads of farming-units					
1	6	28	45	29	108	108
2	9	14	16	9	48	96
3	2	1	1	—	4	12
No wife(a)	—	2	6	3	11	—
Total	17	45	68	41	171	216
	Men-in-*gandu*					
1	17	18	23	10	68	68
2	2	1	1	—	4	8
3	1	—	—	—	1	3
No wife	1(b)	—	—	—	1(b)	—
Total	21	19	24	10	74	79
			Total			
1	23	46	68	39	176	176
2	11	15	17	9	52	104
3	3	1	1	—	5	15
No wife(a)	1	2	6	3	12	—
Total	38	64	92	51	245	295

(a) Nearly all young men.
(b) A widower.

Numbers of working-sons

The Group 1 farming-units have on average nearly twice as many working-sons as other farming-units (Table IV.1, p. 61), this being connected with the high incidence of *gandu* in that economic-group. About a half (9 out of 17) of the Group 1 farming-units include two or more working-sons (see Table V.10), against about a quarter or a fifth of the farming-units in the other economic-groups. However, the relationship between a man's economic situation and his number of working-sons is far less close than is commonly supposed. Thus, as will be seen (Table XII.1, p. 170), about one-third of the farming-units in Groups 1 and 2 lack working-sons, about a quarter of all farming-units without working-sons being in those economic-groups. Of the 45 farmers who have two or more resident sons (Table v.10), over half are in Groups 3 and 4 and over a third of the very favourably situated farming-units with three or more working-sons are in those two economic-groups.

TABLE V.10. *Farming-units with two or more sons by economic-group*

Economic-group	Two or more resident working-sons[a]	Three or more resident working-sons[a]	Total
		(Number of heads of farming-units)	
1	9	7	17
2	12	6	45
3	14	6	68
4	10	2	41
Total	45	21	171

(a) Sons who have migrated or left *gandu* are excluded.

Acreage of manured farmland per working-man

Nearly all the farming-units with small acreages of manured farmland per working-man are in Groups 3 and 4. Thus (Table v.11) all save one of the 25

TABLE V.11. *Acreage of manured farmland per working-man by economic-group*

Acreage range	Economic-group				Total
	1	2	3	4	
		(Number of farming-units)			
Nil	—	—	4	4	8
Under 1	—	1	6	10 ⎫	17
1–1·9	—	4	22 ⎫	14 ⎬32	40
2–2·9	1	4	13 ⎬46	8 ⎭	26
3–3·9	3	11	11 ⎭	1	26
4–4·9	2 ⎫	10 ⎫	3	2	17
5–5·9	4 ⎪	4 ⎬32	2	1	11
6–6·9	2 ⎬13	7 ⎭	4	—	13
7–7·9	— ⎪	4	2	—	6
8 and over	5 ⎭	—	1	1	7
Total	17	45	68	41	171
Average acreage as per Table IV.2 (p. 62)	5·3	4·1	2·4	1·5	3·2

NOTE. Acreages owned by men-in-*gandu* are included.

farming-units with less than one acre per working-man are in those economic-groups, the corresponding numbers for those with between one and three acres being as high as 57 out of 66.

Although as many as 11 of the 37 farming-units with 5 acres or more per working-man are in Groups 3 and 4, a number of these farmers fail to cultivate all their farmland effectively. As many as 16 out of 17 of the Group 1 farming-units farm more than 3 acres per working-man (many of them also employing labourers, see Chapter VIII); only 5 out of 41 Group 4 units are in this situation.

In the course of presenting all this detailed statistical material, arguments have necessarily been circular, and basic terms have gone deliberately undefined. On the one hand Group 1 farmers have been presumed to be 'richer' than Group 2 farmers, and so on down the scale; on the other hand the subjective nature of the original classification has been constantly stressed. One has even allowed oneself to be surprised by the great degree of *economic inequality* revealed by the various indicators, without in any way justifying the use of such an over-riding term. But now that the members of the four economic-groups have been compared from so many different aspects, and virtually all the statistical evidence has been found to point in the same direction, it is time to drop all this pretence and to assert that the analysis will henceforth be based on the definite idea that, in any meaningful economic sense of the word 'rich', most of those in Group 1 *are* 'richer' than most of those in Group 2 and so forth.

It begins to seem possible that our informants were so successful in assessing relative 'living standards' because in this economy richer men tend to be in a position to pursue all their basic economic activities on a larger scale than poorer men, their farms being larger, their non-farming occupations more remunerative in type.

In the following three chapters the classification by economic-group will be found to be a useful device for analysing farm-selling, farm-labouring and outward migration. The analysis in Chapter IX, which relates to local trading in grains and groundnuts, is a necessary preliminary to Chapters XII and XIII which are concerned with the stability of economic-grouping in the short and long terms respectively. Case material relating to poverty-stricken and richer farmers respectively is presented in Chapters X and XI. Concluding speculations on the causes of general poverty are in Chapter XIV.

CHAPTER VI

The sale of manured farmland

The sale of manured farmland is nowadays very common in Batagarawa and involves close kin (fathers, sons and brothers) as well as non-kin. Detailed enquiries (Table IV.3, p. 64) showed that about one-fifth of the total mapped acreage had been bought by the present owner from persons other than close kin – kin-sales are very common, but their incidence cannot be reliably assessed owing to secrecy and consequent confusion with gifts. Farm-selling was also found to be very common in nearby areas of dispersed settlement: in Kaukai 25%, in Autawa 31% and in Makurdi 40% of the farmland owned by resident farmers was reported to have been bought by the present owner – some kin-sales being here included.

The history of farm-selling in rural Hausaland is briefly dealt with in the Commentary – see **Farm-selling**. Here it is only necessary to remark that selling is not necessarily 'something new' (it was common in some localities in the nineteenth century) and that the general freedom of resident farmers to sell established farms to each other, *as though their individual rights over these farms were absolute*, is taken for granted by the whole community. Wider questions of land tenure can safely be ignored in this context, especially as bush-farms are seldom sold.

Very little, if any, formality attends the actual sale: transactions in farmland and in house property are similar, the former perhaps being the more casual, each of them requiring official permission if the buyer is a newcomer. As farms are owned by individuals and as it is of the nature of the case that there is no concept of lineage land, the seller is not obliged to consult any of his relatives – and, indeed, sales sometimes occur in the teeth of bitter opposition from sons. Secluded women are often ignorant of their husbands' intentions and have much less influence nowadays than when they were themselves farmers. There are no written documents; there are not necessarily any witnesses to the transactions; and the whole affair may be shrouded in secrecy, both to save the feelings of the seller and to ensure a quick sale advantageous to both parties. If the Hamlet Head is notified, or happens to learn, of the transaction, then he may be present when the sale is made, possibly in the presence of witnesses appointed by each party, who receive a commission; if the transaction involves a farm-portion, then the boundaries should be marked at that time. The official registration fee, known as *shaidi* (q.v.), which is payable to the Hamlet Head and passed on to higher authority, may or may not be levied. The buyer pays the seller the whole of the agreed sum, in cash, at the time of the sale.

But even if secrecy is often preserved at the moment of the sale, the interesting news that a certain farm has been sold soon leaks out. Everyone, including the schoolboys, knows who owns each of the farms bordering the paths on which they habitually walk and there are many farmers whose minds hold a complete ownership picture of large portions (if not the whole) of the complicated mosaic of nearly 600 plots in the manured zone. So everyone gossips about the details of the latest transaction and the seller's sons may be painfully teased by their schoolmates.

Until about ten years ago there was one important limitation on the freedom of resident farmers to sell farms to one another; farmers who migrated to farm elsewhere were obliged to hand over their farms to the District Head who could dispose of them as he wished. Nowadays migrating farmers, or other permanent migrants, are free to sell their farms to other residents when they depart, and migration has become one of the main causes of selling.

Although, as has been seen, there is no scarcity of land *as such*, the existence of a flourishing market in conveniently situated manured farmland is easily explained. The closer the farm to the residence, the less the time that is wasted in walking to and fro, often with burdens, for the purposes of cultivation, inspection, harvesting, removal of crops and manuring; and a manured farm is a piece of 'improved' or 'tamed' land (see Plate 3), free of all stumps and requiring no clearing before it is planted. The Batagarawa farmers conform very well to the 'rules' formulated by locational geographers regarding rural settlement and land-holding (see p. 306) and rich and poor alike have a preference for farming in the manured zone (*karakara*). The price of a manured farm may be regarded as a very rough measure of its superiority (over un-cleared bush-land, which may be freely appropriated) in terms of its location, cleared condition and manurial content – higher than average prices, per unit of area, being commanded by the sellers of larger farms. Men are unequal and are apt to die and migrate, and at any moment of time some farmers' effective demand for manured farmland will exceed that of others, with resultant transfers.

Our enquiries relating to 'farm pedigrees' (see 'Notes on Table IV.3', p. 64) revealed a most remarkable distinction between richer and poorer farmers; whereas farmers in Groups 1 and 2 had bought at least a quarter of their total acreage of manured farmland, the purchases of poorer farmers had been trivial in comparison. So most farm-buyers are richer farmers. But are most richer farmers farm-buyers? And who are the farm-sellers? (For the sake of the present analysis relative economic-groupings are regarded as fixed in the short-run – this being a matter which will receive attention in Chapter XII.)

In our painstaking endeavour to trace back the history ('pedigree') of each farm our informants had been asked to move backwards in time in their imagination, providing the names of each buyer and seller whenever a transaction had occurred. Certainly, the list of sellers which was compiled on the basis of these recollections was very incomplete; certainly, it was impossible to relate the list to any fixed period – in some cases, recollections went back some twenty-five years or so, in other cases not so long; even more importantly, the fact that the pattern of plots had not remained fixed over time like a jigsaw puzzle, but had constantly changed as a result of farm sub-division, consolidation, bush clearance, and so forth, meant that our informants were often being burdened with unanswerable questions. But despite all this, it seemed worth relating the list of sellers to the classification by economic-group.

Many of the farmers recorded as having been farm-sellers had meanwhile died or migrated. After removing their names from the list, as well as those of a few farmers who had sold farms which they were known to have bought earlier 'in order to help people', the names of 45 surviving, resident, heads of farming-units remained on it.

So far as concerned the list of farm-buyers, it was decided to include only those who had bought farms which still remained in their possession in 1967, for buyers often quickly dispose of their acquisitions. The list of buyers, which included 42 names, was not, therefore, directly comparable with the list of sellers, the latter including those who had resold bought farms.

Most surprisingly, there were found to be only 3 farmers (one in Group 2, two in Group 4) whose names were on both lists. (To simplify the presentation in the following Table VI.1, the Group 2 farmer is classified as a farm-buyer and the two Group 4 farmers are shown as farm-sellers – appropriately enough, for it was later learnt that they had subsequently resold their bought farms.) Farm-buyers and farm-sellers (as defined) were, thus, two distinct groups. About a quarter of all heads of farming-units had bought farms which they had retained; another quarter were known at some time in the past to have been farm-sellers; therefore about a half of all heads of farming-units were recorded as being 'neither buyers nor sellers'.

Although the list of farm-sellers was incomplete, the figures in Table VI.1 are sufficient to establish that most farm-sellers are poorer farmers, 39 out of 45 of them being in Groups 3 and 4. Over a half of all the Group 4 farmers and nearly a quarter of all the Group 3 farmers had sold farms.

As for the farm-buyers, 12 out of 17 Group 1 farmers were recorded as having bought farms which they had not resold, compared with 19 out of 45 farmers in Group 2, and 11 out of 68 farmers in Group 3.

The figures will be examined further below. Meanwhile it is concluded that much farm-selling evidently involves the transfer of farmland from poorer to richer farmers – a conclusion which does not allow for some degree of causal connexion between farm-selling and poverty (and farm-buying and relative wealth), especially as some of the transactions occurred some time ago.

TABLE VI.I. *Farm-buyers and farm-sellers by economic-group*

Economic-group	Farm-buyers (farms retained)	Farm-sellers[a]	Neither buyers nor sellers[d]	Total
		(Number of heads of farming-units)		
I	12	I	4	17
2	19	5[b]	21	45
3	11	15	42	68
4	—[c]	24	17	41
Total	42[c]	45[b]	84	171

(a) Incomplete figures – see text.
(b) Excluding one seller, who was also a buyer.
(c) Excluding two buyers, who were also sellers.
(d) Inflated figures – see (a).

The farm-buyers

Our whole analysis is based on the presumption that those who wish to expand their scale of farming usually prefer to buy manured farmland if they can afford to do so, and if any suitable plots are available. So there is no need to examine the general motives of farm-buyers, who were never asked why they had bought farms. But our statistics enable us to examine the relationship between farm-buying and inheritance.

Richer farmers with insufficient inherited farmland are able to overcome this disability by buying manured farmland – though not to any appreciable extent by renting it, as *aro* (q.v.) is always on a very temporary basis and mainly concerns bush-farms. Two of the 12 farm-buyers in Group 1 and 5 of the 19 buyers in Group 2 had in fact inherited no farmland. It was found that those with large inherited acreages tend not to be buyers: thus all the 7 farmers in Groups 1 and 2 who had inherited more than 11 acres were 'neither buyers nor sellers'. That, in general, there is a definite inverse relationship between farm-buying and the area inherited is also shown by these figures: the estimated average area inherited by the 19 farm-buyers in Group 2 was 3·4 acres, against an estimated average of 6·2 acres for the 21 farmers in that economic-group who are 'neither buyers nor sellers'.

Some richer farmers buy farms adjoining their own plots in order to increase farm-size – and sometimes they exchange farms for this purpose. Farmers do not necessarily idly wait for the farms they covet to fall into the market, but try to ingratiate themselves with the owners of neighbouring farms, hoping to persuade them to sell.

This process of consolidation is illustrated by the following two examples, the second of which also shows how some plots constantly change hands. (A few interesting details have had to be omitted to conceal the identities of those concerned.)

A farm of 12 acres (plus unmapped marshland – *fadama*) is an amalgamation of the following six portions: (i) given to the present owner by his father; (ii) bought from a man who had successfully claimed a portion of a farm which had been inherited by a woman relative; (iii) bought from a farmer who had migrated, his son having died; (iv) bought from the brother of the seller of (iii) who as a 'servant' (*bara*) was probably persuaded to sell – he has since migrated; (v) bought from the widow of a late brother of the sellers of (iii) and (iv) who was holding the land on behalf of her sons, the senior of whom had died; (vi) bought from one or more of a set of brothers who are drummers and uninterested in farming.

A farm of 8·4 acres is an amalgamation of two portions: (i) inherited from the grandfather through the father; (ii) acquired from a man who had originally pledged (*jingina*) the farm as he was in debt through gambling, and who had been unable to redeem it, having meanwhile got further into debt through his inability to repay a loan granted by the co-operative society. (The original owner of (ii) had migrated and the farm had passed to another farmer who had resold it; the latter owner had become indebted and was forced to sell to a fourth owner who resold to a fifth; this fifth owner had exchanged it for another farm owned by the gambler.)

The farm-sellers

What are the various reasons for selling farms? Why do many poor farmers sell farms while others do not? These two questions will now be examined.

To ask a farmer 'Why did you sell that farm?' is almost as ridiculous as to enquire 'Why are you poor?'. The matter of farm-selling is usually a very painful one to all but the brashest sellers – reasonably enough in a society where sellers are apt to be dubbed 'failures' by others. Although it is often a conjunction of unfavourable circumstances which causes selling, so that a man could fairly retort that he sold a farm because he was so poor, embarrassed informants commonly mention the first contributory cause which enters their heads (provided it is not too painful), or hastily provide the foolish questioner with the kind of simple answer they imagine him to be expecting. While certain types of information, such as the number of farms sold by individuals, must be obtained from other people by direct, or indirect, means – it is on the basis of such information that we have already concluded that most farm-sellers are (or have become) poor – some statements should be obtained from sellers themselves, if only because in lying about themselves they sometimes speak the truth about others. So the following list of 'contributory causes' of farm-selling takes some account of what sellers themselves said. In such a situation it is impossible to indicate the relative importance of different causes, though sale on migration is one of the commonest and most isolable. In numerous cases the seller had originally had some hope of raising the cash received for the farm from another source, so that in the first instance he had pledged the farm (*jingina*) not sold it: as this prelude is soon forgotten (see *Jingina*), no account could be taken of it here.

Contributory causes of farm-selling

1   *Migration.* As has been seen, migration is a common cause of farm-selling – see also Chapter VII. However, as migration often results from indebtedness, or 'trouble' of various kinds, this is not necessarily an isolable cause. Often a migrant's brother takes advantage of his right of first refusal to buy the farmland; but as many migrants lack brothers, or have brothers who are too poor to seize the opportunity presented, many sales to outsiders result from migration.

2   *'No food'.* Although informants volunteered that in the past farm-selling often resulted from famines (q.v.) – those with grain stocks buying from those less fortunate – nowadays the explanation 'no food' implies extreme poverty, which is unrelievable by other less drastic means than farm-selling, for instance by borrowing.

3   *Particular forms of indebtedness.* Some examples of types of indebtedness which lead to farm-selling were provided by outsiders: (i) the farm-seller was in debt to a notorious money-lender who always went to extreme lengths to claim sums outstanding; (ii) the seller's debt resulted from gambling; (iii) the seller had absconded with a sum entrusted to him for trading; (iv) the seller had been unable to repay a loan granted to him by the co-operative society.

4   *Threat of confiscation.* As farms are sometimes confiscated (*kwacewa*) owing to debt (and possibly for other reasons) and as migration may follow, this cause connects with (1) and (3) above. Farms may be hastily sold because it is feared that they will otherwise be confiscated.

5   *Inability to meet obligatory expenditure.* Informants often mention the need to raise marriage expenses as a precipitating cause of farm-selling: fathers have an obligation to assist their sons-in-*gandu*, at least in connexion with their first marriages, and young fatherless men may themselves incur much expenditure, unless they have 'rich' mothers. (See **Marriage expenses** and p. 151.) But the extent to which fathers sell farms to meet these expenses is quite unclear: it may be that they seldom go to this length in assisting their sons unless they had contemplated selling in any case. Besides, as will be seen, farm-prices are so low relative to conventional marriage expenses, that a poor man with a badly manured farm might find that its sale was of little assistance, even when the expenses actually incurred were far below the 'conventional minimum'. The same doubts arise in connexion with the very heavy conventional ceremonial

expenses associated with the birth of a son's wife's first child – see **Naming-ceremony**. On the other hand, there is no doubt that farms are sometimes sold to meet levies which are totally unavoidable, such as the community tax (*haraji*) and fines.

6 *Need to pay for something else with the proceeds.* The following examples were mentioned by informants: donkey purchase, expenditure on 'magic', house-building, plough hire.

7 *Sales following death.* The death of a poor father who (like many such) had an aversion to selling his farms, often results in the immediate selling of most or all of his farmland by his sons, who have become demoralized by long attach-ment to a broken-down *gandu*, or who have lost interest in farming. Sons of richer farmers sometimes sell farms at this juncture – see pp. 143–4. (Farms inherited by resident children are not sold, but are usually farmed by a relative until they are transferred to them on adulthood.) Non-resident sons who have maintained good contact with Batagarawa sometimes inherit farmland on their father's death, which they may then sell, after giving their brothers the right of first refusal.

8 *Too much farmland in relation to resources available.* As will be seen, many farmers who inherit substantial areas of manured farmland fail to evolve into successful farmers; such farmers may be obliged to meet their farming-expenses by selling part of their inheritance. Thus, if a man's father dies when he is too young to have working-sons, he may sell one farm in order to finance the em-ployment of labourers on the others. Similarly, if a farmer lacks manure, he may sell one farm in order to manure another.

9 *Ill health or old age.* Some poor farmers sell their farms when they become ill or old, even though they have working-sons who could take charge of their farming: they cannot find it in their hearts to hand over gracefully to their sons, who may anyway have become demoralized by their poverty. The inevitable collapse of the *gandu* may then effectively precede the father's death.

10 *Deliberate contraction of scale of farming.* Richer farmers never sell farms because of their increasing success as traders or craftsmen; if they wish to spend more time on their non-farming work the possibility of employing additional farm-labourers is always open to them. In the rare cases where poorer farmers deliberately opt out of farming, the non-farming occupation is always a menial one, such as local authority road work, or they are drummers or *barori* – though most of the latter (see *Bara*) are obliged to farm to maintain their families. It is *because* of their lack of success as farmers, that some poor men fall into despair to the point of selling most of their farmland, being then obliged to work increasingly as *barori*, farm-labourers, firewood-collectors, sellers of 'free goods'. As will be seen (Chapter VIII), most of the more energetic farm-labourers (*'yan kwadago*) are also active farmers.

11 *Impulsive or spiteful sales.* There being little to inhibit impulsive sales,

farmers sometimes angrily sell farms to spite their sons, their wives – or them-selves. One such sale involved a son's refusal to work; in another the son was a thief; in a third a wife had refused to cook. (Occasionally sons or brothers are able to stop, or even to revoke, such selling; they never appeal to the *alkali's* court in Katsina city in such connexion, and not necessarily to the *masu-sarauta*, if private sympathisers prevail on the buyer to return the farm. As farms may be casually sold, so they may be casually resold to the original seller.)

But such an analysis of the causes of selling cannot adequately explain why some farmers are much more 'at risk over selling' than others. As many as 8 of the 45 farm-sellers have sold all their manured farmland and 20 are known to have sold at least two or more farms – as an elementary Hausa grammar *(Yau da Gobe)* has it, there are those 'who keep on selling their farms, to the degree that they lack a space to farm' *(suna ta sai da gonakinsu har sun rasa wurin noma)*. Incomplete though our list of sellers undoubtedly is, there is no doubt that a large number of equally poor farmers have never sold a farm. Detailed examin-ation of the individual circumstances of poor farmers is deferred until later chapters: but a few cursory comparisons between the sellers and 'non-sellers' are made here.

The age-structure of the two groups was found to be quite similar, except that 10 of the non-sellers were estimated to be under thirty, compared with only 1 of the selling class. Omitting these 10 young men, on the grounds that they had had little time to sell, and omitting also 8 farmers who had not sold any manured farm for the simple reason that they had none to sell, we are left with 41 farmers in Groups 3 and 4 who were not recorded as being sellers, compared with 39 sellers in these two economic-groups. The average area of inherited farmland still owned by the 39 farm-sellers is 2·1 acres, the corresponding area for the 41 non-sellers being 2·9 acres. So it is probable that the farm-sellers as a group had inherited considerably more farmland per head than the non-sellers – having subsequently disposed of a considerable proportion of it. In which case it is not necessarily the very poorest people who have the greatest propensity to sell.

Many of those who do not sell farms are not only very poor, but also own more farmland than they can possibly cultivate. Perhaps there are many poor farmers who would not even sell their farms in the last resort? Perhaps many of those who do not sell are trusted as borrowers, or have many *biki* partners?

Farm-prices

Reliable information on farm-prices is very hard to collect. It is best obtained from well-informed outsiders who check what they hear by continually gossip-ing with their friends – but, of course, there is much genuine forgetfulness even over recent sales and the parties concerned may agree to conceal the real price. Much price data is valueless, owing to the impossibility of relating price and area when changes in boundaries have been made since the sale. The prices in Table VI.2, which relate to recent sales only, were obtained both from reliable farm-buyers and from third parties. Rough though they are, they would appear to justify the conclusion that prices are usually low in relation to potential yield, while covering a wide range.

TABLE VI.2. *Farm-prices*

Approximate price per acre	Number of farms
Under £1	1
£1 and under £2	8
£2 and under £4	11
£4 and under £6	9
£6 and under £10	5
£10 and over	6
Total	40

In 1967 observation indicated that the gross yield per acre of a millet (*gero*) farm which had been very well manured might have been about £9 at harvest prices, or (say) £18 if the grain were to be stored for later consumption or sale – see Chapter IX. The value of the net yield at harvest prices would vary greatly according to the cost of manure, expenses of farm-labourers, and so forth, but let us put it as low as £4. Yet £4 an acre (the value of a single year's crop at the low prices ruling at harvest-time) would not have been a low price at that time: the price was actually estimated at less than £4 in as many as half of the cases to which Table VI.2 relates. Whatever the condition of the farm at the time of the sale, a buyer who could inject capital into it in the form of manure, could be certain of recouping his outlay in a couple of years or so – and he would have acquired an asset which, owing to its position, could never lose all value.

It seems likely that these very low prices reflect the economic weakness of most farm-sellers, partly because their ill-manured farms are useless (*salla-cewa*): significantly, a badly manured farm may be referred to as *matatta* – lit. 'the dead one'. Sellers often need to raise cash at a moment's notice: they are obliged to sell, as buyers very well know. The buyer, for his part, is able to take his time and to wait until a farm falls into the market. A seller who is angry, panic-stricken, despairing, or bent on a quick sale, is unlikely to spend much time bargaining over price. If he is intent on raising £*x* immediately, he will sell the farm to anyone secretly offering him that sum. And insofar as he takes account of the net yield of the farm in 'fixing' his price, this is likely to be very low, owing to lack of manure and the need to sell or consume the grain at low harvest prices.

The wide dispersion in farm-prices is unlikely to be related to the fact that farmers lack a mathematical concept of area (see **Farm-size**), for they are very good judges of relative areas. The likelihood is that most of the highly-priced farms were either sold by men, such as departing migrants, who could afford to take their time over selling (and whose farms might be well-manured), or were bought by those who especially coveted them, being large, situated near another farm owned by the buyer and so forth. Only then do market forces operate convincingly.

Investigations elsewhere in rural Hausaland provide no evidence of there being anything notably peculiar about farm-selling in Batagarawa and neighbouring dispersed Hamlets: in all the localities studied there was some degree of selling by private farmers, though the incidence (the proportion of farmland which had been bought by the present owner) varied very greatly – variations which are misleadingly wide if a significant proportion of the mapped farmland in the localities with least selling consisted of bush-farms, and if such farms are seldom sold.

Perhaps the incidence (as defined) is highest in the Kano Close-Settled Zone, where selling has been extremely common for many decades – but there are no recent figures. The highest incidences so far recorded are: 40% among resident farmers in Makurdi (q.v.), 39% in Bindawa (Grove, 1957), 32% in Kadandani (Luning, 1963a), 31% in Autawa (q.v.) and 29% in Kaura Kimba, 5 miles west of Sokoto city (Goddard, 1971) – these figures do not compare directly with an incidence of 27% for Batagarawa (Table IV.3, p. 64), which relates to purchases of manured farmland from non-kin by heads of farming-units. In Bindawa and Kaura Kimba, but not in the other localities, bush-farms had been virtually eliminated from the agricultural landscape.

Low incidences, such as 5% to 10%, have been recorded in Zaria villages (Norman, 1967), in the extreme north of Katsina Emirate (Luning, 1963a), in Gulumbe (q.v.) and by Nicolas in Maradi – see, for example Nicolas (1968a, p. 18).

Most investigators, notably Nicolas in the Niger Republic, suggest that farm-selling is on the increase, but the peculiar case of northern Zaria, where prohibitions on selling may have been stronger after the British occupation than earlier, should be noted in this connexion – see Cole (1949, Appendix D).

Fragmentary material on farm-prices has been provided by Grove, Luning, Mortimore and Nicolas – see **Farm-prices**. Apart from Mortimore and Wilson's brief reference (1965, p. 52) to rapidly rising prices in one locality in the Kano

Close-Settled Zone, prices generally appear to be low, uncompetitive and rising slowly over time.

Our enquiries have established that in Batagarawa most farm-selling (other than that which occurs on migration) involves the transfer of farms from poorer to richer farmers: clearly, the incidence of selling is likely to be greater, 'other things being equal', the greater the degree of economic inequality. But what might those 'other things' be?

So far as our information goes, it may be presumed that the incidence of farm-selling is always likely to be high in very densely-populated areas where bush-farms are lacking. On the other hand, it is clear that a high incidence of selling does not necessarily imply land shortage. (See Hill (1970a, p. 157) for a brief discussion of size of settlement in relation to the preference for cultivating manured farmland.) It is to be presumed – *ibid.*, p. 158 – that low incidences of selling are likely in newly-settled localities where farmers are in process of establishing their manured farms.

As for possible sociological variables, there is no limit to the list that might be compiled. Are there any localities where sons have so strong a wish to set up as independent farmers that fathers are often obliged to buy farms for them on marriage? Is a high rate of outward migration for farming usually associated with much farm-selling? Is farm-pledging (perhaps for a term of years) a genuine alternative to selling in some localities? Is the renting (*aro*) of manured farmland to non-kin ever a common practice? Has the practice of selling bush-farms developed extensively in some areas? If so, are the vendors always private farmers?

CHAPTER VII

Migration

Little of the scanty historical information about Batagarawa has any bearing on migration. In the middle of the last century Henry Barth included the town in his list of the 'chief places' in Katsina Province – see **Batagarawa**. According to Abubakar Labo (q.v.) of Kaukai, the town was 'filled up with people' in the 1880s and 1890s, when he was young. Perhaps it was in 1907–8, when there was widespread grain scarcity (see **Famine**), that 'hunger' caused a large-scale exodus from Batagarawa, and more migration may have followed the terrible famine of 1914 (*malali*). However this may have been, the town fell into a decline in the early years of this century, from which it did not begin to recover until it became the seat of the District Head of Mallamawa (q.v.) in 1928. There is no means of judging whether the present-day population of the *gari* is larger or smaller than in the nineteenth century – or whether, indeed, the town occupies the same site as in Barth's time.

When studying the historical development of cocoa-growing in southern Ghana, the present writer was greatly helped by many elderly farmers whose memories went back some fifty to sixty years or more – Hill (1963). But, unfortunately, in Batagarawa there are few very old men, and our information on such matters as outward migration during the first decades of this century is sadly deficient. Most of this outward migration, which may have been on a large scale, was probably westward into Ruma District, then even more sparsely populated than it is today, and Ruma continues (see p. 101 below) to be one of the main receiving areas. Only one of the twelve Ruma localities mentioned could be found on a map, but certainly there is a large and prosperous community of Mallamawa migrants at Zanko, south of Yandaka, some twenty-five miles west of Batagarawa. The general opinion is that as the fear of widespread famine has receded, so the compulsion to migrate to take up virgin land has diminished – but there is said to have been a considerable exodus following the famine known as Uwar Sani in 1954. Before dealing with present-day outward migration, the question of inward migration will be considered.

Migration into Batagarawa

The great majority of migrants into Batagarawa are women who have come, mainly from neighbouring Hamlets, to marry Batagarawa men. (Presumably this inflow is roughly matched by a corresponding outflow, the sexes being equally balanced – certainly, many Batagarawa girls marry men in neighbouring Hamlets.) Table VII.1, which relates to very nearly all the wives of heads of farming-units and men-in-*gandu* in Batagarawa in 1969, shows that 57% of the wives are Batagarawa women, that 29% are from neighbouring Hamlets, that 2% (only) are from Katsina city and that 11% are from other Districts – nearly all of them in Katsina. There seems to be little significant difference as between economic-group in the place of origin of wives, except that a high proportion of the wives of Group 3 husbands are from other Districts.

TABLE VII.1. *Places of origin of Batagarawa wives by economic-group*

Husbands	Batagarawa Hamlet (1)	Other Mallamawa Hamlets (2)	Katsina City (3)	Other Districts (4)	Total
		(Number of wives)			
Heads of farming-units by economic-group					
1	15	12	2	3	32
2	36	18	1	6	61
3	44	18	3	13	78
4	26	18	1	1	46
N.A.	7	3	—	4	14
Total	128 (55%)	69 (30%)	7 (3%)	27 (12%)	231 (100%)
Men-in-*gandu*	46 (64%)	20 (28%)	—	6 (8%)	72 (100%)
Grand total	174 (57%)	89 (29%)	7 (2%)	33 (11%)	303 (100%)

NOTES

The place of origin of the wife is the 'home hamlet' of her father, i.e. usually the place where she was living at the time of her marriage. As husbands are often reluctant to discuss the affairs of their 'in-laws' (*surukai*), the information was obtained, by M. S. Nuhu, from a group of 5 very well-informed farmers who, in discussion, had no difficulty in providing the name, father's name (if a Batagarawa man) and place of origin of all wives.

Col. (1)   Including those living in Kauyen Yamma and in other dispersed houses in the Batagarawa Hamlet Area.

Col. (2)   Twenty-eight different hamlets were listed, most of them within 5 miles of the *gari*. Four hamlets (Autawa, Tsauni, Makada and Agama) were the places of origin of more than a third of the wives. See, also, notes on col. (4).

Col. (4)   All save 2 of these wives (who were from Kano city and Sokoto) were from 4 nearby Katsina Districts, viz. Kaura, Magajin Gari, Dutsi and Kaita. (There were no wives from Ruma, whence many Batagarawa farmers were said to have migrated in the past.) It is to be noted that a few of the neighbouring hamlets included in column (2) were probably in Yandaka or Kaura Districts, not in Mallamawa; there was no map showing the new (1967) boundaries of Mallamawa.

Few of the neighbouring Hamlets (column 2 in the table) include nuclear settlements of any size and, as already noted, Batagarawa *gari* may be regarded as the nucleus of a considerable area of dispersed settlement within which there is much inter-marriage.

Although male immigrants are made welcome in Batagarawa and may buy, or otherwise acquire, farmland once their residence has been established, there are nowadays few who arrive in the capacity of farmers, this being perhaps as much due to the shortage of house-sites as to the scarcity of farmland within a mile or two of the *gari*. Ten of the 171 heads of farming-units are immigrants, of whom 3 originally came as 'servants' (*barori*), one is the Sanitary Inspector (who is a well-known farmer), one is the Chief Imam (who came from a neighbouring hamlet on his appointment), leaving only 5 who arrived in the capacity of farmers. Of these 5 farmers, one is a young unmarried man who arrived to claim a farm which had been owned by his mother (he mainly works elsewhere as a ploughman and lodges with another farmer); the other 4 men came from neighbouring hamlets (3 of them because of some unspecified 'trouble' there) – 3 of them have their own houses, 3 have acquired small manured acreages (by purchase, by gift, or on *aro*) and 3 retain farmland in their native areas. (The members of the ruling-class, who are of Katsina city origin, are of course, excluded from the above figures, as are such immigrant *barori* as are not classified as heads of farming-units.)

As no more than about 9 of the 171 heads of farming-units had had fathers who were immigrants, it seems that there has been little permanent movement into Batagarawa during the past few decades.

Migration of men from Batagarawa

There are numerous reasons why, on the basis of enquiries made of relatives, it is very difficult to make any reliable estimates of the volume of outward migration over any definite period, or to obtain sound opinions on motivation. Relatives are often forgetful, reticent or embarrassed and are usually vague about dates. Also, there were some men who departed leaving no relatives behind. However, on the basis firstly of a statistical analysis of the whereabouts and occupations of 138 ex-schoolboys in 1968–9 (whose present age-range lies between about 15 and 35 years) and secondly of other material collected in sundry different connexions, such as the enquiry on the history of transactions in farmland, some conclusions on the nature and approximate volume of migration have emerged.

In the following summary (after which there are more detailed notes) most of the statistics are analysed by economic-group, this having proved very illuminating. The migration of sons of the *masu-sarauta* is dealt with on

p. 103 below, where migration for higher education and of highly qualified men is also generally mentioned. See p. 101 for a note on seasonal migration – *cin rani*.

1   *The volume of outward migration is quite considerable*

(a) At least 36 of the sons of present-day heads of farming-units were recorded as having migrated as adults, this number representing about 19% of the total recorded number of surviving adult sons – both figures are most certainly under-estimates. (This information was collected before the enquiry mentioned in 1(b) had been conducted; the two groups of migrants largely overlap.)

(b) Of 113 surviving Batagarawa ex-schoolboys (excluding sons of the *masusarauta*), 9 were in higher education, 41 were working away from home in other capacities and 63 were following normal farming and non-farming occupations at home.

(c) The 171 heads of farming-units were known to have had 42 brothers who migrated as adults – a figure which is certainly an under-estimate; as many as 16 of these men were brothers of farmers living in dispersed farmhouses.

(d) As many as 11 heads of farming-units are known to have migrated between about 1966 and 1969 – 5 of them removed before the compilation of the list of 171 farming-units. (It was later learnt that 3 of these 11 men returned to Batagarawa, having failed to make an adequate living.)

2   *Most outward migration of middle-aged men with families is for farming*

(a) In 32 cases the occupations of the 42 migrant brothers – 1(c) – were known; as many as 25 of them had migrated as farmers.

(b) At least 7 of the 11 heads of farming-units who departed recently – 1(d) – migrated for farming.

3   *Few younger men migrate for farming*

(a) Only 6 of the 41 migrant ex-schoolboys – 1(b) – are known to be occupied in farming, 3 of them having migrated with their fathers.

(b) Of the 36 migrant sons – 1(a) – only 4 were recorded as having migrated for farming.

(As the brothers of heads of farming-units are a generation ahead of their sons, a comparison of these figures with those in (2) clearly shows that most migrants for farming are middle-aged men with growing families.)

4   *The sons of poorer farmers have a much higher propensity to migrate than the sons of richer farmers*

Only 10% of the adult sons of Group 1 farmers – 1(a) – are known to have migrated, compared with 30% of the sons of Group 4 farmers.

5 *Virtually all those younger men who migrate to follow 'traditional style' (non-farming) occupations, which are unconnected with modern education, are sons of poorer farmers*

Of the 19 ex-schoolboys who migrated as house-servants, labourers, butchers, lorry-mates, etc., and who were classifiable by economic-group, 17 were either in Groups 3 or 4 or had fathers who were house-servants in Batagarawa.

6 *The sons of richer farmers seldom migrate when they are young except in connexion with higher education*

Of 18 migrant ex-schoolboys classified in Groups 1 and 2, only 2 were known to have 'traditional style' jobs; 8 were scholars in higher education, one was a government official, 4 were teachers, 2 were soldiers and the occupation of one was unknown.

7 *Especially so far as younger men are concerned, the general economic pull of the big cities is weak*

(a) With the exception of house-servants, very few of the migrant ex-schoolboys in 'traditional style' occupations – (5) – went to cities such as Katsina or Zaria; nearly all of them went elsewhere in Katsina Emirate.
(b) A few poverty-stricken men of all ages, as well as itinerant drummers and beggars, drift to Katsina city – most of them temporarily.

8 *Most migration for farming is to localities within about forty miles of Batagarawa, except for that to Gombe*

See p. 101 below.

9 *Migration for farming is usually permanent*

See p. 101 below.

10 *There are many poor heads of farming-units who do not contemplate migrating as farmers, presumably often because their poverty prevents this*

See p. 103 below.

11 *Notably successful farmers never migrate spontaneously*

See p. 102 below.

The following material is added to the points summarized above:
1(a) The total number of adult sons of heads of farming-units was roughly estimated as at least 190, of whom 144 were working with their fathers, 36 were recorded as having migrated (certainly an under-estimate) and 10 had left *gandu* (and were therefore both 'sons' and heads of farming-units) – see (4) below.

1(b) In 1968 and 1969 M. S. Nuhu collected information – see Hill, 1969a – relating to the occupations and whereabouts of 184 ex-schoolboys (138 from Batagarawa Hamlet – including sons of the ruling-class – and 46 from neighbouring Hamlets) being the complete membership of 8 classes – Classes I (1946, 1947, 1955, 1957, 1959, 1961), Class II (1954), Class IV (1954) – at Batagarawa primary school between 1946 and 1961. As (at least in recent years) a high proportion of boys of school age attend school (see School), the ex-schoolboys are probably a reasonably representative cross-section of young men aged from 15 to 30 (or so), with the addition of a few who are older because their schooling was belated. Seventy-nine of the 184 boys had migrated, 96 were still farming in their home areas, and 9 had died.

1(d) In at least 3 (out of 11) cases the primary reasons for the migration of a head of a farming-unit was indebtedness. See, also, p. 102 below.

4 Detailed figures of the whereabouts of adult sons by economic-group are given in Table VII.2, those who have migrated for higher education and Koranic schooling being excluded. Information obtained from fathers was supplemented from other sources – as already noted, the numbers of migrants (and hence the totals) are certain to be under-estimates.

TABLE VII.2. *The whereabouts of adult sons by economic-group*

Economic-group of father	Working with father	Left *gandu* (still resident) (Number of adult sons)	Migrated	Total
1	33	2	4 (10%)	39 (100%)
2	41	2	6 (12%)	49 (100%)
3	38	3	11 (21%)	52 (100%)
4	42	3	15 (30%)	50 (100%)
Total	144	10	36 (19%)	190 (100%)
	76%	5%	19%	100%

5 In most instances the economic-group is that of the father (or of the brother, in the rare cases of fraternal *gandu*), but when the father is dead, the classification relates to the ex-schoolboy himself. (It is, of course, a weakness of this classification for present purposes that economic-group is regarded as fixed over time – see, however, Chapter XII.)

7(a) Of 11 ex-schoolboys (including boys from other hamlets) who migrated as butchers, labourers, lorry-driver's mates, etc. (domestic service excluded), 1 went to Lagos (as a butcher) and 1 to Kazaure Emirate; the remaining 9 all went to places in Katsina Emirate – 2 to Funtua, 2 to Katsina city, 1 to Malumfashi and 4 to localities in Mallamawa, Magajin Gari, Tsagero and Kankiya Districts.

7(b)   Some drummers migrated to Katsina city recently, but are excluded from 1(d) above, not being heads of farming-units.

8   Figures relating to 39 men who migrated as farmers show that: 6 went to neighbouring Hamlets, 7 to nearby Magajin Gari (the Katsina Home District), 9 to the two western Katsina Districts Tsaskiya and Ruma, and 9 to five other Katsina Districts; the remaining 8 men (of whom as many as 7 lived in dispersed farmhouses) went to Gombe Emirate ('Bima') – see **Migration**. Although it seems likely that many migrants hope to cultivate more land very near to their houses than is possible in Batagarawa, it does not follow that the population density within (say) a five-mile radius in the new locality is necessarily lower than in the Batagarawa Hamlet Area, though this is likely in Tsaskiya and Ruma Districts.

9   *The permanency of migration*

Seasonal migration (*cin rani*, q.v.) is quite uncommon in Batagarawa. In January 1969 it was reported that only 8 heads of farming-units and 7 sons-in-*gandu* were temporarily away from home: 5 of this total of 15 had gone no further than Katsina city, 3 were merely visiting relatives, the remaining 7 men were all in Katsina Province, working as butchers, traders or labourers, and only one had gone outside the Province – to Kano. During the 1966 farming-season, 56 heads of farming-units were asked if they intended to go on *cin rani:* of the 8 men who said that there was a possibility of this, 3 have since migrated permanently. Even though many men are very poor and have little to occupy them at home in the dry season, there is no evidence which would justify a conclusion that Batagarawa men are unusually sedentary.

Most migration for farming is intended to be permanent, as shown by the frequency with which farms are sold on departure. Certainly there is no tendency, as in many West African societies, for migrants to return to their homeland on their retirement – or to re-establish themselves as farmers in anticipation of their old age. The crucial point in this connexion is, of course, the lack of lineage land, such that rights of cultivation may be automatically resumed at any time (see **Migration**).

As the temporary departure and return of young men, who owned no farms, could not be recorded, opinions were sought on this question. Somewhat evasive replies were usually returned to the general question of whether sons or brothers who break *gandu* and depart would be likely to be welcomed back, although it is always emphasized that those who migrate for Koranic studies, or who make the pilgrimage to Mecca the hard way (as no young Batagarawa men do nowadays) should retain their farming rights, however long they may be away. Young men who migrate in non-farming capacities, such as house-servants, and who keep in constant touch with their homeland while they are away, are probably usually welcome on their return; but as their fathers are often poor, they usually have to start *ab initio* as farmers. However, general opinion has it that those who have seen the world are usually reluctant to return permanently, finding *gandu* irksome.

At least 10 heads of farming-units are known to be returned migrants, the list excluding those who had travelled for Koranic studies. Among those who returned were two brothers who had sold their farms on migration as road workers, one farmer who had removed to a neighbouring hamlet but fell into such poverty that he was brought back by friends, and one man who after spending many years in Sokoto returned to see his father before he died. In a different category are several drummers who sold all their inherited farms on their departure and did not attempt to re-establish themselves as farmers on their return.

As for the three poverty-stricken farmers who migrated after the 1967 farming-season only to return by 1970, one (a butcher) has a house but no farms, the second (a barber–drummer) owns no farms or house (but has rented a farm), the third returned from Gombe Emirate after a couple of years and had to rent a house – he had even sold a bush-farm on his departure.

10 and 11   *Motives for migrating for farming*

Occasionally, as in cases of dramatic indebtedness, a specific occurrence precipitates migration, but usually farmers contemplate migrating for some years before taking the plunge. Direct enquiries about motives usually receive uninformative replies, such as that the farmer was short of (manured) farmland, or 'did not get on with his father'.

No notably successful farmers were reported as having migrated in recent years, with the possible exception of one man who had fallen massively into debt. A rich farmer who wishes to expand his production may do so by buying additional manured farmland, by establishing new bush-farms, by converting bush-farms into manured farmland and by additional investment in manure or imported fertilizers. For those with money, the situation is always under control; there is no long-term, ineluctable, irreversible, tendency for yields to fall: there is no need to migrate.

But a moderately successful, middle-aged farmer, whose family labour-force is growing, may find that migration offers him the best opportunity of matching his land and labour supplies.

It is only very rarely that the son of a successful farmer migrates in order to escape from *gandu:* as constantly emphasized, many such sons are successful farmers in their own right, having no more need to migrate than their fathers. Although the sons of unsuccessful farmers often migrate as servants, labourers, etc., they lack the finance to establish themselves as farmers, particularly as few of them own more than a very small acreage of saleable manured farm-land.

It is probable that very poor farmers seldom migrate for farming, except in the rare cases where they can join friends or relations who are prepared to sustain them during the first year or two, while they are establishing their farms – or unless they drift into neighbouring hamlets. Rather curiously, it seems that short distance migration seldom involves farmers resident in the *gari*, perhaps owing to their strong attachment to their home-town. Although the sample is small, it is worth mentioning the possibility that those living in dispersed farmhouses have a higher propensity to migrate for farming than those in the *gari:* many very poor farmers in the *gari* never contemplate migration, even to nearby vacant land, as a solution to their problems.

Migration for higher education

It is because Batagarawa is in the unusual position of being a District capital that as many as 35 of the 130 surviving ex-schoolboys covered by our sample enquiry were reported to be in 'the modern educational sector', being either students in universities, secondary schools and similar institutions, or holding posts as teachers, government or local authority employees, or professional men for which higher education had qualified them. For no fewer than 15 of these 35 ex-schoolboys are sons of members of the ruling-family including the late District Head. (Only 3 ex-schoolboys from the ruling-class have not migrated – 2 of them are teachers in Batagarawa and one is unwell.)

The fathers of 17 of the remaining 20 ex-schoolboys in the 'modern sector' are classifiable by economic-group or are *barori:* 10 of them are in Group 1 – of whom no fewer than 5 are sons of Alhaji Nuhu (see p. 158) – 3 are in Group 2, and 4 are either in Groups 3 or 4 or are *barori*. In 1970 when 6 schoolboys passed their examinations and proceeded to higher education, one was a son of the District Head, 3 were sons of fathers in Groups 2 or 3 and two were from neighbouring hamlets. These numbers are clearly too small to enable any conclusions to be drawn relating to higher education and economic-group.

The unrepresentativeness of Batagarawa in this connexion is not only due to the presence of the District Head, but also to the fact that its highly success-ful primary school was founded as long ago as 1946; most Katsina villages of this size, and many which are much larger, still have no primary school (see **School**).

So great is our ignorance concerning rural migration within Hausaland and the socio-economic factors that influence it, that conclusions, or ideas, derived from the detailed study of a single village, even over a very short period, may be useful in a much wider context, both enabling one to call in question certain widely held conventional beliefs (such as that, nowadays, most West Africans 'migrate in search of wage labour' – Morgan and Pugh (1969, p. 462)) – and provoking the formulation of testable hypotheses. Excluding migration connected with pastoralism, seasonal migration and migration into, or out of, special areas (such as the Kano or Sokoto Close-Settled Zones, frontier areas, very infertile localities, or especially magnetic or fertile areas – such as parts of Gombe Emirate – where there is a sudden rush for farmland), then (for example):

it *may be* that most migration for farming involves middle-aged men with families, who either have sufficient capital (derived, for instance, from selling their farms, if sale on migration is nowadays permitted in many localities) or who join relatives or friends who assist them during the first year or two;

it *may be* that heads of farming-units under about 35 years old, seldom migrate as farmers, except for very short distances;

it *may be* that most outward migration from rural areas is for farming, the pull of urban life being relatively weak;

it *may be* that those living in dispersed areas of settlement have a higher propensity to migrate than those in towns, even small towns like Batagarawa;

it *may be* that most young men who migrate as house-servants, labourers, etc. are the sons of poorer farmers;

it *may be* that notably successful farmers and their sons-in-*gandu* seldom migrate;

it *may be* that the 'dissatisfaction' which sometimes triggers migration is often partly non-economic;

it *may be* that most (non-seasonal) migrants, other than those concerned with Koranic studies, never return to settle in their homeland.

So little do we know that the reasonableness of such hypotheses cannot be gainsaid. The notes in the Commentary (see **Migration**) both survey our ignorance and offer some support, on general grounds, for a few of these hypotheses.

CHAPTER VIII

Farm-labouring

In 1925 slave labour was still common in Hausaland, but hired labour was beginning to take its place on a small scale, the wage being 'perhaps 700 cowries a day' – Meek (1925, p. 133). According to Abubakar Labo (q.v.), labour employment did not become really common in Mallamawa until 1942 when the famine called 'Yar Balange made many farmers destitute. Before the war the daily wage was about 3*d*. or 4*d*.; it rose to about 1*s*. in 1948 – Pedler (1948, p. 267).

In Batagarawa the farm-labouring system is known as *kwadago* (q.v.), the labourers as *'yan kwadago* – there is also a relatively unimportant system of contract labour (*noman jinga*, q.v.) with which this chapter is not concerned. The *'yan kwadago*, who provide their own tools, are paid a 'standard' wage, which varies somewhat seasonally, for some 5 to 6 hours' work during the morning and are served with free porridge (*fura*) while at work; the wage for working some 2 to 3 hours in the afternoon or evening is always half the morning (or, as it will be denoted, 'daily') rate. As has been seen (p. 47) sons-in-*gandu*, as well as unmarried sons, usually hand over a large part of their morning earnings to their fathers, but retain their evening earnings. The employing farmer, provided he is not very old or decrepit, usually works alongside his labourers, as do his sons.

Labourers are mainly employed on weeding (ploughs cannot be used for the first weeding), on ridging by means of the hoe (or 'hand-plough') known as *galma* (see **Farm-tools**) and on groundnut harvesting; larger farmers sometimes employ labourers on grain harvesting. Very few labourers are employed on sowing, a task which is accomplished extremely quickly in the sandy soil of Batagarawa; and not many are engaged on bush-clearing. As will be seen, a small number of richer farmers, together with a few of their sons-in-*gandu*, provide a high proportion of all employment; but there are many farmers who are occasional employers.

A high proportion of all the labouring work is performed by a small number of fairly regular labourers, about one-third of whom are heads of farming-units in Groups 3 or 4, the remainder being dependent men in those economic-groups.

Numerous other men and youths work occasionally as labourers, many of them in the evenings only.

As it appears that *kwadago* is seldom undertaken at the expense of 'own-farming', the system increases the effective labour force of richer farmers as a group, without leading to a corresponding reduction in the number of man-days worked on the farms of the poorer farmers. This, and other conclusions, are derived from the statistical analysis which follows.

The wage-rate

On any day in Batagarawa there is a standard wage which is paid as a matter of course, without bargaining. From June until the middle of September 1968 the wage was consistently 2s. (with *fura*) for a long-morning and 1s. for an evening – the corresponding rates in 1967 having been 2s. 6d. and 1s. 3d. Although this standard rate is a reality, which fully reflects the widespread desire to put order into the economic system by 'price-fixing' (q.v.), enquiries showed that there is no formal 'machinery' by which it is established and certainly no organized discussion among farmers. Circumstances at the time of the reduction of the rate from 2s. to 1s. 6d. in the third week of September, show the 'process of conformity' at work. (In 1967 the rate had fallen from 2s. 6d. to 2s. at about the same time.)

During the week ending 15 September (Table VIII.1) the volume of employment fell abruptly, the weekly index dropping from 120 to 82. During the following week, as many as 10 of the 24 employers for whom information was available lowered their wage rate from 2s. to 1s. 6d., and in the fourth week of the month all but one of the remaining farmers followed suit – the exception being a man who consistently employed the same labourer.

Except when the general rate is in process of changing, as in mid-September, our wage statistics suggest that daily rates are rigidly standard – to the point that if a farmer wishes to give an extra reward to a regular labourer this is likely to take the form of a loan, or of gifts in kind such as grain or second-hand clothing. (However, in the fairly rare cases when the wage is paid in grain, not in cash, the grain-value may be above the standard rate.) Non-Batagarawa labourers, from neighbouring hamlets, sometimes receive higher daily rates, as do local labourers employed on more distant farms – the addition presumably compensating for the extra time spent in walking to the farms. The fact that such cases were reliably reported, and that several labourers independently admitted that one particular employer paid the above-standard rate of 2s. 3d. for work on nearby farms, suggests that labourers would have had no strong inhibitions over reporting deviant wage-rates, had such been paid.

If the standard wage-rate is not 'fixed' or 'agreed' by employers, how then is it determined? The first point to note in this connexion is that Batagarawa

TABLE VIII.I. *Total employment offered by 40 farmers (Employers' returns)* [a]

Week ending (1968)	'Days' [b][c]	% of 12-weekly average [d]
July 14	184½ (46)	100
21	177½ (42)	96
28	164½ (41)	89
August 4	182½ (54)	99
11	213½ (45½)	116
18	189½ (41½)	102
25	208½ (51½)	113
September 1	210 (43½)	114
8	221½ (36½)	120
15	152 (31)	82
22	146 (37)	79
29	168½ (34)	91
Total	2218½ (503½)	

(a) Returns relating to farm-labourers employed by 40 farmers (see p. 108).
(b) A 'day' is a 'long morning equivalent', evening work being counted as half a 'day'.
(c) The figures in parentheses are 'days' worked by non-Batagarawa labourers.
(d) An estimate for the two weeks (taken together) preceding 14 July is equivalent to an index of 86.

is not an island: some Batagarawa men seek work elsewhere (notably with farmers living in Katsina city, who offer higher rates) and about a quarter of the total Batagarawa labour-force in 1968 was drawn from neighbouring hamlets. Batagarawa wage-rates are, therefore, directly related to those prevailing in a somewhat wider area – one which is small enough to be fairly homogeneous so far as weather, harvest dates and crop variations are concerned. Clearly the farmers are right in their assertion that wages in this wider area are not determined by discussion.

The second point of importance is that farmers are unanimous in their insistence that plentiful supplies of labour are available at standard wage-rates – an assertion which is amply confirmed by our own statistical enquiries. Perhaps, then, the process of 'wage-fixing' can be approached in terms of the question – 'Why do these rates not fall?' It seems that our analysis in terms of economic inequality explains this apparent paradox. The wage-rate, which 'establishes itself' without discussion, is effectively determined by the small number of richer farmers who account for the bulk of the demand for labour; by actually testing the market, these farmers ascertain the level of wage adequate to ensure *instant* recruitment of sufficient supplies of *high-quality* labour – it is erroneous to regard 'labour' as a homogeneous factor. In September 1968 when, as we have seen, the standard wage fell, employers were less short of funds than they had been earlier, for the millet (*gero*) harvest had been completed by the end of August; the process of wage-reduction, which occurred over 2 to 3 weeks, must have been associated with the farmers' awareness of a general falling-off in the demand for labour.

When farmers were asked why wages (in the wider area) were only 2s. in 1968 when they had been 2s. 6d. in 1967, their reply to the effect that there was 'less money about' in the later year was, at first, incomprehensible, considering the bumper harvest of 1967. But on reflection it became obvious that the employers, most of whom are grain-sellers, would indeed have had less money, owing to the astonishingly low level of grain prices during the 1968 farming-season – see Chapter IX. Furthermore, the employers would have had no difficulty in attracting adequate supplies of good quality labour at this lower wage, considering that most labourers were dependent on bought grain at that time, and that the purchasing power of 2s. in 1968 was far higher than that of 2s. 6d. in 1967 – see p. 164.

The standard wage having been thus determined, it was then payable by all farmers, as a matter of course, being demanded by labourers. In their implicit acceptance of this rate, the entire community was effectively paying obeisance to the 'higher forces' responsible for price-fixing.

For numerous reasons which are discussed in the course of this book, the marginal productivity of the labour employed by the richest farmers is far higher than the average: their labourers have a greater output of much higher average value than the average labourer – and this irrespective of the capacity of these farmers to attract the most efficient labourers owing to their offer of more regular employment. In other words, the richest farmers are much more likely than other farmers to find that labour employment 'pays'. For many farmers the marginal productivity of labour would be less than the standard wage, even if they could raise the cash to pay this: indeed it may be so low that employment at any wage is out of the question.

Although labour is plentiful (in the sense that any farmer who can offer the standard wage can recruit all the labour he requires) and although land is not scarce, the demand for labour is severely limited by shortage of working capital, especially that suffered by poorer farmers whose farms are inadequately manured.

Our statistics on farm labour employment, which will now be presented, come from two separate, complementary, sets of enquiries, which were organized by M. S. Nuhu in 1968. One survey (denoted 'employers' returns') related to the numbers of labourers employed during 14 weeks (24 June to 29 September) by 40 richer farmers – these being 16 Group 1 farmers, certain of their sons-in-*gandu*, together with a one-third sample of Group 2 farmers. The other survey (denoted 'eighteen labourers') covered the daily occupations, during July, August and September, of 18 well-known labourers – who, as the employers' returns later showed, amounted to two-thirds of all those 27 labourers (the 'prominent labourers') who worked a minimum of 20 'days' in 12 weeks on

Batagarawa farms. Although our statistics do not relate to the whole farming season, which began on 20 April, many firm conclusions may be drawn from them.

The employers and labourers

The conclusion that much of the employment is provided by certain richer farmers who employ certain poorer farmers and their dependants, is derived from the four tables VIII.2 to VIII.5 read in conjunction. The 7 largest employers, in the sample of 40, were responsible (Table VIII.2) for as much as two-fifths

TABLE VIII.2. '*Days*' *of employment offered by farmers*[a] (*Employers' returns*[b] (*12 weeks*))

Farmers	Under 20 'days'	20–49	50–99	100–49	150 'days' and over	Total
			(Number of 'days'[c])			
Heads of farming-units	57 (8)	208½ (7)	556 (8)	563 (5)	356½ (2)	1741 (31)
Dependent men	—	152 (4)	325½ (5)	—	—	477½ (9)
Total	57 (8)	360½ (11)	881½ (13)	563 (5)	356½ (2)	2218½ (40)
	3%	16%	40%	25%	16%	100%

(a) Numbers of employers shown in parentheses.
(b) See Table VIII.1, note (a).
(c) See Table VIII.1, note (b).

(41%) of the total employment provided by the sampled farmers, the 20 largest employers for as much as four-fifths (81%). As the labourers' returns suggest that: (i) there were no more than about 4 significant employers (excluding the *masu-sarauta*) outside the sample of 40 (unless there were some who relied almost entirely on non-Batagarawa labourers, or who very seldom employed any of the 18 labourers); (ii) that employment provided by Group 1 and 2 farmers (and by sons-in-*gandu* with the former) accounted for about four-fifths of total employment – it may be that no more than about 10 richer farmers accounted for about half the total employment.

If the 18 labourers had reasonably representative employers, then Table VIII.3 suggests that about a third (37%) of all employment was provided by Group 1 farmers, about a quarter (26%) by Group 2 farmers, under a tenth (8%) by Group 3 farmers, about a sixth (17%) by sons-in-*gandu* and about a tenth (10%) by the 4 *masu-sarauta* on their local farms only – most of the latter's farms were worked by labourers resident in the hamlets where they were situated. Over half of the total employment by Group 3 farmers was accounted for by 2 employers only. The employment of labourers by women farmers was trivial – accounting for only 2% of the total.

TABLE VIII.3. '*Days*'[a] *worked by 18 labourers*[b] *for Batagarawa*[c] *farmers*

Employer	Number of 'days'	%	Number of farming-units	Average number of 'days' per farming-unit
Masu-sarauta[d]	100	10	..	..
1	386½	37	17	23
2	272½	26	45	6
3	78½	8	68	1
4	2½	—	41	—
Dependent men	172½	17	..	..
Women	19	2	..	..
Total	1031½	100	..	..

(a) See Table VIII.1, note (b).
(b) Returns relating to work done by 18 well-known labourers (see p. 108).
(c) Exclusive of the 140½ 'days' worked for non-Batagarawa farmers.
(d) Most of the farms owned by the *masu-sarauta* are situated some distance from Batagarawa, being worked by labourers from nearby hamlets.

The average Group 1 farmer (Table VIII.3) provided the 18 labourers with 23 'days' employment during 3 months (a long morning counting as one 'day', an evening as half a 'day'), the corresponding average for Group 2 farmers being 6 'days'. But such averages must not be allowed to obscure the very great variation within Groups 1 and 2 in the volume of employment provided by individual farmers – as well as in the extent of their reliance on labour employment. The employment provided by 16 Group 1 farmers during 12 weeks ranged from 220½ 'days' to nil – with 11 farmers each providing more than 60 'days'. As many as 6 Group 1 farmers relied almost entirely on family labour.

TABLE VIII.4. *Classification of labourers by economic-group* (*Employers' returns*[a])

Classification of labourers[b]	Number of labourers[c]	%	Number of man-'days'[d]	%
Dependent men	113 (183)	72	1179½	69
Heads of farming-units:				
Group 1	— (15)	—	—	—
2	2 (40)	2	11	1
3	24 (65)	15	309½	18
4	13 (40)	8	207½	12
N.A.	3 ..	2	7½	—
	43 (160)	28	535½	31
Total	156 (343)	100	1715	100

(a) See Table VIII.1, note (a).   (b) Batagarawa labourers only.
(c) Total numbers of working-men in each category in parentheses.
(d) See Table VIII.1, note (b).

TABLE VIII.5. *'Days'(a) worked by labourers by economic-group (Employers' returns(b)) (12 weeks))*

	Number of labourers Economic-group						Number of man-'days'(a) Economic-group						Total man-'days' %
	1	2	3	4	N.A.	Total(c)	1	2	3	4	N.A.	Total	
A: Labourers who are heads of farming-units													
Less than 10	—	3	15	6	3	27	—	11	52	12½	7½	83	
10–14½	—	—	1	—	—	1	—	—	10	—	—	10	
15–19½	—	—	3	2	—	5	—	—	54	32½	—	86½	
20 and over	—	—	5	5	—	10	—	—	193½	162½	—	356	
Total	—	3	24	13	3	43	—	11	309½	207½	7½	535½	31
B: Labourers who are dependent men													
Less than 10	11	22	22	10	4	69	15½	71½	103	29½	14	233½	
10–14½	1	—	5	9	—	15	11	—	60½	114	—	185½	
15–19½	—	4	6	5	—	15	—	67½	102½	85½	—	255½	
20 and over	1	2	6	4	1	14	21	52½	273	138½	20	505	
Total	13	28	39	28	5	113	47½	191½	539	367½	34	1179½	69
C: All labourers													
Less than 10	11	25	37	16	7	96	15½	82½	155	42	21½	316½	18
10–14½	1	—	6	9	—	16	11	—	70½	114	—	195½	11
15–19½	—	4	9	7	1	20	—	67½	156½	118	—	342	20
20 and over	1	2	11	9	1	24	21	52½	466½	301	20	861	50
Grand total	13	31	63	41	8	156	47½	202½	848½	575	41½	1715	100

(a) See Table VIII.1, note (b).
(b) See Table VIII.1, note (a).
(c) Exclusive of non-Batagarawa labourers.

As for the structure of the labour-force, the first point to make (Table VIII.4) is that nearly three-quarters of all dependent men sometimes work as labourers: most of them are in Groups 3 and 4, and many of them seldom do this work. Forty-three heads of farming-units, nearly all of them in Groups 3 and 4, accounted for about a third (31%) of the total number of 'days' worked. Only 3 heads of farming-units in Group 2, and none in Group 1, were recorded as doing any labouring work – the number of 'days' being trivial.

Information relating to the 27 'prominent labourers' mentioned above (p. 108) confirms the findings presented in Table VIII.4. All of these labourers were members of Groups 3 and 4: 11 of them were heads of farming-units (6 in Group 3, 5 in Group 4) and 16 were dependent men – of the latter, as many as 9 were unmarried youths.

Much more detail is provided in Table VIII.5. The 36 labourers in Groups 3 and 4 who worked for 15 'days' or more, during the 12 weeks, accounted for 61% of all the work performed by Batagarawa labourers for the 40 farmers. Of the 68 heads of farming-units in Group 3, only 8 were recorded as doing

TABLE VIII.6. *Distribution of individual farmer's employment between labourers* (*Employers' returns*[a])

Farmer	First labourer[c]	Second labourer[c]	7 'days' or more[c]	Under 7 'days'[c]	Non-Batagarawa labourers[d]	Total[e]	Total number of Batagarawa labourers employed
A	22	16	14	22	25	100 (220)	32
B	7	6	10	45	31	100 (188)	36
C	8	5	5	32	50	100 (158)	28
D	64	32	—	4	—	100 (138)	8
E	15	10	19	54	2	100 (116)	29
F	17	15	13	32	23	100 (116)	17
G	19	—	—	25	70	100 (114)	12
H	10	7	—	2	81	100 (112)	4
I	21	13	17	33	17	100 (99)	24
J	—	—	—	8	92	100 (91)	6
K	16	15	36	11	22	100 (88)	7
L	12	11	9	64	4	100 (81)	29
M	11	—	—	71	19	100 (80)	24
N	24	20	—	57	—	100 (78)	21

The header above reads: % of employment[b] — Others: 7 'days' or more[c], Under 7 'days'[c], Non-Batagarawa labourers[d].

(a) See Table VIII.1, note (a). The figures relate to periods varying between 14 and 17 weeks for different farmers.

(b) The table shows, for each farmer, the distribution of employment between labourers in percentages of 'days'.

(c) The 4 columns show the percentages of total 'days' worked by: the most important labourer, the second most important labourer, other labourers who worked either 7 'days' or more, or under 7 'days'.

(d) Labourers resident outside Batagarawa in neighbouring hamlets.

(e) Total numbers of 'days' employment are shown in parentheses.

15 or more 'days' work for the 40 employers – the corresponding figures for Group 4 being 7 out of 41. Of the 53 dependent men in the Group 3 farming-units (Table XII.2, p. 171) only 12 were recorded (Table VIII.5) as working for 15 or more 'days', the corresponding figures for dependent men in Group 4 being 9 out of 35.

It is interesting that many of the dependent men in Groups 1 and 2 have no objection in principle (unlike their fathers) to working as occasional labourers – mainly in the evening, to pick up a little pocket money. About a quarter (11 out of 46) of all Group 1 dependants, and nearly a half (22 out of 49) of Group 2 dependants worked for under 10 'days' during the 12 weeks.

Much of the employment provided is essentially 'casual', many labourers being recruited for a single day at a time or for the duration of the short-term work on hand. Table VIII.6, which relates to the 14 largest employers in the sample, shows that most substantial employers engaged an enormous number of different labourers in relation to the volume of employment they provided: thus 8 of these employers each engaged between 21 and 36 different Batagarawa labourers during periods varying between 14 and 17 weeks. In only one case (D in Table VIII.6) did an employer depend to the extent of more than 25% of the total number of 'man-days' on a single employee and in only 3 cases (A, D and N) was the corresponding percentage for the first and second labourers taken together more than 35%. The farmers' preference for employing several labourers on any occasion (see p. 114 below) partly explains their inability to rely on one or two labourers only.

However, many regular labourers would find no difficulty in naming their principal employer. As Table VIII.7 shows, 6 of the 18 labourers worked 40%

TABLE VIII.7. *Distribution of labourers' work between employers (Eighteen labourers[a])*

	Under 20%	20%–39%	40%–59%	60%–79%	80% and over	Total
			(Number of labourers)			
'Days'[b] worked for single[c] largest employer	5	7	5	—	1	18
'Days'[b] worked for all employers offering 7, or more 'days' work[d]	2	6	5	3	2	18

(a) See Table VIII.3, note (b).
(b) See Table VIII.1, note (b).
(c) Thus, in the case of 5 labourers, their largest single employer engaged them for less than 20% of the total number of 'days worked; at the other extreme 1 labourer devoted more than 80% of his total 'days' to working with one employer.
(d) Thus, in the case of 2 labourers, over 80% of the total number of 'days' worked were spent with those farmers who employed them for less than 7 days.

TABLE VIII.8. *Size of work-group* (*Employers' returns*[a])

Farmer[d]		1	2	3	4	5	6 or more	Total number of occasions [e]
		Number of (i) labourers or (ii) all working-men[b] engaged on any occasion[c]						
		(% of total number of occasions[e])						
A	(i)	14	36	29	14	7		100
	(ii)		14	36	29	14	7	
B	(i)	4	17	24	22	15	19	54
	(ii)	4	17	24	22	15	19	
C	(i)		3	8	46	32	11	37
	(ii)			3	8	89		
D	(i)	61	38	1				123
	(ii)		61	38	1			
E	(i)	25	34	28	11	2		61
	(ii)		25	34	28	11		
F	(i)	10	52	17	19	2		52
	(ii)			10	52	38		
G	(i)	2	32	41	17	5	2	41
	(ii)				2	32	65	
H	(i)	28	29	24	16	3		58
	(ii)		28	29	24	19		
I	(i)	19	35	37	9			43
	(ii)			19	35	46		
J	(i)	22	54	24				67
	(ii)		22	54	24			

(a) See Table VIII.1, note (a). (The figures relate to 14 weeks in some cases and 12 in others.)
(b) Including the working employer himself and all his working dependants, as well as his hired labourers.
(c) Mornings and evenings are treated as separate occasions. The table relates only to those occasions on which labourers were employed.
(d) The ten largest employers (heads of farming-units only).
(e) On which labourers were employed.

TABLE VIII.9. *Size of work-group by economic-group* (*Employers' returns*[a])

Average work-group per occasion[b]	Family manpower only			Family manpower plus labourers		
	Group 1	Group 2	Total	Group 1	Group 2	Total
	(Number of farming-units)					
1 under 2	3	6	9	1	6	7
2 under 3	3	7	10	1	4	5
3 under 4	3	1	4	4	4	8
4 under 5	3	1	4	4	1	5
5 under 6	1	—	1	3	—	3
6 under 7	—	—	—	—	—	—
7 under 8	1	—	1	1	—	1
10	1	—	1	1	—	1
Total	15	15	30	15	15	30

(a) See Table VIII.1, note (a).
(b) See Table VIII.8, note (c).

or more of the total time they were employed (long-mornings only) for one employer; and only 5 labourers devoted less than 20% of their mornings to working with their principal employer. It might have been that there were some 15 to 20 labourers (no more) who could rely on one employer offering them employment for a third or more of their mornings.

Many labourers are recruited the evening before they are required, often through the agency of a few well-known 'recruiters', who are usually labourers themselves; larger farmers sometimes engage several labourers for several days. Farmers say that, despite the short notice, they are usually able to recruit as many men as they require, though not necessarily those individuals whom they prefer; and one well-known recruiter said that the over-supply of labour was such that labourers would even work during heavy rain.

The size of the work-group

The preference for employing several labourers at a time, rather than one man on more occasions, results from such considerations as that the labourers are stimulated by team-work, the task is achieved more quickly while the weather remains suitable and that the necessary supervision is not wasted on a single man. Only one of the ten largest employers – (D) in Table VIII.8 – preferred to employ a single labourer, all the others having chosen to engage 2 or 3 men at a time. When account is taken of the family labour available to each employer, as many as nine out of the ten farmers are shown as favouring work-groups of 4 or more men when they employed labourers – the evidence is that farmers usually concentrate their entire labour force on one farm at a time.

The same question is dealt with in Table VIII.9, which relates to 30 employers: it shows that without hired labourers, the work-groups of 19 out of 30 farming-units would have consisted, on average, of between 1 and 3 men; with the addition of hired labour the work-groups of 18 of these farming-units averaged between 3 and 8 men.

From both sets of figures it can be seen that the distinction between Groups 1 and 2 is very marked, the Group 1 work-groups being much the larger: whereas (Table VIII.9) the average work-group, including labourers, of 13 out of 15 of the Group 1 farming-units had between 3 and 8 members, the corresponding figures for Group 2 were only 5 units out of 15. By means of labour-employment 4 out of the 6 Group 1 farmers with family work-forces averaging less than 3 men, were able to raise this figure to 3 men or more – the corresponding figures for Group 2 being only 3 out of 13.

The various occupations of the 18 labourers

The eighteen labourers as a group (Table VIII.10) devoted about half of all their mornings during the three months to farm-labouring: 9 of them (Table

TABLE VIII.10. *Time spent by 18 labourers*[a] *on different occupations:* (*A*)

	Number of 'long mornings'[b]	%
Kwadago – for Batagarawa farmers	758	46
for other farmers	128	8
	886	53
On own farm – minimum figure[c]	312	19
maximum figure[c]	549	33
On *gayya*[d]	63	4
Non-farming occupations[e]	111	7
Totally idle – minimum figure[f]	27	2
Ill	20	1
Total	1656	100

(a) See Table VIII.3, note (b).

(b) Excluding evening work. The total number of evenings spent on *kwadago* was 572 – 35% of the possible total.

(c) Unfortunately, work on 'own farm' was recorded only when no paid work at all was done on that day, this total representing the minimum figure; included in the maximum figure are all those days on which the labourer was recorded as having had no other paid work except *kwadago* in the evening. The correct figure is likely to be much nearer the maximum than the minimum. The term 'own farm' includes work on both *gandu* and private farms.

(d) See Commentary.

(e) Representing days spent on remunerative work such as firewood-collection, building work, trading, etc.

(f) See (c) above.

TABLE VIII.11. *Time spent by 18 labourers*[a] *on different occupations:* (*B*)

	Proportion of 'long mornings' worked over 3 month period (Number of labourers)					
	Under 20%	20%–39%	40%–59%	60%–79%	80% and over	Total
Kwadago	—	4	9	4	1	18
On own farm						
minimum[b]	10	7	1	—	—	18
maximum[b]	3	9	6	—	—	18
Non-farming occupations	15[c]	3	—	—	—	18
Evening-*kwadago*[d]	2	9	7	—	—	18

(a) See Table VIII.3 note (b).

(b) See Table VIII.10 note (c).

(c) In 14 cases the number of days was 5 or less – in 3 cases nil.

(d) These percentages represent the proportion of the total number of evenings on which the labourer undertook *kwadago*.

VIII.11) spent 40% to 59% of their mornings on this work and 5 of them 60% or more. Our statistics on the time the labourers devoted to their own farming are unfortunately deficient (see note (c) on Table VIII.10), but it is probable that most of them (Table VIII.11) spent at least a fifth of their time on their own, or their father's, farms.

The labourers as a group (Table VIII.10) devoted only 7% of all their mornings to non-farming occupations (mainly firewood-collection and sale, building work and trading) – only 3 labourers (Table VIII.11) spent 20% or more of their time on this work. Communal farmwork (*gayya*) was undertaken on 4% of all mornings (Table VIII.10). The degree of total idleness cannot be accurately assessed but, for these particular labourers, was almost certainly very small; illness accounted for a trivial loss of time. In this connexion it should be noted that there were very few days indeed when rain made farm work altogether impossible – and our statistics show that there was a negligible degree of variation in the volume of employment offered on different days of the week.

For their morning and evening work the 18 labourers earned a total of £125 during the three months. (Evening work was common as Table VIII.11 shows.) The distribution of these total earnings between the labourers is shown in Table VIII.12: 13 of the 18 labourers earned between £6 and £10 monthly, or between about 10s. and 15s. weekly.

TABLE VIII.12. *Labourers' earnings from 'kwadago' (Eighteen labourers*[a])

Total earnings during 3 months	(Number of labourers)
£3 and under £4	1
£4 and under £5	1
£5 and under £6	3
£6 and under £7	5
£7 and under £8	2
£8 and under £9	4
£9 and under £10	2
	18

(a) See Table VIII.3, note (b).

Farm-labouring and 'own farming'

The 11 heads of farming-units included in the list of 27 'prominent labourers' (see p. 108) had the following characteristics in common: none of them was the head of a paternal *gandu*, had more than one working-son, or was in Groups 1 or 2.

But the circumstances which caused these men to work as farm-labourers were very variable, being summed up as follows:

Reason for working as a labourer	Number of heads of farming-units
Had sold his farms, or otherwise lacked farmland	4
More interested in labouring than in farming	3
Labouring wages financed 'own farming'	3
An eccentric who enjoys mixing farming, labouring and other occupations	1
	—
	11

In no case did the labouring work appear to conflict with 'own farming'. Only one of the men cultivated more than 3 acres of manured farmland and the wages he received assisted him to buy groundnut seed. Heads of farming-units work as labourers because they lack food, reckon to make more money than by farming, or require finance for their own farming.

Turning to the 16 prominent labourers who were dependent men, 13 out of 16 of them were in Groups 3 and 4, 9 out of 16 were unmarried young men (without farms of their own) and only one was a married member of an effective paternal *gandu* – and he mainly worked during his off-time in the evening. Two labourers were members of paternal *gandaye* with retired heads and 3 were members of weak paternal *gandaye*. The varying circumstances of some of the men concerned is shown by the following list:

(a) Younger brother gave 1*s*. 6*d*. from his daily earnings to his elder brother who was in charge of their retired father's *gandu*.

(b) Two brothers agreed that one of them should work as a labourer to assist in maintaining their retired father.

(c) Younger unmarried man sent out to work by his elder brother.

(d) Both brothers in fraternal *gandu* were labourers, their own farmland being insufficient.

(e) Son of a *gandu* head who had lost all authority over his sons and who worked secretly as a labourer in nearby hamlets.

(f) and (g) The married sons of two desperately poor fathers, who enjoyed working together as labourers.

(h) An unmarried man, an only son, who did his utmost to care for his ill father.

The evidence is, then, that few sons undertake farm-labouring on any scale in order to escape from their obligations under paternal *gandu*. Most sons in the poorer *gandaye* do little labouring: 10 of the 15 *gandaye* in Group 3 included no dependants who were prominent labourers, the corresponding figures for Group 4 being 5 out of 8.

The prominent employers

The two sets of statistical returns, read in conjunction, suggest that the number of farmers whose labourers worked for 30 or more 'days' during 14 weeks was little more than 28 – all these farmers (see p. 108) being included in the list of 40 farmers. Fifteen of the 28 men were heads of farming-units who could be regarded as having been very dependent on labour employment: in each of these cases the volume of employed labour was equal to half or more of the volume of family labour – on the very arbitrary assumption that family workers farmed on the average for as many as 5 'days' a week. (Five of these men had no working-son; eight had one working-son; and two had 2 working-sons.) The remaining 13 men were 4 heads of farming-units who enjoyed a useful addition to their family labour-force and 9 men-in-*gandu* – the sons of only 4 fathers, all of them in Group 1.

The largest employer was a young man who had left *gandu* and who had no adult sons. The owner of some 16 acres of manured farmland and several bush-farms, his dependence on his labourers was very great: on the average day, they provided him with the equivalent of 2·7 'days' of work during 14 weeks. Also very dependent were Alhaji Nuhu (q.v.) and Mukaddas (see p. 157) with corresponding averages of 2·1 'days' and 1·9 'days'.

The employment provided during 12 weeks by the 9 sons-in-*gandu* varied between 78 and 36 'days'; in nearly all cases, most of the employment was in the evening when these sons were free to supervise the work on their private farms.

Estimate of total labour-employment

Heads of farming-units in Group 1 were recorded (employers' returns) as having provided, in 12 weeks, about 850 'days' of employment for Batagarawa labourers – and about 370 'days' for non-Batagarawa men. If the 18 labourers were representative in this regard, about a third (37%) of the total volume of employment (Batagarawa labourers only) was provided by Group 1 heads of farming-units (Table VIII.3). Total employment of Batagarawa labourers during the 12 weeks may, therefore, be put at about 2,300 'days' – corresponding to a daily average of about 27 'days' (long-morning equivalents). The total number of working-men being 343, employment on any day represented 8% of the total potential labour-force, and a much higher proportion of those actually at work on any day.

On the basis of these estimates (and again assuming a 5-day week for family workers), the *kwadago* system is seen (Table VIII.13) to have resulted, during this period, in an expansion of the labour force utilized by heads of farming-units in Groups 1 and 2 respectively of about 21% and 6%, the labour *available to* (though not all utilized by) farmers in Groups 3 and 4 consequently contracting to the extent of about 15%. When account is taken of non-Batagarawa labourers, the total expansion in the Group 1 labour-force was about one-third – 14·5 labourers having supplemented an estimated family labour-force of 43 on the average day. But such totals of course conceal much variation as between Group 1 farmers, as many as 6 of whom employed hardly any labourers.

TABLE VIII.13. *The transfer of labour between economic-groups* (*Estimated daily employment*)

Farmers	Labourers employed[a]	Labourers provided for employment[b]	Family workers[c]	Change resulting from *kwadago*	
				No.	%
Masu-sarauta[d]	3	—	—	+3	..
Group 1	10	1	43	+9	+21%
Group 2	7	3	65	+4	+6%
Groups 3 and 4	2	23	139	−21	−15%
Dependent men	5	..	..	(+5)	..
Women	..	..	..	..	..
Total	27	27	247	—	..

(a) See p. 119 for the basis of these estimates.
(b) Estimate based on Table VIII.5. *Exclusive of non-Batagarawa labourers.*
(c) Estimate based on the arbitrary assumption of a 5-day week.
(d) The *masu-sarauta* employ regular 'farm-servants' on their farms (see **Bara**), in addition to 'yan kwadago. See also Table VIII.3, note (d).

In 1968 (see **Harvest-dates**) the first planting rains fell as early as 18 April, so that much weeding would have been done in May and June before our statistical enquiries started. Had our statistics related to 5 months (rather than 3) it is probable that the Group 1 farmers would have been shown to be somewhat more dependent on labourers than our estimates suggest.

There is, unfortunately, a possibility that 1968 was a very unrepresentative year, owing to the extremely low level of grain prices during the farming-season – see p. 108 above. It may be that much more employment is offered in more normal years, when prices rise steeply in pre-harvest months.

Employment on bush-farms

According to the eighteen labourers' returns, about one-sixth of the work they did for Batagarawa farmers was on unmapped farms. The employers' returns yielded similar results, about one-seventh of the time worked by the labourers employed by this sample of farmers having been spent on unmapped farms. For 8 heads of farming-units (all in Group 1) the volume of employment on unmapped farms varied between 51% and 25% of total employment – in all other cases the proportion was nil or negligible. (Most employment on unmapped farms involved morning not evening work, owing to the time wasted in walking to these farms.) These statistics certainly show that *most richer farmers who employ labour produce the bulk of their crops on manured farmland.*

Summing up the results of these statistical enquiries for the farming-season of 1968 (which may be atypical):

(i) About 10 richer farmers accounted for about half of total employment of *'yan kwadago* (p. 109).

(ii) About 37% of all employment was provided by Group 1 heads of farming-units, about 26% by heads of farming-units in Group 2 and about 17% by 9 sons-in-*gandu* (Table VIII.3).

(iii) Of 27 prominent labourers, all were members of Groups 3 and 4, 11 were heads of farming-units and 16 were dependent men – of whom as many as 9 were unmarried (p. 117).

(iv) Most poorer farmers did not, however, work to any significant extent as labourers. Of the 68 heads of farming-units in Group 3, only 8 were recorded as doing 15 or more 'days' work, during 12 weeks, for the 40 employers (Table VIII.5), the corresponding figures for Group 4 having been 7 out of 41. Similar results were obtained for dependent men.

(v) Many men occasionally worked as labourers (Table VIII.5) and many farmers employed large numbers of different labourers (Table VIII.6).

(vi) However, there were some 15 to 20 regular labourers who depended to a significant extent on one employer (p. 112).

(vii) Most larger employers preferred to hire several labourers on any occasion (Table VIII.8). The work-groups (including labourers) of Group 1 farmers were notably larger than those of Group 2 farmers (p. 113).

(viii) *The work of the regular labourers was seldom undertaken at the expense of their own, or their father's, farming.*

(ix) About 15 heads of farming-units (the *masu-sarauta* excluded) were very dependent on labourers (p. 119). Several sons-in-*gandu* were notably large employers (p. 119).

(x) Very rough estimates suggest (Table VIII.13) that the *kwadago* system resulted in an expansion of the labour-force of farmers in Groups 1 and 2 by about 21% and 6% – the potential (though not actual) labour-forces of farmers in Groups 3 and 4 contracting by about 15%.

(xi) The labourers employed by Batagarawa farmers spent about six-sevenths of their time on manured farmland (p. 120).

'Falle'

Labourers are sometimes paid in advance for their work under a system known as *falle* (q.v.), a word with other connotations. Although some farmers and labourers insisted that *falle* was quite common, much detailed enquiry failed to throw up many certain cases, possibly because of informants' reticence about this, as about other, forms of indebtedness. The sum borrowed seldom exceeds more than 5s. to 10s. Although it may usually be the labourer who applies for *falle*, one informant said that if there is a prolonged drought employers may contract in advance to secure the services of certain labourers when the rains come, and a very temporary labour shortage develops. Usually, it would seem, employers are reluctant to grant *falle* except to those they particularly like and trust.

The word *falle* has the general sense of 'eating something one has not got', and repayment does not necessarily take the form of farmwork for the creditor: thus, a labourer may repay the creditor in cash earned by working with someone else; he may repay in kind (an example was locust beans); or he may repay by means of non-farming work. Although he is a craftsman not a labourer, Sule Magini (see p. 158) mentioned that he often received *falle* in respect of future building work.

Farm-labour employment in Hausaland generally

All other investigators in rural Hausaland (see *Kwadago*) have reported on systems of daily-paid employment for which there are a variety of words in different regions. There is nothing in the literature significantly at variance with findings in Batagarawa and much to suggest the existence of a 'standard system' in Hausaland. Certainly, wage-levels, which are always 'fixed', vary somewhat from place to place; certainly, the volume of employment is very variable; possibly, there are some areas where many labourers are temporary migrants from elsewhere: but our main conclusions, including the finding that 'labour is not scarce', are likely to be of very wide application.

The fullest statistics are provided by Nicolas. In 16 Kantché villages he found (NK, p. 252) that 109 out of 241 farmers sometimes employed labourers (most of them only occasionally) – though wider enquiries revealed lower proportions of farmer-employers. An enquiry covering 3,132 man-days of farm-labour in the Maradi area (NM, p. 38) showed that about two-thirds of all labour was engaged on the first and second weedings, 17% being on harvesting, 8% on sowing and 3% on clearing. Another enquiry in that area, which covered 5,375 man-days of non-family farming work, showed the proportion of *kwadago* (there known as *barema*) to be 70%, of *gayya* 30%.

It is possible (if Batagarawa is not notably atypical) that the farmers' preference for employing young dependent men, especially those as yet unmarried, has been overlooked in the literature. Younger heads of farming-units may also be willing, efficient workers: in Batagarawa they do not suffer from the same fear of social stigma as older men, which makes one doubt the general applicability of M. G. Smith's finding that *kwadago* 'is practised only as a last resort by independent farmers' (1955, p. 161). Luning refers, in this connexion, to 'the extent of paid labour and the creation of a landless class' (1963a, p. 63). It is obvious that in Batagarawa paid employment is no cause of landlessness, though it may sometimes relieve its consequences – in any case, most of those who are very short of land do not work to any significant extent as *'yan kwadago*, perhaps because they have altogether lost interest in farming.

Although material relating to variations in labour-employment within the farming-season is very scanty, there is certainly no reason to accept the widespread belief in the inevitability of 'labour bottlenecks' at certain points in the farming cycle, the existence of which was emphatically denied by Batagarawa farmers, who insisted that labour was always plentiful. The main crops are harvested at different times, the general farming programme varying greatly from year to year according to the weather. However, Norman's finding (1969, p. 10, fn. 2) that the total volume of labour-employment in three Zaria villages was *not* greatest at times of peak farming activity, requires further analysis.

Perhaps there are some localities to which young men migrate as *'yan kwadago* during the farming-season. Although there are no published references to such migration, the present writer was informed that there were immigrant labourers in Gulumbe (q.v.) and has learnt, from Mary Tiffen, of their existence in richer villages in Gombe Emirate, where farming has expanded very rapidly.

CHAPTER IX

Local trade in grains and groundnuts

Considered as an island economy, Batagarawa is probably always a net 'importer' of grain, the main counter-balancing export being, of course, groundnuts. Local farmer–traders, known as *'yan kwarami* (sing. *dan kwarami*) are responsible for procuring most of the imported grain from producing areas which lie to the south and west.

The type of trade known as *kwarami* has been wholly ignored in the literature, except by the compilers of dictionaries who casually define it as, e.g., 'trading in corn, buying in villages and selling in towns' (Bargery) – see *Kwarami*. The essential features of *kwarami*, as it exists in Batagarawa and nearby localities, are: that it is relatively localized (in contrast to *fatauci*), the trader usually making the return journey to the supplying area in one day; that the traders are mainly concerned with provisioning their home area; that the traders operate on a moderate scale, buy frequently and usually lack the financial strength to hold produce for a price rise for more than a week or so; that other produce (such as groundnuts, cowpeas, locust beans) may be handled besides grains; and that the traders are non-specialists in the sense that farming takes up most of their time during the farming-season, when the demand for grain may be highest. *Kwarami* is to be distinguished from those types of trade which necessarily involve long-term storage for a price-rise – for which there are many Hausa words, but see *Soke*. Nor is it to be confused with itinerant trading, within a small radius, sometimes known as *jagale* or *jaura*.

In 1967 there were about a dozen regular *'yan kwarami* in Batagarawa and a few others who traded spasmodically. Nearly all of them were youngish men in Group 2, sons-in-*gandu* as well as heads of farming-units. Most of them handled a variety of produce, which they bought either at rural periodic markets in 'grain surplus' areas (never in Katsina city) or directly from farmers' granaries. The most commonly frequented market was at 'Yar Gamji (see Fig. 3, p. 10), a small centre some ten miles south of Batagarawa (near Tsanni), to which about half of the regular traders travelled weekly by lorry; also commonly attended was Bakiyawa market, some ten miles to the west. Other local markets where supplies were obtained included Batsari, Gangara, Tsauri and (occasionally) Dutsin Ma.

Many *'yan kwarami* buy some of their produce from agents or friends (*abokan arziki*), who obtain supplies from other farmers and store on their behalves. One *dan kwarami* reported having four such agents, one at 'Yar Gamji, two at hamlets south of Batagarawa and one to the north-west of Katsina city – the latter three bought all their supplies outside markets; he sent his son with a donkey to collect the produce. These agents received their expenses, which they reported in detail, and a commission of perhaps 5*s.* a bag (or sack) of grain or cowpeas – a low margin, corresponding to less than 2*d.* a *tiya*.

Another *dan kwarami* had agents first at Zakka, west of Kurfi, a place about thirty miles south-west of Batagarawa where grain was reported to be cheap as there was no road, and second in a roadless western area nearer Batagarawa. Not being as short of finance as most *'yan kwarami*, he gave his agents sums such as £10 and £20 at harvest-time to spend on his behalf.

The Batagarawa *'yan kwarami* also buy small quantities from a few farmer–traders, from grain-surplus areas, such as Kurfi and Tsauri, who themselves transport the produce to the *gari*, as well as from a small number of Batagarawa farmers who prefer to sell their own produce through local intermediaries, rather than disposing of it for themselves.

The '*honeycomb-market*'

Although a few of the *'yan kwarami* dispose of their surpluses in the nearby markets at Abukur and Katsina city, their main business is that of provisioning the people of Batagarawa, including the women purveyors of cooked foods: there being (as it was reported) 'some *'yan kwarami* in every hamlet', few outsiders come into Batagarawa to buy. The produce is retailed from the traders' houses, mainly by their secluded wives, though to a small extent by the men themselves. These wives constitute a species of 'honeycomb-market', the separate cells of which are mainly linked by children who 'shop around' on behalf of their mothers – see **House-trade**. It will now be shown that there is truth, not mere aspiration, in the common assertion that the prices of each type of produce are 'fixed' in this 'market' on any day. (See also **Price-fixing**.)

The price information which circulates through Batagarawa, almost as though it were a stock exchange, is always expressed in terms of a standard enamelware bowl known as a *tiya* (q.v.), which holds about 6 lbs of grain, with some variation according to type and moisture content, and which is used for measuring grain issued by husbands to wives for household consumption, as well as in trading.

Statistics of prices charged were collected from 4 *'yan kwarami* for 5 months

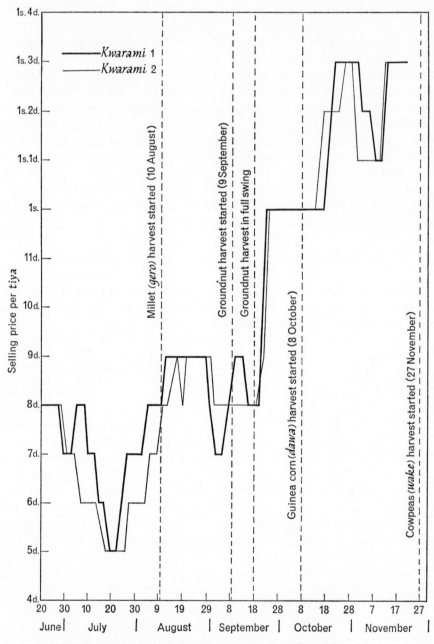

Fig. 10. Retail selling price of early millet (*gero*), 1968 (after Hill, 1969b)

in 1968 (June to November). The separate graphs of these prices showed such a close correspondence that they could not be clearly plotted on the same sheet, and Fig. 10 relates to the prices charged by 2 *'yan kwarami* only. The two graphs are shown to be strikingly similar – a similarity which would have been even more pronounced had it not happened that the price information was obtained from each trader on different days. Additional information was collected from 11 *'yan kwarami* on three separate dates. On 28 October 1968, when the price trend was strongly upwards, 4 of these *'yan kwarami* charged 1s. 1d. per *tiya* of early millet, 3 charged 1s. 2d. and 2 charged 1s. 3d. – no quotations were obtained from the other 2 traders; on 6 and 16 November all 11 *'yan kwarami* were charging 1s. 2d. and 1s. 3d. respectively.

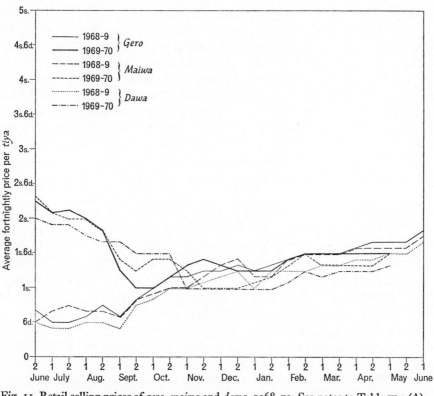

Fig. 11. Retail selling prices of *gero*, *maiwa* and *dawa*, 1968–70. See notes to Table IX.1 (A)

Such a degree of price uniformity is easily explained. When instructing their wives as to the prices per *tiya* that they should charge, the *'yan kwarami* are mainly guided by the prices they themselves paid for the produce – usually quite recently, owing to their inability to lock up their capital in stored produce. These buying prices, according to information obtained from the traders themselves, show little variation on any day, the same being true of trading margins.

Statistics relating to the reported trading margins of 2 traders for sixteen months ending May 1970 showed that each of them usually charged 2*d.* per *tiya* over his buying price for guinea corn, 2*d.* or (half as often) 3*d.* for early millet and 2*d.* or (somewhat more often) 3*d.* for cowpeas – there being no clear relationship between margin and price so far as any produce was concerned. In the case of shelled groundnuts, in November 1969 to March 1970 both traders reported that their margins were nil; at other times margins were most commonly 2*d.*, though sometimes 1*d.* or 3*d.* When retail grain prices were of the order of 1*s.* 6*d.* per *tiya*, as they were for about half the period (see Fig. 11), margins were about 10% to 15% of retail prices.

Paradoxical though it may seem, such a 'honeycomb-market' may serve a rural community more efficiently than a conventional open market-place, this being mainly because it is in constant session, unlike a rural periodic market which in northern Katsina would seldom function more often than once in seven days – and then usually in the evening only, unless it were large enough to attract outside traders – see **Market-place.** The 'fixed price for the day' is as competitively determined as in an open arena, for much enquiry established that buyers do not have their regular suppliers, but rather instruct their children to buy anywhere at a certain price. Before these and other matters affecting the local trade in grain and groundnuts are further considered, the important question of seasonal price fluctuations will be examined.

Price fluctuations

Such a competitive market provides ideal opportunities for studying the neglected subject of rural seasonal price fluctuations. The prices charged by the Batagarawa *'yan kwarami,* who hold no stocks, and operate competitively, clearly reflect those prevailing in the main supplying markets – as enquiries in those markets in 1966 and 1967 confirmed. The *'yan kwarami* make it their business to be well informed with regard to relative price movements in different markets, and endeavour to buy where prices are lowest. Furthermore, enquiries made in several large markets outside the range of the Batagarawa *'yan kwarami,* such as Jibiya and Mai-Aduwa (both very near the frontier with the Niger Republic), suggested the possibility of there being a vast northern area of the North Central State within which grain prices tend to fluctuate similarly. In short, so far as supplies of essential produce are concerned, Batagarawa is merely a small part of a wide economic community, being at the mercy of economic events in a large area, over which she has absolutely no control. The *'yan kwarami* are efficient and the village is not isolated: there is every reason to suppose that Batagarawa prices follow a very similar course to those in hundreds of hamlets and villages in the same 'catchment area'. This being so, it seems worth following, in some detail, the movement of prices in the honeycomb-market.

Grain prices

In the pre-harvest months of 1966 it was the unanimous opinion of both traders in northern Katsina markets and of ordinary consumers in Batagarawa that grain prices were higher than ever before. The 1965 harvest having been considered reasonably good, people were puzzled by these soaring prices – which might easily have been accounted for (though no one suggested this) by the farmers' unwillingness to deplete their granary stocks to the usual degree as the harvest approached, owing to political uncertainties and the riots following the military *coup* in January. However this may have been, grain prices remained consistently high, and very stable, for some four months, reaching a peak in Batagarawa of about 2s. 6d. a *tiya* in August – about £47 a ton of early millet (*gero*).

In August of the following year (1967) grain prices were only slightly lower than in the same month of 1966. As new season *gero* became available at certain supplying markets, prices began to fall; by the middle of September the *gero* price was about 1s. 6d. (all prices are per *tiya*); and throughout October it stood at 1s. At that time it had seemed reasonable to assume that the pattern of seasonal price fluctuations for grains involved a rough halving of prices during the weeks immediately preceding the early millet harvest (when farmers were sufficiently sure of the harvest-date to risk disposing of their surplus stocks) and a gradual build-up of prices following the guinea-corn harvest which, according to planting dates and weather, might be up to two months or more later than the millet harvest. Seasonal price fluctuations on this scale evidently had such important socio-economic implications in a community where many households were partly, if not mainly, dependent on bought grain, that it was decided to arrange for the collection of regular price statistics over a term of years. Figures for nearly two years, beginning June 1968, are presented here – for groundnuts, cowpeas and locust beans (*kalwa*), as well as for the three types of grain.

The results were astonishing for two reasons: on the one hand they indicated that seasonal price fluctuations (which are clearly related to harvest-dates) are apt to be even more severe than one's preliminary enquiries (together with scanty material from other sources) had led one to suppose; on the other hand they showed that prices sometimes move so erratically and unpredictably as to reverse the normal seasonal trend. Given prices of over 2s. in July 1966 and July 1967 it had not been regarded as conceivable that the price of *gero* in the pre-harvest month of July could stand as low as 6d., as it did in 1968. The prolonged fall of grain prices after the 1967 harvest surprised the farmers of Batagarawa, as well as the present writer; one man, who lacked storage capacity, suffered severe financial loss on several tons bought soon after harvest for 1s. a *tiya*, for quick resale (as he had hoped) at a profit.

TABLE IX.1. *Retail selling prices of produce per 'tiya': (A)*

Date	Early millet (gero)		Guinea corn (dawa)		Late millet (maiwa)	
	1968–9	1969–70	1968–9	1969–70	1968–9	1969–70
June (2)	8d.	2/3	6d.	2/-	6d.	2/4
July (1)	6d.	2/1	5d.	1/11	8d.	2/1
(2)	6d.	2/2	5d.	1/11	9d.	2/-
Aug. (1)	7d.	2/-	6d.	1/9	8d.	2/-
(2)	9d.	1/10	6d.	1/8	8d.	1/10
Sept. (1)	7d.	1/3	5d.	1/8	7d.	1/5
(2)	10d.	1/-	9d.	1/6	10d.	1/3
Oct. (1)	1/-	1/-	10d.	1/6	11d.	1/5
(2)	1/2	1/2	1/-	1/6	1/-	1/5
Nov. (1)	1/2	1/4	1/-	1/-	1/-	1/3
(2)	1/3	1/5	1/1	1/-	1/2	1/-
Dec. (1)	1/3	1/4	1/2	1/-	1/4	1/-
(2)	1/4	1/3	1/3	1/-	1/5	1/-
Jan. (1)	1/3	1/3	1/-	1/-	1/2	1/1
(2)	1/4	1/3	1/3	1/-	1/2	1/2
Feb. (1)	1/5	1/5	1/3	1/1	1/5	1/4
(2)	1/6	1/6	1/3	1/3	1/6	1/6
March (1)	1/6	1/6	1/4	1/2	1/6	1/4
(2)	1/6	1/6	1/4	1/3	1/6	1/4
April (1)	1/7	1/6	1/5	1/3	1/7	1/4
(2)	1/8	1/6	1/5	1/3	1/7	1/4
May (1)	1/8	1/6	1/6	1/4	1/7	1/6
(2)	1/8	..	1/6	..	1/7	..
June (1)	1/10	..	1/8	..	1/9	..

NOTES

(i) The prices are rounded averages of several quotations for each half-month, for a single Batagarawa *dan kwarami*. (The statistics were, in fact, obtained from two *'yan kwarami*, but were so similar that it seemed unnecessary to include both sets.)

(ii) See Figs. 11, 12 and 13 which are based on this table.

(iii) For quantities of the various produce per *tiya*, see **Tiya**.

Our graphs – see Fig. 11 on p. 127 and Figs. 12 and 13 on pp. 131 and 132 – and statistics (Table IX.1) show that the price fluctuations of the three grains, which for convenience are here referred to as *dawa* (guinea corn), *gero* (early millet) and *maiwa* (late millet), usually (though not invariably) follow very similar patterns and that (allowing for the fact that a *tiya* of *gero* or *maiwa* weighs about 6 lbs, compared with about 5½ lbs for the coarser-grained *dawa*) the prices of the three grains are usually about equal. (The three grains are to a large extent substitutes: although *dawa* is the preferred grain for *tuwo*, *gero* is often an acceptable alternative.) Price movements for the three grains will therefore be considered together.

To the bewilderment of the farmers, who regard seasonal price fluctuations as a phenomenon to be taken for granted, the low prices prevailing after the 1967 harvest, showed a persistent, prolonged tendency to fall and to go on falling. Retrospectively reported figures show them as dropping from 10*d*. to 9*d*. in January 1968, to 7*d*. in March and to 6*d*. in April – the level at which the *dawa* price stood when the systematic collection of price figures started in June.

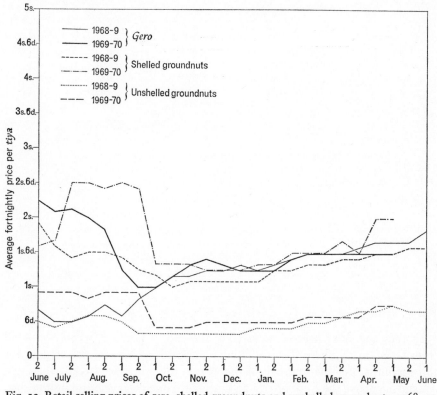

Fig. 12. Retail selling prices of *gero*, shelled groundnuts and unshelled groundnuts, 1968–70. See notes to Table IX.1 (A)

Almost unbelievably, prices continued to fall for a further month (see Fig. 11), the lowest recorded prices being 4*d*. for *dawa* and 5*d*. for *gero* – which informants considered were the lowest for some thirty years. The price of *dawa* at 'Yar Gamji market fell to 3*d*. and news was received in Batagarawa that it had gone down to 2*d*. at Safana market, west of Dutsin Ma.

Slight rises then occurred and 'normal seasonal movements' were soon reasserted – see Fig. 11 and Table IX.1. A very steep rise occurred in September, after the *gero* harvest and before the *dawa* harvest; thereafter prices moved gradually upwards. By June 1969 the *gero* price had reached its peak of 2*s*. 3*d*. – over three times as high as in the same month of 1968. Prices of all grains then began to fall slowly. In the second half of August the fall became rapid, *gero* prices being halved by mid-September.

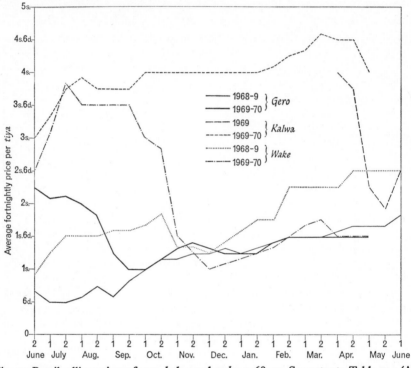

Fig. 13. Retail selling prices of *gero*, *kalwa* and *wake*, 1968–70. See notes to Table IX.1 (A)

In 1969 the *dawa* harvest occurred at the end of October, when prices fell from 1*s*. 6*d*. to 1*s*., thereafter remaining remarkably stable at that level for over three months. For the first half of this period the *gero* price stood at between 4*d*. and 6*d*. above the *dawa* price – an unusually large proportionate discrepancy – falling slightly thereafter. From the beginning of February 1970 the *gero* price remained completely stable at 1*s*. 6*d*. for 3 months, when our price series ends; during this period the *dawa* price fluctuated a little, around a mean of 3*d*. below the *gero* price. These long periods of price stability reflected similar stability in the supplying markets – or so the *'yan kwarami* reported.

Groundnut prices

Although during the Marketing Board (q.v.) season (which usually lasts for about six months from about November to May) prices of groundnuts for local consumption are fairly stable, reflecting the slowly rising prices offered by licensed buying agents (prices which are above the minimum fixed by the Marketing Board), our figures suggest that they normally show marked seasonal trends during the remainder of the year – though they are also subject to unpredictable variations, perhaps mainly in response to such variations in grain prices.

TABLE IX.2. *Retail selling prices of produce per 'tiya': (B)*

Date	Groundnuts (gyada)				Cowpeas (wake)		Locust beans (kalwa)	
	Shelled		Unshelled					
	'68–9	'69–70	'68–9	'69–70	'68–9	'69–70	'68–9	'69–70
June (2)	1/11	1/7	6d.	11d.	11d.	2/6		3/-
July (1)	1/7	1/8	5d.	11d.	1/3	3/1		3/4
(2)	1/5	2/6	6d.	11d.	1/6	3/10		3/9
Aug. (1)	1/6	2/6	7d.	10d	1/6	3/6½		3/11
(2)	1/6	2/5	7d.	11d.	1/6	3/6		3/9
Sept. (1)	1/5	2/6	6d.	11d.	1/7	3/6		3/9
(2)	1/3	2/5	4d.	11d.	1/7	3/6		3/9
Oct. (1)	1/2	1/4	4d.	5d.	1/8	3/-		4/-
(2)	1/-	1/4	4d.	5d.	1/10	2/10		4/-
Nov. (1)	1/1	1/4	4d.	5d.	1/4	1/6		4/-
(2)	1/1	1/3	4d.	6d.	1/4	1/3		4/-
Dec. (1)	1/1	1/3	4d.	6d.	1/3	1/-		4/-
(2)	1/1	1/3	4d.	6d.	1/5	1/1		4/-
Jan. (1)	1/1	1/4	5d.	6d.	1/7	1/2		4/-
(2)	1/3	1/4	5d.	6d.	1/9	1/3		4/-
Feb. (1)	1/3	1/6	5d.	6d.	1/9	1/4		4/1
(2)	1/4	1/6	6d.	7d.	2/3	1/6		4/3
March (1)	1/4	1/6	6d.	7d.	2/3	1/8		4/4
(2)	1/5	1/8	7d.	7d.	2/3	1/9		4/7
April (1)	1/5	1/6	8d.	7d.	2/3	1/6	4/-	4/6
(2)	1/6	2/-	8d.	9d.	2/6	1/6	3/9	4/6
May (1)	1/6	2/-	9d.	9d.	2/6	1/6	2/3	4/-
(2)	1/7	..	8d.	..	2/6	..	1/11	..
June (1)	1/7	..	8d.	..	2/6	..	2/6	..

NOTE. See Notes to Table IX.1.

During the three years ending May 1970 the lowest recorded price for shelled groundnuts in Batagarawa was 10d., in the post-harvest month of October 1967. When the Marketing Board season first opened in 1967 the Batagarawa co-operative society paid 11s. 3d. a *bokiti* (q.v.), corresponding to about 1s. 3d. a *tiya* (or about £29 a ton) and the price of nuts for local consumption rose correspondingly. As the season progressed the price offered by the co-operative rose slightly, until at the season's close it was 12s. 6d. a *bokiti*, about 1s. 4½d. a *tiya*. Local prices then began to rise steeply, reaching 1s. 11d. in June 1968 – see Fig. 12 and Table IX.2. Thereafter groundnut prices followed a course at variance with normal seasonal trends, falling rapidly in the pre-harvest months of July and August, when grain prices were so unusually low. The groundnut harvest began on about 9 September 1968, when prices were about 1s. 5d.; thereafter prices continued to fall, declining to 1s. in the latter half of October.

When the official buying season opened in November, it was found that the Marketing Board price had been cut, the co-operative offering only 10s. a *bokiti*, corresponding to 1s. 1d. a *tiya*. Local prices remained constant at this level for over three months, rising in sympathy with the licensed buying agents' price to 1s. 3d. in January 1969. The price then moved gradually upwards to 1s. 8d. in June, when it suddenly bumped up to 2s. 6d. (compared to 1s. 6d. in the same month of 1968), staying at this level for nearly three months until harvest, when it dropped to 1s. 4d.

The 1969 Marketing Board season opened on 13 November, when a higher price, corresponding to 11s. 6d. a *bokiti*, or about 1s. 3d. a *tiya*, was announced. Thereafter prices followed much the same, gradually rising, trend as in the previous season, until in March 1970 they rose to 1s. 6d., by which time the licensed buying agents had stopped buying (in advance of the official closure) owing to their inability to pay the local price; in April (still in advance of the official closure in mid-May) the price shot up further to 2s.

The pattern of price fluctuations of unshelled groundnuts (*shanshera*) is similar to that of shelled nuts, but the range of fluctuations is somewhat greater: thus in September 1968 and September 1969 the prices of unshelled nuts were 4d. and 11d. respectively, compared with 1s. 5d. and 2s. 6d. for shelled nuts. (The price per *tiya* of shelled nuts is usually some $2\frac{1}{2}$ to 3 times that of unshelled, the ratio tending to be lower during the sowing season when the demand for unshelled seed is high.)

Prices of cowpeas

Seasonal price fluctuations of cowpeas (*wake*) appear to be even more pronounced than those of grains. During the two years ending May 1970 the lowest price was 11d. (June 1968), the highest having been 3s. 10d. in July 1969 (see Fig. 13 and Table IX.2). During the farming season of 1968, when grain prices were so depressed, *wake* prices were low also, though (unlike grain prices) they showed a consistent upward trend. Reaching 1s. 10d. in the pre-harvest month of October 1968, the price fell to 1s. 3d. immediately following the harvest which began on 27 November. Thereafter the price gradually rose to 1s. 9d. in January 1969. In February it rose to 2s. 3d., then remaining quite constant until April when it rose to 2s. 6d. at which figure it remained until June. Prices then rose further and remained very high until the harvest month of November, when the price dropped abruptly to 1s. 6d. Thereafter the upward trend of prices was similar to that in the previous season (the level being somewhat lower) until April 1970, when they fell from 1s. 9d. to 1s. 6d.

Prices of locust beans

Reliable price statistics for locust beans (*kalwa*) were collected for 13 months only – see Fig. 13 on p. 132 and Table IX.2 on p. 133. In April 1969 the price stood at 4s., falling to 1s. 11d. in May when the main harvesting season occurred. Prices rose rapidly after harvest to 3s. 9d. during late July; they then remained remarkably constant until February 1970 when they showed a slight rise, reaching 4s. 7d. in the latter half of March. If 1969–70 is a typical year, it seems that although *kalwa* is subject to about the same degree of seasonal price variation as grains, this may be of little significance as prices stand at a high stable level for a large part of the year.

Useful and thought-provoking though our price statistics are in terms of their implications in a single village economy (see Chapter XII, pp. 162–3), they can obviously be of little assistance in analysing the main causal factors determining the price fluctuations in the wide area of which Batagarawa is a fragment. Any fundamental analysis should take account of variations in farmers' granary stocks, information which would be extremely hard (if not impossible) to obtain, owing to farmers' reticence and to quantification difficulties: it is even doubtful whether those with large stocks would be able to make reliable estimates without emptying their granaries to count the bundles of grain! However, it does seem certain that the dramatic fall in grain prices which persisted during the 10 months after the 1967 *gero* harvest was caused by very good grain harvests in a large area which does not attract many long-distance grain-traders, perhaps because of its inaccessibility and/or because a sufficient grain surplus is seldom achieved.

Price fluctuations in rural Hausaland

Insofar as any thought is given to the subject, it is probably usually presumed that price fluctuations are much less severe in rural than in urban areas: a presumption which cannot be checked owing to the notorious unreliability of official market price statistics, which in any case usually cover only a very few markets in large urban centres – see, in this connexion, Jones (1968). Indeed, it may be that some of the blame for high urban pre-harvest prices is often mistakenly attributed to stubborn stock-holding farmers, to those who ought rather to be praised for their enterprise in investing millions of £s in granaries in which much of the grain required for provisioning urban centres is stored for most of the year. It may even be that the following citation reliably sums up some aspects of prevailing folk-lore: 'Unfortunately there is a tendency in Northern Nigeria, as in many other parts of Africa, to feel that it is necessary to husband stocks of food crops in the areas in which they are grown so that supplies are adequate and prices low. Such a parochial attitude is incompatible with economic development' – Baldwin (1957, p. 196).

But there is, also an entirely contrary belief to the effect that *farmers generally* are so profligate, ignorant and poor, as to unload all their stocks on the market immediately after harvest, being unable to take advantage of seasonal price fluctuations. The 500-page FAO *Report* (1966) devotes but two pages to the marketing of staple food crops in Nigeria, two excerpts from which provide the most bizarre distillation of conventional wisdom:

Owing to lack of farm storage facilities and, primarily, to the ever-prevailing need for cash amongst farmers, practically all farm surpluses appear on the market immediately after the harvest, thereby depressing prices.

Producers cannot, by and large, store more than 20 per cent of their marketable surpluses on their farms, and even this quantity for only short periods. It would be useless to ask them to increase this share in order to take advantage of seasonal price fluctuations, since they just do not have the necessary holding power. They must convert their crops into cash at the earliest possible opportunity. In addition, producers are ignorant of market conditions, outside their immediate neighbourhood and the individual quantities available are much too small to have any impact upon prices.   (*ibid.*, p. 352)

The FAO *Report* proceeds to argue that 'since individual production is too small to make modern storage facilities on the farm economic, it is rather difficult at this stage to improve farm-storage facilities'. It therefore urges the establishment of 'centralized storage facilities in the producing as well as in the consuming areas'. Let one comment suffice. Until levels of storage-costs in traditional granaries, have been established by scientific research, and methods of improving such granaries have been explored, the superiority (in cost terms) of centralized long-term storage in producing areas must remain doubtful in the extreme.

The non-Batagarawa evidence, scanty though it is, suggests that it is reasonable to suppose that severe seasonal price fluctuations affecting, in varying degrees, all types of farm produce, always tend to be a feature of trade conducted in market-places – and, as we may also presume, of house-trade nurtured by such *'yan kwarami* as either frequent market-places themselves or buy from farmers who act on market information. So long as farmers continue (as we presume they do at present) to undertake most of the long-term grain storage in Hausaland in their traditional granaries, and so long as transport remains so primitive (in terms of lack of lorries as well as of roads) – so long as these and maybe other conditions are satisfied, price fluctuations will persist, in towns and countryside alike.

This hypothesis has been cautiously expressed, so as not to exclude the possibility of relatively stable prices in localities which are poorly linked to open market-places, either because they are remote, or because there is little 'external trade'. But this is not to say that the probability of the existence of large 'stable-price areas' is rated at all highly – no more highly, perhaps, than that of the existence of communities (of any size) such that most farmers produce for self-consumption only, no more and no less than their requirements.

Most references to rural seasonal price fluctuations, whether historical or contemporary, are entirely casual – the writer taking the phenomenon for granted, like the weather. Thus Henry Barth at Kukawa in Bornu: 'Of course, the price of corn varies greatly according to the season, the lowest rates ruling about a month or two after the harvest, when all the corn in the market has been thrashed, and the highest rates just about the harvest time' (1857, vol. ii, p. 313). Only when prices soared during famines did writers occasionally expostulate. The official *Annual Report* for the Katsina Division (1927) stressed that following the bad harvest of 1926 prices of grain in Katsina market rose as high as 3*d.* a lb (the equivalent, for millet, of about 1*s.* 6*d.* a *tiya*) falling to 0·7*d.* by the end of the year.

In 1915 the price of *gero* in Birnin Kebbi was recorded by C. B. Smith (see **Gulumbe**) as being 9 to 10 lbs per penny at harvest-time (the equivalent of about 0·6*d.* a *tiya*), against 4 lbs per penny before harvest. In 1937 L. C. Giles, cited by Forde (1946, pp. 144–5), noted grain prices as ranging from 3*s.* to 8*s.* per sack in various places in Zaria Emirate. Smith (1955, p. 136) noted grain prices in 1949–50 as ranging between 25*s.* and 50*s.* a sack in rural areas in Zaria and between 30*s.* and 65*s.* in Zaria city. While a rough doubling of price between harvest and pre-harvest dates is often regarded as 'normal', an example being statements about the northern Katsina tobacco trade in the late nineteenth century and today – see Hill (1970a) – with especially fragile produce, such as onions (q.v.), much greater rises are common.

Statistics presented by Nicolas in various volumes, notably that on Kantché, show pronounced seasonal price fluctuations per *tiya* in markets in the Niger Republic.

Finally, it must be stressed that in rural West Africa generally prices are apt to fluctuate significantly seasonally. Although for any type of produce these fluctuations are not necessarily more severe in Hausaland than in southern forest country, in the sense that differences between maximum and minimum prices may be just as great, *the economic consequences of such fluctuations are much more far reaching*. In Hausaland consumers cannot switch away from grains when prices rise, in the way that southern consumers switch (say) from yams to plantains, when relative prices vary. Furthermore the fact of there being a single rainy season in the savannah compared with two such seasons in the south, is likely to mean that prices stand at a high level for a much larger proportion of the year.

Nadel's comments on price variations and fluctuations in Nupe country might happen to relate to Hausaland:

Regular variations and fluctuations in price must, to some extent at least, be based on a systematic common knowledge of the conditions which determine supply and demand in the country and which can thus sustain definite expectations of price developments at a given moment. Such a body of common knowledge indeed exists in Nupe. It is embodied in the universal experience that certain commodities are always plentiful in the dry season and get more and more scarce towards the close of the rains.   (1942, p. 316)

The house-trade in grain

In Batagarawa in 1967 there was no market-place and most consumers and women processors of cooked foodstuffs bought their supplies of grain, groundnuts and other essential produce from secluded women house-traders. Numerous attempts had been made within living memory to establish a market; sometimes the market had survived for a few years, but ultimately it had always failed. On 27 May 1968 a further attempt was made – see **Batagarawa Market** – and a small market was thereafter held every Monday evening. But according to detailed enquiries made by M. S. Nuhu on four market days in September to November 1968, no grain, groundnuts or cowpeas were sold in the market, the women's house-trade continuing undisturbed. It is our hypothesis – see **House-trade** – that in Katsina Emirate generally the final consumers of bought grains (and of other essential farm produce) obtain much, if not most, of the supplies required for day-to-day consumption from women house-traders.

This hypothesis has been dealt with in some detail by the present writer – Hill (1969b and 1971) – the latter source including a map of nearly all of the market-places in Katsina Emirate. It is based on two premises: first (see p. 128 above) that consumers find a perpetual honeycomb-market much more convenient than a 'stop-go' periodic market (where such exists in the village) and second that a considerable proportion of the population lives, in any case, more than two or three miles from a market-place which, experience suggests, is the maximum distance which men farmers are prepared to walk in the evening (after their day's work is done) to buy weekly grain supplies either for their households or for their secluded wives who sell cooked foods. Contrary to general belief, there are many sizeable towns which lack market-places; and it is quite likely (see **Migration**) that a considerable proportion of the rural population lives in marketless hamlets or dispersedly.

Therefore, in places where the quantity of grain sold locally by farmers from their own production is inadequate to meet the demand from other households and from sellers of cooked foodstuffs, there may be presumed to be a strong tendency for local farmer–traders, the *'yan kwarami*, to fill the gap by bringing in supplies, bought in market-places or from houses which are within 'daily donkey or lorry distance', which are then mainly sold by secluded women. Nor would such reliance on house-trade, nourished by *'yan kwarami*, necessarily be anything new. Such scanty evidence as exists, suggests that in the last century rural Hausa women, who were not then in Muslim seclusion, were little in evidence in rural periodic markets. Hausa farmers are averse to retailing grain in market-places – hence their reliance on the market measurers (*ma'auna*) and house-selling must have been practised for generations.

Prohibition on groundnut purchase

Although there are no references in the literature to the *'yan kwarami* in their capacity as suppliers of essential produce to their local community, many of these traders also function as local buyers of groundnuts for ultimate export overseas through the Marketing Board. In this latter capacity they may then be generally known as *'yan baranda – baranda* (q.v.) being one of the many Hausa words for buying for a quick resale. Some of the groundnuts bought by the Batagarawa traders, especially at harvest-time, may happen (whether or not this had been the trader's original intention) to be destined for export overseas.

In the weeks immediately following the groundnut harvest many poor farmers are obliged to sell their crop at the low prices then prevailing, being unable to wait for the official opening of the buying season, which may not occur for a month or more after a substantial proportion of the crop has been harvested and dried: they may even find it necessary to sell unshelled nuts (*shanshera*) to the traders, who arrange for drying and decortication before reselling. Although there is a flourishing demand for groundnuts for local consumption at that time, both for making oil for immediate consumption and for storage (by women oil-makers and others), some of the nuts will ultimately be exported: terminological inexactitudes (see **Trading-terms**) reflect the impossibility, in this instance, of distinguishing these two types of transaction, which involve the same produce and the same traders.

But in 1966 and (to a much lesser extent) in 1967, it was embarrassing to enquire about this subject owing to a so-called 'prohibition' (which apparently had no legal force) on the sale of groundnuts before the opening of the Marketing Board season, which had been 'imposed' by the Katsina Native Authority in 1965 and which was still in force. This extraordinary restriction, which had been widely publicised, had caused much hardship in 1965, when it had greatly frightened traders and farmers alike. Gradually, however, it had come to be more honoured in the breach than the observance – inevitably so, since it took no cognisance of the necessary existence of a flourishing local trade in groundnuts, but was based on the presumption (which was not made explicit, since nearly everyone knew it to be false) that groundnuts are bought for export only. A translation of parts of the official proclamation relating to the prohibition is given in the Commentary (**Proclamation on farm produce**). In brief it was laid down that: the buying of groundnuts for resale (*baranda*) was prohibited; the Marketing Board price (which is a legal minimum applicable to licensed buying agents) was to be 'adopted everywhere' – 'no more no less'; and that groundnuts were not to be sold (for export) at official buying stations until the season had opened. (The opportunity was also taken of insisting that creditors who had lent money in advance of crop in return for a promise of produce at harvest were entitled to no interest!)

This proclamation is no more bizarre than many other official regulations which, however well-motivated, aggravate the symptoms of poverty, without effecting a cure – see **Economic regulations**.

CHAPTER X

Individual poverty

The lot of a poverty-stricken farmer in Batagarawa may be likened to that of a solitary cyclist invariably peddling up hill and against the wind, while certain others speed by in the opposite direction: to travel a given distance he has to expend much more effort than a richer man, and the wind will always be contrary. Some of the special reasons for this will be explored in Chapter XII. Meanwhile, in order to give a general impression of the economic way of life of the very poor, some brief case material relating to 28 (of the 41) Group 4 heads of farming-units is presented here. The present concern is with *individual impasse*, not with general poverty – see Chapter XIV. Just as past experience shows that about x individuals will be bound to commit suicide in England in the course of the next year, so we are here assuming that about 40 Batagarawa farmers are bound, for the time being at least, to be in grievous economic predicament.

Although the causes and effects of extreme poverty are so often indistinguish-able, and although an individual's plight commonly results from a conjunction of unfavourable circumstances, the following case notes are rather arbitrarily classified under a number of descriptive headings, a few of which might be regarded as 'causal'. The need to conceal the identity of individuals partly accounts for the brevity of these notes – much interesting detail having, un-fortunately, to be omitted. Also, to avoid overmuch repetition, and because the main concern is with circumstances special to the individual, certain common features of extreme poverty, such as the inability to borrow cash (as such), are not mentioned again and again.

A *No proper start in life*

Some individuals' prospects have always looked hopeless because they had no proper start in life.

A(1) A man in his fifties, his father was a drummer who owned no farms. His one small farm is rented (*aro*) from an influential friend. Other friends give him second-hand clothing. He has a humble occupation connected with butchering. For long unmarried, his present wife provides her own food and lives separately. He once hopefully migrated to a nearby hamlet, but was rescued by friends, having been 'caught by hunger' there. He sold part of his house to raise his tax and later disposed of the remainder – now lodging alone. He has no resident brothers.

A(2) A man in his fifties, his father, who died only recently, had been a great trial to him: the latter had sold all his farms, except for a fragment which he had given directly to his grandson. Himself a farm-seller, he owns no manured farmland and hardly cultivates his bush-farm. Little food is cooked in his house. He maintains himself mainly by firewood-collection. His married son is in *gandu* only in the sense that he has not formally departed. This son recently succeeded in reclaiming a farm which, it was said, his father had sold to spite him – acting out the sins of his forefathers in so doing; being a serious farmer on his own account, and also a *dan kwadago* and earth-collector for builders, he (unlike his father) would seem to be emerging from his plight.

A(3) Ground down by poverty owing to his father's death when he was a child, it is only now that he and his poverty-stricken brother (who are both in their thirties) are beginning to emerge from their worst distress – another brother is farming elsewhere. He is a very active *dan kwadago*, does not neglect his own farming, and is an eager firewood collector. He was once a farm-seller. Although he has insufficient grain, he cultivates no bush-farm. His regular employers help him with clothes and grant *falle* (q.v.). His plight is considered worse than his brother's owing to his wife's unhelpfulness. (He has since migrated to Katsina, selling a farm.)

A(4) His father, who had migrated to Batagarawa, left insufficient land for his 3 sons, 2 of whom later migrated, one as a farmer. A man in his forties, he has sold all his own farmland and relies on a farm still owned by a migrated brother – which he could not sell without incurring public odium. His only bush-farm is rented for him by his daughter's husband. His pride will not permit him to collect firewood. Lack of finance has forced him to abandon his previous humble trading occupation. He has 2 unmarried working-sons who work as *'yan kwadago* outside Batagarawa and who are, also, active farmers. His wife helps greatly with household expenses.

B *Farm-sellers who inherited considerable farmland*

In contradistinction to those who had a poor start in life, are those who were well-favoured initially, at least so far as inherited farmland was concerned.

B(1) Although this man in his thirties inherited a considerable acreage, he sold it all and is now mainly dependent on a portion of a farm he had formerly owned, which had been rebought by his late senior brother and which he holds in trust for that brother's young son. He cultivates his bush-farm desultorily. He miserably sells bundles of grain at harvest, and unripe groundnuts for later harvesting by the buyer (*cinikin tsaye*). He is a meat-seller, and goes to Katsina as such for *cin rani*. All his affairs are in hopeless disorder and he is on the brink of migration. His wife is a hairdresser and makes groundnut oil.

B(2) The father of this man in his forties was a very well-known farmer, and his only brother is in Group 1, but he himself is (and was) abysmally poor, to the point that he could not retain the services of his eldest working-son who recently migrated. While chronic bad health may be the main cause of his present plight, his situation was presumably aggravated by earlier farm-selling, perhaps (since it is unrecorded) to his brother, whose inherited acreage is far larger than his own. Although his farm of $2\frac{1}{2}$ acres is far too small for his family and he has working-sons, he has no bush-farm. He has no non-farming occupation and begs for alms. (He has since sold part of his remaining farm.)

C *Formerly much better off*

A few of the poorest farmers were once much better off.

C(1) One of two brothers in their forties (the other is in Group 3) who inherited large acreages in the manured zone from their father (who died long ago), but whose farms are now unmanured. Once much better off, he now imposes his poverty on others, and shows a helpless dependence on his mother, who formerly cultivated her late husband's farmland with the help of labourers. After his father's death he remained for some time in *gandu* with his brother who 'helped him to marry'. Two of his sons have migrated in discontentment, and his relationship with the third fluctuates uneasily. Both he and his son do non-farming *kwadago*. (He has since sold a large inherited farm.)

C(2) One of Batagarawa's most notorious farm-sellers – he is renowned both for selling bush-farms in other hamlets over which he has temporary usufructuary rights only, and for disposing of the same farm to two buyers – he was formerly quite well off, but having failed as both trader and farmer he has resorted (a man in his fifties) to working secretly elsewhere as a *dan kwadago*. His *gandu* having virtually collapsed, several of his sons migrated. His wife, once rich, has lost everything; and his dependants are numerous and hungry. (He has since sold another farm.)

C(3) One of several brothers (two of them in Group 2), whose father had distributed most of his farmland to his sons before his death, although they had left *gandu*. Now in his fifties, he was much better off until recently when he became greatly impoverished, partly (or so he complained) as a result of meeting the marriage expenses of several daughters whose mother had died – he was also indebted to the co-operative society (q.v.). Although his financial difficulties caused him to sell some farms, this hardly affected his plight, particularly as he has no working-sons. He has now resorted to collecting firewood and working for builders, as well as to manure-spreading (for payment) during the dry season. He produced no millet in 1967. His present wife is an active trader, who largely maintains his household and holds him in contempt.

C(4) One of several brothers, the others being better off; his inherited acreage is possibly the smallest owing to sales to his brothers. In his fifties, he has fallen on hard times, possibly mainly through ill-health, having formerly had occupations appropriate to Groups 1 or 2, in which he had failed. His 2 sons-in-*gandu* are mainly engaged in outside work, one being a ploughman; 2 other sons have migrated, one of them giving him financial assistance – as do his brothers. His womenfolk cultivate his bush-farms, as his sons neglect them. His very numerous dependants are hungry.

D *Poverty closely associated with farm-selling*

As has been seen (Chapter VI), many of the poverty-stricken have sold much of their farmland, selling being both a cause and an effect of poverty. Farm-selling seems to have contributed greatly to the individual's plight in the following cases.

D(1) The son of a prominent farmer, he (like his numerous brothers, all of whom are in Groups 3 or 4) is a well-known farm-seller, having sold at least 4 farms. Although only in his thirties, he has been married successively to no fewer than 5 women, 2 of whom died,

2 of whom he divorced and later remarried: several of these marriages were partly financed by selling farms. He owns one manured farm and cultivates a bush-farm. His working-son does not get on with his step-mother and constantly threatens to assert his independence by working as a *dan kwadago*, earth-collector, etc., rather than on his father's farm. He is a firewood-collector and goes to Katsina for *cin rani*. (He has since sold his only remaining farm for about £15.)

D(2)   Brother of D(1). He has sold at least 3 inherited farms, 2 of them owing to trading debts, and his manured acreage is very small. He does his best to cultivate his bush-farms, but spends more time on *kwadago*, some of it outside Batagarawa. He is a thatch-maker. He buys on commission for others in markets and is trusted by his creditors generally. He shares a house with a brother.

D(3)   Brother of C(3), he has sold all his inherited farm-land and relies solely on a plot which he had bought with the aid of a loan which he cannot repay – so that he is likely to lose the farm. He has no bush-farm. Once hard-working, now in his forties, he scrounges a living as best he may with the spasmodic help of an influential friend. Creditors no longer help him. His wife is an active trader.

D(4)   Like his numerous brothers, he has sold most of his farms. Although still in his thirties he has successively married 5 Batagarawa women, of whom he has divorced 4. He financed these marriages mainly by borrowing and by selling livestock, but partly by farm-selling. Friends in a nearby hamlet help him with clothes and with grain, of which he has insufficient through failure to cultivate his large bush-farm. He is well-liked and trusted by his creditors.

D(5)   One of 3 sons of a well-known farmer, he has sold most of his manured farmland, to meet many expenses including those connected with his second marriage and a naming-ceremony, and now he has the utmost difficulty in providing for his family of 8 dependants, including 2 working-sons, one of whom works as a *dan kwadago*. One of his 2 wives assists in financing the household – he sold her a farm which she cultivates; and his senior sister helps him. He sells firewood at all seasons and is a carpenter.

E   *Poverty aggravated by migration of sons*

As has been seen (Chapter VII), the sons of poor farmers sometimes regard migration as the only possible way of escaping from their father's poverty, and their departure may then aggravate their father's plight.

E(1)   One of several brothers who were officially prevented from dividing their late father's large bush-farm; as 3 of his brothers subsequently migrated for farming, he was left with more land than he could possibly cultivate and has now sold a large acreage. The vicious circle is tightening, his *gandu* having collapsed on the migration, for non-farming work, of his 3 working-sons. He does not cultivate his bush-farm. Now in his forties, he does his best to earn daily cash for the sustenance of his large family by collecting firewood and by road work during the farming-season. He is trusted by his creditors.

F   *Returned migrants*

A man who leaves Batagarawa, selling his farms on his departure, can claim no rights of cultivation of family farmland on his return, such as are automatically

1 Mallamawa, the District Head, Alhaji Dalhatu Shawai

2 *Below left:* Magaji Batagarawa, the Village Head, standing by a bundle of bulrush millet (*gero*)

3 *Below right:* Audi Mai Gida (see p. 156), sowing grain

4 *Left:* Malam Tukur, District Scribe of Mallamawa

5 *Right:* Alhaji Barau, with a background of guinea corn (*dawa*), August 1966

6 Small clay granaries mounted on stones, with steps for thatch-lifting

7 The District Scribe peers inside a large granary owned by Alhaji Barau; M. S. Nuhu is second from the left, and Kaura (see p. 244) is on the right

8 Cornstalk granary

9 Fellow-students on vacation at Batagarawa: M. S. Nuhu (*left*) and Malam Dikko (son of Mallamawa)

10 A family group including three of Mallamawa's four wives and a married daughter

11 The road into Batagarawa

12 *Below left:* A walled street in the miniature city of Batagarawa; only the thatch of a woman's sleeping-hut is visible

13 *Below right:* Two types of entrance-hut (*zaure*) – thatched and square

14 At last the rains come: ploughing on 15 June 1967

15 Ploughing

16 *Left:* The 'hand-plough' or *galma*; note the desolate farmscape of mid-June 1967

17 *Right:* A labourer weeding Mallamawa's official farm on 20 June 1966

18 Drought in mid-season: dust rises during weeding

19   Supervised labourers weeding Mallamawa's official farm

20   Bent backs for weeding

21 View of part of Batagarawa, with labourers weeding (June 1966)

22 *Below left:* Groundnuts interplanted with guinea corn (*dawa*), September 1967

23 *Below right:* Bulrush millet (*gero*) ready for harvesting

24 Dressed in their best, men and boys celebrate the Prophet's name-day, 28 June 1967

25 Secluded women openly celebrating the Prophet's name-day

26 An earthenware tray (*tanda*) with twelve indentations, used for cooking *waina* and other snacks sold by secluded woman

27 *Below left:* At last the rains come: dropping the seeds in prepared holes, 15 June 1967

28 *Below right:* Woman grain-measurer (*ma'auniya*) at 'Yar Gamji market, south of Batagarawa; she is holding a *tiya*

29   The once-famous Katsina market has a desolate air in June 1966: the wares are
peppers and natron (to the left)

30   Oceans of onions bought by long-distance traders (*fatake*) at Ajiwa market

31   The standard measuring bowl, the *tiya*, in use in a market

32   Plough parts in Batsari market, both imported and blacksmith-made

33   Some indication of the extent of the bush farmland to the west and north-west of the *gari* is
given by this aerial photograph – see also Plate 35. Two unfarmed forest reserves lie to the extreme
north and south-west. (Plates 33–5 are based on a photograph kindly lent by the Federal Survey
Department, Kaduna – See p. 63.)

34 Aerial view of part of the dispersed Hamlet of Autawa (A): showing the narrow belt of (cultivable) bush which divides its manured farmland from that of Batagarawa (B) to the north. See also Plate 35 and Fig. 9.

35 Aerial photograph (March 1966) of Batagarawa and neighbouring farmland on the scale of about three inches to the mile (see also Fig. 6). The white (weedless) manured farmland (*karakara*) contrasts sharply with the grey (weedy) farmland which had lain uncultivated in 1965. Farm boundaries and footpaths may be clearly seen, and the black blobs of locust-bean trees. Note: (C) bush with isolated farms to the west of the town (*egari*); (D) the dispersed farmsteads of Kauyen Yamma; (E) other dispersed farmsteads

accorded in communities where land-owning lineages exist. So those who return home, perhaps driven back by poverty, are sometimes in a serious plight.

F(1)   One of the 3 sons of a relatively well-off farmer, all of whom had earlier left Batagarawa, selling their farms, although their migration, which was not for farming, had not been intended to be permanent. He has no manured farmland and grows *maiwa* (only) on his one bush-farm. He maintains himself mainly by firewood-collection. His daughter sometimes helps him, as he cannot afford to buy clothing. His only son has migrated as a butcher. His former wives having died or been divorced (he is in his fifties), he has recently contracted a *silkiti* (*surkute*) marriage, his wife providing his food.

G   '*Refugees*'

The possible plight (at least in the short term) of those few farmers who take refuge in Batagarawa, owing to 'trouble' (such as debt) in their native hamlet, is illustrated by G(1).

G(1)   One of two brothers who, together with their mother and numerous dependants, recently arrived in Batagarawa (where their father had formerly lived for a time), having sold all their farms in the nearby hamlet where they had lived. The grain produced on his bush-farm – he owns no manured farmland – is quite insufficient for his large family and he is a very active firewood-collector. His 2 wives (he is in his fifties) are believed to contribute largely to the household finances, being keen traders. His 4 working-sons only farm when they feel like it and his only married son is a very active *dan kwadago*. He lives in a separate section of a house owned by a non-relative.

H   *Poverty not alleviated by leaving '*gandu*'*

When the son of a poor farmer leaves *gandu* he sometimes fails to better himself or becomes even more distressed.

H(1)   Under thirty years old, he and his brother both left *gandu*, by agreement with their father, though he still lives in his father's house. He hardly cultivates the manured farm which his father gave him on his departure, but is a hard-working *dan kwadago* and a general labourer. His father has stopped helping him, but he is (for the time being) the protegé of an influential man. His marriage expenses were met by his senior sister who owns many small livestock. His wife is not a house-trader.

H(2)   Now in his forties, with 2 wives (who are active house-traders), a large family and only 1 working-son, he was given only one small manured farm on his departure from *gandu* (at his father's request), but cultivates 2 large bush-farms. He is a hut-builder. Friends in a nearby hamlet assist him and he is trusted by his creditors. When short of food he occasionally works as a *dan kwadago*. He is a non-teaching Malam.

J   '*Little interest in farming*'

There are a few men who seem to have little interest in farming, although their non-farming occupation provides a poor income.

6

J(1) This elderly man is a semi-retired, formerly active, butcher. Although he has 3 working-sons and his manured farm is much too small to provide for his large family, he cultivates no bush-farm. His *gandu* is very weak, perhaps partly because his only married son has little time for farming being an active butcher. He has the utmost difficulty in paying tax for himself and his sons. He is well-respected, can readily borrow and is given clothing by 2 rich friends.

J(2) One of several brothers, 2 of whom migrated. He sold most of his inherited farmland and relies on renting a farm from his sister's husband. A butcher in his forties, he has one unmarried working-son, another son having migrated as a servant. He has no bush-farm. He has stopped taking much interest in either farming or butchering and ekes out a meagre living by trading in small livestock. (He has since pledged the remnant of his inherited farmland.)

J(3) One of 3 brothers, this man in his thirties probably inherited sufficient farmland, but he sold this land by degrees and, having no bush-farm, he has virtually stopped farming. He has been twice married and on both occasions his expenses were met by 4 male relatives. His second wife succeeded in reclaiming one of the farms he had sold and makes some attempt at cultivating it; she and his 4 children suffer greatly from poverty. He is a ploughman and earth-collector.

J(4) A brother of D(5), this man in his forties sold several farms, at least one of them to meet his marriage expenses. His one (unmarried) working son is a *dan kwadago*. He himself prefers firewood-collection to farming. He neglects his bush-farm. His 2 wives cultivate his manured farmland: 'They are not suffering, but they do not help him.' He is addressed as 'Malam'. (He has since migrated.)

J(5) One of the 3 sons of a prosperous farmer (one in Group 2, the other dead), it is not clear why the brothers owned so little inherited farmland following their father's death – one of them improved his position by purchase. Although his inherited farmland is far too small for his family, his bush-farms are poorly cultivated; a man in his fifties, he prefers to work as a *dan kwadago* in neighbouring hamlets, and is also a thatch-maker and firewood-collector. His married son, though nominally in *gandu*, refuses to obey him, but works very seriously as a *dan kwadago* on his own account. His wife is not a house-trader.

J(6) One of 2 poverty-stricken brothers, he prefers farm-labouring (including *jinga*) to working on his own farm – he is also a general labourer. A man in his thirties he has already divorced 2 wives. He borrowed money and sold farms to finance the first 2 marriages and then contracted a *sadaka* marriage. He assists his widowed mother. His poverty partly resulted from the death of his father when he was young.

K   *'Barori' and beggars*

Nearly all *barori* (clients or servants) are either classified in Groups 2 or 3 or are not regarded as heads of farming-units; but one farmer who renders personal services to members of the ruling-class is included here, as is one beggar. (Some of the professional drummers were classified as Group 4 heads of farming-units, but are too readily identifiable to be included here.)

K(1) One of several brothers (sons of a successful farmer), 2 of whom migrated, selling most of their farmland. He is inhibited from selling 1 of the 2 farms he is cultivating as it belongs to an absent brother. His forebears were dependent on the ruling-class, from the time of the latter's first arrival – as he is himself. His father met the expenses of his first 2 marriages, but he financed the 3rd by borrowing and selling farms. One of his present 2 wives is one of Batagarawa's most prominent house-traders and she assists him – it is thought unlikely that anyone else would lend to him. (He has since sold the last farm that he owned.)

K(2) An old and decrepit beggar who no longer does any farming, having handed over full responsibility to an unmarried son. His father was a well-known farmer, but he, like his two brothers, sold his inherited farmland and is now dependent on a 3-acre manured farm which he originally cleared for himself and on a bush-farm which is not well cultivated. He has one wife and many young children, who suffer severely from poverty. He is given second-hand clothes, bundles of grain at harvest and threshed grain at other times.

This case material makes it clear that the victims of extreme poverty are not a separate group of under-privileged men, whose circumstances were hopeless from the start. Many of them have reasonably well-off brothers; a considerable proportion of them inherited unusually large acreages; several of them were once notably prosperous; a number of them have large numbers of sons of working age; and so forth. The general impression given is that in terms of their origin the very poor are a fairly representative cross-section of the population.

It is also clear that 'poor men do not starve, they only suffer'. Nor would they starve if the safety valves of *kwadago* and firewood-collection were lacking. The conscience of the people and the tradition of Muslim alms-granting would not permit this. Before a man reaches his 'last resort', he can always rely on the *masu-sarauta* and the general public for support.

But poor men are the victims of unfortunate happenings which seldom, if ever, afflict the better off. Their *gandaye* effectively collapse because their sons migrate, concentrate on outside work, or fail to obey them (see p. 172). Their wives stop trading and even cooking and drag their husbands down; other husbands find themselves becoming almost entirely dependent on their wives' trading. Poor men find themselves obliged to sell crops before harvest, and bundles of grain when prices are lowest. Much needed farmland is suddenly sold for a song.

The case material shows that a considerable proportion of the wives of the poorest farmers were not in as serious a predicament as their husbands – which suggests that those responsible for the classification by economic-group did find it feasible to detach the affairs of men and women (see p. 59). At least ten of the 28 men – A(4), B(1), C(3 and 4), D(3 and 5), G(1), H(2), J(3 and 4) – had wives who were reasonably active in house-trading (q.v.) or in some other occupation which insulated them to some degree from their husband's poverty: some of these wives were regarded as particularly helpful to their husbands, sometimes assisting them with farming, others led their own lives to the degree that their husbands bought their own cooked meals. On the other hand, there were several cases of wives who were dragged right down by their husband's poverty, doing no house-trading – e.g. the wives of C(1) and H(1) – or having 'lost everything' as a result of his indebtedness, as with C(2). The situation of a poor man who is so fortunate as to have a wife who contributes significantly to the household expenses, or who lends him money or assists him in other ways, is similar to that of a man who has helpful friends – except that his wife is perhaps more likely to abandon him.

Old age, ill-health, the death of a father when a man is young, lack of enthusiasm for farming in a society where this occupation is virtually 'compulsory' – if we conclude that these are some of the primal causes of poverty, we have not got very far. Nor can we ask the victims themselves for an explanation. When a man's plight is extreme, he cannot remember how it all started – the anatomy of poverty is least comprehensible to those in the worst predicament. Those few men who moan about their poverty to outsiders are seldom truthful and the numerous sincere sufferers endure their miseries silently. Insofar as poverty is inactivity, it cannot be studied by participant observation. The way of life of richer people makes far more sense than that of poorer. *Unless village surveys cover the entire population, the poor are usually unobserved.*

There is also another difficulty. Although third parties are sometimes prepared to be much more forthcoming than the victims themselves, the general fear of extreme poverty, coupled with the moral attitude to hard work, results in stereotyped analysis, denigration and condescension: the contemplation of other people's suffering is only endurable if it is demonstrably 'their fault'.

However misleading the stereotyped judgments of third-party informants may be in relation to particular indigent individuals, they are interesting in themselves as indicating the kinds of situations which richer people try to avoid. So before turning (with much relief) to the affairs of some of these richer people, it seems appropriate to list some of the comments that were volunteered on 'other people's poverty' – hardly any of which could conceivably apply to richer farmers in Groups 1 or 2.

Farms and farming
'His situation is hopeless because he has no manured farmland.'
'Having no manured farmland, he is just like somebody drowned in a river, trying to catch the weeds.'
'He is always earning daily money for food and finds no time for cultivation.'
'He sold a farm to pay his tax.'
'Oh, he who cannot afford to cover his body with a cloth during sleeping, how is it possible for him to have a pillow?' – i.e., he has no manured farmland, so how could be possibly cultivate a bush-farm?
'He sold all his farmland to meet his marriage expenses.'
'He grew 6 bundles of *maiwa* last year, but was not serious about bringing them home, so cattle ate them.'
'His bush-farm is still neglected; he has no means of expanding his farming.'

Crops
'He grows no groundnuts or cassava to get money.'
'He grew *maiwa* last year on one of his bush-farms, but he sold the farm before the crop had ripened. People believe that he will sell anything that comes his way, except his wife and son.'
'He sold standing crops before harvest.'
'He grows no *gero* because he has no manured farmland and everyone knows it.'

Wives
'His wife left him because she was hungry.'
'His wife buys most of his food.'
'He is pathetically dependent on his wife.'
'His wife lives in a separate house.'
'No food is cooked in his house.'
'He married an old woman recently for her wealth.'
'His wife ran away last year, for more than 3 months, together with her small baby, because he had failed to rebuild a room that had collapsed in the rains.'
'His wives, not his sons, do his farming.'

Working-sons
'Three of his sons have left him and this is because of lack of food.'
'His sons do what they like.'
'He never gives his sons any clothing.'
'The *gandu* is not serious.'
'The *gandu* group is too poor to cultivate more land; they have not cultivated their bush-farm for two years.'

Manure
'He sold all his compound sweepings.'

Clothes
'He never buys new clothes.'
'He begs for second-hand clothes from his friends.'
'He sells all the clothing he is given.'

Farm-labouring
'He has to work secretly as a *dan kwadago*.'

Livestock
'No one in the house owns any small livestock.'

Taxation
'He pays his tax by collecting firewood.'

Road work
'He does road work during the farming-season.'

Borrowing
'He is never given *bashi* or *ramce* except by fools or strangers.'
'He even went on receiving *bashi* from his migrated son's wife, and as he never repaid that was the end of the marriage.'
'He got second-hand clothes on *bashi* for 30s., but could not pay.'

Postscript on marriage expenses

There is such an entire lack of reliable information on marriage (and naming-ceremony) expenses, and on the ability of poor men to raise the sums involved, that the following note on this subject, which incorporates information relating to the marriages of 13 young men in Group 4, is attached as a postscript.

If the expenses incurred in connexion with an 'ordinary marriage' conform to the formula regarded as 'obligatory' by informants (see **Marriage expenses**), the gross outlay (excluding the cost of marriage feasts) of the bridegroom and/or his parents in the case of a girl's first marriage, would amount to some £30 to £40. The gross outlay of the bride's parents (again excluding the cost of marriage feasts) was put at about £10 to £15 as counter-payments to the bridegroom and his parents, plus the substantial costs of the bride's dowry. It is important to note that the counter-payments made by the bride's parents might be roughly equal to the payments which had been made to them earlier by the bridegroom and his kin, since the latter's gross outlay includes substantial gifts for the bride herself. But even so, the bridegroom and/or his kin are faced with the need to raise some £30 to £40, no postponement being permitted. The main beneficiary, when all is concluded, is likely to be the bride herself, who may have received gifts amounting to some £20 from the bride's side, apart from her dowry.

The heavy expenses associated with the birth of the wife's first-born child (but not with later births) may be considered as postponed marriage expenses – see **Naming-ceremony**. With this ceremony, the counter-payments made by the wife's kin are very small in comparison with the expenses incurred by the husband and/or his parents, and the conventional formula would involve the latter in a net outlay ranging between some £15 and £35 or more. The lack of a large counter-payment by the wife's kin is comprehensible on two grounds: in the first place, a large proportion of the expenses incurred by the husband's side benefits people other than the bride's kin; in the second place the payments received by the wife's kin are in the nature of compensation for the responsibilities and expenses involved during the long period their daughter resides with them.

If the wife's first pregnancy occurs within a year or two of her marriage, the husband and/or his parents will have been obliged to raise a net sum of some £35 to £55 during that short period – of which some £20 will be of some indirect benefit to the husband, having been gifts to his wife. Additionally, the husband's side may have incurred heavy expenses on two marriage feasts.

Were it not for the existence of the contribution system linking partners which is known as *biki* (q.v.), one would have been justified in regarding these heavy expenses as representing an ideal which no ordinary husband could achieve – the formula for richer farmers involves even heavier expenditure. But a man (or woman) of good repute, with many reliable *biki* partners, is effectively in a position to borrow large sums of money, in return for the undertaking to repay larger sums at some unspecified future date when his (her) partners find themselves in like situation. *Biki* is a non-usurous device, facilitating borrowing from trusted partners at moments of crisis or celebration. Although a person with many partners is effectively shackled by long-term debt, a participant's failure to pay is tolerated in the short run, and indebtedness never results in official disgrace. Rich and poor alike participate in *biki*, poor men sometimes having richer partners who willingly give more than they receive.

Nevertheless, many men lack sufficient *biki* partners to raise the sums required, so that if they also lack other means of borrowing, they may be obliged to resort to such irrevocable action as farm-selling in order to marry the girl of their choice. The fact that farm-selling commonly occurs for this reason, although farm-prices are so low, suggests that many poorer men either incur expenses which are far lower than the conventional 'minimum', or that they contract cheaper marriages with widows or divorcees (preferably mothers, whose 'naming-expenses' will be much lower), cousins, or girls with no suitors – 'marriages of almsgiving' (*auren sadaka* – see **Marriage-types**) are not common in Batagarawa. It may be that many poor men are obliged to marry the daughters of poor fathers (see Table XIII.3, p. 180) owing to their inability to meet the sums demanded by richer fathers. (See Taylor and Webb (1932, pp. 69 ff.) on the divorce law.)

As has been noted, the richest husbands have, on average, more wives than other men. But it does not follow that, on average, they contract more marriages in the course of their lives. It may be that one of the particular problems that besets poor men is a pronounced inability to remain married to their wives, who commonly seek divorces on the grounds of their husbands' poverty. Perhaps the large group of poor farmers who never sell land (see Chapter VI) have a low rate of divorce? None of these questions can be answered. But summary information collected by M. S. Nuhu in 1969, relating to the marriages of 13 young fatherless men in Group 4, indicates a fairly high rate of divorce during the short period since they had first married.

The total number of marriages contracted by these young men (all of whom were in their thirties, save one in his twenties) was reported to have been 27; 7 men had contracted one marriage, the others having contracted two, three or five marriages (2 men in each case). Only 15 of the 27 unions were still extant, 10 had been broken by divorce and 2 wives had died. (Several of the divorced wives had remarried their husbands several times before their departure was final.) At the time of the enquiry, only 2 of the husbands had more than 1 wife – they each had 2 wives. Five of the husbands had been divorced at least once.

Only one of the unions was a *sadaka* marriage: it had been contracted by a man who had been twice divorced. None of the marriages involved the children of brothers and the number of cross-cousin marriages was certainly very small. According to informants, 4 of these young men had been assisted to marry by their fathers before they had died; 5 had been assisted by their mothers (after their father's death); 1 had been assisted by his senior sister; and 1 by unspecified male relatives. As for the 2 men who had each contracted 5 marriages, they were reported to have financed their later marriages themselves by borrowing money, and by selling grain, farmland and part of a house.

In our present state of ignorance, there are no grounds for concluding that the system of marriage expenditure results in a net transfer of funds from poorer to richer families – it may do the opposite. But by enhancing the general precariousness of life and by creating indebtedness, it exacerbates the situation of many poorer farmers, and of others who happen to have more sons than daughters.

CHAPTER XI

Individual viability

The last chapter was concerned with individual impasse – with the economic affairs of those who are trapped by their penury. This chapter deals, correspondingly, with *individual viability* – with the situation of men who possess some power of manoeuvre in unfavourable conditions, whether or not they might be termed 'relatively prosperous'. There are 62 heads of farming-units in Groups 1 and 2: this case material relates to 21 of them, 8 in Group 1 and 13 in Group 2. As in Chapter x, the cases have been rather arbitrarily classified under a number of headings. Some of the farmers whose affairs are outlined here are so well known that it would have been impossible to write about them at all without revealing their identities, so that it has seemed best to name them; in these and some other cases it has been necessary to omit certain interesting details, relating for instance to loan-granting or other ways of 'helping people'.

The case material makes it clear that while it is often a conjunction of favourable circumstances which accounts for a man's economic success, there is nothing to prevent an energetic, efficient and intelligent man (whether he be in or out of *gandu*) who has inherited no land and has no working-sons from becoming a notable farmer. Such matters will be dealt with in Chapters XII and XIII.

A *The crucial significance of trading*

As has been constantly reiterated, there is no man of any economic standing in Batagarawa (other than a few drummers and *barori*) who neglects his farming for the sake of his non-farming occupation. But there are some men whose work as *'yan kwarami*, or as traders of other types, is a crucial element in their viability.

A(1) This man in his thirties is much better off than his 2 brothers, one of whom has migrated. His father owned 7 farms at the time of his death, only the largest of which was actually divided between his sons, each of the others having been appropriated by one or other of them. He owns some 13 acres of manured farmland (much of which he bought) and 3 unmapped farms. He is a well-known *dan kwarami* in grains and groundnuts. His wife is a hairdresser (*makitsiya*) and makes groundnut oil. Having only one (unmarried) working-son, he sometimes employs *'yan kwadago*.

A(2)   One of 4 brothers, 2 of whom are notably poor. A man in his forties, his reasonably secure position depends on his work as a *dan kwarami;* he buys groundnuts in Mallamawa villages at harvest-time and grains at all times at markets. He claims that the capital for this business came from farming, particularly from the sale of cassava in Katsina city. He owns some 5 acres of inherited manured farmland and 1 bush-farm. Having only one (unmarried) working-son, he sometimes employs *'yan kwadago.*

A(3)   This middle-aged son of a well-known farmer, who has 2 brothers in Batagarawa, is steadily improving his economic position through his work as a *dan kwarami* in grains and groundnuts and also as a trader in cowpeas, which he buys locally and sells elsewhere. He was reported as never running short of grain or groundnuts and as being 'a perfect *dan kwarami*, who vigorously searches for supplies'. He has 7 acres of manured farmland, of which 5½ acres had been inherited: as he has no bush-farms, this area may be adequate for his small household, which includes one working-son. He is addressed as 'Malam'.

A(4)   The youngest of the 4 sons of a very well-known farmer, he was much better off than his brothers at the time of their father's death and, unlike them, has retained the large acreage he inherited, a considerable proportion of which he has since made over to his 2 sons-in-*gandu*. He is a well-known trader in grains, groundnuts and cowpeas, often buying at villages at harvest-time and storing there for some months, before selling the produce, mainly outside Batagarawa. He is a big groundnut producer; probably sells much grain of his own production; and grows cassava for sale. He is in charge of a plough, one of his sons acting as ploughman. He owns a groundnut decorticator. His 2 wives are prominent house-traders, one of them buying groundnuts for a price rise – see **House-trade.** One of his 2 sons-in-*gandu* owns nearly as large an acreage as he does himself: he is a *dan kwarami* and lives in a separate house.

A(5)   A man in his thirties, he is one of 3 brothers in Group 2, whose late father was a well-known farmer. He has a large inherited farm and another farm which he bought following pledging (*jingina*). Too young to have working-sons, he is assisted by a young relative. He is primarily a trader, not a specialist *dan kwarami* as defined in Chapter IX, though groundnuts may be bought from him at all seasons. He buys cowpeas in Batagarawa and neighbouring villages and may transport quantities up to 2 tons to Katsina, Kano, Funtua. He buys rice at Birnin Kebbi and Bida, which he sells at Katsina, Daura and elsewhere. He buys grain at various local markets, and from farmers who store on his behalf, selling much of it in Katsina market through the agency of an Alhaji, on whose behalf he sometimes makes purchases. He is also a groundnut buyer. He was formerly a long-distance trader (*farke*) in locally bought fowls which he sold at Lagos. His wife is not a house-trader. (He has since bought 3 more farms.)

A(6)   This elderly man was formerly, for many years, a dry-season long-distance trader (*farke*) who bought groundnuts and cowpeas at markets and villages (the latter from as far away as Ruma) which he carried (originally by donkey and later by lorry) to Yorubaland; he claimed that the capital for his business, which had built up gradually, had been derived from farming. He is now a *dan kwarami*, buying in markets and villages and selling mainly from his house, though also in Katsina and Abukur markets. He has one large manured farm (part of which is *fadama*) which, as his father's only son, he inherited without division; he has bought a bush-farm. Having 2 working-sons, one of them married, he seldom employs *'yan kwadago.* He has one wife and many children. Groundnuts may be obtained from him at all seasons; he buys for resale and stores in his house. His wife makes groundnut oil. Members of his household own many goats.

B *No non-farming occupation except cattle-rearing*

Although this successful farmer is very unusual in having no non-farming occupation, he is a well-known cattle-owner and rearer and also sells much non-staple produce, such as sweet potatoes and tobacco.

B(1) One of several brothers, the inherited acreage owned by this successful middle-aged farmer, who left *gandu* before his father's death, is some 6 acres only and he is generally considered to owe his present favourable position, which is far superior to that of his brothers, to hard work and enterprise. His 'bought farm' of about 7 acres is a consolidation of purchases from several farmers. He produces unusually large quantities of grain and groundnuts and is a prominent grower of sweet potatoes (*dankali*), tobacco and cassava. He is a cattle-owner and also rears cattle for others. He owns a plough. He has only 1 working-son and is a considerable employer of *'yan kwadago*. He has 2 wives, neither of whom is a house-trader.

C *Farming and non-farming activities develop simultaneously*

Quite often, as in the case of Alhaji Shekarau, farming and non-farming activities develop simultaneously and their relative importance and inter-relationship cannot be assessed retrospectively – it should be noted, in this connexion, that no farmer admitted to any concept of separate capital funds for different types of farming or non-farming enterprise. From whatever angle Alhaji Shekarau's economic affairs are considered, he is seen as one of the most prominent and successful men in the *gari*, who is well known for 'helping people'.

C(1) *Alhaji Shekarau* (Alhaji Mai Goro). The son and grandson of Batagarawa farmers, he had at least 2 brothers, of whom one died, one migrated. His inherited farmland was insufficient and he set about buying farms long ago, now claiming that his manured acreage is entirely adequate, so that he will buy no more – he has no interest in owning bush-farms. His large house, with its vaulted entrance hall, is the home of 25 people, and includes 4 separate sections which are occupied by 2 married sons, and 2 brother's sons, one of the latter being in *gandu* with him. His 3 wives are all prominent house-traders. He operates a plough; he owns a groundnut decorticator (*sarkin aiki*); he is a cattle-owner and grows much tobacco on heavily manured land. He and his 2 married sons (who are both prominent farmers, having bought much of their farmland) are on the short list of those from whom groundnuts may be bought at all times. He produces large quantities of grain. Having a work-force of 4 (himself excluded) he employs few *'yan kwadago*, but one of his 2 sons-in-*gandu* is a notable employer, mainly in the evenings. He is much the largest kola-trader in the *gari* (hence his nickname 'Mai Goro'), buying wholesale by the *huhu* from a certain merchant in Katsina city (these large packages being one of the few wares, other than the grains bought by the *'yan kwarami* at 'Yar Gamji market, which are delivered by lorry to Batagarawa) and selling in large and small quantities, often through boys; he is believed to supply most of the kola required for ceremonial purposes.

D *Many working-sons*

Audi Mai Gida (as he is always addressed) is the most respected farmer in Batagarawa and has the largest family labour-force. The well-known blacksmith

Idi Makeri has been a prominent farmer for some years, but the scale of his farming is increasing as his 6 working-sons approach adulthood.

D(1) *Audi Mai Gida.* Generally respected as Batagarawa's most notable farmer, this elderly retired butcher possibly ultimately inherited most of his father's farmland, though he was a posthumous son. He has bought a considerable acreage of manured farmland and also has under his management three large farms owned by a fatherless boy, related to him maternally, who lives with him. In 1967 he had the services of 9 family workers, of whom 4 were sons-in-*gandu*. He has no need to employ *'yan kwadago*, but engages boys with donkeys to carry manure to his farms and sometimes hires a plough. Although he has delegated much responsibility for his farming to his 2 eldest sons, he is very active in overseeing the work. In 1969 he owned 11 *gandu* granaries, and 20 other granaries were owned by 6 of his dependants. He is a prominent tobacco grower, paying Fulani cattle-owners to manure his fields. One of his 2 wives is a midwife (*ungozoma*). Despite (in several cases) the large scale of their private farming, all his sons are loyal and efficient workers on the *gandu* farms, taking Wednesday as their off-day and also being allowed other periods of time (such as 4 days in succession) for their own farming. The eldest son (a groundnut trader) bought a large farm and also has a *gayauna;* together with his 3 wives (one of whom is a very prominent house-trader and an *uwar adashi*), he lives in a separate house, bought by his father, which is also occupied by the second son, who is a trader in hides and skins and a *dan tebur.* These 2 sons regularly employ *'yan kwadago.*

D(2) *Idi Makeri.* The middle-aged head of a household of 17, this well-known blacksmith followed his father's craft, which is also being pursued by 3 of his own sons. Both of his brothers having migrated, all his father's farms passed to him and he has expanded his acreage in the mapped zone by clearing bush, to the point that he is one of Batagarawa's largest farmers – he is also extending his cultivation in neighbouring hamlets and (most unusually) has one farm further afield. As he has 6 working-sons and owns a plough and 4 oxen, he is only an occasional employer of *'yan kwadago.* As a maker and repairer of farm-tools, he spends much time in his forge during the farming-season, but he is also an active farmer.

F *No working-sons*

To contrast with the foregoing, are three examples of successful farmers who have no working-sons.

F(1) One of several brothers, some of whom are very poor, 'he has got stored grains, and animals, and things to sell to get money'. Although he and his brothers had all left *gandu* simultaneously, their father subsequently distributed most of his farmland to them during his life-time. Unlike his brothers, he increased his farmland by purchase. A middle-aged man, he has no working-sons, one wife and a small household. He is well known for lending grain to those whom he trusts. He owns a groundnut decorticator. He is a local trader.

F(2) A young man who left *gandu* (receiving no farm from his father) and who, in the space of a few years, has become the largest employer of *'yan kwadago* in Batagarawa – he is too young to have working-sons. Apart from his two main farms in the mapped area (one of which is on *aro*, the other having been bought), he has 7 farms elsewhere, 3 bush-farms and 4 manured farms in a neighbouring Hamlet Area. He is a very active *dan kwarami;* a buyer of grains and groundnuts for storage; a trader in cowpeas (*wake*) – buying mainly in the *gari* and selling elsewhere; a kola-seller; and a maker of *alewa.* He owns a *sarkin aiki* and hires a plough.

In 1969 he had 3 wives, 2 of them from neighbouring hamlets; they sell many types of ware on their husband's behalf. His farming and non-farming activities progress *pari passu*. He is regarded as one of the hardest-working men in the town: 'no one sees him sleeping or walking slowly'. (Four more farms have since been sold or pledged to him.)

F(3)   A young man, who was given no farms by his father when he left *gandu*, he has bought 6 farms in the mapped zone, also having one on *aro* and another on *jingina*. He is a well-known teaching Malam, having no other non-farming occupation, and in 1968 several of his students worked on his farms, making the employment of *'yan kwadago* unnecessary. He owns bicycles for hiring.

G   *An elderly farmer who has handed over responsibility to his eldest son*

Even before they become decrepit, some elderly fathers hand over all responsibility for their farming to their eldest son-in-*gandu*.

G(1)   This Malam in his sixties stopped farming some years ago, delegating most of his authority to his eldest son, who considers that his 2 brothers are effectively in fraternal *gandu* with him. (This eldest son consults his father on many matters – e.g. when he sells cowpeas from a *gandu* granary.) He owns a plough, his sons acting as ploughmen. He employs considerable numbers of *'yan kwadago*, though only for the first weeding. He owns a few cattle which are in the charge of a Fulani cattle-owner in a neighbouring hamlet. The 3 manured farms are all *gandu* property, but the two eldest sons own no fewer than 6 bush-farms.

H   *Koranic teachers*

H(1)   A well-known Koranic and Arabic teacher, this man in his thirties is a successful farmer, who owns a plough and oxen and is one of the largest employers of *'yan kwadago*. His married brother, who was an infant when their father died, is in *gandu* with him. His father was a Fulani cattle-owner who had settled down to farm at Batagarawa – and his descendants still own a few cattle. His mapped farms were inherited: one of them is very large, having been his father's grazing area. He owns 3 bush-farms.

H(2)   A Koranic teacher, whose father recently migrated for farming, this man in his thirties is a well-known employer of *'yan kwadago*, who are mainly young men on evening work. He and his brother broke *gandu* some 2 years after their father's departure, dividing his farms and sharing his house. Part of his manured farmland was possibly bought from his father on his departure. His brother is much less well off and has let off 2 farms on *aro*. His small household includes one working-son. He sells grain from his own production.

J   *Two Batagarawa notables*

J(1)   *Mukaddas Ibrahim.* Mukaddas is the title of the Hamlet Head (*mai unguwa*) of Batagarawa Hamlet, the present office-holder being a son of Mukaddas Tanko, who was the Hamlet Head at the time when the District Head (Ibrahim) first made his headquarters in Batagarawa. (The first successor to Mukaddas Tanko had been his younger brother Isyaku.) When Mukaddas Tanko died his 3 surviving sons at first continued to work together on his extensive *gandu* farms, but they soon decided to separate, dividing the farms between them. Mukaddas Ibrahim later bought two large farms, one from a departing Fulani who was in search of larger grazing grounds, the other from a woman with no sons. Mukaddas, and his younger brother

Mati Na'ida – K(1) – have continued to occupy their late father's house, each living in a separate section. He has 3 wives, but no working-sons, his only surviving adult son holding an official position elsewhere: he is, however, assisted by a late brother's son. He is a large employer of *'yan kwadago* and also sometimes calls *gayya* – giving wages and food when so doing. He owns a plough and 4 oxen and employs a ploughman. He is a notable producer of grains and groundnuts. He grows rice on his *fadama* farm. Despite his numerous official duties, he is himself a very hard-working farmer.

J(2) *Alhaji Nuhu.* This prominent head of an extended household of 20 people (a group which is unique in Batagarawa as including both a son and a brother in *gandu*) has been the Arabic teacher in the primary school since its foundation in 1946. He does no farming, relying wholly on *'yan kwadago*, whose work is supervised by his son-in-*gandu*. Partly because his father had sold farmland during a famine, he owns a relatively small acreage in the mapped zone, his labourers (he is one of the largest employers) working largely on his unmapped farms, 2 of which are on *haya* (q.v.). He does not aim at self-sufficiency in grain, which he buys by the sack in Katsina city at all seasons. Both of his wives are active traders, his senior wife, in particular, being a very well-known producer of groundnut oil, from nuts which she buys (so far as possible) at harvest. His senior wife has 6 surviving sons (one of them M. S. Nuhu), and 5 surviving daughters; in 1967 no fewer than 4 of these sons were in higher education, 2 of them being students at Ahmadu Bello University. His senior son, who is in *gandu* with him, is a Koranic teacher, who spent many years pursuing his studies in Bornu, and another son is in Koranic work at Birnin Kuka. Both men-in-*gandu* are prominent farmers on their own account, employing *'yan kwadago:* his son owns a large manured farm, which is a consolidation of portions bought from numerous people. An elderly woman renders much domestic assistance, and his wives pay other women for pounding grain, groundnuts, etc. (*aikatau*). He hires a plough. He is a prominent sheep-rearer, buying much fodder. Entirely indifferent to many conventional notions of economic wisdom, he is one of the most revered men in the town. (His senior son, Malam Sa'adu, has since unfortunately died.)

K *Three other prominent men*

K(1) *Mati Na'ida.* A younger brother of Mukaddas – J(1) – with whom he shares a house, he likewise added to his inherited farmland by means of purchase and bush clearance. In 1967 he had 2 wives and 9 other dependants, apart from 2 sons-in-*gandu*, each with his own house – another son was a soldier. Having 4 working-sons, he has no need to employ *'yan kwadago* – especially as he no longer troubles to cultivate any bush-farms. He grows and sells cassava. Formerly a *dan tebur* in local markets, and a trader in second-hand clothing, he now buys henna, snuff, 'vegetables', ropes, baskets, mats, *makuba* and other goods as occasions arise, for resale in Batagarawa, often with the help of his 2 wives, who are also very active traders on their own accounts; he is also a builder and pigeon-rearer. He has given, or lent, a considerable acreage to his married sons.

K(2) *Sule Magini.* This very well known house-builder and prominent, gay, personality had the misfortune to lose one of his legs, in the course of his work, so that he is unable to farm, though he visits his farms constantly. His father came from the neighbouring Hamlet of Autawa, where most of his farmland is situated. His unmarried son works on his farms and he employs *'yan kwadago*. Despite his disability, he is an extremely active builder, constantly found perched in the most unlikely places; he employs assistants to collect and transport earth.

K(3) The eldest of 3 brothers, whose father died recently, he either inherited a larger acreage than his brothers, or bought portions of farms from them – he has also bought farms from non-kin. He and his brothers and sisters are cattle-owners, most of the beasts having been inherited, all being in his care. He is a plough-owner. A relative's son is in *gandu* with him (he works as ploughman) and he has one unmarried working-son. He employs many *'yan kwadago*, most of them in the evenings only. A man in his forties, he has 2 wives and many children. He is a tobacco trader, buying locally and selling at frontier markets. He has several personal (non-*gandu*) granaries, which are presumably used for storing produce bought for resale.

This is not the place in which to sum up the general circumstances of farmers in Groups 1 and 2, which are clearly very variable. Some have many working-sons, some have none – see Tables v.10, p. 82 and xii.1, p. 170. Some inherited large acreages of manured farmland, others inherited none.

Like nearly all farmers, the 21 men in this sample all have some non-farming occupation – save one man who is a cattle-rearer. It is interesting (see, however, p. 186) that as many as 12 of these 20 men are traders (including one retired butcher) and that 5 are Koranic or Arabic teachers – the others being Mukaddas, Sule Magini (the builder) and Idi Makeri (the blacksmith).

CHAPTER XII

Short-term stability

This long excursion into the field of economic inequality has not been under-taken as an end in itself but as a means to an end. The whole method of approach is based on the belief that in the present state of our ignorance of the workings of rural economies of this type, it is necessary to acquire some knowledge of the economic behaviour of individual farmers (*qua* individuals) and of the relation-ship between them. Insofar as economic behaviour shows much diversity, as it does in Batagarawa, our findings cannot be expressed as overall statistical averages or as behavioural norms. The problem is to find some other organized method of expressing diversity.

The farmers of Batagarawa vary greatly in the extent to which they are successful in achieving the universal aim of insuring themselves, by means of farming, against the uncertainties of their harsh economic environment. No farmer is so secure that he deliberately chooses to dispense with the services of all his sons-in-*gandu* – or even to abandon the cultivation of millet; with a few exceptions, all those who do little farming are derelict. The chief value of the classification by economic-group was that it facilitated the practical study of the kinds of economic behaviour associated with 'success' and 'failure'.

The classification was, also, useful in isolating the acutely poverty-stricken as 'differently situated people'. It served to show that a considerable proportion of farmers are so poor that their economic behaviour is apt to be different in kind from that of the rest of the population. Obliged as they are to live from hand to mouth, and to ignore the future rather than to guard against it, the 'failed farmers' do not deviate from the norms but live in a looking-glass world of contrariety.

Of course, if our enquiries had led to the conclusion that the farmers of Batagarawa are 'class-stratified', in any common understanding of that term, then the classification by economic-group would have provided a structural framework for further sociological analysis – insofar as 'economic-groups' and 'classes' tended to correspond. But (questions of higher education apart), there is no evidence that this is so. However, before discussing this provocative assertion further in Chapter XIII, it is necessary to consider the stability of the pattern of economic-grouping in the short run.

In a short run of (say) 10 years there is arguably considerable stability in the pattern of economic-grouping, so that, for instance, relatively few farmers would move from Group 4 to Group 2, or *vice versa*, during such a period. Of course this is not to say that the circumstances of a particular individual, whose poverty could be mainly attributed to his having no working-sons, might not improve dramatically in this period; of course, there are not many richer farmers whose security would be unaffected by dire family calamity. Then, over a ten-year period, many heads of farming-units would have died and have been succeeded by their sons. The contention is merely that, in the short run, the number of surviving heads of farming-units whose relative position remains fairly stable is likely to be much larger than the number whose position drastically worsens or improves.

As a preliminary to much more general discussion, it is to be noted that the only statistics with any time depth which it was possible to collect in Batagarawa, namely those relating to migration and transactions in farmland, confirm our contention. The classification by economic-group would not have been such a useful tool in analysing the sale of farmland (Chapter VI) and migration (Chapter VII) had there been extensive switching between the two upper and the two lower groups during the past ten years or so, when most of the recorded farm-selling and migration had occurred.

Over a really short period, such as 3 years, the evidence is that the economic-grouping is sufficiently fixed to have prognostic value in relation to the sale of farmland. During such a period very few of those originally classified as 'rich' are obliged to sell farmland. Information collected by M. S. Nuhu in 1970 showed that at least 39 farmers had sold (or pledged) manured farmland to non-kin since 1967. In 6 cases the farms had been sold following the owner's death and in 2 cases the owner had migrated. Of the remaining 31 farmers, as many as 29 were in Groups 3 or 4; one of the 2 sellers in Group 2 had sold a small farm very cheaply to help a friend – leaving only one case of a straightforward pledge by the head of a Group 2 farming-unit, who may, in any case, later redeem the farm.

As for the farm-buyers, it was to be expected that they would be mainly, though not entirely, in Groups 1 or 2 – see Table VI.1 (p. 87). Of the 28 farmers who had bought (or had pledged to them) one or more farms between 1967 and 1970, 2 were *masu-sarauta* and 2 were women; 16 of the remainder were heads of farming-units in Groups 1 and 2; 5 were heads of farming-units in Group 3; and 3 were sons-in-*gandu* in Groups 3 and 4. As many as 3 of the 5 Group 3 farmers were those border-line cases, who ought to have been classified as Group 2 (see p. 60 above) and one of their sons-in-*gandu* was also a farm-buyer.

A small economy like Batagarawa provides, in the short term, no exception to the general rule, applicable to economies of any size (even to the world as a whole), that where most economic decisions are taken, self-interestedly, by individuals, the rich are bound to win, the poor to lose, so that the gap between the two groups is always tending to increase. An attempt will now be made to justify the assertion that the basic mechanism of the Batagarawa economy, at least in the short run, is such as to promote the affairs of the rich and to inhibit those of the poor – thus stabilizing the relationship between the two groups.

The workings of this general rule can be seen most clearly in relation to crop-storage. Most long-term storage of grains and groundnuts (either self-produced or bought) for sale to other farmers is undertaken by richer men; most of the poorer farmers subsist on bought grain for most of the year, many of them having been obliged to sell grains (and groundnuts) when prices are lowest. In the conditions of pronounced seasonal price fluctuation, which prevail over a wide area of northern Katsina (Chapter IX), the poor are obliged to pay the rich a high price for storing produce on their behalf.

In this connexion two kinds of storage may be distinguished. On the one hand there is a small number of richer farmers (the number is not known, but may be tentatively put at between ten and twenty) who deliberately engage in the storage of produce for a price rise in order to make a cash profit – most of these farmers are in Group 1. (There are, also, a few women who store for a price-rise: see **House-trade**.) On the other hand there are those who in fact sell some grain before harvest when prices are high, although their basic reasons for undertaking such storage had been precautionary: the grain had been stored owing to the possibility that it might be required for self-consumption, or as a convenient form of liquid savings, which is less subject to theft, or dissipation, than cash. So even if there happened to be no storers in the first category (none who make a regular business out of storing for resale), the other category of storer, most of whom are in Groups 1 and 2, effectively stores grain on behalf of the poorer farmers, and usually makes a profit in so doing.

But do most grain-storers in fact make a profit when selling? Might it not be that seasonal price rises inadequately cover the costs of long-term storage, including the building of granaries (q.v.), inevitable wastage due to crop deterioration, insect attack and so forth? Clearly these costs are very variable, depending on type and size of granary, the length of time the grain is stored (grain stored for more than one year may rapidly deteriorate in quality) and on the incidence of numerous types of risk. But despite our ignorance of the magnitudes involved, there is no doubt that, by and large, returns must cover costs. Were this not the case, the *business* of storing grain for a price rise, would not be regarded by the community as one of the standard aspirations of richer farmers – *being constantly spoken of as such*.

The present writer has sometimes heard it argued that the *business* of storing grain for resale at a price rise to the local population cannot be generally profitable, for otherwise it would immediately be undertaken on a much larger scale, with a resultant ironing out of local seasonal price fluctuations. Although, unfortunately, it is impossible in Batagarawa, as it would be anywhere else in savannah West Africa, to obtain statistics on granary stocks, so that the number of farmers who deliberately engage in this business cannot be reliably estimated, or the scale of their operations assessed, yet the reasons why this business is necessarily undertaken on a very limited scale are easy to understand. The number of farmers who own as much as £50 of trading-capital which they are prepared to invest in grain is, in any case, very small; and not all of these men would be able to avoid serious loss by holding on to stocks for a second season if prices were to fall as unpredictably low as they did in the farming-season of 1968 – see Chapter IX. Farmers vary greatly in their preferences for different types of non-farming occupation. The business of large-scale grain storage does not necessarily appeal to those with funds available – and, owing to its riskiness, is best carried on in conjunction with other types of non-farming occupation.

It may indeed be that most of the grain sold to poor farmers during the farming-season comes from the granaries of the precautionary stockists. But if grain storage is a profitable business for those who have alternative ways of putting their capital to work, it is even more profitable to the precautionary stockists who lack these alternatives. Hence the conclusion that poorer farmers render positive economic assistance to those who store grain on their behalves.

For their part the poorer farmers are well aware that this is the case. Lacking all power of manoeuvre, it is only too obvious to them that self-sufficiency in grains is a sensible aim – as is not necessarily the case with richer farmers. On the one hand most of them produce much too little grain to last for the whole year; on the other hand, post-harvest poverty and indebtedness cause them to sell their stocks at the worst possible time. Through grain-selling they mortgage their future, becoming the owners of larger and larger sums of negative capital.

Owing to the timing of sales and purchases, the poor pay more for their purchased grain and receive less for their sold grain than do the rich – they are also dependent on bought grain for more days in the year. But this is not all. Despite the fact that their farming techniques are similar, the poor get lower returns per unit of effort than the rich, owing to their inability to manure their farms adequately. The poorer a farmer gets, the greater the likelihood that he will sell his compound sweepings, thus increasing the supplies available to richer farmers. (See **Manure, Permanent cultivation.**)

Then, poor farmers seldom store groundnut seed – see **Groundnuts.** They are often obliged to borrow their seed in return for an undertaking to repay a larger quantity at harvest, or the equivalent in cash (see *Falle*). Their net return after this deduction is made is considerably lower than that of the rich farmer, who usually stores groundnut seed.

Although poor farmers are often obliged to borrow grain for consumption during the farming-season under a system known as *dauke* (q.v.), which often, though not invariably, involves them in repaying twice the quantity borrowed, this is not necessarily more disadvantageous to them than buying grain for consumption at peak prices, for prices are likely to have fallen greatly by the time repayment is made. If prices fall by more than 50%, *dauke* may even be a means by which a richer farmer 'helps' a poorer farmer.

Finally, there is the question of whether poor farmers always stand at a disadvantage, so far as their outside activities are concerned. Are there any occupations they can pursue which will insulate them from the worst effects of soaring grain prices?

Certainly farm-labouring is not one of these. Poor farmers and their sons, *who are subsisting on bought grain*, comprise the great bulk of the hired farm labour-force. But the fixed daily wage (Chapter VIII) bears no relationship to the fluctuating price of grain. In June 1967, the standard daily wage of 2s. 6d. would have purchased about 7 lbs of grain (see Chapter IX); in June 1968, when the standard wage was 2s., about 24 lbs of grain could have been bought. (But the normal seasonal pattern may have one saving grace: it is possible – see Chapter IX – that grain prices, unlike wages, usually tend to fall some weeks *before* harvest, when poverty is most acute.)

Poor farmers get a lower return from rearing goats than rich farmers, owing to their greater need to sell these animals before harvest, to finance grain purchase, when goat-prices (according to all accounts) are far lower than at other times. (Owing to variation in animal size, reliable statistics of price variation could not be obtained; nor can price variations of butchers' meat be studied, there being no weighing.) Although the animals owned by rich and poor have equal access to grazing, rich farmers are better able to afford supplementary foodstuffs for their animals – and poor farmers may sell their bran (*dusa*).

As has been seen (Tables V.1 and V.2, pp. 72 and 74) the main non-farming occupations pursued by poorer farmers (other than *barori*, drummers, etc.) are the production of 'free goods' (including firewood), general labouring, building and butchering – certain other specific occupations cannot be mentioned, or the identity of individuals would be revealed. Inasmuch as firewood is mainly used for cooking – there are better uses for dried dung – demand is likely to be well maintained at all seasons; providing a donkey was owned or could be borrowed, the return from collecting and selling firewood (q.v.) in Katsina city in 1967 was somewhat higher than the daily *kwadago* wage, though the hours of work were certainly longer. But the demand for many types of 'free goods' (such as mats, cornstalk beds and thatches) slumps during the farming-season, when money is tight, and new building is at a standstill – prices presumably being lowest at that time. (For the same reason demand for general labourers and for the services of hut-builders is then at a low ebb.) There is also the important point that new supplies of cornstalk do not become available until the guinea-corn harvest is over, perhaps not until November.

The only type of trading undertaken on any scale by poor farmers is butchering and meat-selling. In August and September 1967, at the time of maximum seasonal hunger, the demand for meat in Batagarawa was very low indeed – on most days goats only were slaughtered.

Finally, the poorest farmers own little that they can advantageously sell or pledge when grain prices are highest. Prices of small livestock are then at their lowest; there is no demand for manure at that season; stocks of crop residues are probably exhausted; standing crops may not be available for pledging, the owner often being committed to hand over part of the harvested crop to his creditors; and the demand for farmland (for which, as has been seen, poor farmers often get very low prices) must then be at its lowest, potential buyers being preoccupied and short of cash.

The developmental cycle

Insofar as each head of a farming-unit is a member of a domestic group which 'comes into being, grows and expands, and finally dissolves' – Fortes (1949, p. 60) – he can be seen as involved in a developing domestic process which will accord him considerable short-term stability, given some degree of overlapping of the three main phases of the conventional three-generational development cycle. These phases, as summed up by Fortes (1958, pp. 4–5), are first the expansion 'that lasts from the marriage of two people until the completion of their family of procreation'; secondly the stage of 'dispersion or fission' which 'begins with the marriage of the oldest child and continues until all the children are married'; and thirdly 'the phase of replacement' which ends with the parents' death and 'the replacement in the social structure of the family founded by the families of their children'.

However, for reasons which will be discussed below, the notion of a standard domestic cycle, with three distinct phases, is of rather limited application in a society like Batagarawa. Perhaps it may be partially replaced by the concept of an 'ideal type life-cycle', involving a viable *gandu*. To make the discussion as realistic as possible, such a life-cycle is exemplified by the following invented, life-like, case history, of Tukur, the son of Ibrahim, which will be useful for both short- and long-term analysis.

Tukur, a man in his early twenties, marries a girl aged fourteen who joins him in his father's house. His father (Ibrahim) being a Group 2 farmer in his forties, and his mother having an independent income, his marriage expenses (q.v.) are largely met by his parents, who succeed in raising some £40 to enable him to marry the girl of his (not their) choice. On the birth of Tukur's first child, his parents again meet most of the heavy ceremonial and other expenses (see Naming-ceremony), though he makes certain contributions from his private income, which is derived partly from selling groundnuts grown on the *gayauna* given to him by his father – he is, of course, in *gandu* – and partly from his work as a labourer in the dry season.

Tukur being the eldest of four sons, his father's farming prospers increasingly as the sons all reach adulthood, and he (Tukur) is content to remain in *gandu*. The expenditure on the naming-ceremony for Tukur's second child is much lower than it was for his first-born, and his parents therefore have little difficulty (assisted as they are by their *biki* partners) in meeting these expenses as well as the marriage expenses of their second son. Tukur expands the scale of his private farming, having bought a second farm from the proceeds of selling boiled cassava in Abukur market. He moves into a nearby house, which is vacant owing to the migration of the owner, his father lending him the purchase price, which he repays over a period.

Having moved house, Tukur's wife is responsible for cooking the evening meal for her household, at least during the dry season: she had previously taken all her meals with her husband's mother, rendering assistance as though she were a junior co-wife. Although the guinea corn for this meal was grown on the *gandu* farms, having been allocated to Tukur at harvest-time (for storage in his own granary), he now has to buy meat and to give money to his wife for the purchase of soup ingredients (*kudin cefane*). His wife now urges him to increase his income by becoming a *dan kwarami*: starting with a capital of £4 (half of which has been lent to him by his wife who processes and sells various snacks), he gradually expands the scale of his trading, his secluded wife retailing the grain on his behalf. He marries a second wife and meets most of the marriage expenses himself.

Tukur's father Ibrahim continues to prosper, both as a farmer and a tailor, and he buys additional farmland. When he is 55 he marries for the third time, his young wife soon bearing him 3 children, who are between 10 and 15 years younger than Tukur's first-born. When Ibrahim is 60, Tukur's eldest son leaves school and joins the *gandu* group, which now includes 6 working-men of 3 generations. Gradually Ibrahim hands over much responsibility for his farming to his son; though he still enjoys supervising the farming work, his son is in full charge of the *gandu* granaries. Ibrahim's second wife dies and two years later he marries for the fourth time, at the age of 65, the children of that marriage being a generation younger than Tukur's first-born son who has recently married.

Five years later Ibrahim dies, leaving 7 sons, whose ages vary from 45 to 2 years. The *gandu* immediately breaks, the manured farmland of 28 acres being divided between the sons (the daughters having renounced their claim), who receive between 3 and 5 acres each – the shares are unequal it being unwise to divide the smaller plots, each of which passes intact to one or other son. The farms inherited by the younger unmarried sons are placed on trust with the older sons. As for the other types of property owned by the deceased, these are shared out, by amicable agreement, between the sons: Tukur assumes charge of the 3 cattle owned by his father, the proceeds to be divided between the brothers when an animal is sold; a son trained as a tailor has the use of Ibrahim's sewing machine; and two younger sons of Ibrahim's senior wife continue living in their father's house together with their mother.

Tukur finds that his standard of living has been little changed by his father's death. His holding of manured farmland has increased by one-third, from 12 acres (which he had formerly cultivated with the help of *'yan kwadago*) to 16 acres. Although his 2 working-sons are now able to devote themselves fully to cultivating his farms, he often employs *'yan kwadago* to increase the size of the work-group. On the other hand, Tukur's 2 married junior brothers, who had acquired less private farmland than he had, find their standard of living reduced. As for the 2 sons of Ibrahim's second wife, who will soon leave school, one decides to join Tukur's *gandu*, while the other goes to live, in due course, with his widowed mother's new husband. Ibrahim's third wife removes to a neighbouring hamlet on her remarriage, taking her 2 infant sons with her.

Whereas Tukur's life-cycle continues, as the years go by, to resemble his father's, his two youngest brothers derive little advantage from having been the sons of a successful farmer. Being fatherless, they are both obliged to sell their inherited farmland, when it is duly handed over to them on their adulthood, in order to finance their marriage expenses.

Although this ideal type of life-cycle makes no mention of family calamity, such as the death of young wives and children, or of family trouble, such as divorce – events which afflict virtually all domestic groups – it yet realistically portrays the steady progression through life enjoyed by a fair number of richer farmers who, as members or heads of successful *gandaye*, are assured of the support of their fathers when they are young, and of their sons when they are middle-aged and old. So, for sociological (as well as general economic) reasons, a farmer who is well set on such a life path may expect to benefit from gradually increasing security as he gets older.

The concept of the developmental cycle was originally formulated in connexion with the study of societies with unilineal descent groups – the domestic group being the source from which the unilineal descent group is 'continually replenished' – Fortes (1958, p. 6). The particular concern was with the feeding-in process 'by which the differentiation of persons in the domestic domain by generation, filiation, and descent, is projected into the structure of the unilineal descent group to generate the modes of collocation and segmentation so characteristic of lineage systems' (*ibid.*). Numerical data were regarded as 'essential for the analysis of the developmental cycle of the domestic group' (*ibid.*, p. 13).

In Batagarawa where there are no unilineal descent groups; where nearly all domestic groups are built round one married man with or without working-sons; where many heads of farming-units have no working-sons; where security in middle and old age depends on the endurance of a stable, paternal *gandu;* where *gandu* is non-cyclical to the point that 'everything collapses' on the death of the *gandu* head; where many men die in the prime of life, their 'physical death' preceding their 'social death' – see Stenning (1958, p. 117); where divorce is common at all ages; where many older men have more than one wife (see pp. 80–1); and where (as in the case of Tukur's father) old men often marry young women, so that the different 'phases' of a man's life-cycle are merged, not merely overlapping – in such a society one must search for regularities of a statistical nature, reflecting certain demographic characteristics, including the matter of *gandu*, rather than imposing the concept of one standard developmental cycle.

Perhaps it is partly because our statistics are, in a few respects, so unusually complete (most West African studies of domestic organization are based on selected families in the community), that it has become apparent that any attempt to formulate a model development cycle represents a starry-eyed approach – a dismissal of many of the problems, such as extreme poverty arising from the early death of fathers, which it is our particular concern to study. Insofar as there are statistical regularities, enabling comparison of one life-cycle with another, this is because men die, marry, etc., at the 'expected ages', and enjoy at some stage the services of married sons. As for our ideal type life-cycle, it cannot even be divided into distinct phases, though a 'phase of replacement' would have existed had Tukur's father been decrepit and handed over all responsibility to his son before his death.

Our statistics reveal the existence of two sets of men whose affairs cannot be analysed with the assistance of the above ideal type of life-cycle: the young fatherless men and the older men who lack the assistance of married sons, nearly all of whom are poor. As many as 14 out of 16 of the heads of farming-units under thirty years old are in Groups 3 and 4 (Table v.7, p. 79), the corresponding figures for those aged fifty or over who have no sons-in-*gandu* being 13 out of 15.

Some of the fathers of the younger heads of farming-units died before completing the expected life-span; others had children born to them when they were old. However this may have been, their sons stand isolated and insecure, as yet uninvolved in any socio-economic time-process which will tend to enhance their security as they get older.

Indeed the seriousness of the predicament of many young fatherless men partly results from the community's failure to modify certain conventional practices – notably those involving the payment of large marriage and naming-ceremony expenses – which evolved at a time when domestic groups were much larger than they are today. In former times a fatherless son could presumably have expected some assistance in meeting his ceremonial expenditure from his paternal kin: nowadays he is often obliged to meet it himself, though sometimes with his mother's assistance (see p. 152). It is as though these young men were victims of the community's unconscious belief in the continued existence of an obsolete patrilocal residence pattern, such as persists with certain Maguzawa, according to which young men could be assured of familial support. Furthermore, marriage expenses have recently been rising much faster than the general level of prices.

This matter of the non-viability of households headed by young men has been little discussed in the West African literature. But fortunately Stenning's analysis (1958) of household viability among certain pastoral Fulani (the Wodaabe of Bornu) is quite relevant here, domestic units in that community being based on individual married men. Young men establish separate households and assume full charge of herds of cattle allocated to them by their fathers, following the return of their wives after the birth of their first child. But such households are non-viable for some years, during which the son leans on his father for support. But many fathers die before their sons have married: in the case where none of the sons has married, 'it is a principle that the dead man's brother or patrilateral parallel cousin, usually a junior, shall act as the guardian of the dead man's children and supervise their betrothals... He should inherit at least one of the dead man's widows, particularly when of child-bearing age...' (*ibid.*, p. 117); but where a 'family head dies leaving some sons married with families, homesteads and herds, and others without, this substitution in the collateral line is not practised... The guardianship of minors and the custody of the herd falls to the dead man's eldest son'. While in Batagarawa an un-married man with no married brothers may adhere to his father's brother's *gandu* on his father's death, this is a temporary arrangement, which never involves his mother's incorporation in the household to which he is attached. In the case of the other alternative, also, the young sons who join their elder brother are in a much more precarious situation than their Fulani counter-parts: Hausa fathers do not aim at establishing their sons as viable economic entities following their marriage, so that elder and younger sons may all be in similar, unestablished, plight.

As for the older men without *gandaye*, many of them find difficulty in sup-porting their families, which often include young children; it seems that poor men in their fifties often suffer from advancing decrepitude, as though they were much older. Just as it was argued that there are *both* sociological and general economic reasons for expecting that the successful middle-aged farmer whose life-cycle conformed to the ideal type was likely to continue to enjoy a measure of security in the short run, so it can likewise be concluded that the insecurity of the old and sonless, as well as of the young and fatherless, is likely to prove somewhat persistent.

In terms of statistical frequencies, there are several standard life-cycles applicable to this community, not merely one. (The main reason for preferring the term 'life-cycle' to 'development cycle' in this context, is the common merging of the three conventional phases of the latter.) The Tukur model applies only to prosperous men who enjoy the security of their father's *gandu* during his life-time and who form another viable *gandu* on his death. Many poor men find it impossible to extricate themselves from their poverty as their sons reach adulthood; owing to their consequent inability to retain the services of their sons, their situation in late middle age, when they have infant children only living with them, may resemble that of a young fatherless married man, so that their life-cycle may then be regarded as having repetitive phases. Another type of cycle, applicable to young fatherless men, would portray them as slowly emerging from their poverty with the help of their adult sons and ultimately forming a viable *gandu* – but yet never flourishing sufficiently to enable their sons to establish private farms of any size, such as would ensure their economic viability on their father's death.

But what of those middle-aged farmers who do not prosper although they are heads of paternal *gandaye*? Table v.7 (p. 79) shows that as many as 7 of the 32 heads of *gandu* aged fifty and over are in Group 4, another 9 being in Group 3. Are these farmers likely to remain poor as they get older?

In an attempt to answer this question, the 40 paternal *gandaye* were classified in four groups, according to whether they were 'strong', 'weak', 'collapsed', or headed by a father who had retired from active farming. The strength, or viability, of each *gandu* was assessed in terms of such factors as the degree of

TABLE XII.1. *The 'strength' and incidence of 'gandaye' by economic-group:* (*A*)

| Type of farming-unit | Economic-group | | | | Total |
| | 1 | 2 | 3 | 4 | |
	(Numbers of farming-units)				
Gandaye					
paternal	8	10	13	9	40
paternal and fraternal	1	—	—	—	1
fraternal	2	3	2	—	7
Total *gandaye*	11	13	15	9	48
Paternal *gandaye*					
(a) strong (or viable)	7	6	8	—	21
(b) weak	—	—	4	5	9
(c) 'collapsed'	—	—	—	2	2
(d) father retired	1	4	1	2	8
Total paternal *gandaye*	8	10	13	9	40
Non-*gandaye*					
with unmarried working-sons[a]	3	15	15	13	46
without unmarried working-sons	3	17	38	19	77
Total non-*gandaye*	6	32	53	32	123
Grand total	17	45	68	41	171
Percentage of farming-units which					
are *gandaye*	65	29	22	22	28
include unmarried working-sons[a]	18	33	22	32	27
lack working-sons	18	38	56	46	45
	100	100	100	100	100

(a) A few relatives other than sons, e.g. brothers or brothers' sons, are included.

authority exerted by the father over his sons; the extent to which the *gandu* head concentrates on farming; the sufficiency of the area of manured farmland in relation to available family labour; the willingness to cultivate bush-farms – and so forth. The results (see Table XII.1) were very striking – illustrating, incidentally, the impossibility of generalizing about attitudes to *gandu* without taking account of economic inequality. None of the Group 4 *gandaye* could conceivably have been classified as strong (or viable); and none of the *gandaye* in Groups 1 and 2 could possibly be regarded as 'weak' or 'collapsed' – only with certain Group 3 *gandaye* did classificatory doubts arise. Thus, although (see Table XII.2) 10% of all working-men (married and unmarried) were members of Group 4 farming-units which were nominally classified as *gandaye*, hardly any of these men were pulling their weight as members of effective farming-groups – many of them doing little work of any kind during the farming-season.

TABLE XII.2. *The 'strength' and incidence of 'gandaye' by economic-group:* (B)

Type of farming-unit	Economic-group				
	1	2	3	4	Total
	(Numbers of working-sons[a] and brothers)				
Gandaye					
paternal	36	24	28	19	107
paternal and fraternal	2	—	—	—	2
fraternal	3	5	5	—	13
Total *gandaye*	41	29	33	19	122
Paternal *gandaye*					
(a) strong (or viable)	31	15	18	—	64
(b) weak	—	—	7	12	19
(c) collapsed	—	—	—	4	4
(d) father retired	5	9	3	3	20
Total paternal *gandaye*	36	24	28	19	107
Non-*gandaye*					
unmarried working-sons	5	20	20	16	61
Total – all farming-units	46 (25%)	49 (27%)	53 (29%)	35 (19%)	183 (100%)
Percentage of all working-men in					
gandaye	22	16	18	10	66
non-*gandaye*	3	11	11	9	34
All farming-units	25	27	29	19	100

NOTES

(a) See note (a) to Table XII.1.

(i) The statistics relating to the *gandaye* include unmarried as well as married working-sons.

The case material presented in Chapter X is relevant here: the following middle-aged farmers are certainly heads of *gandaye* which should be classified as weak or collapsed. (There are, also, several other Group 4 farmers, such as E(1), F(1) and J(2), who would have been *gandu* heads had their sons not been so dissatisfied that they migrated for non-farming work.) Any hope that these men might once have had of enjoying increasing security as they get older, has vanished for ever, unless they live to a very ripe old age.

A(2), p. 142   He has no manured farmland and scarcely farms his bush-farm, though his son is a serious farmer. (Classified as 'father retired' in Tables XII.1 and 2.)

B(2), p. 142   He has only 2½ acres of manured farmland; he fails to cultivate his bush-farm, although his family is hungry, his sons insufficiently occupied.

C(2), p. 143   He himself has stopped farming, having sold most of his farms; several of his sons have migrated.

C(4), p. 143   Two of his sons have migrated, and those who remain are mainly engaged in non-*gandu* work.

G(1), p. 145   He owns no manured farmland and his working-sons 'do what they like'.

J(1), p. 146   His farm is too small and his son is mainly occupied as a butcher.

J(5), p. 146   He himself prefers (secret) *kwadago* to 'own farming'; his son refuses to obey him, his farms are too small.

On the other hand, if poverty is not so extreme everything does not necessarily work out for the worst in all possible worlds, the following being three examples of middle-aged Group 3 farmers who enjoy the support of married sons, and who may well emerge from their poverty within a few years. Our general thesis regarding short-run stability is obviously not affected by the existence of a few such cases.

(i)   Although he himself is not notably successful either as a farmer or in his other occupations, he enjoys much support from one of his wives who is among Batagarawa's most successful house-traders (she stores produce for a price rise); he also has 4 working-sons, the eldest of whom has a very high reputation as a farmer and washerman.

(ii)   A trader who sells locally-grown vegetables at various markets (where he then buys cotton for sale to Batagarawa spinners), he has a large semi-manured farm and also large bush-farms, providing much opportunity for his sons-in-*gandu*, one of whom works very hard as a *dan kwadago*, in order to raise finance for his private farming. His 2 wives are successful house-traders.

(iii)   A butcher, in his fifties, who has minor official functions such that he might be classified as *bara*. He has 2 outstanding sons-in-*gandu*, one of whom privately farms more than 8 acres, although also a butcher. Both sons probably own more farmland than their father, who was formerly a farm-seller; they both help their father sufficiently, he having the good sense to allow them a great deal of freedom for their private farming.

Contrary to much implicit belief about 'poor farming communities', men are not born equal in their capacity to farm efficiently, so that relative economic-groupings to some extent reflect innate variations in farming aptitudes. In a hostile natural environment like northern Hausaland, the soil does not complacently yield its fruit to those who meekly follow traditional techniques, but poses an ever-changing series of challenging problems, which it is the business of the efficient man to solve by innovation, foresight, experimentation and so forth. Systems of permanent cultivation of manured farmland may be old, but they are not 'traditional agriculture'. There are few rigidly standard practices, certainly none involving crop rotation. Virtually every farmer has his own opinion on the merits of different crop mixtures. Every farmer has to take quick decisions when there are sudden changes in the weather. Many men obtain low yields because they are poor, others because they are bad farmers. As in Genieri in the Gambia, 'any assumption that there is fair uniformity in the economic behaviour and farming abilities of individual families or compounds would be wholly wrong' – Haswell (1953, p. 57).

In Batagarawa men are never insulated from the consequences of their own incompetence by virtue of their ownership of scarce resources. An incompetent man is bound to fail and to go on failing. A competent man, who has already established himself, and whose family circumstances are favourable, stands a good chance of continued success. As we shall see (p. 185) the concept of economic 'luck' (*arziki*) is a positive one, involving both prosperity and good fortune. Either a man possesses this attribute (being *mai arziki*), or he does not. It is a personal matter.

Nowadays there is less occupational specialization in Batagarawa than there was formerly, when crafts flourished and the opportunities presented by long-distance trade (*fatauci*) might take a man away for most of the year. Hardly any occupations, other than school-teaching and (in a few cases) drumming, are sufficiently lucrative and time-absorbing to free a family man from his obligation to farm, especially as there are none who enjoy the support of a large extended family. Almost every farmer, other than the old and decrepit and two or three famous Malams, is effectively a farm-labourer (on his own farms) as well as a farm-manager – as might not have been the case in the days of farm-slavery. Those whose gifts and inclinations lie in directions other than farming and who do not migrate, may eke out their lives as Group 3 farmers.

But where, some readers may be impatiently asking, is the scientific evidence that farmers vary so greatly in their efficiency? Here the present writer insists that, as a non-agronomist, it was not within her competence to explore such scientific matters: she is even insistent that amateur attempts to measure yield-variations per acre tend to discredit social scientists, especially in a situation where manurial applications are of crucial importance, and could not be measured without an army of workers – and then only roughly, insofar as they consist of the dung of grazing cattle (see **Manure**). Of course the author regrets her incapacity to compare the technical achievements of different farmers, but she is quite unrepentant in insisting that scientific evidence is not required to establish the general case.

It is not possible to live for long in Batagarawa without realizing that farmers spend a great part of their spare time comparing notes on the relative efficiency of their fellows – and not necessarily arriving at any conclusion insofar as there are no standard cultural practices. On one's walks through the farmland it was only too obvious that X, whose sons-in-*gandu* had little to do, had neglected the weeding of his farms. But it is not necessary, or indeed desirable, to list points of this type. In a society where a man has no choice but to strive to be a working-farmer on his own account (with or without the help of his sons) and where organizing ability, good judgment, financial aptitude, timing, man-management, and so forth are just as important as in business life, it is obvious that innate characteristics, such as intelligence, will bear some relationship to farming efficiency.

Men are born with widely different energies and abilities, with an acquisitive instinct of very variable strength. Some have a flair for 'getting on' and fortune smiles upon them regardless of merit or ability, while others are dogged by inscrutable and undeserved bad luck. All those things tend to bring about inequality even in such a comparatively equal and stable society as the medieval village...   Hoskins (1957, p. 141)

If this was so in an English village in the fifteenth and sixteenth centuries, where much land had been held freely from early times, why not also in present-day rural Hausaland?

In our present state of ignorance the case for short-term stability in economic-grouping cannot, of course, be proven. In this chapter we have sought to justify the reasonableness of our hypothesis by: (a) presenting evidence of actual stability in the form of statistics relating to migration and transactions in farmland over a term of years; (b) arguing that the economic system works in a way which constantly tends to widen the gap between rich and poor – to 'confirm' a man's security or poverty; (c) showing that certain richer middle-aged farmers with a number of working-sons are involved in a developing life process such as tends to enhance their already existent security as they get older; (d) emphasizing the special precariousness of the situation of certain poorer farmers – notably younger fatherless men and older men who are either sonless or have broken-down *gandaye;* and (e) by insisting that innate variations in individual efficiency are likely to bear some relation to relative living standards.

CHAPTER XIII

The absence of 'class'

However stable the pattern of economic-grouping in the short run, it does not follow that there is sufficient long-term stability to justify regarding the community as actually, or even incipiently, 'class-stratified' in any conventional understanding of this term. In a society in which neither labour nor land is scarce, where there is no slavery or serfdom, or landowning or landless groups, where there are no craft guilds, and where little physical property of any value (other than manured farmland, houses and granaries) escapes sale on the death of its owner – in such a society it would be necessary to call on very special circumstances in support of any case for the existence of economic stratification. Rural West African society being commonly 'classless', the onus of proof lies on those who would find this village a special case.

The general conviction that rural Hausa are somehow 'different' rests, of course, on a belief in the significance of status-stratification, which derives almost entirely from the early work of M. G. Smith. In his *Hausa Communities of Zaria* Smith had listed (1955, p. 16) various 'occupational classes' in eleven grades in order of prestige (*girma*). Aristocrats by birth and by appointment came first and second, followed by Malams (and Koranic students) and 'successful merchants' (*attajirai*); then came craftsmen (*masu sana'a*) – other than those to be mentioned – and 'smaller traders' (bracketed fifth), brokers (*dillalai*) and 'farmers with unimportant subsidiary occupations' (seventh); finally came blacksmiths, hunters, musicians, with butchers bring up the rear. Although in a later article (1959) Smith emphasized the differences of opinion about the ranking of certain craftsmen, including blacksmiths, and was generally concerned to emphasize (see below) the limitations of his 'three- or four-class model of Hausa society', his earlier classification has continued to this day to have a profound influence on other scholars.

But even if such a model were to be regarded as applicable to a village such as Batagarawa (or to the wider rural community including many hamlets and dispersed homesteads, of which the *gari* is the social centre), it would not follow that the community were 'class-stratified'. In formal terms 'stratification systems' are usually regarded as having three separate dimensions, economic-class, status and power, which according to a clear exposition by Runciman

(1968, p. 41) are 'both conceptually and empirically distinct'. A society cannot be considered as 'class-stratified' merely because its members are 'status ranked'; it is necessary to examine ranking within the economic dimensions as well. If this ranking shows much long-term instability then whatever the conclusions on status (or indeed on the third dimension – power) there is no class-stratification.

Before concentrating on the proper purpose of this chapter – which is that of demonstrating the universal validity of the popular motto, painted on lorries, that 'no condition is permanent' – it will be as well to attempt to apply Smith's 'status model' to Batagarawa, though not in any spirit of regarding the village as typifying rural Hausaland. To the notion of status, we are told (*ibid.*, p. 30) are linked such terms as 'esteem, gentility, exclusiveness, deference, condescension'. (To the notion of economic-class, terms such as 'wealth, income, price, capital, market' are correspondingly linked.)

In his well-known article on the Hausa system of social status (1959), Smith concluded that in Hausaland generally there were three status groups – which were confusingly denoted as 'social classes'. The upper class (which some might prefer to divide into two) consisted of the chiefs and high officials on the one hand and the wealthier merchants and Malams on the other; the lowest (fourth) class included 'the musicians, butchers, house-servants and menial clients, porters and the poorer farmers who mostly live in rural hamlets' (p. 249). Everyone else was in the 'middle' (third) class.

Batagarawa is an exceptional village in being the seat of a District Head (Mallamawa), whose status is so high that he bears comparison with no one else. However, insofar as it is necessary to refer to a top 'status-class', the two other members of the ruling-family who have been classified as *masu-sarauta* (Magaji – the Village Head – and Alhaji Barau), should also be included in it, together with the District Scribe. There is no one in the village who could be accounted a 'rich merchant' (*attajiri*). The only men who might qualify for inclusion in the second status-class are those three Alhajai who are not members of the ruling-class (being the Chief Imam, Alhaji Shekarau and Alhaji Nuhu) together with the very small number (say 2 or 3) of eminent practising Malams.

Turning next to the lowest (or fourth) status-class, the number of 'menial clients and house-servants' who can be classified with any certainty as members of this class is quite small, most lowly house-servants (see *Bara*) being young farmers (or dependent sons), who live in their own houses and who seek domestic work from time to time and do not remain in it permanently – most of them are not the sons of servants. (Smith states explicitly – *ibid.*, p. 249 – that 'clients who live in their home and remain economically independent of their patrons' would belong to 'the moderately prosperous middle-class'.) Small though these numbers are, they would be even smaller were it not for the presence of the ruling-class, to whom very nearly all such men are attached.

If (following Smith) all butchers and musicians be placed in the lowest status-class (even if they are successful farmers), then at least 14 heads of farming-units in these occupations (see Table V.1, p. 72) fall in this class, together with one other musician who does not farm. Therefore, unless a fair number of the 'poorer farmers' are to be placed in this class, it would consist of no more than about a tenth of the 200 (or so) male household heads (other than dependent sons) in the village.

In referring to the 'poorer farmers who mostly live in rural hamlets', Smith shows that he is considering status from the aspect of those who do not live in 'rural hamlets' – for he is surely not implying that there are not many 'poorer farmers' in larger centres. Perhaps townsmen tend to regard 'villagers' with condescension – though there is no evidence that residents of a small *gari* like Batagarawa think slightingly of those in Mallamawa hamlets. However this may be, two variables, poverty and 'urban versus rural' residence, are involved in Smith's classification. It may be, indeed, that he would agree with Yeld (1960, p. 115) that occupational-status is only significant in Hausa villages with populations of 'several thousands'.

Fortunately, however, there is no formal need to consider such a question as whether all Group 4 farmers should be placed in the lowest status-class. A close relationship between a man's success or failure as a farmer and his general economic standard has been shown to exist. If the 'failed farmers' are to be regarded as having low status, then it is not possible to regard the dimensions of economic-class and of status as distinct and it will be sufficient to concentrate attention on the former. If, on the other hand, non-farming occupations are to be regarded as the sole determinant of status then, had Batagarawa not happened to be the seat of a District Head, some nine-tenths of the population would have fallen in the middle status-class, virtually all active farmers, other than a few butchers, being of equal rank. If economic-ranking were shown to be unstable in the long term, such status-ranking would provide an uninteresting framework for the erection of a stratification system.

In his most recent statement on this subject (1969) Smith makes it clear, beyond doubt, that his fascinating analyses of 'overlapping social strata based on hereditary occupational classes' (p. x) which had existed 'for centuries before the Jihad', relate to town-life, for his long list of non-farming occupations concludes with this anti-climax: 'Then as now, the mass of Hausa people lived in rural villages and hamlets, farming the sorghum and millet staples and the cotton they wove for cloth...'.

These people, of course, were the *talakawa*, presumably an undifferentiated group, the general mass of peasantry, the men in the fields (not the street) – everybody in fact except the *masu-sarauta*. Lacking *sarauta* (this being indeed their only disability), the *talakawa* were poor because they were insecure and at the mercy of the rulers: indeed *talaka* (q.v.) is a word for a 'poor man', *talauci* being poverty as such. 'We the *talakawa...*' is a common (shrugged) prefix today: it implies no lack of differentiation within the rural community, but a general inability to comprehend the ways of the *masu-sarauta* in the cities, who stand aloof. (As for the Malams, eminent Koranic scholars were somehow not supposed to flourish in the deep countryside.)

But even had the stratification of individuals and their families in terms of occupational class formerly corresponded with 'a prestige scale which they use for one another in rural areas' – Smith (1960, p. 251) – then insofar as this stratification had involved 'occupational inheritance' and been 'inherently static', it would be likely to be of little significance today, except possibly in those villages where a considerable proportion of adult men are engaged in some craft, such as weaving (q.v.). It would seem possible that in most villages only a very small proportion of men are nowadays engaged in hereditary craftwork (*karda*, q.v.), the prime example of which is smithing, and that nearly all craftsmen (including builders, carpenters, and even well-diggers) acquire their expertise for themselves, while working for wages with non-relatives. Craftwork is being ousted by cheap manufactured goods, and most of those whose prestige (*daraja*) is notably enhanced by their non-farming occupation are successful traders.

In emphasizing the limitations of his model based on the occupational system, Smith listed many variables which it ignored:

It ignores the status placement of women entirely. It ignores the widespread practice of occupational combinations. It ignores the status difference between *karda* and *shigege* [hereditary and non-hereditary occupations respectively]. It ignores the factors of ethnic difference, descent, seniority, and household headship and the difference between freeborn and slave. It entirely ignores the way in which these variables are related to one another or to the occupational system which is treated as here dominant...   (1959, p. 249)

While it is entirely outside the scope of this book to consider either what non-occupational criteria should be involved in rural status-ranking, or the significance of any status-ranking system, it seems worth presenting some rudimentary statistics suggesting that the variable of imputed slave origin may often be safely ignored in economic contexts.

With the assistance of M. S. Nuhu, a few prominent citizens were asked to state which heads of farming-units were commonly regarded as being descended from slaves in the male line and which were of 'free descent'. Although it is certain that such a procedure could not yield meaningful estimates of the proportion of the population which is of actual slave origin (a vague enough concept, in any case, in a society in which slaves constantly evolved into free men), the resultant figures had their uses.

The most important finding was the lack of any significant relationship between economic-grouping and imputed slave descent – Table XIII.1. Richer farmers (in Groups 1 and 2) are just as likely as poorer farmers (Groups 3 and 4) to be regarded as of slave origin.

As for the matter of the relationship between imputed slave origin and non-farming occupation, the numbers in most occupations were too small for detailed conclusions to be drawn. But given the general lack of any association between economic-grouping and imputed slave origin, and the fact that most occupations are not 'inherited', it is unlikely that such relationships exist, except in the cases of butchering (for which the incidence of imputed slave origin was extremely high), musicianship and possibly one or two other crafts. As for the *barori*, they are a general cross-section of the population, except that a fair proportion of them are immigrants or sons of immigrants.

TABLE XIII.1. *Imputed slave origin by economic-group*

Economic-group	Slave origin	'Free origin'	Total
	(Number of heads of farming-units)		
1 and 2	26	36	62
	(42%)	(58%)	(100%)
3	33	32	65
	(51%)	(49%)	(100%)
4	14	27	41
	(34%)	(66%)	(100%)
Total	73	95	168
	(43%)	(57%)	(100%)

TABLE XIII.2. *Marriage and imputed slave origin*

Husbands	Both parties of slave origin (1)	Neither party of slave origin (2)	Husband only of slave origin (3)	Wife only of slave origin (4)	Total
		(Number of marriages)			
Heads of farming-units	29	29	27	27	112
	(26%)	(26%)	(24%)	(24%)	(100%)
Men-in-*gandu*	6	19	11	7	43
Total	35	48	38	34	155
	(23%)	(31%)	(46%)		(100%)

NOTE. Assuming that 43% of this sample of heads of farming-units were of imputed slave origin (see Table XIII.1), then if the variable of slave origin were 'neutral' the *expected* proportions falling in columns (1), (2) and (3) + (4) would have been $18\frac{1}{2}\%$, $32\frac{1}{2}\%$ and 49% respectively – figures which correspond very closely to the actual proportions. Marriages involving women from neighbouring hamlets are excluded, their father's origin being unknown.

Nor is there any evidence that the matter of imputed slave origin has any significant influence on the choice of marriage partner: men of imputed slave origin contract as great a proportion of marriages with women of imputed 'free origin' as do men of imputed 'free origin'. The incidence of each of the four possible types of union is shown (Table XIII.2) to be very closely in accordance with chance expectations. (The figures relate to all extant marriages involving wives whose fathers were Batagarawa men of known origin.)

Assuming that in Batagarawa, as among the Hausa in Ibadan, marriage 'is not involved in issues concerning status' – A. Cohen (1969, p. 88) – this demonstration of the 'neutrality' of the variable of imputed slave origin should occasion no surprise, even among those who insist that it is still a necessary component of any concept of status.

TABLE XIII.3. *Economic-groupings of husbands and of wives' fathers*

Economic-group of husband	Economic-group of wives' fathers		
	1 and 2	3 and 4	Total
	(Number of marriages)		
A: Marriages involving men-in-*gandu*			
1 and 2	13	3	16
3 and 4	5	11	16
Total	18	14	32
B: Marriages involving heads of farming-units			
1 and 2	13	9	22
3 and 4	6	9	15
Total	19	18	37
C: All marriages			
1 and 2	26	12	38
3 and 4	11	20	31
Grand total	37	32	69

NOTE. The table relates to all marriages involving wives whose fathers were living Batagarawa men who had been classified by economic-group.

But the present writer would have been very surprised if the 'economic dimension' had been shown to be neutral in the same context. The statistics in Section A of Table XIII.3 which relate to extant marriages of men-in-*gandu*, show that, in fact, there is a fairly strong tendency for unions to involve the offspring of fathers of roughly the same economic-group: thus 13 out of 16 of the husbands in Groups 1 and 2, and 11 out of 16 of those in Groups 3 and 4, married daughters of men in Groups 1 and 2 and Groups 3 and 4 respectively. (As the incidence of unions involving brothers' children is low – see p. 23

above – economic position, not kinship, appears to be the significant variable.) The fact that a much higher proportion of the marriages of heads of farming-units than of dependent sons were contracted some time ago, since when changes in economic-groupings have occurred, might well account for the lack of such a close relationship between the economic groupings of the spouses in the former case – see Section B of Table XIII.3.

We now turn to the question of whether the economic-ranking of men in this community is sufficiently stable in the longer run to provide the framework of a system of class-stratification.

Whether conventional notions of economic-class are ever held to apply to communities in which there is no inter-generational economic continuity, so that rich and poor sons are equally likely to have had rich or poor fathers, is quite unclear. However this may be, we may start by enquiring whether the sons of rich farmers are apt to be better endowed than the average man following their father's death.

In this polygynous society richer men probably have (on average) more sons than poorer men, and they are certainly much more successful in retaining the services of their sons of working age. However this may be, it is an extraordinary fact – see Table XIII.4, cols. (4) and (5) – that the average acreage of manured farmland per working-son actually shows little variation as between Groups 1, 2 and 3, though it *is* lower for Group 4. It is certainly clear from these figures that many sons of richer farmers are bound to inherit relatively small acreages.

TABLE XIII.4. *Acreage of manured farmland per working-son*

Economic-group	Number of working-sons (1)	Total acreage of manured farmland		Average acreage of manured farmland per working-son	
		Including *gayauni* (2)	Excluding *gayauni* (3)	Including *gayauni* (4)	Excluding *gayauni* (5)
1	39	331	270	8·5	6·9
2	42	378	328	9·0	7·8
3	40	287	253	7·2	6·3
4	33	114	103	3·5	3·1
Total	154	1,110	954	7·2	6·2

NOTES

(i) Col. (1): working-men other than sons of heads of farming-units are excluded.
(ii) Cols. (2) and (4): including farms privately owned by sons-in-*gandu*.
(iii) Cols. (3) and (5): excluding farms privately owned by sons-in-*gandu*.

TABLE XIII.5. *Number of brothers sharing inheritance at father's death*

Economic-group of head of farming-unit	Sole inheritor	One brother	Two brothers	Three or more brothers	Total
		(Number of heads of farming-units)			
1 and 2	16	8	16	7	47
3	15	10	16	10	51
4	3	7	7	12	29
Total	34	25	39	29	127

NOTES

  (i) The table relates to the number of brothers (other than the head of the farming-unit himself) between whom (so far as our information goes) the father's farmland is believed to have been divided on his death. As heads of farming-units were not expressly asked to provide this information, which was deduced from various records, including those relating to the history of transactions in farmland, the number of brothers was certainly under-estimated in some cases. Such men as were known to have sold their farmland to their brothers on their migration, were regarded as non-inheritors.

 (ii) Although no account has been taken of brothers who are currently too young to farm, much of their farmland is held in trust for them by their elder brothers, who are consequently benefiting from its use as though they had inherited it.

(iii) The following heads of farming-units are excluded from the table: 22 men who are thought to have inherited no farmland; 10 who left *gandu*, their fathers being alive; 7 who are heads of fraternal *gandaye*; and 5 for whom information on the numbers of brothers was lacking.

That the 'number of sons on death' is a significant variable in relation to inter-generational continuity, at least so far as extreme poverty is concerned, is indicated by Table XIII.5 which is based on estimates, for 127 heads of farming-units, of the number of brothers between whom their father's property had been divided on his death. Nearly half of the farmers who had been their father's sole inheritors are in Groups 1 and 2, the corresponding proportion for those who had had 3 or more brothers being only a quarter. Then, one third of all the farmers in Groups 1 and 2 and in Group 3 had been their father's sole inheritors compared with only about one-tenth of those in Group 4. If (as seems reasonable to presume) a high proportion of fathers who had had 3 or more (inheriting) sons at their death, would themselves have been classified in Groups 1 or 2, then it seems likely that many of these sons are in lower economic-groups than their fathers. Certainly, the case material presented in Chapter X showed that many of the poorest farmers had had rich fathers.

But although many of the sons of rich farmers may be badly situated following their father's death, there are some who will be exceptionally well placed. As under systems of primogeniture, it may be that one son (or perhaps two or more) is effectively his father's heir and successor, while his brothers are not. This is not because of any blatant inequality in the division of physical property at the time of the father's death (see **Inheritance**), but because a man's eldest son (or elder sons) may have had special opportunities, like our imaginary Tukur, of establishing a secure position in life, while under his father's wing, partly owing to gifts of farmland in advance of death. Insofar as this son (or sons) had been relieved of part of the customary obligation to work on the *gandu* farms, so that he might devote more time to his private farming and non-farming occupations, this would have been to the disadvantage of his younger brothers – who were, in any case, less favourably situated than he.

The fact that no account is taken of *inter vivos* gifts when the property is divided on death (so that, for example, a younger son who has remained in *gandu* to support his father gets no greater a share of the farmland than a brother who left *gandu* at his father's suggestion, being given a portion of the (then) *gandu* property) illustrates our contention that rural Hausa communities may lack a systematic attitude towards inheritance, despite (or even because of) the formalism of the official Muslim attitude.

This heterodox assertion is discussed in the Commentary, and further aspects of inheritance are dealt with below. Suffice it, meanwhile, to insist that the last sentence of the following citation (the whole of which is not necessarily relevant) illustrates our general contention:

Broadly speaking, we may say that in Muslim communities inheritance of real property and fixtures is bound up with the customary system of land tenure, and is, in consequence, governed by customary law, while that of personal property is subject to the provisions of the Muslim Shari'a. Thus if a man dies his eldest son usually takes possession of such houses, wells and fixtures as he considers fit and native custom allows. The remainder he can apportion among his other male relatives according to their condition.   Meek (1925, vol. I, p. 282)

Continuing with the presentation of our detailed statistical material, it must now be noted that there are few men as well situated as our imaginary Tukur (pp. 166–7), who owned 16 acres of manured farmland after his father's death. Only about 5 heads of Group 1 farming-units are believed to have owned more than about 8 acres of farmland following their father's death, the corresponding number of Group 2 farmers being about 9. (Comparable figures for farmers in Groups 3 and 4 cannot be presented, owing to the sale of inherited farmland.) If more prosperous men lived to a ripe old age, there would be greater continuity between the generations, and more chance of the emergence of a small peasant aristocracy, such as may have existed in the nineteenth century, if (as may not have been the case) rural slave-ownership was mainly concentrated in a few hands.

The inheritance of a substantial acreage is not a necessary condition of success as a farmer (see Chapter XI): it seems that about one-third of all Group 1 farmers inherited no farmland, or very small acreages indeed. There is no evidence that a progressively larger proportion of farmland is falling under the control of a small number of rich people. Although it is possible that the proportion of 'failed farmers' has tended to increase during the last half century, it may be that improved opportunities of local trading, and widespread plough-hiring, have improved the position of many middle-range farmers relative to the 'top 10%'.

The well-known tendency for West African businesses to collapse on the death of their owners is often said to be particularly pronounced in Hausaland – see Smith (1962, p. 318). As a species of business organization, an effective paternal *gandu* is no exception, for even if Batagarawa brothers are atypical in their reluctance to form fraternal *gandaye* on their father's death, such organizations are always temporary.

The hiatus which occurs on the death of a *gandu*-head is a period of disarray, rather than of reorganization according to accepted procedures. Sons often exert their new-found freedom to sell their father's farmland, perhaps to finance their migration as farmers. Granary stocks often run down severely in this period of dissolution, and not only because of the widows' right to full maintenance during the mourning period (*takaba*). Most of the livestock owned by the deceased is apt to be sold. The lack of any inheritance *system* is shown most clearly in regard to house property (including granaries), which may be casually allocated in a way which benefits some sons much more than others. It is partly because one brother may compensate another whose share of the fixed property seems unfairly small, that movable property is so likely to be sold for cash at this juncture.

The 'one variable diagnostic approach' which would regard inexorable inheritance systems as the cause of all ills, is peculiarly inappropriate to a village like Batagarawa. In a society where men are obliged to earn their living mainly by farming, and where there are no land-owning lineages, each dependent son must necessarily receive some portion of his father's farmland on his death: even if, as in former times, the senior male agnate administered the deceased's property, the results would be the same. Insofar as the brothers farm less efficiently as individuals, following their father's death, than they did as a group, the causes are sociological and organizational and not the result of the workings of 'the system' as such. In densely populated localities, where there is no uncultivated bush fit for farming, it is the growth of the population, not the inheritance system, which would account for any reduction in the size of average holdings over time.

Nor do conventional notions regarding the 'evils of fragmentation' necessarily apply to a community where brothers endeavour, so far as possible, to distribute the separate farm-plots among themselves, without division, possibly compensating one another if the shares are then unequal. (Insofar as the right of daughters to receive a share of their father's farmland is accorded any respect, this also involves cash compensation by their brothers – see **Inheritance, Women farmers.**)

How, then, does it come about that as many as 123 of the 530 mapped farms (Table II.11, p. 37) are under one acre? Detailed analysis of the material relating to farm-ownership yields most interesting results in this connexion – see Table C.3 on p. 234. Only about 7 of the 123 small farms had been divided between brothers at the time of the death of the present owner's father. As many as 32 of the farms had been given to their owners as *gayauni*, 26 were owned by women and 14 had been bought by men. Nor had more than about 10% of the farms between 1 and 2 acres been divided between brothers. It is not division on inheritance, but the practice of giving away farm *portions* to sons-in-*gandu* and women, and of selling and renting portions to kin and non-kin, which largely accounts for the existence of so many small farms. Furthermore, few small farms (see Table C.4, p. 234) are owned by richer heads of farming-units.

So much for death as the great leveller. We turn now to the Hausa philosophy of *arziki* (a word with the double sense of prosperity and good fortune), which sees life as a game of chance, which some men are more likely to win than others – though they, too, *may* lose. Both Smith and Nicolas have expounded this philosophy most interestingly.

Nicolas (1964, p. 105) sees the gift of *arziki* as the basis of a man's personality: a man is defined by the power of his *arziki*, which may be increased or diminished without reason. He may be loaded with the good things of this world, enjoy good health, be the head of a large family and yet if he loses his *arziki* he will be stripped of all he possesses. Anyone who lacks *arziki* must abandon all hope of enhancing his economic standing, his prestige, his enjoyment of life. He who is endowed with *arziki* must risk everything in the game of chance.

Smith's formulation is similar:

It is not mere possession of money...nor ownership of rights to land; nor simply numerous offspring; nor is it social prestige...*Arziki* is a combination of these qualities, and with them something more...It is essentially a quality of the present, though continued future enjoyment is also desired. A *mai arziki* of today may, and often does, return to his former obscurity tomorrow, in both the political and economic fields. It is essentially also a non-transmittable quality. Despite the greatest will in the world, fathers cannot transmit *arziki* to their favourite sons, or even foretell who will or will not achieve it. For it is not simply a matter of achievement. The struggle to achieve *arziki* is too universal and the issue too varied...Fortunate combination of circumstances as well as individual effort, acumen and personal charm are together, the essential prerequisites of *arziki* – while they continue together, *arziki* continues; when they cease to cohere, *arziki* withdraws, and left to his own individual resources, the formerly fortunate man rapidly loses the last traces of his fortune.   Smith (1955, p. 15)

In 1955 Smith asserted (*ibid.*, p. 14) that political power and trade were 'the only two avenues to *arziki* in Zaria at the present'. As eligibility for political power is greatly limited by birth, 'those so unfortunate as to lack this qualification seek fortune through clientage or trade'. He sought to apply the notion of an 'appropriate type and degree of *arziki*' to each 'occupational class' – this being an approach which was dropped in his later analysis (1959) of the Hausa system of social status. Nicolas, also, mainly discusses *arziki* in reference to traders, as this enabled him the better to pursue his analogy with games of chance. But in noting that whole 'local communities' might be endowed with particular *arziki*, he specifically mentions successful farming as one of their attributes.

In 1955 Smith explicitly ruled out the idea that a successful farmer, who was not a trader, might be *mai arziki*. 'Before the British occupation there was a third source of wealth based on slave-owning, and the master of many slaves was the enjoyer of fortune...But this source is no longer open' (*ibid.*, p. 14). Good farming might be one of the 'elements', or consequences, of the enjoyment of a high degree of *arziki*, but it was not a necessary pre-condition. Indeed, large-scale slave-owning had 'usually depended on former success...by a man or his father' in political or trading activities.

Whatever the evidence may be for this last assertion, a *mai arziki* in Batagarawa today may be a successful farmer, who is not a trader: indeed, he may have no non-farming occupation – see Chapter XI. It happens that many successful farmers are (or were) traders and that most of them, other than the most learned Malams, sell goods or services of some kinds; but in many cases, such as that of Audi Mai Gida (p. 156), their *arziki* is closely associated with their farming. In this connexion it should be mentioned that the lexicographers, Bargery and Abraham, who so far as is known are the only other literary sources of any significance on this question, do not imply that *arziki* (or *azziki*) is necessarily associated with luck in trading. *Ya auna azziki* is a very general expression meaning (according to Bargery) '(a) he had a stroke of good luck, was very fortunate and prospered; (b) he tempted Providence, he made an experiment' (see *Arziki*). Thus it is that the concept of *arziki* – of life as a lottery, which some are bound to lose and others may win – is very relevant to our notions of long-term instability in economic-grouping, both during a man's life-time and (since *arziki* is non-transmittable by father to son) after his death.

Perhaps in the old days most long-distance traders (*fatake*) were younger men, who were better able than their fathers to endure the rigours of the journey; however this may have been, the much less arduous types of trade which are nowadays based on Batagarawa seldom involve older men. All but one of the 7 heads of farming-units whose principal occupation is shop-keeping (or 'table-selling') – Table V.1, p. 72 – are in their thirties; only 2 of the 8 *'yan kwarami* included in this table are aged fifty or over, and one of these is in any case virtually retired. Of the 35 men classified as 'traders', only 5 are not in their thirties or forties, one of whom is Alhaji Shekarau (p. 155), whose business as a kola-wholesaler is based on his house. Local trading is the characteristic occupation of energetic, intelligent, younger men who are seeking to build up capital for farming, and it is probably during this phase of their lives that poor men stand the best chance of radically improving their economic standing, provided they can borrow a few £s of trading capital. But such goodwill as may gradually be established is personal to the trader (or to the trader and his wife) and vanishes on his retirement from this occupation in his middle years, when he may turn to a former subsidiary occupation, such as hut-building, or Koranic studies, which makes less demand on his time during the farming-season.

In fact most older *masu arziki* are primarily occupied as farmers: there are not many lucrative types of occupation which continue to sustain a prosperous farmer throughout his working life. Apart from several specialist traders, there are only a few craftsmen, notably blacksmiths, tailors and skilled house-builders, who flourish increasingly in their occupations as they pass through their middle years. Farming-businesses tend to collapse on death: many other types of business collapse (or are abandoned) in the prime of life. This is another reason why, in Batagarawa, we are not witnessing the emergence of a 'peasant aristocracy', owning 'substantially larger farms and capital resources than the general run of village farmers' – Hoskins (1957, p. 141) – such as evolved in Wigston, a medieval English village.

Land was a scarce factor in Wigston, as it is not in Batagarawa. Might it not be that economic-classes are tending to crystallize out in those Hausa villages where uncultivated bush is lacking? What about the factor of labour?

In Wigston there emerged in the seventeenth century a 'rudimentary class-structure out of the hitherto rather amorphous and generalized peasant community of earlier days' (*ibid.*, p. 213). The upper class consisted of some half a dozen 'peasant gentry' – successful families which had, in the course of time, accumulated up to 200 or so acres of land in the parish –, the lowest class of 'the able-bodied poor' who, being short of land, provided the gentry with a convenient pool of labour. At first sight, there is no reason why such a development should not be paralleled in Hausaland. But this is in fact unlikely so long as the system of farm-labour employment remains as rudimentary.

This matter will be further discussed in Chapter XIV. Here it will only be noted that, in accordance with the conclusions of Chapter VIII, the need to supervise casual daily labour severely limits the scale of an individual's farming – and hence his capacity to bequeath large estates to his sons. Although from what Batagarawa farmers report about other districts, it seems that there are a few very large farmers living in fully rural surroundings, it may be that *nowadays* most of those who farm (say) 100 acres or more live in large towns or cities, where the opportunities of earning a significant income from non-farming occupations are much greater than elsewhere. In West African conditions stable systems of farm-labour employment seldom exist unless the labourers partly maintain themselves by their own farming, as did the slaves in former times. So that densely populated localities, which lack a 'pool of land' potentially exploitable by labourers, are those where a dependent labouring-class is least likely to emerge.

Much the largest farmers in Batagarawa are the *masu-sarauta* who, unlike anyone else, are able to delegate much (or all) of the responsibility for the day-to-day management of their farms to clients or to Hamlet Heads. They, alone, escape the limitations of the labouring system.

Finally, it must not be forgotten that the position of some poorer farmers changes out of all recognition as their sons reach adulthood, this being one obvious reason for the instability of economic-grouping in the longer run. Whereas (Table XIII.6) only 30% (22 out of 73) of heads of farming-units under forty years old are in Groups 1 and 2, the corresponding proportion for those aged forty or over who have 2 or more resident working-sons is 55% (23 men out of 42).

TABLE XIII.6. *Working-sons, age and economic-grouping*

		Forty years and over		
Economic-group	Under forty years old	With 2 or more resident working-sons	Other	Total
	(Number of heads of farming-units)			
1	3 }22	11 }23	3 }17	17 }62
2	19	12	14	45
3	35 }51	12 }19	21 }39	68 }109
4	16	7	18	41
Total	73	42	56	171

NOTE. Ages as in Table v.7, p. 79.

The hiatus caused by death; the general riskiness of life; the dearth of re-munerative non-farming occupations especially for older men; the lack of durable physical capital; the rudimentariness of the farm-labouring system – these are some of the reasons for the lack of a peasant aristocracy, despite the existence of a fair degree of economic inequality.

As for the poor, although the dice are always weighted heavily against them ('luck' invariably being bad not good), they are at least not institutionally trapped by their poverty, or necessarily prevented from exerting their energies and intelligence to good effect in the longer run, or from enjoying increasing security as their family labour-force increases.

CHAPTER XIV

Concluding speculations

So much for our relentless pursuit of the theme of economic inequality in Batagarawa. With the aid of the remarkable classification by economic-group which was invented by our eager informants, we have been able to avoid some of the limitations of a static approach based on the concept of a single 'modal farmer'. As it has been our purpose to study the workings of the economy in terms of the relationship between richer and poorer farmers, it is to be hoped that no reader will suppose that we have merely replaced one modal farmer with four other dummies.

Our analysis has shown that while a farmer's short-term prospects are greatly dependent on his relative economic position, this is not necessarily true of his longer-term situation. So far as 'mobility' between economic-groups is concerned, the system is sticky but not set, there being no 'peasant aristocracy', nor institutionally under-privileged group. Nor (an associated point) is the economic system in some kind of natural stable balance, such as would automatically stultify all outside attempts to raise living standards – either by resisting all change, or by toppling in chaos when this balance was disturbed. Batagarawa is an economy in unstable equilibrium which is ripe for development.

There is nothing in the least mysterious about the general level of poverty, which mainly results from capital shortage at village, state and national levels. Of course, as in all under-developed communities, a whole conspiracy of environmental and socio-economic circumstances accounts for, and aggravates, this capital shortage (which is itself self-perpetuating); however, there is most emphatically no need to identify all of these factors in order to understand the general situation or to appreciate that it may be getting worse.

As should be obvious enough to the reader, the picture of socio-economic life in Batagarawa which has been painted in this book is partly abstract, partly impressionistic, partly realistic. Such a picture cannot be summarized: nor, indeed, can the numerous attempts which have been made (as much in the Commentary as in the main chapters) to relate it to the situation in rural Hausaland generally. But as it is hoped that some of the ideas generated in this book will appeal to students of economic under-development, certain of the main elements in the 'conspiracy of circumstances' which may account for general (not individual) poverty in rural Hausaland are arbitrarily listed and discussed in this concluding chapter in a brief and practical way. Some of these circumstances apply to other West African savannah peoples, as well as to the Hausa; others, such as the seclusion of women, are peculiar to rural Hausaland. Factors such as the 'inheritance system' which have been found 'not guilty' in Batagarawa (p. 184) are omitted from the list, though the general applicability of these findings cannot be assessed. Also omitted is the matter of land scarcity in very densely-populated localities, for our ignorance regarding the socio-economic consequences of such scarcity is profound. The politico-economic environment in which village life is set is here taken entirely for granted.

'Causes' of general poverty

(i) The brevity of the farming-season.

(ii) The unreliability of the climate, especially as concerns annual variations in the dates of planting rains, and erratic distribution of rainfall within the farming-season.

(iii) The under-utilization of labour resources during the farming-season resulting from:

    (a) the inability of many poor farmers to farm on a scale which matches their labour resources;

    (b) the rudimentary nature of the system of farm-labour employment;

    (c) the Muslim seclusion of women.

(iv) The dire shortage of working-capital, which severely limits the scale and productiveness of farming, especially where permanent cultivation of manured farmland is the preferred agronomic system.

(v) The shortage of cattle manure derived from Fulani-owned herds.

(vi) The dearth of remunerative non-farming occupations during the long dry season, this being connected with the declining demand for craft goods and with the decreased opportunities for rurally-based long-distance trade (*fatauci*).

(vii) The inability of many poorer men to finance migration for farming.

(viii) The 'balance of payments' difficulties from which village communities are apt to suffer, owing to the small range of produce and craft goods which is sold 'abroad', the obstacles to increasing groundnut production, and the need to 'import' many types of goods, including grain.

(ix) The burden of assisting in the maintenance of many poverty-stricken people, which is borne by the community generally.

(i) The short farming-season

The brevity of the single farming-season (especially in *northern* Hausaland) results in under-utilization of labour resources, as it does in the northern savannah generally – except possibly where fertile *fadama* is extensive. Given the small range of basic crops, *all of which are harvested within a short period*, economic life in the savannah is much riskier, in terms of the consequences of variations in crop size, than in the southern forests, where most farmers subsist on a greater variety of crops which are harvested at different seasons. Then, far more capital is tied up in crop-storage in the savannah, which is much longer term than in the south. The risks of mortgaging the future by unfortun-ately-timed crop-selling would thus be great in rural Hausaland, even if in-dividual farmers did not nowadays stand so solitarily, unsupported by the farming services of their wives or by corporate lineages.

(ii) *The unreliability of the climate*

The dates of the first planting rains, and (accordingly) of the millet (*gero*) harvest, are so variable that grain requirements between one harvest and the next may vary by (say) 20%, making long-term planning difficult. Considerable quantities of seed may be lost in abortive sowing (see *Binne*). In 1967 most Batagarawa men were very idle for about two months, while waiting for the rains which fell as late as 15 June. General uncertainty lasts throughout the farming-season, when the rain does not fall regularly, but in fits and starts, lengthy periods of drought often occurring within the rainy season. Such un-certainties aggravate seasonal price fluctuations, which may be more pronounced in northern than in southern Hausaland – famines (q.v.) were always worst in the north.

(iii) (a) *The under-utilization of labour resources*

Our analysis of the causes of extreme rural poverty, which is summed up in the concept of 'too poor to farm', suggests that some degree of destitution is likely to occur in most communities where permanent cultivation (q.v.) is the preferred agronomic system, and where poorer farmers have few opportunities of significantly supplementing their income either by growing special crops (other than grains or groundnuts), or by pursuing remunerative non-farming occupations. Young fatherless men, and older men who lack the services of working-sons, are certain to exist in all communities – though they will be more at risk in some than in others. Our analysis of the general obstacles which hamper poor men in their struggle against poverty, is likely to be of wide application where most farmers gain their livelihood mainly by growing basic crops: 'With abundant land and reasonable fertility, a very considerable pro-portion of farming households fail to produce crops sufficient to build up reserves of the food staple to meet their regular subsistence needs' – L. C. Giles on Zaria farmers, cited by Forde (1946, p. 168).

(iii) (b) *The farm-labouring system*

The rudimentary nature of the Hausa farm-labouring system (*kwadago*) has already been discussed – see Chapter VIII and pp. 173, 187–8; as this presents the

Hausa farmer with one of his most intractable organizational problems we revert to the question here.

The *gandu* system provides the married sons of richer farmers (as likewise the slaves in former times) with the opportunity of establishing themselves as private farmers within the framework of the security provided by their father's farming. The fathers (and slave-owners) not only give their sons *gayauni*, but by maintaining them from the proceeds of the *gandu* farms, by providing seed and tools, by meeting their marriage expenses and so forth, they effectively invest capital in their sons to enable them to develop their farming – and, consequently, their non-farming occupations. Even with the best organized *gandaye* it is impossible, owing to the unpredictability of the weather, to plan the various agricultural operations in advance, so as to ensure that team-work is regularly performed for five (or so) days a week throughout the farming-season. When the fathers do not require the services of their sons, the latter are not idle, but can fall back on their private farming and other occupations – as could the slaves in former times. The sons resemble a permanently-hired labour-force in that they are always instantly available for farmwork as required – but at the same time they are men who regularly supplement their own earnings.

It seems likely that in West African conditions large-scale farming by rurally-based farmers (farmers resident in cities may be differently situated) depends on the presence either of stranger–labourers who return home during the dry season, or of fully-resident labourers (whether strangers or local men) who are partly occupied in cultivating their own farms in order to supplement their food supplies. There seems to be no example in the literature of the emergence of a 'class' of landless, permanently-resident labourers, as a consequence of the development of a basic export crop – though specialized irrigated crops might be an exception. Thus, the rapid development of cocoa-growing in southern Ghana seventy years ago – see Hill (1963) – was greatly dependent on stranger–labourers who were usually rewarded with a one-third share (*abusa*) of the cocoa crop and who were always allocated portions of farmland on which they grew food crops; although daily-paid labourers were sometimes also employed, they were stop-gaps only – their work, unlike that of the labourers, requiring constant supervision.

There are at least four reasons why it is beyond the power of Hausa farmers to offer such attractive conditions to resident labourers. First, they lack lineage (or family) land, portions of which are commonly made available to cocoa-labourers; secondly, they cannot buy large tracts of uncultivated land (in the manner of the migrant cocoa-farmers of southern Ghana); thirdly, farming is only possible during the single short rainy season, whereas in the southern forests cultivation of one crop or another is possible for many months; fourthly, labourers would require finance for seed and manure, unless they were content to cultivate bush-farms only – planting material for perennials such as plantain and cocoyam and also for cassava, may be made freely available in the southern forests.

While a 'labouring-class' may exist in Hausa cities, where regular employment is on offer throughout the year, it is difficult to see how a 'class of resident landless labourers' could ever emerge in the countryside, except possibly where dry-season crops are grown or where there were special opportunities of non-farming employment. However regular his employment during the short farming-season, a landless labourer's earning would always be insufficient for the maintenance of himself and his family during the long dry season, for poor men lack the finance to pursue the more remunerative trading occupations.

The limitations of the labouring system provide a reason, additional to those usually advanced, for the extreme importance of the plough (q.v.), especially in those districts of Katsina and Kano where the readily-ploughed sandy soils are so suitable for groundnut cultivation. (But, unfortunately, there is (as yet) no alternative to hand work for the first weeding.)

(iii) (c)   *Wife-seclusion*

Presumably Muslim wife-seclusion is becoming increasingly strict throughout rural (Nigerian) Hausaland. However, for present limited purposes there is no need to speculate about the proportion of wives who still enjoy any day-to-day freedom of movement (perhaps because they live in dispersed settlements, or are required to carry water), the likelihood being that, in any case, Nigerian Hausa women (unlike many of their sisters in the Niger Republic) undertake little cultivation proper, though they may have responsibility for special tasks such as cotton picking. (But see *Kulle*.)

The Nigerian Hausa thus stand in great contrast to many other peoples – including their neighbours the Kanuri of Bornu, with whom – R. Cohen (1960, p. 274) – the number of wives a farmer has available for work is a 'major factor in crop production'. Perhaps it is usually only in certain forest-dwelling societies, such as the Akan of Ghana, that women do most of the food farming. Yet, according to Haswell's excellent study (1953) of the economics of agriculture in a savannah village in the Gambia, the men farmers' efforts at cultivating late millet were so 'pitifully inadequate' (p. 25) that they were wholly dependent on the women's cultivation of rice, which work was maintained at a 'high pitch of activity' throughout the period May to January.

(iv) and (v)   *Capital shortage and permanent cultivation*

The shortage of working-capital in Batagarawa is associated with the general level of poverty; with the failure of 'farming-businesses' (*gandaye*) to survive the shock of the death of the *gandu* head; with the fact that there are few other types of business enterprise which enable an individual to build up capital during the course of his working-life (most traders being younger men – p. 186); with the lack of durable equipment; with high levels of celebratory expenditure; and so forth. Such factors are likely to have general relevance to many Hausa communities where the farmers mainly grow basic crops, and where few men are engaged in hereditary crafts.

It has been concluded that irrespective of population density, permanent cultivation (q.v.) of manured farmland is often the preferred agronomic system: there is much general evidence in favour of this hypothesis, and it is our presumption that where, as in Batagarawa, the incidence of farm-selling is high, the bulk of basic produce is grown on permanently cultivated farmland.

As noted by Netting (1968) in his valuable examination of the cultural ecology of the Kofyar of the Jos plateau, whose primary dependence is on staple crops grown on permanently cultivated farms, land cannot be viewed as a really valuable resource unless it is being kept in production by its owner – this involving the expenditure of working-capital. Most richer farmers in Batagarawa buy some types of manure (q.v.), such as compound sweepings and imported fertilizers (q.v.), and are able to attract visiting Fulani to herd their cattle on their farms after harvest, if they are not themselves cattle-owners.

But whereas a farmer with sufficient working-capital is always in a position to increase his supplies of manure, his increased production may be at the expense of that of poorer farmers in his own community. This is the situation in Batagarawa, where no one except a single member of the ruling-class is reported as 'importing' compound sweepings; where supplies of imported fertilizers are limited (as they are throughout the northern states owing to Nigerian balance of payments difficulties); where there is much competition for the dung provided by locally-based Fulani-owned herds (there is no nearby cattle route); and where the Hausa farmers themselves own no more than about 100 cattle (q.v.). The situation could presumably be alleviated by rearing (and penning) more sheep and goats (q.v.) and the manurial contribution of the donkey has been neglected; but whether the limited grazing would support more cattle is not known.

The two main variables (apart from working-capital) determining the capacity of rural communities to 'import' more manure, are the availability of Fulani-owned herds (whether locally-based, on trade routes, or transhumant), and the possibilities of bringing in compound sweepings and other material of manurial value from neighbouring communities with surpluses available – such as the donkey-loads of sweepings which are 'imported' from Kano city by farmers in the Close-Settled Zone. Published material on the geographical distribution of Fulani-owned herds and on transhumant (as distinct from trade) routes is very scanty – see **Fulani**. So even if it be presumed that many communities are likely to be much more favourably situated than Batagarawa with regard to the possibilities of investing working-capital in increased supplies of cattle manure, there is little detailed information as to where these communities might be, especially as there are secular as well as seasonal changes in the geographical distribution of herds – for instance, out of Katsina into Bauchi and Bornu. (Unreliable official figures of the numbers of cattle in Katsina Province published in the Northern Nigerian *Statistical Yearbook*, *1965*, showed a drop of over a half between 1957 and 1964.) There is such a paucity of published information on cattle-ownership by Hausa farmers, on whom the cattle-tax (*jangali*) is not levied, that there is no means of checking whether (as is possible) such farmers are substantial owners in some localities.

(vi) *The decline of craftwork and rurally-based 'fatauci'*

Remarkably little has ever been recorded about traditional craftwork in rural Hausaland – see the entries in the Commentary on the various crafts. A few crafts are known to continue to flourish – an example is smithing, for traditional-type farm-tools (q.v.) have not been replaced by manufactured tools, and blacksmiths are learning to repair imported ploughs and to make spare parts (see Plate 32); but many skilled craftsmen, such as weavers and dyers, are suffering from the competition from manufactured goods, and in many hamlets, such as Autawa (q.v.), few crafts are pursued. However, there are presumably still many rural communities which continue to specialize in certain crafts, including weaving, mat-making and potting: dry-season idleness will be a less serious problem there than it is in Batagarawa.

The idea that rurally-based *fatauci* (q.v.) is decreasing in importance, chiefly as a result of switching from donkey-caravans to lorries, but also owing to the decline in craftwork, requires investigation. Whereas most caravan-donkeys were owned by farmer–traders resident in the countryside, lorries (most of which are much larger than in some West African regions, such as southern Ghana or Yorubaland) are owned by rich men in cities, where the only large lorry-parks are situated. Certainly *fatauci* provides few men in Batagarawa and neighbouring hamlets with lucrative dry-season opportunities, such as existed in former times – it is much cheaper to transport natron by lorry than by donkey-caravan.

It is possible that the decline of craftwork has resulted in a lower incidence of dry-season migration (*cin rani*), for craftsmen sometimes transfer to urban centres during the dry-season, the better to sell their wares: but such is the lack of information that this is sheer surmise.

(vii) *Migration for farming*

Although it might be thought that poor farmers are always able to escape from their poverty by migrating as farmers to localities where fertile farmland, which does not require manuring, may be freely cultivated in the neighbourhood of their farmsteads, our findings in Batagarawa – Chapter VII – suggest that most of those who are 'too poor to farm' in the home village, are also 'too poor to migrate for farming', unless they have relatives or friends in the reception area who are prepared to maintain them. As many of the vacant lands to which Batagarawa people migrated in former times lie not far to the west and are not 'full up', it may be that the concept of 'too poor to migrate for farming' commonly applies even more strongly in less favourably situated localities. It is possible that young fatherless men without working-sons (who are particularly likely to be poor), seldom migrate for farming, except to join relatives.

(viii) *'Balance of payments' difficulties of rural communities considered as 'island economies'*

The exceedingly rough estimates of Batagarawa's 'imports' and 'exports' which follow should not even be regarded as indicative of the orders of magnitude involved (which anyway vary greatly from year to year), but rather as realistic hypothetical figures.

On a number of heroic assumptions, Batagarawa's groundnut exports (see **Groundnuts**) have been very roughly estimated at 100 tons in 1968, worth (say) £2,500 to the farmers – production by the *masu-sarauta* is excluded. A few local traders export cowpeas and there is a little 'external trade' in such produce as sweet potatoes, cassava, fruit and small vegetables – as well as in tobacco. A few farmers 'export' small quantities of grain, which they sell in local markets such as Abukur, but our presumption is that 'net imports' of grain (see below) are always substantial. Most craftsmen and traders (other than firewood-sellers) nowadays mainly rely on local demand and do not 'export' their goods – though some blacksmith's tools are sold 'abroad', as also small quantities of embroidered caps, mats and other 'free goods'. Excluding the *masu-sarauta*, it may be that Batagarawa's total annual 'exports' do not exceed some £3,500 or (say) £10 per adult man.

Again excluding the *masu-sarauta*, what might the value of grain 'imports' be? The total area of manured farmland is some 1,200 acres, of which some 500 acres is estimated to be under groundnuts. As little early millet (*gero*) is grown on bush-farmland, and as the total area of bush-farmland which is under cultivation at any time is likely (see p. 120) to be much smaller than the area of manured farmland, it may be that the equivalent of some 1,000 acres of farmland is under grain. Then, if yields average a quarter of a ton an acre (a high figure), and if (see Chapter IX) average annual grain prices are arbitrarily set at 1s. 6d. per *tiya* (i.e. 3d. per lb or £28 per ton), the gross value of 250 tons of grain would be some £7,000. If grain requirements (q.v.) were put as high as 2 lbs per head per day, then a total of about 400 tons would be required annually, necessitating net 'imports' of 150 tons, at a value of (say) £4,000 – a rate of 'import' which, with groundnut exports at £2,500, could not be financed. Although in an exceptional year like 1968 (when grain prices were much lower relative to groundnut prices than is here assumed), grain consumption might have been as high as 2 lbs per head, it is clearly not beyond the bounds of possibility that consumption rates might often be much lower. Certainly, the shortage of 'foreign exchange' for other purposes is likely, always, to be acute.

Clearly, Batagarawa's 'capacity to import' manufactures often varies greatly from year to year. Many of these goods are very expensive, having passed through a long chain of traders, and being packed in small quantities, such as tiny packets of detergents. Apart from cloth, which is 'imported' in huge quantities, at competitive prices, and some other manufactures, like kerosene, which is handled in large tins, Batagarawa's 'terms of trade' tend to be markedly unfavourable. Insofar as these imports are not manufactured in the northern states, heavy transport costs from the distant seaboard enhance prices. The very high price of kola-nuts (q.v.), especially at certain seasons, is also a serious drain on the 'balance of payments'.

In many West African communities, for instance in southern Ghana and Yorubaland, women trade largely with the outside world, often travelling long distances in lorries. But Muslim attitudes preclude most Hausa women from 'exporting' in this way: the dozen (or so) older women in Batagarawa who trade in Katsina market, are most of them wives of poorer farmers, for husbands are put to shame when their wives do this work.

As for the 'invisibles' in the 'balance of payments', two points about remittances will be made. Batagarawa is at present passing through a stage when outgoings on expenditure on higher education probably exceed incoming funds from those in the modern sector of the economy: it is as yet too early to say whether the well-educated young men who leave the town will do much to assist development there. But remittances from other migrants are likely to remain at a lower level than with many other West African ethnic groups, as migration (q.v.) is often more permanent.

While many of these 'balance of payments' difficulties will obviously affect Hausa rural communities generally, some communities are certain to be much more favourably situated than others. Large exports of both grains and groundnuts may be achieved by communities which are well supplied with cattle manure; communities with much rich *fadama* land, or with access to irrigable farmland on river banks, may derive a large income from special, highly-priced crops, such as vegetables, onions, wheat; there may (as already noted) be some communities where traditional craftwork for export continues to flourish on a large scale. On the other hand, there are some localities, such as northern Sokoto, where high population densities combined with low soil fertilities have produced a situation such that local communities could not survive there at all were it not for the high incidence of dry-season migration.

(ix) *The burden of poverty*

Some measure of 'exploitation' of the rich by the poor is inevitable in every community where economic inequality is pronounced: thus, profits from grain storage would be lower if there were none who were 'too poor to farm' and farm-labour employment would be a less advantageous stop-gap. But on the other hand, the richer members of the community are obliged to give food, clothing and money to the under-employed: to provide partial maintenance for those who, for financial reasons, they are unable to set to work. Rich merchants in cities do not carry the burden of maintaining unemployed labourers generally, many of whom are strangers cared for by their 'countrymen' in the city. *Village responsibilities for providing social security are much wider and inhibit capital growth.*

But this book on a delightful, vital, village – a village which effervesces with merry children who form nearly half the population – must not be allowed to end on such a sad note. The mystery is not poverty, but how such splendid and proud communities can flourish in such unpropitious circumstances. 'Look here, upon this picture [Plate 8], and on this' – Plate 22. How is it that with no modern devices, other than a few ox-ploughs, the desert can be forced to yield, and to go on yielding year after year, vast quantities of grain and groundnuts. As in 1911, the puzzling and unanswered question, is how '...land which for centuries has been yielding enormous crops of grain, which in the spring is one carpet of green, and in November one huge cornfield "white unto harvest", can continue doing so' – Morel (1911, pp. 115–16).

COMMENTARY
including
Hausa Glossary

INTRODUCTION

This alphabetical Commentary serves three purposes: first, it is a repository for reference material; secondly, it is the place where generalization about rural Hausaland has been attempted under different headings (such as 'Inheritance' or 'Usury'), without interrupting discussion of the main themes relating to Batagarawa; thirdly it serves as a glossary of such Hausa words as have been used in the chapters of this book.

Although this system of compilation has made it possible to dispense with footnotes to the main text, it is hoped that readers (particularly those who lack detailed knowledge of Hausaland) will find that this procedure enhances readability: the author has endeavoured to make the chapters generally comprehensible, without constant reference to these back pages, which may be dipped into on another occasion. (See, also, pp. XI–XII.)

It must be strongly insisted that the Commentary has been designed to relate to the chapters of this book, in that it altogether lacks comprehensiveness. To emphasize this point, many entries on important subjects which happen not to be relevant to Batagarawa, have been left deliberately brief – e.g. those on cotton and rice. On the other hand, a fair quantity of historical reference material has been included, mainly to emphasize the continuity in rural economic affairs over many decades (that rural cash economies were not the consequence of Sir Frederick Lugard), but also because Henry Barth, who was in Hausaland 120 years ago, is often the most up-to-date observer of the rural scene. The general justification for the inclusion of so much bibliographic material in the Commentary is the hope that it will be useful to future research workers.

Most Hausa words that appear in the main text are in the Commentary. In order to facilitate easy reference, isolated nouns are usually given their singular forms in the text, even when the sense demands the plural. When an important Hausa or English word is mentioned in the running text for the first time, or when there is some special reason why readers may care to refer to the Commentary, the letters 'q.v.' may appear: otherwise 'q.v.' is generally omitted. When an important Hausa or English word is not actually mentioned in the running text but may be looked up in the Commentary, it appears in parentheses in semi-bold type. The same system (in addition to straightforward cross references) applies to the text of the Commentary itself.

In dealing with Hausa words the author has taken the same liberties as all glossary-compilers. Thus, many Hausa words have numerous separate meanings, but one meaning only is usually given here. (In the rare cases where two or more meanings are given, these are denoted as (i), (ii), etc.) Then, many Hausa nouns have several different plural forms, one of which has been arbitrarily selected – when no plural is shown, this is usually because the word is both singular and plural. Again, the 'hooked' forms of 'b', 'd' and 'k', have not been distinguished from the 'ordinary' letters – see p. xv above. Finally, dialectical variations are virtually ignored.

ARRANGEMENT OF MATERIAL

Many entries have two separate sections denoted as (a) and (b): where this is so, (a) relates to Batagarawa in particular; and (b) to rural Hausaland generally.

ABBREVIATIONS

'Abraham' is R. C. Abraham's *Hausa Dictionary*
'Bargery' is G. P. Bargery's *Dictionary*
'Barth' is Henry Barth's *Travels and Discoveries* (1857)
'Dalziel' is J. M. Dalziel's *Useful Plants* (1937)
FAO *Report* (1966) is *Agricultural Development in Nigeria (1965–1980)*, by the Food and Agricultural Organization of the United Nations, Rome
'NK' is G. Nicolas' major work on the rural Hausa in the Kantché area of the Niger Republic (1965); NK2 his minor work (1962b)
'NM' is the same author's corresponding major work (jointly with G. Mainet) on the Maradi area (1964)
(Further details on all these works are provided in the Bibliography.)

Abakuru (Bakuru). Tiny cakes made from groundnuts, bean flour, etc.

Aboki – f. *abokiya*, pl. *abokai*. A friend or companion; also one who shares in something, e.g. *abokin aiki*, a fellow-worker. See *Arziki, Kawa*.

Abokin wasa. The 'joking-relationship' between certain friends, occupational groups, and categories of kin, the latter including cross-cousins, grandparents (and grandchildren) and a younger brother of a husband or wife. See Smith (1955, pp. 43–5).

Abubakar Labo. Abubakar Labo of Kaukai (q.v.) who was a most valued informant in 1967 and 1968 on long-distance trading (*fatauci*), the tobacco trade, slavery, the cowry currency, the history of markets, and other historical matters, was in Damagaram (Zinder) with his father (Geshe), who was a famous caravan-leader, during the reign of Sarki Ahmadu (1893–9). His father was himself the son of a rurally-based *farke*, who had lived in Makurdi (q.v.): he had been on *fatauci* to Lagos before 1900, knew Agadez well, and regarded Damagaram as a 'second home'.

Acacia: see *Gawo*, Mimosa.

Acakwa. Raphia (*gwangwala*) tray for carrying a load.

Acca. 'Hungry rice' (*Digitaria exilis*), known as *intaya* in Zaria. The evidence is that this grain is seldom cultivated by the Hausa.

Adada – pl. *adadai*. Rectangular thatched house or room.

Adashi.

(a) A 'rotating credit association' (or contribution club) such that each member undertakes to pay, usually weekly, a certain sum of money into a common pool for a fixed period, a different member drawing the total fund on each occasion, until each has had her share. Nearly all *adashi* members are women and each group is run by a woman (*uwar adashi* – lit. 'mother of the *adashi*') who collects the contributions (sometimes through the medium of children), selects the weekly beneficiary and generally organizes affairs, in return for a small commission payable by each beneficiary. When contributions are payable weekly (as they often are) the *adashi* usually lasts for 30 weeks, having the same number of members. The weekly contributions (*zubi*) vary between 1*d*. and 2*s*. The last person to receive the weekly pay-out (*kwasa*) is known as *kutal* (the end of a queue) – she may be compensated by drawing the first *kwasa* in the next *adashi*. When a member fails to pay the *zubi* due, the *uwar adashi* herself becomes liable. About four-fifths of all Batagarawa women participate in *adashi*. Nearly every woman aspires to coagulate her savings in this way and membership of several groups is common.

(b) In Hausa towns certain men (e.g. junior civil servants) form *adashi* groups. The existence of women's *adashi* groups is briefly noted by Smith (1955) and Nicolas (NM, etc.). (The Batagarawa variety of *adashi* is very similar to the Nupe *dashi* reported on by Nadel (1942); Nupe farmers, unlike urban men in other occupations, are never members.) Rotating credit associations are a world-wide institution, the Hausa variety being very common – see Ardener (1964).

See *Biki*, Women – economic position of.

Agama. Oppression of market vendors by a chief – Bargery. 'Illegal market impost on goods other than meat' – Hiskett (1960, p. 573).

Agazari. The hot season immediately following the cessation of the rains, which is followed by *dari*. See *Kaka, Rani*.

Age-structure. According to the 1952 population census, only 5% of all males in Mallamawa District were aged over fifty years, the corresponding proportion for females being 10%. Owing to the difficulties of age-estimation, little significance would have been attached to these percentages, had it not been that the proportion of males over fifty was found to be 5%

or less in 21 out of 22 Districts in Katsina Emirate. Unless the statistics had been centrally 'adjusted', or abnormal instructions given to the numerous Katsina enumerators, the figures certainly suggest that life expectancies for Katsina males were lower than in northern Nigeria generally. (In 8 out of 12 Northern Provinces the proportion lay between 9% and 11%: it was 4% in Benue and Katsina and 7% in Kabba and Plateau.)

Agola – pl. *agolai*. A wife's child by an earlier marriage who lives with her (his) mother. See Smith (1955, p. 21).

Agushi. The seeds of various types of water melon. Known in West African markets generally by the Yoruba word *egusi*, the seeds are used as medicine, in soups and for oil, etc. – they have a considerable food value, but much labour is involved in de-husking them. See Dalziel (p. 55). See **Melon**.

Aikatau. Working for wages or payment – from *aiki* (work). Also a (male or female) worker for wages.

   (a) In Batagarawa the word is usually only applied to paid work performed by one woman for another; types of work include grain-grinding (*nikau*), grain-pounding (*dakau*), threshing, winnowing, as well as other assistance in processing foodstuffs, including groundnut oil. About a half of all women reported that they sometimes did this work – the corresponding proportions for wives of heads of farming-units varied between one-quarter for Group 1 and two-thirds for Group 4. See *Indikya, Koda, Yima*.

Aiki. Any kind of work, including farming, whether paid or not; *abokin aiki* = a fellow worker. See *Aikatau*.

Ajali. An agreed time-period – e.g. for repayment of debt.

Alaro. Carrying loads for payment; *dan alaro* = carrier.

Albasa. Onion (q.v.).

Albasar kwadi (*Crinum yuccaeflorum, Haemanthus rupestris*). These and other lily species are known as *albasar kwadi*, lit. 'frogs' onions'. *H. rupestris* may correspond with the boundary plant known as *hurar-kiba* in Batagarawa (see **Farm-boundary Plants**), for Dalziel notes (p. 487) that Fulani pastoralists sometimes use that plant in that way. It is fortunate that *hurar-kiba* is little used as a boundary plant in Batagarawa, for many boundaries would otherwise have been missing from the farm maps based on air photographs taken during the dry season, when the plant lies invisibly latent.

Albashi. Monthly salary, *dan albashi* being a person on a monthly salary.

Alewa. A type of sweetmeat made from honey, sugar or sugar cane, often flavoured with a fruit such as *dinya*.

   (a) *Alewa* is made and sold by men in Batagarawa.

Alhaji – f. *alhajiya*, pl. *alhajai*. The title of one who has made the pilgrimage to Mecca; also the *name* of certain people, such as those born on various dates – e.g. the day for starting the pilgrimage, etc.

   (a) In 1967 there were 3 *alhajai* in Batagarawa – the District Head's eldest son (Alhaji Barau), the Chief Imam and Alhaji Shekarau. In 1969 there were 3 others who made the pilgrimage by air; they were the District Head (Mallamawa), Alhaji Nuhu, and the widow of the late Sarakin Fada – whose origins were in Katsina city. The minimum cost of the expedition is now over £200. See *Haji*.

Alkali – pl. *alkalai*. A judge. See **District Courts**.

Alkama – (*Triticum durum* and *T. vulgare*). Soft wheat, mainly grown in Hausaland **as an** irrigated dry-season crop, on *fadama* and on river-banks, as it was in Clapperton's day (1829, p. 218). Although much more expensive than imported wheat flour, *alkama* is the main ingredient of various cooked foodstuffs purveyed by secluded women, including *alkaki* (a cake) and *taliya* (a kind of macaroni). Cultivation being highly localized (e.g. in parts of northern Sokoto), wheat is much handled by long-distance traders. It is reported by Nicolas (NM, p. 187) that much wheat grown by Hausa in Niger is sold at Jibiya in northern Nigeria.

Alkarya: see **Gari**.

Amarya – pl. *amare*.

(i) A bride; also, a man's junior wife, however long she may have been married.

   (ii) Anything new – thus *amaryar wata* is the new moon.

Aminiya – pl. *aminai*.

(a) A woman's female bond-friend, to whom confidences may be entrusted, and whose help (by means of *biki* or otherwise) may be relied on. See **Kawa**.

Area courts: see **District Courts**.

Arne (Azne). Any pagan – i.e. non-Muslim and non-Christian. See *Maguzawa*.

Aro. 'A loan of something which is itself to be returned' – Bargery. This entry refers only to the loan, or renting, of farmland.

(a) In Batagarawa the two words for the renting of farmland, *aro* and *haya* (q.v.), are used somewhat interchangeably, though when informants are pressed for a definition, they may explain that *aro* is the more flexible arrangement, *haya* the more fixed. *Aro* often involves relatives or friends and/or the idea of 'helping' the tenant, so that rents are usually very low, often a few shillings only; *haya* which, according to one informant, is 'fixed money and no love', is much the rarer of the two. Owing to the practice of letting off portions of manured farms, the proportion of manured farmland under *aro* cannot be accurately assessed, but it is likely to be much less than 10%. Most cases of *aro* involve bush-farms.

As owners of manured farms are nervous of long tenancies (suspicions are immediately aroused if a tenant is seen manuring a farm), the stereotyped notion of *aro* involves letting a farm for one season for a small cash rent payable before harvest plus 'something extra' (*goro*) at harvest; however, if the parties are close relatives, 'in-laws' (*suruki*, q.v.), or good friends, the rent may be nil and the tenancy longer. Occasionally the tenant pays rent in terms of farm-labour – e.g. assisting the owner on the whole farm in return for the produce of certain of its ridges. Another interesting arrangement involves 2 farmers in renting the same farm, each planting a different crop.

As for bush-farms, when they are put out on *aro* this is usually after a period of fallow, the tenant having to clear the land, and being allowed to remain there until the next fallowing. Perhaps about a quarter of all cultivated bush-farms are under *aro*. Short-term allocation of bush-farms to strangers by Hamlet Heads (in return for a consideration) is not *aro*, which necessarily involves two individuals.

(b) *Aro* (termed such) is common in rural Hausaland. It has been reported on by Rowling (1952) – who noted that in Revenue Survey areas (q.v.) the tenancy might have been granted in consideration of the payment of the tax on the farm; by Smith (1955); by Luning (1963a); by Norman (1967); and by others. It is possibly of very variable incidence, though definitional difficulties and the failure to distinguish manured and bush-farms obscure the general picture. Rents are always reported as being low.

  See *Bashi*, **Bush-farm**, *Haya, Jingina, Rance*.

Arziki (Azziki) – pl. *arzuka*. Used in the double sense of prosperity and good fortune, this important concept is considered on pp. 185–7 above. See also *Dukiya*.

  yana cikin arziki = (i) he is prosperous; (ii) he holds an official, or an assured position.

  yana cikin arzikin Audu = he's in Audu's employ.

  abokin arziki = (for example) (i) a trading partner or associate; (ii) one who assists another with finance for trading; (iii) one who buys and stores produce for a *dan kwarami*.

mai arziki = a fortunate *and* prosperous man; *mara arziki* = a poor man.
arzikinsa ya karai = his luck has broken.

Asali – pl. *asalai*. Ancestral home; pedigree; origin.

Asurkumi. A dressed skin bag with a small mouth, formerly for carrying cowries.

Attajiri – f. *attajira*, pl. *attajirai*. A wealthy trader or merchant who is usually city-based. See p. 176. See Smith (1955).

Aunaka. From *auna* – measured or weighed.
(i) The periodic distribution of household supplies of grain, rice etc. by the household head.
(ii) A supply of grain and money given by a bridegroom to his bride before she joins him.

Autawa. A Mallamawa Hamlet situated a few miles south of Batagarawa, not far from Abukur. Most of the residents live in dispersed houses – see Fig. 9 on p. 14 and Plate3 4. See also **Farm-size**.
The following notes relate to a brief survey undertaken in 1967, when the farms were mapped using an air photograph:
(1) although most farms were under permanent cultivation, the proportion of bush-farms was somewhat higher than in Batagarawa;
(2) the institution of *gandu* was found to be very strong. Of 51 tax-payers, 11 were heads of paternal *gandaye* and 2 of fraternal *gandaye*; only 3 tax-payers had left *gandu*, being sons of resident farmers;
(3) economic inequality appeared to be as pronounced as in Batagarawa. Of a sample of 33 heads of farming-units, at least 10 were extremely poor; 3 of them were butchers and 4 were firewood-collectors;
(4) the Hamlet Head (*mai unguwa*) was the sole plough-owner – he owned 2 ploughs and 5 plough-oxen; he managed a large herd of cattle, probably owning many of the animals himself;
(5) there were no blacksmiths, tailors, dyers, carpenters, weavers, or skilled builders in the Hamlet. There were 2 *'yan kwarami*, 2 tobacco traders and 1 kola trader;
(6) although women are not as strictly secluded as in Batagarawa, very few of them owned farms.

Awo. Corn bought by measure (in a market or a house) for immediate consumption.

Aya. Tiger-nut (q.v.). See *Dakuwa*.

Ayari – pl. *ayarori*. A trading caravan. See *Fatauci*.

Azahar. The period for rest and prayer between about 2 and 3 p.m. See Taylor and Webb (1932, p. 95) for a chart of obligatory prayers (*salloli na farilla*).

Azumi. The fast of the month of Ramadan (*watan azumi*).

Baba. Father. See *Uba*.

Bachelor. A bachelor who has not been married is *tuzuru*, but a man who is no longer married, or whose wife is absent, may be referred to as *gwauro*, though not in his presence.
Gwauro ya fi tuzuru barna = 'A man no longer married is more dangerous than one not yet married' – Kirk-Greene (1966b, p. 7).

Ba-cucane – f. *bacucaniya*, pl. *cucanawa*. One born in slavery of slave-parents. See *Dimajo*.

Baduku – pl. *dukawa*. Leather worker.

Bafada – pl. *fadawa*. A chief's courtier or household official. See Smith (1960). See *Bara*, *Fada*.

Baitulmal (*Beit-el-mal*). Native Treasury. See **Taxation**.

Bako – f. *bakuwa*, pl. *baki*. A guest, visitor, or stranger. The leader of a group of resident stranger-traders, such as the Buzu headman in Katsina market, may be known as Sarkin Baki.

Balbela (*Belbela*) – pl. *balbelu*. The ubiquitous cattle-egret (*Bubulcus ibis*), great colonies of which roost on trees at night, resembling white blossom. See **Onions**.

Balma. Salt from Bilma in the Sahara.

Bambara groundnut: see *Gujiya*.

Bango – pl. *bangaye*. A wall of a hut, or house, or round a compound.

Baobab: see *Kuka*.

Bara – f. *baranya*, pl. *barori*. A 'servant' (domestic or other), a client, or a retainer. Since a chief's courtier or household official (*bafada*) may be regarded as a *bara*, the following notes refer to both types of 'client'. See Smith (1955, 1960, etc.) for much valuable material. See also Nadel (1942, p. 123).

(a) In Batagarawa, in 1967, there were about 20 men and youths who could be classified as either *bara* or *bafada* (there were also some borderline cases), nearly all of them being attached to the *masu-sarauta*. Most of the men had families and houses of their own, as well as farms which they were free to cultivate. About 4 of them were mainly engaged in domestic tasks (such as issuing grain to wives, clothes-washing, arranging for firewood and water supplies, and house maintenance); about 9 were primarily 'farm-servants' (supervising the work, recruiting labour, or working themselves) or concerned with horses or cattle; the remaining 7 men had specific posts connected with the administration of the District – some having titles such as Shamaki or Makama, most also having some connexion with their patron's farming.

Domestic servants are usually given some food, as well as a little money (such as 1s. a day) to buy such meals as are not provided and most of the 'farm-servants' receive 1s. a day when they work, in addition to *fura* and *tuwo*: in both cases the master's duty to pay the community tax (*haraji*) and to 'help' in adversity over obligatory ceremonial expenditure, etc., are the main compensations for the loss of personal freedom involved. Such servants are apt to fall in and out of favour, the relationship often involving much quarrelling. Most of those with official duties are indirectly remunerated in the course of their work: 2 of them are well-known farmers and were classified as Group 2.

Only one of the 4 domestic servants was the son of a *bara* – the other 3 had originally taken up the work when they were boys. Only one of the 'farm-servants' was known to have had a father who had been a *bara* (he had also been a butcher): it was poverty and/or insecurity which had driven most of these men into this work. As for those with official duties, one was the son of a farmer/dyer; one held the same office as his late father (who had migrated to Batagarawa as a *bara*); one was a brother of the foregoing; two had migrated to Batagarawa as *barori*; one was the son of one of the foregoing; the origin of one was unclear. Thus 5 out of 7 of these men were immigrants or immigrants' sons. (It is to be noted that immigrants who arrive as *barori* often become independent farmers in due course.)

In 1967 there were at least 8 middle-aged or elderly women classifiable as *barori*, 7 of whom were attached to one or other of the *masu-sarauta*. These women were mainly engaged in threshing, grinding, pounding, water carrying and other heavy tasks, and might assist with cooking. Most of them were given all their food and small sums of money: as with the men, it was the general security of the position which was appreciated. Six of these women were widows (4 of their husbands had been *barori*); one was a divorcée who had not remarried; and one was the wife of a farmer whose poverty drove her to work in this way.

See **Barau (Alhaji), Magaji, Mallamawa**, *Shamaki*, **Zagi**.

Baranda. Buying goods for resale, the trader being *dan baranda* (pl. *'yan baranda*). According to Bargery this type of trade involves 'buying goods to sell again, but not paying for them until the re-sale has been effected': it 'is not irksome to the agent, as if he sees no chance of profit he merely returns the goods to the owner'. But (see Chapter IX) this is not the sense in which the word is nowadays employed (at least in some areas) in connexion with local purchase of groundnuts for ultimate export. See *Bilkara*, *Kwarami*, **Trading-terms**.

Barau, Alhaji. Alhaji Barau is the senior son of the District Head of Mallamawa; he is the Batagarawa Village Scribe. He and his father both farm on a larger scale than anyone else in the *gari*.

In 1967 there were 11 people living in his house, including 3 wives, 1 schoolboy and 6 other children. His senior wife was an important house-trader handling kerosene and cigarettes (her husband arranging for supplies to be procured for her in Katsina city), as well as cooked foodstuffs and groundnut oil; she also bought groundnuts for storage. One of his wives was the daughter of his father's father's junior brother and 2 were non-relatives.

Apart from a relatively large area of *fadama*, he owned three farms in the mapped zone. One of these (about $4\frac{1}{2}$ acres) had been acquired from a man who had migrated; it was entirely planted with cassava. Another farm of about 12 acres was a consolidation of numerous portions bought from at least six other farmers. He also had farms in at least four other Hamlets, including Makurdi (some 7 acres which he had bought from a relative) and Dabaibayawa, where he sometimes goes to stay to supervise the farming – he himself never farms.

He employs many *'yan kwadago*, who are recruited locally on his behalf by those in charge of his farms in the neighbouring hamlets. He also greatly relies on both *taimako* and *gayya*. In July 1968 he 'called *gayya*' at Dabaibayawa and 103 men attended; he sent the workers 3 donkey-loads of *fura* from Batagarawa. In September 1967 as many as 32 men, many of them youths from neighbouring Kabakawa, were seen on his large farm near the *gari*, collecting and bundling the millet, which had earlier been reaped, into 187 bundles – see Plate 2.

In 1968 he owned 2 ploughs, acquired through the Native Authority, and 4 plough-oxen which he had bought privately.

He produces great quantities of groundnuts, which he also buys for storage, and is an important producer of tobacco, which (like all substantial growers) he stores for a price rise.

In 1967 his economic life tended to centre round the co-operative society (q.v.), of which he was President. The society would scarcely have survived as long as it did (and would certainly have operated on a much smaller scale), had it not been for his enthusiasm and initiative.

He is a cattle-owner and his wives own sheep and goats.

In 1967 two youths, who might be regarded as *barori*, were regularly employed by him to care for his cattle and to assist in farming, and numerous other men were partially dependent on him. He also employed a regular plough-man. Two full-time women servants assisted his wives.

As an enterprising innovator, who sets an example to other farmers, and is always in the process of expanding the scale of his farming and the range of his crops, Alhaji Barau holds a unique position in the community.

Barbarta. The leaves, and sometimes the fruit and roots, of the shrub *sabora* (*Guiera sene-galensis*), which are much used medicinally. *Barbarta* was one of the few wares (apart from *kanwa* and livestock) transported southwards by the northern Katsina *fatake*. See *Fatauci*.

Barber-Surgeon – *wanzami*, pl. *wanzamai*. Apart from men's hair-dressing, shaving, etc., barber-surgeons have numerous specialized functions (see **Circumcision**, **Naming-cere-mony**) and also dispense medicines and give medical advice. Barbers may be addressed as Sarkin Aska – *aska* being a razor.

(a) In Batagarawa there are 5 heads of farming-units who are active barbers, and a few others who are skilled in this work. Each family is said to have 'its own barber' for ceremonial occasions.

(b) See Mary Smith (1954, pp. 139, 141–2) on the operation for the removal of a baby's uvula which is performed by barber–doctors. See Taylor and Webb (1932, p. 33).

See Nadel (1942, pp. 298–301) for a detailed account of the function of barber–doctors in Nupe – there being no comparable description for Hausaland.

Barema: see *Kwadago.*

Barkono: see **Pepper.**

Barter: see **Exchange.**

Bashi – pl. *basusuwa.* The most usual and general term for a loan or, more particularly, a debt; *bashi da ruwa* is a loan with interest. Formally, *bashi* is a debt which is not repayable for some time, short-term debts or loans being *rance* (q.v.) – but the terms are often used interchangeably (at least in Batagarawa), though most large loans are *bashi.* The borrowing of something which is itself to be returned is *aro* (q.v.) – see also *Dauke* and *Falle. Bashi* usually, though not necessarily, takes the form of money.

biya bashi = to pay a debt.

biyo bashi = to recover a debt.

ya karbi bashi = he incurred a debt.

ya cinye bashi = lit. 'he ate up the loan' – i.e. he borrowed and failed to repay.

ya ba ni bashin riga = he sold me a gown on credit.

bashi hanji ne, yana cikin kowa = debt is like intestines, everyone has them.

The following notes summarize the preliminary results of a recent enquiry on traditional credit-granting (*bashi*) in rural areas near Maradi (Nicolas, 1970):

(1) two-fifths of all those questioned were borrowers;

(2) nearly half of all debts were incurred during the farming-season (*damuna*), one-fifth during the previous season (*bazara*); three-quarters of all repayments were made at harvest-time, or when groundnuts were sold for export;

(3) most lenders (84% of them) were non-kin;

(4) loans consisted as to: 34% of money, 20% of millet, 16% of groundnuts and 11% cloth; 75% of repayments were in cash;

(5) between 2% to 3% of the adult population were lenders, most of them rurally-based farmers and traders; nearly half of them were aged between 40 and 50. Most creditors lent to a number of debtors. Very large town-based creditors accounted for a large proportion of total loans;

(6) interest-charging is an ancient practice. One-fifth of loans were interest free; of the remainder, four-fifths involved interest 'rates' of between 10% and 70% (whether such rates were in fact paid is another matter);

(7) the main reasons for borrowing were: need for food (27%), ceremonial expenditure (22%, of which marriage expenditure 9%), trading stock (20%), seed acquisition (13%).

See **Butchers, Usury.**

Batagarawa. The small town (*gari*) together with surrounding dispersed homesteads, the socio-economic life of which is the main concern of this book. See Chapter II, pp. 10 ff. and Chapter I, pp. 8–9.

The town was included in Barth's list of 'the principal places belonging to the province of Katsena' (vol. II, p. 557); though spelt 'Atagarawa', its identity is not in doubt, as several present-day neighbouring hamlets, one of them Kabakawa, occur before and after it in the list. Barth, like Clapperton before him, commented on the wild state of the country south of Katsina city (vol. II, p. 84) – which greatly impeded communication between the *gari* and the *birni* until quite recently. See also Falconer (1911, p. 268). In March 1953, Barth must have passed very near to the *gari* after spending a night at Kabakawa, a couple of miles to the north-east. He then proceeded to the village of Doka, at present a Mallamawa Hamlet some 5 miles south of Batagarawa, where the country was 'well populated and well cultivated' (permanent cultivation?), extensive tobacco grounds and large fields of cocoyam being seen. But it was

8

at Maje, some eight miles south of Batagarawa, where he was most impressed with the 'fertility and beauty' of the country – vol. IV, p. 107.

In the early years of the century Batagarawa was in Yandaka District, of which the capital is now Dutsin Ma – see Fig. 3, p. 10. According to Abubakar Labo the *gari* was very populous until Yandaka Zubairu left for Tsauri – a market-town to the south-west – but subsequently fell into a decline. (See Chapter VII, p. 95.)

In 1916 the Village Head of Batagarawa was recorded (National Archives, Kaduna, Acc. 1280) as being Dan Sanebbi, the son of the District Head of Yandaka, who had 11 Hamlet Heads under him, and whose monthly salary was £2.

According to the 'Intensive Census' conducted in this locality in 1931 (see p. 309 below) the total population of Batagarawa was 1,084, but whether of the *gari* only or of the whole Hamlet Area (*unguwa*) was not stated. In 1967 (see p. 17 above) the population of the *unguwa* was 1,395. (Unfortunately, certain later figures extracted from the National Archives, Kaduna are highly suspect.) The 1952 census recorded 6,520 persons as resident in the Batagarawa *Village Area*. See **Mallamawa District**.

Batagarawa Market. In 1967 Batagarawa was the only capital of a Katsina District which lacked a market-place, the nearest market being at Abukur, some 3 to 4 miles away by foot and some 5 miles by lorry. Informants mentioned the numerous attempts which had been made (with varying success) to establish a market in the past forty years or so, since the town had first become a District Head's seat. On 27 May 1968 (see p. 138 above) a further attempt was made – see also Hill (1969b). (This market failed in 1970.)

The market, which was under the authority of the chief butcher (*sarkin pawa*), operated on a small scale. According to surveys made by M. S. Nuhu, an average of only 70 sellers (excluding a few men who were there in the capacity of tailors, barbers, or drummers) attended the market on three days in September to November 1968, about half of them coming from neighbouring hamlets. As many as 32 of the traders were either butchers and their assistants, or male petty traders ('*yan tireda*), nearly all of whom had merely shifted their selling-points from the village streets and paths where they usually conducted their business. Ten of the traders were women and girls who sold cooked foods. No grain, groundnuts or cowpeas were sold and few of the other wares handled by men traders were of a type sold by secluded women (see **House-trade**), whose business continued undisturbed – it may, indeed, have increased owing to the influx of buyers from nearby hamlets. The other wares sold by men included: sugar cane, kola, cooked cassava, guava, secondhand clothes, donkeys, cloth, mats, cornstalk beds, honey, hoe handles, perfumes and enamelware, etc. See **Market-place**.

Batagarawa *unguwa*. The Batagarawa Hamlet (*unguwa*) consisting of Batagarawa *gari* together with the dispersed farmhouses, within a mile or so, which is under the authority of Mukaddas (see p. 157).

Bawa – f. *baiwa*, pl. *bayi*. A slave, either literally or figuratively. See *Dimajo*, *Rinji*, **Slavery**.

***Bazara*.** The hot dry season just before *damuna*, the rainy season; the length of this season, and its dates, vary with latitude and from year to year. See *Rani*.

Bazawara – pl. *zawarawa*. A formerly married woman who, following the collapse of her marriage, usually remains at home for a short time with her parents or other relatives and who is not a prostitute (*karuwa*); also a widow.

Beans: see **Cowpeas**.

Beggar: see *Mai bara*, *Maroki*, *Masarci*.

Bicycles – *keke*, pl. *kekuna*; *basukur* (from English).
(a) About 17 men (other than the *masu-sarauta*) owned about 24 bicycles in 1967; most of these men owned one cycle, but 2 owned 4 each; 21 of the cycles were owned by men in

Groups 1 and 2, as many as 7 of them by 2 sons-in-*gandu*. Most cycles are acquired with a view to hiring out – poorer men sometimes buy machines at harvest-time and resell them before the next farming-season: bicycle ownership (and repair) is considered a gainful (and distinct) *occupation*. A new cycle may cost as much as £25. The cost of hiring for a full day was 2s. 6d. to 3s. While in many regions of savannah West Africa, e.g. parts of Northern Ghana, farmers commonly cycle to their farms, this is not so in Batagarawa, the paths being too narrow and sandy, the ubiquitous donkey being a much more efficient load-carrier.

Biki – pl. *bukuwa*.

(i) A feast, e.g. in celebration of a marriage or name-day.

(ii) 'Any gift or contribution of food, cloth, or money to a friend who is celebrating a special occasion' – Bargery. Such a contribution is not a true gift (*bikin sa'a ba kyauta ba ne*) 'as it will have to be recompensed when occasion offers' – Bargery.

(a) *Biki* as a contribution system linking partners is a very important socio-economic institution in Batagarawa involving, so it is said, virtually the entire adult population, most contributions being made in connexion with marriage, naming-ceremonies, funerals and *gayya*. No formality attends the initiation of a *biki* relationship, one party simply making a contribution on a certain occasion on the understanding that the recipient will make a larger counter-contribution (will hopefully double the sum) when the original donor is in like need of funds. Especially as *biki* often involves poorer people, there is considerable flexibility and a participant's failure to pay may be tolerated on up to three occasions. Nowadays literate people often keep records of contributions. When, through doubling, the sum reaches what is considered an intolerably high level, say £10, it is halved in the sense that the next party to pay contributes only £5 (the sum which he received on the last occasion) – the contribution may then be fixed at that sum. Total sums received from all sources may be quite large if an individual has several *biki* partners: thus, recently, a popular woman got £20 on the occasion of the marriage of her grand-daughter. No dispute regarding *biki* ever reaches the *masusarauta*, so that although passions often rise high, particularly between co-wives, over the failure to pay sufficiently, or at all, the parties must settle their own affairs. On the death of a *biki* partner, relatives such as sons may accept the obligation to continue the relationship. If a participant who makes a contribution to a naming-ceremony has no children, then one of his relatives may receive his partner's counter-gift. No *biki* occurs between parents and children or between brothers and sisters.

Biki commonly occurs between: (i) friends (preferably of the same age-group); (ii) masters and servants; (iii) rich and poor; (iv) women including co-wives; (v) certain close relatives, but not others such as fathers (or mothers) and sons. Partners are commonly motivated by feelings of friendliness, love and trust. Although, as in the cases of (ii) and (iii), the richer partner may be deliberately helping the poorer, who is not expected to double the contribution, *biki* is usually clearly differentiated from *gudummawa* (a donation made with no expectation of a return gift), some counter-contribution being required.

Contributions are not necessarily in cash, but may take such forms as clothes, threshed grain, bundles of grain, small livestock, food together with money, or enamelware; but like must always be 'exchanged' for like, so that, e.g. a donor of threshed grain must be given such produce in return. Contributions tend to be higher at harvest-time and lower during the dry season.

(b) See Mary Smith (1954, pp. 191–2, etc.).

See *Adashi, Aminiya, Kawa.*

Bilkara. 'Buying in bulk without weighing or numbering, trusting to luck to make a profit, but not used with regard to corn' – Bargery.

Binne (*Bizne*). The practice of sowing grain before the expected date of the first rains. (If slight rains fall causing premature germination the seed may be lost, as happened in Batagarawa in April 1969.) See *Shuka.*

Birni – pl. *birane.* A city; the seat of an Emir. Formerly a *birni* was distinguished from other towns by its earth wall (*ganuwa*). 'This distinction is no longer valid today, and *gari* [q.v.] has assumed a generic title to cover city (walled or unwalled), town or even large villages' – Kirk-Greene (1969, p. 265).

(a) In Batagarawa (which had once been walled) neighbouring Katsina city is always referred to as *birni.*

(b) Kirk-Greene (*ibid.*) makes the point that proximity may determine whether a city is referred to as a *birni* – thus Kano city is the only *birni* to the inhabitants of Kano Province, but people living elsewhere may refer to it as *garin Kano.* (In 1904 (Cd 2684, p. 32) it was reported that there were some 40 walled towns within a 30-mile radius of Kano city.)

Blacksmith – *makeri,* pl. *makera.*

(a) There are 3 forges (*makera,* pl. *makerai*) in Batagarawa owned by 3 skilled men, each of whom is descended from a line of blacksmiths. (The paternal grandfathers of two of them were brothers and the father of the third had a brother who was a blacksmith.) Two of them are notable farmers – one being Idi Makeri (p. 156), the other farming more than 13 acres. All of them are in Groups 1 or 2. It is not without significance that two of them are heads of fraternal *gandaye,* the third heading a paternal *gandu.* They specialize in making (and repairing) farm-tools (q.v.), their raw material being scrap iron. Much of their selling is done from their forges, which are attached to their houses. One smith makes his own charcoal, others buy their supplies. Each is assisted by a son or brother, who is paid for this work, and who is permitted to work on his own account when the forge is available. Their simple working tools are mainly forged by themselves. Their bellows are of the simple split-bag type described by Nadel (1942, p. 260) in the course of his admirable description of smithing in Nupe country.

(b) Brief descriptions of smithing are provided in Taylor and Webb (1932) and Ibrahim Madauci (1968), and Nicolas makes reference to Hausa blacksmiths in Niger (NK, p. 60; NM, p. 66): otherwise the literature is extremely scanty. See Smith (1960) on the traditional taxation of blacksmiths. According to Forde's summary of the findings of L. C. Giles in Zaria Emirate – (1946, p. 136) – smiths were largely paid in kind and did little farming: perhaps, as in Batagarawa, they are often nowadays full members of the cash economy and prominent farmers. (Research on Kano blacksmiths is in train by P. Jaggar.)

See **Ploughing.**

Bojuwa. 'Rapid travelling on foot to a distant town to buy easily portable goods to sell in the home market, taking on the outward journey money or a small load of local goods' – Bargery. Hence *dan bojuwa,* a trader in such business.

Boka – pl. *bokaye.* A native doctor; a wizard. Nowadays usually associated with treating madness and 'spirit troubles' generally.

Bokiti – pl. *bokitoci,* from the English word 'bucket'. Licensed buying agents, and others buying groundnuts, commonly employ the *bokiti* as a measure, there being 9 *tiya* (q.v.) of shelled groundnuts to the *bokiti,* 4 *bokitoci* to the bag (or sack) and 13 bags to the ton.

Boko. From 'book'; *makarantar boko* = any school or similar establishment where a secular (i.e. non-Arabic) education or training is given. See **School.**

Bori. Hausa possessive spirit cult, originally associated with sickness-curing, now more often 'play'. 'The bori is an old, indigenous, pre-Islamic Hausa cult which involves the belief in spirits known as *isokoki,* which under certain conditions can possess men and harm them' – A. Cohen (1969, p. 58). Cohen points out (*ibid.*) that in fighting against *bori* 'the malams have admitted their existence, and hence their mystical power, by identifying them as the wicked among the many categories of *jinns* whose existence and characteristics are discussed in the Koran'.

Prostitution (*karuwance*) is closely associated with *bori*. See Jacqueline Nicolas (1967) on *bori* among Hausa women in the Niger Republic and the bibliography therein. See also Onwuejeogwu (1969), Tremearne (1913).

Boundary – *iyaka*, pl. *iyakoki*. *Iyaka* may denote any kind of boundary, or limit, including a frontier, farm-boundary, etc. See **District boundaries, Farm-boundary plants, Hamlet boundaries.**

Building – *gina* = built with clay, brick or cement; *magini*, pl. *magina* = builder or potter.

(a) Six heads of farming-units (see Table v.1, p. 72) had building as their main non-farming occupation, and there were many other men who sometimes undertook the building, or repair, of huts (*daki*), granaries (*rumbu*), or compound walls (*bango*), etc. The ordinary householder lacks the skill to repair the damage, which occurs almost annually, as a result of heavy rains.

The building material is red earth, of a somewhat clayey texture, which has considerable adhesive powers and binds well, after mixing with water and with straw, hay or grass, and after exposure to the sun. Builders are usually paid an agreed sum for a certain task; alternatively, their pay may be related to the time taken – e.g. 7s. to 10s. for a 'long-morning'. The labourers who collect, mix and carry the earth, receive 2s. to 3s. daily, according to the task, plus food and possibly 'something extra' on completion; those who mend walls may receive 4s. to 5s. If a hut is built on contract for a sum such as £1, then it may be that the owner is expected to arrange for the supply of earth. Building and earth-carrying etc. are probably much the most important type of occupation during the dry season – only emergency repairs can be carried out during the rains.

(b) *Magini* is a potter or a builder – a habitation being 'une grande poterie entièrement faite à la main' (NK, p. 249). Nicolas deals adequately with building processes and costs (NK, pp. 60, 249–50; NM, pp. 66, 70, 246). See Taylor and Webb (1932, pp. 169–91). See Prussin (1969) on building technology in northern Ghana.

See *Gida*, **Granary, Potters.**

Bundle: for a bundle of grain see *Dami*.

Burdumi – pl. *burduma*. A wrapping made of dum palm (*kaba*), used for packing broken natron (q.v.).

Burgami (Birgami) – pl. *burgamai*. 'A dressed goat-skin made into a wide-mouthed bag the shape of the animal being retained' – Bargery. Formerly used for carrying cowries.

Burtali. A Fulani word for a cattle track running between farms; it is often hedged.

Bush – *daji, dawa, jeji*, etc. Uninhabited, lightly cultivated thinly wooded, country. To be distinguished from *kurmi* (forest) and *karakara* (q.v.). See **Bush-farm, Fallow.**

Bush-farm – *gonar daji*, pl. *gonakin daji*. An unmanured farm which is cultivated for a term of years and then put to fallow.

(a) For the sake of convenience, see p. 21, all farms cultivated by Batagarawa farmers which lay outside the mapped area surrounding the *gari*, which broadly corresponded with the zone of permanent cultivation (Plate 35), were classified as bush-farms, though a few of these farms are, in fact, known to have been manured. Nearly all these farms are situated within a radius of about 1½ to 4 miles of the *gari* (but a few, see below, are much closer), many of them in localities where there is much land which may be freely cultivated.

It having been quite impracticable to map the bush-farms, which were widely dispersed, and had not necessarily existed when our air photograph had been taken in March 1966, all heads of farming-units and sons-in-*gandu* were asked to state where each of their bush-farms was situated, and to provide information on the means of acquisition. While the resultant statistics have some uses, attention must be drawn to some of their many defects. Thus: (i) some informants included farms which were in fallow, while others did not, this being partly dependent on whether the farmer was sure to resume cultivation of the plot; (ii) plots are of very varying size – some informants regarded all plots in a certain locality as 'one farm', others did not; (iii) for the foregoing reasons, there was considerable arbitrariness about statements relating to numbers of farms.

As noted in Table IV.2 (p. 62), the average number of bush-farms per head of farming-unit was actually higher for Group 1 than for other farmers – 1·5 farms, against 0·9 or 1·0 farms for the other economic-groups – although these farmers own much more manured farmland than the average farmer. It was interesting to find that there was little variation as between economic-groups in the proportions of farmers who owned no bush-farm – 29% for Group 1, against 42%, 31% and 37% for Groups 2 to 4 respectively. Many poor farmers with small acreages of manured farmland owned no bush-farm. To compare with the 62 farmers who said they owned no bush-farm, were 67 farmers who owned one such farm, 28 who owned 2 farms and 13 who owned 3 farms – otherwise there was 1 (Group 1) farmer who owned 7 farms. Twenty-three men-in-*gandu* were recorded as owning a total of 36 bush-farms. Heads of *gandaye* owned more bush-farms than other heads of farming-units: three-fifths of all such farmers owned bush-farms, the proportion showing little variation as between economic-groups.

About a half of all the farms were stated to be in the Batagarawa Hamlet, the others all being in other nearby Hamlets in Mallamawa District, most of them in the Batagarawa Village Area. Nearly all these farms lay south, south-west, west or west north-west of Batagarawa, where population densities are lower than to the east and north-east; the most commonly mentioned Hamlet Areas were, Autawa, Dabaibayawa, Gwamatawa, Jilawa, Kwami, Makada and Turuma. About one-sixth of the farms were reported as being rented (*aro*): most of the remainder had been cleared by the present owner.

Although the total acreage of bush-farms under cultivation at any time is clearly inestimable, the fact (see p. 120) that a sample of farm-labourers was recorded as spending only one-seventh of their time on bush-farms, is evidence that farmers are correct in their assertion that the bulk of their production comes from manured farmland. Most groundnuts are grown on manured farms (it is considered that the crop does not flourish so well on bush-farms); the only crop which is mainly grown on bush-farms is late millet (*maiwa*). One well-informed farmer estimated that about one-half of bush-farms were planted with *maiwa*, about one-quarter with groundnuts, the remaining one-quarter being planted with both cowpeas and guinea corn – hemp (*rama*) was another crop. Early millet (*gero*) is hardly ever grown on bush-farms. There is no standard rotation of crops. Farms are commonly cropped for 2 or 3 years before being fallowed.

Although bush-farms are usually not considered as formally heritable, a son may happen to continue to work on his deceased father's farms. Bush-farms are seldom sold, but in the rare cases where this happens the price is very low; there have been a few recent instances of farmers clearing bush during the dry season in order to sell the 'farm' – such men are effectively being paid for their labour only. When a farm is situated in a Hamlet other than that in which the farmer lives, the farmer usually gives the Hamlet Head a few bundles at harvest – at least for the first few years; the Hamlet Head may object if he sees manure being applied to the farm, this being regarded as equivalent to permanent appropriation.

In 1966 and 1967 a fair number of bush-farms were being established in an area just west of the *gari*, which had previously been reserved as a grazing ground – see Plate 33. The fact that there was no rush for this land, which was being gradually taken up, is proof (if such be needed) that land is not a scarce factor.

(b) See Hill (1970a, p. 159) on the question of the critical population density – perhaps 150 to 200 persons per square mile – such that the outermost zone of bush-fallow farming is eliminated from the land-use pattern.

See **Fallow, Inheritance, Permanent cultivation.**

Butchers – *pawa* (*fawa*); *mahauci*, pl. *mahauta*.

(a) There are about 9 heads of farming-units and about 5 men-in-*gandu* whose principal occupation is (or was formerly) butchering (or meat-selling); virtually all of them are sons of butchers and many are related in the male line; most of them (see Tables v.1 and v.2, pp. 72 and 74) are in Groups 3 or 4; all of them save Sarkin Pawa (the chief butcher) are farmers as well as butchers.

The present Sarkin Pawa is a young man who was appointed on the retirement of the former chief butcher, who is not his father. He was put in charge of the Batagarawa market (q.v.) when it was established in 1968. There is no other trade or craft which is organized under an appointed head. Although each butcher is free to act independently, butchers often join together to buy a 'cow', or to share the meat. One of the butchers is the official slaughterer (*mai yanka*) – he receives 1s. per cow and 3d. per sheep or goat as his fee; certain Malams are also prepared to slaughter small livestock for their owners. The meat is sold in a central place, known as *fage* – see Fig. 4 – where such delicacies as *tsire* are also cooked, the main customers being young men who partake of their meals in the street. (See also *Kilishi*.)

A few local Fulani cattle-owners are prepared to grant short-term credit when selling their beasts, and at least one Batagarawa cattle-owner extends longer-term credit to buyers; but as most cattle-sellers insist on full payment in cash at the time of sale, and as most butchers are very poor, there is need for outside credit, which is said to be granted by some 12 Batagarawa farmers, of whom 3 are particularly prominent. Interest may be charged, or the profits may be shared; credit is sometimes granted for some 2 to 3 weeks, during which time the butcher may be able to turn the capital over several times in purchasing animals. Both butchers and creditors sometimes store cattle for short periods before slaughter.

Owing to lack of purchasing power, especially during the farming-season, the slaughter of a 'cow' is often quite an event, entailing the sending of messengers to neighbouring hamlets. If it is known that visitors are arriving or that important building works will be in progress, butchers will foresee additional demand and slaughter accordingly. On many days goat meat only is on sale.

Traders in small livestock are apt to be butchers – active or retired. They either extend credit themselves or guarantee payment to the seller.

In every Mallamawa Hamlet there are several farmer–butchers – there are, for example, 4 in Autawa (q.v.).

(b) Although this is not the place to deal with the general position of Hausa butchers (either in Hausaland or elsewhere in West Africa, where they are found in many widely dispersed large and small centres), reference may be made to an interesting unpublished report on 'butchers' guilds' (National Archives, Kaduna, File 17,009, 1932), based on information sought from the various emirates. All respondents insisted that head butchers did not hold up the public to ransom, as is still often supposed. Thus:

Bornu   the organization of butchers is 'autocratic in form but entirely democratic in practice'.

Kano   'The Sarkin Pawa has now been given a small salary by the Administration and is responsible for seeing that correct butchering and flaying is carried out at the abattoir... There is no evidence of the existence of a guild with powers of the nature suggested – public opinion would not tolerate it.'

Sokoto   'Speaking generally I believe that the Sarkin Pawa is an extremely useful institution.'

Zaria   '...The Sarkin Pawa is not despotic, neither is his guild a closed community.'
See pp. 176–7 above, on the low status of butchers. However, especially in large centres
butchers may be notably prosperous. See A. Cohen (1965 and 1969) and Hill (1966) on the
position of Hausa butchers in Ibadan and Kumasi respectively. See, also, Smith (1962,
p. 307) on Sarkin Pawa as Sarkin Kasuwa (q.v.). Nicolas discusses the position of butchers
in various publications; in the Maradi area the average consumption of meat per head per
annum is put as high as 14 kg.
    See **Cattle-ownership**, *Dauke*, **Hides and skins**.

Calabash: see **Gourds**, *Kwarya*.

Calabash-mender – *gyartai*. The trade of calabash-mending (also *gyartai*, or *laskare*) is
considered very lowly.

Camels – *rakumi*, f. *rakuma*, pl. *rakuma*. It seems probable that there are only a few regions,
such as north-western Sokoto, where camels are much used, like donkeys, as draught-animals
for local farmers or traders. Camels are sold at all the very large markets in northern Katsina,
such as Jibiya and Mai Aduwa, the buyers sometimes being butchers. There is no information
on the extent to which camels (other than those which are Tuareg-owned) are utilized by
long-distance traders in remote areas of Hausaland.
    (a) Tuareg-owned camels sometimes visit Batagarawa to manure the farms after harvest.

Capital. Words for trading-capital include *jalli* (q.v.), *uwar kudi* (lit. 'mother of money'),
doki and *dukiya* (q.v.); both *digi* and *gugu* may be used to mean 'the first beginning or foundation of anything, especially the capital with which a man starts trading' – Bargery (p. 404).

Caravan tax: see *Fito*.

Carpenter – *masassaki*, pl. *masassaka*; *sassaka* is carpentered. Any wood-worker, including
those who make tool-handles, mortars, pestles, drum-bodies, furniture, etc.
    (a) A considerable number of Batagarawa men have some skill as carpenters.

Cassava – *rogo* (*Manihot utilissima*).
(a) This non-staple, surprisingly prestigeous crop, grows all the year round and thus requires
fencing against small livestock: the fencing being visible on the air photograph, it was surprising to note that most plots (*garka*) which had existed in March 1966 had vanished 15
months later – this belying some farmers' statements that successive crops are often taken from
manured land. Many farmers have small plots and there are some farms of several acres. As
cassava can be harvested at any time, stocks of growing tubers resemble savings-bank deposits,
being available for cashing for special purposes, such as buying groundnuts for a price rise,
or for financing trade or labour-employment. As elsewhere in West Africa, fresh cassava is very
perishable, and farmers commonly sell the tubers in the ground to men or to women traders,
who usually postpone paying until they have sold the crop (either boiled or raw) in Batagarawa,
Katsina city or elsewhere. (The types of cassava grown are non-toxic and, after peeling and
boiling, the spindly tubers are much relished as a snack. No cassava meal (*gari*) is made.)
Owing to the heavy costs of fencing and planting material, cassava is not typically a poor man's
crop, though some enterprising sons-in-*gandu* accumulate capital for trading etc. by its
cultivation. The two main varieties are known as *gama gari* and *dan wari*, the former growing
more quickly.
    (b) Although it is often stated – e.g. by W. O. Jones (1959, p. 80) – that cassava is a new
crop in Hausaland, it has in fact been cultivated for a very long time in many areas, '*rogo*'
having been noted by Barth in northern Sokoto in 1853 as 'enlivening' the ground, contributing greatly to the beauty of the scenery, and as growing in fields bordered by 'living hedges'.
In Katsina Emirate there was a tax on cassava before the British occupation. Robinson (1896a,
p. 156) noted that it was 'extensively cultivated' and Staudinger (1889, p. 634) that it was

'more widespread than yams'. In 1914 in Gulumbe (q.v.) it was very commonly cultivated, fetching a price of 6*d*. a basket of 65 lbs. The general lack of literature on cassava in Nigerian Hausaland is astonishing. Nicolas reports its recent introduction into, and rapid spread in, the Niger Republic.

Cattle-ownership – *sa*, pl. *shanu* = bull; *saniya* = cow. This brief entry relates to the ownership of cattle, other than plough-oxen, by Hausa farmers only. The original policy of 'mixed farming' was partly based on the false belief that all the cattle in Hausaland are owned by pastoral Fulani: in fact, in Batagarawa, as presumably in many other localities, the number of cattle reared by Hausa farmers for sale to butchers far exceeds the number of plough-oxen – successful though the policy of 'mixed farming' (see **Ploughing**) has been there.

(a) Detailed enquiries indicated that the total number of cattle owned by Batagarawa residents (excluding plough-oxen, calves and cattle permanently boarded outside Batagarawa, where there is better grazing) is probably of the order of 100 to 120 – but these figures could not be checked by reference to the local herds, some of the cattle in which are owned by men in Katsina city. (The cattle-tax, *jangali* (q.v.), is not payable by Hausa owners – a little-emphasized fact, which has misled some investigators.) A large proportion of the total is probably owned by 6 'rich' farmers, but there are also some 10 men, including sons-in-*gandu*, who own a few beasts, and women own about 20 head.

A few farmers maintain their own herds, but in order to save labour on herding most owners board out their animals. One settled Fulani (a Batagarawa farmer) tends a large herd which is mainly (if not entirely) owned by others; he sells milk, and also butter, in the *gari*. When owners board their animals outside Batagarawa, cattle manure may be the main perquisite of the Fulani, but the owner is entitled to claim the animals for manuring his farm whenever he wishes, and it is notable that most cattle-owners are tobacco farmers, the crop requiring much cattle-manure.

(b) See Grove (1957, pp. 41–2) and Luning (1963(a), pp. 45–9) on ownership of cattle by Hausa farmers elsewhere in rural Katsina. Luning, whose observations on grazing and other matters are most interesting, states that few cattle are kept in the neighbourhood of the towns where their owners live, but are taken to surrounding hamlets. Owing to the severe competition for fodder with other animals, the cattle may be sent even further away during the farming-season, with a resultant serious loss of organic matter to the home districts. He makes the point that there is less waste of dung with plough-oxen, which are kept in round huts during the farming-season.

See also **Butchers, Inheritance, Manure, Ploughing, Tobacco.**

Cattle tax: see *Jangali.*

Cefane. 'Buying the odds and ends which go to the making of soups and gravies' – Bargery; *cefanad da* = to sell something (maybe by degrees) to provide the means of getting daily supplies. See *Kudin cefane.*

Ci (or *Bi*) *ni da zugu* (*Jatrophra Curcas*). A very common farm hedge-plant, which can be easily propagated from stakes; its Hausa name derives from the belief that it is dangerous – *zugu* meaning 'shroud'.

Ciko. 'Buying to sell again at another price, or to put aside until market prices have risen' – Bargery. See also *Soke.*

Ciniki. Trading, a trading transaction, the process of bargaining; *cinikin tsaye* = trading in standing crops.

Cinkoso. Superabundance; *hatsi yana kasuwa cinkoso* = the market is full of corn.

Cin rani. A shorthand expression for dry-season (*rani*) migration; *ya tafi cin rani* = he went on dry-season migration (in order to eke out his grain supplies).

(a) While it is often supposed that a high proportion of rural Hausa migrate in search of work during the dry season (*rani*), this is (see p. 101) an uncommon practice in Batagarawa and neighbouring hamlets, even though the ideal of closing the *gandu* granaries during *rani* is quite persistent. Batagarawa is, in fact, a reception area for many farmers on *cin rani* who come in, from some distance east, to produce (and trade in) grindstones (q.v.) there.

(b) The ancient Hausa practice of travelling (or even wandering about) in the long dry season is regarded by Nicolas (personal communication) as pre-dating long-distance trade and travelling for Koranic studies; in the Maradi area it is still associated with a traditional ritual cycle, starting as late as January and ending at the first rains, when the *gandu* granary is closed – though privately-owned granaries are nowadays open. In the nineteenth century *cin rani* became associated with war, slave raiding, *fatauci*, Koranic learning, craftwork (requiring a nearby market) and with farming, productive, or labouring opportunities such as do not exist at home. Nowadays, available information (which is remarkably scanty) does at least establish that *cin rani* is of very variable incidence. Very common in northern Sokoto, where Prothero undertook his well-known study in 1954–5 – see Prothero (1957a) as well as Forde (1946, p. 153) – and also in the extreme north of Katsina – Luning (1963a) – its unimportance in Batagarawa and certain other Katsina areas – Luning (*ibid.*, p. 75) – is presumably not exceptional, strange though such sedentariness may seem to be, considering the extreme poverty endured by many people. Perhaps in some localities its incidence is much higher after bad harvests: as in an instance reported by Rowling (1952, p. 61) of a rate of 60% of all families in part of the Kano Close-Settled Zone. Informants at Jibiya and Batsari markets spoke of the dry-season influx of farmers from Kano Emirate for the purpose of growing onions on nearby river-banks.

For an account of the earlier dry-season wanderings of Koranic scholars see Mary Smith (1954, pp. 131 ff.). See *Galbaro.*

See *Dandi,* **Gulumbe, Migration.**

Circumcision – *kaciya.* The operation, which is enjoined by Islam, is performed by barber–surgeons (*wanzamai*) when boys are some seven to nine years old. See Ibrahim Madauci (1960) and Taylor and Webb (1932).

Citta (Aframomum melegueta). 'Guinea grains': a small fruit containing aromatic seeds used as spice and medicine.

Cloth. Hundreds of words for different types of woven cotton cloth, and clothing made therefrom, are given in Bargery. White woven strips are *fari*; when indigo-dyed they are *baki. Zane,* pl. *zannuwa,* is a woman's body-cloth. *Gwado* (or *farin gwado*) is a type of hand-woven white cloth, or sleeping-rug, often with blue stripes. See **Weaving.**

Cocoyam – *gwaza, mankani (Colocasia esculentum).*
(a) Cocoyams are not now grown at Batagarawa, although Barth (vol. IV, p. 107) referred to the 'large fields of yams or gwaza' not far south of the *gari.* (Barth was always apt to confuse yams and cocoyams.)

(b) In Clapperton (1829) there are a number of references (e.g. p. 218) to *gwaza* in Hausaland and Barth, also, was interested in the crop. Recent literature is extremely scanty. Oyenuga (1967, p. 173) suggests that it is mainly grown on *fadama* in N. Nigeria, which is certainly not true in southern Katsina, e.g. in the area of Funtua, where large fields of cocoyam can be seen.

Communal labour: see *Gayya.*

Community tax: see *Haraji.*

Confiscation – *kwacewa.* Nowadays farms are still occasionally officially confiscated (*kwacewa*) perhaps usually owing to debt, this sometimes amounting to the banishment of the owner.

Palmer (1907) stated that 'much arbitrary dispossession' took place; in his evidence to the N. Nigeria Lands Committee in 1908 (Cd 5103, p. 68) he added that although the practice was regarded as 'contrary to the sense of the community', it often occurred.

Co-operative society
(a) In 1967 the Mallamawa co-operative marketing society, under the presidency of Alhaji Barau (q.v.), had 2 branches, one at Batagarawa, the other at Sabon Gari – but it ceased to operate at the end of that year. The explicit purpose of the society was that of encouraging 'good' (i.e. richer) farmers to produce more groundnuts for export, to which end loans were granted and supplies of groundnut seed and imported fertilizers distributed. The society also acted as the equivalent of a licensed buying agent for groundnuts for the Marketing Board (q.v.).

It is no secret that the smaller farmer's attitude to the society was at best luke-warm, at worst hostile, this being mainly owing to the ruthless treatment of those who defaulted over loan repayment – whose property, including farmland, was apt to be seized (*kwacewa*). The strategy of loan-granting was indeed bewildering. In 1967 the Batagarawa branch received no money for loans for groundnut seed until 7 August, nearly 2 months after the seed had been sown, when a total of about £700 was lent to certain members (individual sums varied, but £13 may have been a rough median), for repayment after harvest, preferably in groundnuts, but alternatively in cash, at an interest rate (for less than 6 months) of 10%. The government official who distributed the money generally exhorted the recipients, who were assembled at a meeting held in the school, to put it to the best possible use, without specifying what this might be – and there was no discussion. Needless to say, no social or other sanctions would have prevented the borrowers from re-lending at higher interest rates to others in greater need.

Members of the society paid minimum entrance fees of £2 2s. 6d. – but might be asked for more. They were then entitled to an allocation of groundnut seed, to be paid for after harvest – in 1967 it was said that 300 sacks of shelled nuts (say about 25 tons) were so distributed – and imported fertilizers were also made available to them. In 1967 the number of members of the Batagarawa branch was put at about 70, many of them from Mallamawa hamlets.

The quantity of groundnuts purchased for export rose from very small quantities in the first 2 years of operation (1963 and 1964) to perhaps 130 tons in 1967 – by which date most sellers were non-members, it having been put about that all farmers were obliged to sell through the society.

(b) This is no place to review the history of the official policy regarding co-operative marketing societies in northern Nigeria since the 1956–7 season when, for the first time, pre-season loans (of £140,000) were granted – mainly in an endeavour to keep groundnut and cotton farmers out of the clutches of 'money-lenders'. By 1964–5 credit issues had risen to nearly £2½m. Thereafter, the machinery was tightened up and there was a marked reduction in the number of societies which received loans. In 1963 co-operative unions (which are groupings of primary societies) were estimated to have bought about 24,000 tons of groundnuts for export.

See **Groundnuts.**

Cornstalk: see *Kara.*

Cotton – *auduga* (*abduga*), the plant and also raw cotton with the seeds (*Gossypium*). See Dalziel for numerous vernacular names; and Bargery for many terms connected with cotton picking, processing, etc. As little attention has been given to cotton-growing by those who have published socio-economic reports on rural Hausaland, and as no cotton is grown at Batagarawa, this entry on this important crop is extremely brief – see p. 201 above.

See Dalziel (p. 124) for fascinating historical speculation regarding 'indigenous' species of cotton; he states that Kano has been a cotton market since the ninth century. See Barth for many references to cotton. The extensive literature (including in particular, Morel – 1911, pp. 167–8, 222–44) on the development of cotton-growing for export from northern Nigeria by the British Empire Cotton Growing Association, which established ginneries, has recently been supplemented by Hogendorn (1970), who regards (p. 44) the development of groundnut growing for export in 1912–13 as having dealt a 'shattering double blow' to the BCGA, by increasing the demand for locally-woven cloth and by causing farmers to abandon cotton-growing except on very fertile land. However, the FAO *Report* (1966, p. 167) states that there is nowadays 'little actual competition between the two crops', groundnuts being better suited to light sandy soils, cotton to heavier soils.

Until recently cotton production in northern Nigeria was mainly concentrated fairly near to the two railway lines running north-west and north-east from Zaria (particularly the former); but it has recently greatly increased in Bauchi and elsewhere in the north-east – *ibid*. See **Dyeing, Spinning, Weaving.**

Courts: see **District Courts.**

Cowpeas – *wake*, pl. *wakaikai*, is the general word for 'bean' (*Vigna unguiculata*). Hausa words for 24 different varieties, the seeds of which vary greatly in size, shape and colouring, are listed by Bargery; see also Dalziel.

(a) Cowpeas (*wake*), which are never grown as a sole crop, are usually interplanted with early millet (*gero*), spreading over the whole field after the grain has been harvested: sown 30 to 40 days after the millet, the cowpeas are harvested some 5 to 6 months later, always some weeks after the cessation of the rains, sometimes as late as December. As nearly all farmers grow some *gero*, so many of them grow cowpeas also – thus ensuring the utilization of their farmland well into the dry season.

As well as being an extremely useful source of protein for the people (consumed in the form of cooked whole beans or flour), cowpeas are 'exported' from Batagarawa to places such as Kano, Katsina and Funtua, probably mainly by local traders, though a few outsiders may come in to buy.

Cowpeas, like grains and groundnuts, are sometimes stored for a seasonal price rise (in pods in granaries) by richer farmers. The haulms (see *Harawa*) and pods are most valuable fodder, and unripe pods are eaten as a vegetable.

Older, semi-secluded, women are responsible for much of the harvesting: the husband is entitled to all the pods picked before a certain time of the day (such as *azahar*), the women retaining all those picked later – which they may store and later resell to their husbands. Women may also be paid for shelling beans for traders.

See Dalziel (p. 258) for a list of some of the numerous snacks made of bean flour – such as *dan wake* (q.v.) and *kosai* (q.v.) – which are produced and sold by secluded women.

(b) When north of Katsina city in 1853, Barth noted 'the whole of this country' to be 'rich in beans', the tressels of which (*harawa*) afforded a 'most excellent food' for camels (vol. IV, p. 90). Having low water requirements and being drought-resistant, cowpeas are a northern savannah crop (principally grown in Kano, Bauchi and Katsina), which is much 'exported' to southern regions, nowadays mainly by rail and lorry – see Hay and Smith (1970). In some localities the crop is grown mainly for fodder. According to Anthony and Johnston (1968, p. 38) insect pests severely limit yields, which are reported as being generally 'low' – FAO *Report* (1966, p. 187) – though most statistics are misleading owing to inter-planting with other crops. See Nicolas (NM, p. 182) for a reference to cowpeas in the Maradi area.

Cowry shells – *wuri*, pl. *kudi* (q.v.). According to the *Kano Chronicle*, the cowry-currency reached Hausaland in the first half of the eighteenth century – Johnson (1970a, p. 33) – and the shells were certainly circulating in Katsina in 1790. As (see *Fatauci*) there is every reason to believe that much long-distance caravan trade was rurally-based, it is quite probable that many village areas like Batagarawa also utilized the shells as a convenient form of cash for purely local transactions throughout the nineteenth century. Indeed, by the end of the century, when the currency had practically lost its value for trading purposes as a result of massive inflation – see Johnson (*ibid.* and 1970b) – so that Robinson (1898, p. 700) could describe it as 'a perfect caricature of what a currency should be, lacking...intrinsic value, scarcity and portability' (ten shillings worth of currency weighing a hundred pounds), its persistence as a medium of exchange might have been due to its popularity with the people, considering that many pounds of grain could then be bought for the equivalent of one penny. If cowries were more commonly used as a local currency in savannah West Africa than in the south, this might be one explanation of why they were not strung, as they were on the coast, but counted individually, by the fingers of one hand, in groups of five – see Barth (vol. II, pp. 28–9).

The great cowry inflation having been recently dealt with by Johnson, little needs to be added here, except the suggestion that the difficulties and dangers of counting thousands of unstrung cowries in open market-places might partly explain why so much long-distance trade was house-based – see Hill (1966). Abubakar Labo volunteered that it was only when buying sheep or goats that the cowries could be carried to market; when buying a bigger animal only the *la'ada* (commission) was paid there, the seller then going to the buyer's house. Units of the *hauya* (of 20 cowries – see Bargery) were often used for computing; a *keso* (or mat) of 20,000 shells was equivalent to a head-load – though see Johnson (*ibid.*, p. 42).

Lugard – see Johnson (1970a, p. 48) – wisely thought that the cowry would always remain a medium of exchange for very small values: he might have been right had prices of basic commodities not risen so greatly in terms of minted coin. In 1904, in an attempt to control the cowry inflation, he prohibited further importation of the shells (*ibid.*), but British coin was accepted even more quickly than he had expected. *See Asurkumi, Burgami.*

Creditor. A common word for creditor is *mabarci*, f. *mabarciya* (pl. *mabarta*), which also means debtor. For 'credit' see *Bashi, Dauke.*

Cukurfa – pl. *cukurfai.* A long narrow bag made of palm-leaves, for holding produce, such as grain and natron (q.v.), which is transported long distances by lorries, camels, etc.

Dabino – pl. *dabinai.* The date palm (q.v.) and also the fruit.

Daddawa. Strongly-smelling, blackish, cakes, which are made from fermented seeds of the locust-bean tree (*dorawa*), being used for flavouring soup: 'The odour is destroyed by frying or roasting, and its place in culinary economy is much the same as that of cheese among Europeans' – Dalziel.

(a) Thirty-two secluded women house-traders were recorded as handling *daddawa*. It is doubtful whether *daddawa* is ever made for 'own consumption' only.

The following method of making *daddawa* was noted in Batagarawa. The seeds (*kalwa*) were cooked in water for over 6 hours; they were then pounded, but were still so hard that they retained their shape; after cooking over water (in another pot), the beans were placed on a mat and fermented under a broken calabash for 3 to 4 days, being then uncovered and left to dry for 1 day. On further pounding, the beans were reduced to a powder to which pounded and sieved leaves of *gwandar daji* were added. Water was then added and the mixture formed into a big ball; after dipping their hands in groundnut oil, the women processors then formed small balls, which were flattened in the palms of their hands into small flat, black, cakes.

(b) Clapperton (1829, p. 219) described the making of *daddawa*, and commented on the 'disagreeable smell' of the cakes, the taste of which 'was rather pleasant than otherwise when put on roast meat or fowls'. According to Barth the tree was unknown in Bornu and comparatively rare in Kebbi and Gobir – though abundant, as today, in many regions of Hausaland. Whether *daddawa* remains an important item of long-distance trade is not known:

Barth (vol. IV, p. 117) saw a caravan of 100 traders whose donkeys were entirely laden with these cakes – 3,000 of which constituted a load: on another occasion he commented on the 'very strong and not quite aromatic smell' which proceeded from the luggage of the *fatake*.

See **Locust bean.**

Daddawar batso. Cakes similar to *daddawa* (q.v.) but made from the fermented seeds of *yakuwa* (q.v.) or of hemp (*rama*). Both the seeds and the cakes are important market wares – the former are sometimes stored for a price rise.

Dagaci – pl. *dagatai.* One of the various titles by which Village Heads (q.v.) are known.

Daji. Bush-land. See **Bush.**

Dakau. Pounding grain etc. for payment. See *Aikatau.*

Daki – pl. *dakuna.* A hut, room, or 'house': usually a round, thatched sleeping-hut, with walls of either baked clay or cornstalk and a beaten-earth floor. As each wife has her own hut, the children of one mother may refer to themselves as 'of one hut' (*dakimmu daya*). A husband may refer to his wife as *mai-daki.* See Nicolas (NM, pp. 140–2) for details of construction of clay-walled huts.

(a) In Batagarawa there are a considerable number of men with the subsidiary occupation of 'hut-builder'.

(b) Whereas in fully rural surroundings round sleeping-huts are the rule, in large towns, such as Kazaure, some women sleep in *soro* (q.v.).

See **Building,** *Gida.*

Dakuwa.

(a) A sweetmeat made from tiger nuts or groundnuts and sold by secluded women traders.

(b) Barth noted (vol. II, p. 10) that *dakkwa* was a very palatable sort of sweetmeat made of pounded rice, butter and honey – but (see Bargery) this may have been *nakiya.*

Dami – pl. *dammuna.* A bundle of unthreshed millet or guinea corn, such as is stored in a granary. It may be (see below) that minimum grain requirements per head of a mixed population are equivalent to about 10 *dammuna* of early millet annually – corresponding to 1 lb of grain per head per day (see **Grain requirements**).

(a) In Batagarawa, where *gero* bundles vary considerably in size, they are often notionally regarded as the equivalent of 6 *tiya* of threshed millet – say 35 lbs.

(b) Smith (1955, p. 240) found that the 'threshed yield' of 10 bundles of *gero* varied between 20 and 45 lbs, the average being 32 lbs. Nicolas (1968a, pp. 44 ff.) reported that in Maradi bundles yielded between 5 and 6 *tiya* (*gero*) and 6 *tiya* (*dawa*); average bundle size was smaller for grain from *gayauni* than from *gandu* farms. The general indication is that guinea corn bundles are much more variable in size than millet bundles.

Damuna (*Damana*). Strictly the rainy season, but sometimes identified with the farming-season, which is longer.

(a) According to the date of the first rains, *damuna* in Batagarawa usually lasts for 4 to 5 months.

See **Rainfall.**

Dandi. The generic term for places south of Zaria, the latter being called *zauran Dandi* (Abraham). Kirk-Greene (1969, p. 274) points out that nowadays the word has taken on a more general meaning in relation to migration, so that *ya tafi dandi* might refer to a dry-season migrant. See *Cin rani.*

Dangi (*Dengi*). Kinsfolk. A cognatic term which can be qualified to denote father's or mother's kin (*dangin uba* or *dangin uwa*), though *danuwa* also means any relative. See Smith (1955, p. 41). See **Kinship terminology.**

Dankali – sweet potato (*Ipomoea batatas*). There are Hausa words for a number of varieties.

(a) Sweet-potato (like cassava) plots require fencing during the dry season when they must be protected from marauding livestock. Propagated by sprouts or cuttings, the tubers take about 6 months to mature and are harvested in January to February. Sons-in-*gandu* expect payment for harvesting, for which work labourers are sometimes employed. The potatoes are stored in shallow pits, covered with light soil, where they may remain for up to 3 months. Although only a few of the richer farmers grow *dankali* on any scale, there are 3 or 4 farmers who sell local production in Katsina city and elsewhere. The vines are a useful fodder, the young leaves a vegetable. A prestigeous crop: expensive, rather than 'not very popular' as the FAO *Report* (1966, p. 186) asserts.

(b) Robinson (1896, p. 156) noted that *dankali* was a common crop throughout Hausaland.

Dan kasuwa – pl. *'yan kasuwa*. Any male trader, whether he frequents a market (*kasuwa*) or not.

Dan kira – pl. *'yan kira*. A professional panegyrist who does not blow a horn or drum like a *maroki* (q.v.).

Dantada (Dandauda) – pl. *'yantada*. A man who dresses as a woman, speaks in a high voice and trades mainly with women, perhaps living with prostitutes. See *Karuwa*.

Dan tebur – pl. *'yan tebur*. Men petty-traders who set up tables (*tebur*) in the open air, in street or market-place, from which they retail such durable wares as soap, sugar, torch batteries, matches, etc. Sometimes known as *dan tireda* – from the word 'trade'.

Dan wake. A snack, being eaten flavoured or with a soup. 'Portions of dry bean [*wake*] meal mixed with *kanwa* are dropped into boiling water to form balls or lumps...' – Dalziel (p. 268).

(a) Nearly a quarter of all Batagarawa's women house-traders are apt to sell this snack.

Daraja. Status, rank, value. See *Karda*.

Dari. Cold weather caused by wind – often the cold dry weather associated with the harmattan (q.v.).

Dashi (Commiphora africana). African myrrh. A common farm hedge-plant. It grows well in arid districts, like Batagarawa.

Data. Bitter native 'tomato', used in soups etc. See also *Gauta*.

Date palm – *dabino*, pl. *dabinai (Phoenix dactylifera)*. Although sometimes planted ornamentally, the palms rarely produce good fruit (*dabino*) in northern Nigeria. The fruit is imported into Katsina from the Niger Republic. See also *Kajinjiri*.

Dauke. As a term meaning 'credit', the word is most commonly applied to the practice of borrowing one bundle (*dami*) of grain during the farming-season in return for the promise to repay two bundles after harvest (see p. 164). However, *dauke* is loosely applied to many forms of (not very short-term) borrowing for a fixed period. Thus, butchers who sell meat on credit terms (payment being required in one or two weeks) speak of *dauke*, as do women who sell cotton to one another on credit. *Dauke* may involve a certain value (not quantity) of produce – 5s. worth of groundnuts lent, 12s. worth promised at harvest. As a sop to Muslim notions of usury (q.v.), money may be lent and produce returned, or *vice versa*. *Dauke* means 'give one and it multiplies' said one informant; another insisted that its 'unlawfulness' was justified by most borrowers having 'no food'. But the more rigorously the term was pursued, the more vaguely elusive its usage became: *ya ba ni dauke* = 'he gave (or sold) me produce [unspecified] on credit terms [unspecified]'. See *Aro, Bashi, Falle*, Proclamation on farm produce, *Rance*, Usury.

Dauki. Issuing the share of various foodstuffs due to each member of a household or to servants. (See Abraham for variations in meaning.)

Dauro. A slow-maturing variety of millet. See *Maiwa*.

Dawa – pl. *dawoyi* (Sorghum). The general word for guinea corn. There are numerous different varieties and types (see Dalziel) and even more names, many of them being peculiar to certain localities – 85 such names are listed in Bargery. See also Nicolas (1962b, p. 35). The grains are very variable in size, shape and colour, being white, yellow, orange, red, etc. – see Oyenuga (1967, p. 177). The stalks (see *Kara*) have many important uses; many varieties have long stalks (up to 20 feet), but there are also dwarf types. Most varieties probably take from 4 to 5½ months to mature. According to Faulkner and Mackie (1933, p. 138) seed is planted at the rate of 15–20 lbs per acre. When the seedlings are some 5 inches high they are weeded and thinned to 2 or 3 plants per stand, blanks often being filled by transplantation (*dashe*).

On the geographical distribution of guinea corn and early millet, the two basic food crops of Hausaland, see *Gero*. Guinea corn is less drought-resistant than millet and is said to flourish best where annual rainfall is between 25 and 50 inches; but it will grow very far north and is one of the major crops of the Hausa in the Niger Republic, both on upland (*tudu*) and *fadama*. Although average yields are commonly put at about 700 lbs per acre, there is great variation, the crop being very responsive to manure (q.v.). *Tuwo*, the basis of the main evening meal, is best made from *dawa*. The type of beer known to the Maguzawa as *fito* is brewed from this grain.

(a) *Dawa* is a very important crop in Batagarawa – the numbers of *dawa* and *gero* granaries being about equal (Tables 11.9 and 11.10, p. 36). If (see p. 196) total grain production (which varies greatly) had been roughly 250 tons in 1967, when production of *gero* (q.v.) was estimated at nearly 100 tons, it might be that *dawa* production somewhat exceeded 100 tons, *maiwa* making up the balance. The grain is commonly interplanted with groundnuts, which are then harvested first, in most pleasant shade; it is, also, often interplanted with *gero* or grown in a pure stand. The crop is not usually harvested until a month or more after the cessation of the rains. See Chapter IX on seasonal price fluctuations.

See *Dami*, Granary, Harvest-dates, Manure, *Tuwo*.

Debt: see *Bashi*.

Debtor: see **Creditor**.

Dillali – f. *dillaliya*, pl. *dillalai*. A broker. In Hausa markets certain types of goods, notably livestock (and formerly slaves), are commonly sold through intermediaries (*dillalai*), who receive a commission (*la'ada*). See *Kasuwa, La'ada, Ma'auni, Mai gida*, **Market-place**.

Dillanci. The brokerage trade. See *Dillali*.

Dimajo – pl. *dimajai*. One born in slavery of slave parents. According to Smith (1960, p. 253), the *dimajo* 'laboured on the master's farm and received food and housing in return, his marriage was arranged by his master; he was from birth incorporated in the Muhammadan population, and addressed his master as father (*baba*). . . '. While it is usually believed that *dimajai* could not be sold, Abubakar Labo (q.v.) reported that slave-owners who were short of money would sell their slaves' children. See **Slavery**.

Dinya (*Vitex Cienkowskii*). The black plum-like fruit of a tree of the same name. *Madi*, a sweet drink, may be made from this fruit mixed with others.

(a) Batagarawa women traders buy this fruit from the tree-owner, paying for it after selling in Katsina city.

District – *kasa* and other words. For administrative purposes Emirates are divided into Districts, each under a District Head (q.v.). In large, populous Emirates, such as Kano and Katsina, some Districts are very large and populous while others are small. Thus, the population of Malumfashi (Galadima) District in Katsina Emirate was estimated at 182,000 in 1965, against an estimated 15,000 for Mallamawa in 1966. Districts are administratively divided into Villages (q.v.).

District boundaries. Partly because territory is still sometimes transferred from one District to another, in 1967 there were no official maps of Districts published by the Survey Department at Kaduna. District boundaries are usually well known to the local populace, whose information is apt to be more accurate than that available to the compilers of unofficial sketch maps. A 'Political Map of Northern Nigeria' compiled at the Intelligence Office, Zungeru, in 1907, made some attempt to show District boundaries in certain Provinces, the 30 Districts of Kano Province (then including Katsina Emirate) being fully defined. The creation of states may lead to publication of District maps, as in Kano. See **Hamlet boundaries.**

District Courts. Although District Heads nowadays lack formal judicial powers in most emirates – but see Smith (1955, p. 9) with regard to the limited powers formerly exercised by 'community chiefs' – it was the aim of the British administration to set up subordinate Native Courts in District capitals only, with the result that a large proportion of the population of certain Hausa Emirates, such as Katsina, lives far away from a Court, so that many matters which in other regions of West Africa would require reference to such a Court are necessarily dealt with locally on an *ad hoc* basis – or, occasionally, by a touring *alkali*. Only 20 Area Courts, to replace Native Courts, were established in Katsina Emirate in 1969 (of which 3 were in Katsina city): with an estimated population of 1·8 m., this would be 90,000 persons per Court, a high figure in relation to Lugard's original aim, as expressed in his *Political Memorandum on Native Courts* – see Kirk-Greene (1965a, p. 136) – that the number of Courts should be adequate to ensure that complainants could 'obtain redress without travelling prohibitive distances'. Were any appreciable proportion of disputes relating to inheritance or land matters (for instance) to be referred to the Courts, they would be overwhelmed with business. Lacking formal judicial powers, the local chiefs are obliged to 'administer justice' as best they may. They, too, would be crushed by the weight of their responsibility were it not that individuals and families have so long been accustomed to minding their own business, without reference to higher authority (for whom they feel a mixture of awe and respect), and were it not also for the buffer provided by the Hamlet Head – who, so far as one knows, is seldom a member of the 'Fulani ruling-class' – who may often be encouraged to arbitrate unofficially at his level. There can be no conflict between local and Islamic law when the latter goes unadministered: and the unfamiliarity of the city-bred *alkalai* with the life of the countryside, see Nadel (1942, p. 172), does much less damage than might be expected.

See Smith (1955, p. 96) on the 'jural powers' exercised by District Heads; Smith (*ibid.*, pp. 90 ff.) on the weakness of the ordinary citizen in relation to the administration; Smith (1960) on the history of the judicial system in Zaria; and Smith (1965, pp. 254 ff.) on 'official inheritance procedure'. See also Anderson (1954) and *Northern Nigeria Local Government Yearbook*, 1965. See **Inheritance.**

District Head – *hakimi, uban kasa*, etc. A salaried 'chief' who is immediately responsible to the Emir for administering a District in which nowadays he always resides, though before the British occupation he often administered it through a *jakada*, or agent. As may be judged from the summarized material provided by Hailey (1951, pp. 52 ff.), most District Heads in Hausaland were usually Fulani who belonged either to the Emir's own family, or to 'other leading local families' (*dangin sarauta*), though in a few emirates there were some who were designated 'Habe'. While it follows that most (though not all) posts were 'inherited', no individual was automatically preferred and nowadays the choice often falls on administratively experienced and well-educated men. District Heads lack judicial functions – see **District Courts.** See Smith (1955, pp. 8 ff.).

District Scribe (Mallamawa). Malam Tukur, the District Scribe, lives in a large house in the centre of the town, his section of which was occupied by 15 people in 1967, including 3 wives and 11 children – Sarkin Fada (who had recently returned from Ghana) was in another section with his wife and child. His 3 wives are daughters of the late Sarkin Fada, and of non-relatives from Batagarawa and a neighbouring hamlet respectively. In 1968 one of his daughters was in teacher-training and one of his sons in secondary school.

His senior wife (*uwar gida*) is a very active house-trader, who mainly sells such manu-factured goods as cloth, sheets, pillows, soap, salt, kerosene, cigarettes, enamelware, as well as kola-nuts and a few types of cooked food. She buys and stores groundnuts, groundnut oil and locust beans, some of her supplies coming from neighbouring hamlets. She has taught herself hand embroidery. She is assisted by a woman servant.

Malam Tukur is an active tailor, who is skilled in machine-embroidery. He owns 8 farms. His main farm at Batagarawa is about 7 acres and is a consolidation of several farms bought from, or obtained by exchange with, other farmers. His other farms are in the Mallamawa Hamlets of Dabaibayawa, Komi, Makada and Makurdi – in the last-named place he has inherited a manured farm of some 8 acres. He employs many *'yan kwadago*: although they are always recruited on his behalf (both in the *gari* and elsewhere) by a certain Batagarawa farmer, he himself takes a keen personal interest in farming. (He has since been transferred to a larger District.)

Divorce – *kashe aure, raba aure*. Divorce is extremely common in Hausaland generally; although it may be initiated by either party, the wife suffers from the disability that she retains no rights over her children (see p. 24). A divorced wife may not remarry for three months (*idda*). Only in the event of a further marriage and divorce may a wife remarry her original husband – such remarriages commonly occur. If the couple have had no children, then in the case of first marriages a wife who has sought a divorce is supposed to be under obligation to repay part of the sum received from her husband on her marriage, after deduction of her parents' counter-payments – according to Smith she usually achieves this with the help of her prospective second husband. As pointed out by Smith (1969, p. xi), it is because women are 'minors at law' under the guardianship of their senior male kinsman, that they enjoy sufficient support from their kin to enable them to divorce their husbands at will.

The fact of high average divorce rates must not be allowed to obscure the fact that many women contract life-long unions. Of a random sample of 164 Hausa wives in Ibadan, over half (91) had never been divorced – A. Cohen (1969, p. 57).

See Anderson (1954, pp. 209 ff.), Ibrahim Madauci (1968), Smith (1955, pp. 21, 62–4), Mary Smith (1954), Taylor and Webb (1932) and Jacqueline Nicolas (1967, pp. 80 ff.). See **Marriage expenses.**

Donkeys – *jaki (jakki)*, f. *jaka*, pl. *jakuna*.

(a) In 1967 there were some 100 donkeys (worth perhaps £300 to £500) in the *gari*, about two-thirds of them owned by farmers in Groups 1 and 2 (Table IV.5, p. 67). Not all richer farmers own donkeys, some of them (especially if their households lack children) preferring to hire; on the other hand, many poorer farmers are aspirant owners, if only because of the significant income that can be gained from hiring out – the rate to Katsina city being as high as 2s. As in rural Hausaland generally, donkeys are used for transporting loads of many types, notably farm produce from farm to house, manure from house to farm, trade-goods, fodder, firewood: they are seldom ridden unless relieved of their loads. Their droppings enrich the manurial content of compound sweepings. Muslim taboo prevents the consumption of donkey meat.

(b) Although donkeys are the local camels of Hausaland, and are a most valuable source of manure (q.v.), their importance has been neglected in the literature – for instance by the FAO *Report* (1966, p. 352), which regards head-loading as the only alternative to road, rail and water transport. In a society where women, whether secluded or not, largely refuse to perform their traditional function as beasts of burden, farmers' productivity would be greatly reduced were donkey-transport unavailable. These small, sturdy, tax-free, beasts, can manage loads of 200 lbs and upwards – about half that of a camel and double that of a man. Barth noted (vol. v, p. 29) that 5,000–6,000 kola-nuts constituted an ass-load. The leather *taiki* (q.v.) may hold the equivalent of 1½ bags (sacks) of grain. Mortimore and Wilson (1965) reports that a *mangala* (q.v.) of manurial sweepings from Kano city might weigh 260 lbs. (As for cowries (q.v.), they were so weighty that as many as 3 to 5 donkeys were required to transport 100,000 of them.)

For transporting produce from (and manure to) farms, and for evacuating produce from the vast roadless areas, the donkey will remain indispensable. But for longer distances, donkey-transport costs more than road transport – where such exists – except with very bulky loads, such as raw cotton, hay etc. Several writers – including Luning (1963a, p. 40), McDonnell (1964, p. 368) – estimated the costs of donkey-hire for short distances at about 2s. per ton mile: and Nicolas (1964, p. 80) states costs are even higher in the Niger Republic. Laden donkeys move rather slowly, seldom emulating the Hausa porters who could head-load 60–120 lbs or more along twenty miles of road in a day – Meek (1925, vol. i, p. 21).

Such reliable donkey-counts as exist (official village livestock statistics are most inaccurate), suggest that the size of the human population is often somewhere between about 5 and 15 times that of the donkey population – see, e.g., Luning (1963a and 1963b), Nicolas (NM, p. 129), unpublished archival material collected by D. G. H. MacBride relating to 9 villages in Ruma District (Katsina Emirate). Nash (1948), who is one of the few writers to praise the donkey, stated (p. 18) that if as much were known about the ailments of donkeys as of cattle, the donkey population would be much greater.

The donkeys owned by long-distance traders were presumably mainly males, which are much stronger and less truculent than females. See *Fatauci*, **Manure**.

Dorawa: see **Locust bean**.

Drummer: see *Makadi, Maroki*.

Dubu. A ceremony involving 'les maîtres de culture' among the Hausa in Niger. See Jacqueline Nicolas (1967).

Dukanci. Working in leather. *Baduku* is a leather worker. See **Tanning**.

Dukiya – pl. *dukoki*. Wealth, property, goods, riches. Thus, *mai dukiya* is a wealthy person, *kan dukiya* is trading capital. See *Arziki*.

Duma – pl. *dumame*. The common white-flowered cultivated gourd (*Lagenaria vulgaris*) with variously-shaped fruits known by different names according to their shape and use. See Dalziel. See **Gourds**.

Dusa. The bran which is a by-product of making flour: it is a useful fodder for livestock.

Dyeing – *marini*, pl. *marina* = dyer; *rina* = dyed with indigo; *karofi, marina* = dye-pit; *shudi* = the act of dyeing blue.

(a) Only 2 men practise the craft of dyeing in Batagarawa and they work spasmodically, handling cotton thread (*zare*) only.

(b) The general literature on dyeing, as on weaving, is astonishingly scanty. The technique of dyeing and glazing was described by Clapperton – see Bovill (1966, part 3, p. 659) – and, in much chemical detail, by Dalziel (pp. 244–5). See also Taylor and Webb (1932, pp. 195–207) and Ibrahim Madauci (1968, pp. 57–8). 'It is principally this dyeing, I think, which gives to many parts of Negroland a certain tincture of civilization, a civilization which it would be highly interesting to trace, if it were possible, through all the stages of its development' – Barth (vol. ii, p. 31). Barth noted (*ibid.*, p. 136) that some of the calico imported into Kano was re-exported after dyeing, back to Ghadames. Dyers still flourish in some rural areas, such as Kura (south of Kano) – current research by P. Shea. See **Indigo, Weaving**.

Economic-group. For the purposes of studying economic inequality in Batagarawa, the 171 farming-units (q.v.) were classified into four economic-groups, those in Group 1 being better off than those in Group 2 and so on progressively. See Chapter IV for the means of classification.

Economic regulations. Although under Sections 37 and 43 of the Native Authority Law, 1954, Native Authorities (now Local Authorities) have wide powers to make Rules or issue Orders on a great range of subjects – the latter, unlike the former, may be issued by the N.A. in its own right, see Campbell (1963, p. 29) – few Rules or Orders which impinge on the ordinary day-to-day economic life of the farmer are in fact introduced and most of them tend, in any case, to be dead letters from the start.

The hardship caused by the Katsina Proclamation on Farm Produce of 1965 has been noted – see p. 139. But as long ago as 1957 the Katsina N.A. had made a Rule under paragraph 55 of Section 37 of the N.A. Law – which paragraph empowered N.A.s to regulate, control or promote 'trade or industry' – which had laid down that no person should: (1) buy or sell groundnuts (other than for export) except in a market; or (2) buy or sell groundnuts either for export (or for resale for export) except 'over a scale' and at an approved buying point established by a licensed buying agent. This meant that the '*yan kwarami* had since 1957 always been acting illegally in buying groundnuts directly from farmers, whether the nuts were resold for local consumption or for export. Perhaps it was considered necessary to issue the Proclamation of 1965 because no proceedings against those infringing the regulations of 1957 had ever been taken.

Similar Groundnut Marketing Rules had been made in 1955 and 1956 by most of the N.A.s in the groundnut exporting zone – these commonly took the form of standard Close Season for Groundnut Purchasing Rules, which prohibited all purchase of groundnuts for resale between 1 August and the date of opening of the official buying season; according to these Rules it was only permissible to buy groundnuts 'intended for personal and immediate consumption' or for 'making groundnut oil by the purchaser or his family'. Such Rules were designed to assist in curtailing rural indebtedness, by providing N.A.s with the power to take proceedings in cases of forestalling, or the purchase and pledging of standing groundnuts: but there is, in fact, no evidence that such proceedings were ever taken. There being a flourishing local trade in new crop groundnuts for some two months before the opening of the groundnut season (which is always a month or more after the harvest has been completed), it is obvious that such Rules are so unrealistic that knowledge of their existence does not percolate through to rural communities, untroubled as they are by court action.

In rural communities where farmers borrow from each other, and where there is no 'class' of professional money-lender whose activities should be controlled in the interests of the poverty-stricken (see *Bashi*, Usury), Rules designed to reduce the total volume of indebtedness by prohibiting specific types of lending, would be likely to do more harm than good were any attempt made to enforce them. If a man is prohibited from borrowing or raising money in one way (e.g. by selling unshelled groundnuts before the opening of the buying season, or by pledging his crop – see *Dauke*), he will usually be obliged to mortgage his future in another way, for instance by selling grain when prices are lowest: presuming that his chosen method of borrowing is the more advantageous (he is seldom under compulsion), his poverty would be exacerbated by regulations which forced him to resort to another method.

Another example of subsidiary legislation based on the philosophy that buying for resale is liable to be anti-social (even when practised by the humble, non stock-piling, '*yan kwarami*) was the Control of Grain Rules made by the Katsina N.A. in 1961, which (*inter alia*) prohibited traders from purchasing guinea corn and millet elsewhere than in a market except with the written permission of the N.A. – only purchase for 'self-consumption' being permitted.

Both Rules and Orders – see Wraith (1966, p. 31) – have to be published in the official Gazette (with the exception of Orders to individuals) and must also be made known to the public 'in such manner as is customary' in the area in question. It seems that regulations resembling Orders are often issued, although they are not published and are therefore unenforceable in the courts. Section 43 of the N.A. Law was amended in 1955 by the insertion of para. 7A which required: 'any native to cultivate land to such extent and with such crops as will secure an adequate supply of food for the support of such native and of those dependent on him'. Whether any N.A. ever issued an Order under these powers (or a similar informal regulation) is not known: if so, it might have been suitably entitled the Prohibition of Poverty (Lazy Farmers) Order.

Under Section 41 of the N.A. Law, N.A.s have wide powers to make Rules concerning markets: while standard (model) Rules on a few subjects, such as times of opening, cleanliness, official rents, have been widely made, it seems that most N.A.s have been uninterested in assuming unenforceable powers such as those 'prescribing the weights, scales and measures to be used in the sale of any particular produce' or by fixing maximum retail prices.

In former times Emirs in Council would sometimes make concerted pronouncements designed, for instance, to draw attention to interpretations of Muslim Law, or to prevent over-rigid adherence to it. Thus – see Anderson (1954, p. 190) – the Emirs agreed in 1939 that where the application of the Islamic law on inheritance would result in uneconomic sub-division of land, or insanitary conditions in compounds, the property might be sold and the proceeds divided among heirs or legatees; and in 1940 they asserted that individual N.A.s might determine the minimum area into which any estate might be divided on inheritance. However, 'little effect was given to these agreements in practice' (*ibid.*). At some date before 1937 (National Archives, Kaduna, File No. 38133) the Emirs issued an (unofficial) 'Order', drawing attention to the Muslim Law – Ruxton (1916, p. 169) – preventing harvesting of immature produce. But when in 1945 draft Rules, under Section 25(1)(a) of the N.A. Ordinance 1943, were circulated to N.A.s, certain of the most influential Emirs were found to be opposed to the Rules, as being against the interests and present practice of many farmers, and the matter was accordingly dropped.

The N.A.s have been reluctant to assume any of the more sweeping powers to control farmland allowed under para. 22 of Section 37 of the N.A. Law 1954, but under the N.A. (Control of Soil Erosion) Rules 1958, which were made in Katsina, and elsewhere, they have sometimes provided themselves with limited powers which are occasionally used. (These Rules direct that farms on hillsides or ridges should be contoured and that land lying within 15 ft of the verge of 'any road, trade route, cattle track, river, stream or watercourse' should not be cultivated without permission.)

The Land Tenure Law 1962, which repealed the Land and Native Rights Ordinance, followed earlier legislation in declaring that, with certain exceptions, 'the whole of the lands of Northern Nigeria, whether occupied or unoccupied', were 'native lands'. Ignoring the history of farm transactions in the past century or more, Section 27 continued to assert that – 'It shall not be lawful for any customary right of occupancy or any part thereof held by a native to be alienated by sale, assignment, mortgage, transfer of possession, sublease, bequest or otherwise howsoever...' to a non-native without the consent of the Minister, or to a native without either the consent of the Minister (in certain special cases) or the approval of the Native Authority – presumably the N.A. would usually be expected to delegate its powers *via* District Heads to Village Heads. However, Section 30 of the Law stated that 'the devolution of the rights of an occupier upon death shall be regulated, in the case of a native, by the native law or custom existing in the locality in which the land is situated'.

In sum, so far as this type of legislation is concerned, it seems that Anderson (1954, p. 177) is right to stress that 'most Nigerian Ordinances seem to have little impact on the day to day life of the Muslims of the North outside urban areas – drafted, as such legislation often is, by those whose experience of the powerful native authority, native court and native authority police systems of the Northern Emirates is strictly limited'.

See **Farm-selling, Inheritance, Native Authority, Proclamation on farm produce, Usury**, etc.

Exchange (Barter). There are several Hausa words which may be used to mean exchange (or barter), including *furfura, musaya, rangama, sauya*.

(a) Such exchange of produce as occurs in Batagarawa usually involves women exchanging equal quantities of millet and guinea corn, irrespective of relative prices. Although convention has it that such exchange should not involve grain allocated by a husband for domestic consumption, it often does. It is said that groundnuts are never exchanged for other produce – but that one type of groundnut might be exchanged for another. Cowpeas may be exchanged for grain.

(b) There appears to be no literature on the extent to which barter formerly occurred in market-places, where it is probably very rare today. See Nicolas (NK, p. 274) in this connexion.

See also *Karba*.

Fada. A chief's residence, including precincts.

Fadama – pl. *fadamu*. Low-lying land in valleys and depressions, which is subject to flooding or water-logging during the wet season.

Unlike *tudu* (q.v.), *fadama* may be cultivable during the dry season, and is often (though not necessarily) exceptionally fertile, being suitable for such special crops as rice, wheat, onions, sugar cane, tobacco, tomatoes, etc. – and, also, for tree crops, such as mango and guava. *Fadama* farms are seldom irrigated unless they lie along river-banks – see **Shadoof**.

(a) The area of *fadama* in the Batagarawa mapped zone is small – see Fig. 6 – perhaps some 30 acres. The farms there could not be mapped (see p. 63); most of the farms are owned by richer farmers (see Table IV.2, p. 62), including *masu-sarauta*, as they command a high price relative to *tudu*.

(b) The availability of fertile *fadama* is apt to be a variable of great significance in rural Hausaland, and population densities in some localities, e.g. the Sokoto river basin, are closely related to this. It is a matter of particular importance to the rural Hausa of the Niger Republic – see, in particular, NM (pp. 163–4) and Nicolas *et al.* (1968b, pp. 71–3). The literature on *fadama* cultivation is very scanty, but Norman (1967) makes a statistical distinction between *fadama* and *tudu* farms. Variations in proportions of *fadama* farms sometimes invalidate comparisons of farm-size in different localities, as such farms are usually small – see Goddard *et al.* (1971). However, the evidence for the assertion by Morgan and Pugh (1969, p. 364) that they average half an acre is not known. See Nadel (1942, pp. 205 ff.) on 'marsh-land farming' in Nupe.

See *Lambu, Rafi*.

Fadanci. 'Obsequiousness; the flatteries and lip-homage, etc., paid by office seekers and others [sometimes professionals] to a chief...' – Bargery.

Fage – pl. *fagage*.

(i) Any cleared open space – e.g. the central place where butchers sell their meat in Batagarawa.

(ii) A farm, when referring to certain crops other than grains.

Falle.

(a) Although one informant defined *falle* simply as 'eating something one has not planted', this elusive word (see pp. 121–2) usually (though not invariably) involves the specific notion of the borrower repaying the lender in terms of work to be performed at a later date – e.g. farm-labouring, building, ploughing, or firewood-collection. In the case of farm-labouring (*kwadago*) the sums involved are usually quite small – even as little as 6*d*. and seldom more than 10*s*.; although considerable secrecy attaches to the granting of such *falle*, it is safe to say that its prevalence varies considerably from year to year according to economic circumstances. While a number of informants associated the word only with *kwadago* (sometimes even insisting that farm-labourers had formerly always demanded *falle*, not wages), others regarded it as a means by which capital could be raised for production – thus tobacco growers in Morawa (near Batagarawa) denoted as *falle* their system of selling tobacco for delivery in some months time, at a pre-determined price.

One dictionary definition of *falle* concerns the time-honoured practice of demanding 'very early payment of taxes by a district head or a minor chief who may be hard up' – Bargery.

Fallow. The verb *huta* or *futa* (rest) is often employed in sentence construction to mean 'fallow'; the nouns *kuba*, *sagagi*, *saura*, and *sunkuru* (q.v.) tend rather to refer to disused (surplus) farmland, than to farms which had required fallowing. *Zan noma gyada a gonan nan har shekara biyu, san nan im bar ta ta huta* = I shall grow groundnuts on this farm for two years, and shall then allow it to rest.

(a) In Batagarawa there are no standard beliefs regarding the desirable period of fallow, this no doubt reflecting varying soils, fertilities, crops etc., as well as the entire lack of standard rotational practices. However, it is sometimes said that a farmer with 2 bush-farms is in a position to farm them alternately for three-year periods. (Opinion differed even more on the length of time that should elapse before a bush-farm is considered abandoned, and thus freely appropriatable by another farmer: some said 'anyone may come after three years', while others considered this period much too short.)

(b) See Nicolas (1968a, p. 43) for statistics showing that most farms in his sample in the Maradi valley had been fallowed during the previous three years.

See **Bush-farm, Permanent cultivation.**

Famine – *yunwa*, i.e. famine or hunger. There are other Hausa words for grain scarcity or 'hunger'.

(a) Although, every year, there are many who suffer some degree of real hunger, especially in the weeks before the early millet harvest, a condition of famine resulting from the failure of crops (usually as a result of low rainfall), is clearly distinguishable. The people of Batagarawa have vivid memories of four famines: *Malali* (1914), *Kwana* or *Kona* (1927), '*Yar Balange* (1942), and *Uwar Sani* (1954) – the dates all relating to the pre-harvest months of the year following the crop-failure.

Earlier this century, at some indeterminate date, the population of Batagarawa appears to have fallen sharply, perhaps because of migration following *Malali*; certainly, many migrated following *Uwar Sani* – it being 'after suffering that you migrate'. Those whose grain stocks were exhausted were obliged, as a last resort, to sell their farms to others more fortunate – farm prices fell very low during '*Yar Balange* and *Uwar Sani*.

It is the general opinion in Batagarawa that the advent of the long-distance lorry has greatly reduced the risk of real famine.

(b) People starve quietly, and the word 'famine' scarcely appears in the history books. According to W. F. Gowers (National Archives, Kaduna, K 2151, 1926) the following famines occurred in Hausaland: *Dawara* (1847); *Banga-Banga* (1855) – 'For 30 days at a time no *gero, dawa*, wheat or rice' were to be had at Kano, and people ate vultures; 1863, 1864, 1873, 1884, 1889 ('slight famines'); 1890 ('fairly severe'); 1907–8 ('widespread scarcity'); *Malali* (1914). (An average of one famine per 7 years.) According to the *Annual Report* on Northern Nigeria for 1904 (pp. 6–7), there was, also, in 1903 a serious famine caused by drought in much, though not all, of the country – 'and, also, to some extent in 1902'. See *Report on Famine Relief in the Northern Provinces in* 1927, Government Printer, Lagos.

See *Malali*.

Faranti – pl. *farantai*. Plates, particularly of decorated enamel, such as wives affix in large quantities on the walls of their sleeping-huts, though the practice is becoming less common.

Farke – pl. *fatake*. A long-distance trader. See *Fatauci*.

Farm-area. Throughout this book the word 'farm' – which corresponds to the Hausa word *gona* – denotes a field or plot cultivated (though not necessarily owned) by a farmer; contiguous areas in the same ownership, even if under different crops, or acquired in different manners, constitute a single farm. A 'holding', or 'farm-holding' (q.v.), comprises all the separate farms owned by an individual.

Although there are many non-sociological (as well as sociological) factors influencing farm-area, such as the proportion of *fadama* (q.v.) and of bush-farms (q.v.), average areas do not show very great variation between localities if the following statistics (Table C.1) are reasonably representative – at least of long-settled communities: in 14 out of 17 cases average farm-area is between 1½ and 3½ acres.

TABLE C.1. *Average farm-areas*

Source[a]	Locality	Average acreage
(6)	Bindawa	2·2
	Ilale and Makera	2·7
	Kadandani	2·9
	Bugasawa and Landa	2·8
	Kasanki	6·6
	Birnin Kuka	3·0
(9)	Dan Mahawayi[b]	1·8
	Hanwa[b]	1·6
(10)	Batagarawa	2·5
(11)	Autawa	3·5
(12)	Makurdi	5·1
(13)	Kaukai	3·3
(14)	Gidan Karma	2·4
	Kaura Kimba	1·0
	Takatuku	1·5
Luning (1963b)	Sokoto/Rima Valley	1·7
Luning (1963c)	Tulluwa	0·7

(a) See table on p. 236.
(b) *Tudu* farms only.

The following Table C.2, shows that Batagarawa and neighbouring hamlets are not exceptional in having such high proportions of small farms – that the proportion is indeed much higher in 2 selected localities in rural Zaria. But this should not be allowed to obscure the fact that in Batagarawa (as well as in the Zaria Hamlets) as much as half of the *total acreage* consists of farms of 3 acres or more – the proportion being as high as 70% in the neighbouring Hamlets of Kaukai and Autawa.

About three-fifths of all the mapped farms in Batagarawa are under 2 acres. However, the analysis in Table C.3, p. 234 of the means by which the present owner had acquired the farm shows that few of these farms had been divided between brothers on the death of the present owner's father. See also pp. 22 and 185 above.

TABLE C.2. *Size–distribution of farms*

I. Number of farms

Farm area	Batagarawa[a] Total		Batagarawa[a] Excluding women		Kaukai		Autawa		Hanwa[b]	D. Mahawayi[b]
	No.	%	No.	%	No.	%	No.	%	%	%
Under 1 acre	123	23	98	20	13	15	20	23	52	56
1–1·9 acres	199	38	179	37	23	26	21	24	27	20
2–2·9 acres	89	17	87	18	20	23	18	20	7	11
3–3·9 acres	48	9	48	10	5	6	4	5	7	6
4–6·9 acres	49	9	49	10	17	19	14	16	5	5
7–9·9 acres	13	2	13	3	9	10	4	5	1	1
10 acres and over	9	2	9	2	1	1	7	8	—	1
Total	530	100	483	100	88	100	88	100	100	100

II. Total acreage

Farm-area	Batagarawa excluding women %	Kaukai %	Autawa %	Hanwa[b] %	D. Mahawayi[b] %
Under 1 acre	5	3	4	16	16
1–1·9 acres	22	11	10	28	19
2–2·9 acres	19	17	14	12	18
3–3·9 acres	14 ⎫	6 ⎫	4 ⎫	16 ⎫	13 ⎫
4–6·9 acres	22 ⎬ 53	31 ⎬ 70	23 ⎬ 70	19 ⎬ 44	17 ⎬ 48
7–9·9 acres	7 ⎪	27 ⎪	10 ⎪	7 ⎪	10 ⎪
10 acres and over	10 ⎭	6 ⎭	33 ⎭	2 ⎭	8 ⎭
Total	100	100	100	100	100

(a) Excluding 49 tiny plots of less than about 0·2 acres which were abandoned house-plots (*kufai*).
(b) Computed from Norman (1967).

It is very interesting to note (Table C.3, p. 234) how little of the manured farmland owned by richer heads of farming-units consists of small plots under 1 acre, there being a close relationship between economic-grouping and farm-area. Nearly two-thirds of the farmland owned by the most successful farmers consists of plots of 5 acres or more – the corresponding proportion for Groups 3 and 4 being less than one-fifth.

Although a quarter of the smallest farms (under 1 acre) are *gayauni*, it does not follow that the practice of giving farm-portions to sons-in-*gandu* necessarily leads to the creation of progressively more and more small farms, since the owner may ultimately inherit the farm of which the *gayauna* was originally a portion.

See also **Farm-size**.

TABLE C.3. *Means of acquisition of small farms, Batagarawa*

Means by which owner acquired farm	Farms under 1 acre		Farms of 1–1.9 acres	
	No.	%	No.	%
		(Number of farms)		
(1) Inherited				
no division between brothers	7	6	25	12
division between brothers	17	14	38	19
	24	20	63	31
(2) Bought	14	11	41	21
(3) *Gayauni*	32	26	17	9
(4) From wife or mother	8	7	9	5
(5) *Kufai*	8	7	—	—
(6) Made from bush	—	—	14	7
(7) Rented (*aro*)	4	3	10	5
(8) Other and not known	7	6	26	13
Total owned by men	97	79	180	90
(9) Owned by women	26	21	19	10
Grand total	123	100	199	100

NOTES

Although entire accuracy is not claimed for the figures, informants' statements were checked against the farm-map and all cases of ownership of contiguous farms by brothers were regarded as having involved division on their father's death. See p. 63 above and Table 11.11 (p. 37).

Line: (1) 'No division between brothers' means either that the present owner had had no brothers or that his brothers received other farms on their father's death.

(3) Farms which had been given to the present owner before his father's death are included here if this information was volunteered.

(5) The farms were so small because they were *kufai* – i.e. abandoned house-sites.

(9) Very few of these farms had been inherited from the woman's father.

TABLE C.4. *Farm-area by economic-group, Batagarawa*

Acreage-range of farm-plot	Heads of farming-units							
	Economic-group				Economic-group			
	1	2	3+4	Total	1	2	3+4	Total
	(Number of farms)				(Total acreage – per cents)			
0.3–0.9	5	18	47	70	1	3	9	5
1.0–1.9	21	42	71	134	12	18	30	21
2.0–4.9	23	48	55	126	26	43	45	39
5 and over	20	16	9	45	61	35	16	35
Total	69	124	182	375	100	100	100	100

Farm-boundary plants.

(a) Among the plants used for marking farm-boundaries in Batagarawa are: (1) *gamba* (q.v.) – a grass; (2) *hurar-kiba*, a lily – see *Albasar kwadi*; (3) *jema* – a grass (*Vetiveria nigritana*); (4) *karan masallaci*, or *hidda-tarutsa*, a leafless plant, something like a cactus (*Caralluma Dalzielii*); (5) *yakuwa* (q.v.) – sorrel.

(b) See Grove (1957, p. 33) on farm-hedges. Henna is a common boundary-plant near Kano.

Farm-holdings. This entry is concerned with the size of farm-holdings in Hausaland, and also with average acreages per head of population and per working-man. Although a farm-holding may be readily defined as comprising all the separate farms (plots) cultivated by a farmer, numerous practical difficulties arise in the statistical application of this definition, chief of which are: 1 – the difficulty of defining a farmer; 2 – the treatment of farms which are in fallow; 3 – the widespread dispersal of bush-farms in some localities.

Although it is one of the main contentions of this book that most statistical averages relating to the socio-economic life of farmers are of little value (even if they are not positively misleading), a brief survey of the literature on the size of farm-holdings must deal first with average areas, if only because some investigators have presented no size-distribution figures. Table C.5 on p. 236 lists, in chronological order, the main recent sources and a few older sources. Certain notes on this Table follow – See also p. 237.

1 – *The definition of the farm-holding unit.* Two questions arise here: whether men-in-*gandu* are included in the list of farm-holders; and whether, if not, farms owned by men-in-*gandu* are included with the holding of the head of the farming unit. Neither of these questions can be answered in respect of Surveys (1) and (3); in the case of Survey (7) a literal interpretation of 'random selection from the tax list' would imply (perhaps wrongly) that men-in-*gandu* are regarded as farm-holders – whereas with Surveys (5), (6) and (8) the terminology implies the opposite (the incidence of *gandu* may, in any case, be low in some areas); Surveys (4) and (9) adopted the same definition as (10) to (13), farms owned by men-in-*gandu* being included in the holding acreages.

2 – *Inclusion of farms under fallow*
    Fallow explicitly excluded: Survey (4)
    Most fallow excluded: Survey (10)
    Separate figures with and without fallow: Survey (5)
    Fallow presumably included: Survey (6)
    Fallow certainly included: Surveys (2), (8), (9), (11–13), (14)
    No information: Surveys (1), (3), (7).
3 – *Inclusion of bush-farms*
    Bush-farms definitely included: Surveys (2), (6), (9), (11–13)
    Bush-farms presumably included: Surveys (3), (4)
    Bush-farms explicitly excluded: Surveys (8), (10)
    Few bush-farms: Surveys (5), (14)
    No information: Surveys (1), (7).

The only conclusion that can be drawn from the summary, Table C.6 (p. 237) is that average holdings in the survey areas commonly lay within the range of 4.3 to 8.0 acres, if farms owned by men-in-*gandu* are excluded. As for the 3 cases with the highest averages, Survey (2) was a special case, in that there was a large proportion of fallow; Survey (6) was based on rough mapping; and Survey (11) was based on a small sample which happened to include some unusually large holdings.

Table C.7, on p. 238, relates to most of the surveys for which reliable statistics on the size-distribution of holdings are available. It shows that in these localities the proportion of holdings of under one acre is of the order of 5%: no mention is made of 'nil holdings' in any

(*Continued on page 239*)

TABLE C.5. *Average acreage of farm-holdings, Hausaland: (A)*

Source	Date of enquiry	Locality	Farm-holding unit	Average acreage of holding	Number of holdings
(1) Official	1917	Katsina Emirate	'Compound'	4·3	N.A
(2) Nash (1948)	1938–9	Gata, N. Zaria	Household	15	25
(3) Rowling (1952)	Before 1949	Kano Emirate	Units headed by tax-payers	4·3–5·1	N.A.
(4) Smith (1955)	1949–50	N. Zaria	'Work-unit'	4·5	109
(5) Grove (1957)	1952	Ilale, Katsina Emirate	'Land-holding unit'	7·2 (exc. fallow) 7·9 (inc. fallow)	92
(6) Luning (1963a)	1960	Katsina Emirate	'Family'		
		Bindawa		6·1	41
		Ilale and Makera		7·9	71
		Kadandani		8·7	70
		Bugasawa and Landa		7·3	75
		Kasanki		15·0	57
		Birnin Kuka		5·8	70
(7) Rural Economic Survey	1963–4	N. Nigeria	Households headed by 'tax-payers'	4·6	2,880
(8) Mortimore and Wilson (1965)	1964	Dame Fulani, Kano Emirate	Family	4·4	103
(9) Norman (1967)	1966	Zaria Emirate	'Gandaye'		
		Hanwa		6·0	64
		Doka		8·7	153
		Dan Mahawayi		10·1	103
(10) Hill	1967	Batagarawa	Heads of farming-units only	5·6	171
			Total, inc. men in *gandu*	6·5	171
(11) Hill	1967	Autawa	Farming-units (inc. sons)	12·2	22
(12) Hill	1967	Makurdi	Farming-units (inc. sons)	10·2	21
(13) Hill	1967	Kaukai	Farming-units (inc. sons)	6·5	45
(14) Goddard	1967	Gidan Karma	Farming-units	10·6	111
		Kaura Kimba		5·6	46
		Takatuku		5·6	129

See notes on facing page.

Notes on Table C.5

(1)   From 'Assessment *Taki*, Katsina Division', National Archives, Kaduna, File no. 1938. Relating to an area of 30 sq. miles near Katsina city, the reliability of these acreages, which were based on rough pacing (see **Revenue Survey**), cannot be assessed.

(2)   This very reliable survey was carried out by D. R. Buxton long before the report was published; it was based on a map of all the farmland in the Hamlet of Gata, near Anchau, which had a population of 180 people. See Hill (1970a, p. 158).

(3)   The Revenue Survey (q.v.) was the source of the statistics. Rowling notes that the figures he cited were unchecked in the field.

(4)   Averages computed from figures on pp. 226–9. Farms were measured along the boundaries and checked by triangulation of a sample: 'an attempt to measure fallow farms was soon abandoned' (p. 128). Random sampling based on tax-lists was employed. A 'work-unit' is identical with a 'farming-unit', farms owned by men-in-*gandu* being included.

(5)   The farm-maps were based on aerial photographs. The 'land-holding unit' was not defined.

(6)   The account given by the author of his fieldwork methods inspires little confidence in the reliability of the acreage measurements or in the randomness of the sample. Ilale and Makera are near Bindawa (in Dan Yusufu District); Kadandani, Bugasawa and Landa are in Kaura District; and Kasanki and Birnin Kuka are in Mashi District, very near to the Niger frontier. 'Family' is not defined.

(7)   From *Rural Economic Survey of Nigeria : Farm Survey – 1963–64*, Federal Office of Statistics, Lagos, 1966. This survey relates to northern Nigeria, not to Hausaland. Adult male tax-payers were selected randomly from tax lists and the household of each was visited. Whether the statistics related to the holdings of the whole household in cases where the tax-payer did not happen to be head of a farming-unit, is not stated.

(8)   The survey was based on air photographs. The authors note (p. 15) that many farmers probably held farms outside the survey area, so that the average acreage is too low.

(9)   The term *gandaye* in this context is identical with farming-unit. The farm maps were based on large-scale air photographs.

(10)   See Table IV.2, p. 62. Bush-farms, outside the mapped area, are excluded.

(11–13)   All Hamlets near Batagarawa – see Commentary. The statistics relate to resident farmers only, some of the farmland being owned by farmers from neighbouring Hamlets. Several of the Kaukai farmers also had farms in neighbouring Hamlets.

(14)   From Goddard *et al.* (1971); three villages respectively situated 22 miles north, 5 miles west and 11 miles south-west of Sokoto city.

TABLE C.6. *Average acreage of farm-holdings, Hausaland : (B)*

(By survey number)			
4·3 to 6·0	6·1 to 8·0	8·1 to 10·6	12·2 to 15
1[b]	5[c]	9[a], [b] (exc. Hanwa)	2[a]
3[c]	6[d] (exc. Kadandani and Kasanki)	12[b]	6[c] (Kasanki)
4[a]	10*[b]	14[c] (Gidan Karma)	11[b]
(7)			
8[c]	13[b]		
9[c] (Hanwa)			
10†[b]			
14[c] (Kawakimba)			
14[c] (Takatuku)			

Population densities per square mile
  (a) Probably under 100.
  (b) Possibly in the range of about 100 to 200.
  (c) Over 200.
  (d) Variable densities.
  (e) Not known: possibly low.
   * Men-in-*gandu* included.
   † Heads of farming-units only.

TABLE C.7. *Size-distribution of farm-holdings, Hausaland*

Percentage of holdings by acreage range

Acreage range	Survey (4)	Survey (10) (A)	Survey (10) (B)	Dawaki ta Kudu§ Dawaki	Yargaya	Runa	Survey (14) Gidan Karma	Hanwa	Survey (9) Doka	D. Mahawayi	Surveys (11) and (12)	Survey (13)
Under 1 acre	7	4	4	5	4	3	3	5	3	6	—	7
1–1.9	14	15	15	12	9	9	4*	28*	8*	9*	2	9
2–3.9	33	28	23	30	20	20	21†	19†	22†	20†	16	20
4–5.9	18	16	18	19	19	18	29‡	25‡	34‡	34‡	16	11
6–9.9	19	22	21	20	23	27					28	42
10 and over	10	16	19	13	23	22	42	23	33	31	37	11
	100	100	100	100	100	100	100	100	100	100	100	100

Survey (10) (A) Exc. men-in-*gandu*; 13 'nil holdings' excluded.
(B) Inc. men-in-*gandu*; 8 'nil holdings' excluded.

Surveys (9) and (14) * Range of 1 to 2½ acres.
† Range of 2½ to 5 acres.
‡ Range of 5 to 10 acres.
§ Three villages in Dawaki ta Kudu District, Kano Emirate. National Archives, Kaduna, possible date about 1930, Kano Provincial Office File, no. 6551/S1.

of the surveys, and the figures for Batagarawa are, therefore, omitted. There is much variation (10%–37%) in the proportion of holdings over 10 acres. In Batagarawa about half of the *total (mapped) acreage* consists of these large holdings, the corresponding proportion for Autawa and Makurdi being 70%.

Average acreage per head of population and per working-man
Such statistics as seem reasonably reliable are listed in the following table C.8.

TABLE C.8. *Average acreage per head and per working-man, Hausaland*

Survey number and locality	Per head of population	Per working-man
(2) Gata	2·1	N.A.
(6) Ilale	1·3[a]	N.A.
Bindawa	1·2	N.A.
(8) Ungogo	0·6[b]	2·6[b]
(9) Hanwa	0·7	3·1[c]
Doka	1·2	3·6[c]
D. Mahawayi	1·7	5·5[c]
(10) Batagarawa	1·0[d]	3·2[d][e]
(11) Autawa	1·5	5·9
Luning (1963b) Sokoto Rima Valley[f]	0·9–1·3[g]	3·3–4·6[g]
Luning (1963c) Tulluwa[h]	0·5	N.A.

(a) Estimate – Grove (1957, p. 46).
(b) From Mortimore (1967, p. 683). Exclusive of acreage owned outside survey area.
(c) Acreage per available working-man, allowance being made for those in occupations in Zaria.
(d) Bush farms excluded.
(e) Making no allowance for movements of labourers in and out of the Hamlet.
(f) Acreages based on farm-pacing.
(g) Six separate villages.
(h) A small village west of Sokoto city.

Omitting Survey (8), *average acreages per head of population* vary between 0·7 in Hanwa, where population density is very high, and 2·1 in Gata. It should be noted that fallow land was included in the three surveys with the highest averages, viz. Autawa, D. Mahawayi and Gata. (The estimated proportion of fallow land in D. Mahawayi was 19%: the corresponding figure for Doka, which had a lower average acreage per head of population, was 24%.) There is virtually no fallow land in Hanwa and little in the mapped area of Batagarawa, or in Bindawa – in Autawa the proportion of fallow was low, though higher than in neighbouring Batagarawa. Average acreages of *cultivated* farmland per head of population vary within the range of 0·6 to 1·3.

Estimates of *average acreage per working man* necessarily relate to the number of men available for agricultural work, taking no account of the degree to which the potential labour supply is actually so engaged, or of immigrant labour. Omitting Survey (8), averages vary between 3·1 and 5·9, or between 3·1 and 4·4 for cultivated land (allowing for fallow at D. Mahawayi). Such a degree of uniformity is quite striking considering the great variations in Batagarawa as between economic-groups (Table IV.2, p. 62) – 5·3 acres for Group 1 against 1·5 acres for Group 4. The range corresponds remarkably closely with estimates relating to cultivated land in large areas of northern Nigeria made by Baldwin (1963, p. 68).

Farm-prices. Data on farm-prices (excluding *fadama*) are given in the following sources:

Grove (1957, p. 45) – the usual price in Bindawa in 1950–2 was put at about £3 an acre, but a farm near a *gari* might have fetched £6–£7; Luning (1963c, p. 180) – a summary table provides statistics of average prices relating to Tulluwa in Western Sokoto (where prices were highest at £9 an acre), 3 places in Katsina and 3 in Eastern Sokoto; Mortimore and Wilson (1965, p. 52), where it is suggested that prices were commonly £10–£20 per acre (or more) in the Kano Close-Settled Zone, and where they were clearly rising fast; Nicolas (1968a, p. 19) where farm-prices (unrelated to area) are commonly between £2 and £6. See, also, Chapter VI, p. 92.

Farm-selling. This entry is mainly concerned with historical references to farm-selling – see also **Inheritance**, and Chapter VI.

The opinion, as expressed by Anderson (1954, pp. 185 ff.) and others, that local custom, not Muslim law, usually governs transactions in farmland is here taken for granted and 'conflicts' (potential or actual) between 'custom' and 'law' are not, therefore, discussed.

> When Northern Nigeria was conquered in 1902–3, each of the present Emirs was appointed by me on terms embodied in a 'Letter of appointment'...in which *inter alia* the ultimate rights in the land, *in so far as they were held by the Fulani dynasty as conquerors*, were transferred to the British Crown. No attempt was made at the time to define those rights...It may be argued that under the law of Islam, the right of the conqueror to unrestricted ownership of the land is recognised, but Mohammedan law in Nigeria has been modified by Native Law and Custom, though to what extent it is impossible to define. I left this delicate question for solution when much fuller knowledge of local conditions should have been acquired.   Lugard (1918) *Political Memorandum* 10 – *Lands*

Following the findings of the 1908 Lands Committee, Lugard's original scruples were overlooked and 'all lands in the Northern Provinces' were declared by Ordinance to be held in trust for the people by the Governor: the assumption was that ownership had merely been *transferred* from one authority to another – that all land had formerly been vested in 'chiefs' who allocated rights of user to occupants, in return for payment of tax, in the sense that, for instance, migrants could retain these rights indefinitely by means of tax-payments, but could not sell their farms. This philosophy of continuity held sway for many years, thus strengthening the original misconception that permanent transfers of farms, for a consideration, from one individual to another, were in no sense 'sales': when such transactions were observed to occur, they were commonly regarded as new-style or anomalous.

But such views overlooked the evidence for the existence of 'individual ownership' and 'farm selling' in some districts in the nineteenth century. Clapperton and Barth commented on the neatly fenced and hedged plantations seen near Kano, Katsina and Gulumbe (Gwandu Emirate) – which must surely have been in permanent private ownership. In the early nineteenth century Abdullahi, whose *Diya-al-hukkam* is cited by Hiskett in his introduction to Temple (1968), declared that any grant of land to an individual 'became his property' to sell, give away, or bequeath: 'there is therefore no doubt', comments Hiskett (*ibid.*, p. xx), 'that freehold in its most complete form was known in Northern Nigeria', varying in degree from place to place. That selling was commonplace is implied by the delightful nineteenth-century story of the boy and his farm, excerpts from which are given below. In the *Provincial Gazetteer for Sokoto Province* (Part III, 1934, National Archives, Kaduna, Acc. No. 279) it is reported that the Sultan of Sokoto who ruled from 1859 to 1866 'put a stop to the buying and selling of farms' – which twenty years later had again become common. In Lugard's *Political Memorandum* H. R. Palmer was cited as stating that in Kano 'nearly every farm has been bought at some time'. Again on Kano, Rowling (1952, p. 5) reported that the sale of farms before the British occupation might readily be confirmed by case histories.

But such rights, though well developed, were not necessarily absolute. Farm-owners were often not entitled to sell farms on their migration (even though their rights would expire did they not pay tax); permission had to be sought from the 'chief' before selling to a stranger; and (a strangely neglected subject) 'chiefs' could (as they still do) confiscate (*kwacewa*) farmland, thus effectively banishing the owner for reasons such as indebtedness, whether or not this involved non-payment of tax. There being no concept of lineage land, migrants had no 'natural rights' of user on their return to their homeland – unless they had departed temporarily (paying their tax in their absence) or had gone to Mecca. But practice varied greatly. According to information provided by Alkalin Sokoto in 1929 (Memorandum on Rural Land Policy in the North prepared in Kaduna, 1929, National Archives, Kaduna, File No. 1724) the rights of returning migrants had diminished since the British occupation. In general, see Meek (1949, p. 150), such rights might only be resumed had the farm happened to be vacant.

So, 'whatever radical right the chief may have in legal theory [or in custom] it does not amount in practice to anything more than administrative control over vacant lands in the interests of the whole community' Meek (*ibid.*, p. 149): to which may be added the point that no two people in any community ever agree on the definition of 'vacancy'.

See also *Aro*, **Farm-prices**, *Haya*, **Inheritance**, *Jingina*, *Kyauta*, **Migration**, **Permanent cultivation**.

The following story (which has been abbreviated at the beginning) is drawn from a book of Hausa texts and translations, edited by J. F. Schön (1885, pp. 120–1). Most of the tales, though not necessarily this one, had been related to Schön by Dorugu who had been brought to England by Barth in 1856 – see Hair (1967). Though entirely fanciful in detail, it is surely likely that the narrator was familiar with the practice of selling manured farmland.

The story of the boy and his farm

A boy of fifteen was advised by his father to do farm work or keep a shop. Choosing the former, the boy took money which was in his possession and 'went to the proprietor of a large farm, and said to him I wish you to sell me half of your farm. The proprietor went, together with him, and measured and marked off the half of his farm' and said to the boy that he might have it for 200 gold pieces. 'Then the boy gave him one hundred pieces of gold, and said to the proprietor, when I have worked your farm and raised much corn, I shall pay you the rest. So the farmer left it to him. He cultivated the land. One year he reaped a great abundance of corn; he went and sold his corn. When he had sold all, he got five hundred pieces of gold; he came to the proprietor and paid him. The farmer said to him, as to this farm I know that it is a good one; and if you will listen to my advice you will manure it. So the boy went, and called the Fulanis together with their cows, and they dwelled on the farm, and manured it for him. He gave them a hundred silver pieces. Next year working his farm he earned four hundred pieces of gold; and, year after year cultivating his land, he received more. But in the seventh year his money began to decrease, and in his dream something said to him. Sell some cows, sell some sheep, and offer them as sacrifices; take some of the money and give it to the poor in the streets together with the blind; and of the flesh, too, you must give some both to rich and poor. If you will do these things your property will not decrease. So the boy got up and did as he was told. Cultivating his land during that year his money was not diminished. In this way he continued to act to the end of his life.'

Farm-size. This entry deals only with the Hausa farmer's concept of farm-size.

(a) The size of a farm (or plot) may be assessed by the farmer in terms of: (1) the number of bundles of grain, or bags of groundnuts, it produces; or (2) the number of *mangala* (q.v.)

9

of compound sweepings required to manure it; or (3) the number of man-days required for its first-weeding; or (4) the quantity of seed-grain required for sowing it; or (5) the number of ridges (*kunya*) made when it is ploughed. Although farmers do not think in terms of the lengths of their boundaries, division of farms (on inheritance or sale) often involves pacing (*taki*), if not counting of ridges. As pacing is ideally along the points of the compass, farms tend to have a north-south/east-west alignment, as can be seen from Fig. 6. See **Farm-area**.

Farm-tools – *kayan aiki*; *ma'aikaci*, pl. *ma'aikatai*.

(a) Farm-tools are bought from blacksmiths (either directly or from markets), the handles being made by carpenters. The main types in use in Batagarawa are:

masassabi = a short-handled hoe for clearing land or reaping grain – resembling a bent axe;

sungumi = a long-handled hoe used when sowing corn (price with handle 1*s.* 6*d.*, without handle 1*s.* 3*d.*);

galma (*garma*) = the 'hand plough' used for ridging (it is too heavy for clearing); it is perforated, being made of metal strips, and bells may be attached to add to the merriment of teamwork; the farmer wields the hoe with both hands, moving backwards with great gusto down the furrow (price 4*s.* to 7*s.*) – see Plate 16;

fartanya, haiwa (*hauya*) = small hoes, with long or short handles, used for weeding and for harvesting groundnuts (price 2*s.* 6*d.*, without handle);

adda = the cutlass or matchet, which may be used when clearing wooded land.

The *gandu* head provides all tools (except, sometimes, the *galma*) and is responsible for paying for all repairs: sons-in-*gandu* may, however, use these tools on their *gayauni* or for *kwadago*. When a son leaves *gandu* his father should give him tools. Tools pass to the sons on the death of a father.

(b) Clapperton (1829, p. 221) refers to the '*gilma*' (*galma*) which 'has a short bent handle, with a large head, and is used in all the heavy work instead of a spade'. Nicolas (NM, p. 158) provides illustrations of farm-tools – not all of which resemble those in use in Batagarawa. Ahmadu Bello University holds a very good collection of some 50 different hoes at Samaru.

See also **Farming-operations, Ploughing.**

Farming-operations. Some of the numerous Hausa terms are:

noma = farming in general, also weeding;

toyi = setting fire to the bush when clearing farms before the rains;

sassabe = the clearing of land of bushes to make a farm;

kafce = hoeing up deeply the whole of a plot;

bangaje = making ridges and furrows and sowing afterwards;

kufurtu = preparing ground with the *fartanya* (hoe) before sowing;

gwarzo banza = making ridges (*kunya*) for sowing;

shuka = sowing;

dashi = the transplantation of seedlings – from *dasa* (transplanted);

firi (*huri*) = first weeding of a grain farm;

maimai (repetition) = second weeding of a grain farm, perhaps adding fresh soil to the base of the plants;

sassarya = the third weeding (if performed);

huda = ridging – e.g. *huda dawa* = to bank up grown guinea corn after completion of *firi* and *maimai*;

girbi = the reaping of grain;

girbe = reaped completely – e.g. cowpeas after millet;

farta = hoed up groundnuts;

rora = 'Gather in harvest of beans, groundnuts, etc. (i.e. where the crop has to be picked separately from each plant)' – Bargery.

See Clapperton (1829, pp. 216–17). See Meek (1925, vol. I, p. 122) and Taylor and Webb (1932) for descriptions of Hausa cultivation methods.

Farming-unit. A farming-unit is defined for the purposes of this book as comprising the man (or men) who cultivate any set of farms, together with their dependants. Excluding the *masu-sarauta* and a few households headed by men who do not count themselves as farmers (they are mainly *barori* or drummers), there were reckoned to be 171 farming-units in Batagarawa, of which 48 are organized as *gandaye*. A farming-unit may, or may not, consist of several separate households, or cooking units. All *gandu* heads are, also, heads of farming-units. A son-in-*gandu* who cultivates a set of privately-owned farms is not the head of a farming-unit. See **Economic-group,** *Gandu.*

Fatauci. Although the dictionaries define *fatauci* as 'itinerant trading' and although nowadays any man who trades outside his home area is apt to denote himself, however jocularly, as *farke* (pl. *fatake*), the word is best confined to the type of long-distance trade which was formerly conducted by members of trading-caravans (*ayari*). It is most certainly to be distinguished from such types of itinerant trading within a small circuit, as *bojuwa* (q.v.), *gurumfa*, *jagale* (q.v.) *koli* (q.v.), etc. See **Trading-terms.**

It is here contended that in former times most long-distance traders (*fatake*) were farmers who were rurally-based. For this reason, and also because the literature on Hausa trading is remarkably slight, this entry is mainly concerned with the former Hausa caravan-trade; it includes a little material obtained from elderly retired *fatake* in the neighbourhood of Batagarawa.

During his second expedition in 1826 Clapperton loosely attached himself to a Hausa caravan which was passing through Kaiama (in Borgu) on its return to Kano from Gonja and Ashanti. The caravan consisted of upwards of a thousand men and women and as many beasts of burden. The principal 'cargo' consisted – Clapperton (1829, p. 68) – of kola, which had been received 'in exchange for natron, red glass beads, and a few slaves, principally refractory ones which they cannot manage'. 'They carry their goods on bullocks, mules, asses, and a number of female slaves are loaded; even some women hire themselves to carry loads to and from Nyffé [Nupe]. Some of the merchants have no more property than they can carry on their own heads.' The caravans (*ibid.*, p. 75) 'occupied a long line of march: bullocks, asses, horses, women and men, to the amount of a thousand, all in a line, after one another, forming a very curious sight; a motley group, from the nearly naked girls and men carrying loads, to the ridiculously and gaudily dressed Gonja traders, riding on horseback'. Having crossed the Niger river, by means of canoes of about 20 ft long and 2 ft broad, they reached 'Koolfu', where the caravans from Bornu and Hausaland always halted, the former never going further south. Their wares on the southward journey included (*ibid.*, p. 137) horses, natron, unwrought silk, beads, 'clothes made up in the Moorish fashion' and slaves. Clapperton referred to the 'head man' of the caravan (with whom he negotiated to carry his goods to Kano), but made no other mention of organizational matters. Barth's references to Hausa caravans were also those of a spectator – though at one stage he joined a salt-caravan bound for Kano: at Zakka (south-south-west of Katsina), for instance, he saw (vol. IV, p. 117) a troop of about 100 *fatake* with asses laden entirely with *daddawa* (q.v.).

Later writers include: Staudinger (1889), who referred (p. 613) to *fatake* as small traders (in salt, natron, leather goods, etc.) who attached themselves to large caravans; Monteil (1895), who joined a Hausa caravan from Say to Hausaland and who referred (p. 209) to the caravan leader's 'absolute authority', and to his function of assessing the share of the tolls to be paid by each member; Robinson (1896) who (p, 137) met a caravan of about 1,000 men with many donkeys, who were carrying kola (of estimated value some £100,000) towards Kano; and Lugard (1904) who referred to the 'wonderful caravan road' between Zungeru and Zaria – 'I have seen nothing like it in Africa. The track is often 50 feet wide, and one meets ceaseless caravans of laden donkeys, men, women and live stock along its whole length. I must have passed many thousands in the 250 miles we traversed to Kano.' See also Morel (1911, Chapter IV). After the British occupation, however, officialdom took little interest in the caravan trade, though a caravan tax (*fito*, q.v.) was briefly imposed.

What, then, is known of the organization of these caravans? How was the *madugu* (the caravan-leader) appointed? What were his powers? How was discipline established? What other officials were there? Did each trader (*farke*) trade on his own account? Who did the selling? Were there restrictions on who could accompany a trader? Who paid the caravan tolls and on what basis were they levied? (Barth stated, vol. V, p. 29, that tolls (*fito*) were levied per donkey.) Did caravans have any effective corporate identity – except, for example, when crossing the Niger river? Could any trader join? Most of these questions cannot be answered from literary sources.

However, in Goody and Mustapha (1967) there is a translation of one of the Krause papers (Krause, 1928), relating to the organization, departure and march of a Hausa caravan from Kano to Salaga. This caravan had an official known as *ubandawaki* (lit. 'head of the horses'), whose duty it was to sell goods; although an elaborate method of sharing the so-called 'proceeds' (*garama*) is partially described, this is puzzling as Bargery defines *garama*, in this context, as 'money paid by the head of a caravan to any chief who might demand it'. Another official was *jagaba* (the guide), one of whose duties was to help the women in carrying their loads.

Before the departure of the caravan the *madugu* 'consulted a malam for two or three days'. In reference to malams, Lander commented that 'every caravan is furnished with one or more of these corpulent drones, who loll at their ease, while their employers are at the same time, perhaps, killing themselves with over-exertion' (1830, p. 275).

The present author's enquiries relating to the history of the long-distance tobacco trade based on Kabakawa (a dispersed hamlet near Batagarawa) – see Hill (1970a, Chapter 6) – has persuaded her that much significant economic enterprise has long been rurally-based, an idea which is confirmed by the Krause manuscript which insisted that whereas in Katsina and Zaria there were not many *madugai*, in the Kano villages they were numerous. Perhaps around 1890–1910 many of the smaller caravans were similar to those originating in the rural areas of northern Katsina, about which a little information was obtained, mainly from two former *fatake* – Abubakar Labo of Kaukai and Kaura of Batagarawa.

The first stage of the expedition, involving the trading of tobacco (which had been stored for a price rise) in Damagaram (Zinder), will not be described here – see Hill (*ibid.*). Returning home from Damagaram with purchased livestock and natron, the farmer–traders waited for a few weeks to fatten their animals before setting out, in October or November, on the south-ward *fatauci*, with their pack-donkeys loaded with natron, and with some food for the journey. The *madugu* was a well-known local man with trading experience who, like all the members, was a farmer–trader, working on his own account. He alone was permitted to take his wives with him. Slaves did not go as servants, but ordinary caravan members might travel with a son or other assistant. The *madugu* might have 20 servants who would erect tents for his wives, and as many as 20 or 30 donkeys. The 'very rich' were those who rode horses, with their donkeys in front of them; the less rich had boys to drive their donkeys and other livestock; following behind on foot, the poorest drove their livestock themselves.

Starting, perhaps, at Abukur (see Fig. 3, p. 10) they moved southwards towards Malumfashi where the routes divided, one passing through Zaria, the other through Bakori and Maska. As they progressed they might fall in with other caravans, making up a procession several miles long; but they did not necessarily amalgamate until, after passing through Bida, they crossed the Niger, below its confluence with the Kaduna river. Which *madugu* would then lead the whole group?

If there was one who could not defend his own group and had to consult the other, the latter would become the leader. It is not sufficient for a *madugu* to know the route, but he must also handle all problems when they reach the Kwara [Niger]. When they get to Kwara the *madugu* will be asked how many donkeys are in his caravan; the canoe man will tell the *madugu* how much is to be paid; this money will be paid by the *madugu* who will decide how much is owing by each caravan member. The less clever *madugu* will approach the other one with his problem, saying how much he was asked to pay; if, then, each of his members is to pay a certain amount the money will be insufficient; but if they were to pay more than this the money would be too much; the clever *madugu* will work out what sum should be paid by the owner of each donkey load, so that the total money will be correct. And from that day the one who could solve that problem would be the 'elder'. If the one with the better personality or appearance could not deal with the money problems, the cleverer man would be the elder.   (Abubakar Labo)

Sometimes the cattle were driven into the water and the Yoruba canoe-men moved along-side to prevent them being carried away by the current; sometimes they were carried in the canoes. The donkeys and their loads were carried (separately) in the canoes, the charge for a donkey being the same as for a man. At this stage their loads might include onions (bought perhaps in Zaria market) – the only commodity apart from natron and *barbarta* (q.v.). Immediately after the ferry crossing they started selling sheep; but they would endeavour not to sell cattle before reaching Lagos or Ibadan, because the cowries (q.v.) were too heavy.

The westward path to Ilorin crossed uninhabited country, but they stayed in many Hausa *zongo* en route. In order to meet the caravan tax in Ilorin they had to sell small livestock – the *madugu* sent advance messengers saying that some of his members would be visiting villages for this purpose. At Ilorin much of their natron and many of their animals were sold with the help of brokers (*dillalai*); they lodged with 'landlords' (see *mai gida*) who sometimes intercepted them in the bush. If any livestock or natron remained they would go to Ibadan, otherwise they went straight to Abeokuta. Each caravan member looked after his own cowries, sometimes having to head-load them. Although, by this time, the cowries were a great burden, at least they were relieved of the heavy natron.

Finally they proceeded to Lagos (Ikko) where they stayed with Yoruba landlords in order to buy kola. They also bought Yoruba cloth, and those with plenty of money might buy an ambulatory ware – a female slave (*kuyanga*). The sellers came to the houses where they were lodging to count and receive the cowries.

The same group of people returned home together by the same route, lacking only those who had died on the way. In Ilorin they had to produce the receipt for the caravan toll to avoid being charged anew. They often had to open their kola packages (*huhu*) en route, to water, air and inspect the nuts, deteriorating nuts being sold. The speed of the return journey depended on the donkeys, who usually took some 20 days from Lagos to the Niger river.

On returning home with the kola, the *fatake* endeavoured to hold it for a price rise. They took it gradually to Katsina city, selling (say) 400 nuts at a time to kola-retailers ('*yan terere*). There were no big kola-traders in Katsina at that time, though there was one in Morawa hamlet, near Kabakawa.

(a) In Batagarawa today there are very few men who might be denoted *fatake*. One retired *farke* used to buy such produce as sugar at Jibiya and cowpeas at Ruma, and transport them by donkey (together with some 10 other traders) to Kano – hence his nickname 'Dan Kano'. His son-in-*gandu*, Bila, is following in his father's footsteps by buying fowls locally and selling them in a market at Lagos. (In 1967 he reckoned that on one expedition, taking 80 birds in baskets, he might make a profit of some £6, after meeting costs of lorry transport etc.). One trader who bought cowpeas locally sold them in Kano and elsewhere. About 3 men are tobacco traders, mainly selling at frontier markets. (Although there are many more tobacco traders in neighbouring hamlets, and in Sabon Gari, this is a declining trade.) In Mallamawa hamlets there are a few men who occasionally undertake small expeditions selling local produce, such as mats, in centres such as Funtua.

(b) There is no information as to whether traders nowadays form donkey-caravans – though this is surely likely in roadless areas. (In February 1958 Miner – (1965, p. 117) – reported a daily average of 100 men going north and south on trading trips, on an old Kano trade route, just to the east of Zaria Province.) Certainly, most long-distance traders nowadays travel by lorry – which means that it is very advantageous for traders to live in large centres.

The literature on present-day *fatauci* is very slight, but see Smith (1962, pp. 317–18), where it is stated that most traffic is with southern Nigeria, involving moving cattle, groundnuts, cotton, locust beans, handwoven cloth and other products southward, the traders returning with kola, ginger, Yoruba cloth and 'such European manufactures as are cheaper at southern markets'. The successful trader eventually establishes sufficient business to be able to retain an agent at the southern market, while he himself remains mainly at his northern headquarters. See A. Cohen (1965) on the Hausa cattle trade in Ibadan. Until quite recently many Hausa traders who were engaged in large-scale, long-distance trade in cattle, kola, onions, etc., were to be found in numerous West African countries; but such difficulties as exchange control and restrictions on stranger–traders (which have recently been imposed in Ghana) are reducing their numbers.

Much long-distance trade within Hausaland is conducted outside markets, being based on the 'landlords' (*mai gida*, or *fatoma*) who maintain houses where the traders can lodge and store their wares and who render assistance over selling. See A. Cohen (1969, etc.) and Hill (1971). Long-distance traders in livestock of all types, and in kola, natron, salt and preserved fish, are very dependent on these landlords – and those who handle such storable wares as onions, grains, cowpeas, groundnuts, locust-bean cakes and rice, may also depend on them.

See **Donkeys**, *Fito*, **Kola-nuts**, *Madugu*, **Market-place**, **Natron**, **Trading-terms**.

Fatoma – pl. *fatomai*. A word of Kanuri origin which is often used in Hausaland as an alternative to *mai gida*, to denote a 'landlord' for long-distance traders.

Fertilizers. Imported fertilizers were first introduced in northern Nigeria in 1950 when a free distribution of 750 tons was made. A few years later superphosphate was sold at £24 a ton, rising to £34. Sales being disappointing, it was decided that superphosphate prices should be subsidized (from Marketing Boards funds, so that farmers as a group paid their own subsidy) – the price of a 40-lb bag being reduced from 12s. to 5s.; demand increased from 416 to 1,778 tons, and exceeded supply in some localities. Subsequently a subsidy was introduced for sulphate of ammonia, and demand rose dramatically. So adequate was the response from farmers that since 1966 subsidies have been reduced.

In Batagarawa in 1966 superphosphate only was available. Anthony and Johnston (1968) reported that knowledge of fertilizer use was universal in Kadandani and Bindawa (in Katsina Emirate), where superphosphate was applied to food crops as well as to groundnuts; sulphate of ammonia, which is not applied to groundnuts, had made but a slight impact. According to fertilizer response data summarized by Anthony and Johnston (*ibid.*, Table 20), groundnuts yield a higher *benefit to cost ratio* than other crops, unless the price of millet is very high – as it may often be for farmers who make a business of storing for a price rise.

See Oyenuga (1967, p. 152) on research work on fertilizers in northern Nigeria which he reports as having made 'great strides': he refers to Greenwood (1951) and Goldsworthy and Heathcote (1963). But owing to shortage of finance (national, state and individual), many years must elapse before fertilizers will be of more than trivial significance for most grain farmers, compared with compound sweepings. See **Manure, Permanent cultivation**.

Firewood - *itace* (wood), or *itacen wuta* (lit. wood for the fire), *kirare* or *bubu* (twigs or kindling wood).

(a) Firewood for cooking was formerly collected by women, but nowadays it is a husband's duty to provide it for his wives, by collecting it himself or by buying from others.

Many poorer men derive a large part of their income from selling firewood either locally or in Katsina city; of the 13 heads of farming-units (see Table v.1, p. 72) whose main non-farming occupation was judged to be firewood-collection, many go frequently to Katsina city to sell donkey-loads of firewood (worth between 3s. 6d. and 4s. during the farming-season) either directly to householders or to extra-market dealers. Although firewood-collectors should hold official licences, many try to evade this heavy expense. Most firewood is collected outside the permanently-cultivated zone.

(b) The problem of obtaining adequate supplies of firewood for cities, is a cause for much concern, especially in Kano where virtually all the farms within donkey-range are permanently cultivated. Despite its great bulk, firewood is sometimes sold in markets. In parts of the extreme north of Hausaland supplies are almost unobtainable – cornstalks (*kara*) and dried dung being substitutes. During the cold harmattan period firewood prices rise, fires then providing warmth.

Fito.

(i) The caravan-tax levied by chiefs in former times.

(ii) A similar tax imposed by the colonial administration in 1902 and abolished in 1907.

(iii) Guinea-corn beer – see *Giya*.

(i) and (ii) In his 1900–1 *Annual Report* on Northern Nigeria (No. 346), Lugard stated (p. 16) that it had been his policy to open up southern trade routes by abolishing all caravan-tolls levied by Emirs. He hoped that it would be feasible for the government to impose a reasonable toll, in return for the safety of the roads secured by the government and the cost of road works and bridges. The toll imposed in 1902 (which became payable early in 1903) was in principle a 5% levy in each Province traversed up to a maximum of 15%, on both the downward and upward journeys – but it was not until 1904 that tolls on the latter journeys were actually imposed. Payment must have been largely evaded, total yield in 1905–6 having been no more than £5,891. The toll was abolished in 1907. Orr argued (1911, pp. 148–9) that great benefits were derived from traders' evasion of the toll stations: new routes were opened up and 'knowledge of the Administration' carried into the remotest pagan villages.

Fowls: see *Fatauci*, **Poultry ownership**.

'**Free goods**'. The term is used in this book to denote non-edible materials for selling or goods made from such materials which may be freely collected by the producer, including: baskets, beds, doors, fans, fences, hats, mats, nets, panniers, rope, sieves, string, thatches – as well as firewood. (Buildings, granaries, pottery, etc. are excluded.) The raw materials (which sometimes enter trade, so that the producer of 'free goods' is not necessarily obliged to collect his own material) include: bark, cornstalks, grass, hemp, leaves, palm fronds, straw, twigs, wood, etc. See Tables v.1 and v.2, pp. 72 and 74. See Meek (1925, vol. 1, pp. 168–9) on straw-plaiting and mat-making. See **Firewood**, *Gamba*, **Hemp**, *Kaba*, *Mangala*, **Mat**, **Thatches**, etc.

Fulani (Filani). The Fulani (Filani) people. Although 'Filani' is the plural of Bafilace, in English contexts it is usual to regard 'Fulani' as both singular and plural. Such Fulani as are Hausa-speaking and non-pastoralists are included under the general term 'Hausa' – see p. 3. Smith distinguishes (1955, p. 3): the *Filanin daji* or Bororo (bush Fulani) 'who are nomadic cattle keepers showing very variable Moslem influence'; the *Agwai* 'who are semi-nomadic cattle keepers practising agriculture, are poorer in cattle than the true nomads, farm for partial subsistence, sell milk' and sometimes tend cattle for others; and the *Filanin gida* the fully-settled group, including the ruling-class. But there are many other classifications: thus the ruling-class may be *Filanin soro*, other settled Fulani then being *Filanin zaure* (urban) and *Filanin gida* (rural). See Last (1967, p. lxxii). See **Hausa**.

See Morgan and Pugh (1969, p. 366) for a map of the principal regions of Hausaland in which pastoral Fulani are to be found. The regions were difficult to delimit

> because within them the pastoral Fulani live side by side for at least part of the year with Hausa cultivators and settled Fulani, because the pastoral Fulani migrate seasonally, and lastly because, although the migration pattern has certain elements of regularity, it may change from year to year, according to variations in pastoral and water conditions, and according to changing relations with the settled peoples.   (*ibid.*, p. 367)

The movements of the Bororo –

> follow the seasons in a broad way; during the rains they move north to the area of less rain, and during the dry season they move in a southerly direction in search of good grazing. Their dispersal and movements in smaller or larger groups brings supplies of meat, manure, sour milk and butter to the Hausa settlements, in return for which they purchase supplies of grain, salt, cloth and other goods and services.   Smith (1954a, p. 17)

There are no reliable estimates of the numbers of Fulani pastoralists in Hausaland, the figures relating to 'Cattle Fulani' in the 1952 census being ridiculously incomplete. So far as concerns the settled Fulani, the Census Report gives no indication as to how enumerators were expected to distinguish the two (so-called) 'tribes', the Fulani and the Hausa; the recorded numbers of Hausa and Fulani respectively in Katsina Province were 527,000 and 480,000.

The only substantial book on the pastoral Fulani in any area of Nigerian Hausaland is Hopen (1958), but see Dupire (1962) and Stenning (1959) on certain Fulani in the Niger Republic and Bornu respectively. See also St Croix (1944). See **Cattle, *Jangali*, Manure**.

Fuloti. From the word 'plot', *fuloti* is the usual term (both in Nigeria and the Niger Republic) for the 'buying stations' where groundnuts (or cotton) are bought for export. See **Marketing Board**.

Funeral expenses – *biso* (burial), *janaiza* (funeral).

(a) In Batagarawa, where funeral expenses are much lower than in the Niger Republic – see (b) below – the main types of expenditure for an ordinary adult's funeral are:

(1) the shroud (*likkafani*) of cotton cloth, which might cost from 12s. 6d. to 25s.;

(2) scent for the shroud, 3s. to 5s.;

(3) those who perform the ritual bathing of the corpse are given calabashes and the clothes the deceased was wearing;

(4) after 3 days alms (*sadaka*) are presented to Malams, Koranic students, the ill and the poor etc., and food and kola are served to those well-wishers who make monetary contributions: the whole scale of this ceremonial is nowadays greatly reduced;

(5) a similar ceremony, on a much smaller scale, occurs 40 days after the death;

(6) in the case of a deceased husband, there is a final ceremony, after about 5 months, in connexion with the end of the widow's period of formal mourning (*takaba*, q.v.). Money, food, clothes etc. are given to the widow by both men and women and counter-gifts are often made – see *Biki*.

Formerly, grave-diggers were usually given about 2s. to 5s., but nowadays they receive nothing; the Chief Imam, who used to receive about 3s., officially gets nothing today. (Burial-places are no longer in, or near, the house compound, as they were formerly.)

(b) Much the most useful source on Hausa funeral expenses is Nicolas (NK, pp. 115–23): on the basis of information relating to the funeral expenses of 83 adults, it is there estimated that the 'help' (*gudummawa*) given by participants covered, on the average, about half of the total expenses incurred, this being about equal to the total sum presented to the Malams. Average total disbursements in connexion with the burial and the distribution of alms (*sadaka*) 7 days after the death, were 7,136 Frs. See also Nicolas (NM, pp. 105–6).

See Taylor and Webb (1932, pp. 137–47) on burial.

Fura (*Fura-fura*). The millet porridge which constitutes the usual midday meal and which is very often served to workers on the farms.

(a) The quality varies greatly, much labour being involved in preparing well-cooked *fura* – for instance. The millet is washed, dried and pounded and then repounded; it is then sieved, such part as will not pass through the sieve being repounded yet again. The flour is then moistened and formed into a large ball, which is boiled in water for about half an hour. This ball is then pounded again, being remade into a ball after the addition of more water. If the *fura* is to be sold this large ball is formed into small flour-covered balls. Sour milk (*nono*) and/ or water is used in mixing the porridge, which is consumed cold and very liquid, as a drink; some people add sugar to taste. Ginger or other flavours may be added in cooking. *Fura* will keep for at least 3 days. See *Kunu*.

Fure – pl. *furanni*. Any flower, but more usually the tobacco flower (*furen taba*), which is used to clean or stain the teeth and which may be chewed with kola.

Furfura (*Hurhura*). The exchange of one thing for another. This term may be employed in connexion with the exchange of farms. See **Exchange**.

Gaba. A measure of length. Defined as a person's 'height' as measured by his full arm stretch, a *gaba* is usually thought of as equivalent to a fathom. Wells, cloth, etc. are measured in *gaba*, but not farm-boundaries.

Gabaruwa – pl. *gabari*. The Egyptian mimosa (q.v.)

Gabu. Cakes of dried, pounded (onion-tasting) onion-leaves, which store well.

Gado.

(i) Inherited property – *na gado* = hereditary. See **Inheritance**.

(ii) – pl. *gadaje*, a bed.

Galbaro. One of many words meaning wandering from place to place, perhaps in search of work.

Galla.

(i) Synonymous with *murgu*.

(ii) Money received as rent.

Galma (*Garma*) – pl. *galmuna*. The hoe known as the 'hand plough'. See **Farm-tools**.

Gamba (*Andropogon Gayanus*). A thick grass used for making *zana* mats, circular bands of conical thatches, hut enclosures, etc. It grows very rapidly in large tufts – hence, presumably, its very common use, in Batagarawa as elsewhere, as a farm-boundary plant.

Gambling – *caca*, and numerous other words for different types. Though proscribed by the Koran, gambling is very common and, as in other parts of the world, is often regarded as a regular occupation – a way of *earning* money. Five varieties of gambling with cowry shells are described by Fletcher (1912). Nowadays card-gambling is usual.

Gandu – pl. *gandaye*. The origin of this word of many meanings (for which see Chapter III, p. 38) is unclear, but Skinner (1968, p. 256) has suggested that it might be a loan-word from Songhai, *ganda/gando* being 'land, earth'.

For *gandu* in Batagarawa see Chapter III. This brief entry is concerned with (1) listing references to *gandu*, as a type of farming organization, in Nigerian Hausaland and (2) providing a brief summary of Nicolas' findings on *gandu* among the Hausa of the Niger Republic.

The main sources relating to Nigerian Hausa include: M. G. Smith (1955 and 1965) –

rural Zaria; Goddard (1969) – northern Sokoto villages; and Buntjer (1971) – rural Zaria. See, also, **Gulumbe**. Mortimore and Wilson (1965, p. 45) make brief reference to *gandu* in the Kano Close-Settled Zone. The two main authorities on the pagan Hausa, namely Greenberg (1946 and 1947) and Krusius (1915), pay much attention to *gandu* – both in Kano Emirate; and Reuke (1969), whose main interests lay in mission work, reports briefly on *gandu* among Maguzawa in southern Katsina Emirate. All writers on land tenure have ignored *gandu* and the considerable literature on Revenue Survey (q.v.) makes no reference to it. As with the Nupe, the community tax system (*haraji*) takes no cognizance of it: 'whereas the traditional productive unit among the Nupe peasants is embodied in the family, taxation takes into account only the individuals'; 'taxation thus ignores and even denies in its own powerful province the existence of the family unit' – Nadel (1942, pp. 164, 165).

In examining the function of *gandu* among the rural Hausa of Niger, a distinction must be made between the Maradi and Kantché areas – see Nicolas (NM, pp. 164–5, 167, 244; NK, pp. 24–5, 57). According to a private communication from Nicolas, the situation in Maradi is often such that the *gandu* is little more than a farm cultivated for the purposes of maintaining the wives and (to some small extent) the sons or brothers living in the same house as the *gandu* head; in Kantché, on the other hand, all members of the household are entitled to a share of millet (*gero*) from the *gandu* farm according to their needs, women receiving less than men. Thus, in Maradi women work for 3 or 4 days weekly on the *gandu* farm, while dependent men scarcely work there at all if they have large private farms; unlike the situation as reported among Muslim Hausa in Nigeria, the *gandu* head often has personal farms, the proceeds of which may be disposed of as he wishes – it is interesting that Krusius (1915, p. 301) also referred to the existence of such farms among the Maguzawa. In Kantché women often do little work on the *gandu* farms, concentrating most of their energy on their personal farms, but the sons are bound to work very regularly there; the sons receive temporary allocations of farms (*gamana*) for their private use; the *gandu* usually breaks on the father's death. See *Gayauna*, **Inheritance**.

Ganuwa.
(i) A wall of earth, or a rampart, such as formerly encircled many Hausa settlements, both towns (*gari*) and cities (*birni*).
(ii) A mound round a farm.

Gari – pl. *garurruka*. A town or compact village – see *Birni*. See Kirk-Greene (1969, p. 265).
Alkarya (pl. *alkaryai*) is defined by Abraham as 'any unwalled town', and (more specifically) by Bargery as 'the principal town of a district, where travellers have no difficulty in obtaining food'.
(a) In this book '*gari*' often refers to the densely-populated village of Batagarawa (which was formerly walled), exclusive of the dispersed farm-houses which are also in the Batagarawa Hamlet (*unguwa*).

Garka – pl. *garaka*. A fenced or hedged plot on which a crop (such as cassava or tobacco) is grown at times, other than the main farming-season, when animals may graze freely.

Garwa – pl. *garewani*. The standard 4 gallon kerosene tin, which is so useful for storage of liquids such as groundnut oil.

Gata. Sustenance, support – e.g. *uba gatan dansa* = 'a father is the support of his son'. *Dan gata* = son of rich parents.

Gauda. A bean food wrapped in *kargo* (q.v.) leaves and boiled.

Gauta (*Solanum incanum*). According to Dalziel, *gauta* is sometimes synonymous with *data* (q.v.), while at other times referring to the white 'garden egg'.

Gawo. The useful tree, *Acacia albida*, which is found in inhabited areas.

(a) Following a Native Authority campaign (of perhaps some 20 years ago) many of these useful trees were planted on the farmlands of Batagarawa, and in 1970 a sample count indicated that there were about 270 trees in the manured zone.

(b) The tree has the peculiarity of being leafless during the rains and of producing leaves and long pods towards the end of the dry season, both of which provide a most useful fodder for livestock at the time of maximum scarcity – to the extent that, in part of Senegal, Pelissier (1966, p. 252) regarded the tree and the cattle as having achieved a real symbiosis. It acts as a 'nutrient pump' which much encourages the growth of grains and groundnuts. The leaves, which are shed at the onset of the dry season, provide a useful manure for the crops which flourish beneath the leafless tree. The tree is sometimes known as *butulu* – 'the ungrateful one'. See also Luning (1963a, p. 37), Morgan and Pugh (1969, p. 95).

Gayauna – pl. *gayauni*; the word has several variants, including *gamana*.

A private farm belonging to a dependent member of a *gandu* group (including slaves in former times), the owner being free to work there on his off-days and in the evenings and to dispose of the proceeds as he (she) wishes. In strict parlance (at least in former times) a *gayauna* is a farm allotted, perhaps temporarily, by the *gandu* head to a dependant; as nowadays sons-in-*gandu* often buy or otherwise acquire farms for themselves, it is often impossible to sustain any distinction between their various private farms, especially as fathers often secretly sell farms to their sons.

(a) See Chapter III, especially pp. 45 and 51. Nowadays, no *gayauni* are owned by women.

(b) In some parts of rural Niger (see **Gandu**) many *gayauni* are owned by married women, having been given to them by their husbands. In some areas, including parts of Sokoto, private farms are known as *kurga* (q.v.).

Gayya. 'Collecting together of a number of people to assist another in some piece of work' – Bargery.

(a) Nowadays an elusive word, used somewhat interchangeably with *taimako*, *gayya* signifies collective farmwork performed for cash remuneration lower than the prevailing wage-rate (see *Kwadago*), for reasons of obligation, friendship, pity, enjoyment, etc. Formerly common, and at times compulsory, *gayya* is nowadays unimportant in relation to *kwadago* and always voluntary: thus, 18 labourers who worked 886 days of *kwadago* during 3 months in 1968 performed only 63 days of *gayya* during that period, although *gayya* was considered unusually common that year owing to the low price of grain. The *masu-sarauta* and certain other prominent men still 'call *gayya*' on occasions (usually single days) when a large team is required, and plough-owners are called on to render communal assistance to the District Head, but there is no obligation on anyone to attend and the reward in the form of cash, food, kola (and even tobacco) might happen to exceed the *kwadago* wage. The practice whereby a suitor endeavoured to impress his prospective wife's father by assembling many friends (and perhaps a drummer) to work on his farms is dying out, as is the obligation of married men to work for some days each year on their wife's father's farms. Insofar as reciprocal obligations are generated by *gayya*, a father will usually send a son in his stead – the *gayya* labour-force essentially consisting of young men. *Gayya* is still sometimes performed to assist old or ill men who are in need. *Biki* (q.v.) may take the form of *gayya*.

(b) Although all recent investigators have regarded *gayya*, which takes the form of farmwork, as of declining importance, it is possibly still common in some localities – e.g. in Koko (Gwandu Emirate) where the present writer was informed that *gayya* was usual for the last hoeing and for groundnut harvesting; in Gulumbe (q.v.); and in the Kantché area of the Niger Republic (see NK, pp. 137, 260, 265 and NK2, pp. 20 ff.), where it is sometimes the practice for non-attenders to send a small gift. (However, *gayya* is generally unimportant in the Maradi area.)

In Kantché (as in Batagarawa) *gayya* does not necessarily take the form of farmwork, but may be for building, roadwork, or other heavy work for which a large team is required.

See **Barau, Alhaji.**

Gero. Bulrush millet (*Pennisetum*). There are several varieties of *Pennisetum* in Hausaland – see Bargery and Dalziel; this entry relates to *gero* (early millet) only – see also *Maiwa* (late millet).

Although the botanical reference books often suggest that the peculiarly drought-resistant *gero* (which matures in about 90 days) and the later-maturing (less drought-resistant) sorghums (see *Dawa*) are to a high degree alternative crops – *gero* being cultivated further north than sorghum – in northern Katsina, as well as in Maradi further north, the two grains together form the staple diet. Individual farmers have a common preference for growing both crops (maybe interplanted), perhaps mainly as an insurance against drought, which (according to date) may affect one grain more than the other. The FAO *Report* (1966, p. 178) regards *gero* as a crop of the 'marginal lands', where it is 'a question not of economics but of survival'. The yield potential of *gero* was considered to be so low that (quite unbelievably) it was recommended that, in the long run of at least 25 years, 'the northernmost part of the present cereal belt [which, presumably, includes most of Katsina Emirate] should revert mainly to pasture' (*ibid.*, p. 178), the inhabitants being persuaded to migrate hundreds of miles south to the 'middle belt'!

Whether or not *gero* is the first crop to be sown, it is always the first to be harvested. The resemblance of the head, or spike, to the common bulrush accounts for its English name. The leaves are a valuable fodder and the stalks have many uses.

(a) Considering that *gero* is always stated to be far less responsive to manuring than sorghum, it is a curious fact that virtually the whole crop is grown on manured farmland – *maiwa* being grown on bush-farms. Nearly all farmers, except some of the very poorest, produce some *gero* – richer farmers growing much more than poorer (Table v.5, p. 77). The crop is often interplanted with cowpeas, which spread over the farm after the millet is harvested. In 1967 (when the harvest was considered 'good'), the total production of *gero* by Batagarawa farmers (excluding the *masu-sarauta*) may have been very roughly of the order of 6,000 to 7,000 bundles which, on the rather arbitrary assumption that the average bundle yields 35 lbs of threshed grain (see *Dami*), would have corresponded to some 230,000 lbs of grain – i.e. about ½ lb daily for the Batagarawa population (see **Dawa** and p. 196 above). It is said that *gero* can be satisfactorily stored for periods of up to 8 years or more, though with gradual deterioration in quality. See Chapter IX on seasonal price fluctuations.

(b) Official estimates for the northern states as a whole indicate that millet and sorghum are produced in roughly equal quantities; but reliable published information relating to the relative importance of the two grains in different localities is very scanty. Nicolas (in numerous publications) is the authority for the assertion that the two grains together form the staple diet in the Maradi area.

See *Binne, Fura,* Granary, Harvest-dates, *Kara, Shuka, Shura.*

Gida – pl. *gidaje.* A house, or compound. A rural *gida* often consists of a clay-walled or fenced, open, rectangular living area, within which the various rooms and/or thatched huts comprising the whole habitation are set – and where small livestock roam at all times in the farming-season. The head of the house is the *mai gida* (lit. 'house-owner') and his senior wife is *uwar gida* (lit. 'mother of the house'). The open compound, in which the secluded women spend nearly all their waking time, unless it is raining, is usually approached by a *zaure* (the man's entrance-hut) and sometimes by another room (or series of rooms) designed to ensure the privacy of the women. The women's sleeping-huts (*daki*), in which they keep all their possessions, are scattered about and there is often a shack or shelter (*dakin girki*) which serves as a kitchen when it rains, cooking usually being done out of doors. If a married son of the *mai gida* lives in the house, he may live in a separately fenced-off section (*shiyya*, q.v.).

(a) See Chapter II, pp. 17–19 and Tables II.6 and II.7, pp. 34 and 35 for statistics relative to houses and house-sections in Batagarawa. In the *gari* nearly all houses have clay walls (*katanga*), but most of the dispersed houses have cornstalk fences (*darni*). Many houses in the *gari* have wells and nearly all of them have interior pit-latrines (*salga*). Most granaries are inside compounds. In Batagarawa hardly any husbands, other than *masu-sarauta*, have interior rooms or huts (*turaka*) of their own.

Houses and house-sections are commonly bought and sold. In 1970 particulars of 18 recent transactions were reported, of which 6 had involved sale on migration, 2 sale on death; in 5 cases the seller did not live in the house he sold. In 10 cases the price was £5 or less (in 4 cases £2 10s. or less); in 4 cases the price was £7, in one (quite exceptional) case it was as high as £45. The sale of 13 house-plots for building was also reported – in 10 cases the price ranged between £1 and £2 5s. (see *Shaidi*).

(b) See Mary Smith (1954) or Smith (1955, p. 17) for diagrams of houses in rural Zaria. As M. G. Smith notes in his introduction to the latter: 'Despite the great variation between Hausa compounds, they follow a basic pattern, elaborations of which merely indicate differences of wealth and status of the household head, or structure of the domestic group' (p. 23). See Nicolas (NM, pp. 143–4) on habitations in the Niger Republic.

See **Building, Inheritance,** *Soro.*

Giginya – pl. *giginyoyi*, deleb-palm (*Borassus aethiopum*). The fronds (*kari*) are used for thatches, panniers, mats, hats, etc. See Dalziel for much information on the uses of other parts of the palm, including the fruit. The germinating radicle may be eaten boiled (*muruci*), and is said to have been very useful in famines. Barth took a great interest in the geographical distribution of the palm in West Africa – see, e.g. vol. II, p. 427.

Ginger – *cittar aho* (*Zingiber officinale*). Much used for flavouring and medicinal purposes. It is produced in certain areas of northern Nigeria, mainly in Zaria, and is an export crop.

Girma. Having the literal meaning of 'bigness', this word is employed in many connexions in reference to prestige (status) as well as to superiority by virtue of age. See Abraham. See *Daraja, Karda.*

Giya. Beer brewed from any grain – *fito* being made from guinea corn. Subject to the Muslim taboo on alcohol. In Maguzawa areas women may derive a large income from selling beer they have brewed.

Goats: see **Sheep and goats.**

Gona – pl. *gonaki.* A farm (individual plot) or field. All the farms (*gonaki*) cultivated by an individual farmer comprise his farm-holding; *gonar daji* = bush-farm (q.v.). See *Fage,* **Farm-area, Farm-holding,** *Garka, Noma.*

Goro – pl. *gwarra.* Kola-nut (see **Kola**). The word '*goro*' has many meanings associated with the ceremonial uses of the nut and its exchange as a gift: it is often used to mean something extra offered as thanks, or for ingratiatory purposes.

Goruba – pl. *gorubai*, (*Hyphaene thebaica*) the dum-palm or ginger-bread palm. See *Kaba* for the uses of dum-palm fronds. The stems are used as hut posts, rafters, door frames etc., where *Borassus* is unobtainable. See Dalziel for other uses. When travelling near Tessaoua (Tasawa), Barth saw a long troop of men head-loading baskets filled with dum-palm fruit, 'which seasons many dishes very pleasantly' (vol. II, p. 13).

Gourds. Numerous types, based on use, include: *kwarya* (the ordinary calabash); *masaki* (a very large calabash used at market, and for separating grain from husk); *koko* (a small calabash, a cup); *kololo* (a variety of bottle gourd and a ladle made from it); *buta* or *gora* (a water-bottle gourd). 'The names of the various gourd fruits...are often confused in the literature' – Dalziel (p. 57). See *Duma, Kabewa*.

Grain: see *Dawa, Gero, Hatsi, Maiwa*.

Grain requirements. It is commonly stated, though on what foundation is unclear, that a mixed population (of men, women and children) in Northern Nigeria requires about 1 lb of unthreshed grain per head per day – an adult man about 2 lbs. According to the FAO *Report* (1966, p. 392) grain consumption (after allowing for seed requirements) in Northern Nigeria was (on the basis of an assumed population of 30 m.) 174 kilo of guinea corn and millet together (roughly equal quantities of each) – or about 1 lb per head per day, equivalent (*ibid.*, p. 395) to about 1,600 calories per day. (The figure would clearly be higher in Hausaland where grains provide the bulk of calories, as they do not in certain southern areas of Northern Nigeria where yams are the basic foodstuff.) But some experts have put requirements very much higher - e.g. Nicolas (1968a, p. 47) who works on the basis of 1 kilo per head (of mixed population) per day, and Dr I. G. Thomson, Senior Medical Officer in Kano, cited by McDonnell (1964, p. 365, fn. 31), who concluded, following research on local diets, that requirements were 750 lbs annually. According to Clark and Haswell (1964, p. 61), *minimum* grain requirements for 'small-bodied people in a hot climate' are 230 kg 'wheat equivalent per head per year'.

If actual *consumption* is of the order of 1 lb per head (of mixed population) per day, and if the high degree of extreme poverty in Batagarawa is nothing exceptional, it is obvious that *requirements* are far higher than 1 lb – and this irrespective of the crying need for forage. It is, therefore, impossible to accept the following statement (which has met a dangerous degree of acceptance) that consumption is 'already very high': 'In Northern Nigeria consumption of cereals is already very high (estimated at 412 lbs or 136 kg per caput) and it is not expected that there will be much increase as incomes rise' FAO *Report* (*ibid.*, p. 21). Why, if everyone is eating sufficient, is the FAO *Report* so much concerned about low grain yields per acre?

Granary – *rumbu*, pl. *rumbuna*, the usual word for any form of outdoor granary, whether of clay, wicker or grass work; *rufewa*, pl. *rufeyi*, a clay granary (*rumbun kasa*); *kudandami*, also a clay type, often very large with a small circular opening. There are other Hausa words for particular types – see Bargery. It is to be noted that, irrespective of whether produce other than grain is stored in the bin, all 'granary type' structures are here denoted as 'granaries'.

(a) See Tables 11.8–10 and IV.6, pp. 35–6 and 68, on granary ownership. As many as 571 granaries were counted in Batagarawa, 445 of them owned by heads of farming-units, 108 by men-in-*gandu*, 13 by the *masu-sarauta* (most of whose storage is done outside Batagarawa) and only 5 by women – who nowadays own hardly any corn-bins, not even the small indoor types for threshed grain (*rahoniya*, q.v.), which were formerly common. (See (b) below.) Most of these containers are made, by builders, of sunbaked earth; others are constructed of cornstalk, *zana* etc.; all are thatched. (See Plates 6 to 8.) Mainly used for storing bundles (*dami*) of grain and unshelled groundnuts (Tables 11.9 and 11.10, p. 36), some of them contain cowpeas, tobacco or fodder; although produce, other than groundnuts and cowpeas, is commonly mixed, many farmers have separate guinea corn and millet granaries. While granaries are usually regarded as strictly private places to which no one save the owner has access, sons (and occasionally wives) sometimes have access to *gandu* granaries: it is almost unnecessary to add that no one is prepared to reveal the quantity of produce stored – see pp. 162 and 163. Raised off the ground on stones, the clay bins are dry and airy containers in which sun-dried bundles of grain may be satisfactorily stored for years, especially if there is a small expenditure on insecticides. Despite overcrowding, most granaries in the *gari* are situated inside compounds – but some farmers own, or use, granaries elsewhere and grain-traders ('*yan kwarami*) often ask their outside suppliers to store on their behalf. The bins are of variable capacity, ranging from about 30 to 100 bundles of grain, the price (including the thatch) ranging from about 25s. upwards for the cornstalk type, with clay types costing more. Nowadays threshed grain (*tsaba*) and shelled groundnuts are always stored indoors, usually in sacks.

(b) Considering that most grain for consumption in Hausaland generally (though see *Soro*) is stored for several months (at least) in farmers' granaries, the paucity of recent descriptive literature, either scientific or aesthetic, is astounding. But the earliest explorers were not so neglectful, Clapperton having written as follows when travelling in the neighbourhood of Sokoto:

> Their granaries are made in the form of a large urn or pitcher, raised from the ground about three feet by stones. They are made of clay and chopped straw, and are raised to the height of eleven or twelve feet. The thickness of the sides is not above four inches, though in any part it will bear a man's weight: the diameter in the widest part may be from seven to eight feet, at the top about three or four feet, and is overlapped at the mouth like a wide-mouthed earthen jar. When the grain is put in, a conical cap of thatch is put over to keep out birds, insects, wet and moisture. The doura [*dauro*] amd millet will keep well in these jars for two or three years; after that period it perishes, and is destroyed by worms and insects. The jar itself will last seven or eight years, if taken care of, by matting round the lower part with straw during the rainy season; if not, two or three years is the period it will stand unimpaired.   Clapperton (1829, p. 217)

Barth also was appreciative of granaries, noting (vol. IV, p. 29) that the 'architecture' of the corn-stacks imparted 'so decided a character of peace and repose to the villages of Hausa', such as is 'sought for in vain in the whole of Bornu' – where grain is still often stored under-ground.

Clay granaries are large pots or urns and the distinguished potter, Michael Cardew, has written lyrically (1960) of Gobir granaries, quoting Clapperton's description as still accurate. These granaries are made in the form of a large urn and, nowadays, are raised to a height of about 16 feet, their widest girth being over 55 feet, while the walls are nowhere thicker than $3\frac{1}{2}$ inches. 'The skill of these builders must compel admiration...; they model a perfect dome entirely by eye and hand, unaided by any form of gauge' (p. 223). A large granary will hold more than 300 bundles, equivalent to about 8 to 10 tons. (But not all the urns in Gobir villages are granaries – some are the domed dwellings known as *kudandan*.)

> During the long dry season, a traveller in the Northern Region can hardly fail to notice the corn-bins and granaries in every village. In the rains they will be covered with thatch, but at this season they stand naked, like huge unfired pots; and the shapes vary with each district. In some places they form the core or centre of the house, surrounded by the living-space of the family; elsewhere they stand separate from the house itself. They are a feature of the landscape everywhere, but they reach their most imposing dimensions in the fertile corn-growing districts of the far north. From about Gusau northwards they gradu-ally become larger and more numerous, until in Gobir, north of Sokoto, they dominate every village. From a little distance, the whole village looks rather as if some gargantuan potter had been assembling his work ready for the oven.   (*ibid.*, p. 216)

A brief survey of Northern Nigerian granaries was made by Giles (1964) who provides a rough sketch map of the geographical distribution of the 'dried earth' and 'plant material' types; his experiments showed that unthreshed sorghum suffered a mean weight loss of 8% when stored for 9 months, and he reported that this grain may be stored for as long as 6 years.

Postscript. An interesting short article by L. M. Bungudu, on granary-storage of grains and cowpeas has recently appeared. (*Samaru Agricultural Newsletter*, 1970, Vol. 12, No. 1, Zaria.)

Grinding mill.

(a) There is one mechanical grinding mill in Batagarawa, owned by a merchant in Katsina city, who employs a young farmer (with an assistant) to operate it. In 1966 it was out-of-order (through neglect in use), but in 1967, after a long interval, it had been repaired. The charge for grinding a *tiya* of grain or groundnuts was 3*d*. – this compared with 2*d*. a *tiya* for women who pound and grind for payment (*aikatau*).

(b) In rural areas generally grinding mills appear to be far less common than in some southern West African regions, though hand food processing methods are even more arduous.

Grindstone – *dustan washi*; lower grindstone, *dustan nika* or *maredi*; upper grindstone, *dam maredi*.

(a) Wives usually own their own grindstones (which they may originally bring with them on marriage) and some households own a considerable number, owing to the practice of reserving certain of them for special uses, such as the processing of groundnut oil.

Some 50 or more men come to Batagarawa in the dry season from Mani (about 20 miles east) either to make grindstones from a small outcrop of suitable rock which has been recently discovered, or to act as itinerant grindstone traders – a few Batagarawa men also act as traders, though none are makers. Techniques are fast improving and an active man can make some 5 stones a day worth about 2*s*. 6*d*. each – the corresponding price in market-places may be 5*s*. Only 4 stones can be carried by a donkey.

(b) As there are few mechanical grinding mills in rural Hausaland and as guinea corn for *tuwo* should always be ground (after pounding), many millions of grindstones must be in use.

See also **Grinding mill,** *Nikau*.

Groundnuts – *gyada*; there are numerous other words for different varieties, see Bargery and Dalziel (*Arachis hypogaea*). The first section of this entry relates to a statistical estimate of groundnut acreage and production in Batagarawa.

(a) As groundnuts are sold at intervals over a long period following harvest, and are stored in shell, the ordinary farmer is usually ignorant of the annual quantity of shelled nuts he produces. Even had the total quantity sold for export by Batagarawa farmers (through the Marketing Board's licensed buying agents) been known – as it was not – this would have been a poor indication of total production, owing to sales for local consumption, mainly for making groundnut oil. It was, therefore, necessary to resort to assessing production on the basis of groundnut acreage.

In 1968 M. S. Nuhu arranged for a sample of over 300 mapped farms (corresponding to about two-thirds of the total acreage) to be inspected after harvest to determine the number of farms which had been planted with groundnuts, with or without interplanting; rough estimates of the proportion of the farm area which had been under groundnuts were made in those cases where other crops had been planted on part of the farm. In cases of interplanting, the acreage under groundnuts was arbitrarily set at two-thirds of the total farm acreage. Assuming that the farmers for whom estimates were made were representative of those in their economic-group, the following estimates (Table C.9) of total acreages under groundnuts were made.

Women farmers were estimated as having only 24 acres under groundnuts. Allowing for the acreage farmed by the *masu-sarauta* and by other farmers not included in the list of 171 farming-units, the total mapped acreage under groundnuts (or, rather, 'acreage equivalent', owing to the allowance made for interplanting) was estimated at some 500.

If average yields per acre were of the order of $\frac{1}{4}$ ton of shelled nuts, and if prices were arbitrarily put at £25 per ton, the value of production (from manured farmland) might have been of the order of £3,000 – no deduction having been made for seed. As farmers insist that the bulk of production comes from manured farmland (the sandy soil of which is more suitable than the harder soil of bush-farms), the total value of groundnut production on all farms in 1968 is unlikely to have exceeded (say) £4,000 (the gross value of 160 tons) – or (say) £3 per head of the population.

TABLE C.9. *Estimated groundnut acreage per farming-unit, Batagarawa*

Economic-group	Heads of farming-units	Men-in-*gandu*	Total	Average acreage per farming-unit
1	118	30	148	8·7
2	136	13	149	3·3
3	90	15	105	1·5
4	40	4	44	1·1
Total	384	62	446	2·6

The discrepancy between the higher and lower economic-groups in the *net value* of ground-nuts produced is very much greater than is suggested by the statistics relating to average groundnut acreage, for the following main reasons: (1) yields per acre are higher on the better manured, and better cultivated, farms of the richer farmers; (2) poorer farmers (see below) seldom store seed, being obliged to borrow or buy it when prices are highest; (3) richer farmers are in a position to plan their selling in order to take advantage of seasonal price fluctuations, whereas poorer farmers are often obliged to sell their crop, unshelled, during the period of low prices before the opening of the official buying season.

If the average farming-unit consumed as little as one beer bottle of groundnut oil (q.v.) per week, then over 20 tons of nuts would be required for oil annually, on the basis of 6 lbs of shelled nuts per bottle. Seed-nuts (plus nuts which deteriorate in storage) might account for 10% of production (16 tons). It is possible, when account is taken of other local selling, that Batagarawa produces less than 100 tons of nuts for export. (See p. 196 above.)

The following table, C.10, shows that about a fifth of all the sampled farmers produced no groundnuts on mapped farmland – very nearly all of them were in Groups 3 and 4; it also suggests that about half of all farmers (sons-in-*gandu* being included with their fathers) had between 1 and 4 acres under groundnuts. (In reading this Table it must again be remembered that net value of production shows much more variation than acreage.)

TABLE C.10. *Size–distribution of groundnut acreage by farming-unit, Batagarawa*

Average range	(Heads of farming-units and men-in-*gandu*) Economic-group				Total	%
	1	2	3	4		
Nil	—	2	16	10	28	22
under 1	—	2	5	7	14	11
1–1·9	—	5	16	10	31	24
2–3·9	3	14	12	5	34	26
4–9·9	7	11	2	—	20	15
10 and over	2	—	—	—	2	2
Total	12	34	51	32	129	100

According to this enquiry, groundnuts were grown in a pure stand on about 28% of the farms; interplanting with guinea corn was about twice as common as interplanting with millet (*gero*).

Most groundnuts are stored (unshelled) in granaries; it was, however, reported that unshelled nuts may be safely stored in big piles covered with earth, for as long as 3 years – though they are usually stored for no more than 1½ years. According to an enquiry made in April 1969 (Table 11.10, p. 36), heads of farming-units and men-in-*gandu* respectively owned 50 and 7 granaries in which groundnuts were being stored – in about one-third of these cases other crops, also, were stored in the granary.

(b) Groundnuts have long been an important crop in Hausaland. There are many references to this crop in Barth (e.g. vol. II, pp. 432–3): in reporting on his journey between Kukawa and Zinder, he asserted that groundnuts and beans constituted 'a large proportion of the food of the inhabitants' (vol. IV, p. 29). Staudinger (1889, p. 631) regarded groundnuts as the most important crop after grains. Baba of Karo – Mary Smith (1954) – had early recollections of groundnuts being grown by slaves. Certainly, there is no evidence for the common belief that groundnuts were formerly merely a 'women's crop' – there would hardly have been a pre-colonial tax on groundnuts in Katsina Emirate (and elsewhere) had this been the case.

The colonial administration was early aware of the possibilities. In 1907 it was reported that groundnuts were produced throughout Northern Nigeria 'and could be grown for export in immense quantities' (*Colonial Reports, Annual*, Cmd 3729); but this was not possible until the completion of the railway link to Kano in 1911. According to Hogendorn's graphic account of the origins of the trade (1966 and the brief summary of 1970), 6,000 tons of nuts were exported from Kano from the 1912 crop – presumably, mainly at the expense of local consumption. After the chaos and suffering which resulted from the severe famine of 1914 (*Malali*), exports from Kano (according to Hogendorn) settled down at around 40,000 tons a year until 1921. If 2 million people had been living within easy reach of Kano at that time, and if (before the growth of exports) average consumption of groundnuts had been as low as 2 lbs per head per week, local consumption would have absorbed about 100,000 tons of nuts – see **Groundnut oil.**

The great expansion in exports did not occur until the mid-twenties. Total Nigerian exports in 1925–9 averaged 117,000 tons annually, rising to 189,000 tons in 1930–4 and 211,000 tons in 1935–9. Thereafter, owing to the development of exports of factory-made groundnut oil, it is necessary to refer to total purchases (not exports) of nuts by the Marketing Board. Such purchases rose from 426,000 tons in 1951–2 to 872,000 tons in 1962–3 to a maximum of 1,026,000 tons (purchases from the Northern States) in 1966–7. Though the trend is upwards, there is much annual variation, and purchases for export from the northern states were much below the maximum in the following three seasons: viz. 679,000 tons, 764,000 tons and 634,000 tons (provisional figure for 1969–70). Kano State accounts for about half the total.

The development of groundnut exporting has been dealt with in many publications, e.g. Helleiner (1966), Middleton (1924). Here it is appropriate to draw attention, under several headings, to the extraordinary paucity of information on production, storage and marketing at the local level. Almost any general statement, such as that groundnut production often suffers from late planting – FAO *Report* (1966, p. 163) – is necessarily guesswork – see (3) below: it is indeed the case that 'little information appears to be available on the economics of groundnut production in Northern Nigeria' (*ibid.*, p. 165).

(1) *Seed storage*

'Peasant producers in Nigeria...do not individually employ significant quantities of domestic intermediate inputs. Seeds are usually self-furnished' – Helleiner (1966, p. 145). This is incorrect in its application to groundnuts, the evidence being that in Hausaland generally (as in Batagarawa) poorer farmers make no attempt to store groundnut seed after harvest, but obtain it at planting time (when prices have risen) by purchase, on credit (possibly involving a lien on crop), or by gift. Information obtained by a questionnaire circulated by the Agricultural Department in 1944 (National Archives, Kaduna, 4206), suggested that the proportion of farmers who sold all their seed was everywhere high. In Kano:

> Many middlemen and even some of the richer farmers buy the groundnuts at harvest time and store with the set purpose of disposal as seed at planting time. The seed merchants may sell the seed for cash down, sell on credit with a view to repayment in cash or kind at harvest time, or alternatively provide seed against a mortgage on the crop produced...The exchange of other crops for groundnut seed is exceptional.

Similar results were obtained by K. D. S. Baldwin in an enquiry conducted for the Agricultural Department in 1957. Enquiries in Gulumbe (q.v.) in 1966 suggested that only about a third of all farmers stored groundnut seed.

(2) Leisure

'The expansion of [groundnut] acreage...was achieved, as elsewhere in Nigeria, through the foregoing of more and more leisure by more and more peasants in response to improved prices for work' Helleiner (*ibid.*, p. 112). For this general assertion there is no evidence whatsoever, which is not to say that it is everywhere necessarily false. Insofar as part of the expansion was accounted for by migrant farmers, it might be that yields per man-day increased. Farmers may increase their groundnut production with the intention of buying grain with the proceeds – which grain may be 'imported' from areas where few groundnuts are grown. Besides, according to Helleiner's own figures (Table 11–B–4), both real and money 'producer prices' were lower in 1961–4 than in 1952–6, although exports were higher.

(3) The question of late planting

It is generally believed that: (i) groundnut yields would be greater if seed were planted earlier; (ii) that it is because the farmer 'gives first priority to his food crops' – FAO *Report* (1966, p. 163) – that groundnuts are planted 'too late'; and that (iii) labour shortage at grain planting time accounts for the delay. On (i), *Strategies and Recommendations for Nigerian Rural Development 1969/1985*, a report to the Federal Ministry of Economic Development made by the Consortium for the Study of Nigerian Rural Development (CSNRD) in 1969, states (p. 89) that research at Samaru (about which no further details are given) indicates that early planting of groundnuts in June would increase yields by 20–25%. On (iii), the same report (p. 91) regards one of the three major constraints on groundnut production as 'labour shortage in the planting season which results in groundnuts being planted after food crops'; and the FAO *Report* (p. 163) notes the 'farmer's inability to prepare and plant a larger area in time'. But these assertions (*taken together*) are most puzzling for the following reasons: firstly meteorological statistics make it clear that in most years, in most areas, grains are sown earlier than June; secondly, in the chief groundnut areas of Kano and Katsina, the bulk of the crop is probably grown on manured farmland which requires no clearing before sowing; thirdly, the present writer's evidence is that most grain sowing is completed instantly, within 2 or 3 days of the planting rains, hardly any labourers being employed (such larger farmers as are apprehensive lest their sowing will not be achieved immediately, tend to resort to *binne* – sowing in anticipation of the rains); fourthly, no evidence is ever presented of substantial groundnut planting in Kano and Katsina after June; fifthly, by postponing groundnut sowing, whether to June or July, farmers would usually be increasing the demand for labour at a peak period, weeding having then started – see Norman (1969). That labour shortage is not the crucial factor is suggested by the fact that in Batagarawa in 1967, when the first rains came as late as 15 June, groundnuts and grains were planted simultaneously, as they had not been in

1966 when the rains came in April. One reason for delaying the sowing of groundnuts, when the rains come early, is the greater risk of drought, and thus of seed-loss, than when rains come late – seed cost being much higher for groundnuts than grains.

(4) *Marketing for export*

Despite the great interest that is taken by many economists all over the world in the general operation of the West African Marketing Boards, the lack of systematic research on purchase of groundnuts for export at the local level is astounding. The rise in the price paid by licensed buying agents as the season progresses (see Chapter IX) is an interesting, neglected phenomenon – related as it is, to the neglected question of local consumption of groundnut oil (q.v.). See Bauer (1954, pp. 235 ff.) on competition between buying agents as a cause of 'above minimum' producer-prices.

Nicolas has presented much interesting material on groundnut production, trading and export in the Niger Republic. In the Maradi area he estimated (1968a, p. 50) that a quarter of 'farming-units' derived more than a third of their farming income from groundnuts, taxation being conventionally paid from the proceeds. Although, since independence, groundnut buying for export has become increasingly regulated by the government, there is (of necessity) a flourishing pre-buying-season 'market' in groundnuts, when seasonal poverty is greatest (see NK, pp. 198 ff.); the official buying season (*traite*) is shorter than in Nigeria.

See *Malali*, **Marketing Board, Proclamation on farm produce.**

Groundnut decorticators.

(a) Always known as *sarkin aiki* (i.e. 'chief of work' or 'the best of workers'), the hand-operated machine for decorticating (shelling) groundnuts is capable of handling as many as 40 sacks (bags) of unshelled nuts per day, say 1½ tons. In Batagarawa *gari* in 1967 there were about 15 machines in good working order, all of them owned by better-off farmers. Priced at about £14 and now manufactured in Nigeria, new machines were obtainable only through the local authority, which granted interest-free loans, nominally of 3-months duration, though many remain outstanding for years. The Marketing Board, which is concerned about nut breakage (and which buys shelled nuts only), organized repair of the machines in Katsina city – £1 for a new handle with cracking points.

The machines were constantly hired out by their owners, the standard charge being 6*d.* a sack of unshelled nuts. Men hired to operate the machine also received 6*d.* a sack. Women winnowers (they were hired by the nut-owner, not the hired operator) received 4*d.* a sack – if there were a strong wind a woman's daily output might have been 7 to 8 sacks (a daily wage of 2*s.* 4*d.* to 2*s.* 8*d.*); if wives of the nut-owners did the work they received only 3*d.* a sack. (At a groundnut decorticating 'factory' near Katsina city in 1967, men operating the *sarkin aiki* were paid 6*d.* per sack of *shelled* nuts, women 9*d.* per sack for winnowing and picking out bits of shell; a team of 2 men and 3 women working for 10 to 12 hours a day would together have earned as little as 12*s.* 6*d.*) The payment for pounding a sack of unshelled nuts in a mortar was 1*s.*; as many nuts break when pounded, seed nuts are always shelled by hand. Sons-in-*gandu* are not paid for shelling nuts but may receive *goro* (q.v.). '*Yan kwarami* commonly find it profitable to buy unshelled nuts and to get them shelled by the *sarkin aiki* before resale.

(b) In 1967 it was officially declared that most decorticating machines were 'worn out and in need of repair': the government decided that 18,000 machines should be supplied to farmers at subsidized prices in the 3 seasons 1967 to 1970, and 2,000 annually thereafter. (*White Paper* on the Government's policy regarding the Northern Nigeria Marketing Board, Government Printer, Kaduna, 1967.)

According to Anthony and Johnston (1968, p. 60) the *sarkin aiki* is capable of shelling 300 lbs of nuts an hour, compared with 80 lbs an hour for a woman at a mortar: they encountered one farmer in Katsina Emirate who owned 8 machines for hiring. In the Niger Republic, as well as in Nigeria, a large proportion of nuts for export is decorticated with the aid of the machine, which is there distributed by official agencies – Nicolas (NK, p. 206).

Groundnut oil – *man gyada*. This entry relates only to local production of groundnut oil, not to production for export.

(a) In Batagarawa, where groundnut oil is the sole edible oil available, about 75 secluded women produce *and* sell this oil (no one produces for 'own consumption' only) and a few others buy from these producers (and also from others in neighbouring hamlets) for resale from their houses. About a third of all women in Groups 1 and 2 are in this business, the corresponding proportions for Groups 3 and 4 being only 14% and 6% respectively. Assistants are sometimes employed in the extremely arduous production process which is briefly as follows: the groundnuts are first pounded (or sometimes mechanically milled); the resulting mass is then placed in a mortar, hot water being gradually added while further pounding and stirring (with a pestle) is proceeding; the oil begins to separate; when a certain stage is reached the mass is removed to a special hollowed grindstone and kneaded at an angle, the oil flowing into a bowl; when much of the oil has been extracted the mass is formed into small balls (*kulikuli*) which are boiled in the extracted oil for about 15 minutes.

The producers are very well aware of the possibilities of profit arising from seasonal price fluctuations: one woman was known to have bought 10 sacks of groundnuts (three-quarters of a ton) at harvest for storage; some buy oil at harvest and store it in kerosene tins – it is said that it will keep for up to 6 months, by which time the price may have doubled. Perhaps a dozen or more of the better-off producers store part of their groundnut requirements. Wives often buy groundnuts from their husbands, the latter not quarrelling with statements that they charge something near the market price. Using the *kudin cefane* a wife may buy oil from herself. Groundnuts for oil may be bought on short-term credit.

In May 1967 when the Batagarawa groundnut price was 15*s*. per *bokiti* of 43 lbs (£39 per ton) or 2*s*. per *tiya* (£46 per ton), a woman who processed a *bokiti* could make a profit of roughly 7*s*., if the yield were as high as 20 cigarette tins (selling at 9*d*.), which was equivalent to about 6½ beer bottles (each at 2*s*. 3*d*.), the value of the *kulikuli* being 7*s*. (The oil is normally measured in beer bottles or cigarette tins.)

Many households are too poor to buy groundnut oil, especially when prices are high, and no palm oil or shea butter is 'imported' into Batagarawa. (However, bought 'snacks' which are consumed by poorer people are often fried in oil.) In Batagarawa local consumption of groundnuts consists almost entirely of groundnut oil and its by-product *kulikuli* (or *guru*); groundnuts are not used in stews and do not form the basis of cooked snacks (*marmari*); there is, however, a small consumption of 'roasted' nuts, especially by children. There is, therefore, so far as this village is concerned, no truth in Helleiner's statement (1966, p. 108) that about one-third of Nigeria's groundnut output is eaten locally as the nut 'can be consumed without further processing'.

(b) See Abraham (p. 654) on different types of groundnut oil. As local oil production accounts for a large part of the difference between total production and total exports of groundnuts, and as no endeavour has ever been made to measure oil production, it is indeed true that 'there are no firm figures for total production of groundnuts' – FAO *Report* (1966, p. 161) – one person's guess being as good as another's. The FAO *Report* estimated 'domestic consumption' at 197,000 long tons annually in 1962, when exports were 673,000 long tons, their forward projections for 1980 having been 375,000 and 1,000,000 tons respectively. Deducting 70,000 tons for seed, it may be that local consumption of 197,000 tons would correspond to usage of about 100,000 tons for groundnut oil (viz. the equivalent of about 35 m beer bottles of oil) at 350 bottles per ton of nuts. In Hausa cities southern palm oil (*man ja*) is commonly much cheaper than groundnut oil: but supposing some 10 m. rural Hausa to be entirely dependent on the latter, would the consumption of 3·5 bottles per head per year be a low figure? Postscript: When visiting Faifaiku (see p. 279) in 1971, the author was surprised to find that no groundnut oil (or palm oil, or shea butter) was consumed there.

There is no information on the continued usage of groundnut oil as a lamp fuel.

See **Marketing Board.**

Group. In this book 'Group 1', 'Group 2', etc. relate to the economic-group in which heads of farming-units were classified. See **Economic-group, Farming-unit.**

Guava – goba (Psidium Guajava).

(a) A much-relished fruit in Batagarawa, where there are small guava 'orchards'.

Gudummawa. Help, such as monetary gifts, given by participants to those responsible for funeral and other ceremonies; any spontaneous help given to a friend in difficulty. Such help is to be clearly distinguished from *biki* (q.v.).

(a) Richer people often help the poorer by means of these gifts.

Guga – pl. *guguna.* A well-bucket of hide, skin, gourd, rubber, etc.

Guinea corn: see *Dawa.*

Guinea fowl – *zabo* (m.), *zabuwa* (f.), *zabi* (pl.).

(a) Batagarawa people own very few guinea fowl.

Gujiya – pl. *guzaye* – Bambara groundnut (*Voandzeia subterranea*). Not an oil-seed, it is classed as a pulse by Dalziel, who considers the possibility of its having existed in a wild state. The seeds require soaking before cooking. Traditionally a woman's crop – as today in the Niger Republic. Mainly cultivated in the Middle Belt.

Gulbi – pl. *gulabe.* The usual Eastern Hausa and Sokoto word for a river – elsewhere usually *kogi.*

Gulumbe. The town of Gulumbe, where the present author (assisted by M. S. Nuhu) undertook a rapid survey in 1966, is situated in Gwandu Emirate, North Western State, near the swamps of the Shella river about 10 miles east of Birnin Kebbi. In 1966, according to the tax register, the town had a total population of about 3,240.

Gulumbe was visited by Barth on 5 June 1853, who reported (vol. IV, p. 209) that it was a walled town 'of considerable size and densely inhabited', there being 'extensive fields cultivated with yams' [presumably cocoyams]. 'The banana [presumably plantain] constituted the chief ornament of the narrow border enclosed between the *faddama* on one side and the wall of the town on the other, and gonda or Erica Papaya [papaw], raising its feathery foliage on its slender, virgin-like stem, towered proudly over the wall.' The fields 'were fenced with great care' and 'horses and asses were grazing on the rich pasture-grounds'. Over a year later (Tuesday, 15 August 1854), on his return journey to Sokoto, Barth revisited Gulumbe, finding the market (which is still held on Tuesday) so badly provisioned, that he had great difficulty in obtaining sufficient corn for his horse (vol. V, p. 323).

In August to September 1915 an excellent survey of Gulumbe was made by C. B. Smith, who had been seconded from his work as a Junior Superintendent of Schools, to make a Re-assessment Report on the Birnin Kebbi Home District, in which Gulumbe is situated (National Archives, Kaduna, 17,765). The total population was then put at 2,367, the number of male tax-payers being 485, compared with 690 in 1966. The number of grain farms was put at 1,132, the number of rice farms at 472. Cotton was grown on 232 plots, maize (*masara*) on 198 plots, cassava (*rogo*) on 87 plots and tobacco on 83 plots: prices 'per basket' stood at 1s. 6d. per 10 lbs of cotton, 6d. per 45 lbs of maize, 6d. per 65 lbs of cassava, and 4d. per 8 lbs of henna (all obviously rough quantity figures); and yields per acre (on the basis of these prices) were estimated as ranging between about 18s. (cotton) and 26s. (cassava). Around

Gulumbe, in a season of heavy rains, the yield of millet (*gero*) was put as high as 900 to 1,000 lbs per acre.

The author recommended a tax rate of 7s. (estimated as being 10% of 'total wealth') for those with *tudu* farms in the District. He had recently been buying millet at 10 lbs for 1d. (His statistics of seasonal price fluctuations suggested a rough doubling between harvest and pre-harvest.) He stated that there was not the slightest doubt that 'all recognise the value of manuring farms'. It seemed that a farm of 2½ acres would 'benefit anything up to 20 bundles by grazing 50 head of cattle for a week, at a cost of about 8 bundles'.

He was in no doubt that the *taki* system of taxation (see **Revenue survey**) was resented, commenting that it took the farmer at a disadvantage, 'for he selected his farm without the thought of paying *taki* and it mattered little whether he included a bad bit of land in his farm or not'. Whereas a Resident (unnamed) later commented that the *taki* system would 'educate the native farmer to accept the system of real land rents and prepare a way for the hoped for cadastral survey', C. B. Smith was right about the Birnin Kebbi Home District: in 1916 rice cultivation was drastically reduced and immediate tax reductions were approved.

Fifty-one years later, in 1966, the general situation in Gulumbe seemed remarkably unchanged. There was no school and there were only 2 ox-ploughs owned by residents of the Village Area under the authority of the Gulumbe Village Head. The market was still small, and without permanent stalls, and was seldom visited by lorries. A good road, linking Gulumbe with the Birnin Kebbi to Jega road, had recently been made and the town had been rebuilt on a grid-iron pattern in about 1950 following a fire. Few of the compounds had clay walls – so the women, now rigidly secluded, did not enjoy total privacy. Groundnut production had presumably increased. A great variety of crops was still grown on the vast expanse of *fadama* – rice, cassava, sweet potatoes, maize and *malle* (a type of guinea corn), being the most popular. Henna continued to be a useful source of income to growers and traders who travelled to Birnin Kebbi, Makera and other markets.

A survey covering 58 heads of farming-units suggested that they owned about 195 *tudu* farms, of which some 106 had been inherited, 24 were rented (*aro*) – about half of them from close relatives or affines – 16 had been pledged (*sufuri*), a total of 26 being regarded as bush-farms. So few cases of farm-buying were reported, that the reliability of the figures is suspect. (All the figures are rough, being based on informants' statements, not on farm maps.) In addition these farmers owned some 94 *fadama* farms, of which about 70 had been inherited. Farms were commonly manured with compound sweepings (which, as in 1915, were never wasted) and by Fulani herds, but the proportion of farmland which was under permanent cultivation could not be assessed.

The incidence of paternal *gandu*, as assessed on the basis of 58 sample farming-units, appeared to be somewhat lower than in Batagarawa. A farm given by a father to a son-in-*gandu* is known as *kurga* (q.v.). Grain is not normally allocated to married sons at harvest, but weekly allocations (*aunaka*, q.v.) are made to wives and sons' wives alike, at least during the farming-season.

About a third of all the farmers in the sample reported that they sometimes employed farm-labourers (*ga noma*). Some of the labourers were local men (probably mainly farmers' sons), others were young Hausa strangers who sometimes arrived (but did not work) in groups. The daily wage varied somewhat seasonally, but at harvest-time was about 3s.

About a quarter of all heads of farming-units reported that they were accustomed to go on dry-season migration (*cin rani*). Of the 14 cases in the sample, as many as 6 went to Yorubaland as fodder-collectors or porters; 3 worked on *fadama* farms elsewhere in Sokoto; and 2 worked as fishermen. The 58 farmers (and members of their households) reported that they owned 58 donkeys, 125 goats, 25 sheep and only 4 cattle. There were many cattle-owning Fulani living in hamlets in the Gulumbe Village Area with its total population of

4,077; 3 out of 8 of the Hamlet Heads were Fulani and one was Zabrama. According to the *jangali* figures, these Fulani owned 829 cattle, compared with 46 (untaxed) animals owned by Hausa farmers. (No Fulani lived in Gulumbe town.) About two-fifths of all heads of farming-units in the sample reported that they bought their groundnut seed and nearly a fifth said that they obtained it on credit; fewer than one farmer in three stored his own seed. In July 1966 many households were dependent on bought grain, much of it obtained from houses.

Gunduma – pl. *gundumomi*. Originally a fief under a *hakimi* (now District Head), the word now sometimes has the meaning of a piece of territory transferred from the jurisdiction of one *hakimi* to another. See **District**.

Gutta-percha tree – *ganji* (*gamji*) (*Ficus platyphylla*); *danko* = any rubber or gutta-percha latex. Niger gutta, also known as red Kano gum or rubber, was an important item of trade prior to the British occupation, growing as far north as Sokoto, Katsina, Kano. See Brand (1940).

Gwangwala. Midrib of raphia palm (*tukuruwa*), used for roofing, etc.

Gyara. A small extra amount thrown in free by a seller to ingratiate a buyer. Synonyms include: *dadi, jefa, nashi, yafa*.

Gwan-Gwan – pl. *gwangwaye*. Any small metal (unenamelled) measuring-bowl for grain etc., or a small tin, e.g. for tinned milk or cigarettes. The word often expressly refers to a cigarette tin (*gwangwanin sigari*) as a measure.

Habe – sing. *Kado*. The original Hausa-speaking inhabitants of Hausaland, regarded from the point of view of the 'settled Fulani'. (Hausa people call themselves Hausawa.) See Chapter 1, p. 3. See **Hausa, Hausaland**.

Haji. The pilgrimage to Mecca. Since the end of the civil war there has been a great increase in the number of pilgrims, many of whom live in rural areas. In 1971 Nigeria Airways were reported as having had a turnover of nearly £3m. from the pilgrim traffic, having transported some 36,400 people to Saudi Arabia. Partly because of the trading and purchasing opportunities presented, many rich men travel repeatedly to Mecca. *Alhajai* continue to enjoy great prestige.

Haifa. To give birth to, or to beget. The relationship of one person to another is very often analyzed with the use of '*mahaifi*' – 'he (or she) who begot'. In questioning, it is often impossible to establish physiological paternity without employing this word. See **Kinship terminology**.

Hakimi – pl. *hakimai*. A high official, usually nowadays a District Head.

Hamlet. For administrative purposes rural Villages (q.v.) are divided into Hamlets (*unguwa*), each under the authority of a Hamlet Head (*mai unguwa*) whose responsibilities include those of collecting *haraji*. (The unfortunate term 'Hamlet' is apt to be confused with 'hamlet'.)

(a) The Batagarawa Village area, which is under the authority of a Village Head (*Magaji*) who lives in the *gari*, was divided in 1966 into 16 Hamlets of which one was Batagarawa. See **Hamlet boundaries, Hamlet Head**.

Hamlet boundaries. If Batagarawa is typical in this respect, Hamlet (*unguwa*) boundaries are usually indeterminate where they cross uncultivated bush-land and not necessarily closely determinate in well-cultivated areas: however, it must be added that the notion of indeterminancy is usually thoroughly repugnant to the parties concerned, each of whom claims to have his own view as to exactly where the boundary runs. In very densely populated areas, with little bush, Hamlet boundaries may usually be well known and 'fixed'; in a memorandum written for the Northern Nigeria Lands Committee (1910, Appendix 1, p. 13)

H. R. Palmer stated that for 'practical purposes the whole of Kano Province has settled village boundaries, which are well known and in many cases have been in existence for hundreds of years'.

Hamlet Head – *mai unguwa*, pl. *masu unguwa*. As the third level of 'chief' in the hierarchy under the Emir, Hamlet Heads (or Ward Heads in towns) are appointed by the District Head, and (so far as the scanty published information goes) are usually, though not necessarily, sons, brothers or grandsons of former Hamlet Heads – see Smith (1954a, p. 28). While District and Village Heads are often outsiders (being members of the Fulani aristocracy), the Hamlet Head (by contrast) is usually the representative of the Hausa 'indigenes'. Having authority for tax-collection, his (low) official salary is based (at least in some areas, see *Haraji*) on the number of tax-payers in his Hamlet; however, as Hamlet Heads are free to allocate unutilized farmland to farmers from other Hamlets in the same District without reference to higher authority, this salary may be supplemented by gifts of grain made at harvest by farmers receiving such allocations. (These allocations are not necessarily temporary; but if they are long-term, the payment of grain usually lapses after some years.) Having an important practical role in land matters, the Hamlet Head is often the official most likely to be concerned with transactions in farmland, including division of inherited land among the heirs, though he is by no means necessarily consulted by the parties involved. Unlike many higher 'chiefs', Hamlet Heads are working farmers.

Haraji. Local community tax. For the history of this tax, see **Taxation**.

(a) In Batagawara, as elsewhere in Hausaland, the annual community tax is levied on all able-bodied males aged 16 and over (see below for exemptions); only those women who are in employment proper (e.g. as sanitary inspectresses or teachers) are regarded as liable to tax (see below). While (see below) each individual should be assessed according to his wealth (by the Village Head in consultation with the Hamlet Head and others), the task of making relative assessments is an impossible one and, for this and other reasons, many poor farmers pay above-average rates and *vice versa*. Although in 1966 the highest rate (45s.) was paid by one of the richest men in town, others who were notably well off paid low rates – excluding the *masu-sarauta*, there were only 4 tax-payers who paid over £3. The average rate for heads of farming-units was about £2, compared with £1 12s. for dependent men. The lowest rate was £1. There was little variation in the average rates paid by members of the 4 economic-groups: there is never any question of relieving extreme poverty by tax remission. Here as elsewhere, taxes payable by sons-in-*gandu* or servants (*bara*) are levied on fathers or masters, though the tax register gives no indication of this.

District and Village Heads are salaried, but in 1966 the official reward of Hamlet Heads was £1 per 100 tax-payers: there having been about 300 taxpayers in the Batagarawa Hamlet, Mukaddas was entitled in 1966 to the princely sum of £3 annually – or less than 1% of the total sum raised (nearly £550).

The tax is payable between about November and January – i.e. after the groundnut and guinea-corn harvests. Although many of the poorest farmers have the utmost difficulty in raising the money (especially if they have several adult sons), punishment for default is severe.

(b) The Personal Tax Law 1962 (with amendments up to April 1964) laid down that it was the Provincial Commissioner who, in consultation with the Native Authority, fixed the whole amount to be paid by each community, having regard to the amount paid in the preceding year and to any changed circumstances. The District Head has the responsibility, acting in co-operation with others, for determining the 'amount of the commodity tax as may be just and equitable for each individual...to pay having regard to his wealth'. Women are not expressly exempted – it is merely conventional to excuse all women save those who draw salaries in the modern sector. Formally exempted are: (1) those 'indigent persons who by reason of bodily infirmity or disease are unable to earn more than the bare means of subsistence, or persons who by reason of old age, infirmity, permanent or partial disablement cannot be reasonably called upon to pay'; (2) full-time students; (3) persons under 16 – this often being a bone of contention, especially where ages are not known or sons are not earning; and (4) those holding various British awards, including the Victoria Cross!

See *Northern Nigeria Local Government Yearbook*, 1965 (pp. 42–3) for community tax rates by Native Treasury for certain years between 1953–4 and 1964–5, during which period many rates rose by 100% or more. (Curiously, a single rate, not a range, is given for most areas – suggesting that there is little variation according to wealth.) It is believed that rates have tended to rise sharply in the last few years. See Last (1967, p. 104), Smith (1960, p. 244).

See *Jangali*, **Marketing Board, Revenue Survey, Taxation.**

Harawa. Stalks and leaves of such plants as cowpeas, groundnuts and sweet potatoes, which are used as fodder. *Harawa* has a cash value.

When in Sokoto in April 1853, Barth had to spend cowries on buying '*harawa* or bean-straw' for his camels, owing to the lack of pasture. See *Karmami*.

Harmattan – *hunturu* (*tunturu*). The 'cold season', with its dusty harmattan wind from the Sahara (*Hamada*), which may last from about December to January or February, may be denoted *hunturu* or *dari*.

'The harmattan that leaves in its wake from Libya to Lagos a shroud of fog that veils the walls and trees like muslin on a sheik' – Ekwensi (1962, p. 1). See *Dari*.

Harvest-dates. Although this goes unrecognized by most botanical and other writers, harvest-dates for different crops in any locality vary considerably from year to year, depending mainly on the date of the first planting rains and also on such factors as the distribution of rainfall during the farming-season and on whether grains and groundnuts are planted simultaneously, which may happen when the rains are very late.

(a) In 1968, when the first rains came on 18 April, the early millet, groundnut, guinea corn and cowpea harvests began on about 10 August, 10 September, 6 October and 27 November respectively. In 1967, when the first rains came on June 15, the early millet harvest was delayed until mid-September, and was followed almost immediately by the groundnut harvest.

See *Kaka*, **Rainfall**, *Shuka*.

Hatsi – pl. *hatsaitsai*. Grain. According to Bargery, in some localities *hatsi* includes both millet (*gero*) and guinea corn (as in Batagarawa), in others it is millet (*gero*) only. See *Tsaba*.

Hausa. The Hausa language or people – see p. 3. The name Hausawa is used in a general way to denote Hausa-speaking people of Northern Nigeria and Niger, being mainly Habe and Fulani. As (see **Fulani**) the report on the 1952 census gives no inkling as to whether enumerators received special instructions enabling them to distinguish Hausa-speaking (settled or semi-settled) Fulani from the Hausa (proper); and as (in any case) a high proportion of the Hausa-speaking population is of mixed Hausa–Fulani origin – the statistics relating to the numbers of Hausa and Fulani respectively are of little practical value in those regions where both 'tribes' are numerous. However, it is worth noting that the geographical distribution by Province of the total recorded Hausa population of 5·5 m. in N. Nigeria in 1952 was Kano (38%), Sokoto (33%), Katsina (11%), Zaria (7%), Bauchi (5%), other (6%); and that the corresponding percentages for the Hausa plus Fulani population of 8·5 m. were Kano (36%), Sokoto (27%), Katsina (13%), Zaria (5%), Bauchi (10%), other (9%). It is therefore nearly certain that some four-fifths of Hausawa resided in Kano, Sokoto and Katsina Provinces. (It must be remembered that there was substantial under-counting in the census.)

Nor (as is so often supposed) are Hausa and Fulani men necessarily distinguishable by stature, the latter being taller. According to the medical census conducted in 4 villages in 1931 (see **Population censuses**) most Hausa as well as most Fulani men were between 5 feet 3 inches and 5 feet 8 inches tall, average heights for the two groups being roughly equal.

As for emigrant Hausa, it is interesting to note that A. Cohen (1969, p. 49) states that in order to qualify as 'Hausa' in the Hausa Quarter of Ibadan a man has to: (1) speak Hausa as a first language; (2) name a place of origin in one of the Hausa Bakwai (q.v.); (3) be a Muslim; and (4) have no tribal mark indicating affiliation to another tribe.

According to the 1963 census (see **Population censuses**), there were 11·7 m. Hausa and 4·8 m. Fulani in Nigeria, on which basis it may be very tentatively suggested (see p. 3) that there are some 15 m. Hausawa in the northern states today. (The recorded number of Yoruba in Nigeria in 1963 was 11·3 m., of Ibo 9·2 m.)

See Skinner (1968) on the origin of the name Hausa.

See **Fulani**, *Habe*, **Hausaland.**

Hausaland. The vast area of Northern Nigeria and Southern Niger which is mainly inhabited by Hausa-speaking people. See p. 1 and Fig. 1, p. xvi.

Hausa Bakwai. The seven original, or 'legitimate', Hausa states – viz. Daura, Kano, Zaria, Gobir, Katsina, Rano (south of Kano) and Biram – the latter usually identified with Garin Gabas north of Hadejia. See Fig. 1. The seven 'false' or 'upstart' states (Banza Bakwai) developed to the south and west of the original states; they were Zamfara, Kebbi, Nupe, Gwari, Yauri, Yoruba (or Ilorin) and Kwararafa, the latter five being outside present-day Hausaland.

Haya – being derived from 'hire'. Rented, hired, etc. This entry relates only to the renting of farmland.

(a) *Haya* is a more formal relationship than *aro* (q.v.), involving higher 'fixed' rents and an economic, rather than a friendly, attitude. The case of a large planted farm which was rented for £5 before the first weeding was regarded as *haya*, as was that of a farm which had been rented at £1 a year for 8 years.

(b) While other investigators have reported on the existence of *haya*, they (also) have been hard put to define it.

Hemp – *rama* (*Hibiscus cannabinus*). Hemp-leaved hibiscus, or Indian hemp; there are many Hausa words for different types.

'The fibre is comparable with jute and can be used for the same purposes. In the open country from Senegal to Nigeria it is the most widely cultivated fibre plant, and next to cotton the most used for local needs. In N. Nigeria it is the commonest source of cordage except the Baobab. Some of the usual applications are for tying the rafters used for roof-binding, plaited ropes for drawing water, hobble ropes, fishing lines, caulking canoes, women's coiffures, etc.' – Dalziel (p. 127). The leaves are a useful vegetable.

(a) Hemp is grown on a small scale in Batagarawa, mainly on bush-farms.

See *Daddawar batso.*

Henna – *lalle* (*Lawsonia inermis*). The dried leaves of this cultivated perennial shrub (Egyptian privet), which may flourish for many years, are pounded and made into a paste which, usually by bandaging (but sometimes by immersing the arm in a cylindrical gourd), is applied as a reddening cosmetic to women's hands, nails, arms, legs, feet, etc., both in everyday life and in marriage and childbirth rituals.

(a) The shrub is mainly grown in small fenced plots. The dried leaves are easily storable during the dry season, but not during the rains when very severe price fluctuations are apt to occur; a quantity costing 1s. 6d. at the time of eid-el-Maulud (the prophet's birthday, June 1967) was worth only 1d. a few weeks later.

Sometimes sold on the bush, the leaves are plucked by men and traded after drying. While a small number of secluded women sell the leaves, most supplies are traded by men, some of whom are strangers.

(b) Although an important commodity in many market-places, there is little mention of *lalle* in the literature – but see Mary Smith (1954). In Gulumbe (q.v.) there were said to be more than 30 people who traded henna in Birnin Kebbi market. *Lalle* is subject to most severe price fluctuations in the Niger Republic – see graph in NK (p. 192). In rural areas near Kano, where *lalle* is the commonest farm-boundary plant, the bushes often form high hedges.

Hides and skins – *fata*, any skin (person, animal, etc.); *kirgi kilago* – respectively untanned and tanned cattle hides.

(a) In Batagarawa there is one trader in both cattle hides and sheep and goat skins, who sells mainly to tanners in Katsina, Abukur and Cheranchi, but also to a trader in Katsina who handles export grades. He obtains his supplies (which are both wet and dry) directly from butchers and villagers and also from nearby markets. Not all skins are converted into leather – some are bought for eating.

(b) Barth noted (vol. II, p. 130) that tanned hides and dyed red sheepskins were exported in great quantities 'even as far as Tripoli'. On the present-day marketing of hides and skins for export see United Africa Company, *Statistical and Economic Review*, Sept. 1951 and FAO *Report* (1966, pp. 356–7).
See **Tanning**.

Honey – *zuma* (*zummuwa*).
(a) There are about 6 serious honey-collectors in Batagarawa, their grass hives (*amya*) being placed in trees during the farming-season, charged with a variety of costly concoctions, such as a meat broth (*romo*). One active collector, with some 20 to 30 hives, claimed to collect about 25 *tiya* of honey, worth £7 or more, in a season. Honey will keep indefinitely, if sealed, and is often stored for a price rise. There are honey dealers in Katsina city. Honey is considered very nourishing, being given, for example, to women after childbirth. See **Naming-ceremony**.

Horse – *doki*, f. *godiya*, pl. *dawaki*.
(a) According to the official figures, there were 8 stallions and 6 mares in the Batagarawa Hamlet Area in 1966. Most of them were owned by members of the ruling-class – they were seldom ridden except on ceremonial occasions and by certain functionaries (*bara*).

House: see *Gida*.

House-trade – *saina*, *saide-saide*. This entry is concerned with the retail trade conducted in their houses by Hausa women, most of whom are in strict Muslim seclusion.

(a) About two-thirds of all the women in Batagarawa – see Hill (1969b) – are engaged in house-trading on their own account, a small number of whom also sell produce (grain, groundnuts and cowpeas) on behalf of their husbands who are *'yan kwarami*. According to enquiries made in 1968, the most frequently traded foodstuffs were: groundnut oil (and its by-product *kulikuli*); *fura*; various cakes, or snacks (*marmari*) made of grain, bean or tiger-nut flour; roasted groundnuts; *daddawa*; boiled cassava; *tuwo*; and *koko*. The secluded women also conduct most of the retail trade in essential condiments, such as salt and natron (*kanwa*), supplies of which have to be bought outside Batagarawa on their behalves. Other wares include 'vegetables', such as dried baobab leaves (*kuka*), locust beans (*kalwa*), pepper, as well as sour milk supplied by nearby Fulani pastoralists. Although the scale of trade could not be measured, it is worth noting that the wives of poorer farmers are just as apt to participate in this trade as those of richer farmers (including the *masu-sarauta* – see **District Scribe**, etc.): no finance is required to enter this business as the raw foodstuffs, such as grains, may be paid for after the processing and selling have been completed. However, those women (there are 14 or more or them) who buy produce at harvest for later processing or resale when prices have risen, require capital, most of them being the wives of better-off farmers. See **Groundnut oil, Women – economic position of.**

The various 'cells' of this 'honeycomb-market' (*ibid.*, p. 396) are entered and linked by children buying on behalf of their kin, as well as by older women. (See Chapter IX above.) As customers 'shop around' the various houses and as there are many suppliers of most wares, highly competitive conditions exist, similar to those in an open market-place. The demand for cooked and processed foodstuffs is very great, snacks being much consumed by women and children, and 'meals' being bought by many young men and youths, as well as by members of households in which no cooking is done; there is an important trade in groundnut oil. There is a heavy demand for grain, groundnuts etc. from households which lack supplies, as well as from the women who sell processed food.

When a small market was established in Batagarawa in 1968 the women's house-trade continued undisturbed. See **Batagarawa market.**

(b) As (so far as is known) Nigerian Hausa women of child-bearing age seldom attend markets (and this irrespective of whether they are in full Muslim seclusion) so it may be presumed that they are strongly inclined to retail from their houses such wares as processed foodstuffs, which they would be certain to handle in open market-places did custom permit their attendance, and which (in their absence) are not handled by men. Nor is this likely to be anything new: seventy or more years ago, Baba of Karo's mother – Mary Smith (1954, p. 54) – produced millet-balls, bean cakes, groundnut cakes, roasted salted groundnuts, and groundnut oil, *entirely for selling*; the wares would doubtless have been sold from her house, had there not happened to have been a nearby market-place attended by children. Nicolas has recorded (1964, p. 70) that in Hausa areas of Niger (where rural women are seldom secluded) most women vendors in market-places handle cooked foodstuffs. He has also noted (NM, p. 77) that irrespective of whether there is a market-place, a great part of the food consumed by any domestic unit is often prepared and bought at other houses – and that women sell cooked foodstuffs even though members of their households must themselves buy food.

It would also be surprising if Batagarawa were a special case so far as concerns the house-trade in wares other than cooked foods. It is our hypothesis – see Hill (1971) and p. 138 above – that in Katsina Emirate a great proportion of grain retailing necessarily occurs in houses. Then, in a part of the world where markets are usually held only once in seven days – see **Market-place** – it is only to be supposed that such produce as locally grown vegetables would be sold from houses, along with other wares – and this irrespective of whether there were a nearby market-place. In Gulumbe (q.v.) where there is an old-established market, it was said that all groundnut oil was sold in houses, as were cooked foods. Baba of Karo – Mary Smith (1954, p. 119) – said that in her youth women had their own granaries, in which they stored produce for a price rise: 'At harvest time we would buy grain and put it by; at the end of the dry season when the Cattle Fulani came we took out our grain and sold it to them and made money.' (Their husbands bought the grain on their behalves.)

A. Cohen (1969, pp. 64–5) has reported that in Ibadan virtually all Hausa women are 'engaged in business from behind their seclusion' – as though they were in Hausaland. About a third of them dominate the business of retailing kola, oranges and plantain, the others running the 'cooking industry' of the Hausa quarter, supplying thousands of bachelors, streams of strangers and other Hausa households. (Muslim Toruba women are not secluded.)

Huhu. Wrapping for kola-nuts; hence a leaf-lined package containing kola-nuts for long-distance transport. There are at least 5 standard sizes of *huhu*, containing 1, 1½, 2, 2½ and 3 *fakani* (each of 2,000 nuts). One *fakani* equals 20 *kwarya* (each of 100 nuts). See A. Cohen (1966, p. 24). See *Fatauci*, **Kola-nuts.**

Hula – pl. *huluna*. A cap.

(a) The making of embroidered caps is a common hobby, or craft, with young men.

Hurumi – pl. *hurumai*. Land outside a town, or in the countryside, which is reserved for commnual purposes, such as grazing, forest-reserves etc., or for cemeteries.

Idda. The period of three months during which a divorced woman may not remarry. *Iddar takaba* (see *Takaba*) is the corresponding, though longer, period for a widow.

Igiya – pl. *igiyoyi*. 'Any kind of rope, whether of grass, hemp, fibre, bark, etc.' – Bargery. There are numerous other words for rope or string.

Ilmi. Koranic knowledge, especially of theology and law; knowledge or ability generally.

Imam: see *Limam*.

Indigo – *baba* (*Indigofera*). The indigo plant from which indigo dye (*shuni*) is prepared.

(a) The plant is still grown on a very small scale in Batagarawa.

(b) An account of the method of cultivating indigo is given by Clapperton (1829, p. 220), who notes seasonal price fluctuations. See Dalziel (pp. 244–5).

See Dyeing, *Shuni*.

Indikya. 'Farming, cutting wood, or doing other hard work for payment' – Bargery. See *Aikatau*.

Inheritance – *gado* (*gada*, *gaje*, verbs): *ya gado ubansa* = he inherited his father's property; *magaji*, f. *magajiya*, pl. *magada* = an heir.

(a) This entry summarizes and supplements certain material presented elsewhere, but reference should also be made to Chapter XIII, pp. 181–5. In Batagarawa property is distributed on death in a manner which is not at variance with the general conclusions which might be formed from reading the scanty literature on the transmission of property between the generations in rural Hausaland. Thus: (1) inheritance is nearly always a family matter, very few cases indeed being referred to the alkali's court in Katsina; (2) manured farmland is divided in a rough and ready way between the sons: insofar as daughters get a share (a point which cannot be checked) they presumably usually sell it to their brothers – see **Women farmers**; (3) bush-farms (q.v.) are seldom regarded as formally heritable – though they may of course be appropriated by the sons; (4) women's movable property (goods and chattels) passes mainly to daughters; (5) houses are not divided on death but usually pass to one of the sons who may compensate his brothers in respect of the shares to which they are entitled; (6) much property, such as small livestock and grains, is sold on death, partly to avoid embarrassment arising from valuation, but also to meet *ushira* (the 10% death duty); (7) the inevitable 'conflict' between customary practice and 'the law' is partly resolved by the payment of *ushira*, as needs be, to the District authority – there is often a long delay before the division occurs, and meanwhile much of the property may have been consumed by those living in the deceased's house.

These various points will be somewhat expanded below. But first it is necessary to emphasize that 'custom' and 'law' diverge not so much because of any 'conflict' of principle, but because of the unreality of the latter, which (for instance) takes no cognisance of *gandu* (or of the changing *gandu* situation) and which is concerned only with that portion of the total property of the deceased which happens to be mentioned to the court (or other authority) – and this hardly ever includes farmland. When considering the transmission of property between the generations, it is as necessary to take account of the *gandu* system as of inheritance proper – a matter which is neglected in the literature.

If, formerly (as is often assumed, though not necessarily correctly), sons usually remained together in fraternal *gandu* on their father's death, no division of farmland would have occurred until that *gandu* broke – and such a distribution is not inheritance. Brothers might leave the *gandu* by degrees, each one being allocated a portion of farmland on his departure – see also (b) below.

Nowadays in Batagarawa much farmland passes to sons during their father's life-time, either as *gayauni* to sons-in-*gandu*, or as gifts on departure from *gandu*: although both types of gift are usually regarded as 'outside inheritance' (they are as much the son's 'permanent property' as any farms he may buy), yet custom, it seems, has had no time to catch up with events, so that no one can say whether a son who has remained in *gandu* to help his father 'ought' to receive a greater share of the inheritance than his brothers who were given portions of land on leaving *gandu* – doubt on this point being as much due to uncertainty as to 'conflict with law'.

Expanding the points on inheritance above: (1) the distribution of property is effected in the presence of those directly concerned (including women), either a senior relative or Mukaddas usually presiding; (2) practice with regard to absent sons is variable – if they receive a share of the farmland, this is often sold, a resident brother having the right of first refusal; a share may be allotted to the sons of any deceased son provided they are still living in Batagarawa (this may be effectively owned by a surviving son, until his nephew marries); in general the division between sons often involves no sub-division of plots, especially when these are small (see p. 185); (3) bush-farms are inherited slightly more often than formerly; (4) when elderly women die, they often own little property, having given it away to their daughters on marriage and at other times; (5) any son who is living in his father's house on his death usually remains there, and occasionally (though not often) two sons who are not in fraternal *gandu* both remain there – questions of prestige are little involved; (6) little squeamishness is felt about selling a deceased father's property, even his cattle; (7) as the property is seldom valued (even notionally), *ushira* is determined by bargaining – it may be deducted before the division is made, or each beneficiary may pay separately; the wives are always allowed to consume grain from the granaries during the mourning period (*takaba*).

(b) The main published sources on inheritance of land in rural Hausaland are: Anderson (1954); Hailey (1951); Lugard (1918); Meek (1957); Michie in Cole (1949); Rowling (1952); Smith in Derrett (1965); Nicolas (NM, p. 84) – Lugard's contempt for the expert evidence given to the Northern Nigeria Lands Committee justifies one in ignoring that source. There is also some useful material in the National Archives, Kaduna – notably *A Memorandum on Inheritance of Land* by the Katsina Resident, 1914, Ref. 1694; and *Memorandum on Rural Land Policy*, 1929, File no. 1724.

The earlier authorities were agreed that, formerly, the senior male agnate inherited all rights in land, with or without an obligation to compensate the remaining male heirs and accordingly there was little discussion of the degree of actual division on death – see reference to fraternal *gandu* in (a) above. (Succession to the headship of the compound operates similarly with the Maguzawa today, descending from elder to younger brother and later to the oldest surviving son of the oldest brother, and so on; this principle is said – Greenberg (1946, p. 17) – 'to be quite automatic in its operation', disputes being unknown.) More recent discussions of 'fragmentation' often refer to the Emirs' pronouncement in 1939 that 'where the application of the Islamic law of inheritance would result in uneconomic subdivision of land', 'the property might be sold and the proceeds divided among heirs', Anderson (1954, p. 187) – but some of them make rather heavy weather of this point considering that in most Hausa Emirates the number of courts per head of the population is so small that they would be inundated with business, were they even to handle more than a tiny proportion of the cases involving inheritance-disputes. In any case, there is nothing in Maliki law which compels inheritors to refer to the court, and every reason why they should do their best to avoid paying *ushira*.

Whether the finding that in Batagarawa only about one-fifth of the farm-plots under 2 acres had been divided on inheritance (see p. 234) is of wide application is not known: it may be that in localities where land is scarce more importance is attached to equal division of plots. (The writer is grateful to D. Goddard for the information that in the densely-populated localities he studied near Sokoto town – see p. 237 for their location – farms, however small, are meticulously and formally divided between brothers.)

The only writer to have discussed inheritance of land in relation to *gandu* is M. G. Smith in Derrett (1965). Some of his findings, such as that 'sons already established on their own in their father's lifetime have claims on the *gandu* land only if it includes surplus fallow' (p. 243), or that 'most of the inherited property' is distributed during the holder's life-time (p. 244), are at variance with findings in Batagarawa.

See **District Courts, Farm-selling,** *Tirka.*

Iri. Seed(s) or seedlings for transplantation. (The word has numerous other associated meanings, such as tribe or stock.)

Iska – pl. *iskoki.*

(i) Wind.

(ii) Evil or benign spirits, especially those causing hysteria.

See *Bori.*

Iyali – pl. *iyalai.* A man's domestic family – i.e. his wife (or wives) and children. Sometimes *iyali* denotes all those who are dependent on a man for food. See **Kinship terminology.**

Jagale. 'Itinerant training within a small circuit, the trader carrying his own load' – Bargery.

Jalli (*Jali, Jari*). Trading-capital. The word sometimes signifies a very small sum of capital, such as the starting capital of a woman trader. See **Capital.**

Jangali. Cattle tax. Since before the *jihad* – see Last (1967, pp. 51, 103) and Hiskett (1960, p. 567) – the purpose of levying *jangali* has always been to raise revenue from the pastoral Fulani. The Native Revenue Proclamation of 1906 distinguished *jangali* from the 'general tax'; and under the Personal Tax Law 1962 – see *Haraji* – it is expressly laid down that no individual shall be assessed for cattle tax 'in respect of cattle the value of which has been taken into account by the Provincial Commissioner when determining . . . the tax [*haraji*] payable by the community of which such individual is a member' – so that, consistently with this, Hausa cattle-owners are considered exempt from *jangali.*

According to both Last (1967) and Smith (1960) an official known as Sai was responsible for collecting the tax which in Zaria at the end of the last century was 'nominally a tithe of the herds, but actually very much less' – Smith (1960, p. 353). Lugard in his survey of taxation before the British occupation (Northern Nigeria Lands Committee, Appendix III) stated that *jangali* had been 'payable to the chief from whose stock the herd first emanated', but that if the herdsman 'settled down and built a village' it would be payable to the Emir.

Under the 1962 Personal Tax Law, the rate of tax in most areas was 7s. per head of cattle – although calves were explicitly included, they are presumably usually excluded from the cattle count. (The law fixed 2s. as the rate for sheep (and lambs!): while sheep go untaxed in most areas, Kazaure is one known exception.) It was laid down that (as with *haraji*) 12½% of the revenue should be credited to central funds, 87½% to Native Authorities.

In most areas *jangali* is mainly collected in July to October, but where many cattle are on transhumance at that time collection may be delayed. Tax evasion is always assumed to be common – thus in Northern Nigeria in 1961–2 only 4.5 m. cattle were taxed compared with 5.4 m. which were vaccinated for rinderpest. But when evasion is discussed there is seldom any mention of the extraordinary harshness of this tax compared with community taxation: a Fulani pastoralist with 50 cattle in his herd would, at 1961–2 rates, have usually been liable to pay about £17 annually, four or five times as much as was ever paid as community tax by rich Hausa farmers, who are exempt from *jangali*, however many cattle they may own. (Furthermore, *settled* Fulani pastoralists are often deemed liable to pay both *jangali* and community tax.) The formal legal penalities for non-payment of *jangali* and *haraji* are equally harsh – £100 or 6 months imprisonment or both.

See Sharwood Smith (1969, p. 193) on D.J. Muffett's supervision of the cattle count on which *jangali* is based: this annual contest between District Heads and pastoralists 'had acquired many of the characteristics of an international sporting event'. See **Cattle-ownership**, *Haraji*, **Taxation**.

Jariri – f. *jaririya*, pl. *jarirai*. An infant under about 6 months old.

Jeji. 'Bush'-land. See **Bush**.

Jigawa: see **Soil types**.

Jihad. This Arabic term is virtually untranslatable into English: it denotes the stage in a struggle, in an Islamic context, at which recourse is made to arms. The *jihad* called by 'Uthman dan Fodio in 1804 was the climax of two or three decades of progressively intensified political agitation against the Hausa rulers (*sarki*): intricate scholarly attempts were made to establish that, because of the excesses of their rule, these men had virtually abandoned any claim to be regarded as Muslims. There is considerable disagreement among historians as to the nature of the 1804 *jihad*. For various accounts see: H. F. C. Smith (1961), M. G. Smith (1966b), Hodgkin (1960), Last (1967), H. A. S. Johnston (1967), Waldman (1965), Hogben and Kirk-Greene (1966). For the notion of *jihad* in a West African context, in its spiritual as well as its military sense, see Willis (1967).

Jinga. Wages; *mai jinga* = a wage-earner. See *Noman jinga*.

Jingina. Pledged or pawned; this entry relates to the pledging of farms only.

(a) Manured farms are usually pledged for one, two or, at most, three years. The creditor is entitled to claim the farm failing repayment of the sum borrowed (or purported to have been borrowed) on the due date and there are no subsequent rights of redemption. No documents record the transaction. Bush-farms are not pledged. If a farm with standing crops, such as henna, is pledged, the right to sell the crop may remain with the debtor.

Pledging is so often the prelude to outright sale that informants are usually reluctant to admit to a state of affairs which is more painful than straightforward selling, in that it is always hoped to redeem the farm. It is, thus, impossible to estimate the proportion of manured farmland that is under pledge at any time – though as pledging is usually for such short periods it is certainly small. However, of a total of 39 transactions in farmland (involving non-kin) which were reported as having occurred during 1968 and 1969, as many as 16 had involved pledging in the first instance, the remainder selling only.

(b) Perhaps sometimes because of the reticence of debtors, nearly all recent investigators have reported pledging as rare or non-existent – the highest incidence being found by Norman (1967) in Hanwa (12% of total acreage). In Gulumbe (q.v.) where farm-pledging is known as *sufuri* (hiring), 16 out of 195 farms were reported as under pledge; sums lent were much lower than in Batagarawa, and pledge-periods were often longer; documents were sometimes drawn up. Rowling (1952, p. 50) reported that in Kano Province the sum borrowed appeared to bear little relation to the value of the land; in one District manuring of the farm was expressly prohibited, being regarded as an assertion of ownership; as elsewhere, pledging was a common cause of dispute. See Goddard *et al.* (1971) for the low incidence of pledging in the Sokoto Close-Settled Zone.

Pledging is an old practice, though frowned on in some emirates. According to *Memorandum on Land Policy*, 1929 (National Archives, Kaduna, 1724) in Sokoto Emirate pledged farms were, in principle, redeemable by a man or his heirs within a period of 10 years – but practice was, presumably, harsher than this. *Jingina* is common in the Maradi area – see Nicolas (1968a, p. 19). See **Usury**.

Jirge: see *Zamiya*.

Joking-relationship: see *Abokin wasa*.

Kaba – pl. *kabobi*. The fronds of the dum-palm (*goruba*) which are used in plaited strips to make mats, hats, baskets, bowls, panniers, fans, rope etc. Bundles of *kaba* may be sold in markets or (as in Kano) directly to secluded women in the countryside who make *mangala*.

Kabewa (*Kabushi*) – pl. *kabeyi* (*Cucurbita Pepo*). Pumpkins. The pulp is eaten as a vegetable and in soup, and the gourds are common domestic utensils.

(a) Grown by women in Batagarawa.

See **Gourds**.

Kadi. Spinning (q.v.).

Kado: see *Habe*.

Kaikayi. Corn chaff.

Kajinjiri (*Kijinjiri*) – pl. *kajinjirai* (*Phoenix reclinata*). The wild or dwarf date palm. 'Strips of the young unopened fronds and their midribs are used to weave fine mats...also, waistbands, sieves, bags, hats, etc.' Dalziel (p. 509).

Kaka. Harvest, harvest-time (*lokacin kaka*). 'Harvest time, used in reference to the time of the ripening of any crop, but when no particular crop is mentioned it refers to...[the time] when guinea corn, beans, groundnuts, etc. ripen' – Bargery. See **Farming-operations, Harvest-dates**.

Kaka gida. 'Children born to people who have left their homes for trading purposes and settled down in some distant place' – Bargery. In Ibadan – see A. Cohen (1969) – recent Hausa immigrants regard the bilingual descendants of earlier immigrants as a special ethnic category.

Kalwa. Seeds of the locust-bean tree (*dorawa*). See Chapter IX, pp. 133, 135 on seasonal price fluctuations of *kalwa*. See **Locust bean**.

Kantu – pl. *kantuna*. A conical or tubular block of salt, natron, etc.

Kanwa. Natron (q.v.).

Kanya – pl. *kanyoyi*. The very sweet fruit of the West African ebony tree (*Diospyros mesipiliformis*) of the same name.

(a) Women traders (non-secluded) sell the fruit in Katsina city. *Kanya* (unlike *dinya*) may be freely collected from any tree.

Kara – pl. *karare*. A stalk, usually a corn stalk. Dried guinea corn stalk is used for fences, palisades, beds, walls (for huts, granaries, etc.), the radiating bands of conical thatches, etc., etc.; it may be used as fuel and the resulting ashes as manure. The value of guinea corn stalks (which are usually much longer and stronger than millet stalks) may be as great as 10% of the value of the grain.

Karakara (*Karkara*). 'Land, near a city, which is covered with hamlets and farms' –Bargery.

(a) In Batagarawa the term *gonar karakara* is used to denote a manured farm – or, sometimes, any farm within the manured zone, whether it happens to be manured or not.

(b) When nearing Sokoto, Barth referred to the 'fields or "karkara"' adjoining a certain village (vol. IV, p. 132).

See **Permanent Cultivation**.

Karawa. A fence of cornstalks or stakes. See **Shinge**.

Karba. Any article handed over in part-payment for another. See **Exchange**.

Karda. Although, according to Smith (see p. 177 above), there is an important distinction between occupations or crafts (*sana'a*) which are 'inherited' (ascribed) and those which are achieved – respectively *karda* and *shigege* (q.v.) – the word *karda* appears in none of the dictionaries and, according to Kirk-Greene (1965b, p. 376), is unknown to younger men. '*Karda*, an hereditary occupation, enjoys greater *daraja* (prestige) than *shigege*, a freely and individually chosen metier' (*ibid.*, p. 376).

However, according to Yeld (1960, p. 117) –

> The only sense in which this distinction between hereditary and acquired crafts can be applied among the independent Hausa of Kebbi is in the higher prestige of traditional craftsmen as against the modern type of petty traders, sellers of kola nuts, cigarettes, scent and the like ... who are often the sons of traditional craftsmen preferring this easier way of obtaining profits.

Kargo (*Kalgo*) – (*Bauhinia Thonningii*). A tree with many uses. Its bark is used for cordage; its root-bark is used for reddening women's lips; and its leaves are used for wrapping certain cooked foods.

Karkashi. A herb (*Ceratotheca sesamoides*) the leaves of which are used in *miya* (soup).

Karmami. Millet or guinea-corn leaves used as fodder.

(a) According to Abraham *karmami* (unlike *harawa*) is not saleable, but both types of fodder are in fact sold in Batagarawa.

Karuwa – pl. *karuwai*. Women of child-bearing age who do not marry after being widowed or divorced, and who are usually, though not always, prostitutes who live with other women. Such women 'are deviants from the Islamic norm of marriage for all adults, and as social deviants they are the traditional custodians of religious deviance in the spirit-possession [*bori*] cult'. Smith (1954a, p. 25). See A. Cohen (1969, pp. 55 ff.) on Hausa prostitutes in Ibadan. 'Prostitutes frequently marry and slip into the anonymity of wifehood, and wives frequently divorce and emerge into the freedom and independence of prostitution' (p. 57). See **Bori**, **Dantada**.

Kasa. Earth, soil, country, land, etc. Also a District (q.v.).

Kasuwa – pl. *kasuwoyi*. The word '*kasuwa*' denotes either 'market-place' or 'market' in the general sense in which the word is employed by economists: accordingly, *kasuwanci* is a general word for 'trading' (otherwise *ciniki*), whether or not the business is conducted in a market-place and a man trader known as *dan kasuwa* may, or may not, frequent a market-place. (However, women's house-trading (q.v.) is not known as *kasuwanci*.) Thus –

ya ci kasuwa = he sold goods (anywhere) at a profit;
kasuwa ta fadi = prices have fallen;
kasuwar gyada ta fadi = groundnuts are not in demand.

See **Market-place**, **Sarkin kasuwa**.

Katanga – pl. *katangu*. The wall of a house or compound.

Kauda. Any kind of *dried* fruits, marrows, kola-nuts, meat, etc. See Bargery.

Kaukai. A Mallamawa Hamlet situated 2 to 3 miles east of Batagarawa on both sides of the Katsina/Kano road. Many of the residents live in dispersed houses (see Fig. 7), but some have been resettled to the west of the road. The following brief notes relate to a survey undertaken in 1967, when the farms were mapped using an air photograph. (See also statistics shown under the entries **Farm-area**, **Farm-holdings**.)

(1) It is said that there were few farmers resident in the mapped area until they began to

migrate there from neighbouring hamlets, some 30 years ago – some of them buying farms at the time of the famine 'Yar Balange, when prices were low.

(2) Resident men farmers owned some 300 (mapped) acres; resident women farmers owned some 15 acres only, though most women are not in strict purdah. About 25% of the acreage owned by resident farmers had been bought. Most of the farmland was under permanent cultivation.

(3) *Gandu* is strong in Kaukai. Of 44 resident tax-payers, 22 were heads of *gandaye*, these being 15 paternal *gandaye*, 1 paternal/fraternal *gandu*, and 6 fraternal *gandaye*. In most of the latter cases the father had died when some of the sons were young.

(4) In great contrast to the position in Batagarawa, a large proportion of the farmland cultivated by resident farmers was owned by a small number of sets of brothers and their male descendants. In fact, 6 such sets of brothers (none of whom had formed a fraternal *gandu*) owned two-thirds of the manured farmland, and 2 owned as much as one-third.

Kaura. Migration (q.v.). Hence *makaurace* – one who migrates.

Kauye – pl. *kauyka*. A village. An administrative area – i.e. Village Area. Country as opposed to town.

(a) At Batagarawa the dispersed settlement to the west of the *gari* is known as Kauyen Yamma – lit. 'Western village'.

(b) Smith has noted (1957, p. 28) that while Hausa who live at the state capital regard all other settlements as *kauyuka*, those in 'village capitals reserve this depreciatory term for their daughter-hamlets'.

See *Gari*, Village.

Kawa – pl. *kawaye*. A woman's female friend, used loosely for any friend, but more specifically for one with whom she has established a formal bond-friendship by exchange of gifts' – Mary Smith (1954, p. 255). However, in Batagarawa '*kawa*' means any female friend, *aminiya* (q.v.) being a bond-friend; *Kawa* does not necessarily involve a *biki*-partnership, nor women of the same age.

Kaya – pl. *kayayyaki*. The general word for a load; also goods, or property.

Kaza – pl. *kaji*. A hen. Cock is *zakara* – pl. *zakaru*'. See **Poultry ownership**.

Kerosene – *kalanzir, kananzir*.

(a) Kerosene is much used as a lamp fuel in Batagarawa and to some extent for cooking; women commonly have to buy their own supplies, which are measured in beer bottles. See *Garwa*.

Kifi. Fish. Owing to the seasonal drying of all save the largest rivers in Hausaland, little fish is consumed in most areas.

Kilishi. Thin strips of meat which are dried in the sun, and redried and cooked after sprinkling with *kulikuli*, or pounded groundnuts, etc.

Kinship terminology. *Zuri'a* (*zuriya*) – lit. 'descendants' – may be used as a term for a genealogically-traced descent group. *Kakani* (pl. of *kaka*) are ancestors. *Dangi* is the general and collective term for maternal and paternal relatives, other than parents or children, *dangantaka* being 'relationship'. *Danuwa*, though literally a mother's son, is commonly used as a general term for any brother, relative or fellow-countryman. A man's domestic family, viz. his wives and children, is *iyali*. The system of 'kinship terminology and relationship' is set out diagrammatically by Smith (1955, p. 42); he states that the system uses as its 'differentiating and classifying principles' factors of 'generation, sex, seniority of birth and patrilateral and matrilateral relationship'. Terms of reference include: *uba* (father), *uwa* (mother), *da* (son), '*ya* (daughter), *wa* (elder brother), '*ya* (elder sister), *kane* (younger brother), *kanwa* (younger sister), *kaka* (grandparent), *jika* (grandchild), *kawu* (mother's brother), *inna* (mother's sister, etc.), *baba* (father's brother, etc.), *goggo* or *gwaggo* (father's sister, father's wife other than one's mother, etc.). A husband is *miji*, a wife *mata*. See *Asali, Haifa*.

Kiri. Peddling; *dan kiri* = peddler.

Kiriga.

(i) A stack of firewood.

(ii) A pile of groundnuts made on a farm.

Kishiya – pl. *kishiyoyi*. A co-wife – from *kishi*, jealousy.

Koda. Any household or farm work done for small payment; according to Abraham the word refers to women's work only. See *Aikatau*.

Kodago: see *Kwadago*.

Kogi – *koguna*. A river. See *Gulbi*.

Koko. A kind of gruel made with any grain flour.

(a) Usually made of guinea-corn flour in Batagarawa, the gruel is sold by secluded women.

Kola-nuts – *goro*, pl. *gwarra*. (See Bargery for the Hausa names of numerous varieties and for much other valuable information.) The red, pink or white nuts of the kola tree (*Cola acuminata* or *Cola nitida*), which flourishes only in forest country, often in areas where cocoa also grows; the nuts have been an important item of West African long-distance trade for many centuries, and are one of the few stimulants permitted to Muslims.

Despite the importance and antiquity of the trade, 'there is no comprehensive work on kola in English and although frequent references to it are to be found in colonial reports and agricultural textbooks, many are misleading as well as incomplete ...' Russell (1955). The most authoritative work is Chevalier and Perrot (1911): although the principal author was a botanist, this work deals with trade and history as well as with scientific matters. The wholesale trade in kola (like that in such West African export crops as cocoa, palm-produce and groundnuts), is mainly conducted outside market-places.

(a) Kola-nuts are much consumed in Batagarawa, both as stimulants and in connexion with numerous ceremonies and gift exchanges – see **Naming-ceremony**. The principal supplier (Alhaji Shekarau – see p. 155) obtains his packages (*huhu*, q.v.) from a trader in Katsina city. As many as 27 secluded women were reported to be kola retailers, and numerous children hawk the nuts on behalf of women and men traders. During the farming season small nuts cost as much as 1*d*., larger ones 2*d*. (See *Fatauci* with regard to the long-distance trade in kola formerly conducted by traders resident in Mallamawa Hamlets.)

(b) As research on the Hausa kola trade is currently in train by P. Lovejoy and others, and as historical material on the caravan trade has been presented elsewhere (see *Fatauci*), this entry merely lists a few additional sources.

See Dalziel on the poor keeping qualities of kola in the savannah. Last (1967, p. lxx) refers to kola as a major item of trade in Gobir before the *jihad*. See Arhin (1970) on the Ashanti kola trade with the north. Barth (vol. II, p. 131) regarded kola as 'the chief article of African produce in Kano market', where it was both in transit and sold for local consumption; he estimated supplies as more than 500 donkey-loads annually, which was surely a low figure. For the organisation of Hausa kola traders resident in Yorubaland see A. Cohen (1966 and 1969). See Smith (1955, p. 162) for details relating to kola packages, specialised traders, etc; Mary Smith (1954) for ceremonial uses of kola and other references; Hay and R. M. T. Smith (1970) for estimates of Nigerian inter-regional trade in kola; Nicolas (NK, Tables 7A and 9) for details of expenditure on kola for name-day and marriage ceremonies.

Koli. The peddling of small wares, such as haberdashery, a peddler being *dan koli*.

Koranic schooling – *makarantar Alkuran, makarantar allo*.

(a) In 1970 there were 10 Koranic classes in Batagarawa, the largest having 55 pupils, the smallest 4; total attendance (which included many pupils who attended the primary school) was 152 boys and 38 girls. Apart from those running these classes, there were 4 other prominent Koranic teachers.

See Taylor and Webb (1932) for an account of Koranic schooling; see, also, Trimingham (1959, pp. 158 ff.). See *Malami*.

Kosai. A snack. Doughnut-like balls, usually made of a paste of cowpeas (*wake*) and fried in groundnut oil.

(a) Nearly a fifth of all Batagarawa's women house-traders are apt to make and sell *kosai*.

Kuba – pl. *kubabi*. An uncultivated farm or disused farmland.

(a) Synonymous with *sagagi* in Batagarawa.

Kubewa: see Okro.

Kudi – the plural of *wuri* (cowry). Money. Hence, price: *kudinsa nawa?* = 'What is its price?' *ya yi kudi* = 'it is expensive'; *kudaidai* = sum of money; *gidan kudi* = bank – lit. 'money house'; *uwar kudi* = capital – lit. 'mother of money'.

Until Lugard introduced coinage in Nigeria – see Johnson (1970a, p. 48) – cowries (q.v.) were the main currency, although silver dollars had been circulating in Hausaland since the second quarter of the nineteenth century. Among the coins issued was one worth a tenth of a penny. See **Money, *Tsaba*.**

Kudin cefane. The money which a husband gives his wife, probably usually daily, for buying foodstuffs required for household cooking, other than grain and meat.

(a) In Batagarawa, where richer husbands commonly claim to give their wives the notional sum of 1s. daily as *kudin cefane*, all the various foodstuffs are bought at houses. (See **House-trade**.) Wives often supplement the sum given by their husbands from their own pockets. A wife may buy from herself.

See *Cefane*.

Kufai. An old site, whether of house, compound or town.

(a) There are many such old house-sites (now tiny farms) in Batagarawa *gari*, the houses having been destroyed following the collapse of the west wall (*ganuwa*).

(b) Barth defined *kufai* as the site of a former town (vol. II, p. 41).

Kuka – pl. *kukoki*. The baobab tree (*Adansonia digitata*) and also its pods and leaves. The bark is made into rope and strings for musical instruments; the dried leaves are a most valuable soup ingredient; the acid fruit pulp (together with its seeds) is consumed raw or cooked – the tree having countless other uses as fodder, etc. (see Dalziel).

(a) In 1965, according to the official records, there were 96 of these grotesque trees in Batagarawa Hamlet; they were owned by those on whose farms they stood. The leaves are mainly cut by one strong man, who charges the owners 1s. 6d. to 2s. per tree, according to size. Twenty-four secluded women traders were recorded as handling the dried leaves.

(b) The tree has greatly impressed travellers.

The kuka is of immense size, erect and majestic; sometimes measuring from twenty to twenty-five feet in circumference . . . The tree, whether bare of its leaves, in flower, or in full-bearing, has a singularly grotesque naked appearance; and with its fruit dangling from the boughs like silken purses, might, in the imagination of some Eastern story-teller, well embellish an enchanted garden of the Genius of the Lamp.

Denham and Clapperton (1826, p. 10)

Barth was fascinated by the tree, with its pods 'hanging down on slender mousetail stalks' (vol. II, p. 86); he re arded it as the constant companion of human society, the largest trunks marking the deserted sites of the oldest habitations. Pelissier (1966, p. 264) emphasizes the nutritional value of the dried leaves which are very rich in calcium and iron, in which millet is gravely deficient.

Kulikuli. Small fried balls made from the residue after hand-expression of oil from ground-nuts. Much used by butchers for coating pieces of meat before 'roasting'.

(a) Commonly known as *guru* in Batagarawa, this food is sold (very cheaply) by women producers of groundnut oil: in July 1966, when a beer bottle of oil sold for 2*s*. 3*d*., 11 balls of *kulikuli* fetched 1*d*.

See **Groundnut oil.**

Kulle. Wife-seclusion, or Muslim purdah, or keeping a wife in purdah – the verb '*kulle*' meaning 'locked'; *tana kulle* = she is in purdah (*tsare*). 'Islam has always been associated with the seclusion of women, but the nature of this association has not always been clear. The Koran ... is not at all conclusive over this point' – Cohen (1969, p. 59).

(a) Muslim seclusion is nowadays very strict in Batagarawa *gari* – see Chapter 11, pp. 22–4. It is suggested (p. 24) that one of the physical factors favouring rigid wife seclusion is a high water-table; an associated point is that the skilled well-diggers also dig pit latrines (q.v.) in compounds. There are few wells in dispersed homesteads.

See also **House-trade, Marriage types, Women farmers.**

(b) Nigerian Hausaland is unique in Muslim West Africa in the strictness and prevalence of rural wife seclusion, which is not practised in Bornu, or other neighbouring Muslim areas. Such a degree of seclusion is something quite new. Robinson (1896a, pp. 205–6) thought that Hausa women were more favourably placed than in 'an ordinary Mohammedan country': 'with the exception of the wives of the king and one or two of his chief ministers, they are not kept in seclusion, but are allowed to go about as they please'. (He was also impressed by the fact that wives retained personal property, including any slaves, after marriage.)

According to Smith (1955, p. 22), one of the reasons for the increased seclusion of rural women in this century was that on the abolition of the legal status of slavery, those formerly of slave status 'withdrew from the farms and as far as possible from wood-gathering', as an assertion of their freedom. He was of the opinion (*ibid.*, p. 24) that wife seclusion is more easily understood in terms of the economic interests and roles of Hausa wives than of ascribed religious injunctions – although, to the husbands, prestige factors are of great importance. Whether, as is often stated, women indeed 'prefer seclusion' – owing to the freedom it gives them to pursue their own trading and to their dislike of hard work – is a matter which has never been investigated. However, as it is inconceivable that women of child-bearing age would be permitted to engage in trade in open markets, the realistic economic question is whether many women would wish to be free to relieve their poverty by means of farming: probably not, for (as has been constantly reiterated) the evidence is that partially secluded (Nigerian Hausa) women in dispersed farmsteads do little farming and are never *gandu* members. If this is so, the strictness of seclusion in any locality, is an unimportant determinant of living standards. (Postscript. But our ignorance is great: in 1971 the author visited a Hausa hamlet (Faifaiku) near Roni, in Kazaure Emirate, where most women are farmers.) See **Women farmers.**

Rural Hausa women in the Niger Republic are seldom secluded and are active market-traders. But Nicolas reports (NK, p. 287) that a few husbands are starting to prohibit their wives from farming – sometimes compensating them to achieve this.

Kunu. A gruel; usually considered a poor substitute for *fura*. See Abraham.

Kunya.

(i) With the general meaning of modesty, shame, bashfulness, etc., *kunya* specifically denotes the avoidance-shame relationship, particularly such as exists between either parent and their first-born son or daughter (*dan fari*, '*yar fari*) or between husband and wife in public, and which involves name-avoidance. Such avoidance takes fullest expression in the presence of outsiders and has fewer directly economic implications than might be expected. See Smith (1955, pp. 41–4).

Kurga – lit. 'working by night'. The word used, in Sokoto and elsewhere, for the private farm belonging to a dependent member of a *gandu* group, which is more usually known as *gayauna*.

Kurmi – pl. *kurame*. Thickly-wooded country; a forest; *ya tafi kurmi* = 'he has gone south', i.e. to the southern forests. See *Dandi*.

Kuyanga – pl. *kuyangi*. A female slave, usually (but not necessarily) young.

Kwacewa: see Confiscation.

Kwadago. Work done for wages – known as *kodago* in some areas including Zaria; *dan kwadago* (pl. '*yan kwadago*) = wage-labourer; *kudin kwadago* = wage.

Although Bargery defines *kodago* as 'any manual work done for wages', the word commonly denotes daily farm-labour – being defined as such by Abraham; its usage is probably confined to men's work. In Batagarawa where *kwadago* has particular reference to farm-labouring, the word is also applied to many forms of paid work, including earth-handling for builders, building on contract, ploughing for payment. Farm-labouring undertaken on contract is *noman jinga*, not *kwadago*. Other words for daily farm-labouring include: *barema*, *fadim baya*, *ga noma* and *ga aiki*.

(a) Chapter VIII relates to *kwadago* in Batagarawa.

(b) Sources on *kwadago* (see also Chapter VIII) include: Anthony (1968), FAO Socio-Economic Surveys of Peasant Agriculture in Northern Nigeria (mimeographed or unpublished), Hill on Gulumbe (q.v.), Luning (1963a), Mortimore and Wilson (1965), Nicolas (particularly NM and 1968a, pp. 33–9 on *barema*), Norman (1969) and Smith (1955). Norman is the only investigator to have provided reliable statistics of the volume of hired labour relative to family-labour: in 3 Zaria villages – Norman (1969, Table 4) – sample figures showed hired labour as varying between 6% and 29% of total farm-labour during the year ending March 1967 – it should be noted that there was no ploughing in these villages. (This article includes valuable statistics on hours worked per day and per year by family farm-workers.)

Kwalli. Antimony, or (more often) galena; it is applied by both men and women to the edges of the eyelids and to eyebrows and as a general 'make-up'. It is also used as a medicine and in dyeing.

Kwando – pl. *kwanduna*. A large basket.

Kwano. A metal bowl or basin; a headpan; a small tin basin used as a corn measure. Also corrugated iron, which is so rarely used for roofing in the countryside that *mutum mai-kwano* is a synonym for a rich man.

Kwara. The Hausa name for the river Niger.

Kwarami.

(a) Local trading in grains, groundnuts and other produce, buying being effected in markets or directly from farmers, retailing being conducted mainly in houses by the traders' secluded wives. The traders ('*yan kwarami*) are all local farmers, whose main function is that of pro-visioning the local community: they lack the finance to store produce for a price rise. See Chapter IX.

(b) Although *kwarami* (as here defined) has been wholly ignored in the literature, the presumption is (see p. 138) that local farmer–traders commonly take on the function of pro-visioning rural communities with grain, especially where there is 'net importation' of grain. Although nowadays *kwarami* relates to trade in any kind of farm-produce, it may formerly have related only to grain. In 1921 (National Archives, Kaduna, 12676), when the abolition of the Kano Produce Market was under consideration, the Emir considered that most of the Kano men who brought groundnuts into Kano were '*yan kworemi*' (*sic*), who bought ground-nuts in the same way as they were accustomed to buy grain.

See **House-trade, Trading-terms.**

Kwarya – pl. *kore*. Any circular calabash-bowl. The word has many other meanings, most of them connected with measurement in terms of length, volume or number. In reference to kola-nuts a *kwarya* (or *kwaryar goro*) is 100 nuts.

Kyauta – pl. *kyautayi*. A present; a 'dash'. The word is also used in the sense of 'to do a kindness'. Thus, when a farmer takes up bush land he may refer to it as *kyauta* in the sense that it has (though often notionally) been 'given' to him by the Hamlet Head. (Statistics relating to the proportion of farmland which has been 'gifted' – *kyauta* – are, therefore, often misleading.)

La'ada. A commission payable to brokers (*dillalai*) and others when goods are sold with their help. (See Bargery.) When the buyer pays the commission (perhaps reclaiming a portion of the payment from the seller) the expression is *la 'ada waje*; when both sides pay it is *la 'ada ciki*. See *Dillali, Mai gida.*

Labourer: see *Kwadago.*

Lada (*Ladan aiki*). Wages; reward. See *Wankin hannu.*

Lalle. Henna (q.v.).

Lambu – pl. *lambuna*. An irrigated farm, or garden, especially for cultivation during the dry season. See *Fadama.*

'Landlord'. In the sense of a 'landlord' for long-distance traders.

See *Fatoma, Mai gida,* **Market-place.**

Lardi – pl. *larade*. A tract of country. Sometimes a Province or other administrative area.

Latrine – *sarga* (pl. *sarguna*), *masai, bayan gida* (lit. 'the back of the house'), *makewayi* (pl. *makewayai*) – place fenced off as bathroom, latrine, etc. For many other words see Bargery on *sarga.*

(a) Well-diggers are responsible for digging the well-shaped (often very deep) pit latrines (which have a small hole in a 'cemented' top), with which most houses (or compounds) in the *gari* are provided; these screened-off latrines are used by everyone living in the house, or (in some cases) house-section. Latrines are much less common in dispersed farmhouses – where few women are rigidly secluded. See p. 289.

(b) Although pit latrines are presumably very common in Hausa settlements where their digging is practicable, the general relationship between the degree of rural wife seclusion and the prevalence of latrines (as of wells) remains unexplored; Smith comments (1955, p. 18) that they are necessary conveniences in houses inhabited by secluded women. Where the water-table is very high, latrines are apt to flood. If latrines are too close to wells they may pollute the water supply.

See *Kulle,* **Manure, Wells.**

Lawashi. Onion tops for pounding. See *Gabu.*

Leather-working – *dukanci*. Literary references to this important trade are very slight. Barth stated (vol. II, p. 130) that sandals (*takalmi*) were exported from Kano to distant places, in huge quantities.

Limam (*Limami, liman*) – pl. *limamai*. An imam; a leader of ritual prayer; officiating Muslim priest. The imam often officiates on ceremonial occasions, including funerals, betrothals, naming-ceremonies.

Locust bean – *dorawa* (*dorowa*), pl. *dorayi* (*Parkia filicoidea*). The locust-bean tree is very common in N. Nigeria, extending (according to Dalziel) to 14°N, being the most typical tree of the savannah parkland. The elaborately processed and fermented seeds or beans (*kalwa*) are made into strongly smelling blackish cakes or balls (*daddawa*, q.v.) which are an almost indispensable ingredient of Hausa (as of Nupe) cooking. The yellow pulp in which the black seeds are embedded may be made into a yellow meal-like powdered biscuit (*garin dorawa*), which (like *daddawa*) is sold in market-places. The empty pods (*makuba*) are used for making a most valuable 'local cement' (*daurin dabe*), which is used to harden laterite floors, and to form a weather-proof layer on the outside of house walls. See Dalziel for numerous other uses. In inhabited areas, each locust-bean tree has an owner. The abundant leaf-fall is a valuable soil improver.

(a) According to official records there were 227 locust-bean trees in the Batagarawa Hamlet Area in 1966. The huge canopies of the trees are clearly distinguishable on air photographs, providing very useful landmarks. The seeds (*kalwa*) are traded by secluded women and older women buy them for resale in Katsina city. The seeds keep well and 4 women were known to store them for a price rise (see Chapter IX). Barth (vol. IV, p. 105), when travelling near Batagarawa, noted the tree as 'the chief representative of the vegetable kingdom', and 'the principal ornament of the landscape' – *ibid.*, p. 107.

Long-distance trade: see *Fatauci*.

Ma'aski – pl. *ma'aska*. A barber–surgeon (q.v.); *aska* is a razor.

Ma'auni – pl. *ma'aunai*.

(i) A measure, scales, weighing machine of any sort – from *auna* = weighed, measured.

(ii) A measurer (f. *ma'auniya*, pl. *ma'auna*) – commonly someone who sells grain and other measurable foodstuffs in a market-place (q.v.) Measurers, though strictly intermediaries, are not known as brokers (*dillali*, q.v.).

Maciya – pl. *maciyai*. A very small wayside market, or eating place.

Madi. A sweet drink made from the juice of various fruits and sugar-cane.

Madugu – pl. *madugai*. A caravan leader. See *Fatauci*.

Most interestingly, in the Niger Republic the rich merchants who buy groundnuts for export promote their interest in villages by means of local representatives who are known as *Madugai* – see Nicolas (NK, pp. 199, 210). '*Madugu*' also has other modern usages.

Magaji – pl. *magadai*.

(i) An heir – see **Inheritance**.

(ii) An official position and title; often a Village Head (q.v.).

(a) Magaji is the title of the Village Head who resides in Batagarawa, one of whose Hamlet Heads is Mukaddas.

Magaji (Batagarawa). Isa, the present Village Head (Magaji) of Batagarawa, was appointed in 1963, following the death of his father Murtala, who was then District Head and who was succeeded by his younger (paternal) brother, the present District Head.

In 1967 there were 11 occupants of his large house in the centre of the *gari*, including 3 wives, one schoolboy, one schoolgirl, 4 other children and one woman servant. In 1970 he had 4 wives: one was the daughter of his father's mother's junior brother, one was the daughter of a Hamlet Head in Rimi District, the other two (both non-kin) being daughters of Abukur and Kwami men. Only one of his wives did a little house-trading.

In 1967 he had eleven farms in four separate localities. The 10 acres (4 farms) he owned in the mapped zone had mainly been acquired by purchase. His other farms were all in his

Village Area, being at Dabaibayawa, Makada and Gwamatawa – where the District Head also had farms. Magaji himself does no farming. Unlike the District Head, he does not invite other farmers to assist him; he is mainly dependent on the employment of *'yan kwadago* who are recruited on his behalf in neighbouring hamlets. Several of the *barori* who are attached to him work on his Batagarawa farms, being paid for the actual work they perform – they also have their own farms.

One of his *barori* is known as *sarkin gida*: he issues grain to the women, fetches water, buys firewood and generally maintains the house. A woman servant helps with domestic work.

Magini – pl. *magina*. Builder or potter. See **Building**.

Maguzawa – sing. Bamaguje. Pagan (non-Muslim) Hausa, who live in scattered settlements, mainly in Kano, Katsina and Zaria Emirates. In 1952 a generally unsuccessful attempt was made to enumerate the Maguzawa as a separate 'ethnic group' in the census; the only published figures were for Kano Emirate, where 47,874 Maguzawa were enumerated. In 1915 Krusius (p. 289) estimated the total number of Maguzawa at 100,000. Apart from Krusius (1915), sources include Greenberg (1946 and 1947) and Reuke (1969). Smith states (1960, p. 241) that the Maguzawa 'are looked down upon by their Islamic cousins for their attachment to ancient "superstitions" (*tsafi*) and for their tribal organization'. See Chapter III, p. 39. See *Gandu*.

Mai bara – pl. *masu bara*. A beggar for alms, as distinct from a professional 'beggar' such as *maroki* (q.v.).

Mai gida – pl. *masu gida*, literally 'house-owner'. The head of a house, or (in reference) a woman's husband. Widely used as a term of respect, or as denoting one in authority, such as a master, a big 'patron', the owner of a business, etc. In many regions of West Africa the word is especially applied to 'landlords' (whether Hausa or not) who own, or rent, houses where long-distance traders live and store their goods. See A. Cohen (1969) and Hill (1966 and 1971). See *Fatoma*, **Market-place**.

Mai unguwa (Mai anguwa) – pl. *masu unguwa*. Hamlet or Ward head – the lowest 'chief' in the hierarchy. See **Hamlet Head**.

Maiwa. A variety of late millet (*Pennisetum*) which takes from about $4\frac{1}{2}$ to 6 months to mature. Dalziel states that another variety *dauro* 'is probably not differentiated from *maiwa* in most districts'. According to the FAO *Report* (1966, p. 177), a distinction between *maiwa* and *dauro* is that the latter is more suitable for transplantation. Little appears to be recorded of the distribution of *maiwa* in Hausaland: Irvine (1934, p. 108) incorrectly states that it is uncommon north of Zaria. According to Dalziel, millet beer (*giya*) is more often made from *maiwa* than from *gero*.

(a) *Maiwa*, in contrast to *gero*, is planted almost exclusively on unmanured bush-farms. The importance of the crop could not be assessed. Thirty-five heads of farming-units reported storing *maiwa* (which may be known as *dauro*) in one of their granaries (Table 11.10, p. 36), 11 of whom reserved a whole granary for this crop (Table 11.9, p. 36). See Table IX.1 on seasonal price fluctuations of *maiwa*.

(b) *Maiwa* is included under the general heading 'millet' in official production statistics and is generally ignored in the literature. Luning (1963a, p. 28) noted that at Kadandani (not far from Batagarawa) *dauro* was cultivated without manuring and considered that in the extreme north of Katsina Emirate inadequate rains partly accounted for the failure to cultivate this grain.

See *Gero*.

Maize – *masara* (from *Masar*, Egypt), or *dawar masara* (lit. Egyptian guinea corn) (*Zea Mays*). See Dalziel. Maize is not grown as a bulk crop in northern Hausaland, which is too dry, but it is said by Oyenuga (1967, p. 181) to be spreading northwards from Zaria. It is, however, often grown on 'garden plots', or *fadama*, as in Gulumbe in 1915 – p. 262.

Makadi – f. *makadiya*, pl. *makada*. A drummer.

(a) In Batagarawa there is a Sarkin Makada – chief drummer.
  See also *Maroki*.

Makauraci – f. *makauraciya*, pl. *makaurata*. A migrant. Also, a place (particularly a village or hamlet) where a migrant takes up new land. See **Migration**.

Makitsiya – pl. *makitsa*. A woman hairdresser; *kitso* = woman's coiffure.

Makurdi. The Mallamawa Hamlet called Makurdi lies to the east of the Katsina to Kano road, about 3½ miles east of Batagarawa north of Kaukai (q.v.). Nowadays the farmers live dispersedly (see Fig. 8), but formerly there were nucleated villages where the Alkalai of Katsina city, who were the forebears of the present ruling-family of Mallamawa, maintained houses near their farms. Abubakar Labo (q.v.) said that the first of the three villages which he could remember lay astride the old road, which can be seen on the farm map (Fig. 8, p. 14); Alkali Aliyu, brother of the paternal grandfather (Alkali Dalhatu) of the present District Head of Mallamawa, had a house in this village, which he had inherited from his father Alkali Hambali; he lived in this house throughout the rainy season, cultivating large areas with the help of slaves. Later, owing to waterlogging by a stream, the village shifted a quarter of a mile south, where it was situated at the time of the famine *Malali*; it finally shifted further west, 5 Alkalai being said to live there at that time. The village ultimately broke up at the time of the removal of Alkali Ibrahim to Batagarawa as District Head.

About a half of the 50 farmers who owned the 77 farms (totalling 236 acres) which were mapped in the Hamlet in 1967 were resident in other Hamlet Areas or in Katsina city. Many of the resident farmers had been born elsewhere, having moved into the Hamlet to take up land there.

Most of the farmland is under permanent cultivation, though there are rocky outcrops on some of the farms. Although the women in this locality are not strictly secluded as in Batagarawa, only 4 of the 77 mapped farms were owned by women, who do little farming. The resident farmers undertake little craftwork, except for mat-making.

One farmer who owned 42 acres in the mapped area had bought most of his farmland during the last thirty years or so; his father had been one of those who had decided to build a house on his farmland on the departure of the Alkalai. He employs many '*yan kwadago* from neighbouring hamlets; they work for him until a certain task is finished, maybe recruiting their friends to join them. He is the only plough-owner in the Hamlet.

Malafa – pl. *malufu*. Large hats made of the fronds of *kajinjiri* (q.v.) etc., sometimes worn by farmers while working in the sun.

Malali. The terrible famine of 1914 which hit northern Hausaland. Other names (see Bargery) include: *kakalaba, kumumuwa, sude mu gaisa*.

In Kano in 1913 rainfall was only 19 inches—14 inches below the average. Owing to food scarcity in 1914 it actually paid the European firms to bring back from Baro port the ground-nuts which had earlier been bought for export and to 'resell them to natives' – see Hogendorn (1966). Many thousands of people died in Kano Province: in northern Katsina alone at least 4,000 people died – many of them having fled from nearby French territory where the famine was even worse. Thousands of cattle and other livestock perished and many others were slaughtered owing to lack of fodder. In the north and north-east of the Province 'the emaciated appearance of many of the people, especially the women and children was most noticeable'. (*Annual Report, Kano Province*, 1914). The official, A. C. G. Hastings, was one of the few to provide a vivid description of the famine:

This year [1914] the effect of shortage showed itself in all its ghastliness. The gaunt ghost of famine stalked abroad through Kano and every other part. The stricken people tore down the ant-hills in the bush to get at the small grains and chaff within these storerooms. They wandered everywhere collecting the grass burrs of the *kerangia* [*karangiya*, the Bur grass (*Cenchrus biflorus*)] to split the centre pod and get the tiny seed. . . . Not only Nigerians but thousands from French country drifted down across our borders, passing through villages *en route* all bare of food to offer them. They died like flies on every road. . . .   Hastings (1925, p. 111)

(After describing the efforts made by officials to alleviate suffering, the author proceeded (see p. 6, above) to comment on the improvidence of 'Nigerian farmers'.) J. E. Trigge, of the Niger Company, attributed *Malali* to the increased planting of groundnuts (q.v.) for export:

[In 1914] although there was supposed to be a good crop, the natives would not bring in the groundnuts because they said they were going to hold them for a better price. They stored them and fortunately they did. Owing to the groundnut planting, they did not provide their yams (*sic*) and their guinea corn, and were faced almost with starvation and so far as they could they ate the groundnuts and held some over till the next season. *West Africa: Committee on Edible and Oil-Producing Nuts and Seeds, Minutes of Evidence* Cd 8247, 1916, p. 61.

Malam (Mallam). Strictly speaking, 'Malam' is only a form of address or a title, but the word has passed into common currency as signifying the man himself – see *Malami*. Its usage as a courtesy title for any educated man or official, whether or not he has any Koranic knowledge, is now extremely widespread.

Malami – f. *malama*, pl. *malamai*. Although in every Muslim village most men with some smattering of Koranic learning are addressed as Malam (q.v.), the number of active Koranic teachers, functionaries and real scholars is a small proportion of this total.

(a) In Batagarawa about 27 (out of 171) heads of farming-units are commonly addressed as Malam, of whom fewer than one half are practising teachers; fifteen of these men are in Groups 1 and 2 and 12 in Groups 3 and 4. Most of them are active farmers, but nearly one-half have no non-farming occupation; non-farming occupations include trading, building, tailoring and honey-collection – but not smithing or butchering. There are also some ten Malams who are men-in *gandu*. In 1968 there were 5 Malams who had (a total of 9) Koranic students from outside Batagarawa who were temporarily assisting them on their farms.

(b) See Smith (1955, pp. 98–100) on the functions and social position of *malamai* in rural Zaria, and also A. Cohen (1969, pp. 43, 165 ff.) on Hausa *malamai* in Ibadan; Nadel (1942, pp. 378 ff.) is also very relevant. 'Malams may be very ignorant, but one of their main characteristics is continuous learning' – A. Cohen (1969, p. 169).

See *Bori, Ilmi,* **Koranic schooling.**

Mallamawa. The title of the District Head (*hakimi*) of the District of the same name, of which Batagarawa is the capital. This brief entry relates only to the economic and domestic circumstances of the present office-holder, Alhaji Dalhatu Shawai – see Plate 1 (See also Chapter II, p. 16 and **Batagarawa.**)

As a young man Alhaji Dalhatu did not accompany his father when he first transferred to Batagarawa (see **Mallamawa District**), but remained in Katsina working in the Native Authority workshop. On his father's death in 1941 he removed to the *gari*, having been appointed Village Head (Magaji).

In 1967 there were 26 people living in his large house in the centre of the *gari* (see plan of house, Fig. 5, p. 12), including 4 wives, 13 children (of whom 2 were schoolboys, 3 were schoolgirls) and a woman servant – see Plate 10. His senior wife (*uwar gida*) is the daughter of a farmer from a neighbouring hamlet; only one of his wives is a relative (viz. a father's junior brother's daughter), the other two being daughters of a late District Head of Rimi and of a Hamlet Head. Each wife has her own cooking utensils (which she may share with others) and a servant to assist her in cooking. A woman servant has access to the room where guinea corn is stored – in September 1967 she issued 5 *tiya* (some 30 lbs) daily; each wife keeps millet in her own room. The grain is threshed, pounded and ground by women servants, though use may be made of the grinding mill, when in working order. The women servants (see *Bara*) are paid mainly in kind and lead independent economic lives; one of them is the head of many *adashi* groups.

All Mallamawa's wives are well-known house-traders, handling many types of ware, including kola, natron (*kanwa*), salt, sugar, cigarettes, clothes and enamelware, as well as some processed foodstuffs such as *daddawa*.

Apart from the single 'official farm', which attaches to the office of District Head (this is about 7 acres of manured farmland, situated near the school), Mallamawa owns only one other small farm in the mapped zone. All his other privately owned farms are situated in about ten other Batagarawa Hamlets, within a radius of perhaps ten miles of the *gari*, the localities including: Makurdi (q.v.) – the 'home of his ancestors', the *alkalai* of Katsina – where he rents a farm from a daughter's husband (the Village Head of Sabon Gari); Dabaib-ayawa (where he has a large manured farm on which 10 ploughs from Batagarawa *unguwa* worked on 21 June 1967, without completing the ploughing); Gwamatawa, Kawo, Jilawa (including Bado within Jilawa), Makada, Tsauni, which like Dabaibayawa, are all Hamlets in the Batagarawa Village Area; and several other areas. At each of these Hamlets the Hamlet Head is said to be 'in charge of the District Head's farm, as though it were his own, just reporting the expenses'. It is believed that most of the produce from these farms consists of grains for consumption by Mallamawa's large household and the numerous other dependants – he has a large storeroom for bags of threshed grain, but owns few granaries in Batagarawa, the unthreshed grain being mainly stored elsewhere. Several of the *barori* (see *bara*) attached to Mallamawa have duties connected with the official farm, and one of them transports *fura* for workers on outlying farms.

The extent to which Mallamawa relies on farm-labour services (other than ploughing) provided at less than the 'market-rate' (see *Kwadago*) is not clear. Those who are 'called' to work on his farms are mainly young men, who are not obliged to attend; they may receive about 1*s*. in cash plus *fura* and kola-nuts for a long-morning's work (known as *taimako*, not *gayya*). Every man has a notional obligation to work for one day annually on the official farm, but few are called for this work. There are occasions (for instance when bush is cleared during the dry season) when '*yan kwadago*, paid at normal rates, are engaged.

In 1968 Mallamawa's sons included one at Ahmadu Bello University, 3 at secondary schools and one in the Nigeria Police; a daughter who had been trained in Kano was a teacher at Batagarawa school – her husband, also a member of the ruling-family, being the headmaster. See also p. 103.

Mallamawa District. The small District south of Katsina city, of which Batagarawa is the capital.

The earlier history of Mallamawa District is not that of Batagarawa, which was in Yandaka District until the boundaries were altered in about 1928, when Ibrahim, the District Head, transferred his headquarters from Dandagoro (now Sabon Gari) to Batagarawa. The District boundaries have been subject to constant adjustment. In 1927 the District Officer reported (National Archives, Kaduna, 1385) that on the partition of Districts in 1906 an outlying portion of Mallamawa (which District had been 'the *hurumi* (q.v.) of the Katsina Mallamai') had become an island in Yandaka District; so an 'heroic adjustment' was recommended by the Emir, and later approved, this involving the transfer of Batagarawa to Mallamawa in return for the absorption of the 'island' (Kewa) in Yandaka. In 1941 and 1967 the area of Yandaka was again reduced in favour of Mallamawa, the latest adjustment also reducing the area of Kaura (or Rimi) District. However, Mallamawa remains much the smallest rural District in Katsina Emirate – though it is probably considerably larger than Magajin Gari, the Katsina City Home District.

In 1967, following the readjustment, there were 3 Village Areas in the District, the Village Heads residing at Batagarawa, Sabon Gari or Dandagoro (on the main road to Kano) and Tsanni to the south; Tsanni, which had been transferred from Kaura District, appeared to be a larger town than Batagarawa, though then having no primary school. In 1966 there were 16 Hamlet Areas within the Batagarawa Village Area, the largest being Jilawa with a total population (according to the tax register) of 1,979 people, many of them Fulani pastoralists; there were 10 Hamlet Areas under the Sabon Gari Village Head.

The recorded population of Mallamawa District in 1931 was 6,129, a highly suspect figure as the recorded number of adult males (1,190) was far less than the number of adult females (1,720). In 1952 the recorded population was 11,122, of whom 4,602 were recorded as being Hausa, 3,057 as Fulani, 1,474 as Kanuri – 'other Northern tribes' (unspecified) accounting for 1,962. (As Districts are the smallest areas for which 'tribal' breakdowns are provided in the census, no statistics for Batagarawa are available.) (See **Fulani.**). As in Katsina Province generally, the proportion of males over 50 years of age was recorded as being very low – 5% as compared with 10% for females. Eighty-two people (72 of them in Batagarawa) were recorded as literate in 'Roman script' and 230 (148 of them in Batagarawa) in *Ajami*. In 1966 the population was estimated at 15,000. See also **Batagarawa, Mallamawa,** and Chapter II, p. 15.

Mangala – pl. *mangaloli.* A kind of rectangular bag of plaited strips of dum-palm (*goruba*) leaves, which is used as a double pannier for donkeys, for carrying manure (to farms), fodder, and other non-spillable produce. See *Kaba, Taiki.*

Mango – *mangwaro* (*Mangifera indica*). The mango tree and fruit.
(a) In Batagarawa the fruit (which is greatly enjoyed) is traded as well as 'just eaten'. There are early and late ripening varieties, the price range being considerable.

Manure – *taki, takanta* = manuring a farm. These notes relate to types of manure other than chemical fertilizers (q.v.). See also **Permanent cultivation.**

(1) *The droppings of Fulani-owned cattle*

(a) When enquiries were made during the farming-season, the payment to the pastoral Fulani who bring their herds to manure the farms in the dry season was always put at £1 a month for 30 cattle – surely an absurdly low figure, whatever quantity of grain etc. is also given? Although the position is clearly competitive, with the richer farmers attracting most of the herds, the owners of farms near wells and grazing-grounds are also well situated.

(b) There is exceedingly little published material relating to the manuring of farms in Hausaland by herds of cattle owned by pastoral Fulani. Hopen (1958, pp. 154–5) remarks that the principal contact between Hausa and pastoral Fulani in Gwandu Emirate is in connexion with manuring, most of which is done between December and April. He found that most herds moved to different farms each year, but that some herd-owners visited the same farms year after year. There was no fixed fee: most pastoralists were 'quite satisfied' if the farmer provided sufficient grain for his family during the manuring period, together with occasional gifts of kola and salt. In Gulumbe (q.v.) it was stated that the pastoralists (many of whom were settled nearby) were given daily cash as well as food for bringing their herds to the farms – 'it's just like *kwadago*'. Luning insisted (1963a, p. 46) that in the three localities he studied all the Fulani herd-owners were settled farmers – he believed that transhumant pastoralists were confined to the west and south of Katsina Province.

(2) *Other cattle manure*

(a) In Batagarawa (see **Cattle-ownership**) the number of cattle owned by Hausa rearers much exceeds the number of plough-oxen. Many of the cattle are 'boarded out' by their owners to farmer–pastoralists who are usually mainly rewarded in terms of manure for their own farms, the cattle-owner often receiving the milk. Such richer farmers as own no cattle, may pay for Hausa-owned cattle to manure their farms. For only two crops, sweet potatoes (*dankali*) and tobacco, was cattle manure said to be essential.

(b) Published information on this subject is exceedingly slight, there being no statistics (see *Jangali*) of cattle-ownership by Hausa farmers. Luning's cattle-ownership figures (1963a, p. 45) show that in some areas more Hausa than Fulani 'families' own cattle. Cattle are brought to the farms after harvest and fed on crop residues; at night (when most of the dung is dropped) they are tethered, not kraaled, on the farms. Luning stated that owing to the lack of village-grazing during the farming-season many cattle had to be sent elsewhere, with a consequent loss of manure – he made many other useful comments. Meek asserted (1925, p. 128) that 30 cattle would adequately manure a 2½ acre farm in one month. According to Morgan and Pugh (1969, p. 513), 2 plough-oxen could supply sufficient manure for only 4 acres a year.

(3) *Compound sweepings* (farmyard manure)

(a) According to an informant who was unaware of the economic-groupings, virtually all farmers in Group 4 and about half of those in Group 3 were known to be sellers of compound sweepings as manure – he named only 2 sellers in Groups 1 and 2. 'If you have money', he said 'you can always buy manure.' Members of the ruling-class are perhaps the only farmers who regularly buy manure from neighbouring hamlets – none comes in from Katsina city. A *mangala* (q.v.) of ordinary household sweepings was said to be worth 3*d*. to 4*d*., while one rich in sheep or goat droppings might fetch up to 1*s*. Although these small livestock range freely during the dry season, they return to the compounds at night. Compound sweepings are mainly applied to the farms during the dry season: those who do not own donkeys may hire them for 1½*d*. to 2*d*. (according to distance), otherwise head-loading is necessary. Farm-size (q.v.) may be reckoned in terms of the number of *mangaloli* of manure required.

(b) The FAO *Report* (1966) is surely entirely incorrect in affirming (p. 182) that 'good yields' of grain will never be obtained without the use of chemical fertilizers. It seems clear from reports on the Kano Close-Settled Zone that fertility can be permanently maintained without the application of either fertilizers or cattle manure – that compound sweepings alone may be adequate, provided (or so one presumes) that they include a sufficient proportion of the droppings of small livestock or donkeys. Nash (1948, p. 17) found that a donkey could produce from 1 to 1½ tons of manure a year when bedding is added. According to numerous field experiments conducted by the Agricultural Department nearly 40 years ago – see Hartley and Greenwood (1933) – appreciable increases in yields of guinea corn could be expected from the application of 'farmyard manure' at a rate as low as 1 ton per acre; while the application of 2 tons gave greater yields, these were hardly raised by applying 3 or 4 tons. (In a later paper Hartley (1937) concluded that such results could be attributed very largely to the phosphorus in the manure.) It is, therefore, interesting that in a locality situated 5 miles from the Kano urban area it has been reported – Mortimore and Wilson (1965, p. 53) – that about 2 tons per acre of household sweepings, much of it brought from Kano city by donkeys, was applied to the average farm, there being, as one would expect, much variation as between farmers. See **Donkeys, Sheep and goats.**

There have been few reports on the sale of compound sweepings which is presumably very common: Luning (1963a, p. 41) found it was 'very common'; MacBride (1937) reported that a donkey-load of manure was worth ½*d*. to ¾*d*. 'at the dung heap', or 1·3*d*. when delivered to the village farm. Nicolas (NK2, pp. 31–2) noted the sale of manure in markets in the Niger Republic. According to Mortimore and Wilson (1965) the cost of a donkey-load in Kano in 1964 had risen to 6*d*.

Several writers have commented on the inefficiency of the practice of applying household sweepings during the dry season: 'this means that the manure is liable to burning by the heat of the sun, severe attack by white ants and to the blowing away of the finer particles by the strong prevailing winds' – Luning (1963a, p. 42).

(4) *Human excrement*

(a) In Batagarawa some farmers deny using dry latrine manure (*takin masai*) while others use it cautiously in small quantities, especially for guinea corn. March is said to be the best month for its application. The latrines are usually sealed with earth, for up to one year, before removal of the manure, which fetches 1*s*. 6*d*. per *mangala* or more. See **Latrine**.

(b) In fully rural areas, where there are usually no latrines, the fertility of nearby farms is, of course, increased by human defecation. There appears to be little published literature on the application of latrine manure, except for Nash (1948, p. 17) who refers to efforts made to persuade people to use their latrines on a 'battery system': if a full latrine is sealed with earth for a year the contents become 'an inoffensive and pathologically harmless rich black earth', ready to spread on the fields. So is Dumont right in asserting (1966, p. 21) that the farmer's aversion to handling human excreta as manure is justified by the risk of spreading amoebic and other intestinal affections? Why do the experimental scientists neglect this subject.

Postscript. Enquiries made in 1971 in the Kumbotso and Ungogo Districts near Kano, revealed that the utilization of dry latrine manure has long been 'standard practice' in many areas.

(5) *Other types of manure*

(a) In Batagarawa groundnut shells are seldom wasted being commonly used as manure, either dry, or after watering when they become black and rotten. Wood ash may be included with compound sweepings and the clearance of bush farms may involve burning. Old thatching grass, cornstalks, etc. may be used as mulch. Pigeon droppings are sold to nearby onion-farmers by pigeon-keepers.

(b) Other types of manure include the droppings of wild birds especially egrets (*balbela*) and of bats. Certain marshland (*fadama*) or riverside crops, notably onions, require special types of manure. See **Cattle, Ploughing, Sheep and goats**.

Marketing Board. The history and operation of the many West African Marketing Boards, which replaced the West African Produce Control Board established by the British Government during the early years of the war, are dealt with in numerous publications. As sole authorities with powers to purchase produce for export, through the agency of their licensed buying agents, Marketing Boards fix minimum prices for farmers ('producer-prices') which are seldom varied during the course of a buying season. In the course of time the original aim of stabilizing the producer-price over a term of years, by building up reserves in years when world prices were high, and deliberately depleting them when world prices fell, has been forgotten, and Marketing Boards have increasingly been used as convenient devices for taxing farmers, by means of export duties and other similar taxes.

In Nigeria in 1954 the National Boards, which had been organized on a commodity basis, were replaced by Regional Boards, the Northern Nigeria Marketing Board being established to buy groundnuts, cotton and other produce for export abroad – this was replaced in 1968 by the Northern States Marketing Board. Until 1968 minimum prices for groundnuts were not uniform, but varied somewhat according to the cost of transport to the port. Thus, in 1963–4, when the Board's 'guaranteed naked ex-scale port of shipment price for decorticated groundnuts' was £40 per ton, minimum producer prices in Katsina Province varied between

£30 11s. 9d. at Funtua and £26 14s. at Batsari. In 1968 the uniform price, after deduction of produce sales tax, was £26.

In 1962–3, when the producer-price at Kano was £30 6s. 9d., it happened that the Board made a negligible trading surplus on the basis of an average f.o.b. price of £54 2s. 8d. Costs of transport, buying allowances for licensed buying agents (to cover their costs and remuneration) and marketing charges (including costs of produce inspection and storage) accounted for about £17 of the difference betwen the producer-price and the f.o.b. price. The balance was taxation to the tune of about £8 per ton (consisting of export duty – levied at 10% *ad valorem* – and produce sales tax of 30s.), this corresponding to a rate of tax of about 20% of the *gross proceeds* from groundnuts for the Kano farmer and to somewhat more for farmers in northern Katsina. Such tax rates vary significantly from year to year: in 1967–8, when the guaranteed port price was reduced by over £5 per ton compared with the previous year, the producer-price fell by over £6, i.e. to £25 at Kano, where the tax rate possibly rose to about 25%. In 1968 the produce sales tax in the North-Central State was raised to £2 per ton.

Insofar as licensed buying agents are forced by competition to pay farmers more than the legal minimum price for groundnuts (see Chapter IX, p. 133) the rate of tax is reduced; on the other hand the effective rate of tax may be much higher in the case of farmers whose poverty drives them to sell nuts for export through an intermediary whose price is below the minimum. As – see FAO *Report* (1966, p. 350) – there are 'no institutional arrangements' for ensuring that minimum prices are actually paid to farmers by licensed buying agents (Ministries of Agriculture having no supervisory powers, the Board no staff for this purpose), there is an entire lack of official information on whether most farmers who sell directly to buying agents get the sums to which they are entitled.

A *White Paper on the Northern Nigeria Military Government's Policy for the Comprehensive Review of the Past Operations and Methods of the Northern Nigeria Marketing Board* (Government Printer, Kaduna, 1967) was written after consideration of the Report of a Committee of Enquiry into the affairs of the Board which had been appointed in 1966. It dealt with the chaotic situation which had developed following the departure of nearly all members of the Board's executive staff in 1963. On the matter of the fiscal role of the Board it frankly concluded (p. 21) that: 'Government does not accept, but notes and will keep under constant review, the Committee's recommendation that in the long term, producer prices should be increased and export duties decreased as alternative sources of revenue are found.'

For most interesting details of '*la traite*' in Niger, which corresponds to the Marketing Board season in Nigeria, see Nicolas (NK, pp. 195 ff.); minimum buying prices for groundnuts are fixed by the government.

See **Economic regulations**, *Fuloti*, **Groundnuts**, **Price-fixing**.

Market-place – *kasuwa*, pl. *kasuwoyi*. This entry provides brief summarized reference material on rural periodic markets, stress being laid on certain peculiarities of Hausa markets; it is not concerned with markets as focal points for long-distance trade. The fieldwork, on which these notes are partly based, was mainly done in markets in northern Katsina and in Gwandu Emirate in 1966.

(1) *Early history*. The lack of historical material on rural markets is astonishing. Smith asserts (1962, p. 304) that 'exchange by gift and barter among occupationally-specialised clans preceded markets', which did not emerge until the development of 'large-scale caravan traffic'. There is, perhaps, no firm evidence that 'local markets', mainly attended by local buyers and sellers, existed before the introduction of the cowry-currency (q.v.) in the eighteenth century. In a work on Habe kingdoms, attributed to dan Fodio, complaint was made about the market tax called *aghama* – Hiskett (1960, p. 567). Barth was mainly interested in Hausa city markets (such as Kano, Katsina and Sokoto): most of the rural markets he describes in

any detail were in Bornu and other non-Hausa areas or, like Gumel, were centres of lon distance trade, in that case in natron.

(2) *Market taxation.* Information on pre-colonial market taxation is very scanty. 'Traditional market tithes' in Argungu, which were said to have been levied from time immemorial – National Archives, Kaduna, Provincial Office Sokoto, file on Markets – included: the corn tithe (*kanmudu*); the shoulder-bone on all animals slaughtered with a small amount of meat left on it (*kashin sungumi*); one faggot from each bundle of wood; one handful from each basket of cotton and henna; etc. These 'tithes' were paid to market overseers, who appointed women corn measurers (see p. 292 below). The colonial administration was quick to intro-duce market tolls in many markets in the innocent belief that these replaced 'traditional taxation', but the underlying philosophy was unclear. In his *Political Memorandum* on Taxa-tion Lugard pointed out that 'market dues and slaughter fees' (except in townships to which the Townships Ordinance of 1917 applied) were not a source of permanent revenue, but should be devoted to market upkeep and maintenance, anything in excess of these require-ments being 'restraint of trade'. A proposal to abolish market tolls was officially discussed in 1927, but it was decided to leave the matter to Residents. In 1932 tolls were collected from 87 markets in Sokoto Emirate – the levying of traditional taxation (as listed above) still being in full swing. Later that year official 'tolls and fees' were abolished throughout Sokoto Province, except in cities – and it was not until some twenty years later that they were re-introduced. Under the Markets Ordinance each Native Authority might make Rules for any of its mar-kets, uniformity not being required. (However, under the Native Authority Law (1954) a market was defined as 'a concourse of buyers and sellers having stalls or occupying places exceeding twenty in number'.) As a general rule official rates of market taxation are still very low compared with those prevailing in many regions of West Africa, e.g. southern Ghana and Ashanti. Usually taxation takes the form of rents on officially-erected concrete stalls, of which there are very few (or none) in many considerable markets, no 'tolls' being charged on produce entering the market; in many of the smaller markets in Katsina Emirate, no official fees are collected.

(3) *Periodicity.* Most Hausa markets meet once or twice during the seven-day week, except a few in the largest cities which meet daily. In Katsina Emirate, where 182 markets were mapped by the present writer – Hill (1971) – 55% of the markets met once every 7 days, 40% twice every 7 days, and one only (that in Katsina city) was open daily; there were also 5 interesting cases of 'alternate day' markets – see Hill (1969b, p. 403). Markets may continue to meet on the same day of the week for many decades. Thus, Kuraye and Raweo (Rawayau) markets are still held on Wednesdays and Saturdays as they were in Barth's time; and 10 out of 13 markets in Mani-Durbi, Kaura and Yandaka Districts, which were mentioned by Abu-bakar Labo, were still held on the same days in 1967 as at the turn of the century.

(4) *Afternoons only.* A peculiarity of ordinary 'local markets', which drew comment from Barth (1855, vol. II, p. 168), Robinson (1896a, p. 90) and Staudinger (1889, p. 614), is that little business is conducted until the late afternoon – see Hill (1971). This is presumably because most of those who attend markets are men who have spent their mornings working on their farms.

(5) *Women in markets.* Nearly all the Hausa females who attend markets are older women, or girls, the former mainly acting as sellers, the latter as both buyers and sellers. There is no evidence that the increased seclusion of women has led to a reduction in market attendance: semi-secluded women in dispersed hamlets do not go to market. Barth makes several references to small, wayside women's 'markets' (e.g. vol. II, pp. 94, 164) and it may be that even then younger women seldom attended 'town' markets. Many of the grain measurers – see (8) – are older women. See also (10) below.

(6) *'Landlords'* (*mai gida*). Another type of extra-market trade, involves resort to 'landlords' (see *Mai gida*) who accommodate stranger–traders, store their goods, act as brokers and render other services. While certain landlords, such as those in the long-distance cattle trade – see A. Cohen (1969) – are necessarily associated with market-places, there are others – see Hill (1966 and 1971) – who provide facilities which make resort to market-places unnecessary. (See Cowries.)

(7) *Brokers* (*dillali*). It is a peculiarity of Hausa trading (both inside and outside markets), which interested Barth, Robinson and others, that brokers often act as intermediaries between buyers and sellers – see Hill (1971) – receiving a small commission from one or both parties. This reliance on intermediaries, this trading neutrality, is the very antithesis of the situation in the forest zone, where traders (especially women traders) so often form reciprocal 'regular-customer' relationships. Such brokers may introduce the parties, facilitate (or undertake) bargaining, guarantee credit, etc. As brokers are not necessarily at all expert, nor any more familiar with the market-place than the traders themselves, it seems that their function is often merely that of freeing the parties to transact other business during the long period which may elapse before a satisfactory transaction is concluded: however, certain brokers, such as those in large cattle markets, are real professionals.

(8) *Grain measurers* – *ma'auni*, f. *ma'auniya*. Perhaps because most grain-sellers in rural markets are farmers who have better things to do than retailing grain in small quantities, it is usual (though never compulsory) for grain to be measured and retailed by intermediaries (*ma'auna*), who are more often older women than men. Like all other market-traders, the measurers act as individuals, and are not effectively organized under a head (sometimes known as *korama*) – as they may wrongly claim. Rates of commission usually appear to be at the discretion of the seller, not being formally based on the quantity sold; the measurer is entitled to the grain-spillings (*rara*).

(9) *Standard containers.* In Katsina markets a genuine standard, the *tiya*, is used for measuring grain and other homogeneous produce; while the *mudu* (q.v.) is not a reliable standard as between markets, various standard bowls (maybe all of them denoted *mudu*) are likely to be in use in any particular market on any day.

(10) *The functions of rural periodic market-places.* It is our hypothesis that irrespective of whether there is a nearby market-place, most *retailing* of foodstuffs required for day to day consumption is undertaken (at least in rural northern Katsina) by secluded women, whose 'honeycomb-market' is in continuous session – see pp. 125–8, and House-trade. Rural periodic markets (*such as are not focal points for long-distance trade*) are basically places where local farmers 'export' basic foodstuffs (grains, cowpeas, groundnuts) not required by their local community, many of the buyers being *'yan kwarami*; where craft goods (such as mats, pots, blacksmiths' wares, mortars, calabashes, embroidered caps, clothing made by tailors) are sold; where manufactures (such as cloth and all the numerous small wares handled by village *'yan tebur*) may be bought; where *'yan tebur* (who sell their wares outside markets on most days of the week) set up their tables; where certain products originally handled by long-distance traders may be bought for resale by secluded women (e.g. natron, but not kola); where certain 'services' (e.g. barbering) are performed; where livestock change hands (though livestock are often sold outside markets); where butchers do some of their business; where men traders sell bulky or fragile produce (e.g. sugar-cane and cassava) which is not handled by secluded women; etc. While every rural community needs to have a market-place within daily (preferably half-daily) reach, there is no necessity for it to have its 'own market': indeed, in Katsina Emirate, the evidence is that many sizeable communities lack markets – see Hill (1971).

(11) *Hausa/Fulani exchange.* In localities where there are many resident or wandering

Fulani pastoralists, market-places may primarily exist to enable Hausa farmers to sell grains etc. to the pastoralists who in turn sell milk and butter.

(12) *Markets in the Niger Republic.* Nicolas has written extensively and interestingly on market-places in rural Niger – see, in particular, Nicolas (1964 and NK, pp. 175–92) – with special reference to the Canton de Kantché. The local markets, such as are not foci for long-distance trade, seem to be as unimportant as in neighbouring northern Katsina. The ordinary farmer effects only a little business there – preferring to travel further to larger trade centres. Only 20 of the 211 villages in Kantché had a market and at least 12 markets had ceased to function in the last few decades. Markets tend to be situated some 10 kilometres apart. Small markets usually have weak links with larger ones – having 'une grande autonomie'. Although many women attend markets, most of the buyers are men; the women are almost entirely engaged in selling prepared foods (which they may cook in the market) for consumption on the spot. (When Barth visited Tessaoua (Tasawa) market he noted that 'provisions and ready-dressed food formed the staple commodity' – vol. II, p. 21.) Most sellers are men farmers and stock-rearers. Most of those who follow 'hereditary crafts' dispose of most of their goods at their place of work; other craftsmen more often sell wares in the market. Of 17 markets for which the date of origin is given, only 5 were founded before this century, the earliest date being 1843. Many brokers (*dillalai*) are humble people, rewarded with a mere pittance.

See **Batagarawa Market, Butchers, Exchange,** *Fatauci,* **House-trade,** *Kasuwa, Sarkin kasuwa.*

Marmari – *abim marmari* = a snack or delicacy.
(a) Numerous varieties of such snacks are produced and sold by secluded women – see **House-trade.**

Maroki – f. *marokiya,* pl. *maroka.* A professional praise-singer or eulogist, who is usually a horn-blower and drummer. See Smith (1957) and Abraham. Sometimes misleadingly known as 'beggars', *maroka* are (see Bargery) 'often very far from being in necessitous condition', getting part of their living by panegyrizing patrons and those whom they hope to enlist as such, but 'villifying such as refuse to be generous'. *Maroka* may operate in teams, or solo; when the latter 'the declamation consists, briefly, in an application of public pressure to prominent members of the community to validate their status by appropriate role perform-ances within the *roko* (q.v.) situation through the mechanism of gifts to the *maroka*. Praise and shame are the sanctions involved' – Smith (1957, p. 42). See *Dan kira, Masarci.*

Marriage – *aure.* According to Muslim law a man may have no more than 4 wives; although concubines (*kwarkwara*) are, also, permitted, it is nowadays usually considered that this is the prerogative of exalted chiefs, perhaps only of Emirs.

Marriage expenses.
(a) The following particulars relate to the expenses which, according to two expert informants, *ought* to be incurred in connexion with the first marriage of a girl from an ordinary family: detailed accounts relating to the marriage of a daughter of a member of the ruling-class showed that expenses were much higher in such a case, the *lehe* alone – see (6) – amounting to £95.

(1) In the *initial approach* (*farin magana*) to the girl's father or relatives, the suitor, or his representative, hands over £1 to £3.

(2) If the suitor is made welcome, a further sum of £3 to £5 is paid.

(3) If further progress is made, the suitor offers a 'small *lehe*' consisting of garments, cosmetics etc. (worth perhaps £5) for the girl and some money (say £2) for the parents.

(4) Then, if there is a *salla* (q.v.) before the confirmation ceremony – see (5) – the suitor will give further presents (*toshin salle*), worth perhaps £5, to his sweetheart, as well as money

(to her parents) for hairdressing – for any subsequent *salla* that occurs before the marriage, smaller presents, worth (say) £2 to £3 will be made.

(5) The *confirmation ceremony* (*baiko*), or formal betrothal, might cost the fiancé some £7 – this sum including about £1 for salt; 10*s.* for a big enamel bowl; 8*s.* for mats; at least £1 for kola; small sums for the officiating Malams; and further gifts for the girl.

(6) Before the marriage the bridegroom must spend at least £10 on clothes, cosmetics etc. for the bride, the whole being known as *lehe* (*lefe*), the goods having formerly been packed in a basket of this name – nowadays suitcases are sometimes provided: if the bride's parents are apprehensive lest the bridegroom's gifts will be insufficient, they will specify the value required.

(7) The simple marriage ceremony (*daurin aure*) may cost from £1 to £4, including kola, and £1 for *sadaki*, the only legally necessary cash gift to establish the contract and status of marriage.

(8) On the first morning that the bride spends in her husband's house a goat (worth, say, 30*s.*) should be slaughtered (*walima*) and donations made to the Malams.

All the expenses (1) to (8), which might amount to between £30 and £40, would have been incurred by the bridegroom or his relatives – only part of which would be reclaimable in the event of divorce. When it is the girl's first marriage, it is a rule, which is said to be rigidly observed, that none of these payments may be postponed; but part-postponement until after harvest is permitted with widows. See Taylor and Webb (1932, p. 69). Poor men often find it necessary to borrow – and there is a proverb saying that '*bashi*-marriages' are cheap. It was said that thirty years ago expenses might have amounted to only about £2, but gifts in the early stages (such as are not reclaimable in the event of divorce) may be omitted from such statements.

After the *walima* ceremony, it is the turn of the bride's parents to offer their contribution to the bridegroom (*dukiyar aure*), which might be £10–£15 plus a gown (*riga*) and some grain: this may be mainly used to pay off debts incurred by the bridegroom, his father or others. (Sometimes the *walima* ceremony is postponed until after this contribution has been received and found sufficient.) The bride's mother may also give about £1 to the 'best man' (*abokin ango*), in return for which a goat is slaughtered. Finally, the bride's mother makes various personal gifts to the bridegroom and his parents.

The value of a bride's dowry (*gara*), provided by her kinsfolk, varies greatly according to the means of the donors, the generosity of the bridegroom, and so forth. It should include foodstuffs such as grain, salt and groundnut oil, decorated enamel plates (*faranti*) which are plastered on the wall of the bride's sleeping hut, mats, a bed (and mattress etc.), cooking and eating utensils, calabashes etc. (See *koran gaban doki* – Bargery, p. 623 – for the list of gifts from the bride's mother which are carried in front of the bride when she is being taken to her new home.)

Finally there is the cost of any marriage feasts (*biki*): there may be as many as four of these, if the bride's and groom's families celebrate separately, as do men and women. Expenditure on these feasts, if they are held, and the scale of the contributions made by participants, vary so greatly that averages would be meaningless.

This account omits any later help, or gifts, which the husband may give to his wife's kin: although, nowadays, these obligations are much reduced, some respect is still paid, at least in the early years, to the idea that the marriage bond, linking the two families, requires continuous sustenance.

(b) See Mary Smith (1954) for a wealth of material on marriage expenses; see, also, Smith (1955, pp. 53–9), Taylor and Webb (1932). Forde (1949, p. 169 fn 1) cites Giles (1937) as reporting that in rural Zaria 'marriage payments, including the various customary gifts and entertainments as well as the *sadaki* proper', ranged from 15*s.* 'for a poor man's son' to about

60*s*. 'for the sons of the richer farmers, traders and village heads'. Most men had recourse to loans, for instance handing over for sale a gown worth 10*s*., for which 15*s*. had later to be paid. A very detailed analysis of expenditure on 46 first marriages is provided by Nicolas (NK, pp. 91–115), who also presents historical material. Nadel's discussion of the Nupe bride-price is extremely relevant (see, in particular, 1942, pp. 349–54).

Considering the complexity of the payments and counter-payments made, it is here noted almost with incredulity that the Katsina Local Authority (Reporting of Marriages) Rules 1969, which applied to 'all persons contracting marriages according to native law and custom', requires both husband and wife to report particulars of 'bride price, if any' – as well as 'details of previous divorce, if any'!

See **Divorce, Marriage-types, Naming-ceremony,** *Sadaki.*

Marriage-types.

(a) Nowadays in Batagarawa *gari* most wives are in full purdah (*kulle*, q.v.) and there is no practical need to distinguish marriage-types in terms of the degree of seclusion involved – see Smith (1955, p. 50). As for Smith's classification on the basis of non-religious criteria (*ibid.*, pp. 49–53), although the incidence of *auren zumunta* (kin-marriage) was not assessed in Batagarawa, it is doubtful whether unions of parallel and cross-cousins should be regarded as being 'preferred' (*ibid.*, p. 49), except possibly by poorer people who may be obliged to resort to them owing to their cheapness – see p. 151. above. 'Marriages of almsgiving' (*auren sadaka*), which cost the man nothing, occasionally occur; and among the old and poor there are a few *silkiti* marriages, the parties usually occupying different houses, or living in the wife's house owing to the husband's inability to provide for his partner. See Abraham (pp. 42–3), Taylor and Webb (1932). See **Divorce, Marriage expenses.**

(b) Marriages involving relative freedom may be known as *auren fita* – *fita*, being 'go out'.

Marshland: see *Fadama.*

Masa – pl. *masoshi.* A small round cake of flour made of any kind of grain. The word is also applied to anything having as ready a sale as such cakes.

Masarci – f. *masarciya*, pl. *masarta.* A professional 'beggar', whether *maroki* (q.v.) or *dan kira* (q.v.).

Masoro (*Piper guineense*). West African black pepper.

Masu-Sarauta – sing. *mai-sarauta.* Members of the ruling-class – see *Sarauta.*

Mat – *tabarma*, pl. *tabarmi*, a mat for sleeping or sitting on. There are numerous other words for different types of mat.

Mats may be made by either men or women from materials which include: fronds of the dum-palm (*kaba*) and of the palm known as *kijinjiri*; lath-like strips of the stem of the raphia palm (*tukurwa*); coarse grass and reeds, (including *kyara, gamba, tsaure*); and hemp (*rama*). Mats are used for sitting, sleeping, partitioning, fencing, door-covering, praying, etc., etc. Certain types are dyed.

(a) One type of mat made by men in Batagarawa is *tarbarmar hannu* which is plaited in narrow lengths, using fine strips of *kijinjiri*, which are then joined together. Common types of mat, or screen, include: *zana, asabari, kwarakwara* and *karamnu* (see below).

(b) There is much long-distance and market trade in mats, based partly on the availability of the various materials in different localities. A very famous mat market is Ajiwa, near Katsina city, where thousands of *karamnu* (whiteish, or greenish, mats made of young dum-palm fronds) may be seen on sale, covering a large area, and attracting traders from far afield. Traders sometimes buy mats for a price rise. See: Nadel (1942) on mat-making and marketing; Meek (1925, p. 168); and Nicolas (NM, pp. 66–7 and other sources).

See **'Free goods'.**

Maye – f. *mayya*, pl. *mayu*. A sorcerer, wizard or witch. Wizards traditionally 'catch people in market-places'. *Sarkin mayu* – itinerant seller of 'anti-witch medicines', charms, etc.

Mazari – pl. *mazare*. Spindle. See **Spinning**.

Meals. Two Hausa words for a meal taken at any time are *kalaci* and *jibi*. The breakfast, midday and evening meals are respectively: *karin kumallo*, *kalacin rana* and *abincin dare*.

Measuring bowls: see *Mudu, Tiya, Zakka*.

Melon – *guna, kankana* (*Citrullus vulgaris*). The most common form of water melon (*guna*), which has green stripes, is apparently half-wild – it may be given to cattle or grown only for its seeds. *Kankana* is the garden water melon with red pulp and black or red seeds; there are also other forms – see Dalziel. See *Agushi*.

Migration – *kaura*, and other words; *makauraci*, pl. *makaurata*, a migrant or a site for a new home in a village or hamlet.

This entry relates only to certain socio-economic aspects of non-seasonal migration within Hausaland: it is mainly concerned to emphasize how little is known on this subject. See also Chapter VII. For seasonal migration, see *Cin rani*.

Migration and farm tenure

(1) *The forfeiting of rights over farmland by migrants*. According to an official Memorandum on Rural Land Policy of 1929, (National Archives, Kaduna, 1724), it was then a 'general rule' that migrants 'abandoned all claims to any rights of occupancy or user': however, 'in more congested areas', or where the land was *taki* assessed (see **Revenue survey**) a farmer who continued to pay his tax was not as a rule deprived of his rights, but if the land were required by 'another member of the community' the matter would be settled by the Native Authority. It seems that returned pilgrims and Koranic students were always entitled to resume their rights.

(2) *An outgoing migrant's freedom to sell his farmland*. Whether the ban on the sale of farmland by departing migrants has been dropped in most emirates, as in Katsina, see p. 85, has not been officially recorded, but it is believed that in the more accessible Districts of Kano Emirate such sales have occurred since 1953, and that migrants from many Sokoto Districts are permitted to sell. (Post-war official reports on land tenure, such as Rowling (1952), paid surprisingly little attention to migration.)

(3) *Inter-Emirate migration*. This has often been considered 'a problem'. Thus, at the 1934 Conference of Chiefs of the Northern Provinces the Emir of Gwandu stated that 'this problem' was increasingly being 'encouraged by the unwritten law that immigrants should either be exempted from tax for the first year or so, or, alternatively, taxed very little'.

(4) *Inter-District migration*. In the early 1960s the Katsina N.A. sought (probably with little success) to prohibit the ownership of farms in one District by those living in another.

Migration and population density

The geographers – Grove (1957 and 1961), Morgan and Pugh (1969), Mortimore and Wilson (1965), Prothero (1956, 1957a, 1958, etc.) and others – who have sought to study rural migration in relation to population density, have been greatly hampered by the fact that only one of the six population censuses (q.v.), viz. that of 1952, is now thought to have been in the least reliable, so that accurate measures of changes in population density over time can only be made for those localities (and such *do* exist) where reasonably accurate population counts have been made in connexion with the compilation of the tax registers. Although there is some evidence of a general tendency for population densities to even out over such large areas as Katsina Emirate, the general directions of the flow are unknown and it may even be – see Mortimore and Wilson (1965) – that there is little emigration from the most heavily populated of all areas, the Kano Close-Settled Zone. One major difficulty in studying the flow is that densities are apt to vary greatly within quite short distances.

Official records of rural migration
It is not known whether any of the attempts made by Native Authorities to obtain returns from Districts on the 'migration of taxpayers' were successful: the Katsina records related only to migration to 'Bima', i.e. Gombe (see the section below, p. 298) and were very incomplete.

The relative unimportance of the drift to the cities
Although certain cities, such as Kano and Katsina, are growing fast – between 1952 and 1963, if the census figures are to be trusted, the population of Kano rose by 123% to 295,432, that of Katsina by 72% to 90,538 – Hausaland is still one of the least-urbanized major regions of West Africa: according to the 1963 census, only 6% of the total population of Kano Province lived in towns or cities with populations of over 20,000, the corresponding figure for Katsina Province being only 4%. In 1952, according to official opinion, there were only 7 towns in Katsina Province (other than Katsina city) with *compact* settlements of 5,000 or more – and their total population was only 54,000 (1952 Census *Report*, p. 11). Assuming that most men in towns with populations of under 20,000 gain a large part of their livelihood from farming, the incidence of migration out of farming (into wholly urban occupations) cannot be high. Assuming, also, a continuation of the general tendency for population densities to even out over certain large areas such as Katsina Emirate – see Grove (1957) – then most migration within Hausaland must be for farming. If the annual rate of migration for farming in Kano and Katsina Emirates were as low as 1% of adult males, then (if the average migrant had 4 dependants) as many as about 100,000 people would be migrating into new farming areas annually.

Short-distance migration
In the early years of the British administration, officials were much troubled in some localities by the question of *nomi-jide*, defined as 'living in a tax area, other than where one farms': although there was much migration out of walled towns at that time – see, e.g., *Colonial Annual Report*, Northern Nigeria, 1907, Cmd 3729, pp. 75–6 and the section on migration for groundnut farming below – many farmers preferred to travel long distances to their farms, rather than to 'move house'. In 1909 C. L. Temple noted (*Annual Report*, Kano Division) that in Kano the domicile was often 10 to 20 miles from the farm: the 'entire division', he insisted, was 'divided into coadunate groups of farms in place of coadunate groups of habitations'. (In this connexion it may be stressed that it is likely that nowadays a substantial proportion of all Hausa farmers lives dispersedly, or in small clusters, this being a matter which has been entirely neglected by census-takers. The Hausa may thus contrast with the Kanuri who, according to Rosman (1962), never live in dispersed homesteads. Nor is such dispersion anything new. When approaching Kano from the north-west, Barth noted that villages were 'scattered about in the most agreeable and convenient way, as farming villages ought to be, but which, is practicable only in a country in a state of considerable security and tranquillity' – vol. II, p. 94.) In 1907–8 it was reported (*Annual Report, Northern Nigeria*, p. 613) that, due partly to the cessation of Maradi raids, 20,000 people had moved out of western Kano into southern Katsina where the land, which was very fertile, was 'rapidly cleaned and put into cultivation'.

Immigration from French territory (now the Niger Republic)
Although Prothero has estimated (1958, p. 8) that at least 250,000 people moved into Sokoto Province from French territory between 1931 and 1952, little attention has been paid to this question of trans-frontier migration. In the intensive survey conducted in certain areas in the 1931 census (see **Population censuses**) information was collected on birthplace, but unfortunately the material relating to immigration into 200 villages was not published in the Census

Report, being considered 'too detailed'; published figures relating to Dankama on the Katsina frontier with Niger, showed that two-thirds of the population was immigrant.

Migration for groundnut farming

Whether the development of groundnut production for export, following the completion of the Lagos/Kano rail link in 1912, in itself prompted much migration for farming is entirely unknown.

Migration to Gombe Emirate

Since about 1949 (personal information from Mary Tiffen), a great many Hausa (or Hausa–Fulani) men have migrated as farmers to Gombe Emirate, with the result that there is a substantial area south-east of Gombe city where virtually all farmland is permanently cultivated. The attractiveness of this area results mainly from the high fertility of the soil, especially for cotton cultivation. Of a sample of 86 immigrant farmers, half had come from Bauchi and other neighbouring emirates, the other main places of origin being Kano and Sokoto Provinces (12 each). Because the historically famous Bima Hill lies a short distance north-east of the main receiving area for farmers, this movement is often denoted (as in Batagarawa) as 'migration to Bima'.

Milk – *nono*, fresh or sour milk; *madara* fresh milk.

(a) The milk supplies of Batagarawa come from the cattle owned by Hausa farmers as well as Fulani pastoralists: many of the latter are near Dabaibayawa (some 6 miles south of the *gari*) and at Jilawa further west. Some half-dozen Fulani women with large calabashes of milk, selling at 4s. to 5s., came into the *gari* daily in 1967.

Millet: see *Gero, Maiwa*.

Mimosa – *gabaruwa* (*Acacia arabica*). Egyptian mimosa. The pods and roasted seeds of this very common tree have many uses in tanning, pottery, dyeing etc. The original source of gum arabic. See **Tanning**.

Mixed farming: see **Ploughing**.

Miya. A sauce, or gravy, which is served with *tuwo*. There are many different types, the various ingredients including: meat, groundnut oil, pepper, dried baobab leaves, *karkashi*, cowpeas, sorrel, tomatoes, onions, okro, sweet potatoes (and other vegetables), salt, natron, *daddawa* (q.v.). According to Bargery, *romo* is a broth which is not thickened with *karkashi*, *okro*, etc.

Money – *kudi* (q.v.). The Hausa words for different sums are: *anini* (one-tenth penny, no longer in circulation); *kwabo* (penny); *ahu* (1½d.); *taro* (3d.); *sule* (1s.); *fataka* (2s.); *fam* (£1).

Money-lenders: see **Usury**.

Mortar – *turmi*, pl. *turame*. Used for pounding grains, groundnuts, etc. and also for threshing small quantities.

(a) Most households own several large wooden mortars, some of which may be reserved for special uses; while usually nominally owned by individual housewives, they are often used communally within the household and may be bought for household use by husbands. The mortars are made from certain hard woods by local wood-workers. See *Dakau*, **Grindstone**.

Mosque – *masallaci*, pl. *masallatai*.

(a) A 'Friday mosque', which attracts a large gathering, was opened in the *gari* in May 1967. There are 13 privately-owned small mosques, of which 10 are in the *gari* (see Fig. 4, p. 11) and 3 in dispersed houses: they are small rooms with direct access to the street, in which anyone may pray. On a man's death a privately-owned mosque passes to his sons; on the sale of a house an attached mosque passes to the purchaser. For some years after the owner's death the mosque usually continues to be known by his name – e.g. Masallacin Ibrahim.

Muciya – pl. *muciyoyi*. A stick used for stirring when cooking *tuwo*.

Mudu – pl. *mudaye*. A measuring bowl (nowadays usually made of tin or aluminium) with a traditional capacity of 4 handfuls of grain, 4 *mudaye* being equal to 1 *sa'a* or *zakka*. Although the *mudu* has long ceased to be a reliable standard (being subject to the constant 'erosion' of competition), it is still often spoken of as such, and there may be a 'range of standards' in use in any particular market – see (a).

(a) In Batagarawa a *tiya* is regarded as roughly equivalent to 2¼ *mudaye*. In nearby 'Yar Gamji market, 3 of the 10 different bowls used by a trader for measuring pepper were denoted '*mudaye*' – normal, small and smaller.

(b) Vessels denoted as *mudaye* are used for measuring grains, groundnuts, etc. throughout the markets of Hausaland – at least so far as has been recorded.

See *Tiya*.

Mukaddas. A deputy, relief or representative.

(a) The title of the Hamlet Head of Batagarawa Hamlet, his immediate superior being Magaji, the Village Head. See p. 157 on the present office-holder.

Murgu. Payment made by a slave in lieu of service – alternatively *galla*.

Musaya. Barter or exchange. See **Exchange.** The term *musayar kasuwa* (lit. 'market exchange') implies *selling* one thing in order to buy another.

Muslim Religious Orders – *tariqas.*

(a) Both Tijaniyya and Kadiriyya flourish in Batagarawa, of which the former has more adherents.

Nama.

(i) Meat or flesh.

(ii) A wild animal.

Naming-ceremony – *ran suna*. On the seventh day after birth, children are formally named at a Muslim ceremony. See Mary Smith (1954, p. 140), Nicolas (NK, p. 103). The following particulars relate to the expenditure conventionally incurred in Batagarawa in connexion with such ceremonies, as well as in the days immediately following the birth. See Taylor and Webb (1932) for 'an account of birth from its beginning till the weaning'.

Expenditure and ceremonies connected with the birth of a wife's first-born child

When a wife is pregnant for the first time she usually goes to her parents' home, at about the end of the seventh month, to be ready for the delivery there. The first type of outlay by the husband's parents is in respect of firewood required for hot baths for 42 days after the birth; about £1 to £2 is given to the wife's parents for this purpose.

Immediately after the birth the husband's parents buy meat, costing between about 3s. and 5s., to be 'roasted' (*naman gishi*) for the mother during the first three days. To congratulate the wife's parents on the baby's safe arrival, gifts of grain (*kayan barka*), amounting to about 14 to 20 *tiya*, are then made to them by the husband (or his parents), a small party being held. About 10s. to £1 worth of honey is also given. Various condiments (*kayan yaji*) costing about £1 to 30s. are given by the husband (or his parents) to the wife's parents – these may include *citta*, ginger, black pepper (*masoro*), garlic, salt, natron, etc.; a length (*turmi*) of patterned cloth (*atamfa*) should also be given. Richer people also provide sets of clothes for the baby (*kayan jariri*). It is also necessary to pay about £1 to 30s. on *kudin durkushi* – lit. 'money for kneeling to give birth'.

On the fourth or fifth day the husband (or his parents) buy certain meat (*kauri*), costing about £1 to 30s. (it consists of the heads and legs of cattle, goats or sheep) and a party (*shan kauri*) is held, at which the meat is divided into three portions – one each for the husband's and wife's parents and one for other people. The husband's parents (or the husband himself) give the barber (q.v.) a share: he has earlier had a share of the *kayan yaji* and the honey.

The midwife (*ungozoma*) attends the mother at the birth and washes the baby every morning and evening for seven days; she is paid by the mother's parents.

On the seventh day after the birth the naming-ceremony (*ran suna*) is held. On the previous evening the relatives of both parties send out messages about the ceremony, which is held at the mother's house; kola may then be distributed, anyone receiving any nuts being obliged to attend. The Imam, or his nominee, recites the prayers. At least 200 kola-nuts are bought by the husband's parents, and the wife's parents also make a contribution. The main expenditure incurred by the husband and/or his parents is on a ram, which may cost between £2 and £10, or even more. Various special portions of the meat are given to the midwife, the husband's sister (*babani*), the Imam, various beggars, the barber, the blacksmiths, the hairdresser – the remainder being for the wife's parents, the wife and their friends and relatives.

After the naming-ceremony there is much merriment, with drumming and dancing, and the husband's parents give calabashes of grain (*koran haifuwa*) to the wife's parents – 14 calabashes, or about 28 *tiyas*, for a baby girl, 13 calabashes for a boy; condiments (*kayan yaji*, see above) are also provided. The husband's parents also give a calabash of grain to the barber.

The wife remains with her parents until after the husband has made his wife a gift known as *bante*, which may cost as much as £5 to £7; the date of the wife's return varies between about 3 months and 2 years after the birth. On the wife's return, her parents make various gifts of clothing, money and grain (*koran tarewar haifuwa*) to the husband and his parents, which may be worth about 30s. to £3.

On the basis of the above estimates, which relate to conventional expenditure, the 'ordinary husband' and/or his parents ought to pay out at least £12 10s., and might spend as much as £29 10s., plus grain and kola – the value of which varies greatly seasonally, but could hardly be less than £5; receipts from the wife's parents, mainly on the wife's return home, are conventionally small in comparison. Expenditure by members of the ruling class is much heavier. It is almost needless to add that poor husbands, especially those with deceased fathers, have little hope of raising such large funds, though *biki* partners might be there to help.

Subsequent births
Expenses incurred in connexion with a first-born child may be regarded as part of the marriage costs for a virgin, as a species of 'thanks' for her fertility, those incurred for subsequent births being much lower. The wife does not return to her parents' house for any subsequent birth but remains with her husband, even if the child is the first she has borne by him. Whereas the numerous forms of expenditure connected with the first birth are regarded as 'standard', the husband (and his parents) are much freer over later births, though they must be careful to spend sufficient in the opinion of the wife's parents, who in this case are responsible for the *koran haifuwa*, the size of which reflects the scale of the husband's expenditure.

Native Authority (N.A.) The constitution, powers and duties of the former Native Authorities (N.A.s) – now known as (Local Government) Authorities – were laid down in the N.A. Law of 1954 as amended. The most recent literature on Native Administration (also, confusingly, known as N.A.) includes Campbell (1963), Kirk-Greene (1965a) and Wraith (1966) – the latter source including a bibliography. See also, Smith (1960) on Native Administration in Zaria in 1950. In 1965 there were 71 Native Authorities of very varying sizes, in the Northern Region of Nigeria, of which Katsina, with an estimated revenue of over £1m., was the fourth largest (in revenue terms) – see *Northern Nigeria Local Government Yearbook, 1965*. Almost all these authorities had chiefs (in the emirates the emir himself) as their heads: these chiefs (who were graded) were in most cases 'the holders of those traditional posts recognized by the British Government when indirect rule was first established through the traditional rulers sixty years ago' – Wraith (1966, p. 10). The bulk of the revenue of N.A.s came from the community tax (*haraji*). Native Authorities had powers to set up Subordinate Councils in Districts, Villages and other administrative sub-areas. See **Economic regulations**, *Haraji*.

Native Courts: see **District Courts**.

Native treasury: see *Baitulmal*.

Natron – *kanwa*, there are many other Hausa words for particular types and qualities – see Bargery.

Hydrous sodium carbonate, or 'potash', of natural occurrence, which is widely consumed by humans and animals, replacing or supplementing salt, the latter having a less caustic taste; it is also used as a medicine and for soap-making and may be mixed with chewing tobacco and snuff. *Farar kanwa* is for food, animals, soap-making; *jar kanwa* is for medicine.

(a) As many as 39 of the secluded women traders of Batagarawa were recorded as retailing natron, mainly bought on their behalf in Katsina city.

(b) The long-distance trade in natron, which excited the interest of both Denham and Barth, remains very important, though recent references to it are most scanty. Katsina city is a very important *entrepôt*, the main sources of supply being Niger (whence supplies are brought by Tuareg traders with camel transport) and Bornu (supplies being handled by Kanuri and Hausa traders). In Barth's time Gumel was a very large wholesale market (vol. II, p. 169), Kanuri traders seldom carrying their supplies further west; when travelling towards Gumel, Barth counted more than 500 loads of natron on his road in one day (*ibid.*, p. 160). Kano was another large *entrepôt* – *ibid.*, p. 123. The long-distance tobacco traders of Kabakawa – see Hill (1970a) – bought natron in Myrria, east of Zinder, for sale in Yorubaland. Despite its bulkiness, natron must have been one of the most important wares carried by long-distance Hausa caravans from Kano and Katsina, via Nupe, to Yorubaland.

> The Hausa merchants form enormous caravans, chiefly of small donkeys, and transport this potash [kanwa] . . . to Illorin and Lagos. They are unwilling to dispose of it en route (hence the equality of prices at Lokoja, Bida, and Lagos), and trade it in Illorin chiefly for kolas, and for cotton, hardware and other goods. It is . . . an indispensable adjunct to the yam diet of the Yorubas.
>
> *Colonial Annual Report, N. Nigeria, 1902* (p. 120)

See *Burdumi, Cukurfa, Fatauci, Kantu*, **Salt**.

Nikau. Corn grinding done by women for payment. See *Aikatau*.

Noma. Farming, or farm-work generally. Hence, farmer = *manomi*, f. *manomiya*, pl. *manoma*. See **Farming-operations**.

Noman jinga – farming for wages.

(a) Under the employment system known as *jinga*, or *noman jinga*, the farmworker (*dan jinga*) is paid a wage, agreed in advance, for a given task, such as weeding or reaping a manured farm, undertaken at times to suit his convenience. The work (unlike *kwadago*) being unsupervised, trouble arises if it is not up to standard; in Batagarawa only a few trusted men are engaged in this manner, but the system is said to be more common in certain neighbouring areas.

(b) See Nicolas (1968a, p. 33), for the suggestion that *'yan jinga* are often debtors.

Nome (*Nomi*). A variety of benniseed (*Sesamum indicum*). Barth saw fields of *nome* on approaching Kano – vol. II, p. 95.

Nomi-jide. Living in a tax area, other than where one farms. This was a problem which greatly exercised officials during the early colonial days. See **Migration**.

Okro – *kubewa* (pl. *kubeyi*) (*Hibiscus esculentus*). The immature mucilaginous fruit is used in soups, and the leaves may be used as a herb.

(a) Grown on a small scale in Batagarawa, the picking of the crop is men's work, for which sons-in-*gandu* are unpaid. The cutting and drying of the vegetable is both men's and women's work. The vegetable is never cooked when fresh.

Onions – *albasa*, pl. *albasoshi* (*Allium Cepa*). 'Onions often of very large size and reddish tinge are skilfully cultivated in N. Nigeria, in both a round-depressed form and an oblong bulb, raised from seed. These are of mild flavour and can be eaten raw without discomfort as a refresher when travelling' – Dalziel (p. 485). Barth regarded onions (which had been introduced from North Africa) as of great benefit to European travellers and was delighted with the irrigated beds (*lambuna*), producing wheat and onions, which he saw in Hausaland. See also, Clapperton (1829, p. 219).

Onions are an important Hausa export, long-distance traders transporting, or despatching, them in very large quantities to Yorubaland, and onwards to southern Ghana and elsewhere. Hay and Smith (1970, p. 59) estimated onion 'exports' from northern to southern Nigeria in 1964 at 37,000 tons – mainly transported by road.

In northern Katsina onions are mainly grown as a dry-season crop on irrigated river-side plots, sometimes by native farmers (as in the neighbourhood of Ajiwa, on the river Tagwai south-east of Katsina city, where there is a renowned wholesale market which attracts many buyers from distant places), and sometimes by seasonal migrants on *cin rani* – as near Batsari and Jibiya. See Plate 30.

So far as is known, onion-growing (like shallot-growing in the Anloga area of south-eastern Ghana) has been developed entirely by the farmers themselves, with no help from Agriculture Departments. Many different types of manure are used, including the droppings of pigeons, cattle-egrets (*balbela*) and goats, but not cattle dung. Although onions are extremely perishable in the tropics, and rot very rapidly when bagged, farmers have developed storage methods – mainly in 'granaries' resembling grain *rumbuna* – to such a fine art that large stocks are held for 6 months and more, for the purpose of profiting from the very pronounced price rise which starts developing some months after harvest.

The neglect of Hausa onion cultivation in the literature is remarkable; but see Harris (1930) on onion-growing in Yauri, and a most interesting paper on 'The Marketing of Onions and Cowpeas in the Kainji Lake Basin', by I. A. Adalemo, issued by NISER, University of Ibadan, 1970.

Papaw – *gwanda* (*gonda*), pl. *gwandoji* (*Carica Papaya*). Although nowadays uncommon in north-central Katsina, Barth saw a fine specimen of the fruit in Katsina (vol. II, p. 60). See also *ibid.*, pp. 12–13.

Pawa (*Fawa*).

(i) The work of a butcher.

(ii) A butcher or meat seller; Sarkin Pawa is a chief butcher.

See **Butchers**.

Pawning – *jingina*, *dangana*. Trimingham states (1959, p. 134) that the practice of pawning a person to a creditor, until a debt was repaid, was always very rare among the Hausa and certainly there are few (if any) references to it in the literature. For the pledging of farmland, see *Jingina*.

Pepper – the generic word for red pepper is *barkono*: there are numerous other words for different varieties. *Capiscum frutescens* is the pungent, shrubby, pepper of commerce.

(a) The varieties which are sold by many women, and some men, traders, are known as

tasshi; grown on a small scale in Batagarawa, this pepper is picked by women, the farmer's wife (who is herself paid) recruiting assistants at the rate of 1s. for a long morning's work.
See *Masoro*.

Permanent cultivation. This entry reviews the evidence showing that permanent cultivation of manured farmland is an old and (nowadays) common agronomic system in Hausaland – a system which is not necessarily associated with land shortage – and discusses misbeliefs on the matter.

It is to be presumed that much of the extensive farmland within the walls of large Hausa cities (*birni*) has been permanently cultivated for centuries – that, over the course of time, there have been millions of Hausa farmers who have successfully practised agronomic systems, with no fallow, such that yields were not necessarily subject to progressive deterioration. Writing before 1918, Temple (1968, pp. 147–8) noted that there were about one million people living around Kano city 'entirely supporting themselves from the produce of a soil which is none too fertile and which has been under close cultivation for five hundred years at least'.

Assuming, as elsewhere in this book, that farm-selling has normally always involved manured plots, the firm evidence is (see **Farm-selling**) that farmland inside city walls was commonly manured, in some localities at least, as early as the beginning of the nineteenth century – though in that case it is admittedly curious that Barth should have been so astonished by the systematic use of manure by the Musgu (who live south of Lake Chad), exclaiming (vol. III, p. 208) that it was the 'first example of such careful tillage' that he had 'as yet observed in Central Africa, both among Mohammedans and pagans'.

In 1894 William Wallace, 'who had lived for 18 years more or less in the Niger region', travelled to Rogo some 50 miles west of Kano, and then on to Fawa in Katsina Emirate. 'Most of the land', he wrote (1896, p. 212), 'is under cultivation with the exception of perhaps a fourth lying fallow in its turn. Much of the ground in the neighbourhood of the towns is divided into fields by raised earthwork dykes or hedges, mostly of cactus'. That this was rural permanent cultivation in the full sense was made amply clear (p. 213): 'The ground is not cleared [at planting time] . . . for undergrowth is there none . . . the ground is as bare as the palm of one's hand'. The old furrows were 'used again and again'. (In any case, no agronomic system based on fallowing could have involved the cultivation of as much as three-quarters of the total area at any time.)

In 1891 Monteil (1895, p. 281) observed that 'toutes les terres, dans un rayon de plus de 100 kilometres autour de Kano, sont en culture . . .' Travelling between Zaria and Kano on a caravan road (which was, presumably, 'The Great White Road' so lyrically described by Morel – 1911, Chapter II), Lugard observed (1904, p. 22) that the road was 'frequently enclosed between hedges of great age, a very striking contrast to the universal bush path of Africa'; the road led 'for the most part through cultivation and villages'. For the first time in Africa he saw, with surprise, that the fields were manured. According to Mockler-Ferryman (1902, p. 70), the countryside round Kano was a 'perfect garden' for 80–100 miles in all directions: 'the most fertile lands in other parts are mere patches of cultivation compared with the province of Kano'. (An impression worth reporting, exaggerated though it is.)

G. C. Dudgeon, who was Inspector of Agriculture for British West Africa before 1911, noted (1922, 2nd edition, p. 153) that manure was so necessary for the system of cultivating guinea corn in Kano and Zaria Provinces 'that every scrap of material which is of manurial value is carefully preserved, being carried to the fields by men and donkeys'.

Where entirely new plants are to be grown, a shallow bed is made upon the top of the ridge or in the furrow, and the goat, sheep and cow manure mixed with ashes, and accumulated carefully in the villages, is spread thinly upon the bed before the seed is sown. In other places, where old root-stocks occur, handfuls of manure are applied to the growing plants in May.   (*ibid.*)

E. D. Morel visited Northern Nigeria in 1910–11. He considered that in the northern part of Zaria and in Kano 'the science of agriculture' had attained 'remarkable development'. 'There is little we can teach the Kano farmer. There is much we can learn from him.'

Rotation of crops and green manuring are thoroughly understood, and I have frequently noticed in the neighbourhood of some village small heaps of ashes and dry animal manure deposited at intervals along the crest of cultivated ridges which the rains will presently wash into the waiting earth. In fact, every scrap of fertilizing substance is husbanded by this expert and industrious agricultural people.   Morel (1911, p. 115)

He had seen nothing more remarkable in the way of cultivation in either France or Flanders – *ibid.*, p. 234.

Writing in 1913, P. H. Lamb, then Director of Agriculture in Northern Nigeria, was perhaps the first scientific expert to express the pessimistic attitude to Hausa agriculture which has prevailed until recently. Although he classed cowpeas as the third most important crop in Hausaland (1913, p. 626), he yet condemned the farmer for his lack of interest in leguminous crops. He regarded the Hausa as destroying the natural fertility of the soil (he wrote as though they were new arrivals in the country) – as making little or no attempt to induce fertility, but 'drawing upon the bounty of nature' (*ibid.*, p. 629). He was writing on the eve of the great expansion of groundnut exports.

Every available piece of land is being planted up with groundnuts, which yield here at the rate of about 1 ton per acre [?]. What the fixation of atmospheric nitrogen will be it is impossible to say, but its influence on the fertility of the soil will, one would imagine, be at least equivalent in effect to that of a modern cyanamide installation of enormous dimensions.   (*ibid.*, pp. 633–4)

Has the preference for permanent cultivation increased *pari passu* with the proportion of farmland under groundnuts? If so, why have the textbooks – and the FAO *Report* (1966) – ignored the potentialities of the new agronomic balance which has resulted from vastly increased production of groundnuts, especially in Kano and northern Katsina?

There is no means of judging whether in fully rural areas, permanent cultivation was always, or usually, associated with the presence (if only seasonally and briefly) of pastoral Fulani and their herds. One must only suppose that the manurial value of animal dung has been well known for centuries. 'There is not the slightest doubt . . . but that all recognise the value of manuring farms' stated the writer of a re-assessment report on Birnin Kebbi in 1915 (see **Gulumbe**) – astutely adding that distant farms 'received scant attention in this respect', unless they were owned by rich farmers who could afford both to transport manure and to pay for cattle to graze over their land (see **Manure**).

Since becoming motor-borne, travellers have ceased observing the countryside, especially as main roads usually traversed uninhabited country: it seems that during the past half century there have been no published accounts relevant to permanent cultivation outside the Kano Close-Settled Zone – though there is doubtless some unexplored archival material. Certainly, until recently, there was no one to dispute the standard contention, repeated in all the textbooks, that (Kano apart) permanent cultivation was as rare in Hausaland as elsewhere in West Africa. 'Neither farmyard manure nor compost nor fertilizers are applied to most farmers' fields (except in areas where there is land pressure, e.g. Kano) . . .' – FAO *Report* (1966, p. 176).

The new evidence that in many localities farmers *prefer* to cultivate the bulk of their food crops on permanently cultivated farmland, irrespective of the density of population, is derived both from air photographs, and from detailed fieldwork. On air photographs taken during the dry season the weedless farms under permanent cultivation (*gonakin karakara*) are seen to be white in contrast to the greyness of the weedy farms that have been fallowed for a single season only – see Plate 35. Inspection of air photographs covering large areas of Katsina Emirate shows that a high proportion of farmland, even in areas of dispersed settlement, is annually cropped – see Hill (1970a, p. 158). Luning was told by farmers in Kogo District (south-west Katsina), where population density was only 44 persons per square mile, that they had learnt about permanent cultivation from Kano immigrants (1961, p. 34). Nor is that emirate exceptional. Members of the Rural Economy Research Unit at Ahmadu Bello University report the existence of permanent cultivation in Zaria, Sokoto and Bauchi Emirates, as has Luning – 1963b and 1963c – in Sokoto villages.

Although the deep pessimism of the following passage is, perhaps, not widely shared, a failure to appreciate the symbiotic relationship which often exists between the Hausa farmer and the Fulani pastoralist is one important reason for the persistence of beliefs that the farmer is ignorant of the value of manure.

> There can be *no solution* (*sic*) to Northern Nigeria's agricultural problem so long as the cattle population remain divorced from its soil . . . No matter how aesthetically attractive the race [the pastoral Fulani] may be, or how deep its roots in history, they and their cattle must become settled if the large issues in Nigeria are to be solved in the interests of the Nigerian people.   Nigerian Livestock Mission *Report* (1950, pp. 36–7)

Apart from the presumed hiatus between farmer and pastoralist, what other factors might account for the persistent belief that farmers never *prefer* to grow most of their crops on manured farmland? These might include: (1) the conviction that all crops 'grow better' on bush-farms (q.v.) – although in Batagarawa, for instance, farmers choose to grow no early millet and only a small proportion of their groundnuts on such farms; (2) the failure to appreciate that yields may be *permanently* maintained with adequate manuring; (3) the undoubted rarity of permanent cultivation (except in the immediate vicinity of farmsteads) in many well-populated non-Hausa areas, e.g. the groundnut basin of Senegal, and the consequent influence of such eminent authorities as W. Allan who asserts (1965, p. 247) that in the northern savannah of West Africa 'intensive systems' seem 'to be characteristic of refuge areas in which natural conditions afforded some degree of protection against attack and disturbance'; (4) the accident that the most important writer on rural Hausaland in this century (M. G. Smith) was uninterested in agronomy; (5) the accident that the most influential geographical report (Grove, 1957) related to a very densely-populated locality (Bindawa), where there was hardly any bush; (6) the accident that the only published farm-maps until the issue of Norman (1967), related to a small hamlet – Gata, see Nash (1948) – where the farmers were recent immigrants who had had insufficient time to establish manured farms – see Hill (1970a, p. 158); (7) the failure to appreciate the saving in manpower resulting from the entire absence of weeds at planting time when farms are cultivated annually; (8) the general lack of interest in sheep and goats (q.v.) and in donkeys (q.v.) and hence in the manurial application of their droppings – the Nigerian Livestock Commission expressly stated (*ibid.*, p. 30) that the 5 or 6 million sheep and goats in the Northern Provinces 'though belonging to the settled agriculturists have not become integrated into the farm economy'; (9) the recent concentration of agricultural scientists on a 'modern development problem' – viz. the application of imported fertilizers (see **Manure**); (10) the failure to appreciate the great importance of ploughs consequent upon their extensive hiring-out – see **Ploughing** – and hence the advantages of

11

'improved', stumpless land; (11) the fact that the headquarters of agricultural research in the northern states is at Samaru, near Zaria, which may be near the southern limit of the zone where permanent cultivation is widely practised. (See Steele (1967) on agricultural research at the only sub-station in Hausaland, that at Kano, where the very small scientific staff was mainly concerned with plant breeding particularly, of groundnuts: 'When we have a full complement of staff there will be four plant breeders and an agronomist working here.')

Finally, the common conviction that the only agronomical alternatives to 'shifting cultivation' are crop-rotational systems involving fallow and cattle manure, has even resulted in a mis-reading of the literature on the Kano Close-settled Zone, where fertility is often maintained without rotation, fallow or cattle manure:

> Until recently population density was low and land was available in abundance, so that fallow periods were long enough to rebuild soil fertility. *In the more densely populated agricultural area of today, the system is an anachronism.* [Present author's italics.] It must be changed to crop rotation, with cultivated fallow crops, mainly of the leguminous type, giving back organic matter to the soil and thus raising soil fertility. At the same time, the poor physical properties of most Nigerian soils have to be improved by the addition of compost and, if available, farmyard manure. Compost can be obtained from plant residues, *which have so far mostly been burnt* [present author's italics] – e.g. cotton stems, cereals, straw, weeds, etc., with the addition of household residues and animal excrement.
>
> FAO *Report* (1966, p. 176)

> By any measure, land under traditional tenure is farmed most haphazardly and most extensively . . .
> Perhaps the most important problem for solution is finding a suitable substitute for shifting cultivation and the accompanying long fallow periods which keep more than half of the arable land out of cultivation at a given time. (From an unpublished paper on agricultural development problems in West Africa, with special reference to Nigeria, by an expatriate expert who was quite familiar with Hausaland.)

Although the hundreds of thousands of Hausa farmers who practise permanent cultivation are so exceptional within the framework of 'African traditional agriculture', they conform very well to the 'rules' formulated by locational geographers regarding rural settlement and land-holding. Chisholm (1962, p. 148) notes

> the frequency with which the same orders of magnitude keep on recurring among peoples of widely different technical achievements and inhabiting areas with markedly different physical characteristics . . . Over much of the world, the present spontaneous tendency is to modify the patterns of rural settlement and land-holding in such a manner that the distance separating the farmstead from the lands cultivated is reduced to something in the order of 1 or 2 kilometres, if the farmstead is not actually on the farm . . . At a distance of 3–4 kilometres the costs of cultivation necessitate a radical modification of the system of cultivation or settlement – for example by the establishment of subsidiary settlements – though adjustments are apparent before this point is reached.

Pestle – *tabarya*, pl. *tabare*. Pestles are often used for threshing on the ground as well as for pounding in a mortar (*turmi*).

Pigeons – *tantabara*, pl. *tantabarai*.
(a) There are about 6 pigeon-keepers in Batagarawa, whose pigeon-cotes, made of baked clay, contain many compartments for roosting. Fed on grain and sugared water, the pigeons sell

for about 6*d*. each: their droppings are sold to outside onion-growers as a much valued manure.

Pigs – *alade*, pl. *aladai*. Owing to the Muslim pig taboo, these animals are not reared in Hausa villages.

Pledging. For farm-pledging, see *Jingina*.

Ploughing. The ox-plough is known as *galmar shanu* (lit. 'cattle-*galma*').

(a) In 1968 in Batagarawa 13 farmers owned (or operated) 15 imported metal ox-ploughs, the number of plough oxen being 36; nearly a third of the oxen, and 2 of the ploughs were, in fact, owned by non-Batagarawa men. Alhaji Barau owned 2 ploughs; 9 of the remaining owners (or operators) were Group 1 farmers, 3 were in Group 2. Ten of the ploughs and about 14 of the oxen had been obtained through the Katsina Native Authority, payment being made over a term of years; the others had been bought privately. Batagarawa farmers also hired ploughs owned by farmers in the neighbouring Hamlets of Kwami, Tsauni and Autawa. Ploughs are much utilised for the second and third weedings, as well as for ridging. In 1967 there was only one plough which could be used for groundnut harvesting.

In Batagarawa, as elsewhere (see below), the hiring of the services of a plough-team is extremely common and enquiries suggested that most non plough-owners in Groups 1 and 2, as well as some farmers in Group 3, hired ploughs from time to time. (Indeed, a large proportion of the total acreage under groundnuts is ridged by plough.) Nine of the 13 plough-owners regularly employed a son as ploughman, 2 employed heads of farming-units and 2 employed dependent relatives or other farmers. Owners sometimes operate their ploughs themselves.

There are few, if any, Batagarawa farmers who could afford to operate a plough were it not possible to recoup expenditure by hiring out. During the farming-season the oxen, which are kept in huts, do not graze and have to be provided with bran (*dusa*), *harawa* (stored groundnut haulms, etc.), grain, etc., at a cost which may exceed 2*s*. a day.

In 1967 the charge for hiring the services of a plough for some 5 to 6 hours in the morning was put at 12*s*. to 15*s*., but it was probably sometimes higher than this; contracts were sometimes made for the ploughing of certain farms at pre-agreed sums. While plough-owners are sometimes prepared to defer full-payment until after harvest, a farmer who wishes to make sure of obtaining the use of a plough at a peak period may pay part of the money in advance – see *Falle*.

(b) The general failure to appreciate the importance of plough-hiring (which was often formally prohibited by loan-granting authorities) renders much of the Nigerian literature on 'mixed farming' quite unrealistic, and has meant that the great popularity of the plough in, for example, several northern emirates, has gone altogether unappreciated. The FAO *Report* (1966) includes only 3 paragraphs on ploughing. Dumont insists (1966, p. 134) that 'the extended family holding of 8–12 hectares, is the smallest unit that can make animal-drawn implements . . . pay their way'.

It was in 1924 that the Department of Agriculture first contemplated introducing 'mixed farming', which was intended to save labour and to ensure the maintenance of soil-fertility by the use of ox manure. The scheme was unsound from the start if Morgan and Pugh (1969, p. 513) are correct in asserting that 2 oxen would provide sufficient manure for only 4 acres, against the minimum of 20 acres of land for ploughing, which was assumed to be required for meeting costs. The same authors also suggest that the need for rough grazing was officially overlooked. It is certain that the scheme was based on the erroneous assumption that manuring was uncommon, except in very densely-populated areas: one official definition of 'mixed farming', cited by Schneider and Darling (1967, p. 49), involved the notion of a 'mixed farmer' as one 'who does not follow the traditional system of shifting cultivation'.

After a slow start the numbers of 'mixed farmers' in N. Nigeria began to increase significantly following the introduction of official loan-granting in 1933, reaching 621 in 1935 – see King (1939, p. 277) – and 1,447 in 1937; the number of failures up to that date was put (*ibid.*, p. 278) at 178. Thereafter the official figures became increasingly inaccurate, owing to the failure to allow either for the numbers of ploughs for which official loans had been granted which had fallen into disrepair or were disused, or for private plough-purchase.

From 1945 the numbers of 'mixed farmers' rose rapidly, official estimates putting the figures at about 7,000 in 1950, 12,000 in 1954, 20,000 in 1962–3 and 40,000 in 1965–6: in the latter year, according to Anthony and Johnston (1968), about a quarter of all Northern Nigerian ploughs were in northern Katsina. More recently, there were known to be at least 5,000 plough-farmers in Gombe Emirate – personal information from Mary Tiffen. In a few places in Gombe Emirate blacksmiths had taught themselves to make entire ploughs – elsewhere, so far as has been recorded, they make certain spare parts only.

With one exception, all writers on the development of ox-ploughing have failed to grasp its profound socio-economic significance: insofar as the popularity of this innovation is partially appreciated, the conventional corollary regarding the incipient emergence of a 'landless class' is always emphasized, the implications of widespread hiring being invariably ignored. The exception is Nicolas who, in a publication (1968a) on the problems posed by the introduction of new agricultural techniques to the Hausa in the Maradi valley of the Niger Republic, argues that plough-owners are largely influenced by considerations of prestige, often hiring-out their ploughs to such an extent that they themselves continue to rely mainly on farm-labourers. As official efforts to encourage ploughing did not begin in the Niger Republic until 1956, and as the number of ploughs is far fewer (in relation to population) than in certain northern emirates today, the present attitude of farmers in Niger may resemble that in Nigeria in the 1930s and 1940s.

Out of a total of 1,794 'plough-days' achieved in a year by 43 Nigerien plough-owners, 57% involved hiring out, 36% were days offered free to other farmers, and only 6% were days devoted to ploughing the owner's land (*ibid.*, p. 86). Although the charge for plough-hiring in 1967 was high (up to 1,600 Fr CFA per day), many farmers preferred to hire the services of a plough (and ploughman) rather than to employ farm-labourers, one reason being the possibility of postponing part of the payment until harvest-time. (Nicolas states that one 'plough-day' is equivalent, in work achieved, to 8 to 10 man-days.)

The apparent reticence of the Nigerien farmer with regard to this new technique resulted from the irrelevance of arguments affecting his own farming. His object was to acquire an external source of income, analogous to that obtained from craftwork or trade. Above all, he was desirous of deriving prestige from this conspicuous form of capital expenditure. On the other hand, as an important man is one who is surrounded by others who are dependent on him, it follows that a plough-owner will lose face if he replaces his farm-labourers by a modern device. So it was that the acquisition and utilisation of the plough depended on considerations 'étrangères aux vues des propagateurs de matériel' (*ibid.*, p. 126).

The access to modern equipment (ox-carts as well as ploughs) therefore tends to be limited to certain notable persons: a humble person ('*un individu d'humble condition*') feels hesitant about acquiring a tool which he regards as an attribute of a rich man – (*ibid.*, p. 126). In the opinion of Nicolas, the diffusion of such modern tools, far from fostering agricultural development, serves to upset socio-economic relationships.

Much valuable information on such matters as the employment of ploughmen; earnings of plough-owners; costs of ploughs and credit conditions; costs of maintaining oxen; age and losses of oxen; and so forth . . . is provided by Nicolas.

If the situation in Batagarawa is any guide to that in northern Katsina generally, plough-owners there have become well aware of the agronomic advantages of ploughing their own farms, only hiring-out after their own work (and that of their sons-in-*gandu*) is complete. Nevertheless, ploughs are sometimes comparable to bicycles: useful in themselves, but acquired mainly for hiring. Certainly, there is no justification for relating the potential demand for ploughs to the number of large holdings, in the manner of many writers.

Although the official figures of plough-ownership are highly unreliable, those for Katsina Emirate suggest that the largest numbers per head of the population are found in the most densely-populated Districts such as Dan Yusufu (Bindawa) as well as in rapidly developing Districts such as Ruma (Batsari). In 1967 a plough cost about £18 to £21 in northern Katsina and a good pair of oxen might have cost £40 to £50. Ploughs are now manufactured in Zaria and Kano.

Morgan and Pugh (1969) include a useful list of references on 'mixed farming', including Corby (1941) on a Zaria village. See also Faulkner and Mackie (1933 and 1936), Hancock (1940), and Schneider and Darling (1967).

See **Cattle-ownership.**

Population censuses. The first population 'census' of Northern Nigeria, that of 1911, was no more than 'an informed guess' – Prothero (1956, p. 166) – the original total of 8·1 m. having been later raised to 9·2 m. The second census of the Northern Provinces was conducted in 1921, the report being published in a book by the Census Commissioner, C. K. Meek (1925, vol. II, pp. 169–263): the *recorded* population had then risen to 10·0 m. The exact system of conducting the census, outside certain townships, had been 'left to the discretion of each Resident'. (National Archives, Kaduna, 1606). When Residents were unable to accomplish a complete new count they were instructed to 'fill in the gaps from existing figures'. But 'existing figures' were usually most inaccurate:

> Counting by Native Mallami is in most cases, I fear, unreliable. In one district a recent recount by a political officer produced an increase of 17% of adult males on the returns made the previous year by 'Mallamai' sent to count and an increase of no less than 78% in the return of the total population of the district.
>
> From a Circular from the Secretary Northern Provinces, 26 July 1920

The next census, that of 1931, also leant heavily on 'existent data' – i.e. annual figures collected, or estimated, locally in connexion with the compilation of Village Tax Registers. According to the Census *Report* on the Northern Provinces (1932, p. 3), it represented 'a very considerable advance' on the 1921 census, but Prothero (1956) regarded it as having been even worse. No general enumeration was conducted, except in five townships, but an intensive census, in which individuals were separately enumerated on special schedules, was conducted in a number of areas, including 4 northern Katsina Districts. Official embarrassments were not concealed:

> The Census could scarcely have been taken under more unfavourable conditions . . . the funds for Census-taking were bound to be reduced to a minimum. Added to this there was a locust invasion, which affected the whole of the Northern Province and most of the time of the limited administrative staff [who were in charge of the Census] was absorbed in supervising anti-locust measures. Census *Report*, p. 10

> As the details of the methods employed in each case of supplying the figures returned were not always given in the memorandum forwarding the returns, it is difficult to arrive at any entirely complete estimate of their accuracy. (*ibid.*, p. 11)

Owing to tax evasion, numbers of adult males may have been greatly under-estimated in the general census: Kuczynski (1948, p. 596), stated that in certain Katsina Districts 21% fewer men (compared with 4% more women) were enumerated in the general census than in the intensive census.

One of the reports on the 1931 census (vol. v) related to a medical census conducted in 4 Northern Nigerian villages, 2 of which (Kaita and Bakori) were in Katsina Emirate. As adults were not asked to strip for their medical examination, many diseases went undiagnosed. The recorded statistics relating to infant mortality and number of pregnancies are (to the author's own admission) highly suspect.

Owing to the war, the next census was postponed until 1952, when the first general enumeration of the Northern Nigerian population was undertaken. Although this census was much more reliable than that of 1931 and the *recorded* population was shown as increasing from 11·4 m. in 1931 to 16·8 m. in 1952, many people may again have escaped the attention of enumerators.

The results of the next census, that of 1962, were regarded with such (justifiable) suspicion that a further count was made in 1963. Although the Federal Census Officer was reported as having regarded the 1963 totals for Northern Nigeria as 'reasonably reliable' – Okonjo (1968) – grave doubts regarding the possible inflation of the figures must remain, especially so long as the detailed figures remain unpublished. According to Aluko (1965), the original northern total in the 1962 census had been 22 m., later raised to 30 m., a figure which was 'confirmed by' the 1963 census. See **Age-structure, Migration.**

Potters – *magini*, f. *maginiya*, pl. *magina*.

(a) in Batagarawa many pots (large and small) are used for water-storage (*tulu*), cooking (*tukunya*), and for other purposes; there are very few metal utensils and most wives own several cooking pots, the usage of which is usually permitted to their co-wives. There are no potters in Batagarawa, where there is no suitable clay, and pots are either bought directly from markets, or from Batagarawa farmer–traders – one of whom is very active in this business having spent about a fifth of his working-time on it during the 1968 farming-season.

(b) Both men and women are potters. The non-archaeological literature on pot-making is scanty, but see Nicolas (NM, p. 65; 1964, p. 58) and Heath (1962, pp. 41–2). See also, Ibrahim Madauci (1968).

See **Building, Granary.**

Poultry ownership – hen, *kaza*, pl. *kaji*; cock, *zakara*, pl. *zakaru*; guinea fowl, *zabo*, f. *zabuwa*, pl. *zabbi*.

(a) A rough count of fowls in Batagarawa *gari* in September 1967 suggested that there was a total of only about 500 birds (excluding chicks), of which about two-thirds were owned by men. About a half of all heads of farming-units and most women owned no fowls – at least at that time of the year; the largest flock was 19 birds. (Women collect the eggs – *kwai* – which are often sold.). See *Fatauci.*

(b) There appear to be few (if any) reliable statistics of poultry ownership in relation to the rural population.

Poverty. There are many Hausa words for 'a poor person', including *fakiri, matalauci* and *matsiyaci*, the latter 'a strong word which is rarely used of any person to his face' – Bargery. *Gyandai* is a destitute person. To become poverty-stricken or destitute is *talauce* or *tsiyace*. See *Arziki, Talaka.*

Price-fixing. The notion of a 'right price' (a price which should remain stable as long as possible) is very common in West Africa and is not connected with Muslim concepts of usury – see Hill (1970a, pp. 8–9). It is a notion which requires far more sophisticated treatment than it has ever received. It is presumably partly because the supply of labour usually shows much more constancy over time than the supply of farm-produce, that attempts to 'fix' wages are far more successful than attempts at price-fixing, except through Marketing Boards. Throughout Anglophone W. Africa, Marketing Board 'producer-prices' are normally regarded as 'fixed', though they are mere legal minima. In many cases (such as Ghanaian cocoa) actual practice reflects this attitude (minima and maxima corresponding); although Nigerian groundnut prices are often above the minimum, the prevailing belief that they 'ought' to be fixed is well conveyed by para. 3 of the (Katsina) Proclamation on Farm Produce (q.v.) in regard to the so-called 'Government Price' (*Kurdin da Gwamnati*). Except with contract labour (which involves payment for a particular job), all the various types of farm-labour employment in West Africa involve the notion of a standard wage (or share of the produce) in any locality – however defined. Perhaps consultative machinery for rural wage determination is rare, but it exists among certain cocoa-farming communities in southern Ghana, where the chief in consultation with farmers fixes the cash sum paid for plucking a load of cocoa for the coming season. Opportunities of very short-term price-fixing are exceptionally propitious in places like Batagarawa because of the existence of standard containers, homogenous (measureable) farm-produce and a 'honeycomb-market' – not because attitudes are exceptional: Figs. 10, 11, 12 and 13 in Chapter IX show that retail prices sometimes remain remarkably stable for several months. As interest on cash loans bears little relationship to time, and as concepts of area are lacking, interest-rates and farm-prices can never be fixed – unless, in the latter case, small irrigated plots sometimes have standard dimensions. Wishful thinking is involved in assertions about another type of 'price-fixing', that connected with marriage and other ceremonies.

Private farm. A farm owned by a man-in-*gandu*. See *Gayauna*.

Proclamation on farm produce. In the summer of 1965 a proclamation on the sale of farm produce was made by the Public Enlightenment Authority in Katsina to people in markets and other public places and in September a circular was issued by the Natural Resources Office, Katsina Native Authority which, after a preamble relating to the need to improve methods of marketing groundnuts and cotton proceeded to list the precepts (here given in rough translation) which should be followed by every citizen.

(1) No buying for resale [*baranda*] of cotton or groundnuts is allowed; every farmer is requested to take his groundnuts to the buying station [*fuloti*] himself.

(2) The sale of groundnuts or cotton is not permitted except in the buying station.

(3) Nobody is allowed to raise, or lower groundnut or cotton prices. The 'Government Price' [*Kurdin da Gwamnati*, i.e. minimum Marketing Board price] is to be adopted everywhere, 'no more, no less'.

(4) No groundnuts or cotton are to be brought to the buying station in a sack. No buyer of groundnuts or cotton is allowed to issue sacks or money to the farmer.

(5) Nobody is allowed to bring groundnuts or cotton to the buying station, except when the season opens.

(6) If anybody has given money before harvest – e.g. 6s. for a *bokiti* [of groundnuts], or one bundle of grain for two or three bundles, or 1s. worth of produce for 2s. or 3s. worth [*dauke*], then he should repay the exact money he gave out – 'equal for equal', just the same amount as was given . . .

(9a) No one may buy groundnuts or cotton except at the official Buying Stations [which were listed].

In conclusion the hope was expressed that the people would obey these 'laws' (*dokoki* – sing. *doka*) – which were taken by village people as amounting to a prohibition of buying or selling of groundnuts, whether for export or not, before the opening of the buying season. See Chapter IX, pp. 139–40. See **Economic regulations.**

Profit – *riba* and other words; *ci riba*, make a profit; *ya ci riba*, he charged interest on the money (got a profit). See **Usury.**

Prostitutes: see *Karuwa*.

Purdah: see *Kulle*.

Rafi – pl. *rafuka*. An irrigated farm.

Rahoniya – pl. *rahoni*. A small corn-bin in a house, which may be of clay or other materials, used for storing threshed grain (*tsaba*).

Rainfall – *ruwa* (water). Statistics relating to rainfall in Batagarawa are presented here, there being a rain gauge at the school.

(a) There is very great variation in the date of the first planting rains in Batagarawa, which fell on 27 April 1966, 15 June 1967, 18 April 1968 and (abortively, see *Shuka*) on 17 April 1969. (In 1970 it was reported that the rains started in late June and ended in early September – with resultant poor harvests.) The distribution of rainfall during the rainy season is, also, very uncertain. In 1966 recorded rainfall between 27 April and the end of September was 27·9 inches – a figure which would be too low if the gauge had overflowed that year, as had happened in 1967. Rain fell on 40 days, of which 8 were in August and as many as 15 in September – whether any rain fell in October is not recorded. Between May 28 and June 10 and again between June 25 and July 3, no rain fell: grain prices soared as never before (see Chapter IX) and there was much anxiety about the millet harvest. The highest recorded rainfall on any day was $2\frac{1}{2}$ inches and over 1 inch fell on 11 days. Manure being applied during the dry season, the violent winds which frequently darkened the heavens in the weeks before the first rains in June 1967 wrought much damage to the soil. See **Harvest-dates**, *Shuka*.

Rama. Hemp (q.v.).

Ramadan (Ramalan). For an account of the fast (*azumi*) during the month of Ramadan and of the festival (*salla*) which follows it, see Taylor and Webb (1932, pp. 115–31).

Rance (*Ramce*). Correctly used (as it often is not) this term should denote very short-term borrowing, either of cash or of a thing not itself to be returned, to tide the borrower over a period of a few days before he sells some goods, goes home to get his money, earns some wages, or otherwise acquires the means to repay. The distinction between *rance* and *bashi* is conveyed by the following: '*kada rance ya zama bashi* = do not let the loan become a debt about which I have to keep on reminding you' – Bargery (p. 92). See *Aro, Bashi, Dauke, Falle*.

Rangama. Buying something and paying wholly or partly in kind. See **Exchange**.

Rani. Strictly speaking, *rani* is the hot dry season which follows *dari* (when the harmattan blows) and precedes *bazara*. But the word is often loosely applied to the whole dry season. See *Damuna*.

Raphia (or Bamboo) Palm – *tukurwa*, pl. *tukware* (*Raphia vinifera*). 'The particle and midrib (*gwangwala*) of the frond serves most of the purposes of bamboo. They are the commonest material used for roofing poles where available, and for canoe and carrying poles; also for native bridges, etc. Short sections are used for making the framework of stools and bedsteads, filled in with the plaited leaflets, for ladders, carrying cradles for marketing...' – Dalziel (p. 511). The screen *kwarakwara* is made from lath-like strips from the pithy inner portion of the petioles. Raphia fibre provides material for mats, bags (*kwararo*, pl. *kwararai*), ropes, etc.

Revenue Survey. A system of local taxation, now abolished, which was based on farm acreage. As part of the general reform of taxation following the Native Revenue Proclamation of 1906 (see **Taxation**), a tax based on farm-area was introduced in 1909 in parts of Katsina and Kano Emirates, acreages being estimated on the basis of pacing, i.e. *taki*, the name by which the system was known – see MacBride (1938) and Meek (1949, pp. 156–7). By 1911 a total of 2,500 sq. miles had been measured, and it began to be hoped that this system, which replaced all former taxes and tithes (other than *jangali*), would form the basis of assessment throughout the Protectorate; in 1913 it was introduced in the neighbourhood of Sokoto city and Birnin Kebbi (Gwandu Emirate).

In Kano and Katsina, where rates were of the order of 6*d*. to 2*s*. per acre, the system appeared to work reasonably well. But in Sokoto and Gwandu Emirates experience soon showed that it led to declining acreages and production and the scheme was abandoned. In 1914 a Survey School was opened in Kano and in 1916 a simple form of cadastral survey of several village areas was begun. In 1918 the newly-constituted 'Revenue Section' began the systematic survey of farms for reassessment and by 1925 'the annual output of new work' in Kano – MacBride (1938, p. 85) – had arisen to 60,000 acres.

Lugard had originally hoped gradually to introduce a full cadastral survey, but in 1918 he announced that *taki* had rendered this unnecessary for the present. But he was indignant (see his *Political Memorandum* on Taxation) at any suggestion of its being a 'land tax' (how could it be in the absence of official cognisance of individual land ownership?) – insisting that it was a tax on usufruct, or agricultural income.

In the event, the system was never extended outside a few Kano Districts – by 1934 it covered 1,254 sq. miles, about a tenth of Kano Emirate, mainly to the north-east and north of Kano city. One of its several great weaknesses was that the initiative in recording changes in tenure, resulting from transactions in farmland, inheritance, bush clearance, abandonment, etc., lay with the tax-payer, who was supposed to report them to the Hamlet Head. To simplify administration, and to ensure the completeness of the figures, there was even for a time a national embargo on farm sales! (See National Archives, Kaduna, 1708.) As time went by the registers became increasingly inaccurate, and various attempts that were made to study changes in farm ownership over time, e.g. by Rowling (1952, p. 13), are quite unreliable, as their authors readily admitted. Given the dearth of accurate statistics on acreages of farms and holdings, this unreliability is much to be deplored, presumably justifying the ultimate abandonment of the system.

Another weakness arose from variations in soil fertility within any locality – Lugard's assumption of little variation in 'value per acre' (except on irrigated farms) having become discredited. In 1924 differential rates for three *soil classifications* were introduced – *rafi*, *jigawa* and *fako* (see **Soil types**). Later, at least in some localities, a finer classification was adopted. The main merit of the original scheme having been its simplicity, its ultimate abandonment was thus inevitable.

Rowling concluded (1952, p. 19) that Revenue Survey had 'aided the break up of large official estates desired by Lugard' and had prevented 'an accumulation of holdings by rich men from the city'. But why should a tax which notionally corresponded to a flat rate 'income tax' of 10% have operated thus progressively? Surely the abolition of slavery had been a more relevant factor? See **Farm-selling**, *Haraji*, **Taxation**.

Riba. Interest on money, or 'usury'. The word is often loosely used in the sense of 'profit'.

Rice – *shinkafa* (*Oryza*), there are numerous words for different varieties.

(a) A little swamp rice is grown on the small acreage of *fadama* in Batagarawa. The rice is harvested and threshed by men and boiled (to remove the husk) by women who receive 3*d*. per *tiya*. Rice is retailed by men (not women) in Batagarawa; as it is too costly for many households a few '*yan kwarami* sell it in Katsina city and elsewhere. One Batagarawa trader buys rice in Birnin Kebbi and Bida and resells it in Katsina city and Daura. It is usually impossible to buy rice in the *gari*.

(b) 'Northern Nigeria may offer the best ultimate prospects for expansion of rice production, but only after heavy capital investment' – FAO *Report* (1966, p. 180). As rice is the main crop in a few areas (such as floodlands of the Sokoto river) and hardly grows in others, it enters largely into long-distance trade. See Hay and Smith (1970).

Riga – pl. *riguna*. The flowing gown worn by Hausa men, over other clothing, when they are not farming or otherwise labouring. *Riga fara* is a gown of any white material.

Rimi – pl. *rimaye*. The silk-cotton tree (q.v.).

Rina. Dyeing with indigo; *marini* is a dyer. See **Dyeing**.

Rinji – pl. *rumada*. A separate slave-village or hamlet in which the slaves owned by certain important slave-owners lived. In Zaria, according to Smith (1960, p. 91), the *hakimi*'s permission was necessary before a *rinji* was built; after the suppression of slavery, ex-slaves and their descendants (*dimajai*) were often obliged to pay rent (*galla*) for their *rinji* land. 'Fiefs have been replaced by districts, and village areas are now the recognized units of local administration; but *rumada* have not been eliminated [in rural Zaria] and may continue indefinitely' (*ibid.*, p. 259). There is no information on the extent to which *rumada* existed in other regions of Hausaland. See **Slavery**, *Ubangiji*.

Roko. Eulogy, praise-singing. See *Maroki*.

Rufewa – pl. *rufeyi*. A large earth granary which has no thatch; the clay may be continued upwards in funnel shape, being capped with a conical grass mat (*dan boto*) as in parts of Sokoto, or the bins may be urn-shaped as in Gobir. See **Granary**.

Ruga – pl. *rugage*. A Fulani cattle encampment.

Rumbu – pl. *rumbuna*. The most usual word for any kind of outdoor granary used for storing threshed grain and other produce, but perhaps formerly denoting only bins made of cornstalk or grass, not of clay. A granary made of grass mats is *rumbun zana*. See **Granary**.

Rumfa – pl. *rumfuna*. A market stall; a shed or shelter.

Ruwa – pl. *ruwaye*. Water, rain, etc. Also denotes interest on money – e.g. *ruwan kudi*, *bashin ruwa*; and is employed in the general sense of 'inflation' – *na ba shi ruwa* = 'I offered him a high price with no intention of buying'. See **Usury**.

Sadaka – pl. *sadakoki*. Charity or alms. See **Funeral expenses, Marriage-types, *Zakka***.

Sadaki. The word is sometimes used to denote marriage expenses generally, though strictly it is the cash gift which 'legalizes' marriage – see **Marriage expenses**. 'Le sadaki c'est le mariage' – Nicolas (NK, p. 101); its value in Kantché averaged about 1,500 frs, being very variable.

Sagagi. Uncultivated land, which is not densely shrubbed, near a village or town; a disused farm.

(a) Synonymous with *kubabi* in Batagarawa.

See **Fallow**.

Sa'i (Sa'a). A measure equivalent to 16 handfuls.

Saimi (Sema) – pls. *saimomi*, *semomi*. A receptacle made of laced cornstalks, etc. and shaped like a bee-hive (*amya*), for transporting baobab leaves, tobacco leaves, tamarind-fruit, bean-pods, etc.

Saina. '(a) Strictly applied only to such edible things sold in a market as used not to be liable to dues, but it is often applied to any edible things on sale. (b) Preparing the above foods. (c) Hawking the above' – Bargery.

In Batagarawa the word denotes women's house-trade in general.

Salla.

(i) Each of the 5 daily sets of Muslim prayers.

(ii) Each of the 2 great Muslim festivals.

Salt – *gishiri*, any salt – there are numerous kinds of African salt known by different Hausa words (see **Bargery**); *kakanda*, European salt; *jici*, baking *kakanda* into cakes (*kantu*), which are often adulterated.

(a) As many as 45 secluded women house-traders in Batagarawa were recorded as retailing manufactured salt, their bulk supplies being mainly bought on their behalf in Katsina city.

(b) Although, presumably, most salt consumed in Hausaland by humans and livestock is nowadays the manufactured type supplied in bags by commercial firms, there is yet a strong demand for natural salt, which comes mainly from Saharan areas within the Niger Republic, from Bornu and elsewhere. Large quantities of Bilma salt (*balma*) and Asben salt (*gallo*) are still brought into Katsina city by Tuareg camel-caravans, being redistributed by Hausa traders, many of whom also handle natron (q.v.). At Kamba (visited in 1966), which is near the river Niger in Argungu Emirate, large quantities of salt (some of it fit for consumption by livestock only) are wholesaled by traders who come through with camels and donkeys from the Niger Republic; some buyers in this market travel from as far away as Sokoto city. In Hausa markets manufactured salt is often sold in locally processed cakes (*zawara*) which are portions of larger blocks (*kantu*). Salt of all types is now extremely cheap compared with the price of 1s. a lb noted by Robinson (1896a, p. 118) in Kano market. See Barth (1965, vol. 1), Bovill (1958, p. 238). Grandin (1951) and Nicolas (NK, p. 211), on the Sahara salt trade with Hausaland.

Sana'a – pl. *sana'oi*, from the verb *sani* (know). Occupation, trade, profession.

While *sana'a* may denote any non-farming occupation, it more often refers to skilled crafts or specialized occupations (including *sarauta*) – as distinct, for instance, from petty trading or labouring.

Despite the lack of information on craft organisation, it seems reasonable to suggest that groups resembling the Nupe guilds – see Nadel (1942) – are unlikely to exist in rural Nigerian Hausaland; certainly butchers (q.v.) are never so organized. 'Craft production is almost always an individual pursuit, small scale in character, giving small daily returns used mainly in daily purchases of household food and services' – Smith (1955, p. 161). The lack of 'factories' (most craftsmen working in their own houses, or casually out-of-doors) must partly explain the paucity of information on manufacturing industries, even those in Kano city.

See *Arziki, Karda, Shigege* and entries on various crafts. Among the craftsmen who often 'inherit' their craft (*karda*) are: barber–doctors, blacksmiths, butchers and musicians – as well as the *masu-sarauta*.

See Nicolas (NM, p. 53) on the organisation of crafts under chiefs (*sarki*) in rural Niger.

Sansani. A war-camp, or the camp of a travelling Emir. See *Zango*.

Sara. Buying in bulk for later resale, the buyers being *'yan sara* – but see *Soke*. According to Bargery, *sarad da* = selling (*sic*) in bulk.

Sarauta – pl. *sarautu*. Being the ruler; an official position to which someone is appointed. Hence, *mai-sarauta* (pl. *masu-sarauta*) = a ruler.

(a) In this book the Batagarawa *masu-sarauta* are somewhat arbitrarily regarded (see p. 16) as being three members of the ruling-family (the District Head, the Batagarawa Village Head, and the District Head's eldest son) together with the District Scribe who, although not a member of the ruling-family or a 'chief', is a man of non-Batagarawa origin with official functions.

See Barau (Alhaji), District Scribe (Mallamawa), Magaji (Batagarawa), Mallamawa.

Sarki – f. *sarauniya*, pl. *sarakuna*. Any chief (including an Emir), or the head or man in charge of any group, institution or building, however elevated or humble. See Abraham.

Sarkin aiki: see Groundnut decorticators.

Sarkin gandu. A trusted slave who was in charge of the farmwork for his master.

Sarkin gida – lit. 'head of the house'. According to Abubakar Labo, a slave known as *sarkin gida* was often responsible for provisioning a large house with such necessities as firewood, meat, milk, fowls: he might also be *sarkin gandu* (q.v.). To be distinguished from *mai gida* (q.v.).

Sarkin kasuwa – lit. 'market head'. The man in charge of the affairs of a market: nowadays in rural periodic markets he is usually a minor local authority official, but he is still sometimes the chief butcher (*sarkin pawa*). In former times the traditional market-head was sometimes known as *sarkin kurmi*.

Sarkin noma – lit. 'head-farmer'. Nowadays there is usually no office of *sarkin noma* in villages, though the most respected farmer may, in semi-jocular fashion, be referred to by this title.

Sarkin pawa. Chief butcher. See **Butchers, *Sarkin kasuwa.***

Saro (Sari). Buying in bulk for resale; wholesaling.

Saura – pl. *sauruka.* A disused farm, whether manured (*gonar karakara*) or not. The word is sometimes employed to mean a fallow farm. See **Bush-farm, Fallow.**

Sautu. 'A commission [often given to men by women] to purchase something for one at a place to which the person is already going on other business, the money for the purchase being prepaid' – Bargery.

Sauya. Exchanging one thing for another; changing in general; *ya sauya kudi* = he turned over his money in trading. See **Exchange.**

School – *makaranta, makarantar boko.*
(a) The Batagarawa primary school was founded as early as 1946. The school achieved high standards under its first headmaster (Malam Mai Wada, who married a daughter of the (then) District Head), and in due course many young men were enabled to enter higher education. In 1968 it had 8 teachers (5 of them Grade 2), the total attendance being 213 (167 boys and 46 girls), some of the pupils being from neighbouring hamlets. The annual fees for a boy were 10s. – girls being admitted free. Not all fathers who could afford to send their sons to school did so: in 1970 at least 7 fathers in Group 1 and 10 in Group 2 had failed to send one or more of their sons to school. A high proportion of the sons of the poorest fathers manage to attend. See p. 100 on the occupations of ex-schoolboys.

(b) In 1964 there were only 15,780 pupils, of whom 4,189 were girls, in 118 primary schools in Katsina Province – less than 10% of all boys of school age were at primary school. Many large towns in Katsina, as in Hausaland generally, have no primary school. In the Kano State in 1968, with its estimated population of 6 m., only 36,000 boys and 13,500 girls were at primary school. In Muslim areas there are few schools run by voluntary agencies.

See **Koranic schooling.**

Season – *kwanaki.* For the various seasons of the year see *Agazari, Bazara, Damuna, Dari, Kaka, Rani.*

Seed dressings. Anthony and Johnston reported (1968, p. 63) that in 1967 there was 'an extremely good general awareness of the existence of seed dressings, and to a lesser extent of storage insecticides' in Kadandani and Bindawa in northern Katsina Emirate: they commented that this was 'all the more surprising' where 'extension staff are very thin on the ground'.

Servant: see *Bara.*

Sewing machines: see **Tailors.**

Shadoof – *kutara, jigo,* pl. *jiguna.* A simple contrivance for crop irrigation, similar to those used in Egypt and elsewhere, consisting of a pole working on a pivot, with a bucket at one end and a weight at the other. The pole is *kutara* or *jigo* – hence the words for the whole contrivance. See Raynaut (1969).

Shaidi. Mark, sign or evidence – but not in a judicial court.
(a) When a house or a farm is sold, both the buyer and the seller may pay small sums to any witnesses and the buyer should, also, pay a sum (*shaidi*) to the Hamlet Head, who passes on a portion to higher authority: with farms (unlike houses) the payment of *shaidi* is more honoured in the breach than the observance, authority commonly not being informed of the sale. *Shaidi* may be regarded as a kind of registration fee of a transaction.

Shamaki – pl. *shamakai.* Traditionally the head-slave in charge of stables.

(a) One of the few titled *fadawa* in Batagarawa is Shamaki; his duties include travelling every Saturday to oversee 'Yar Gamji market.

Shanshera. *Unshelled* groundnuts, cowpeas, etc.; or *unpounded* dried leaves (baobab, tobacco, etc.).

Share-cropping – *noma mu raba* = lit. 'we divide the farm'.

(a) Systems of tenure involving division of the produce between the farmer and his tenant are unknown in Batagarawa.

(b) Rowling (1952, p. 52) refers to two types of share-cropping, which relate mainly to irrigated land (*fadama*): in the one case the landlord contributes the land and half the seed and labour, the crop being divided in half; in the other case the landlord contributes land only, receiving a variable portion of the crop. However, Smith (1965, p. 263) casts doubt on these findings – see **Slavery.**

Shea-nut tree – *kadanya*, pl. *kadane* (*Butyrospermum Parkii*); *kadanya* (*kade*) = the tree and its fruit; *man kade* = shea-butter.

(a) There are few shea-nut trees at Batagarawa and women are ignorant of the work of shea-butter making.

(b) Barth noted the existence of the tree in northern Katsina. According to Dalziel, shea-butter made in Hausaland (always by women) is invariably yellow, the nuts not being roasted as, often, elsewhere. Bargery records (p. 520) that Karaye in Kano Province was famous for its shea-butter. Oyenuga notes (1967, p. 35) that shea-nuts are crushed at a factory in Zaria. There appears to be little information on shea-butter production or trading in Hausaland – perhaps because, in most localities, production is very small compared with that of groundnut oil. Nicolas reports (1964) that shea-butter is commonly sold in markets in the Niger Republic. In 1905–6 it was officially reported – see Dudgeon (1922, pp. 131–2) – that the shea-nut export trade, which formerly constituted the staple of Northern Nigeria, continued to decrease in an unaccountable way. Morel (1911, p. 167) 'rode for days through woods of shea' finding these trees growing abundantly in many parts of Kano Province, as well as in Zaria.

Sheep and goats – *rago*, pl. *raguna* = ram; *tunkiya*, pl. *tumaki* = ewe; *akwiya*, pl. *awaki*, strictly female goats, but of general usage; *bisa*, pl. *bisashe* = domestic animals generally; *kananan bisashe* = sheep and goats.

(a) These small livestock (whose very sturdiness – see Nash (1948, p. 17) – has led to their neglect in the literature) are of crucial importance in the Batagarawa economy, the manurial application of their droppings being surely associated with the development of permanent cultivation in circumstances where a large, local, settled cattle population is lacking. As the community consumes no fish and can afford only the occasional slaughter of cattle, these animals are an important source of protein (as meat, not milk), sheep, in particular, having many ceremonial (non-wasteful) uses. Owners always allow their goats to wander freely in the dry season (as wicked marauders – see **Cassava** – they are necessarily 'secluded' during the farming-season), so rearing costs may be fairly low, though most owners aim at supplementing natural grazing with (saleable) fodder such as *harawa*, *dusa*, collected grass and tree-foliage.

About two-thirds of both the sheep and goats in the *gari* are owned by women – see Table IV.5, p. 67 and **Women – Economic position of** – (whose husbands, however, are entitled to utilise, even to sell, the compound sweepings enriched by their droppings) – for whom they constitute a secure, expanding, form of investment, maintainable by children, removable on divorce, and safe (by tradition) from seizure by husbands, against whom there would be a right of appeal to the *masu-sarauta*. 'Sooner suffer than sell' being the motto of many owners, who are well aware of the inevitable post-harvest price rise (when £3, not 30s., might be realisable on the sale of a goat), some 700 goats and 300 sheep were still to be found in the compounds of the *gari* (excluding those of the *masu-sarauta*) in the hungry week before the *gero* harvest in 1967.

Animals for slaughter are bought either by traders (for full cash) or directly by butchers, who usually demand short-term credit. Although it is doubtful whether livestock stealing is as common as some insist, such owners as recognise their goat's footprints are reasonably secure.

(b) Although the FAO *Report* (1966) praises *goats*, which 'fit well into the African picture' (p. 223) and which 'have not received the attention they deserve ..., partly because of the strong anti-caprine literature and teaching' (p. 216), their manurial contribution is wholly ignored. In those southern localities of Hausaland where cattle-rearing is difficult owing to trypanosomiasis, goat droppings may be an even more crucial type of manure than in Bata-garawa, though this partly depends on how freely the animals range during the dry season. The high quality of the compound sweepings 'exported' from Kano city for manuring farms in the Close-Settled Zone – see Mortimore and Wilson (1965) – results from the popularity of goat-rearing in the city. Statistics of goat-ownership collected at village level are apt to be unreliable: but certain published and archival statistics suggest that (as in Batagarawa) goat numbers often range between a half and three-quarters of the human population – a high proportion being everywhere owned by women. The FAO *Report* (1966) puts the Northern Nigerian goat population at 14·3 m. (p. 216), and makes no mention of seasonal variation: 'a substantial increase in goat numbers in the next 15 years is proposed (*sic*)' p. xxxv) – but how is this to be achieved? (Goat values cannot be estimated – size is very variable.)

As for *sheep* (all of which are hairy types), the FAO *Report* (*ibid.*) estimates the number in Northern Nigeria at 4·4 m., stating that expansion is hindered by the extent to which they suffer from intestinal parasites. The proportion of sheep owned by women is high, though lower than that for goats.

In the Niger Republic, also, most goats and many sheep are owned by women. In the cercle de Maradi, where the human population is 154,000, Nicolas (NM, p. 129) estimated the goat and sheep populations to be as high as 280,000 and 60,000 respectively.

See **Hides and skins**, *Jangali*, **Manure**, **Naming-ceremony**, **Permanent cultivation**.

Sheka. Winnowed. Hence *masheki*, f. *mashekiya* (pl. *masheka*), a winnower.

Shigege. A person who holds a non-hereditary (non-farming) occupation. For the distinc-tion between *shigege* and 'inherited' occupations see *Karda*. According to Kirk-Greene (1965 , p. 376), few of 'the modern generation' know '*shigege*' in its sense of a 'person who adopts a calling different from that of his ancestors', but only in its secondary meaning of 'interloper'.

Shinge – pl. *shingogi*. A farm fence, whether of sticks or thorns etc. or of living material; thorn fences are prickly (and inedible) to repel marauding livestock.

Shiyya. Direction or place. The word is sometimes employed (as is *waje* which has a similar meaning) to denote a separately fenced-off section of a house (*gida*).

Shuci (Cifci). Any grass for thatching.

Shuka. The sowing of grains, groundnuts, cowpeas, etc.; *ya yi shuka* = he did the sowing.

(a) The first sowing sometimes has to be repeated owing to drought. For example, all the grain seed (*gero, dawa* and *maiwa*) sown in Batagarawa on 17 April 1969, when the first rains fell, failed to germinate owing to a drought which lasted until 18 May: the various grains were then resown, groundnuts being sown on the same day. Cowpeas (*wake*) were sown, following heavy rains, on 15 July. For variation in dates of first rains, see **Rainfall**.

See also *Binne*.

Shuni. Prepared indigo, extracted from the leaves of the indigo plant (*baba*) and sold in cones or lumps; it has many uses apart from dyeing – e.g. in women's hairdressing and as a contra-ceptive and abortifacient. Detailed accounts of the various methods of preparing *shuni* are given in Dalziel (p. 244); see, also, Clapperton (1829, p. 220) – who noted that the price of indigo doubled between spring and summer. In some localities *shuni* is an important market ware. See **Dyeing, Indigo**.

Shura. The first early millet (*gero*) of the season to ripen.

Silk-cotton tree – *rimi*, pl. *rimaye* (*Ceiba pentandra*). The tree from which kapok (*audugar rimi*) is obtained. The floss is used to stuff cushions, mattresses etc., generally without separation of the seeds, though this can be done by hand.

'*Audugar rimi fasu, kowa ya samu*, said of a generous, open-handed person because, when the pods of this tree burst, the contents become scattered far and wide' – Bargery.

Slavery – *bauta*; slave = *bawa*, f. *baiwa*, pl. *bayi*. Brief reference material on slavery in rural Hausaland is presented here under a number of headings.

(1) *Farm-slavery*. See Chapter I, p. 6 and Chapter III, p. 39 above, with regard to the scanty literature on farm-slavery.

(2) *Number of slaves*. Several travellers produced very high estimates of slave-numbers, basing their guesses on impressions gained in cities. Thus, Monteil (1895, p. 287) stated that slaves comprised four-fifths of the population of Kano city, and presumed that, in general, slaves formed the bulk of the population. (So necessary were slaves, in his opinion, that without them 'il n'y aurait pas de société, mais bien des individualités sans cohésion.') Barth estimated (vol. II, p. 144) that the population of the 'province of Kano' was some 400,000, of whom a half were slaves. Robinson (1896a, p. 127) remarked that one out of every 300 persons in the world was a Hausa-speaking slave – presuming that there were 15 m. Hausa of whom one-third were slaves. The difficulties of defining 'slavery' in a society where there was much intermarriage between the enslaved and the free; where slaves were assimilated to Islam; and where second-generation slaves could not be sold (see **Dimajo**) – make it quite certain that the prevalence of slavery will remain forever inestimable. See p. 178.

(3) *The slave-estates* (*rinji*, pl. *rumada*). However, further research might provide some indication of the prevalence of large slave-estates in localities outside Zaria, where they have been studied by M. G. Smith – see, in particular, Smith (1955, pp. 102 ff). The possibilities of such research partly depend on whether it is still common practice (as in some Zaria localities) for the successors of the estate-owner to claim 'rent' from those who now occupy the farm-land. Smith has surmised (1965, p. 263) that the type of 'rent' known as *galla* in some areas, was in origin (as the dictionaries define the word) 'a payment made by a slave in lieu of work' – *murgu* being a synonym; and that Kano share-cropping systems (q.v.) may be of similar origin.

(4) *The treatment of domestic and farm slaves*. Clapperton reported (1829, pp. 213–14) that domestic slaves were 'generally well treated', being 'fed the same as the rest of the family, with whom they appear to be on an equality of footing', and all later observers of the rural scene have arrived at much the same conclusion. However, it must be remembered that rapid processes of assimilation ensured that the demand for such slaves was never satiated, so that slave-raiders may have relied as much on the private demand as on official demands for 'tribute slaves', etc. (Barth was so well aware of this point that he mistakenly concluded – vol. II, p. 152 – that slaves were 'very rarely allowed to marry'!) Several writers, including Smith (1954b), have emphasized the significance of the fact that slave-owners were obliged to provide Koranic instruction for their *dimajai*, seeking to convert them by chastisement if necessary. But the pagan Maguzawa may have assimilated their slaves with equal readiness – see Krusius (1915, p. 299). See Trimingham (1959).

(5) *Slave-markets*. Literary references to Hausa slave-markets are surprisingly meagre, and it may be that, owing to their high value, most slaves were sold from houses – see **Cowries**. Robinson (1896a, p. 124) noted that there were usually about 500 slaves at a time on sale in

Kano market, and that they were sold in just the same way as other merchandise; in Zaria market-place he saw (*ibid.*, p. 88) about 300 slaves, worth from 100,000 to 300,000 cowries each, or from £3 to £9. In 1862 Baikie saw 300 slaves in Zaria market . . . 'whereas three years previously as many as 4,000 might have been seen' – Baikie (1867, p. 95). According to Abubakar Labo (q.v.), in northern Katsina slaves were only sold in the larger markets: slaves, he added, were not like goats, most traders bringing only 1, 2 or 3 to the market.

(6) *The abolition of slavery.* It was in 1901 – see Perham (1960, pp. 51 ff.) – that Lugard made his first Proclamation abolishing the *legal status* of slavery, which meant that no new slaves could be made, and that no owner could restrain or recapture a slave who appealed to the courts: he was following in the footsteps of the Royal Niger Company which had attempted similar action in part of their territory in 1897 – see Mockler-Ferryman (1902, p. 251) and Orr (1911, p. 199). In his *Annual Report* on N. Nigeria for 1902, Lugard stated that he did not 'propose to interfere with the serfdom of the agricultural peasantry, or the house-born domestics of the cities, insofar as avoidance is compatible with the abolition of the "legal status"' – adding, presumably with embarrassment, that 'space precludes the possibility of a fuller examination here of this very intricate question'. As early as 1903 the largest of all public slave-markets, that at Jega, was closed. Although the number of slaves freed by legal processes was always very small, Lugard's policy was generally highly successful, justifying his statement in his *Amalgamation Report* of 1919 – Kirk-Greene (ed.) (1968, p. 120) – that among those who voluntarily remained in slavery 'the old relation of master and slave is practically dead and is replaced by that of master and servant'. See Orr (1911, pp. 200–6) on the effects of Lugard's policy.

Orr expressed the moral view (*ibid.*, p. 202) that 'in order to prevent vagabondage and the occupation of land by a horde of masterless runaway slaves, who sought to profit by the government policy towards slavery by living a life of idleness and lawlessness impossible under native law and custom' – it was necessary for slaves to be denied the right to cultivate land for themselves until they had bought their freedom: this denial of elementary rights was (in principle) made possible by the fact that land was vested in the government.

(7) *The present day.* In Hausaland it is not customary, as it is among the Kanuri of Bornu, for young men to attach themselves as clients to private households. Hausa farmers who are short of family-labour must hire '*yan kwadago*; but it is very common – R. Cohen (1967, p. 50) – for ordinary Kanuri farmers to require their clients to perform farm work (and other tasks), in return for food, maintenance, etc. So it seems to be no accident that there have been no reports from rural Hausaland of the persistence of domestic relationships resembling farm-slavery, whereas among the Kanuri – Rosman (1962) – 'the institution of slavery persists', the slave (who is by no means a degraded individual) being distinguishable by his distinctive scars and his bare head.

See *Fatauci*.

Soil types

(a) In general at Batagarawa farmers consider there is little variation in soil type within the mapped zone and would denote most farmland (other than *fadama*) as *jigawa*. They insist that, except in rare cases, farm buyers assess farm value in terms of the manurial content of the soil (and other factors) rather than by soil type.

(b) MacBride (1937) distinguished 6 soil types in Dawaki ta Kudu District and concluded that the yield (in terms of grains and groundnuts) of *jigawa* and *jangargari* was about double that of the others. Although definitions must vary greatly within Hausaland, a summary of his classification follows:

Jigawa. Light but relatively fertile soil, which is easy to work and extremely sensitive to manure, but which tends to wash out in heavy rains.

Jangargari. Red lateritic soil, more fertile than *jigawa* if both are unmanured, but harder to work and less sensitive to manure; however, owing to its closer texture it retains manure better than *jigawa* when rains are heavy.

Tsakuwa. Light gravelly soil, which requires much manure if it is to grow white guinea corn, being unsuitable for certain other types.

Dabaro. A very heavy soil of uncertain character, which is difficult to work; liked in some localities, disliked in others; may produce good yields of guinea corn with no manure.

Shabuwa. Defined by Bargery as 'any unfertile useless land', in Dawaki ta Kudu it was regarded as a very light soil of low fertility – which might or might not be degenerate *jigawa*.

Fako. Although the word is generally applied to hard barren ground, cultivated *fako* is a heavy black soil of low fertility which quickly dries out if there is a short drought.

See **Manure, Revenue survey.**

Soke. 'Buying from villagers for re-sale in city' – Bargery. Anderson notes that:

> To the practice termed 'soke' different meanings are attached in different localities, for it is sometimes interpreted as an act of intervention in a sale between two other parties, e.g. by disparagement of the goods concerned, for one's own or another's benefit; sometimes as the cornering of some commodity in order to profit thereby; and sometimes as the interception of country people on their way to the market in order to buy their goods cheaply and then sell them at a large profit. On the first interpretation the practice is commonly regarded as disgraceful; on the second as legitimate if only partial and moderate but illegal if carried too far; and on the third as illegal if near the market but legitimate if far afield.   Anderson (1954, p. 217)

Sorghum: see *Dawa*.

Soro – pl. *soraye*. A rectangular mud-built room (or house), with a flat or round roof (may be with a cupola).

    (a) In Batagarawa *gari* nearly all *soraye*, except those owned by the ruling-class, are entrance-huts (*zaure*), some of which are vaulted.

    (b) In Hausa towns and cities, where most dwellings are rectangular, '*soro*' has many connotations; there being little room for granaries, grain and other produce is often stored in *soraye*, mainly bagged but sometimes in bundles – see p. xii above.

Spinning – *kadi*.

(a) Spinning is pursued by some 85% of all women in Batagarawa, as virtually their only craft or pastime; the raw cotton is bought, the thread (*zare*) sold, outside the village, where the craft of weaving is nearly extinct. The primitive clay spindle (*mazari*) being used, output and earnings are very small. A prepared skein (*sulu*) which a woman sold to a trader in Batagarawa at 1s. 6d. might fetch 1s. 9d. in a market.

    (b) References to spinning in the literature are slight. See Meek (1925, p. 166). According to the intensive census conducted in 6 Katsina Districts in 1931 (which provided more reliable occupation figures than any more recent census), virtually all women (i.e. two-thirds of the total female population) regarded their 'occupation' as spinning.

See **Dyeing, Weaving.**

Sufuri (*Sifiri*), Hiring, renting or pledging; transport of merchandise (hence '*yan sufuri*, carriers); money paid to carriers. See *Jingina*.

Sugar cane – *rake*; there are many words for different varieties – see *takanda* in Bargery (*Saccharum officinarum*).

    'Grown in many places and always in low damp situations or near streams . . . The stems are chewed rather as a sweet than as a food; red- and white-stemmed varieties are recognised ' – Dalziel.

(a) Not grown at Batagarawa, supplies from nearby are brought in by local traders.

(b) In reference to the recent Emirs' 'ban' on the sale of immature crops, Anderson noted (1954, p. 190) that it did not apply to sugar cane. Sugar cane is sold in great quantity in Hausa markets in Nigeria, as well as in the Niger Republic, where it is said to be a recent introduction – Nicolas (NM, p. 188 and 1964, p. 44). Barth was surprised when told, near Sokoto city, that the owner of a sugar plantation 'prepared sugar' – (vol. IV, p. 171). See Buchanan and Pugh (1955, pp. 117–18) and Prothero (1957b, pp. 82–3) with regard to sugar-crushing in Zaria, Kano and Katsina.

See *Alewa*.

Sulu – pl. *sulaye*. 'A completed skein of white cotton thread of just the correct length for weaving narrow widths of material, or for being dyed black' – Bargery. See **Spinning**, *Wadari*.

Sunkuru. Uncultivated land; synonymous with *sagagi* (q.v.).

Surkute (*Sulkuci, Silkiti*). A cheap form of marriage, contracted only between the old and poor, such that the husband provides no home for the wife (see **Marriage-types**). Also known as *auran dauki sandanka* – lit. 'marriage of pick up your stick' – and by other words and expressions.

Suruki – f. *suruka*, pl. *surukai*. An affine. See Smith (1955, pp. 48–9) on the relationship of reciprocal avoidance and respect involving *surukai*. The term is often used classificatorily to denote the 'in-laws' as a group.

Sweet potatoes: see *Dankali*.

Tabarya – pl. *tabare*. A pestle used with a mortar (*turmi*) for pounding grain etc.

Tafasa. The senna plant (*Cassia Tora*), the leaves of which are used in soups.

(a) A number of the older women who trade in Katsina market handle *tafasa* leaves.

Taiki (*Teki*) – pl. *taikuna*. A large hide bag used as a double pannier for carrying loose, spillable, produce (particularly threshed grain) which is unsuitable for the *mangala*.

Tailors – *ma'dunki*, pl. *ma'dunka*, also *tela* (from tailor).

(a) In 1968 the 10 sewing machines in Batagarawa *gari* were operated by: the District Scribe (q.v.), 2 machines; a woman teacher – a daughter of the District Head; 4 men in Group 1; and 3 men in Group 3. There were no tailors in dispersed homesteads. Machines which, as noted by Nadel (1942, p. 290), are far the most expensive means of production used by craftsmen, are not necessarily owned by those who operate them; however, some of the poorer owners acquire machines at harvest-time and sell them at the end of the dry season. Machine-tailoring (as distinct from machine-embroidery) does not demand long training or special skill and needs no workshop: anyone may happen to learn the work, if necessary hiring a machine.

As women seldom do any sewing, even the smallest children's garments are usually run up by machine. Most clothing is made after harvest, when money is available; a few richer tailors may then acquire stocks of cloth. Made-up gowns (*riga*) are often bought outside Batagarawa.

(b) The tailor working at his treadle-machine is a familiar feature of the Hausa landscape, sitting in markets, at the road side, under trees, in open sheds. Hausa machine-embroidery is justly famous – it is one of the few examples of a flourishing modern craft. The Hausa migrate to many other West African regions in their capacity of tailor – and may go on *cin rani*, transporting their machines with them. Nicolas (NM, p. 69) notes that men machine-tailors are found in most villages and markets in the Niger Republic. Many rich farmers, traders and craftsmen invest in machines, either hiring them out or themselves employing tailors on commission.

Taimako. Assistance rendered in farm work. See **Gayya**.

Takaba. The mourning-period for a widow, when she may not remarry, but remains in absolute retirement, doing no work, neither borrowing nor lending, seldom washing, wearing no head-scarf and generally 'keeping out of trouble'. In Hausaland generally the length of this period varies between 120 and 150 days – see Trimingham (1959, p. 182): in Batagarawa it is said to be 150 days. See **Funeral expenses**, *Idda*.

Taki.
(i) Manure of all types; *ya yi wa gonarsa taki* = he manured his farm.
  (ii) A pace – or measuring by pacing.
  See **Manure, Revenue Survey**.

Talaka – pl. *talakawa*. An ordinary member of the populace in contradistinction to one who holds office (of any sort) – hence 'the man in the street', a poor person. See p. 177.

Talla. Exposing wares for sale: hawking; *'yar talla* = a girl hawker.

Tallafi.
(i) Adoption.
(ii) An adopted child, or one received for bringing up – usually the child of a close relative. To be distinguished from a wife's child (*agola*).
  See Smith (1955, p. 21) and Mary Smith (1954).

Tamani. Price; *tamani kafaffe* = a fixed price.

Tamarind – *tsamiya*, pl. *tsamaiku* (*Tamarindus indica*). The fruit of the ubiquitous tamarind tree has many medicinal and other uses; a pleasantly acid drink may be made from the pulp. Barth regarded the tree as 'the principal ornament of Negroland', and the fruit as providing the most refreshing drink.

Tanning – *jema* (*jeme*); *majemi*, pl. *majema* = tanner; *majema*, pl. *majemai* = tannery. Although, according to Barth, 'no place in the whole of Negroland is so famous for excellent leather and the art of tanning as Katsena' (vol. IV, p. 99), yet published information on the organisation of the craft appears to be negligible – see, however, brief notes in Ibrahim Madauci (1968, p. 56), Taylor and Webb (1932, p. 193), Meek (1925, pp. 160–1) and Nicolas (NK2, p. 64). See also, FAO *Report* (1966, p. 277). In the Niger Republic tanners, unlike leather workers, are specialist members of certain clans.

  Dalziel states (p. 203) that the pods of *Acacia arabica* – see **Mimosa** – are the commonest tanning material in the Western Sudan being 'the usual article used for tanning the goat-skins known as Kano leather'; he provides information on the chemistry of native dyeing. Many vegetable dyes used in tanning are secrets of particular villages – personal information from D. M. Last. Many leather workers do their own tanning. See **Hides and skins**.

Tarayya. Partnership; political federation; *abokin tarayya* = a partner.

Tariqas: see **Muslim Religious Orders**.

Tasshi: see **Pepper**.

Taxation. This entry is mainly concerned to outline the history of local rural tax-collection in the Hausa Emirates during the early years of the British occupation. See also *Haraji*, *Jangali*, *Nomi-jide*, **Revenue Survey**.

  As in the early years – Perham (1960, p. 165) – the 'very structure of the emirs' government' would have collapsed had the flow of revenue been checked by hasty reforms, it was not until 1904 that Lugard issued the Land Revenue Proclamation, the objects of which were to simplify and to make more uniform, ancient systems and modes of taxation, some of them pre-*jihad* – see, in this connexion, Hiskett (1960, p. 567); this measure was soon superseded by the Native Revenue Proclamation of 1906 which aimed at the substitution of a 'general tax' for the multiplicity of taxes in many (though not all) Hausa Emirates and which established the principle that although the tax was levied by government 'it should be divided at source and a fixed proportion retained by the Native Authority for its own purposes' – Wraith (1966, p. 202). In a country of slavery and serfdom, taxation was to Lugard 'synonymous with economic and moral reform' – Perham (1960, p. 166): 'he claimed for what most men regard as unfortunate necessity a surprising number of advantages, even to the payers' (*ibid.*, pp. 165–6). 'Direct taxation may be said to be the corollary of the abolition, however gradual, of forced labour and domestic slavery' – from Lugard's *Political Memorandum on Taxation* (see below). See Orr (1911, Chapter VIII). See also Crowder (1968, p. 206).

But as was made abundantly clear by H. R. Palmer's somewhat embarrassed evidence to the Northern Nigeria Lands Committee in 1908, it proved quite impossible for the small staff – 'We have had two political officers in Kano Emirate, during the last few years to look after two millions of people' (Cd 5103, p. 76) – to achieve the desired consolidation of taxes, though progress was made (in connexion with the reorganisation and consolidation of Districts) in arranging for tax collection on a territorial basis, rather than through the notorious tax-gatherers (*jakada*) who were centrally based. In fact in Kano in 1908 all the old taxes had been maintained (*ibid.*, pp. 69–70). (The elaborate tax system which had existed before the occupation had been outlined by Lugard in a Memorandum written in 1906, which was published in 1910 (*ibid.*, Appendix III) and by C. L. Temple (*ibid.*, Appendix II).) In Katsina where there was also a great variety of taxes – see Palmer (1908) – the collection of *zakka*, the tithe on grain, presented such difficulty that it was decided in 1907 to introduce a so-called 'farm tax' of 4*s*. a farm; however, as Palmer explained to the Lands Committee (Cd 5103, p. 76), this was really a 'household tax' – 'a farm is rather a vague thing'. Another witness before the Lands Committee (C. W. Orr) considered the Zaria 'hoe tax' to be the 'farm tax' under another name. In 1909 the new acreage tax (*taki*) – see **Revenue Survey** – was substituted for the farm tax in parts of Kano and Katsina.

But if progress over the introduction of the 'general tax' was so slow, one reform was quickly achieved in some localities: following Lugard's prohibition of the importation of cowries (q.v.), coins soon became the medium of tax-collection, to the extent that it was claimed by Palmer (1908) that in Katsina in 1908 replacement was complete.

The *Annual Report* for Northern Nigeria for 1910–11 explained that at that time the two extremes of divergence in taxation systems were represented in Sokoto and Bassa. In Sokoto each village was assessed at a lump sum, after careful enquiries made on the spot by a British official as to the resources of the inhabitants, and determination of the sum payable by each individual was left to 'the village head and his council', who were directed to assess each man in accordance with his wealth from all sources. In Bassa, on the other hand, each individual was required to pay the same rate. In Zaria, Kano and Katsina Emirates the systems were regarded as approximating to that of Bassa inasmuch as there was a fixed rate per farm, and to that of Sokoto inasmuch as tithes on grain (in Zaria on all crops) were payable to the government. It was at about this date that the false hope of widely extending *taki* as *the* consolidated tax began to be expressed.

By degrees a single consolidated tax on each adult male (*haraji*) was introduced in those localities where *taki* did not obtain, its incidence in some localities varying slightly according to local assessment of 'wealth'. In Zaria in 1912 the two taxes *haraji* and *jangali* had, according to Smith (1960, p. 211), completely replaced the old system.

In 1911 the first Native Treasuries were established. The Native Revenue Ordinance of 1917 placed emphasis on village and district 'headmen' as agents of tax-collection; decreed that any form of property or income could be valued for taxation purposes; and established the principle that some portion of the revenue collected by Native Authorities should pass to the central government.

In *Political Memorandum on Taxation* (1918), which was a revised version of instructions issued in 1906, Lugard was concerned to emphasize that the taxation imposed by the Native Revenue Ordinance was an income tax not a land tax. He admitted that in one (unspecified) Province many taxes were still being paid to the Village Head in addition to *haraji*; and the general lack of detail suggests that in many emirates the single consolidated tax was still little more than an ideal.

See Wraith (1966) on the increase through time (ultimately to $87\frac{1}{2}\%$) in the proportion of Native Revenue which was retained by Native Authorities, and not paid over to the central government.

The Personal Tax Law of 1962 established a government income tax on people with ascertainable incomes of more than £350 a year; but it seems that the tax is seldom levied on rurally-based farmers.

See **Marketing Board.**

Thatch (Thatched roof) – *jinka*, *baibaya* and other words. There are numerous Hausa words for the different parts of a thatched roof.

(a) All the sleeping-huts (*daki*) and granaries (*rumbu*) in Batagarawa are covered by thatches (made of cornstalk, grass, rope, etc.) and there are some dozen or so specialist thatchmakers. There are also some other men who collect and prepare grass (*shuci*) for thatching (*yanta*).

(b) *Yantanya* (bundles of grass prepared for thatching) are a common ware in market-places, where complete thatches are sometimes seen.

See Taylor and Webb (1932, pp. 189–91).

See 'Free goods', *Yama.*

Thresh. To thresh grains or to decorticate groundnuts by any means, including pounding in a mortar = *sussuka*; to thresh by beating with a stick = *buga.*

(a) In Batagarawa co-wives often thresh grain together; richer housewives commonly employ other women for threshing.

Tiger-nut – *aya* (*Cyperus esculentus*). A grass-like perennial which produces small underground tubers – or nuts.

(a) Both the nuts themselves (fresh or 'roasted') and *dakuwa* (a snack made from the nuts) are important items of women's house-trade in Batagarawa.

Tirka. The effects of a deceased person; *an yi tirkar kayansa* = the deceased's effects were assessed.

Tiya. A standard measure. The word *tiya*, which is in no dictionary, is probable derived from the English noun 'tare'.

(a) A multi-coloured enamel measuring bowl, of standard capacity, and instantly recogn-nizable, which is manufactured in Kano, originally at the instigation of the Katsina N.A. (which distributes it through traders), and which carries the words TIYA KATSINA NA and the date – 1963 or later – see Plate 31. In 1969 the bowl cost about 2*s.* and could be bought in market-places and elsewhere. The weight of the contents depends on type of produce, variety, moisture content, etc., being very roughly as follows:

	lbs
groundnuts – unshelled	3
cowpeas groundnuts – shelled }	5
guinea corn locust beans }	$5\frac{1}{2}$
millet (*gero*) millet (*maiwa*) }	6
rice	7

The ever-fluctuating prices in Batagarawa are always expressed in terms of *tiya* – or *bokiti* (q.v.) – as are household grain allocations – see Chapter IX. Secluded women house-sellers measure grain and other produce in *tiya*.

(b) No other writer, save Nicolas, having reported on the *tiya*, the extent of its distribution in Hausaland is not known. Its use in the markets, and houses, of Katsina Emirate is extremely widespread – and white bowls, called *tiya* but non-standard, are used in Kano and elsewhere. According to Nicolas, the standard *tia* (*sic*) in use in the Niger Republic is imported from overseas; it has a capcity of about 2 kgs of shelled groundnuts.

See *Mudu, Zakka.*

Tobacco – *taba* (*Nicotiana tabacum*). This entry relates to native tobacco only, not to 'commercial cultivation' for cigarette manufacture, of which there is none at Batagarawa. Nowadays most native tobacco is chewed, with salt or natron, and not smoked, and the use of snuff is diminishing; the leaves also have medicinal uses. The tobacco flower (*fure*) is used for teeth-staining.

(a) in Batagarawa tobacco is a 'rich man's crop', which is grown on a significant scale by no more than about 10 farmers. The crop requires much cattle manure and must be grown on a different plot each year. Successive crops of millet (*gero*) and tobacco may be taken from the same farm, the transplantation of the tobacco seedlings from a nursery plot following the millet harvest. The leaves are picked between December and January by farmers or their sons and, after sun-drying, are packed in bundles (*sanka*) of varying sizes, which are commonly stored for a seasonal price rise, before being sold to local traders.

(b) Clapperton noted that tobacco was one of the wares handled by long-distance Hausa traders (1826, p. 9). At Duncammee (east of Gyaza in Katsina) Lander remarked that 'every inch of spare ground was planted with tobacco' – Clapperton (1829, p. 261). In the first half of the nineteenth century tobacco was grown in Katsina – Daumas and de Chancel (1848, p. 214). Barth happened to note (vol. IV, p. 107) the 'extensive tobacco-grounds' south of Batagarawa, commenting that (outside Musgu country) he had first observed tobacco being 'largely cultivated' near Katsina city; he stocked up with a good quantity of Katsina tobacco 'which is held in great estimation even in Timbuktu' – (*ibid.*, p. 99). See Hill (1970a, Chapter 6) on the neglected history of the northern Katsina tobacco trade with Damagaram (Zinder) in the late nineteenth century, when the most renowned centre of cultivation was Kabakawa, a dispersed hamlet some 2 miles north-east of Batagarawa. Although Kabakawa tobacco has recently lost its pre-eminence, the trade still persists, being mainly handled by a small number of local traders (from Kabakawa, Morawa, Sabon Gari and neighbourhood) who even buy some of their supplies from Kandawa market, the main local outlet for the expanding production of Ruma District. As in the nineteenth century, the farmer–traders endeavour to store for a seasonal price rise.

In the hamlet of Morawa (south of Sabon Gari, west of the Katsina/Kano road) there are still many tobacco growers, some of them financed by outside traders who, as in earlier times, grant loans (*falle*) during the growing season, for repayment in tobacco. All the farms are manured by cattle owned by nearby Fulani pastoralists.

Most of the tobacco grown in northern Katsina is probably exported to the Niger Republic, the four main tobacco markets all being on the frontier – Babura (north-east of Kano), Garke (between Babura and Baure), Zango (east of Daura) and Mai-Aduwa (north of Daura). (Nicolas has recorded that while some excellent tobacco is grown south of Maradi (NM, p. 186), most supplies in the Niger Republic come from Nigeria.) However, poorer farmers, who lack the finance to hold for a price rise, sell tobacco at Ajiwa market, south-east of Katsina city. The great range of seasonal price variation is constantly emphasised by traders and farmers: but it cannot be measured owing to variations in bundle-size.

See *Fatauci.*

Tomato – *tumatur*, pl. *tumaturi*, from the English word (*Lycopersicum esculentum*).

(a) Grown on a small scale in Batagarawa, the fruit are picked by men, sons-in-*gandu* being obliged to help if they are at home. Tomatoes are often cut and dried (*kauda*). An important sauce ingredient, but expensive.

(b) Tomatoes are an important marshland (*fadama*) crop.

See also *Data*.

Tools: see **Farm-tools.**

Trading-terms. Different Hausa trading-terms have different meanings in different localities (see *Soke*); and terms often have several specific meanings in the same locality – perhaps sometimes because one trader may perform several different functions. However, it seems worth-while to attempt to classify common words for types of trade, as in the following list. Specialised trading-terms, e.g. those involving butchering and meat-selling, or milk-selling by pastoralists, are omitted from the list. For all that is known, numerous other unrecorded words for these and other types of trade are in use in particular localities. (Most, though not quite all, of the terms in this list are separate entries in the Commentary.)

any kind of buying:	*saya*
any kind of selling:	*sayar da*
buying and selling:	*saye da sayarwa*
buying soup ingredients:	*cefane, masarufi*
selling off property bit by bit in order to purchase daily supplies:	*cefanad da*
any kind of trading:	*ciniki, kasuwanci*
women's house-trade and girls' hawking:	*saina* (*saisaina*) – more generally 'to offer for sale'
exchange or barter:	*furfura, musaya*
a type of bargain struck by traders who have unsold goods on their hands at the end of the day in the market-place, such that the goods are valued and exchanged, the balance being made up in cash:	*arazan* – noted in certain frontier markets, a word of unknown origin
local buying and reselling of grain and other produce by traders who do not store:	*baranda, kwarami*
buying and storing grain and other produce for later resale, by traders as distinct from farmers:	*cido, ciko, kamci, sara, soke* – commonly defined by the use of such opprobrious (though entirely inappropriate) terms as 'cornering', 'profiteering', 'speculating', some types such as *ciko* being 'worse' than others
as above, but involving produce other than grain:	*bilkara*
'table selling':	the traders are known as '*yan tebur* or '*yan tireda*
groundnut buying by firms:	*kanti* – from the English word 'canteen' (shop)
buying by measure:	*awo*
selling by measure:	*auna*

brokerage:	*dillanci*
a commission to purchase something at a place to which a person is already going, the money being pre-paid:	*sako, sautu* – the former usually applying to men's commissions the latter to women's
retailing small numbers of kola-nuts at a time from a basket known as *terere*:	the traders are *'yan terere*
peddling, hawking, or short-distance itinerant trading, by men:	*jagale, jaura, jemage, kiri, koli, talla*
rapid, unburdened, travelling on foot to buy something:	*bojuwa (bojwa), gurumfa* – also *burabura*, which may be with donkeys
long-distance trading:	*fatauci, safara*

Tribal marks – *shasshawa*. Tribal marks cut or tattooed on the face or body by barbers.

(a) In Batagarawa few babies are nowadays marked on the face.

Tsaba (tsababbe). Threshed grain; *tsabar kudi* = 'cash, as opposed to goods representing its value' – Bargery; *tsabar karfe* = money, contrasted with cowries.

Tsaki. Coarse siftings of flour which may be used to stiffen *tuwo*.

Tsamiya – pl. *tsamaiku*. The tamarind tree or fruit. See **Tamarind**.

Tsara – pl. *tsarori*. One's equal in age, position or wealth.

Tsaure (Cymbopogon giganteus). A tall coarse grass commonly used for *zana* and *asabari* matting and fencing. See **Mat**.

Tsire. Bits of meat spitted on a stick and toasted: an excellent snack, eaten where bought. Barth at Tassawa: 'Every open space in the midst of the market-place was occupied by a fire-place . . . on a raised platform, on which diminutive morsels of meat, attached to a small stick, were roasting, or rather stewing, in such a way that the fat, trickling down from the richer pieces attached to the top of the stick, basted the lower ones' (vol. II, p. 30).

Tsiya. Poverty; destitution.

Tudu. 'High ground (*compared with the level occupied by the speaker, hence* hill, river bank *seen from river*, etc.)' – Abraham. Often used in the sense of dry farmland which is slightly higher than *fadama* (marshland). See **Fadama**.

Tukunya – pl. *tukwane*. Cooking pot.

(a) Clay cooking pots are owned by individual housewives; many wives own several pots owing to the preference for reserving separate ones for making *fura*, *tuwo* and soup. Many pots are supplied by one Batagarawa trader who buys in neighbouring markets. *Tukunyar taba* = tobacco pipe.

See **Potters**.

Tukwici. The return of a small part of a gift, for instance that made by a bride's parents to a bridegroom (or his parents), to indicate that its size is sufficient.

Tulu – pl. *tuluna*. Water pot, pitcher, etc.

Turaka. The private room, or hut, of the householder (*mai gida*), which is inside the compound, unlike the *zaure*. Hence, *'yan turaka* = children of the same father by different mothers.

(a) In Batagarawa very few husbands have a *turaka*.

Turmi – pl. *turame*.

(i) A wooden mortar for pounding grain etc.

(ii) A 'whole piece' (6 yds) of printed cloth.
See *Tabarya*.

Tuwo. The basis of the main evening meal (*abincin dare*), *tuwo* resembles a very well-set pudding, slices of which may be cut and sold. The grain (preferably guinea corn, but millet is a substitute) is elaborately pounded, sieved and ground before being cooked in boiling water. It is served with *miya*, a sauce.

Uba – pl. *ubanni*. Father, whether real or figurative – though *mai gida* or *baba* are more usual terms for the latter. See *Haifa*.

Uban daki – lit. 'father of a hut'.
(i) Master of a servant.
  (ii) A person's immediate superior – e.g. a District Head in relation to a Village Head.

Ubangiji – f. *uwargijiya*, pl. *iyayangiji*. The owner of a slave, or any object. See Smith (1960, p. 258) on the relationship between *iyayangiji* and farmers of slave-origin on former *rumada* (see *Rinji*) in Zaria. 'Unless one understands the basis of the *ubangiji*'s power, it is difficult to appreciate the extent to which servitude continued in Zaria, fifty years after proclamations intended to eliminate slavery . . .' (*ibid.*, p. 258). See **Slavery**.

Ungozoma (Ingozoma) – pl. *ungozomai*. A midwife.
(a) in Batagarawa midwives are engaged for 7 days at the time of the birth, but remain on for a few days after the naming-ceremony (q.v.).

Unguwa (Anguwa) – pl. *unguwoyi*. A hamlet, an area of dispersed settlement, or a ward. An administrative area. See **Hamlet**.

Ushira (Ushura). A tenth part of the estate of a deceased person, or of the sum involved in an action for debt, which is payable as a commission to a court hearing a case. The tax may also be levied by administrative authorities, even when no dispute is involved. See **Inheritance**.

Usury. For the student of the rural scene the difficulty is that of assessing the manner in which prevailing attitudes to, and definitions of, 'usury' (a word without a Hausa equivalent – though see *Bashi*) actually affect the systems, patterns and volumes of borrowing and lending within the local community. In an economic environment where erratically fluctuating prices introduce an element of speculation into all transactions involving a time-lag; where 'time-lag transactions' involve nearly everybody save the destitute ('la societé locale peut apparâite comme un réseau extrêmement touffu [involved] de prêteurs et d'emprunteurs' – Nicolas (NM, pp. 241–2)); where prices are *expected* to double seasonally; where there is a great degree of economic inequality (long-term storage being a specialised function of the better-off); where there is seldom any concept of an interest rate (related to time) but only of the general reasonableness of returning a good deal more than had been received; where the principal 'money-lenders' are 'insiders' (not professional outsiders), being farmers who conform to conventional economic practice, while operating on a larger scale; where successful lenders and borrowers are alike admired – in such an environment, much standard economic behaviour is necessarily, or potentially, 'usurous,' and our question is whether the 'prohibitions' of Muslim law have significant practical effect.

This is not the place to summarise the Muslim attitude to 'usury' the most convenient authoritative interpretation of which is given in the *Risâla* of Ibn Abi Zayd (1960, pp. 201–21), 'Chapitre des ventes et des contrats analogues': 'Allah a déclaré la vente licite et il a interdit l'usure (Coran 2–276)'. Meek provides (1949, pp. 232 ff.) a useful summary of the Koranic prohibitions against usury (interest-taking) and gambling – the latter including the taking of risks in forward contracts and fluctuations in rates of exchange; of the differences between law and practice; of the kinds of sale for future delivery which are recognized by the law; and of the 'numerous devices to evade the prohibitions' which 'have received the sanction of the schools'.

The authorities – Anderson (1954), Meek (1949), and others – are agreed that the prohibition on interest-taking is widely respected in the northern Nigerian courts, in the sense that contracts involving interest are 'nowhere enforceable ... although seldom punished' – Anderson (*ibid.*, p. 217). Although in the event of court action, creditors are likely to lose any claim to interest which the debtor had agreed to pay, it may yet be surmised that most rural debtors would have a deep reluctance to initiating legal action (even were the courts not usually so far away), owing to the extreme importance of remaining credit-worthy in the eyes of the local community, which does not favour such resort to law. But such an attitude does not imply an indifference to the requirements of the law – rather the contrary.

The bewilderment betrayed by farmers who are questioned about different forms of borrowing or indebtedness, or contracts of sale, is often a sincere expression of their wish to conform with Muslim law, if only they could understand what this would entail. Despite the invariable presence of some Koranic scholars in the local community, it is inevitable that particular bafflement should relate to the doctrine relating to 'similars of weight and capacity', such that with a measurable commodity, like grain, any contract of 'exchange' must involve reciprocal and immediate delivery of the same quantity – see the *Risâla*. Informants constantly emphasize that if grain or groundnuts are borrowed during the farming-season, then it is obligatory for money to be returned after harvest and *vice versa*. Although it is doubtful whether anyone conforms to this 'rule', informants sometimes vaguely presume that others are more obedient than themselves. But given the economic environment, such conformity is usually altogether beyond the scope of the individual farmer.

On the other hand, formal interest-granting in certain official spheres is an acceptable fact of life. Of course the co-operative (q.v.) charged a (timeless) 10% on its loans; of course a certain prominent farmer from a nearby hamlet openly charges interest of 25% per month on loans granted to many employees in Katsina city. As there are no licensed money-lenders in Batagarawa, citizens are unaware (though they would not be surprised to learn) that under the Moneylenders Ordinance 1938 interest of up to 48% (9½d. per £ per month) may be legally charged.

Devices for avoiding (or appearing to avoid) the prohibition on interest-taking are legion. 'The fictitious acknowledgment by the borrower of a larger sum than he actually receives' – Meek (*ibid.*, p. 235) – is usually assumed to be one of them. But as such a practice is common in many regions of non-Muslim West Africa (in a study of indebtedness among cocoa-farmers of southern Ghana the present writer came upon many cases), it is doubtful whether it is necessarily evasive, but may be designed merely to ensure the recording of the most crucial sum – that to be repaid. A device which was said in 1939 (National Archives, Kaduna, file on moneylenders) to be especially prevalent in Katsina Emirate, involves the lender in selling goods at exorbitant prices to the borrower, who immediately resells at a much lower price, thus obtaining ready money. Again, if a borrower *voluntarily* happens, when the time comes, to repay more than he borrowed, there is no transgression. But such devices have little relevance within the framework of the local rural economy where the volume of debt (most of it effectively interest-carrying) necessarily ebbs and flows with changing seasons and with individual vicissitudes and where (presumably) most credit, except that granted to a few of the rich, is internally generated. Universal indebtedness is nothing new. When giving evidence to the Northern Nigeria Lands Committee, H. R. Palmer was asked whether there were 'usurers or money-lenders'. 'No', he replied, 'but every native is in debt to another. I have never come across one who was not. They are all in debt.' (All creditors were debtors also.)

Although it is arguable that the lifting of the 'prohibition' on interest-taking would have little direct effect on rural economies, yet the present moral attitude of pretence stands as a barrier between officialdom and farmers, ensuring the continued irrelevance of legislation and official commands on such matters as pre-season crop-marketing and plough-hiring and justifying the refusal to explore such fundamental problems of rural organisation as extreme poverty.

See Nicolas (NK, pp. 263–73) for a full discussion of borrowing with interest (*bashin ruwa*) in the Niger Republic. See Bivar and Hiskett (1962) for an eighteenth-century poem by Muhammad Ibn 'Abd-al Rahman al-Barnawi, which includes much practical exhortation relating to the legality of certain village transactions in Bornu, e.g. grain-selling: 'The selling of food excessive to one's requirements is obligatory in (time of) need at a price suitable to a time of dearth' (pp. 126–7). See *Bashi, Biki*, Butchers, *Dauke*, Economic regulations, Proclamation on farm produce, *Rance, Riba, Soke*.

Uwa – pl. *uwaye*. Mother, whether real or figurative.

Uwar gida – lit. 'mother of the house'. Strictly the householder's senior (or sole) wife, the word is widely used as a term of respect or address.

Village – *kauye*, pl. *kauyuka*. For administrative purposes Districts (q.v.) are divided into Villages under the authority of Village Heads and in many areas such Villages are known as *kauye*, pl. *kauyuka*. A Village is in turn subdivided into Hamlets or Wards (*unguwa*).

(a) Mallamawa (of which the capital is Batagarawa) is administratively divided into 3 Villages.

(b) Villages, like Districts, vary greatly in size and population. However, according to the 1952 census, about half of all the 258 Village Areas in Katsina Emirate (excluding the Katsina Home District) had populations of 3,000–5,000; four Villages had populations of over 10,000; nine large Districts were divided into 16 or more Villages.

Village Head – *dagaci*, pl. *dagatai*; *magaji*, pl. *magada*, and other titles and words. The grade of 'chief' directly below the District Head; the salaried head of a Village (q.v.). While Village Heads, like Hamlet Heads, may be representatives of the local Hausa population, they are perhaps more often of aristocratic Fulani origin – but there are few references to this level of chief in the literature. The Head of a large Village who lives outside the District capital may be very powerful. Smith states (1955, p. 13) that in Zaria most 'village areas' – which he ambiguously defines as 'local communities' – have 'local chiefs drawn from *danginsarauta* [ruling-families] founded by Fulani shortly after the *Jihad*'.

Wada. Wealth; 'a sufficiency of any commodity' – Bargery; *wadata* = to be or to become wealthy; a wealthy person.

Wadari. 'Arranging cotton thread in the required length for weaving, whether for long narrow widths or shorter broad widths of material' – Bargery.

Waina. Small cakes made of cowpeas (*wake*) or grain flour and fried in groundnut oil, often in a *tanda* – see Plate 26.

(a) Nearly a fifth of the Batagarawa women house-traders sell *waina*.

Waje. Direction. See *Shiyya*.

Wake – pl. *wakaikai*. Cowpeas (q.v.). See *Dan wake*.

Wali. The male guardian who has the right of giving a girl in marriage.

Wankin hannu. An extra 'dash', in addition to his wages, given to a building-labourer when he has finished his work – and needs to wash his hands.

Wanzami – pl. *wanzamai*. A barber–surgeon (q.v.).

Wasa. Play, Hence *abokin–wassa* (q.v.), the joking-relationship between certain categories of kin and friends.

Washermen – *wanki* (clothes washing), *mai wanki* (washerman).

(a) Clothes-washing (like sewing) is traditionally regarded as a man's occupation – Smith (1955, p. 60); but in many Batagarawa households the secluded women in fact wash their own and their children's clothes, sometimes with their children's help. Richer men (and some of those engaged in very dirty work) employ a washerman – who may then wash women's, as well as men's, clothes. The washing of men's gowns (*riga*) is very skilled work: as one of the 4 best-known washermen remarked – 'it takes a long time to establish a name'. Two washermen (only) do much of the work (they sometimes employ each other or have other assistants), one being head of a farming-unit the other a son-in-*gandu*: they do much of the washing for the households of the *masu–sarauta* and have many other regular customers. The charge for washing and pressing a *riga* (with a charcoal iron) is about 9*d*. Imported detergents are increasingly bought by richer people.

Wealth: see *Arziki, Attajiri, Dukiya, Gata, Wada, Zarafi.*

Weaving – *saka* (weaving), *masaki* (weaver) – pl. *masuka.*

(a) Although formerly there was a man weaver 'in every house', none remain in the *gari* today and only one man occasionally pursues the craft in Kauyen Yamma. No women weave with the broad loom.

(b) Considering the importance of long-distance trade in Hausa cloth, the lack of literature on weaving, or on the organisation of the trade, is astounding. Dalziel (p. 124) states that the method of weaving is pre-Islamic 'and may have come from India through East Africa'. Early references to the trade with the Fezzan are made by Lucas, reporting the evidence of a Fezzan trader, in *Proceedings of the Association for Promoting the Discovery of the Interior Parts of Africa* (1791, pp. 264–5, 275–8) – special mention being made of the huge quantities of cloth exported from Katsina. Barth regarded cotton cloth as 'the principal commerce' of Kano and neighbouring towns: 'There is really something grand in this kind of industry, which spreads to the north as far as Murzuk, Ghat, and even Tripoli; to the west, not only to Timbuktu, but in some degree even as far as the shores of the Atlantic, the very inhabitants of Arguin dressing in the cloth woven and dyed in Kano . . .' 'As for the supply sent to Timbuktu, this is a fact entirely over-looked in Europe, where people speak continually of the fine cotton cloth produced in that town, while in truth all the apparel of a decent character in Timbuktu is brought either from Kano or from Sansandi . . .' (vol. II, p. 126). Robinson (1896a, p. 113) supposed that Kano might clothe 'more than half the population of the Central Soudan' and reported that travellers had 'no difficulty' in purchasing Kano-made cloth at Alexandria, Tripoli, Tunis or Lagos.

However, search the published literature as one may, little of significance is found on weaving. Meek (1925, pp. 166–8) and Ibrahim Madauci (1968, pp. 65–7) include less technical detail than an earnest search through Bargery's *Dictionary* would reveal. Morel was one of the few writers to relate the internal trade in cotton to the demand from weavers: he considered (1911, p. 239) that virtually the whole of Zaria's cotton crop was bought by the weavers of Kano and Zinder; that Katagum consumed all the cotton it grew; and that Katsina 'exported' a percentage to Kano, consuming the rest.

There appears to be no collated material on the main centres of production. Among those centres are (or were): Kazaure Emirate – Parsons (1934) regarded the craft as the chief non-farming occupation throughout the emirate, the village of Malaganta being the 'Blackburn of Northern Nigeria'; numerous parts of Kano Emirate – see e.g. Mortimore and Wilson (1965, p. 64) on the importance of weaving in the Kano Close-Settled Zone; and Kadandani in Katsina Emirate where Luning (1963a, pp. 110–11) found that 46 of a sample of 77 men were weavers, mainly producing cloth for 'export' to Sokoto by 'financiers' in Katsina city. Weaving probably remains an important craft in many areas of Sokoto and Gwandu Emirates –

Barth (vol. IV, p. 203) regarded Gwandu cloth (which was 'in great demand as far as Libtako') as coarsely dyed compared with Nupe and Kano cloth. In many Katsina Districts it has long been unimportant; thus, in the 6 Districts covered by the 1931 intensive census there were only 244 men weavers (and 318 dyers) – total male population 119,000.

Although the craft is declining greatly in importance owing to the widespread preference for cheaper manufactured cloth, many Fulani pastoralists will continue to wear handwoven cloth and the strong demand for 'blankets' – *gwado*, *luru* and other types – may well be maintained. Nicolas (NK, pp. 62–3) reports a decline in demand as affecting Hausa weavers of Niger, most of whose cloth is now sold to Tuareg and Buzu.

Men weavers usually work on a horizontal loom, producing strips of a width of some 3 to 4 inches. (However, Smith (1955, p. 160) states that men sometimes use a broad loom for weaving a special cloth for sale to the wives of Fulani pastoralists.) If Nadel is correct in his surmise (1942, p. 297) that the women's vertical broadloom came to Nupe from Yoruba, the same may apply to Hausaland: Baba of Karo (Mary Smith, 1954) reported that this loom was unknown at the end of the last century. In the longer run, most weavers may be women.

See **Cloth, Cotton, Dyeing, Spinning**.

Wells – *rijiya*, pl. *rijiyoyi*.

(a) It may be that about a third of all houses in the *gari* have private wells (some of which are dry at times) and the 5 concrete-lined wells with walled tops (Fig. 4), together with other wells constructed or maintained by the local authority, provide sufficient good drinking water for the community. None of the Kauyen Yamma houses have private wells, but there are 3 communal wells. Although there are some wells (old and new) in the farmland, the water is never used for farming, but is drunk by humans and livestock and used for washing.

There are 2 professional well-diggers (who are also farmers) in the *gari*, neither of whom 'inherited' the craft from his father. They charge about £2 to £3 for a well no more than some 7 fathoms (*gaba*) deep, one-third of this sum being for their assistants; half of the price is payable at the start, the balance when the work is completed. For wells of (say) 15 to 20 fathoms the price might be £5 to £6; the buyer has to pay more if the depth proves to be greater than had been expected, but the well-digger must start again without further payment if he strikes rock.

At Kabakawa, just north of Batagarawa, Barth noted (vol. IV, p. 106) that the wells were only 8 fathoms deep. (East of Kano, in Zakara District, he had measured one of 33 fathoms – vol. II, p. 159.)

(b) See Prothero (1958, pp. 3 ff.) on wells in Sokoto. Although little work appears to have been done on the relationship between the density of the rural population and the height of the water-table, Grove and Luning agree that lack of water in the extreme west of Katsina Emirate has retarded settlement. According to D. G. Jones (1957) a significant rise in the water-table had occurred in parts of Daura and adjoining areas of northern Katsina, this being thought to have been due to an increasing proportion of the rainfall percolating to the water-table, as a result of reduced transpiration losses, through clearance of the natural vegetation. He recorded the depths of 87 wells: the average depth was 55 feet; 14 wells were less than 30 feet and 5 were over 100 feet.

The following citation refers to the high water-table in the Kano Close-Settled Zone:

For a radius of 30 miles round the city, the country is closely cultivated and densely populated with some 40 walled towns, and with villages and hamlets hardly half a mile apart. The Kano district proper contains 170 walled towns and about 450 villages. There are many streams, but water is chiefly obtained from wells 15 to 40 feet deep.

Colonial Reports Annual – Northern Nigeria, Report for 1904, p. 32

In reference to the possible relationship between rural wife seclusion and the availability of well-water (see p. 24), it is noteworthy that rural women are seldom secluded in Bornu, where wells are often extremely deep and expensive. According to Prothero (personal information) there is no area in rural Hausaland with wells comparable in depth to those in some parts of Bornu.

As in Barth's time (vol. IV, p. 88) the water, even from the deepest wells, 'is procured by the labour of man alone'.

See Prothero (1962) and Mary Smith (1954); also Nash (1948, p. 10) on methods of preventing guinea-worm infection by providing wells with collars.

Wheat: see *Alkama*.

Wife-seclusion: see *Kulle*.

Women – economic position of. At the outset it had been intended that this enquiry should relate mainly to the socio-economic affairs of men farmers (with particular reference to *gandu*) and the increased scope of the investigation, which partly resulted from the additional fieldwork done by M. S. Nuhu in 1968 and 1969, has made the neglect of women's economic affairs (apart from their house-trade) much more evident. There are, however, four important reasons why, in a Hausa village community like Batagarawa, it is not so preposterous to isolate the economic affairs of men, as it would be in many non-Hausa villages. First, the 'export income' of the community (see pp. 197–8) is almost entirely generated by men farmers: the important trade activities of women are largely conducted within the local community. Secondly, there is the fact that women's economic activities are mainly carried on independently of their husbands: their produce is their own to dispose of, and any loans made to their husbands are recoverable in court – see Smith (1955, p. 115). Thirdly, most of the men are permanent members of the village community, whereas the composition of the female population is undergoing constant change, many Batagarawa women marrying men in other hamlets, many resident wives having been born elsewhere: this is a matter not only of the high proportion of wives of non-Batagarawa origin, but also of the constant ebb and flow resulting from high divorce rates. Fourthly, is the fact that women are physically isolated by their Muslim seclusion, having few dealings with individual men, other than their husbands and sons. Fortunately, however, there is much interesting material on the economic affairs of women in *Baba of Karo* and Smith (1955) – in the latter see p. 115. Although Smith endeavoured to estimate women's incomes, he was greatly hampered by his inability to obtain accurate information. His 'community calculations' in respect of women were seriously incomplete. 'Yet if the majority of women's incomes are spent in the community from which they were earned, and the non-recorded portions mainly in transactions with other women, the accuracy and completeness of our tables for the economic activities of the community's males is not in question – and with that we must be content' (*ibid.*, pp. 115–16).

The main unanswered question, so far as this enquiry is concerned, is whether richer men tend to have richer wives (richer in terms of their independent incomes) than poorer men: assuming that richer fathers give more help to their daughters than poorer fathers, our statistical demonstration (Table XIII.3, p. 180) of the existence of some relationship between the economic-grouping of a man and that of his wife's father provides some general evidence that this is the case. Much detailed analysis of our rudimentary statistics relating to the types of ware handled by individual women house-traders (see **House-trade**) suggested that (apart from the question of storage for a price rise) the relationship between the scale of a woman's trade and the economic-group of her husband was not close. However, the likelihood is that most of the very prominent house-traders have 'rich' husbands: of the 17 women traders who handled 10 wares or more, 5 were wives of the *masu-sarauta*, 5 were wives (or in one case a mother) of men in Group 1, and 3, 3 and 1 respectively were wives of men in Groups

2, 3 and 4; as 2 of the 3 Group 3 husbands had been wrongly classified (see p. 60), only 2 of the husbands were actually 'poor' men. The proportion of wives who do no house-trade varies little between Groups 1 and 4. Older women probably tend to do more house-trade than younger women: three-fifths of the wives of men-in-*gandu* do no house-trading, compared with one-third of all women. Interestingly, there was little difference in the types of ware handled by the wives of richer and poorer husbands, except that the former more often made groundnut oil (q.v.).

The proportion of women who save by means of *adashi* groups (q.v.) varies little according to their husband's economic-grouping – though, of course, the scale of saving may do so. As for *aikatau* (q.v.), this is performed somewhat more often by wives of Group 4 than of Group 1 men.

It was noted (see p. 68 and Table IV.5, p. 67) that women with husbands in Groups 3 and 4 own more goats than wives with Group 1 husbands. However, this is mainly accounted for by the fact that most of those (few) households in which the women own 10 goats or more, are those headed by men in Groups 3 and 4. Excluding these households, goat ownership shows little variation between Groups. So if the wives of Group 1 farmers *are* richer than the average, it seems that their preference for investing their savings in goats is lower than that of other wives. As for sheep-ownership, the figures in Table IV.5 are not misleading: roughly equal proportions of houses headed by men in Groups 1 and 3 include women sheep-owners.

Although the occupational statistics provided by the 1952 population census are crude in the extreme, it is perhaps worth noting that only about 1% of all adult women in Katsina Emirate stated that they had trading or clerical occupations – evidently house-trading was not regarded as an 'occupation'.

Women farmers.

(a) Forty women farmers were recorded as owning 47 mapped farms (Table II.11, p. 37), of which 26 were smaller than one acre, 19 were between 1 and 2 acres – the total area being 47·9 acres. (A number of other farms which appeared to be owned by men were probably owned by their wives). It is possible that a few women also own bush-farms. As many as half of the women were widows; 14 were wives of heads of farming-units; and 3 were servants. Although few women in Kauyen Yamma are rigidly secluded, only 9 of the women farm-owners were resident in Kauyen Yamma, of whom 5 were widows. About one-third of the total acreage had been received by women from their husbands; about a quarter had been inherited from their fathers; and about a tenth had been bought. It is interesting that all the 11 women recorded as inheriting from their fathers had brothers who also inherited – see **Inheritance**. Only 3 women were recorded as owning (a total of 5) granaries (q.v.), most women's produce being stored by sons or other relatives.

As most women farm-owners are semi-secluded older women, they are free to work on their farms if they wish; however, it seems that most of the weeding is done by their husbands or sons: women seldom employ *'yan kwadago* – see Table VIII.3, p. 110.

Although women own so few farms, it should be remembered that some older women assist their husbands with tasks such as sowing or harvesting of certain crops – the same applying to a few younger semi-secluded women in dispersed homesteads.

(b) See Chapter III, pp. 41–3, with regard to the uncertainty as to whether farmers' wives did much farming in the nineteenth century; it may be added here that Staudinger asserted, without further elaboration, that farming was men's not women's work (1889, p. 613). See *Gandu* on the position of women farmers in the Niger Republic. See also *Kulle*.

Wuri – pl. *kudi*. A cowry shell (q.v.).

Yaji. Any type of pungent condiment, such as pepper (q.v.), ginger, etc.

Yakuwa – roselle or Guinea sorrel (*Hibiscus Sabdariffa*). There are several varieties, cultivated for leaf, calyx, seed or fibre.

(a) Sometimes used as a boundary plant in Batagarawa, the succulent calyx is used in soups and the fermented seeds are made into *daddawar batso* (q.v.).

Yama – the grass *Hyparrhenia rufa*. One of the many grasses commonly used for thatching (q.v.).

Yams – *doya* (*Dioscorea*). *Doya* is the general word for yam, there being many other words for different types.

(a) Yams are not grown in Batagarawa. Although yams 'imported' from further south are on sale in Katsina city, they are far too expensive for Batagarawa farmers.

(b) Yams are an important crop in parts of Zaria.

See **Cocoyam.**

Yanta. Preparing grass for thatching; *yantanya* = a bundle of grass ready for thatching. See **Thatch.**

Yaro – pl. *yara*. A boy. By extension the word has many usages (irrespective of age), such as servant, dependant, trading or other assistant, etc.

Yima. 'Sewing, weaving, or any similar work, except dyeing, done for payment' – Bargery. See *Aikatau.*

Zagi – pl. *zagage*. A runner in front of a horseman.

(a) One of the two youths (*barori*) who attend to the District Head's horses.

Zakka.

(i) A grain measure, the equivalent of 4 *mudaye* – see *Mudu.*

(ii) A tithe of grain.

(a) After harvest one out of 10 bundles of grain 'ought' to be set aside for certain malams and for old or poor people of the donor's choice – but 'each according to his own conscience'. At the end of Ramadan the 4 handfuls of grain per household member which are traditionally given to malams, go to poor people (*fidda*).

(b) (i) The *zakka* is a common grain measure in the Niger Republic where Nicolas observed 5 sizes (1964, p. 83).

(ii) See Smith (1960) on *zakka* as a traditional grain-tithe for the benefit of rulers and malams.

Zamiya. 'Deducting the sum a person owes from a payment one is making to him' – Bargery.

Zanganniya – pl. *zangarku*. A head of any kind of corn, such as is stored in bundles in granaries.

Zango.

(i) Camping-place or halting-ground of a trading-caravan – not to be confused with *sansani* (q.v.).

(ii) Lodging-place of travellers who are *en route.*

(iii) 'Any village or ward of a town the inhabitants of which are all Barebari people' – Bargery.

In many non-Hausa regions of West Africa, for instance southern Ghana, villages or wards inhabited by strangers of any ethnic group are known as *zango* – or more often *zongo*. *Zangoma* (pl. *zangomai*) is one who lodges travellers – viz. a *mai gida* (in the sense of 'landlord') or a *fatoma.*

Zarafi – pl. *zarufa*. Wealth: opportunity.

Zaure – pl. *zauruka*. An entrance-hut leading into a compound or house (*gida*) where men commonly sit and meet their friends.

(a) In Batagarawa, where most houses have *zauruka*, there are two main types: rectangular mud-roofed rooms (*soro*) which are all in the *gari* and circular thatched huts, which may be some distance from the compound if it is in the open countryside.

See p. 24 and Plate 13.

Zubi. The periodic contribution under the *adashi* system.

Zumunta.

(i) Relationship by blood or marriage – thus *auren zumunta* is kin-marriage.

(ii) 'Clan feeling, e.g. between two people of the same town or district who meet in a place strange to both' – Bargery.

Bibliography

Abraham, R. C., 1946. *Dictionary of the Hausa Language*. University of London Press; 2nd edition 1962.
   1959. *Hausa Literature and the Hausa Sound System*. University of London Press.
Abuja for *A Chronicle of Abuja: see* Heath (1962).
Adeyinka, S. O., 1966. 'Agricultural Statistics and Food Crops Production in Nigeria'. Rural Economic Survey Division, Federal Office of Statistics, Lagos (cyclostyled).
Agriculture, Northern Nigeria Ministry of, *Socio-Economic Surveys of Peasant Agriculture: see* FAO.
Allan, W., 1965. *The African Husbandman*. Oliver and Boyd, Edinburgh.
Aluko, S. A., 1965. 'How Many Nigerians?'. *The Journal of Modern African Studies*, III, 3.
Anderson, J. N. D., 1954. *Islamic Law in Africa*. Colonial Research Publication no. 16, HMSO, London; reprinted Cass, London, 1970.
Anthony, K. R. M., and Johnston, B. F., 1968. 'Field Study of Agricultural Change: Northern Katsina'. Economic, Cultural and Technical Determinants of Agricultural Change in Tropical Africa, Preliminary Report no. 6, Food Research Institute, Stanford University (cyclostyled).
Ardener, Shirley, 1964. 'The comparative study of Rotating Credit Associations'. *Journal of the Royal Anthropological Institute*, 94.
Arhin, K., 1970. 'Aspects of the Ashanti Northern Trade in the Nineteenth Century'. *Africa*, XL, October.
Arnett, E. J., 1920. *Gazetteer of Sokoto Province*. Waterlow, London.
Awe, B.: *see* Lloyd (1967).
Ayandele, E. A., 1967. *The Missionary Impact on Modern Nigeria, 1842–1914*. Longmans, London.
Baikie, W. B., 1867. 'Notes of a Journey from Bida in Nupe to Kano in Haussa, performed in 1862'. *The Journal of the Royal Geographical Society*, 37.
Baldwin, K. D. S., 1957. *The Niger Agricultural Project: an Experiment in African Development*. Blackwell, Oxford.
   1963. 'Land-Tenure Problems in relation to Agricultural Development in the Northern Region of Nigeria', in Biebuyck (1963).
Barbour, K. M., and Prothero, R. M. (eds.), 1961. *Essays on African Population*. Routledge and Kegan Paul, London.
Bargery, G. P., 1934. *A Hausa–English Dictionary and English–Hausa Vocabulary*. Oxford University Press, London.
Barth, H., 1857. *Travels and Discoveries in North and Central Africa, 1849–1855*. Vols. I to V, London; reprinted in 1965 in 3 volumes, Cass, London.
Bauer, P. T., 1954. *West African Trade*. Cambridge University Press.
Benton, P. A.: *see* Schultze (1968).
Bercher, L.: see Ibn Abi Zayd Al-Qayrawani (1960).
Biebuyck, D. (ed.), 1963. *African Agrarian Systems*. International African Institute, Oxford University Press, London.

Bivar, A. D. H., and Hiskett, M., 1962. 'The Arabic Literature of Nigeria to 1804: A Provisional Account'. *Bulletin of the School of Oriental and African Studies*, xxv, Part I.

Bohannan, P., and Dalton, G. (eds.), 1962. *Markets in Africa*. Northwestern University Press.

Bovill, E. W., 1922. 'Jega Market'. *Journal of the African Society*, October.

1958. *The Golden Trade of the Moors*. Oxford University Press, London.

Bovill, E. W. (ed.), 1966. *Missions to the Niger, II, III and IV, The Bornu Mission, 1822–25*, Parts 1, 2 and 3. Hakluyt Society, Cambridge University Press.

Brand, F. T., 1940. 'The History of the Niger Gutta Industry'. *The Nigerian Forester*, I.

Buchanan, K. M., and Pugh, J. C., 1955. *Land and People in Nigeria: The Human Geography of Nigeria and its Environmental Background*. University of London Press, London.

Buntjer, B. J., 1971. 'The Changing Structure of *Gandu*', in Mortimore (ed.) 1971.

Burdon, J. A., 1904. 'The Fulani Emirates of Northern Nigeria'. *Journal of the Royal Geographical Society*, December.

1909. *Historical Notes on certain Emirates and Tribes in Northern Nigeria*. London.

Caldwell, J. C., and Okonjo, C. (ed.), 1968. *The Population of Tropical Africa*. Longmans, London.

Campbell, M. J., 1963. *Law and Practice of Local Government in Northern Nigeria*. Sweet and Maxwell, London.

Cardew, M., 1960. 'Gobir Granaries'. *Nigeria Magazine*, 67.

Census: *see* Population Census.

Chancel, A. de: *see* Daumas (1848).

Chevalier, A., and Perrot, E., 1911. *Les Végétaux Utiles de l'Afrique Tropicale Française*. Fascicule VI: *Les Kolatiers et les Noix de Kola*. Challamel, Paris.

Chisholm, M., 1962. *Rural Settlement and Land Use*. Hutchinson, London.

Clapperton, H., 1826: *see* Denham.

1829. *Journal of a Second Expedition into the Interior of Africa from the Bight of Benin to Soccatoo*. Reprinted Cass, London, 1966.

1966: *see* Bovill (ed.).

Clark, C., and Haswell, Margaret, 1964. *The Economics of Subsistence Agriculture*. Macmillan, London.

Cohen, A., 1965. 'The Social Organisation of Credit in a West African Cattle Market'. *Africa*, January.

1966. 'Politics of the Kola Trade'. *Africa*, January.

1967. 'Stranger Communities: the Hausa', in Lloyd (1967).

1969. *Custom and Politics in Urban Africa: A Study of Hausa Migrants in Yoruba Towns*. University of California Press, Berkeley.

Cohen, R., 1960. 'The Structure of Kanuri Society'. Ph.D. thesis University of Wisconsin, University Microfilms, Ann Arbor, Michigan.

1967. *The Kanuri of Bornu*. Holt, Rinehart and Winston, New York.

Cohen, R., and Middleton, J. (eds.), 1970. *From Tribe to Nation in Africa: Studies in Incorporation Processes*. Chandler, Scranton, Pennsylvania.

Cole, C. W., 1949. *Report on Land Tenure, Zaria Province*. Government Printer, Kaduna.

Coleman, J. S. (ed.), 1965. *Education and Political Development*. Princeton University Press, Princeton, New Jersey.

Colonial Annual Reports: *see* Northern Nigeria.

Colonial Office, 1947. *Report of the Mission appointed to enquire into the production and transport of Vegetable Oils and Oil Seeds produced in the West African Colonies*. HMSO, Colonial, no. 211.

Colville, G.: *see* Shaw (1950).

Corby, H. D. L., 1941. 'Changes brought about by the introduction of Mixed Farming'. *Farm and Forest*, 2.

Crocker, W. R., 1936. *Nigeria: A Critique of British Colonial Administration*. Allen and Unwin, London.

Crowder, M., 1966. *The Story of Nigeria*. Faber, London (revision of first edition of 1962). 1968. *West Africa under Colonial Rule*. Hutchinson, London.

Dalton, G.: *see* Bohannan (1962).

Dalziel, J. M., 1937. *The Useful Plants of West Tropical Africa*. Crown Agents, London.

Daumas, E. and de Chancel, A., 1848. *Le Grand Désert, ou Itinéraire d'une Caravane du Sahara au Pays des Nègres (Royaume de Haoussa)*. Paris.

Davies, H. R. J., 1964. 'The West African in the Economic Geography of Sudan'. *Geography*, July.

Denham, D., and Clapperton, H., 1826. *Narrative of Travels and Discoveries in Northern and Central Africa in the Years 1822, 1823 and 1824*. London.

Derrett, J. D. M. (ed.), 1965. *Studies in the Laws of Succession in Nigeria*. Oxford University Press, London.

Douglas, Mary and Kaberry, Phyllis M., 1969. *Man in Africa*. Tavistock Publications, London.

Dry, D. P. L., n.d. 'The Family Organisation of the Hausa of Northern Nigeria' (typescript, based on fieldwork in 1948–50).
    1953. 'The Place of Islam in Hausa Society'. Oxford University D.Phil. (typescript).

Dudgeon, G. C., 1922. *The Agricultural and Forest Products of British West Africa*. Murray, London.

Dumont, R., 1966. *African Agricultural Development: Reflections on the Major lines of Advance and the Barriers to Progress*. FAO, Rome.

Dupire, Marguerite, 1962. *Peuls nomades: Étude descriptive des Wodaabe du Sahel Nigérien*. Institut d'Ethnologie, Paris.

Echard, Nicole, 1967. 'L'habitat traditionnel dans l'Ader (Pays Hausa, République du Niger)'. *L'homme*, VII, 3.

Edgar, F., 1911. *Litafi na Tatsuniyoyi na Hausa*, vol. I. Erskine Mayne, Belfast.
    1969: *see* Skinner (1969).

Eicher, C. K., and Liedholm, C. (ed.), 1970. *Growth and Development of the Nigerian Economy*. Michigan State University Press.

Ekwensi, C., 1962. *Burning Grass: A story of the Fulani of Northern Nigeria*. African Writers Series, Heinemann, London.

Falconer, J. D., 1911. *On Horseback through Nigeria*. Fisher Unwin, London.

Faulkner, O. T., and Mackie, J. R., 1933. *West African Agriculture*. Cambridge University Press.
    1936. 'The Introduction of Mixed Farming in Northern Nigeria'. *The Empire Journal of Experimental Agriculture*, January.

Fine, J. C., 1970: *see* Goddard (1971).

Fisher, A. G. B., and Fisher, H. J., 1970. *Slavery and Muslim Society in Africa: The Institution in Saharan and Sudanic Africa and the Trans-Saharan Trade*. Hurst, London.

Fletcher, R. S., 1912. *Hausa Sayings and Folk-Lore: with a Vocabulary of New Words*. Oxford University Press, London.

Food and Agricultural Organisation (FAO), 1965. 'Socio-economic Survey of Peasant Agriculture in Makarfi, Ako, Mallam Madari and Ibeto Districts in Northern Nigeria'. N. Nigeria Ministry of Agriculture (cyclostyled).
    1966. *Agricultural Development in Nigeria, 1965–1980*, Rome.

Forde, D., 1946. 'The North: the Hausa', in Perham (ed.) (1946).

1953. 'The Cultural Map of West Africa: Successive Adaptations to Tropical Forests and Grasslands'. *Transactions of the New York Academy of Scien-es*; also in Ottenberg (1960).

Forde, D. and Scott, Richenda, 1946. *The Native Economies of Nigeria*, vol. 1 (ed. Perham). Faber, London.

Fortes, M., 1949. 'Time and social structure: an Ashanti case study', in Fortes (ed.) (1949).

1958. Introduction to Goody (ed.) (1958).

Fortes, M. (ed.), 1949. *Social Structure: Studies presented to A. R. Radcliffe-Brown*. The Clarendon Press, London.

Geary, W. N. M., 1927. *Nigeria under British Rule*. Methuen, London; reprinted Cass, London, 1965.

Gibbs, J. L. (ed.), 1966. *Peoples of Africa*. Holt, Rinehart and Winston, New York.

Giles, L. C., 1937. 'The Hausa Village and Co-operation'. Unpublished report cited by Forde (1946).

Giles, P. H., 1964. 'The Storage of Cereals by Farmers in Northern Nigeria'. *Tropical Agriculture* (Trinidad), 41, no. 3.

Gilles, Helen T., 1946. 'Nigerian Groundnuts help feed Starving Nations'. *Farm and Forest*, VII, no. 1.

Goddard, A. D., 1969. 'Are Hausa-Fulani Family Structures breaking up?'. *Samaru Agricultural Newsletter*, Ahmadu Bello University, Zaria, June.

Goddard, A. D., Fine, J. C. and Norman, D. W., 1971. *A Socio-Economic Study of Three Villages in the Sokoto Close-Settled Zone*, Samaru Miscellaneous Paper no. 34, Ahmadu Bello University, Zaria.

Goldsworthy, P. R. and Heathcote, R., 1963. 'Fertilizer Trials with Groundnuts in Northern Nigeria'. *The Empire Journal of Experimental Agriculture*, XXXI.

Goody, J. R. (ed.), 1958. *The Developmental Cycle in Domestic Groups*. Cambridge Papers in Social Anthropology no. 1, Cambridge University Press.

Goody, J. R., and Mustapha, T. M., 1967. 'The Caravan Trade from Kano to Salaga'. *Journal of the Historical Society of Nigeria*, III, June.

Gowers, W. F., 1921. *Gazetteer of Kano Province*. Waterlow, London.

1924: *see* Middleton (1924).

Grandin, le Capitaine, 1951. 'Notes sur l'industrie et le commerce du sel au Kawar et en Agram', *Bulletin de l'I.F.A.N.*, III.

Greenberg, J. H., 1941. 'Some Aspects of Negro-Mohammedan Culture-Contact among the Hausa'. *American Anthropologist*, Jan.–March.

1946. *The Influence of Islam on a Sudanese Religion*. Monographs of the American Ethnological Society, New York.

1947. 'Islam and Clan Organization among the Hausa'. *Southwestern Journal of Anthropology*, 3.

Greenwood, M., 1933: *see* Hartley (1933).

1951. 'Fertiliser Trials with Groundnuts in Northern Nigeria'. *The Empire Journal of Experimental Agriculture*, XIX.

Grisman, C. S., 1955. 'West Africans in Eritrea'. *The Nigerian Field*, January.

Grove, A. T., 1957. *Land and Population in Katsina Province*. Government Printer, Kaduna.

1961. 'Population Densities and Agriculture in Northern Nigeria', in Barbour (1961).

Hailey, Lord, 1951. *Native Administration in the British African Territories*, Part III, *West Africa*. HMSO, London.

Hair, P. E. H., 1967. *The Early Study of Nigerian Languages: Essays and Bibliographies*. Cambridge University Press.

Hancock, Sir Keith, 1940. *Survey of British Commonwealth Affairs:* Vol. II, Part 2, *Problems of Economic Policy, 1918–39.* Oxford University Press, London.

Harris, P. G., 1930. 'Notes on Yauri, Nigeria'. *Journal of the Royal Anthropological Institute,* July–December.

Hartley, K. T., 1937. 'An explanation of the effect of Farmyard Manure in Northern Nigeria'. *The Empire Journal of Experimental Agriculture,* V.

Hartley, K. T., and Greenwood, M., 1933. 'The effects of small applications of Farm-yard Manure on the yields of Cereals in Nigeria'. *The Empire Journal of Experimental Agriculture,* I.

Hassan, Alhaji, and Shuaibu Na'ibi: *see* Heath (1962).

Hastings, A. C. G., 1925. *Nigerian Days.* John Lane, The Bodley Head, London.

Haswell, Margaret, 1953. *Economics of Agriculture in a Savannah Village.* Colonial Research Studies, no. 8, HMSO, London.

1964: *see* Clark (1964).

Hay, A. M., and Smith, R. H. T., 1970. *International Trade and Money Flows in Nigeria, 1964.* Nigerian Institute of Social and Economic Research, Oxford University Press, Ibadan.

Heath, F., 1962. *A Chronicle of Abuja,* translated and arranged from the Hausa of Alhaji Hassan and Mallam Shuaibu Na'ibi. African Universities Press, Lagos.

Heathcote, R.: *see* Goldsworthy (1963).

Helleiner, G. K., 1966. *Peasant Agriculture, Government and Economic Growth in Nigeria.* Economic Growth Center at Yale University, Irwin, Homewood, Illinois.

Heussler, R., 1968. *The British in Northern Nigeria.* Oxford University Press, London.

Hill, Polly, 1963. *The Migrant Cocoa-Farmers of Southern Ghana.* Cambridge University Press.

1966. 'Landlords and Brokers: A West African Trading System'. *Cahiers d'Études Africaines,* VI, 23.

1968. 'The Myth of the Amorphous Peasantry: A northern Nigerian Case Study'. *Nigerian Journal of Economic and Social Studies,* July.

1969a. 'Notes on the Occupations of former Schoolboys: the case of a Hausa Village'. *Nigerian Journal of Economic and Social Studies,* July.

1969b. 'Hidden Trade in Hausaland'. *Man,* September.

1970a. *Studies in Rural Capitalism in West Africa.* Cambridge University Press.

1970b. *The Occupations of Migrants in Ghana.* Museum of Anthropology, University of Michigan, Anthropological Papers no. 42.

1971. 'Two Types of West African House Trade', in Meillassoux (1971).

Hiskett, M., 1960. 'Kitab al-Farq: A Work on the Habe Kingdoms attributed to Uthman dan Fodio'. *Bulletin of the School of Oriental and African Studies,* XXIII.

1962: *see* Bivar (1962).

1966. 'Materials relating to the Cowry Currency of the Western Sudan: I. A late Nine-teenth-Century Schedule of Inheritance from Kano'; II. 'Reflections on the Provenance and Diffusion of the Cowry in the Sahara and the Sudan'. *Bulletin of the School of Oriental and African Studies,* XXIX, Parts I and II.

1968: *see* Temple (1968).

Hodgkin, T., 1960. *Nigerian Perspectives: An Historical Anthology.* Oxford University Press, London.

Hogben, S. J., and Kirk-Greene, A. H. M., 1966. *The Emirates of Northern Nigeria: A Preliminary Survey of their Historical Traditions.* Oxford University Press, London.

Hogendorn, J. S., 1966. 'The Origins of the Groundnut Trade in Northern Nigeria'. Un-published University of London Ph.D. thesis.

1970. 'The Origins of the Groundnut Trade in Northern Nigeria', in Eicher (1970).

Hopen, C. E., 1958. *The Pastoral Fulbe Family in Gwandu*. International African Institute, Oxford University Press, London.

Hoskins, W. G., 1957. *The Midland Peasant: The Economic and Social History of a Leicestershire Village*. Macmillan, London.

Hughes, T. P., 1885. *A Dictionary of Islam*. London.

Ibn Abi Zayd Al-Qayrawani, 1960. *La Risâla: ou Epître sur les éléments du dogme et de la loi de l'Islâm selon le rite mâlikite*. Texte arabe et traduction française, by L. Bercher. Carbonel, Alger.

Ibrahim Madauci and others, 1968. *Hausa Customs*. Northern Nigerian Publishing Company, Zaria.

Irvine, F. R., 1934. *A Text-book of West African Agriculture*. Oxford University Press, London.

    1969. *West African Agriculture:* Vol. 2, *West African Crops*. Oxford University Press, London.

Jackson, J. A. (ed.), 1968. *Social Stratification*. Cambridge University Press.

Johnson, Marion, 1970a and b. 'The Cowrie Currencies of West Africa', Parts I and II. *Journal of African History*, XI, 1 and 3.

Johnston, B. F.: *see* Anthony (1968).

Johnston, H. A. S., 1966. *A Selection of Hausa Stories*. Clarendon Press, London.

    1967. *The Fulani Empire of Sokoto*. Oxford University Press, London.

Jones, D. G., 1957. 'The Rise in the Water-table in parts of Daura and Katsina Emirates, Katsina Province'. *Records of the Geological Survey of Nigeria*. Government Printer, Lagos.

Jones, W. O., 1959. *Manioc in Africa*. Stanford University Press, California.

    1968. *The Structure of Staple Food Marketing in Nigeria as revealed by Price Analysis*. Food Research Institute, Stanford University Press, California.

Kaberry, Phyllis M.: *see* Douglas (1969).

King, J. G. M., 1939. 'Mixed Farming in Northern Nigeria'. *The Empire Journal of Experimental Agriculture*, VII.

Kirk-Greene, A. H. M., 1956. 'Tax and Travel among the Hill-Tribes of Northern Adamawa'. *Africa*, XXVI, October.

    1958. *Adamawa, Past and Present*. Oxford University Press, London.

    1962, *Barth's Travels in Nigeria*. Oxford University Press, London.

    1965a. *The Principles of Native Administration in Nigeria: Selected Documents, 1900–47*. Oxford University Press, London.

    1965b. 'Bureaucratic Cadres in a Traditional Milieu'. in Coleman (1965).

    1966a: *see* Hogben (1966).

    1966b. *Hausa ba dabo ba ne: A Collection of Hausa Proverbs*. Oxford University Press, Ibadan.

    1967. 'The Linguistic Statistics of Northern Nigeria: A Tentative Presentation'. *African Language Review*, 6.

    1969. 'The meaning of Place Names in Hausaland'. *Bulletin de l'I.F.A.N.*

Kirk-Greene, A. H. M. (ed.), 1968. *Lugard and the Amalgamation of Nigeria: A Documentary Record*. Cass, London. See Lugard (1919).

    (ed.) 1970. *Political Memoranda by Lord Lugard*. 3rd edition, with a new Introduction by the editor, Cass, London.

Krause, G. A., 1928. 'Haussa-Handschriften in der Preussischen Staatsbibliotek'. *Mitteilungen des Seminars für Orientalische Sprachen zu Berlin*.

Krieger, K., 1954. ' "Kola-Karawanen": Ein Beitrag zur Geschichte des Hausahandels'. *Mitteilungen des Instituts für Orientforschung*. II, 2.

Krusius, P., 1915. 'Die Maguzawa'. *Archiv für Anthropologie*, XIV.

Kuczynski, R. R., 1948. *Demographic Survey of the British Colonial Empire*, vol. I. Oxford University Press, London.

Kuper, Hilda (ed.), 1965. *Urbanization and Migration in West Africa*. University of California Press.

Lamb, P. H., 1913. 'Agriculture in Hausaland, Northern Nigeria'. *Bulletin of the Imperial Institute*, XI.

Lander, R., 1830. *Records of Captain Clapperton's Last Expedition to Africa*, with the subsequent adventures of the author, vols. I and II. Reprinted Cass, London, 1967.

Larymore, Constance, 1908. *A Resident's Wife in Nigeria*. Routledge, London.

Last, M., 1967. *The Sokoto Caliphate*. Longmans, London.

1970. 'Aspects of Administration and Dissent in Hausaland, 1800–1968'. *Africa*, XL, October.

Lewis, I. M. (ed.), 1966. *Islam in Tropical Africa*. International African Institute, Oxford University Press, London.

Liedholm, C.: *see* Eicher (1970).

Livestock Mission: *see* Shaw and Colville (1950).

Lloyd, P. C., Mabogunje, A. L. and Awe, B., 1967. *The City of Ibadan*. Cambridge University Press, Institute of African Studies, University of Ibadan.

Lugard, Flora, 1905. *A Tropical Dependency*, London.

Lugard, F. D., 1904. 'Northern Nigeria'. *The Geographical Journal*, XXIII.

1907. *Memorandum on the Taxation of Natives in Northern Nigeria*. Colonial Reports – Miscellaneous no. 40, Cmd 3309.

1918. *Political Memoranda* 1 to 12. For confidential circulation to Political Officers. (*See* Kirk-Greene (ed.) (1970).

1919: *see* Kirk-Greene (ed.), (1968), which is a reprint, with an introduction, of Lugard's Report of 1919 on the Amalgamation of Northern and Southern Nigeria and Administration, 1912–19.

1922. *The Dual Mandate in British Tropical Africa*, Allen and Unwin, London.

Luning, H. A., 1963a. *An Agro-Economic Survey in Katsina Province*. Government Printer, Kaduna.

1963b. 'The Rural Economy in the Upper Catchment of the Sokoto-Rima Valley'. Ministry of Agriculture, Northern Nigeria (typescript).

1963c. 'An Agro-economic Investigation in the Maramaru-Kasarawa Catchment Area'. Ministry of Agriculture, Northern Nigeria (typescript).

Mabogunje, A. L.: *see* Lloyd (1967).

MacBride, D. F. H., 1937. *Assessment Report* on Dawaki ta Kudu District, National Archives, Kaduna.

1938. 'Land Survey in Kano Emirate'. *Journal of the Royal African Society*, January.

McDonnell, G., 1964. 'The Dynamics of Geographic Change: The Case of Kano'. *Annals of the Association of American Geographers*, September.

Mackie, J. R.: *see* Faulkner (1936).

Mackintosh, J. P., 1966. *Nigerian Government and Politics*. Allen and Unwin, London.

Mahood, M. M., 1964. *Joyce Cary's Africa*. Methuen, London.

Mainet, G. and Nicolas, G., 1964. 'La Vallée du Gulbi de Maradi: Enquête socio-économique'. Documents des Études Nigériennes no. 16, IFAN-CNRS, Éditions du Centre Universitaire de Polycopiage de l'A.G.E.B., Bordeaux, (cyclostyled).

Meek, C. K., 1925. *The Northern Tribes of Nigeria*, 2 volumes, vol. II containing the report on the 1921 census. Oxford University Press, London.

Meek, C. K., 1949. *Land Law and Custom in the Colonies*. Oxford University Press, London.
1957. *Land Tenure and Land Administration in Nigeria and the Cameroons*. Colonial Research Studies, no. 22, HMSO, London.
Meillassoux, C. (ed.), 1971. *The Development of African Trade and Markets in West Africa*. International African Institute, Oxford University Press, London.
Michie, C. W., 1949. 'Notes on Land Tenure in the northern districts of Zaria Emirate', in Cole (1949).
Middleton, H. H., 1924. *Report on the Groundnut Trade in Kano Province*, with Memoranda by W. F. Gowers. Government Printer, Lagos.
Middleton, J.: *see* Cohen, R. (1970).
Miller, R., 1937. 'Katsina, A City of the Desert Border'. *Geography*, XXII, December.
1938. 'Katsina, a Region of Hausaland'. *Scottish Geographical Magazine*, July.
Miner, H. M., 1965. 'Urban Influences on the Rural Hausa', in Kuper (1965).
Mockler-Ferryman, A. F., 1902. *British Nigeria: A Geographical and Historical Description of the British Possessions adjacent to the Niger River*. London.
Monteil, P.-L., 1895. *De Saint-Louis à Tripoli par le lac Tchad: Voyage au travers du Soudan et du Sahara accompli pendant les années 1890–91–92*. Paris.
Morel, E. D., 1902. *Affairs of West Africa*. Heinemann, London; reprinted Cass, London, 1968.
1911. *Nigeria: Its Peoples and its Problems*. Murray, London; reprinted Cass, London, 1968.
Morgan, W. B. and Pugh, J. C., 1969. *West Africa*. Methuen, London.
Mortimore, M. J., 1967. 'Land and Population Pressure in the Kano Close-Settled Zone, Northern Nigeria'. *The Advancement of Science*, April.
1968, 'Population Distribution, Settlement and Soils in Kano Province, Northern Nigeria 1931–62', in Caldwell (ed.) (1968).
Mortimore, M. J. (ed.), 1971. *Zaria and its Region*. Department of Geography, Ahmadu Bello University, Zaria.
Mortimore, M. J., and Wilson, J., 1965. *Land and People in the Kano Close-Settled Zone*, Department of Geography, Ahmadu Bello University, Zaria.
Mouche, M. dan.: *see* Nicolas (1968 and 1970).
Muffett, D. J. M., 1964. *Concerning Brave Captains*. Deutsch, London.
Nachtigal, G., 1879–89. *Sahara und Sudan, Ergebnisse sechsjähriger Reisen in Afrika*, vol. I, Berlin, 1879; vol. II, Berlin, 1881; vol. III, Leipzig, 1889; complete reproduction, Graz, 1967.
Nadel, S. F., 1942. *A Black Byzantium: the Kingdom of Nupe in Nigeria*. International African Institute, Oxford University Press, London.
Nash, T. A. M., 1948. *The Anchau Rural Development and Settlement Scheme*. HMSO, London.
Netting, R. McC., 1968. *Hill Farmers of Nigeria: Cultural Ecology of the Kofyar of the Jos Plateau*. University of Washington.
Nicolas, G., 1962a. 'Un village Haoussa de la République du Niger: Tassao Haoussa'. *Les Cahiers Outre Mer*, October–December.
1962b. 'Problemes agraires en pays Haoussa' (Canton de Kantché), provisional report of 1961–2 mission (cyclostyled) (NK2).
1964. 'La Vallée du Gulbi de Maradi: Enquete socio-économique'. Documents des Études Nigériennes no. 16 IFAN-CNRS, Éditions du Centre Universitaire de Polycopiage de l'A.G.E.B., Bordeaux (cyclostyled) (co-author G. Mainet) (NM).
1964. 'Étude de marchés en pays Hausa (République du Niger): Documents ethno-graphiques. University of Bordeaux (cyclostyled).
1965. 'Circulation des richesses et participation sociale dans une société Hausa du Niger'

(Canton de Kantché), 2nd edition 1967, Bordeaux, Éditions du Centre Universitaire de Polycopiage de l'A.G.E.B., Bordeaux (cyclostyled) (NK).

1968a. 'Problèmes posés par l'introduction de techniques agricoles modernes au sein d'une société africaine: Vallée de Maradi, Niger'. Faculté des Lettres et Sciences Humaines, University of Bordeaux (cyclostyled). (Co-authors Magaji, H. and Mouche, M. dan.)

1968b. *Étude Socio-Economique de deux villages Hausa: enquête en vue d'un aménagement hydro-agricole, Vallée de Maradi*, no. 22 Études Nigériennes. C.N.R.S., Paris. (Co-authors Doumesche, H. and Mouche, M. dan.)

1970. 'Le systeme traditionnel du crédit dans la région de Maradi'. Mission d'études socio-economiques du pays haoussa oriental, Maradi (cyclostyled) (Co-authors Magaji, H. and Mouche, M. dan.)

Nicolas, Jacqueline, 1967. *"Les juments des dieux"*: *Rites de possession et condition féminine en pays Hausa* (*Vallée de Maradi, Niger*). Études Nigériennes no. 21, IFAN–CNRS.

Nigerian Livestock Mission, 1950. *Report: see* Shaw and Colville (1950).

1953, *Proceedings of a Conference called to consider the Report of the Nigerian Livestock Mission*. Government Printer, Lagos.

Norman, D. W., 1967 and 1971. *An Economic Study of Three Villages in Zaria Province:* 1. *Land and Labour Relationships;* 2. *Input–Output Relationships;* 3. *Maps*. Samaru Miscellaneous Papers nos 19, 33 and 23, (no. 33 published 1971), Ahmadu Bello University, Zaria.

1968. 'How hard do Nigerian Farmers work?'. *Samaru Agricultural Newsletter*, Ahmadu Bello University, Zaria, April.

1969. 'Labour Inputs of Farmers: A Case Study of the Zaria Province of the North-Central State of Nigeria'. *The Nigerian Journal of Economic and Social Studies*, II, 1.

1971a. 'Rural Economy with special reference to Agriculture', in Mortimore (ed.) (1971).

1971b: *see* Goddard (1971).

Northern Nigeria, 1900–1 to 1911, *Colonial Annual Reports*, nos. 346, 409, 437, 476, 516, 551, 594, 633, 674, 704, 738. HMSO, London.

1965. *Northern Nigeria Local Government Yearbook, 1965*. Institute of Administration, Ahmadu Bello University, Zaria.

1966. *Statistical Yearbook, 1965*. Ministry of Economic Planning, Kaduna.

Northern Nigeria Lands Committee, 1910. *Minutes of Evidence* and *Appendices*. Cd 5103, HMSO, London.

Okonjo, C. 1968. 'A preliminary medium estimate of the 1962 mid-year Population of Nigeria', in Caldwell (1968).

Oluwasanmi, H. A., 1966. *Agriculture and Nigerian Economic Development*. Oxford University Press, Ibadan.

Onwuejeogwu, M., 1969. 'The Cult of the *Bori* Spirits among the Hausa'. in Douglas (1969).

Orr, C. W. J. (Sir Charles), 1911. *The Making of Northern Nigeria*. Macmillan, London; reprinted, with a new introduction by A. H. M. Kirk-Greene, Cass, London, 1965.

Ottenberg, S. and P. (eds.), 1960. *Cultures and Societies of Africa*. Random House, New York.

Oyenuga, V. A., 1967. *Agriculture in Nigeria*. FAO, Rome.

Paden, J. N., 1970. 'Urban Pluralism, Integration and Adaptation of Communal Identity in Kano, Nigeria', in Cohen and Middleton (1970).

Palmer, H. R., 1907. *Notes on Kano Land Tenure*, attached to a Memorandum on Land Tenure and Land Revenue in Northern Nigeria by P. Girouard. National Archives, Kaduna.

1908. *Changes in the Taxation of Katsina Division: Report on Taxation*. National Archives, Kaduna, 1289.

Palmer, H. R. (ed.), 1908. 'Kano Chronicle'. *Journal of the Royal Anthropological Institute*, 38.

Parsons, F. W., 1934. *A Report on Kazaure Emirate*. Kano Provincial File No. 2007, National Archives, Kaduna.

Pedler, F. J., 1948. 'A Study of Income and Expenditure in Northern Zaria'. *Africa*, October.

Pelissier, P., 1966. *Les paysans du Senegal: Les civilisations agraires du Cayor à la Casamance*. Imprimerie Fabrégue, Saint-Yrieix (Haute-Vienne).

Perham, Margery, 1937. *Native Administration in Nigeria*. Oxford University Press, London.

1960. *Lugard: the Years of Authority, 1898–1945* (being the second part of a life of Lord Lugard). Collins, London.

Perham, Margery (ed.), 1946. *The Native Economies of Nigeria*, vol. 1. Faber, London.

Perrot, E.: *see* Chevalier (1911).

Piault, M.-H., 1964. *Populations de l'Arewa: introduction à une étude régionale*. Études Nigériennes, no. 13, IFAN–CNRS.

Proceedings of the Association for Promoting the Discovery of the Interior Parts of Africa, 1791, London.

Population Census, Nigerian

1921: *see* Meek (1925).

1931, *Census of Nigeria, 1931*, Crown Agents, London: vol. 1, *Nigeria* by S. M. Jacobs, 1933; vol. 11, *Census of the Northern Provinces*, by N. J. Brooke, 1933; vol. v, *Medical Census, Northern Provinces*, by Dr R. C. Jones, 1932.

1952, *Population Census of the Northern Region of Nigeria*. Government Statistician, Lagos 1953.

Prothero, R. M., 1956. 'The Population Census of Northern Nigeria 1952: Problems and Results'. *Population Studies*, x, November.

1957a. 'Migratory Labour from North-Western Nigeria'. *Africa*, July.

1957b. 'Land Use at Soba, Zaria Province, Northern Nigeria'. *Economic Geography*, January.

1958. *Migrant Labour from Sokoto Province, Northern Nigeria*. Government Printer, Kaduna.

1962. 'Some observations on Desiccation in North Western Nigeria'. *Erdkunde*, 16.

Prothero, R. M., and Barbour, K. M. (eds.), 1961. *Essays on African Population*. Routledge, London.

Prussin, Labelle, 1969. *Architecture in Northern Ghana: A Study of Forms and Functions*. University of California Press, Berkeley.

Pugh, J. C.: *see* Buchanan (1955), Morgan (1969).

Rattray, R. S., 1913. *Hausa Folk Lore*. Oxford University Press, London.

Raulin, R., 1963. *Techniques et bases socio-économiques des sociétés rurales Nigériennes*. Études Nigériennes 12, IFAN–CNRS.

Raynaut, C., 1969. *Quelques Données de l'Horticulture dans la Vallée de Maradi*, no. 26. Études Nigériennes, CNRS, Paris.

Reuke, L., 1969. *Die Maguzawa in Nordnigeria*, Bertelsmann Universitätsverlag, Freiburger Studien zu Politik und Gesellschaft überseeischer Länder.

Robinson, C. H., 1896a. *Hausaland: Fifteen Hundred Miles through the Central Sudan*, London.

1896b. 'Hausaland', *The Geographical Journal*, VIII, September.

1896c. *Specimens of Hausa Literature*. Cambridge University Press.

1898. 'The Slave Trade in the West African Hinterland'. *The Contemporary Review*, LXXIII, May.

1900. *Nigeria: Our Latest Protectorate*, London; reprinted Negro University Press, New York, 1969.

Rohlfs, G., 1874. *Quer durch Afrika: Reise vom Mittelmeer nach dem Tschad-See und zum Golf von Guinea.* Leipzig.

Rosman, A., 1962. 'Social Structure and Acculturation among the Kanuri of Northern Nigeria'. Ph.D. Dissertation, Yale.

Rowling, C. W., 1952. *Report on Land Tenure, Kano Province.* Government Printer, Kaduna.

Runciman, W. G., 1968. 'Class, Status and Power?', in Jackson (1968).

Russell, T. A., 1955. 'The Kola of Nigeria and the Cameroons'. *Tropical Agriculture*, July.

Ruxton, F. H., 1916. *Maliki Law.* Luzak, London.

St Croix, F. W. (ed.), 1944. *The Fulani of Northern Nigeria.* Government Printer, Lagos.

Schacht, J., 1964. *An Introduction to Islamic Law.* Clarendon Press, London.

Schneider, R. M., and Darling, H. S., 1967. 'Power in Agriculture in Nigeria: Today and Tomorrow'. *Samaru Agricultural Newsletter*, Ahmadu Bello University, IX, August.

Schön, J. F., 1885. *Magana Hausa. Native Literature, or Proverbs, Tales, Fables and Historical Fragments in the Hausa Language*, to which is added a Translation in English. London.

Schultze, A., 1913. *The Sultanate of Bornu*, new edition with Additions and Appendices by P. A. Benton, Cass, London, 1968.

Sellnow, Irmgard, 1963. 'Der Handel in der Hausa-Literatur des ausgehenden 19. und beginnenden 20. Jahrhunderts'. *Mitteilungen des Instituts für Orientforschung*, IX, 4.

1964, 'Die Stellung der Sklaven in der Hausa-Gesellschaft'. *Mitteilungen des Instituts für Orientforschung*, X, 1.

Sharwood Smith, B. E., (Sir Bryan), n.d. *Sokoto Survey, 1948.* Gaskiya, Zaria.

1950. *Kano Survey.* Gaskiya, Zaria.

1969. *But Always as Friends: Northern Nigeria and the Cameroons, 1921–57.* Allen and Unwin, London.

Shaw, T., and Colville, G., 1950. *Report of Nigerian Livestock Mission.* Colonial no. 266, HMSO, London.

Skinner, N., 1968. 'The Origin of the Name "Hausa"'. *Africa*, 38, July.

1969. *Hausa Tales and Traditions: An English Translation of Tatsuniyoyi na Hausa.* Originally compiled by Frank Edgar: translated and edited by N. Skinner; with a foreword by M. G. Smith. Vol. I, Cass, London.

Smith, H. F. C., 1961. 'The Islamic Revolutions of the nineteenth century'. *Journal of the Historical Society of Nigeria*, II, 2.

Smith, Mary, 1954. *Baba of Karo: A Woman of the Muslim Hausa.* Faber, London.

Smith, M. G., 1952. 'A Study of Hausa Domestic Economy in Northern Zaria'. *Africa*, XXII.

1954a. 'Introduction' to Smith, Mary (1954).

1954b. 'Slavery and Emancipation in Two Societies'. *Social and Economic Studies*, December.

1955. *The Economy of Hausa Communities of Zaria.* Colonial Research Series no. 16, HMSO, London. To be reprinted by Johnson Reprint Company Ltd, London.

1957a. 'The social Functions and Meanings of Hausa Praise Singing', *Africa*, January.

1957b. 'Co-operation in Hausa Society'. *Information*, International Research Office on Social Implications of Technological Change, International Social Science Council, XI, January (cyclostyled).

1959. 'The Hausa System of Social Status'. *Africa*, XXIX, July.

1960. *Government in Zazzau, 1800–1950.* International African Institute, Oxford University Press, London.

1961a. 'Field Histories among the Hausa'. *Journal of African History*, II, 1.

1961b. 'Kebbi and Hausa Stratification'. *British Journal of Sociology*, 12.

1962. 'Exchange and Marketing among the Hausa', in Bohannan (1962).

1964. 'Historical and Cultural conditions of Political Corruption among the Hausa'. *Comparative Studies in Society and History*, VI, January.

Smith, M. G., 1965. 'Hausa Inheritance and Succession', in Derrett (1965).
  1966a. 'The Hausa of Northern Nigeria', in Gibbs (1966).
  1966b. 'The Jihad of Shehu dan Fodio: Some Problems', in Lewis (1966).
  1969. Foreword in Skinner (1969).
Smith, R. H. T.: *see* Hay (1970).
Staudinger, P., 1889. *Im Herzen der Haussaländer*, Berlin.
Steele, W. M., 1967. 'Agricultural Research in Kano'. *Kano Studies*, June.
Stenning, D. J., 1958. 'Household Viability among the Pastoral Fulani', in Goody (1958).
  1959. *Savannah Nomads: A study of the Wodaabe Pastoral Fulani of Western Bornu Province*.
  International African Institute, Oxford University Press, London.
Taylor, F. W., and Webb, A. G. G., 1932. *Al'adun Hausawa: Accounts and Conversations
  describing certain Customs of the Hausas* (In Hausa and English). Oxford University Press,
  London.
Temple, C. L., 1918. *Native Races and their Rulers*, Cape Town: reprinted, with a new intro-
  duction by M. Hiskett, Cass, London, 1968.
Temple, C. L. (ed.), 1919: *see* Temple, O. (1919).
Temple, Olive, 1919. *Notes on the Tribes, Provinces, Emirates and States of the Northern
  Provinces of Nigeria*. Compiled from Official Reports by O. Temple, ed. C. L. Temple;
  reprinted Cass, London, 1965.
Tiffen, Mary, 1971. *Changing Patterns of Farming in Gombe Emirate*. Samaru Miscellaneous
  Paper no. 32, Ahmadu Bello University, Zaria.
Tremearne, A. J. N., 1913. *Hausa Superstitions and Customs*, London; reprinted Cass, London,
  1970.
  1914. *The Ban of the Bori*. London; reprinted Cass, London, 1968.
Trimingham, J. S., 1959. *Islam in West Africa*. Clarendon Press, London.
Turner, R., 1940. 'Some Economic Aspects of the Groundnut Industry of Northern Nigeria',
  The Empire Journal of Experimental Agriculture, January.
Vesey-Fitzgerald, S., 1931. *Muhammadan Law: An Abridgment according to its various
  Schools*. Oxford University Press, London.
Waldman, M. R., 1965. 'The Fulani Jihad: a reassessment'. *Journal of African History*, VI, 3.
Walker, G., 1959. *Traffic and Transport in Nigeria*. Colonial Research Studies, no. 27, HMSO,
  London.
Wallace, W., 1896. 'Notes on a Journey through the Sokoto Empire and Borgu in 1894'.
  The Geographical Journal, VIII, September.
Webb, A. G. G.: *see* Taylor, F. W. (1932).
Werhahn, H. *et al.*, 1964. 'The Cattle and Meat Industry in Northern Nigeria'. A report
  made to the Ministry of Animal and Forest Resources, Kaduna (cyclostyled).
Westermann, D., 1934. 'Some Notes on the Hausa People and their Language', in Bargery
  (1934).
Whitaker, C. S., 1970. *The Politics of Tradition: Continuity and Change in Northern Nigeria
  1946–1966*. Princeton University Press.
Whittlesey, D., 1937. 'Kano, a Sudanese Metropolis'. *Geographical Review*, 27.
Wilks, I., 1970. 'Asante Policy towards the Hausa Trade in the Nineteenth Century', in
  Meillassoux (1971).
Willis, J. R., 1967. '*Jihad fi Sabil Allah* – its doctrinal basis in Islam and some aspects of its
  evolution in nineteenth-century West Africa'. *The Journal of African History*, 3.
Wilson, J.: *see* Mortimore (1965).
Wraith, R. E., 1966. 'Local Government', in Mackintosh (1966).
Yeld, E. R., 1960. 'Islam and Social Stratification in Northern Nigeria'. *British Journal of
  Sociology*, June.

Index

Note. Many of the less important entry words in the alphabetical Commentary are not included in the index. Those entry words that do form index headings have not been broken down into subheadings in the index, e.g. *fatauci* as a Commentary entry word is simply referenced '243–6'. Passing references to subjects in the Commentary have, however, been indexed in the same way as the text – e.g. *fatauci*, mentioned in connexion with natron on p. 301 of the Commentary, appears as a subheading under *fatauci*.